STAFFING ORGANIZATIONS:

Recruitment and Selection in Canada

Canadian Edition

Herbert G. Heneman III
University of Wisconsin–Madison

Timothy A. Judge
University of Florida

Vicky Smith
Fanshawe College

Russel Summers
St. Mary's University

Toronto Montréal Boston Burr Ridge, IL Dubuque, IA Madison, WI New York San Francisco St. Louis Bangkok Bogotá Caracas Kuala Lumpur Lisbon London Madrid Mexico City Milan New Delhi Santiago Seoul Singapore Sydney Taipei

Dedication

To my husband, Rob, and my family – much thanks for their encouragement and understanding.

- V. S.

To Maureen, Shelagh, Gavin and Brody.

- R. S.

Staffing Organizations
Canadian Edition

ISBN-13: 978-0-07-094829-7
ISBN-10: 0-07-094829-1

1 2 3 4 5 6 7 8 9 10 TCP 0 9 8 7

Printed and bound in Canada

Editorial Director: *Joanna Cotton*
Sponsoring Editor: *Kim Brewster*
Marketing Manager: *Joy Armitage Taylor*
Developmental Editor: *Lori McLellan*
Senior Editorial Associate: *Christine Lomas*
Supervising Editor: *Elizabeth Priest*
Copy Editor: *Michael Kelly*
Senior Production Coordinator: *Madeleine Harrington*
Cover Design: *Sharon Lucas*
Cover Image: *MedioImages/Getty Images*
Interior Design: *Greg Devitt*
Page Layout: *S R Nova Pvt Ltd., Bangalore, India*
Printer: *Transcontinental*

Library and Archives Canada Cataloguing in Publication

Heneman, Herbert Gerhard, 1944–
Staffing organizations / Herbert G. Heneman III ... [et al.]. – 1st Canadian ed.
Includes bibliographical references and index.

ISBN-13: 978-0-07-094829-7
ISBN-10: 0-07-094829-1

1. Employees–Recruiting–Textbooks. 2. Employee selection–Textbooks.
I. Title.

HF5549.5.R44H46 2006 658.3'11 C2006-903831-7

Author Profiles

Herbert. G. Heneman III is the Dickson-Bascom Professor Emeritus in the Management and Human Resources Department, School of Business, at the University of Wisconsin-Madison. He also serves as a senior researcher in the Wisconsin Center for Educational Research. Herb has been a visiting faculty member at the University of Washington and the University of Florida, and he was the University Distinguished Visiting Professor at the Ohio State University. His research is in the areas of staffing, performance management, compensation, and work motivation. He is currently investigating the design and effectiveness of teacher performance management and compensation systems. Herb is on the board of directors of the Society for Human Resource Management Foundation, and serves as its director of research. He is the senior author of three prior textbooks in human resource management. Herb is a Fellow of the Society for Industrial and Organizational Psychology, the American Psychological Association, and the Academy of Management. He is also the recipient of the career achievement award from the Human Resources Division of the Academy of Management.

Timothy A. Judge is the Matherly-McKethan Eminent Scholar, Department of Management, Warrington College of Business, University of Florida. Prior to receiving his PhD at the University of Illinois, Tim was a manager for Kohl's department stores. Tim has also served on the faculties of Cornell University and the University of Iowa. Tim's teaching and research interests are in the areas of personality, leadership and influence behaviors, staffing, and job attitudes. He serves on the editorial review boards of *Academy of Management Journal, Journal of Applied Psychology, Personnel Psychology,* and *Organizational Behavior and Human Decision Processes.* Tim is a former program chair for the Society for Industrial and Organizational Psychology, and past chair of the Human Resources Division of the Academy of Management. Tim is Fellow of the American Psychological Association and the Society for the Industrial and Organizational Psychology, and in 1995 he received the Ernest J. McCormick Award for Distinguished Early Career Contributions from the Society for Industrial and Organizational Psychology. In 2001 he received the Cummings Scholar Award for the Academy of Management.

Vicky Smith, CHRP, brings a strong practical influence to this textbook gained through her extensive experience in all aspects of staffing. As chief operating officer of Express Personnel Services (Canada)—a global organization with more than 500 franchises worldwide—from 1994 to 2000, Vicky was instrumental in designing and leading the implementation of best practices in recruitment and selection for a highly successful organization. Since 2000, Vicky has been president of Contact Human Resource Group, providing consulting services to organizations in the business, government, and non-profit sectors from multi-nationals to SMEs (small and medium-sized enterprises). Through her consulting experience, she has gained a "bigger picture" view of the strategic importance of effective staffing practices, thus bringing real life stories to the book. Vicky is a CHRP and has taught the Recruitment & Selection course at Fanshawe College since 2003. She sits on advisory committees at Fanshawe College to ensure that the Recruitment & Selection course covers the Required Professional Capabilities as set out by the Canadian Council of Human Resources Associations. She has been a long-standing member—and is currently vice president—of the Human Resources Professionals of London and District. She has written weekly articles for the *London Free Press* that focused on various human resources topics. Educational qualifications include a Bachelor of Arts degree, Adult Education Diploma, C.H.R.P. (Certified Human Resource Professional) and CPC (Certified Personnel Consultant) designations, and a Human Resources/Organizational Development Practitioner's Practicum.

Russel J. Summers is an Associate Professor of Management in the Sobey School of Business at Saint Mary's University in Halifax. Russ began teaching at Saint Mary's after receiving his PhD from the University of Waterloo in 1987, and during his tenure he has served as chair of the Management Department as well as director of the MBA program. He has also served as a member of the Saint Mary's University Graduate Studies Research Committee, and is currently a member of the Saint Mary's Board of Govenors and an Associate of the Leadership Centre of Excellence. Russ has taught undergraduate, MBA, and EMBA courses dealing with organizational behaviour, human resource management, research methods, staffing, training and development, management skills, and leadership. Outside the classroom he has been involved in projects with the CBC, CIBC, Nova Scotia's Department of Business and Consumer Affairs, Vietnamese Department of Foreign Affairs and International Trade, Employment and Immigration Canada, Nova Scotia Power, and Emera. He has served as a reviewer for the *Journal of Organizational Behavior,* the *Canadian Journal of Behavioural Sciences,* the *Journal of Applied Social Psychology,* and the Social Sciences and Humanities Research Council. His research interests include sexual harassment, employment equity, leadership, cynicism, and organizational justice. Russ has presented his research at conferences for the Academy of Management, the Eastern Academy of Management, the Southern Academy of Management, and the Administrative Sciences Association of Canada, and has published research reports in the *Journal of Vocational Behavior,* the *Journal of Applied Social Psychology, Sex Roles,* the proceedings of the Administrative Sciences Association of Canada, and the *Journal of Social Psychology.*

PREFACE

We believe staffing strategies should be pre-eminent topics of discussions in the boardroom. Organizations can only be vibrant and profitable when progressive staffing practices are endorsed by the executive team.

– The authors

Staffing Organizations, Canadian Edition contains current information that reflects the rapidly evolving terrain of strategic, technological, practical, and legal issues confronting organizations and their staffing systems. We provide relevant references, found within chapter endnotes, as well as listings of Web sites within most chapters that are specific to the subjects discussed in the chapter for the reader to reference when specific issues arise. From our research, we have extracted key examples of best practices or what not to do in staffing practices; tools to assess the effectiveness of staffing practices; and changes in staffing laws and regulations, as well as the interpretation of them by the courts and subject matter experts. The text is rich with examples and stories from a practical perspective of how organizations apply the principles outlined in the text.

ABOUT THIS CANADIAN EDITION

Staffing Organizations, Canadian Edition, has been written in response to a need on the part of Canadian students—and an increasing demand on the part of Canadian faculty—for a student-friendly text that is concise, relevant, and experiential.

Three major features in the text enrich the learning experience and sharpen one's staffing knowledge and skills. The first feature is incorporating staffing ethics into the entire book. This is done by presenting a section on staffing ethics in the first chapter, as well as a set of staffing ethics guidelines. Then at the end of each chapter, we have added two ethical issues to ponder, discuss, and resolve. We hope you will gain a greater appreciation of how complicated ethical issues are to resolve by those responsible for staffing in organizations, because there are few black and white answers. Through the exercises you will gain some practice trying to "do the right thing" when making staffing decisions, even though the ethical dilemmas do not have easy or necessarily correct solutions.

The second major feature is a case study that runs throughout the book, known as the Tanglewood Stores case. Tanglewood is depicted as an up-and-coming retailing organization. Tanglewood emphasizes an outdoor, western theme in its merchandise and stores. It has expansion plans that will allow it to challenge national retail chains. While most of its staffing policies and practices have been centralized to the regional or store level, Tanglewood is in the process of centralizing the human resources function, including staffing, in order to promote consistency in practices and presentation of the Tanglewood brand. At the end of Chapters 1, 3, 5, 8, 10, and 11 you will encounter a brief description of the specific case relevant to that chapter, and the specific tasks required of you to analyze the case material by applying concepts you've learned directly from the chapter. The full text of the case and your assignment is located online at www.mcgrawhill.ca/olc/heneman.

The third feature is Chapter 11 on Retention Management. We include the discussion of issues related to retention when discussing recruitment and selection because if an organization does not implement sound retention practices the vicious circle of "in one door and out the other" squanders precision financial and human resources.

ORGANIZATION OF THE CANADIAN EDITION

Staffing Organizations, Canadian Edition, is divided into five parts:

1. The Nature of Staffing
2. Support Activities
3. Staffing Activities: Recruitment
4. Staffing Activities: Selection
5. Retention and Staffing System Management

The "meat" of each chapter in these parts (12 chapters in total) is interspersed with and followed by additional material provided to supplement the chapter's contents and provide both context and relevance:

- The Staffing Organizations Model, developed by the authors, appears at the beginning of each of the five parts. Notice that a different section of the model is highlighted in each appearance, illustrating where we are in the staffing model for that part of the text.

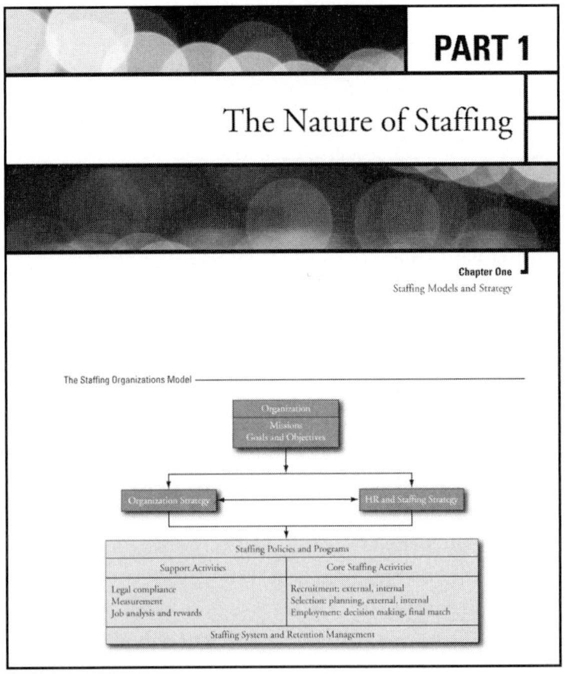

PART 1

The Nature of Staffing

Chapter One
Staffing Models and Strategy

The Staffing Organizations Model

Organization
Mission
Goals and Objectives

Organization Strategy
HR and Staffing Strategy

Staffing Policies and Programs

Support Activities
Legal compliance
Measurement
Job analysis and rewards

Core Staffing Activities
Recruitment: external, internal
Selection: planning, external, internal
Employment: decision making, final match

Staffing System and Retention Management

- Chapter Objectives have been highlighted at the beginning of each chapter, and the chapter's Summary relating to these learning objectives is included at the end of the chapter.

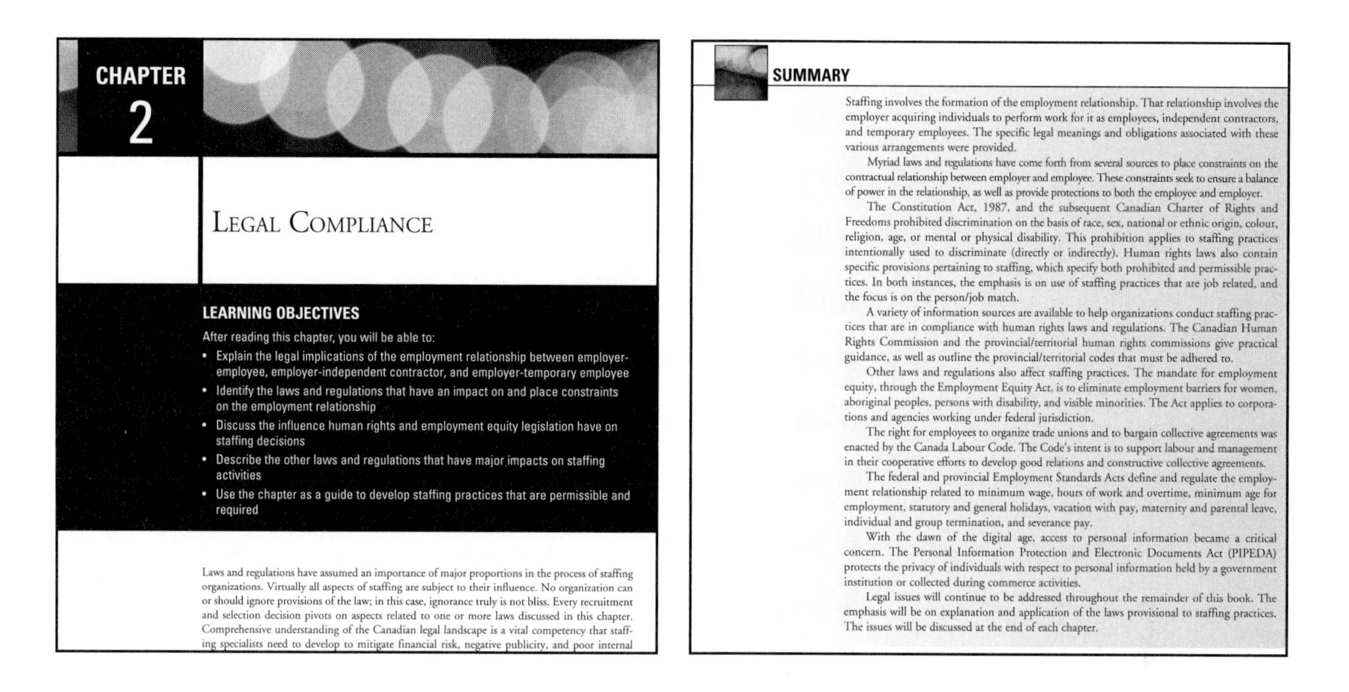

CHAPTER 2

LEGAL COMPLIANCE

LEARNING OBJECTIVES

After reading this chapter, you will be able to:

- Explain the legal implications of the employment relationship between employer-employee, employer-independent contractor, and employer-temporary employee
- Identify the laws and regulations that have an impact on and place constraints on the employment relationship
- Discuss the influence human rights and employment equity legislation have on staffing decisions
- Describe the other laws and regulations that have major impacts on staffing activities
- Use the chapter as a guide to develop staffing practices that are permissible and required

Laws and regulations have assumed an importance of major proportions in the process of staffing organizations. Virtually all aspects of staffing are subject to their influence. No organization can or should ignore provisions of the law; in this case, ignorance truly is not bliss. Every recruitment and selection decision pivots on aspects related to one or more laws discussed in this chapter. Comprehensive understanding of the Canadian legal landscape is a vital competency that staffing specialists need to develop to mitigate financial risk, negative publicity, and poor internal

SUMMARY

Staffing involves the formation of the employment relationship. That relationship involves the employer acquiring individuals to perform work for it as employees, independent contractors, and temporary employees. The specific legal meanings and obligations associated with these various arrangements were provided.

Myriad laws and regulations have come forth from several sources to place constraints on the contractual relationship between employer and employee. These constraints seek to ensure a balance of power in the relationship, as well as provide protections to both the employee and employer.

The Constitution Act, 1987, and the subsequent Canadian Charter of Rights and Freedoms prohibited discrimination on the basis of race, sex, national or ethnic origin, colour, religion, age, or mental or physical disability. This prohibition applies to staffing practices intentionally used to discriminate (directly or indirectly). Human rights laws also contain specific provisions pertaining to staffing, which specify both prohibited and permissible practices. In both instances, the emphasis is on use of staffing practices that are job related, and the focus is on the person/job match.

A variety of information sources are available to help organizations conduct staffing practices that are in compliance with human rights laws and regulations. The Canadian Human Rights Commission and the provincial/territorial human rights commissions give practical guidance, as well as outline the provincial/territorial codes that must be adhered to.

Other laws and regulations also affect staffing practices. The mandate for employment equity, through the Employment Equity Act, is to eliminate employment barriers for women, aboriginal peoples, persons with disability, and visible minorities. The Act applies to corporations and agencies working under federal jurisdiction.

The right for employees to organize trade unions and to bargain collective agreements was enacted by the Canada Labour Code. The Code's intent is to support labour and management in their cooperative efforts to develop good relations and constructive collective agreements.

The federal and provincial Employment Standards Acts define and regulate the employment relationship related to minimum wage, hours of work and overtime, minimum age for employment, statutory and general holidays, vacation with pay, maternity and parental leave, individual and group termination, and severance pay.

With the dawn of the digital age, access to personal information became a critical concern. The Personal Information Protection and Electronic Documents Act (PIPEDA) protects the privacy of individuals with respect to personal information held by a government institution or collected during commerce activities.

Legal issues will continue to be addressed throughout the remainder of this book. The emphasis will be on explanation and application of the laws provisional to staffing practices. The issues will be discussed at the end of each chapter.

- After an introduction in Chapter 1, the end of each subsequent chapter contains a separate Legal Issues section, within which specific legal topics relevant to the chapter's content are discussed. These sections allow for a more focused discussion of legal issues while not diverting attention from the major thrust of the text.

LEGAL ISSUES

Strategic Implications of Legal Challenges

There are compelling reasons why employers need to staff organizations with a diverse workforce. As we move into an era of skill shortages caused by the exodus of the baby boomers, those companies who have solid practices and policies in place to promote inclusion will have the greatest opportunity for economic success.

Best Practice Criteria The rest of this book will discuss in further detail the following best practices in cultivating human rights in the workplace:

- Strategic direction for inclusion needs to be supported by the organization's executive team, both financially and in directing organizational policy.
- Practicing diversity becomes part of the mission statement and core values of the organization.
- A formalized process for staffing is in place, including organizational analysis, job analysis, recruitment planning, structuring the recruitment message, structuring the hiring process, and valid and measurable recruitment tools.
- Staffing policies clearly outline employee expectations.

- Definitions of key terms highlighted in each chapter are provided in the margins, and a list of these terms with page references is provided at the end of the chapter.

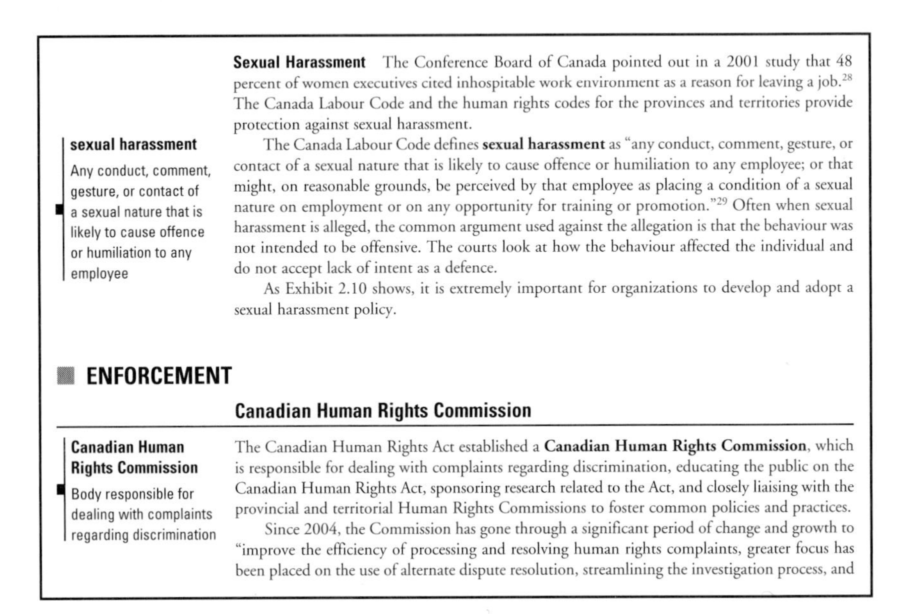

sexual harassment
Any conduct, comment, gesture, or contact of a sexual nature that is likely to cause offence or humiliation to any employee

Sexual Harassment The Conference Board of Canada pointed out in a 2001 study that 48 percent of women executives cited inhospitable work environment as a reason for leaving a job.[28] The Canada Labour Code and the human rights codes for the provinces and territories provide protection against sexual harassment.

The Canada Labour Code defines **sexual harassment** as "any conduct, comment, gesture, or contact of a sexual nature that is likely to cause offence or humiliation to any employee; or that might, on reasonable grounds, be perceived by that employee as placing a condition of a sexual nature on employment or on any opportunity for training or promotion."[29] Often when sexual harassment is alleged, the common argument used against the allegation is that the behaviour was not intended to be offensive. The courts look at how the behaviour affected the individual and do not accept lack of intent as a defence.

As Exhibit 2.10 shows, it is extremely important for organizations to develop and adopt a sexual harassment policy.

ENFORCEMENT

Canadian Human Rights Commission

Canadian Human Rights Commission
Body responsible for dealing with complaints regarding discrimination

The Canadian Human Rights Act established a **Canadian Human Rights Commission**, which is responsible for dealing with complaints regarding discrimination, educating the public on the Canadian Human Rights Act, sponsoring research related to the Act, and closely liaising with the provincial and territorial Human Rights Commissions to foster common policies and practices.

Since 2004, the Commission has gone through a significant period of change and growth to "improve the efficiency of processing and resolving human rights complaints, greater focus has been placed on the use of alternate dispute resolution, streamlining the investigation process, and

- Exhibits are interspersed throughout the text to illustrate concepts and provide a visual framework for students.

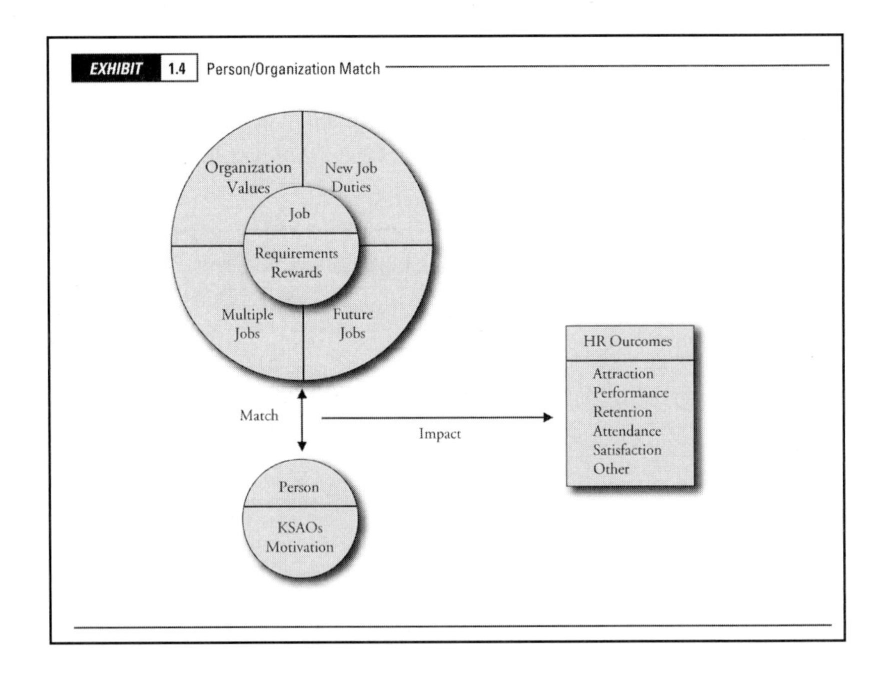

- Other end-of-chapter material to note are the Relevant Web Sites listings, suggested Discussion Questions, Ethical Issues exercises, and Applications cases that require analysis and response or entail small projects and active participation.

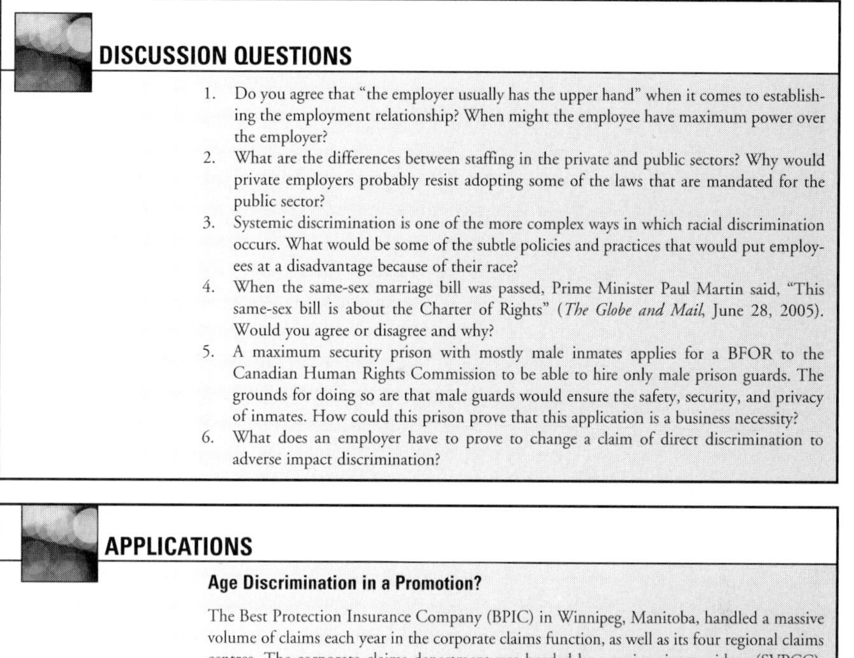

DISCUSSION QUESTIONS

1. Do you agree that "the employer usually has the upper hand" when it comes to establishing the employment relationship? When might the employee have maximum power over the employer?
2. What are the differences between staffing in the private and public sectors? Why would private employers probably resist adopting some of the laws that are mandated for the public sector?
3. Systemic discrimination is one of the more complex ways in which racial discrimination occurs. What would be some of the subtle policies and practices that would put employees at a disadvantage because of their race?
4. When the same-sex marriage bill was passed, Prime Minister Paul Martin said, "This same-sex bill is about the Charter of Rights" (*The Globe and Mail*, June 28, 2005). Would you agree or disagree and why?
5. A maximum security prison with mostly male inmates applies for a BFOR to the Canadian Human Rights Commission to be able to hire only male prison guards. The grounds for doing so are that male guards would ensure the safety, security, and privacy of inmates. How could this prison prove that this application is a business necessity?
6. What does an employer have to prove to change a claim of direct discrimination to adverse impact discrimination?

APPLICATIONS

Age Discrimination in a Promotion?

The Best Protection Insurance Company (BPIC) in Winnipeg, Manitoba, handled a massive volume of claims each year in the corporate claims function, as well as its four regional claims centres. The corporate claims department was headed by a senior vice president (SVPCC). She had two managers reporting to her—manager of corporate claims/life (MCC-L) and manager of corporate claims/residential (MCC-R)—and a highly skilled corporate claims specialist (CCS). Each regional office was headed by a regional centre manager (RCM); the RCM was responsible for both supervisors and claims specialists within the regional office. The RCMs reported to the vice president of regional claims (VPRC). Here is the structure before reorganization:

- Interspersed throughout the text at the end of selected chapters are instructions for completing assignments for the Tanglewood Stores case. The full case and assignments are located at the following Web site: www.mcgrawhill.ca/olc/heneman.

TANGLEWOOD STORES CASE II

Adverse Impact

One of the most significant equal employment opportunity concerns for any organization is when a large class of employees gathers together to propose that they have been discriminated against. In this case, you will assess a complaint of adverse impact proposed by designated-group employees of Tanglewood.

REQUIRED PROFESSIONAL CAPABILITIES (RPCs)

As of March 2003, provincial human resources associations throughout Canada have successfully agreed on a framework for achieving the designation of Certified Human Resource Professional (CHRP). This national accreditation process was launched by the Canadian Council of Human Resources Associations (CCHRA); see www.cchra-ccarh.ca/parc/en/section_3/ss_3/333e.asp for entry-level RPCs and www.cchra-ccarh.ca/parc/en/section_3/ss_3/33X3e.asp for experienced-professional RPCs.

The national CHRP certification program has raised the bar for human resources practitioners across the country who must now meet an even more demanding set of professional performance standards and acquire knowledge and skills covering a wide range of required professional capabilities (RPCs). Specifically, in the area of staffing (which includes recruitment and selection, deployment, retention, turnover, and terminating/outplacing staff), the accredited CHRP must possess the following capabilities to strategically staff an organization:

- Develop and implement programs for recruitment, selection, and orientation of new employees, and monitor the effectiveness of these programs
- Develop and implement programs for the effective allocation of staff, and for any adjustments to staffing due to major organizational changes
- Provide guidance on policies and procedures related to retention, turnover, and termination, as well as how the organization manages turnover

Look to the inside front cover of this text to see the conveniently located set of the specific RPCs required for staffing. You will see these referenced throughout the chapter with the icon shown here in the margin. Whenever you see this icon in the margin beside chapter content, simply look to the inside front cover to link to the required staffing competency. Please note that for the sake of brevity and simplicity, we have included only the staffing competencies upon which students will be responsible for in the CHRP exams, and not cross-referenced to other functional areas.

INSTRUCTOR AND STUDENT SUPPORT

Integrated Learning System

Great care was used in the creation of the supplemental materials to accompany *Staffing Organizations,* Canadian Edition. Whether you are a seasoned faculty member or a newly minted instructor, you will find the support materials to be comprehensive and practical.

Instructor's CD-ROM

The CD-ROM includes electronic versions of the following:

- Instructor's Manual
- Computerized Test Bank
- PowerPoint Presentations

Instructors can use this resource to access many of the supplements associated with the text and to create custom presentations. Most of these supplements are also available for downloading from the Instructor's Resource Centre of the Online Learning Centre, located at www.mcgrawhill.ca/olc/heneman.

PageOut

McGraw-Hill's unique point-and-click course Web site tool enables users to create a full-featured, professional-quality course Web site without needing to know HTML coding. PageOut is free for instructors, and lets you post your syllabus online, assign McGraw-Hill OLC content, add Web links, and maintain an online grade book. (And if you're short on time, we even have a team ready to help you create your site.)

WebCT/BlackBoard

This text is available in two of the most popular course-delivery platforms—WebCT and BlackBoard—for more user-friendly and enhanced features. Contact your local McGraw-Hill *i*Learning Sales Specialist for more information.

Instructor and Student Online Learning Centres (www.mcgrawhill.ca/olc/heneman)

This online learning centre is a text Web site that follows the text material chapter-by-chapter. Students will find custom quizzes for chapter content and a searchable glossary, in addition to the "Staffing Casebook" for the Tanglewood Stores case.

Instructors will find downloadable supplements, including the Tanglewood Stores case instructor manual.

*i*Learning Sales Specialist

Your Integrated Learning Sales Specialist is a McGraw-Hill Ryerson representative who has the experience, product knowledge, training, and support to help you assess and integrate any of the above-noted products, technology, and services into your course for optimum teaching and learning performance. Whether it's how to use our test bank software, helping your students improve their grades, or how to put your entire course online, your *i*Learning Sales Specialist is there to help. Contact your local *i*Learning Sales Specialist today to learn how to maximize all McGraw-Hill Ryerson resources!

*i*Services Program

McGraw-Hill Ryerson offers a unique *i*Services package designed for Canadian faculty. Our mission is to equip providers of higher education with superior tools and resources required for excellence in teaching. For additional information, visit www.mcgrawhill.ca/highereducation/iservices.

ACKNOWLEDGEMENTS

In the preparation of this first Canadian edition of *Staffing Organizations,* we have benefited greatly from the helpful critiques and suggestions of numerous professors across the country. They helped us identify new topics, clarify information, and rearrange and delete material. They also suggested examples that students would identify with. Their assistance was invaluable, and we extend our many thanks to the following:

Genevieve Farrell, *Ryerson University*
Anne Harper, *Humber College*
Maria Rotundo, *University of Toronto*
Nancy Stewart, *Sheridan Institute of Technology*
Carol-Ann Samhaber, *Algonquin College*
Anna Bortolen, *Conestoga College*
Fred McGregor, *Concordia University*
Gordon Barnard, *Durham College*
Krista Uggerslev, *University of Manitoba*
Barbara Lipton, *Seneca College of Applied Arts and Technology*
Glenn Coltman, *Athabasca University* and *Laurentian University*
Geoffrey Smith, *University of Guelph*

We also recognize the excellent parent text from the United States: *Staffing Organizations,* 5th edition, authored by Herbert G. Heneman III (University of Wisconsin-Madison) and Timothy A. Judge (University of Florida) and Mendota House, Inc., of Middleton, Wisconsin, as well as the contributions of the following reviewers of that text, upon which this Canadian edition is based:

Karen Bilda, *Cardinal Stritch University*
James Brakefield, *Western Illinois University*
Dennis Cockrell, *Washington State University*
Randy Dunham, *University of Wisconsin–Madison*
Fred Eck, *Miami University, Ohio*
Lynda Hartenian, *University of Wisconsin–Oshkosh*
Anthony Milanowski, *University of Wisconsin–Madison*
Lori Muse, *Western Michigan University*
Cynthia Ruzkowski, *Illinois State University*

Special thanks for the contributions of Professor John Kammeyer-Mueller at the University of Florida, most notably for developing the Tanglewood Stores case.

Vicky Smith also sends thanks to Denis Gravelle, Manager, Continuing Education at Fanshawe College, "for recommending me to McGraw-Hill Ryerson to co-author the Canadian edition of this text. Because of Denis's faith in my professional acumen, I have had the opportunity to research and write about my passion—best practices in staffing—to stretch my skills and abilities, and to work with amazing people at McGraw-Hill."

Finally, we thank the McGraw-Hill Ryerson publishing team: Kim Brewster, *Sponsoring Editor*; Lori McLellan, *Developmental Editor*; Elizabeth Priest, *Supervising Editor*, and Michael Kelly, *Copy Editor*, for their dedicated work in this collaborative undertaking.

Contents

PART 1

The Nature of Staffing

Chapter One

Staffing Models and Strategy

The Staffing Organizations Model

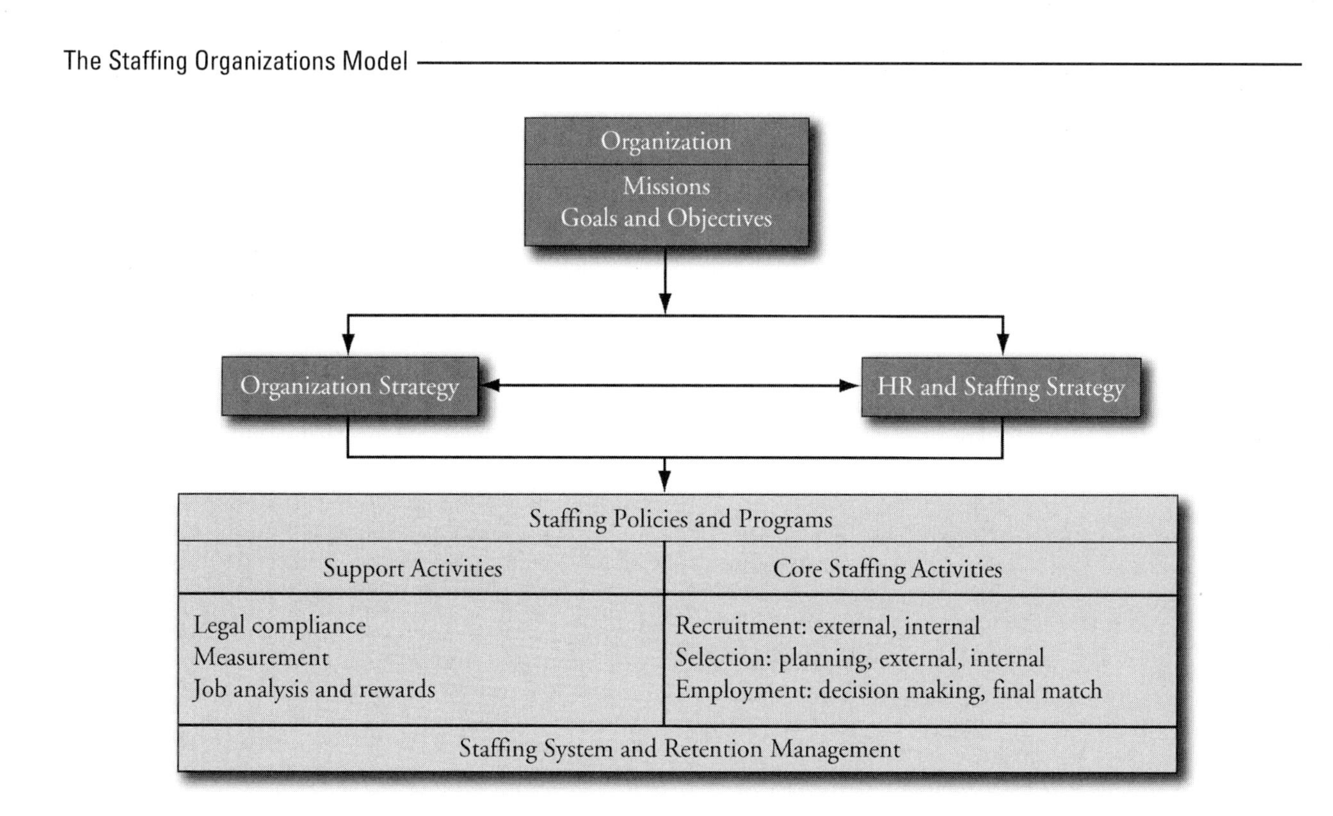

CHAPTER

1

Staffing Models and Strategy

LEARNING OBJECTIVES

After reading this chapter, you will be able to:

- Define staffing and outline the implications of the definition
- Explain how organizational effectiveness is determined by both staffing levels and the quality of labour
- Describe the five models of staffing
- List the 13 strategic staffing decisions that any organization is confronted with
- Understand the complexity of ethics in staffing decisions and use suggestions to assist in making ethical staffing decisions

Staffing is a critical organizational function concerned with the acquisition, deployment, and retention of the organization's workforce. This chapter begins with a look at the nature of staffing. This includes a view of the "big picture" of staffing, followed by a formal definition of staffing and the implications of that definition. Examples of staffing systems for a Canadian Astronaut recruitment campaign, store level human resource managers, and direct sales representatives are given.

Five models are then presented to elaborate on and illustrate various facets of staffing. The first model shows how projected workforce head-count requirements and availabilities are compared to determine the appropriate staffing level for the organization. The next two models illustrate staffing quality, which refers to matching a person's qualifications relative to the requirements of the job or organization. The person/job match model is the foundation of all staffing activities; the person/organization match model shows how person/job matching could determine how well the person will also fit with the organization. The core staffing components model identifies recruitment, selection, and employment as the three key staffing activities, and it shows how both the organization and job applicant interact in these activities. The final model, staffing organizations, provides the entire framework for staffing and the structure of this book. It shows that organizations, human resources (HR), and staffing strategy interact to guide the conduct of staffing support activities (legal compliance, measurement, job analysis) and core staffing activities (recruitment, selection, employment); employee retention and staffing system management are shown to cut across both types of activities.

Staffing strategy is then explored in detail by identifying and describing a set of 13 strategic staffing decisions that any organization is confronted with. Several of the decisions pertain to staffing levels, and the remainder to staffing quality.

Staffing ethics, which involve moral principles and guidelines for acceptable practice, are discussed next. Several pointers that can serve as guides to ethical staffing conduct are indicated, as are some of the common pressures to ignore these pointers and compromise one's ethical standards. Suggestions for how to handle these pressures are also made.

Finally, the plan for the remainder of the book is presented. The overall structure of the book is shown, along with key features of each chapter.

THE NATURE OF STAFFING

The Big Picture

human capital
Refers to the knowledge, skills, and ability of people, and their motivation to use them successfully on the job

Organizations are combinations of physical, financial and human capital. **Human capital** refers to the knowledge, skill, and ability of people, and their motivation to use them successfully on the job.[1] The term "workforce quality" is also a way of referring to an organization's human capital. The organization's workforce is the human capital it acquires, deploys, and retains in pursuit of organizational outcomes such as profitability, market share, and customer satisfaction. Staffing is the organizational function used to build the organization's workforce through such systems as staffing strategy, human resource planning, recruitment, selection, employment, and retention.

At the national level, the collective workforce of organizations totals almost 16.3 million employees spread across more than 1 million worksites.[2] The worksites vary considerably in size, with nearly 98 percent of employees in worksites with fewer than 100 employees, 2.1 percent in worksites with between 100 and 499 employees, and .3 percent in worksites with more than 500 employees.[3] Each of these worksites used some form of staffing process to acquire employees. In 2005, there was on average 20,800 new hire transactions each month, or more than 250,000 annually according to Statistics Canada's December 2005 Labour Force Survey Report (www.statcan.ca/english/Subjects/Labour/LFS/lfs-en.htm). This figure does not include internal transfers and promotions or the hiring of temporary employees, so the total number of staffing transactions is much greater than the 250,000 figure. Staffing is thus a big business for both organizations and job seekers.[4]

For most organizations a workforce is an expensive proposition and cost of doing business. It is estimated that an average organization's employee cost (wages or salaries and benefits) is over 25 percent of its total revenue.[5] The percentage is much greater for organizations in labour-intensive industries—the service-providing as opposed to goods-producing industries—such as retail trade, information, financial services, professional and business services, education, health care, and leisure and hospitality. Since service-providing industries now dominate our economy, matters of employee cost and whether the organization is acquiring a high-quality workforce loom large for many organizations.

A shift from viewing employees as just a cost of doing business to valuing employees as human capital that creates competitive advantage for the organization is gradually occurring. Organizations that can deliver superior customer service, for example, much of which is driven by highly knowledgeable employees with fine-tuned customer service skills, have a definite and hopefully long-term "leg up" on their competitors. The competitive advantage derived from such human capital has important financial implications.

From a financial perspective, human capital is an intangible asset for an organization that is difficult to measure directly and to place a value on. The value of human capital may be estimated, however, by comparing the value of the organization's tangible assets with the value of its stock. The valuation by the market and financial analysts of an organization's stock in excess of its tangible assets represents a premium for the intangible assets that make the organization valuable—such as its human capital. In many organizations, especially those in service-producing industries, most if not all of the premium reflects human capital value.

For example, say an organization's stock has a value of $100 million, and its tangible assets are valued at $60 million. Its potential human capital value is $40 million. If the organization has 1,000 employees, the average employee adds $40,000 in human capital value to the organization ($40,000,000/1,000 = $40,000/employee). For staffing, acquisition of high-quality employees thus has substantial implications for the organization's value. High-quality employees can indeed be value adding.[6]

Organizations are increasingly recognizing the value creation that can occur through staffing. Quotes from several organization leaders attest to this, as shown in Exhibit 1.1.

EXHIBIT 1.1 The Importance of Staffing to Organizational Leaders

"It all starts and ends with people. They are the heart, the soul and the spirit of our company... From a human resources perspective, it starts with selecting the best. The most important decision that we make within our company is who we hire."[7]

Carolyn Clark, vice president, human resources
CP Hotels—hospitality

"Globally, heads of companies consistently rank the ability to find the right talent to deliver on business objectives as one of their greatest challenges ... The investment in capability upfront will have a direct impact on the quality of the talent who come in the door later."[8]

Maureen Neglia, director, RBC recruitment
RBC Financial Group—financial

"I think about this in hiring, because our business all comes down to people.... In fact, when I'm interviewing a senior job candidate, my biggest worry is how good they are at hiring. I spend at least half the interview on that."[9]

Jeff Bezos, chief executive officer
Amazon.com—Internet merchandising

"We carefully select people who have more than one knowledge area, so there is no rigid job description and people can perform more than one function. This strategy is built on selecting highly adaptable employees rather than specialists for one job."[10]

Peter Klein, president
KLN KLEIN Products Development Inc.—custom manufacturing services

"If we talk about people as expendable cogs who are responsible to manage their own careers then we cannot be surprised when they leave for other opportunities. If the strategy is to buy what you need when you need it, then everyone potentially ends up in the contingent workforce—and procurement replaces human resources. You lose the benefits of the cohesiveness, coherence and connectivity that come from a resident workforce."[11]

Teresa Lister,
partner of human capital management
IBM Business Consulting Service—business and IT consulting services

staffing
The process of acquiring, deploying, and retaining a workforce of sufficient quantity and quality to create positive impacts on the organization's effectiveness

Definition of Staffing

Staffing is the process of acquiring, deploying, and retaining a workforce of sufficient quantity and quality to create positive impacts on the organization's effectiveness. This straightforward definition of staffing will be used throughout this book. It contains several implications, which are identified and explained next.

Implications of Definition

acquisition activities
External staffing systems that govern the initial intake of applicants into the organization

 1

Acquire, Deploy, Retain Any organization must have staffing systems that guide the acquisition, deployment, and retention of its workforce. **Acquisition activities** involve external staffing systems that govern the initial intake of applicants into the organization. It involves planning for the numbers and types of people needed, establishing job requirements in the form of the qualifications or KSAOs (knowledge, skill, ability, and other characteristics) needed to perform the job effectively, establishing the types of rewards the job will provide, conducting external recruitment campaigns, using selection tools to evaluate the KSAOs that applicants possess, deciding which applicants are the most qualified and will receive job offers, and putting together job offers that applicants will hopefully accept.

deployment
The placement of new hires on the actual job they will hold

 4

Deployment refers to the placement of new hires on the actual job they will hold, something that may not be entirely clear at the time of hire, such as the specific work unit or geographic location. Deployment also encompasses guiding the movement of current employees throughout the organization through internal staffing systems that handle promotions, transfers, and new project assignments for employees. Internal staffing systems mimic external staffing systems in many respects, such as planning for promotion and transfer vacancies, establishing job requirements and job rewards, recruiting employees for promotion or transfer opportunities, evaluating employees' qualifications, and making them job offers for new positions.

retention systems
Systems that seek to manage the inevitable flow of employees out of the organization

 5

Retention systems seek to manage the inevitable flow of employees out of the organization. Sometimes these outflows are involuntary on the part of the employee, such as through layoffs or the sale of a business unit to another organization. Other outflows are voluntary in that they are initiated by the employee, such as leaving the organization to take another job (a potentially avoidable turnover by the organization) or leaving the organization to follow one's spouse or partner to a new geographic location (a potentially unavoidable turnover by the organization). Of course, no organization can or should seek to completely eliminate employee outflows, but the organization should try to minimize the types of turnover in which valued employees leave for "greener pastures" elsewhere—namely, voluntary-avoidable turnover. Such turnover can be very costly to the organization. So can turnover due to employee discharges and downsizing. Through various retention strategies and tactics, the organization can combat these types of turnover, seeking to retain those employees it thinks it cannot afford to lose.

Staffing as a Process or System Staffing is not an event, such as "we hired two people today." Rather, staffing is a process that establishes and governs the flow of people into the organization, within the organization, and out of the organization. There are multiple, interconnected systems that organizations use to manage the people flows. These include planning, recruitment, selection, decision-making, job-offer, and retention systems. Occurrences or actions in one system inevitably affect other systems. If planning activities show a forecasted increase in vacancies relative to historical standards, for example, the recruitment system will need to gear up for generating more applicants than previously expected, the selection system will have to handle the increased volume of applicants needing to be evaluated in terms of their KSAOs, decisions about job offer receivers may have to be speeded up, and the job offer packages may have to be "sweetened" in order to entice the necessary numbers of needed new hires. Further, steps will have to be taken to try to retain the new hires in order to avoid having to repeat the above experiences in the next staffing cycle.

quantity
Having enough head count to conduct business

quality
Having people with the requisite KSAOs so that jobs are performed effectively

Quantity and Quality Staffing the organization requires attention to both the numbers (**quantity**) and types (**quality**) of people brought into, moved within, and retained by the organization. The quantity element basically refers to having enough head count to conduct business, and the quality element entails having people with the requisite KSAOs so that jobs are performed effectively. It is important to recognize that it is the combination of sufficient quantity and quality of labour that creates an effective staffing system.

Organization Effectiveness Staffing systems exist, and should be used, to contribute to the attainment of organizational goals such as survival, profitability, and growth. A macro view of staffing like this is often lost or ignored because most of the day-to-day operations of staffing systems involve micro activities that are procedural, transactional, and routine in nature. While these micro activities are essential for staffing systems, they must be viewed within the broader macro context of the positive impacts staffing can have on organization effectiveness. There are many indications of this critical role of staffing.

Leadership talent is at a premium, with very large stakes associated with the new leader acquisition. Sometimes new leadership talent is bought and brought from the outside to hopefully execute a reversal of fortunes for the organization or a business unit within it. Other organizations acquire new leaders to start new business units or ventures that will feed organizational growth. The flip side to leadership acquisition is leadership retention. A looming fear for organizations is the unexpected loss of a key leader, particularly to a competitor. The exiting leader carries a wealth of knowledge and skill out of the organization and leaves a hole that may be hard to fill, especially with someone of equal or higher leadership stature. The leader may also take other key employees along, thus increasing the exit impact.

Organizations also recognize that talent hunts and loading up on talent are ways to expand organizational value and provide protection from competitors. Such a strategy is particularly effective if the talent is unique and rare in the marketplace, valuable in the anticipated contributions to be made (such as new product creations or design innovations), and difficult for competitors to imitate (such as through training current employees). Talent of this sort can serve as a source of competitive advantage for the organization, hopefully for an extended time period.[12]

Talent acquisition is essential for growth even when it does not have such competitive advantage characteristics. Information technology companies, for example, cannot thrive without talent infusions via staffing. An Internet start-up called edocs, inc., sold Internet bill presentment and payment software. It doubled its employee ranks to over 100 in five months and sought to double that number in another five months. The CEO said this was necessary or "we won't have the resources we need to keep up the growth and go public. You grow fast or you die."[13] Quantity or quality labour shortages can mean lost business opportunities, scaled-back expansion plans, inability to provide critical consumer goods and services, and even threats to organization survival.

Finally, for individual managers, having sufficient numbers and types of employees on board is necessary for the smooth, efficient operation of their work unit. Employee shortages often require disruptive adjustments, such as job reassignments or overtime for current employees. Underqualified employees present special challenges to the manager, such as a need for close supervision and training. Failure of the underqualified to achieve acceptable performance may require termination of employees, a difficult decision to make and implement.

In short, organizations experience and respond to staffing forces and recognize how critical these forces can be to organizational effectiveness. The forces manifest themselves in numerous ways: acquisition of new leaders to change the organization's direction and effectiveness; prevention of key leader losses; use of talent as a source of growth and competitive advantage; shortages of labour—both quantity and quality—that threaten growth and even survival; and the ability of individual managers to effectively run their work units.

Staffing System Examples

Canadian Astronaut Recruitment Campaign* Alan Davis and Associates was chosen by the Canadian Space Agency to assist in the design and implementation of a recruitment campaign for engineers and scientists in 1992. The only previous recruit occurred in 1983. Alan Davis was the project manager and his role was to manage the design and implementation of the whole campaign. The campaign was divided into the following phases:

> Phase I, planning: Define the job requirements; design the content and layout of advertisements; design the assessment tools, including psychological testing; and develop screening parameters.
> Phase II, preselection: More than 5,300 applicants applied. Resumes were sorted by an initial screening process where all aspects of experience and education were scored by predefined parameters. The best qualified candidates were then immediately identified by discipline.
> Phase III, selection: Five hundred resumes were screened down from the initial applicants to present to the Canadian Space Agency's Selection Committee, and the committee further screened down to 370 resumes. Each of the short-listed candidates was sent an assessment package that included a specially designed application form and medical questionnaire, a psychological questionnaire, and security forms. After receiving the assessment packages back from the applicants, approximately 100 applicants were selected for interviews.
> Phase IV, initial interview: The screening interview was conducted to ensure that each applicant received objective and equal treatment. The initial interviewing process included a batch of psychological tests and interview. The top 50 applicants were then short-listed.
> Phase V, panel interview: A panel of seven conducted the interviews and the applicants were required to take a flight medical at their local Canadian Forces Base.
> Phase VI, final selection: The top 20 finalists completed a 20-hour medical examination at the National Defence Medical Centre in Ottawa, another panel interview, manual dexterity testing, oral presentations, and psychiatric examinations. A scoring system was developed to ensure consistency in the decision-making process. Four finalists were selected.

For Alan Davis, identifying person/organization fit was paramount in the recruitment process: "Never hire if you think there is going to be a mismatch between the candidate and the culture. For a person to be successful in an organization, their behaviours must complement those of the people they are working with. Behaviours are driven by values and you are not going to be able to change a person's values."[14]

Store HR Managers The new executive vice president of human resources for Home Depot (Dennis Donovan) ordered a complete audit of the HR department's capabilities. One weakness discovered was a lack of presence of HR at the store level, so the individual store managers oversaw all of HR themselves, including staffing and training for an average workforce of 400 employees. To provide relief and expertise to the store managers, Donovan decided to expand HR down to the store level by having an HR representative in each store. To achieve this staffing objective, the corporate HR department conducted 97 full-day career forums, processed more than 37,000 applications from external and internal applicants, interviewed 3,000 of these applicants, and selected 1,500 of them for the job. The program has been well received by managers. One regional manager, with over 600 stores, said the "managers used to have to wear multiple hats, but now they are free to run the business. Putting HR professionals in the stores has helped us to hire more efficiently and find better people."[15]

---

*Reprinted with permission: Alan Davis & Associates Inc.

Direct Sales Representatives Avon Products, Inc., uses multilevel direct selling of its many cosmetic products to its women customers. Avon has 25,000 sales representatives who are part of a sales force Avon calls Leadership. The Leadership program was undertaken to reenergize the sales force and boost sales. The sales representatives are independent contractors, not employees. During the selling process and customer exchanges, the representatives use the opportunity to recruit the customers themselves to become sales representatives. The sales representative receives two biweekly cheques: one is for sales commissions and the other is a commission for recruiting and training new sales representatives. The program has helped increase the number of sales representatives by 3 percent, sales have grown by 4 percent, and profits have increased 20 percent. Because the sales representatives are increasing the number of recruits they train and manage, Avon has been able to reduce the number of district managers of the sales representatives. A remaining problem is turnover among the sales representatives, which runs more than 50 percent annually. To improve retention, Avon began investing $20 million in a series of programs (e.g., training) to help sales representatives increase their sales and thus their desire to remain with Avon.[16]

STAFFING MODELS

Several models depict various elements of staffing. Each of these is presented and described to more fully convey the nature and richness of staffing the organization.

Staffing Quantity: Levels

The quantity or head-count portion of the staffing definition means organizations must be concerned about staffing levels and their adequacy. Exhibit 1.2 shows the basic model. The organization as a whole, as well as for each of its units, forecasts workforce quantity requirements—the needed head count—and then compares these to forecasted workforce availabilities—the likely employee head count—to determine its likely staffing level position. If head-count requirements match availabilities, the projection is that the organization will be fully staffed. If requirements exceed availabilities, the organization will be understaffed, and if availabilities exceed requirements, the organization will be overstaffed.

Making such forecasts to determine like staffing levels and then developing specific plans on how to cope with them are the essence of planning. Being understaffed means the organization will have to gear up its staffing efforts, starting with accelerated recruitment and carrying on through the rest of the staffing system. It may also require development of retention programs that will slow the outflow of people, thus avoiding costly "turnstile" or "revolving door" staffing. Overstaffing projections signal the need to slow down or even halt recruitment, as well as to take steps that will actually reduce head count, such as through reduced workweeks, early retirement plans, or layoffs.

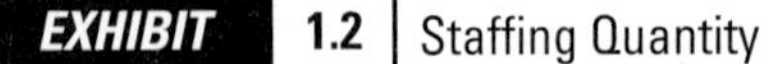
EXHIBIT 1.2 Staffing Quantity

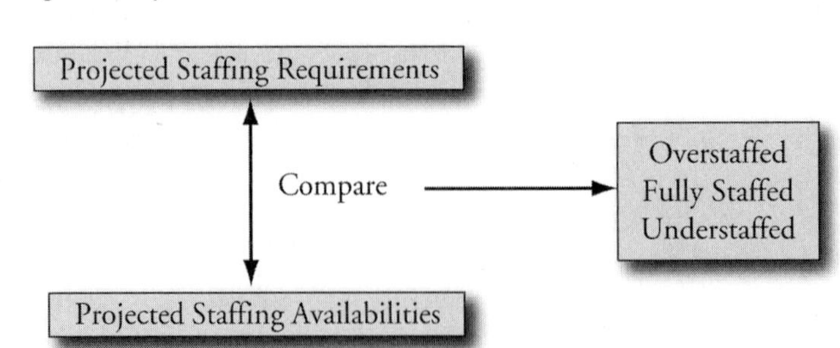

Staffing Quality: Person/Job Match

2.1

person/job match
An alignment of the characteristics of individuals and jobs in ways that will result in desired HR outcomes

The **person/job match** seeks to align characteristics of individuals and jobs in ways that will result in desired HR outcomes. Casual comments made about applicants often reflect awareness of the importance of the person/job match:

> "Clark just doesn't have the interpersonal skills that it takes to be a good customer service representative."
> "Mary has exactly the kind of budgeting experience this job calls for; if we hire her, there won't be any downtime while she learns our systems."
> "Gary says he was attracted to apply for this job because of its sales commission plan; he says he likes jobs where his pay depends on how well he performs."
> "Diane was impressed by the amount of challenge and autonomy she will have."
> "Jack turned down our offer; we gave him our best shot, but he just didn't feel he could handle the long hours and amount of travel the job calls for."

Comments like these raise four important points about the person/job match:

1. Jobs are characterized by their requirements (e.g., commission sales plan, challenge, and autonomy).
2. Individuals are characterized by their level of qualification (e.g., few interpersonal skills, extensive budgeting experience) and motivation (e.g., need for pay to depend on performance, need for challenge, and autonomy).
3. In each of the previous examples the issue was one of the likely degree of fit or match between the characteristics of the job and the person.
4. There are implied consequences for every match. For example, Clark may not perform very well in his interactions with customers; retention may quickly become an issue with Jack.

KSAOs
Job qualifications, including ***k***nowledges, ***s***kills, ***a***bilities, and ***o***ther characteristics, to look for when considering potential candidates

These points and concepts are shown more formally through the person/job match model in Exhibit 1.3. In this model, the job has certain requirements and rewards associated with it. The person has certain qualifications, referred to as **KSAOs** (knowledges, skills, abilities, and other characteristics), and motivations. There is a need for a match between the person and the job. To the extent that the match is good, it will likely have positive impacts on HR outcomes, particularly attraction of job applicants, job performance, retention, attendance, and satisfaction.

EXHIBIT 1.3 Person/Job Match

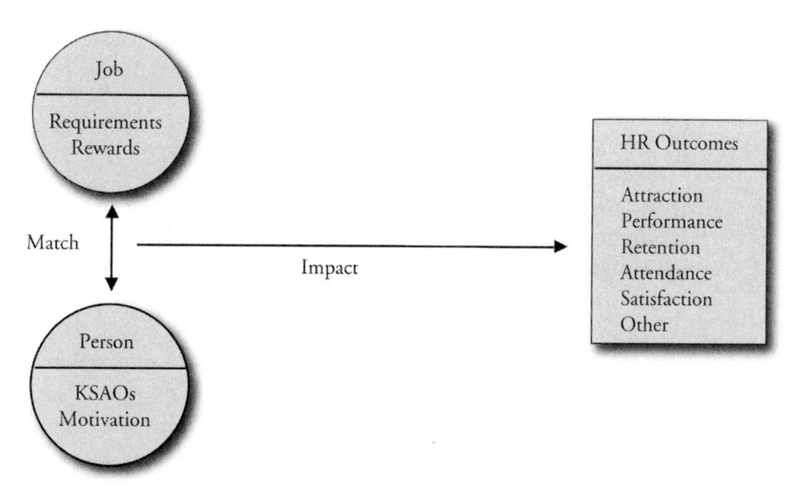

There is actually a need for a dual match to occur: job requirements to KSAOs, and job rewards to individual motivation. In and through staffing activities, there are attempts to ensure both of these. Such attempts collectively involve what will be referred to throughout this book as the **matching process**.

matching process
A process that matches both job requirements to KSAOs and job rewards to individual motivation

Several points pertaining to staffing need to be made about the person/job matching model. First, the concepts shown in the model are not new.[17] They have been used for decades as the dominant way of thinking about how individuals successfully adapt to their work environments. The view is that the positive interaction of individual and job characteristics creates the most successful matches. Thus, a person with a given "package" of KSAOs is not equally suited to all jobs, because jobs vary in the KSAOs required. Likewise, an individual with a given set of needs or motivations will not be satisfied with all jobs, because jobs differ in the rewards they offer. Thus, in staffing, each individual must be assessed relative to the requirements and rewards of the job being filled.

Second, the model emphasizes that the matching process involves a dual match of KSAOs to requirements and motivation to rewards. Both matches require attention in staffing. For example, a staffing system may be designed to focus on the KSAOs/requirements match by carefully identifying job requirements and then thoroughly assessing applicants relative to these requirements. While such a staffing system may be one that will accurately identify the probable high performers, problems may arise with it. By ignoring or downplaying the motivation/rewards portion of the match, the organization may have difficulty getting people to accept job offers (an attraction outcome) or having new hires remain with the organization for any length of time (a retention outcome). It does little good to be able to identify the likely high performers if they cannot be induced to accept job offers or to remain with the organization.

job requirement
The tasks involved in the job and the KSAOs that are necessary to perform those tasks

Third, **job requirements** should usually be expressed in terms of both the tasks involved and the KSAOs thought necessary for performance of those tasks. Most of the time, it is difficult to establish meaningful KSAOs for a job without having first identified the job's tasks. KSAOs usually must be derived or inferred from knowledge of the tasks. An exception to this involves very basic or generic KSAOs, such as literacy and oral communication skills, that are reasonably deemed necessary for most jobs.

Fourth, job requirements often extend beyond task and KSAO requirements. For example, the job may have requirements about reporting to work on time, attendance, safety toward fellow employees and customers, and needs for travel. With such requirements, the matching of the person to them must also be considered when staffing the organization. Travel requirements of the job, for example, may involve assessing applicants' availability for, and willingness to accept, travel assignments.

Finally, the matching process can yield only so much by way of impacts on the HR outcomes. The reason for this is that these outcomes are influenced by factors outside the realm of the person/job match. Retention, for example, depends not only on how close a match there is between job rewards and individual motivation but also on the availability of suitable job opportunities in other organizations and labour markets.

Staffing Quality: Person/Organization Match

Often the organization seeks to determine not only how well the person fits or matches the job but also the organization. Likewise, applicants often assess how they think they might fit into the organization, in addition to how well they match the specific job's requirements and rewards. For both the organization and the applicant, therefore, there may be a concern with a person/organization match.[18]

Exhibit 1.4 shows this expanded view of the match. The focal point of staffing is the person/job match, and the job is like the bull's eye of the matching target. Four other matching concerns, however, involving the broader organization, also arise in staffing. These concerns involve organizational values, new job duties, multiple jobs, and future jobs.

EXHIBIT 1.4 Person/Organization Match

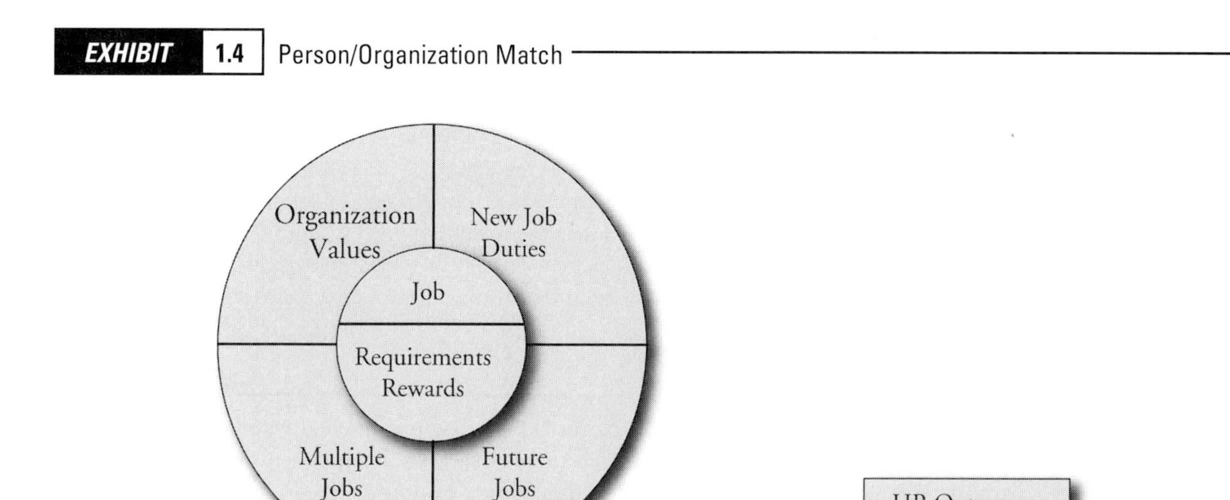

Organizational values are norms of desirable attitudes and behaviours for the organization's employees. Examples include honesty and integrity, achievement and hard work, fairness, and concern for fellow employees and customers. Matching these values as well as the job description has to be assessed during the staffing process.

New job duties represent tasks that may be added to the target job over time. Organizations desire new hires who will be able to successfully perform these new duties as they are added. In recognition of this, job descriptions often contain the catchall phrase "and other duties as assigned." These other duties are usually vague at the time of hire, and they may never materialize. Nonetheless, the organization would like to hire persons it thinks could perform these new duties. Having such people will provide the organization a degree of flexibility in getting new tasks done without having to hire additional employees to do them.

Flexibility concerns also enter into the staffing picture in terms of hiring persons who could perform multiple jobs. Small businesses, for example, often desire new hires who can wear multiple hats, functioning as jacks-of-all-trades; or, organizations experiencing rapid growth may require new employees who can handle several different job assignments, splitting their time between them on an "as needed" basis. Such expectations obviously require assessments of person/organization fit.

Future jobs represent forward thinking by the organization and person as to what job assignments the person might assume beyond the initial job. Here the applicant and the organization are thinking of long-term matches over the course of transfers and promotions as the employee becomes increasingly "seasoned" for the long run.

In each of the above four cases, the matching process is expanded to include consideration of requirements and rewards beyond those of the target job as it currently exists. Though the dividing line between person/job and person/organization matching is fuzzy, both types of matches are frequently of concern in staffing. Ideally, the organization's staffing systems focus first and foremost on the person/job match. This allows the nature of the employment relationship to be specified and agreed to in concrete terms. Once these terms have been established, person/organization match possibilities can be explored during the staffing process. In this book for simplicity's sake we will use the term "person/job match" broadly to encompass both types of matches, though most of the time the usage will be in the context of the actual person/job match.

Staffing System Components

As noted, staffing encompasses managing the flows of people into and within the organization, as well as retaining them. The core staffing process has several components that represent steps and activities that occur over the course of these flows. Exhibit 1.5 shows these components and the general sequence in which they occur.

As shown in Exhibit 1.5, staffing begins with a joint interaction between the applicant and the organization. The applicant seeks the organization and job opportunities within it, and the organization seeks applicants for job vacancies it has or anticipates having. Both the applicant and the organization are thus involved as "players" in the staffing process from the very beginning, and they remain joint participants throughout the process.

At times, the organization may be the dominant player, such as in aggressive and targeted recruiting for certain types of applicants. At other times, the applicant may be the aggressor, such as when the applicant desperately seeks employment with a particular organization and will go to almost any length to land a job with it. Most of the time, staffing involves a more balanced and natural interplay between the applicant and the organization, which occurs over the course of the staffing process.

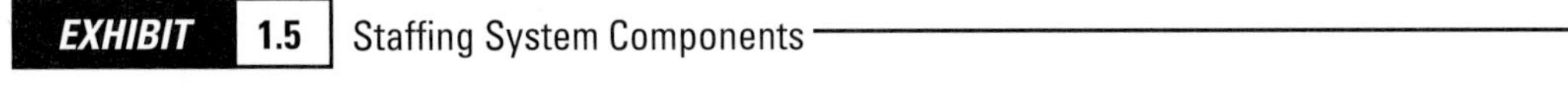

EXHIBIT 1.5 Staffing System Components

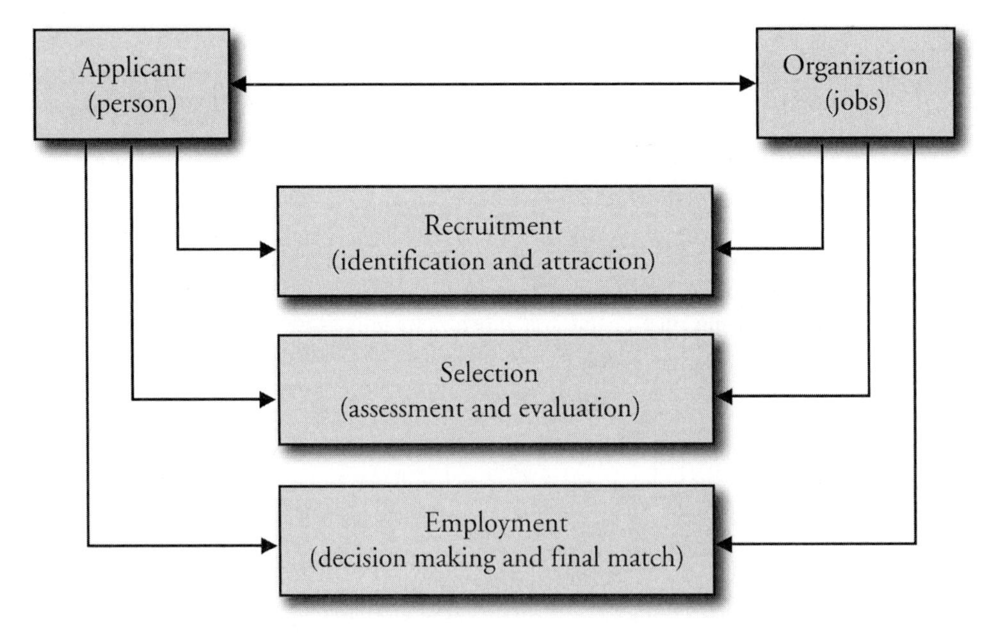

The initial stage in staffing is recruitment, which involves identification and attraction activities by both the organization and the applicant. The organization seeks to identify and attract individuals so that they become job applicants. Activities such as advertising, job fairs, use of recruiters, preparation and distribution of informational brochures, and "putting out the word" about vacancies among its own employees are undertaken. The applicant attempts to identify organizations with job opportunities through activities such as reading advertisements, contacting an employment agency, mass mailing resumés to employers, and so forth. These activities are accompanied by attempts to make one's qualifications (KSAOs and motivation) attractive to organizations, such as by applying in person for a job or preparing a carefully constructed resumé that highlights significant skills and experiences.

Gradually, recruitment activities phase into the selection stage and its accompanying activities. Now, the emphasis is on assessment and evaluation. For the organization, this means the use of various selection techniques (interviews, application blanks, and so on) to assess applicant KSAOs and motivation. Data from these assessments are then evaluated against job requirements to determine the likely degree of person/job fit. At the same time, the applicant is assessing and evaluating the job and organization. The applicant's assessment and evaluation are based on information gathered from organizational representatives (e.g., recruiter, manager with the vacancy, other employees); written information (e.g., brochures, Web site, employee handbook); informal sources (e.g., friends and relatives who are current employees); and visual inspection (e.g., a video presentation, a worksite tour). This information, along with a self-assessment of KSAOs and motivation, is evaluated against the applicant's understanding of job requirements and rewards to determine if a good person/job match is likely.

The next core component of staffing is employment, which involves decision making and final match activities by the organization and the applicant. The organization must decide which applicants to reject from further consideration and which to allow to continue in the process. This may involve multiple decisions over successive selection steps or hurdles. Some applicants ultimately become finalists for the job. At that point, the organization must decide to whom it will make the job offer, what the content of the offer will be, and how it will be drawn up and presented to the applicant. Upon the applicant's acceptance of the offer, the final match is complete, and the employment relationship is formally established.

self-selection
Decision that an applicant makes about whether to continue in or drop out of the staffing process

For the applicant, the employment stage involves **self-selection**, a term that refers to decisions about whether to continue in or drop out of the staffing process. These decisions may occur anywhere along the selection process, up to and including the moment of the job offer. If the applicant continues as part of the process through the final match, the applicant has decided to be a finalist. The individual's attention now turns to a possible job offer, possible input and negotiation on its content, and making a final decision about the offer. The applicant's final decision is based on overall judgment about the likely suitability of the person/job match.

It should be noted that the above staffing components apply to both external and internal staffing. Though this may seem obvious in the case of external staffing, a brief elaboration may be necessary for internal staffing. In internal staffing, the applicant is a current employee, and the organization is the current employer. Job opportunities (vacancies) exist within the organization and are filled through the activities of the internal labour market. Those activities involve recruitment, selection, and employment, with the employer and employee as joint participants. For example, the employer may recruit through use of an internal job posting system. Employees who apply may be assessed and evaluated on the basis of supervisory recommendation, a formal promotability rating, and previous job assignments for the employer. Decisions are made by both the employer and the employees who are applicants. Ultimately, the position will be offered to one of the applicants and, hopefully, accepted. When this happens, the final match has occurred, and a new employment relationship has been established.

Staffing Organizations

The overall staffing organizations model, which forms the framework for this book, is shown in Exhibit 1.6. It depicts that the organization's mission and goals and objectives drive both organization strategy and HR and staffing strategy, which interact with each other when they are being formulated. Staffing policies and programs result from such interaction and serve as an overlay to both support activities and core staffing activities. Employee retention and staffing system management concerns cut across these support and core staffing activities. Finally, though not shown in the model, it should be remembered that staffing levels and staffing quality are the key focal points of staffing strategy, policy, and programs. A more thorough examination of the model follows next.

Organization, HR, and Staffing Strategy Organizations formulate strategy to express an overall purpose or mission and to establish broad goals and objectives that will guide the organization toward fulfillment of its mission. For example, a newly formed software development organization may have a mission to "help individuals and families manage all of their personal finances and records through electronic means." Based on this mission statement, the organization might then develop goals and objectives pertaining to product development, sales growth, and competitive differentiation through superior product quality and customer service.

Underlying these objectives are certain assumptions about the size and types of workforces that will need to be acquired, trained, managed, rewarded, and retained. HR strategy represents the key decisions about how these workforce assumptions will be handled. Such HR strategy may not only flow from the organization strategy but also may actually contribute directly to the formulation of the organization's strategy.

EXHIBIT 1.6 Staffing Organizations Model

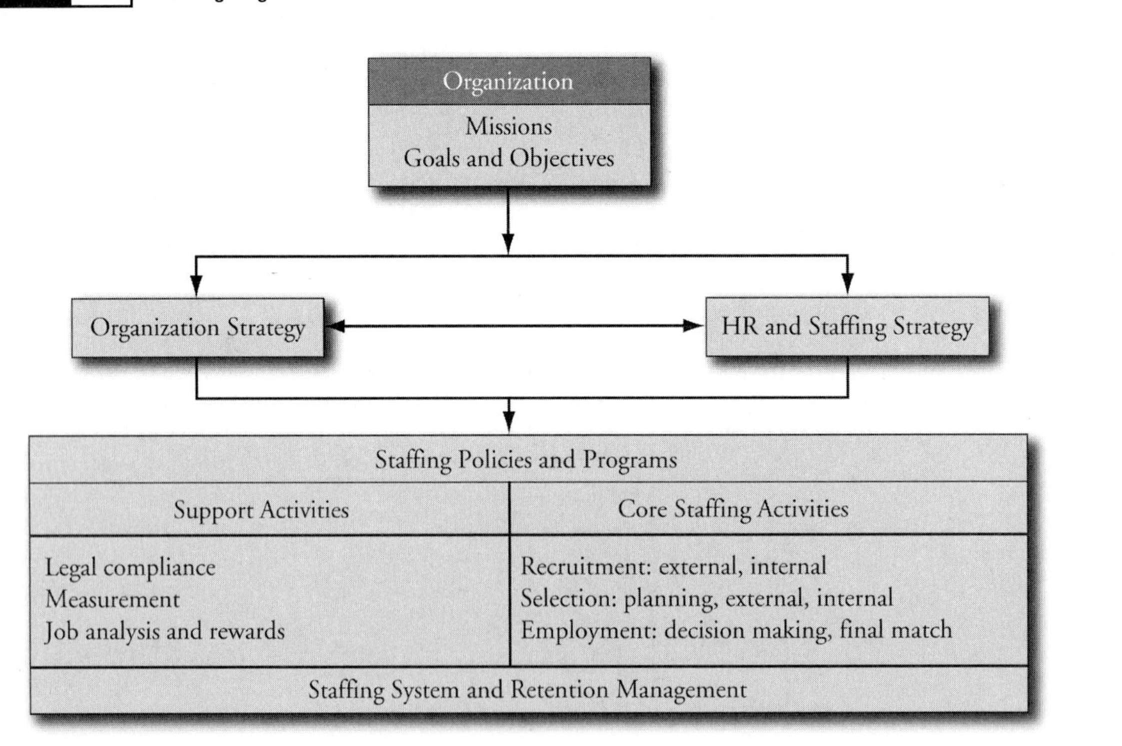

Consider again the software development organization and its objective pertaining to new product development. Being able to develop new products assumes that sufficient, qualified product-development team members are available internally and externally, and assurances from the HR department about availability may have been critical in helping the organization to decide on its product development goals. From this general assumption, HR strategy may suggest:

1. Obtaining new, experienced employees from other software companies, rather than going after newly minted university and graduate school graduates
2. Building a new facility for software development employees in a geographic area that will be an attractive place to work, raise families, and pursue leisure activities
3. Developing relocation assistance packages and family-friendly benefits
4. Offering wages and salaries above the market average, as well as using hiring bonuses to help lure new employees away from their current employers
5. Creating special training budgets for each employee to use at his or her own discretion for skills enhancement
6. Putting in place a fast-track promotion system that allows employees to rise upward in either their professional specialty or the managerial ranks

In all of these ways, HR strategy seeks to align acquisition and management of the workforce with organization strategy.

Staffing strategy is an outgrowth of the interplay between organization and HR strategy described above. It deals directly with key decisions regarding the acquisition, deployment, and retention of the organization's workforces. Such decisions guide the development of recruitment, selection, and employment programs. In the software development example discussed above, the strategic decision to acquire new employees from the ranks of experienced people at other organizations may lead the organization to develop very active, personalized, and secret recruiting activities for luring these people away. It may also lead to the development of special selection techniques for assessing job experiences and accomplishments. In such ways, strategic staffing decisions shape the staffing process.

Support Activities Support activities serve as the foundation and necessary ingredients for the conduct of core staffing activities. Legal compliance represents knowledge of the myriad laws and regulations, especially human rights, employment standards, employment equity, and privacy; and incorporation of their requirements into all phases of the core staffing activities. Measurement ensures the rules applied to staffing decisions are standardized, valid, and reliable thus providing the organization with a systematic staffing process. Determining what measurements will be used in testing the skill levels of potential applicants is a key function in identifying qualified applicants and ensuring that the core staffing activities are equitable and are in legal compliance. Job analysis represents the key mechanism by which the organization identifies and establishes the KSAO requirements for jobs, as well as the rewards jobs will provide, both first steps toward seeking to begin filling projected vacancies through core staffing activities.

Returning to the software development organization, if it meets various size thresholds for coverage (usually 15 or more employees), it must ensure that the staffing systems to be developed will comply with all applicable federal, provincial, and local laws and regulations. Decisions will need to be made about testing procedures, whether tests will be developed in-house or purchased, and how the tests will be administered. Finally, job analysis will be needed to specify for each job exactly what KSAOs and rewards will be necessary for these sought-after new employees. Once all of these support activities are in place, the core staffing activities can begin.

Core Staffing Activities Core staffing activities focus on recruitment, selection, and employment of the workforce. Before recruitment plans can be formalized, planning of staffing levels—both requirements and availabilities—needs to occur. Planning serves as a tool for first becoming aware of key external influences on staffing, particularly economic conditions, labour markets, and labour unions. The results drive staffing planning for the core staffing activities. For the software development organization, planning activities will revolve around first determining the major types of jobs that will be necessary for the new product development venture, such as computer programmers, Internet specialists, and project managers. For each job, a forecast must be made about the number of employees that will be needed and the likely availability of individuals both externally and internally for the job. Results of such forecasts serve as the key input to the development of detailed staffing plans for the core staffing activities.

3.1

The emphasis then shifts to staffing quality to ensure that successful person/job and person/organization matches will be made. Accomplishment of this end result will require multiple plans, decisions, and activities, ranging from recruitment methods to use, communication with potential applicants with a special recruitment message, recruitment media, types of selection tools, deciding which applicants will receive job offers, and job offer packages. Both staffing experts and the hiring manager will be involved in these core staffing activities. Moreover, it is likely that the activities will have to be developed and tailor-made for each type of job.

Consider the job of computer programmer in our software development example. It will be necessary to decide and develop specific plans for such issues as: Will we recruit only online, or will we use other methods such as newspaper ads or job fairs (recruitment methods)? What exactly will we tell applicants about the job and our company (recruitment message) and how will we deliver the message, such as on our Web site or a recruitment brochure (recruitment media)? What specific selection tools, such as interviews, assessments of experience, work samples, and background checks, will we use to assess and evaluate the applicants' KSAOs (selection techniques)? How will we combine and evaluate all of the information we gather on applicants with these selection tools and then decide which applicants will receive job offers (decision making)? What exactly will we put in the job offer, and will we be willing to negotiate on the offer (employment)?

Staffing and Retention System Management The various support and core staffing activities are quite complex, and they must be guided, coordinated, controlled, and evaluated. Such is the role of staffing system management. In our new product development example, what will be the role of the HR department, and what types of people will it need to develop and manage the new staffing systems (administration of staffing systems)? How will we evaluate the results of these systems—will we collect and look at cost-per-hire and time-to-hire data (evaluation of staffing systems)? Data such as these are key effective indicators that both general and staffing managers are attuned to.

Finally, voluntary employee departure from the organization is usually costly and disruptive, and it can involve the loss of critical talent that is difficult to replace. Discharges too can be disruptive. Unless the organization is downsizing, however, replacements must be found in order to maintain desired staffing levels. The burden for such replacement staffing can be substantial, particularly when the turnover was unanticipated and unplanned. Other things being equal, greater employee retention means less staffing, so effective retention programs complement staffing programs.

In our software development organization example, the primary focus will likely be on "staffing up" in order to keep producing existing products and developing new ones. Unless attention is also paid to employee retention, however, maintaining adequate staffing levels and quality may become problematic. Hence, the organization will need to monitor the amount and quality of employees who are leaving and the reasons they are leaving in order to learn how much of the turnover is voluntary and avoidable; monitoring discharges will also be necessary. Based on these data, specific and tailor-made retention strategies and programs to better meet employees' needs can be developed. If these are effective, strains on the staffing system will be lessened. The remainder of the book is structured around and built on the staffing organizations model shown in Exhibit 1.6.

STAFFING STRATEGY

As noted, staffing strategy requires making key decisions about the acquisition, deployment, and retention of the organization's workforce. Thirteen such decisions are identified and discussed below. Some decisions pertain primarily to staffing levels and others primarily to staffing quality. A summary of the decisions is shown in Exhibit 1.7. While each decision is shown as an "either-or" one, each is more appropriately thought of as lying on a continuum anchored at either end by these either-or extremes. When discussing the decisions, continued reference is made to the software development organization involved in developing personal finance software.

Staffing Levels

Acquire or Develop Talent To fulfill its staffing needs, a pure acquisition staffing strategy would have an organization concentrate on acquiring new employees who can hit the ground running and be at peak performance the moment they arrive. These employees would bring their talents with them to the job, with little or no need for training or development. A pure development strategy would lead to acquisition of just about anyone, as long as they were willing and able to learn the KSAOs required by the job. Staffing strategy must position the organization appropriately along this "buy-or-make-your-talent" continuum. For critical positions and newly created ones, such as might occur in the software company example, the emphasis would likely be on acquiring talent because of the urgency of developing new products. There may be no time to train, nor may qualified internal candidates be available.

Lag or Lead System The organization's staffing systems may develop in response to organization and HR strategy (lag system), or staffing considerations may serve as key inputs to organization and HR strategy (lead system). With staffing as a lag system, strategic organization objectives and plans are developed first, and staffing systems are then developed to deliver the numbers and types of employees needed. Using staffing as a lead system involves the acquisition of people and their accompanying skills without a formal blueprint for how many are needed or when. Such people are acquired to come into the organization and make things happen, so organization strategy becomes a reflection of newly acquired employees' talents and ideas. In the software organization illustration, it may decide to use a lead system approach to "staff up" on good programmers whenever they can be found, regardless of whether specific, defined jobs exist for them at the moment.

EXHIBIT 1.7 Strategic Staffing Decisions

Staffing Levels	Staffing Quality
• Acquire or Develop Talent	• Person/Job or Person/Organization Match
• Lag or Lead System	• Specific or General KSAOs
• External or Internal Hiring	• Exceptional or Acceptable Workforce Quality
• Core or Flexible Workforce	• Active or Passive Diversity
• Hire or Retain	
• National or Global	
• Attract or Relocate	
• Overstaff or Understaff	
• Hire or Acquire	

External or Internal Hiring When job vacancies occur or new jobs are created, should the organization seek to fill them from the external or internal labour market? While some mixture of external and internal hiring will be necessary in most situations, the relative blend could vary substantially. To the extent that the organization wants to cultivate a stable, committed workforce, it will probably need to emphasize internal hiring. This will allow employees to use the internal labour market as a springboard for launching long-term careers within the organization. External hiring might then be restricted to specific entry-level jobs, as well as newly created ones for which there are no acceptable internal applicants. External hiring might also be necessary when there is rapid organization growth, such that the number of new jobs created outstrips internal supply.

Core or Flexible Workforce The organization's core workforce is made up of individuals who are viewed (and view themselves) as regular employees of the organization, either full-time or part-time. They are central to the core goods and services delivered by the organization.

The flexible workforce is composed of more peripheral workers who are used on an as-needed, just-in-time basis. They are not viewed (nor do they view themselves) as "regular," and legally, most of them are not even employees of the organization. Rather, they are employees of an alternative organization, such as a staffing firm (temporary help agency) or independent contractor that provides these workers to the organization. Strategically, the organization must decide whether it wishes to use both core and flexible workforces, what the mixture of core versus flexible workers will be, and in what jobs and units of the organization these mixtures will be deployed. Within the software development organization, programmers might be considered as part of its core workforce, but ancillary workers (e.g., clerical) may be part of the flexible workforce, particularly since the need for them will depend on the speed and success of new product development.

Hire or Retain There are trade-offs between hiring and retention strategies for staffing. At one extreme the organization can accept whatever level of turnover occurs and simply hire replacements to fill the vacancies. Alternatively, the organization can seek to minimize turnover so that the need for replacement staffing is held to a minimum. Since both strategies have costs and benefits associated with them, the organization could conduct analysis to determine these and then strive for an optimal mix of hiring and retention. In this way the organization could control its inflow needs (replacement staffing) by controlling its outflow (retention).

National or Global An organization can choose to staff itself with people from within its borders, or it can supplement or replace such recruitment with employees recruited from other countries. As trading restrictions and immigration barriers are lessened, global staffing becomes a more distinct possibility.[19] The organization may seek to overcome quantity or quality labour shortages, or excessive labour costs, by staffing with foreign workers. The software development organization might seek some technology employees from India, for example, because of the large number of technology workers being trained in that country. Or it might outsource some of its jobs to a technology organization in India, where wages are substantially lower than in Canada.

Attract or Relocate Typical staffing strategy is based on the premise that the organization can induce sufficient numbers of qualified people to come to it for employment. Another version of this premise is that it is better (and cheaper) to bring labour to the organization than to bring the organization to labour. Some organizations, both established and new ones, challenge this premise and decide to go to locations where there are ample labour supplies. For example, the growth of high technology pockets such as in Ottawa reflects establishment or movement of organizations to geographic areas where there is ready access to highly skilled labour and where employees would like to live, usually locations with research universities nearby to provide the needed graduates for jobs. The software development organization may find locating in such an area very desirable.[20]

Overstaff or Understaff While most organizations seek to be reasonably fully staffed, some opt for or are forced away from this posture to being over- or understaffed. Overstaffing may occur when there are dips in demand for the organization's products or services that the organization chooses to "ride out." Organizations may also overstaff in order to stockpile talent, recognizing that the staffing spigot cannot be easily turned on or off. Understaffing may occur when the organization is confronted with chronic labour shortages, such as is the case for nurses in health care facilities. Also, prediction of an economic downturn may lead the organization to understaff in order to avoid future layoffs. Finally, the organization may decide to understaff and adjust staffing level demand spikes by increasing employee overtime or using flexible staffing arrangement such as temporary employees. The software development organization might choose to overstaff in order to retain key employees and to be poised to meet the hopeful surges in demand as its new products are released.

Hire or Acquire Rather than hire new talent through normal staffing systems, it might be possible to acquire it en masse through a merger or an acquisition.[21] This acquisition strategy has the potential to quickly deliver large numbers of qualified people, allowing the organization to grow through new or better projects and business units. The downsides to such a strategy are numerous. Staffing costs are greater since the acquired employees may have to be provided special compensation incentives to join the organization. Care will be required during the pre-deal and due diligence stages of the merger or acquisition to ensure accurate KSAO assessments of the to-be-acquired employees. Finally, retention will become an issue, with some individuals refusing to join, some being laid off, and others leaving soon after the acquisition, due to a poor person/job or person/organization fit. Seeking a merger or acquisition for staffing purposes would likely not happen with our software development company, at least in its early growth stages.

Staffing Quality

Person/Job or Person/Organization Match When acquiring and deploying people, should the organization opt for a person/job or person/organization match? This is a complex decision. In part a person/job match will have to be assessed any time a person is being hired to perform a finite set of tasks. In our software development example, programmers might be hired to do programming in a specific language such as Java, and most certainly the organization would want to assess whether applicants meet this specific job requirement. On the other hand, jobs may be poorly defined and fluid, making a person/job match unfeasible and requiring a person/organization match instead. Such jobs are often found in technology and software development organizations.

Specific or General KSAOs Should the organization acquire people with specific KSAOs or more general ones? The former means focusing on job-specific competencies, often of the job knowledge and technical skill variety. The latter requires a focus on KSAOs that will be applicable across a variety of jobs, both current and future. Examples of such KSAOs include flexibility and adaptability, ability to learn, written and oral communication skills, and algebra/statistics skills. An organization expecting rapid changes in job content and new job creation, such as in the software development example, might position itself closer to the general competencies end of the continuum.

Exceptional or Acceptable Workforce Quality Strategically, the organization could seek to acquire a workforce that was preeminent KSAO-wise (exceptional quality) or one that was a more "ballpark" variety KSAO-wise (acceptable quality). Pursuit of the exceptional strategy would allow the organization to stock up on the best and the brightest with the hope that this exceptional talent pool would deliver truly superior performance. The acceptable strategy means pursuit of a less high-powered workforce and probably a less expensive one as well. For the software development organization, if it is trying to create clearly innovative and superior products, it will likely opt for the exceptional workforce quality end of the continuum.

Active or Passive Diversity The labour force is becoming increasingly diverse in terms of demographics, values, and languages. Does the organization want to actively pursue this diversity in the labour market so that its own workforce mirrors it, or does the organization want to more passively let diversity of its workforce happen to it? Advocates of an active diversity strategy argue that it is not only legally and morally appropriate but also that a diverse workforce allows the organization to be more attuned to the diverse needs of the customers it serves. Those favouring a more passive strategy suggest that diversification of the workforce takes time because it requires substantial planning and assimilation activity. In the software development illustration, an active diversity strategy might be pursued as a way of acquiring workers who can help identify a diverse array of software products that might be received favourably by various segments of the marketplace.

STAFFING ETHICS

Staffing the organization involves a multitude of individuals—hiring managers, staffing professionals, potential co-workers, legal advisors, and job applicants. During the staffing process all of these individuals may be involved in recruitment, selection, and employment activities, as well as staffing decision making. Are there, or should there be, boundaries on these individuals' actions and decisions? The answer is yes, for without boundaries potentially negative outcomes and harmful effects may occur. For example, many times staffing is a hurried process, driven by tight deadlines and calls for expediency (e.g., the hiring manager who says to the staffing professional, "Just get me someone now—I'll worry about how good they are later on."). Such calls may lead to negative consequences, including the following actions and outcomes that can raise staffing ethics issues:

- Hiring someone quickly without proper assessment and having them subsequently perform poorly
- Ignoring many applicants who would have been successful performers
- Failing to advance the organization's workforce diversity initiatives and possible legal obligations
- Making an exceedingly generous job offer that provides the highest salary in the work unit, causing dissatisfaction and possible turnover among other work unit members

Ethics involves determining moral principles and guidelines for acceptable practice. Within the realm of the workplace, ethics emphasizes "knowing organizational codes and guidelines and behaving within these boundaries when faced with dilemmas in business or professional work."[22] More specifically, organizational ethics seek to:

- Raise ethical expectations
- Legitimize dialogue about ethical issues
- Encourage ethical decision making, and
- Prevent misconduct and provide a basis for enforcement

While organizations are increasingly developing general codes of conduct, it is unknown whether these codes contain specific staffing provisions. Even the general code will likely have some pertinence to staffing through provisions on such issues as legal compliance, confidentiality and disclosure of information, and use of organizational property and assets. Individuals involved in staffing should know and follow their organization's code of ethics. As pertains to staffing specifically, there are several points that can serve as a person's guide to ethical conduct. These points are shown in Exhibit 1.8 and elaborated on below.

It should be recognized that many pressure points on HR professionals may cause them to compromise the ethical standards discussed above. Research suggests that the principal causes of this pressure are the felt need to follow a boss's directive, meet overly aggressive business objectives, help the organization survive, meet scheduling pressures, be a team player, save jobs, and advance the boss's career.[23]

The suggestions for ethical staffing practice in Exhibit 1.8 are guides to one's own behaviour. Being aware of and consciously attempting to follow these constitutes a professional and ethical responsibility. But what about situations in which ethical lapses are suspected or observed in others?

One response to the situation is to do nothing—not report or attempt to change the misconduct. Research suggests a small proportion (about 20 percent) choose to ignore and not report misconduct.[24] Major reasons for this response include a belief that no action would be taken, a fear of retaliation from one's boss or senior management, not trusting promises of confidentiality, and a fear of not being seen as a team player. Against such reasons for inaction must be weighed the harm that has, or could, come to the employer, employee, or job applicant. Moreover, failure to report the misconduct may well increase the chances that it will be repeated, with continuing

EXHIBIT 1.8 Suggestions for Ethical Staffing Practice

1. **Represent the organization's interests:** Serve as an agent of the organization and remain duty bound to represent the organization first and foremost. This duty brings into being effective person/job and person/organization matches.
2. **Beware of conflicts of interest:** Avoid placing personal interest, or that of a third party (such as an applicant or friend) above that of the organization.
3. **Remember the job applicant:** Even though the HR professional represents the organization, remember that the applicant is a participant in the staffing process. The type of treatment provided to applicants may well lead to reactions by them that are favourable to the organization and further its interests, let alone those of the applicants.
4. **Follow staffing policies and procedures:** Know the organization's staffing policies and procedures and adhere to them.
5. **Know and follow the law:** Be knowledgeable of the myriad laws and regulations governing staffing, follow them, and seek needed assistance in their interpretation and application.
6. **Consult professional codes of conduct:** Seek out professional codes of conduct that pertain to staffing and human resources. The Canadian Council of Human Resource Associations (CCHRA) has a formal code of ethics (www.chrpcanada.com). The Canadian Society for Industrial and Organization Psychology follows the policy statements of the Canadian Psychological Association, which governs the ethical principles followed by its members (www.cpa.ca).
7. **Shape effective practice with research results:** Take advantage of useful research-based knowledge about the design and effectiveness of staffing systems and techniques to guide staffing practice. Much of that research is summarized in usable formats in this book.
8. **Seek ethics advice:** When confronted with ethical issues, it is appropriate to seek ethical advice from others. Handling troubling ethical issues alone is unwise.

harmful consequences. Not reporting misconduct may also conflict with one's personal values and create remorse for not having done the "right thing." Finally, a failure to report misconduct may bring penalties to oneself if that failure subsequently becomes known to one's boss or senior management. In short, "looking the other way" should not be viewed as a safe, wise, or ethical choice.

A different way to handle unethical staffing practices by others is to seek advice from one's boss, senior management, co-workers, legal counsel, ethics officer or ombudsperson, or an outside friend or family member. The guidelines in Exhibit 1.8 serve as a helpful starting point to frame the discussion and make a decision about what to do.

At times, the appropriate response to others' misconduct is to step in directly to try to prevent or rectify the misconduct. This would be especially appropriate with employees that one supervises or with co-workers. Before taking such an action, it would be wise to consider whether one has the authority and resources to do so, along with the likely support of those other employees or co-workers.

PLAN FOR THE BOOK

The book is divided into five parts:

1. The Nature of Staffing
2. Support Activities
3. Staffing Activities: Recruitment
4. Staffing Activities: Selection
5. Staffing System and Retention Management

Following the "meat" of each chapter in these parts, additional material is provided to supplement the chapter's contents. A selection of relevant Web sites, for further research, is followed by a chapter summary, which reviews and highlights points from the chapter. A set of discussion questions, ethical issues to discuss, applications (cases and exercises), the Tanglewood Stores case (in some chapters), and detailed endnotes complete the chapter.

The importance of laws and regulations is such that they are considered first in Chapter 2 (legal compliance). The laws and regulations, in particular, have become so pervasive that they require special treatment. To do this, Chapter 2 reviews the basic laws affecting staffing, with an emphasis on the major federal laws and regulations pertaining to human rights matters generally. Specific provisions relevant to staffing are covered in depth. Each subsequent chapter then has a separate section at its end labelled "Legal Issues" in which specific legal topics relevant to the chapter's content are discussed. This allows for a more focused discussion of legal issues while not diverting attention from the major thrust of the book.

The endnotes at the end of each chapter are quite extensive. They are drawn from academic, practitioner, and legal sources with the goal of providing a balanced selection of references from each of these sources. Emphasis is on inclusion of recent references of high quality and easy accessibility. Too lengthy a list of references to each specific topic is avoided; instead, a sampling of only the best available is included.

The applications at the end of each chapter are of two varieties. First are cases that describe a particular situation and require analysis and response. The response may be written or oral (such as in class discussion or a group presentation). Second are exercises that entail small projects and require active practice of a particular task. Through these cases and exercises the reader becomes an active participant in the learning process and is able to apply the concepts provided in each chapter.

Interspersed throughout the book at the end of some chapters are instructions for completing assignments for the Tanglewood Stores case. The full case and assignments are located on the following Web site: www.mcgrawhill.ca/OLC/heneman. You will see that Tanglewood Stores is an up-and-coming retailing organization. Tanglewood is in an expansion mode, seeking to aggressively grow beyond the current 243 stores. As Tanglewood pursues expansion, numerous staffing issues arise that require analysis, decisions, and recommendations from you. You will receive assignments in the areas of staffing strategy (Chapter 1), measurement (Chapter 3), external recruitment (Chapter 5), external selection (Chapter 8), decision making (Chapter 10), and retention (Chapter 11).

SUMMARY

Nationally, staffing involves a huge number of hiring transactions each year; is a major cost of doing business, especially for service-providing industries; and can lead to substantial revenue and market value growth for the organization. Staffing is defined as the process of acquiring, deploying, and retaining a workforce of sufficient quantity and quality to create positive impacts on the organization's effectiveness. The definition emphasizes that both staffing levels and labour quality contribute to an organization's effectiveness, and that a concerted set of labour acquisition, deployment, and retention actions guide the flow of people into, within, and out of the organization. Descriptions of three staffing systems help highlight the definition of staffing.

Several models illustrate various elements of staffing. The staffing level model shows how projected labour requirements and availabilities are compared to derive staffing levels that represent being overstaffed, fully staffed, or understaffed. The next two models illustrate staffing quality via the person/job and person/organization match. The former indicates there is a need to match (1) the person's KSAOs to job requirements and (2) the person's motivation to the job's rewards. In the person/organization match, the person's characteristics are matched to additional factors beyond the target job, namely, organizational values, new job duties for the target job, multiple jobs, and future jobs. Managing the matching process effectively results in positive impacts on HR outcomes such as attraction, performance, and retention. The core staffing components model shows that there are three basic activities in staffing. Those activities and their fundamental purposes are recruitment (identification and attraction of applicants), selection (assessment and evaluation of applicants), and employment (decision making and final match). The staffing organizations model shows that organization, HR, and staffing strategies are formulated and shape staffing policies and programs. In turn, these meld into a set of staffing support activities (legal compliance, measurement, and job analysis), as well as the core activities (recruitment, selection, and employment). Retention and staffing system management activities cut across both support and core activities.

Staffing strategy is both an outgrowth of and contributor to HR and organization strategy. Thirteen important strategic staffing decisions loom for any organization. Some pertain to staffing level choices, and others deal with staffing quality choices.

Staffing ethics involves determining moral principles and guidelines for practice. Numerous suggestions were made for ethical conduct in staffing, and many pressure points for sidestepping such conduct are in operation. There are some appropriate ways for handling such pressures.

The staffing organizations model serves as the structural framework for the book. The first part treats staffing models and strategy. The second part treats the support activities of legal compliance, measurement, and job analysis. The next three parts treat the core staffing activities of recruitment, selection, and employment.

The last section addresses staffing systems and employee retention management. Each chapter has a separate section labelled "Legal Issues," as well as discussion questions, ethical issues questions, applications, the Tanglewood Stores case (in some chapters), and endnotes (references).

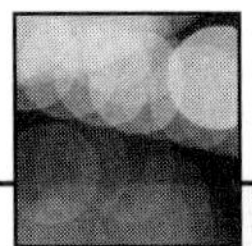

KEY TERMS

acquisition activities 5
deployment 5
human capital 3
job requirement 10
KSAOs 9
matching process 10
person/job match 9
quality 5
quantity 5
retention systems 5
self-selection 13
staffing 4

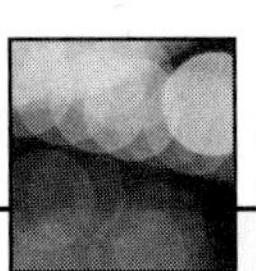

DISCUSSION QUESTIONS

1. What would be potential problems with having a staffing process in which vacancies were filled (1) on a lottery basis from among job applicants, or (2) on a first come–first hired basis among job applicants?
2. Why is it important for the organization to view all components of staffing (recruitment, selection, employment) from the perspective of the job applicant?
3. Would it be desirable to hire people only according to the person/organization match, ignoring the person/job match?
4. What are examples of how staffing activities are influenced by training activities? Compensation activities?
5. Are some of the 13 strategic staffing decisions more important than others? Which ones? Why?

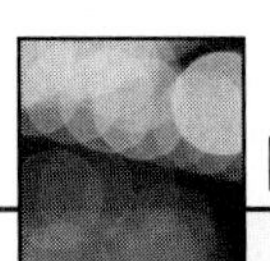

ETHICAL ISSUES

1. As a staffing professional in the department or as the hiring manager of a work unit, explain why it is so important to represent the organization's interests (see Exhibit 1.8). What are some possible consequences of not doing so?
2. One of the strategic staffing choices is whether to pursue workforce diversity actively or passively. First suggest some ethical reasons for active pursuit of diversity, and then suggest some ethical reasons for a more passive approach. Assume that the type of diversity in question is increasing workforce representation of women and visible minorities.

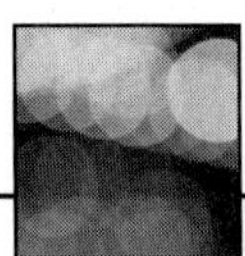

APPLICATIONS

Staffing for Your Own Job

Instructions

Consider a job you previously held or your current job. Use the staffing components model to help you think through and describe the staffing process that led to your getting hired for the job. Trace and describe the process (1) from your own perspective as a job applicant, and (2) from the organization's perspective. Listed below are some questions to jog your memory. Write your responses to these questions and be prepared to discuss them.

Applicant Perspective

Recruitment:

1. Why did you identify and seek out the job with this organization?
2. How did you try to make yourself attractive to the organization?

Selection:

1. How did you gather information about the job's requirements and rewards?
2. How did you judge your own KSAOs and needs relative to these requirements and rewards?

Employment:

1. Why did you decide to continue on in the staffing process, rather than drop out of it?
2. Why did you decide to accept the job offer? What were the pluses and minuses of the job?

Organization Perspective

Even if you do not know, or are unsure of, the answers to these questions, try to answer them or guess at them.

Recruitment:

1. How did the organization identify you as a job applicant?
2. How did the organization make the job attractive to you?

Selection:

1. What techniques (application blank, interview, etc.) did the organization use to gather KSAO information about you?
2. How did the organization evaluate this information? What did it see as your strong and weak points, KSAO-wise?

Employment:

1. Why did the organization decide to continue pursuing you as an applicant, rather than reject you from further consideration?
2. What was the job offer process like? Did you receive a verbal or written (or both) offer? Who gave you the offer? What was the content of the offer?

Reactions to the Staffing Process

Now that you have described the staffing process, what are your reactions to it?

1. What were the strong points or positive features of the process?
2. What were the weak points and negative features of the process?
3. What changes would you like to see made in the process, and why?

Staffing Strategy for a New Plant

Household Consumer Enterprises, Inc. (HCE) has its corporate headquarters in downtown Toronto, with manufacturing and warehouse/distribution facilities throughout the central region of Canada. It specializes in the design and production of nondisposable household products such as brooms, brushes, rakes, kitchen utensils, and garden tools. The company has recently changed its mission from "providing households with safe and sturdy utensils" to "providing households with visually appealing utensils that are safe and sturdy." The new emphasis on "visually appealing" will necessitate new strategies for designing and producing new products that have design flair and imagination built into them. One strategy under consideration is to target various demographic groups with different utensil designs. One group is 25- to 40-year-old professional and managerial people, who it is thought would want such utensils for both their visual and conversation-piece appeal.

A tentative strategy is to build and staff a new plant that will have free rein in the design and production of utensils for this 25- to 40-year-old age group. To start, the plant will focus on producing a set of closely related (designwise) plastic products: dishwashing pans, outdoor wastebaskets, outdoor plant holders, and watering cans. These items can be produced without too large a capital and facilities investment, can be marketed as a group, and can be on stores' shelves and on HCE's store Web site in time for Christmas sales.

The facility's design and engineering team has initially decided that each of the four products will be produced on a separate assembly line, though the lines will share common technology and require roughly similar assembly jobs. Based on advice from the HR vice president, Jarimir Zwitski, it is decided the key jobs in the plant for staffing purposes will be plant manager, product designer (computer-assisted design), assemblers, and packers/warehouse workers. The initial staffing level for the plant will be 150 employees. Because of the riskiness of the venture and the low margins that are planned initially on the four products due to high start-up costs, the plant will be run on a continuous basis six days per week (i.e., a 24/6 schedule), with the remaining day reserved for cleaning and maintenance. It is planned for pay levels to be at the low end of the market, except for product designers, who will be paid above market. There will be limited benefits for all employees, namely, health insurance with a 30 percent employee copay after one year of continuous employment, no pension plan, and an earned time-off bank (for holidays, sickness, and vacation) of 160 hours per year.

The head of the design team, Maria Dos Santos, and Mr. Zwitski wish to come to you, the corporate manager of staffing, to share their preliminary thinking with you and ask you some questions, knowing that staffing issues loom large for this new venture. They ask you to discuss the following questions with them and send them to you in advance so you can prepare for the meeting. Your task is to write out a tentative response to each question that will be the basis for your discussion at the meeting. The questions are:

1. What geographic location might be best for the plant in terms of attracting sufficient quantity and quality of labour, especially for the key jobs?
2. Should the plant manager come from inside the current managerial ranks or be sought from the outside?
3. Should staffing be based on just the person/job match or also the person/organization match?
4. Would it make sense to staff the plant initially with a flexible workforce by using temporary employees and then shift over to a core workforce if it looks like the plant will be successful?
5. In the early stages, should the plant be fully staffed, understaffed, or overstaffed?
6. Will employee retention likely be a problem, and if so, how would this affect the viability of the new plant?

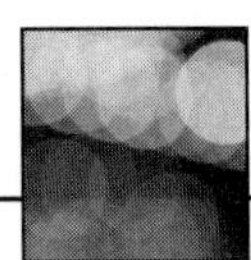

TANGLEWOOD STORES CASE

In this chapter you read about the relationship between organizational strategy and organizational staffing practices. The introductory section of the casebook will give you an opportunity to see how these principles are put into practice. The goal of this section is to help you learn more about how competition, strategy, and culture jointly inform the effective development of staffing strategy.

The Situation

The case involves a series of staffing exercises related to the Tanglewood department stores. You will act as an external consultant for the organization's staffing services department. Tanglewood department stores is a chain of general retail stores with an "outdoors" theme, including a large camping and outdoor living section in every store. The organization's culture is based on a set of core values that includes employee participation and a commitment to being a positive place to work. The context section provides additional details regarding Tanglewood's industry, core jobs, market niche, and other strategic concerns.

Your Tasks

For each of the issues related to strategic staffing levels and staffing quality in Exhibit 1.7, make a statement regarding where Tanglewood should position itself. For example, the first decision is to develop or acquire talent. To what extent should Tanglewood follow either strategy and why? Repeat this process for each of the staffing level and staffing quality dimensions. The background information for this case, and your specific assignment, can be found at www.mcgrawhill.ca/OLC/heneman.

ENDNOTES

1. J. Fitz-enz, *The ROI of Human Capital* (New York: Amacom, 2000), pp. 6–7.
2. "Labour Force Survey," Statistics Canada, December 2, 2005, www.statcan.ca/english/Subjects/Labour/LFS/lfs-en.htm.
3. "Population of businesses with employees," Statistics Canada, *The Daily,* August 22, 2005, www.statcan.ca/Daily/English/050822/d050822b.htm.
4. "Key Small Business Statistics," Industry Canada publication, January 2005, p. 6.
5. Saratoga Institute, *2000 Human Capital Benchmarking Report* (Santa Clara, CA: author, 2000), p. 73.
6. Fitz-enz, *The ROI of Human Capital,* pp. 30–38.
7. R. Langlois, "Carolyn Clark: Business strategy starts with people," *CHRR, Guide to Strategic HR,* November 5, 2001.
8. M. Neglia, "It takes talent to find talent," *Canadian HR Reporter,* December 6, 2004, p. 3.
9. G. Anders, "Taming the Out-of-Control In-box," *Wall Street Journal,* February 4, 2000, p. 81.
10. "The definitive guide to managing human resources for small business owners," *Magazine for Canadian Entrepreneurs,* October 1998, 17(5), p. insert 1–83.
11. S. Singh, "Globalization puts focus on HR," *Canadian HR Reporter,* June 6, 2005, p. 1.
12. J. B. Barney and P. M. Wright, "On Becoming a Strategic Partner: The Role of Human Resources in Gaining Competitive Advantage," *Human Resource Management,* 1998, 37(1), pp. 31–46; C. G. Brush, P. G. Greene, and M. M. Hart, "From Initial Idea to Unique Advantage: The Entrepreneurial Challenge of Constructing a Resource Base," *Academy of Management Executive,* 2001, 15(1), pp. 64–80.
13. J. S. Lublin, "An E-Company CEO Is Also Recruiter-in-Chief," *Wall Street Journal,* November 9, 1999, p. B1.
14. D. Brown, "Fit more important than skills," *Canadian HR Reporter,* July 14, 2003, p. 17.

15. A. R. McIlvaine, "Retooling HR," *Human Resource Executive*, October 2, 2003, pp. 18–24.
16. N. Byrnes, "Avon Calling—Lots of Reps," *Business Week*, June 2, 2003, pp. 53–54.
17. D. F. Caldwell and C. A. O'Reilly III, "Measuring Person-Job Fit with a Profile-Comparison Process," *Journal of Applied Psychology*, 1990, 75, pp. 648–657; R. V. Dawis, "Person-Environment Fit and Job Satisfaction," in C. J. Cranny, P. C. Smith, and E. F. Stone, *Job Satisfaction* (New York: Lexington, 1992), pp. 69–88; R. V. Dawis, L. H. Lofquist, and D. J. Weiss, *A Theory of Work Adjustment* (A Revision) (Minneapolis: Industrial Relations Center, University of Minnesota, 1968).
18. D. E. Bowen, G. E. Ledford, Jr., and B. R. Nathan, "Hiring for the Organization and Not the Job," *Academy of Management Executive*, 1991, 5(4), pp. 35–51; T. A. Judge and R. D. Bretz, Jr., "Effects of Work Values on Job Choice Decisions," *Journal of Applied Psychology*, 1992, 77, pp. 1–11; C. A. O'Reilly III, J. Chatman, and D. F. Caldwell, "People and Organizational Culture: A Profile Comparison Approach to Assessing Person-Organization Fit," *Academy of Management Journal*, 1991, 34, pp. 487–516. A. L. Kristof, "Person-Organization Fit: An Intergrative Review of its Conceptualizations, Measurement, and Implications," *Personnel Psychology*, 1996, 49, pp. 1–50.
19. Society for Human Resource Management, "The Labor Shortage," *Workplace Visions*, 2000; Society for Human Resource Management, "Globalization and the HR Profession," *Workplace Visions*, 2000.
20. C. Turner, "The Morphing of Ottawa," *Time Canada*, March 12, 2001, pp. 1–7.
21. M. L. Marke and P. H. Mirvis, "Making Mergers and Acquisitions Work," *Academy of Management Executive*, 2001, 15(2), pp. 80–94; J. A. Schmidt (ed.), *Making Mergers Work: The Strategic Importance of People* (Alexandria, VA: Society for Human Resource Management, 2001); E. R. Silverman, "Supply for Demand," *Human Resource Executive*, May 15, 2000, pp. 76–77.
22. www.shrm.org/research, Nov. 6, 2004.
23. J. Joseph and E. Esen, *2003 Business Ethics Survey* (Alexandria, VA: Society for Human Resource Management, 2003), pp. 1–10.
24. Joseph and Esen, *2003 Business Ethics Survey*, pp. 10–11.

Online LearningCentre

Visit the Online Learning Centre at
www.mcgrawhill.ca/olc/heneman

PART 2

Support Activities

The Staffing Organizations Model

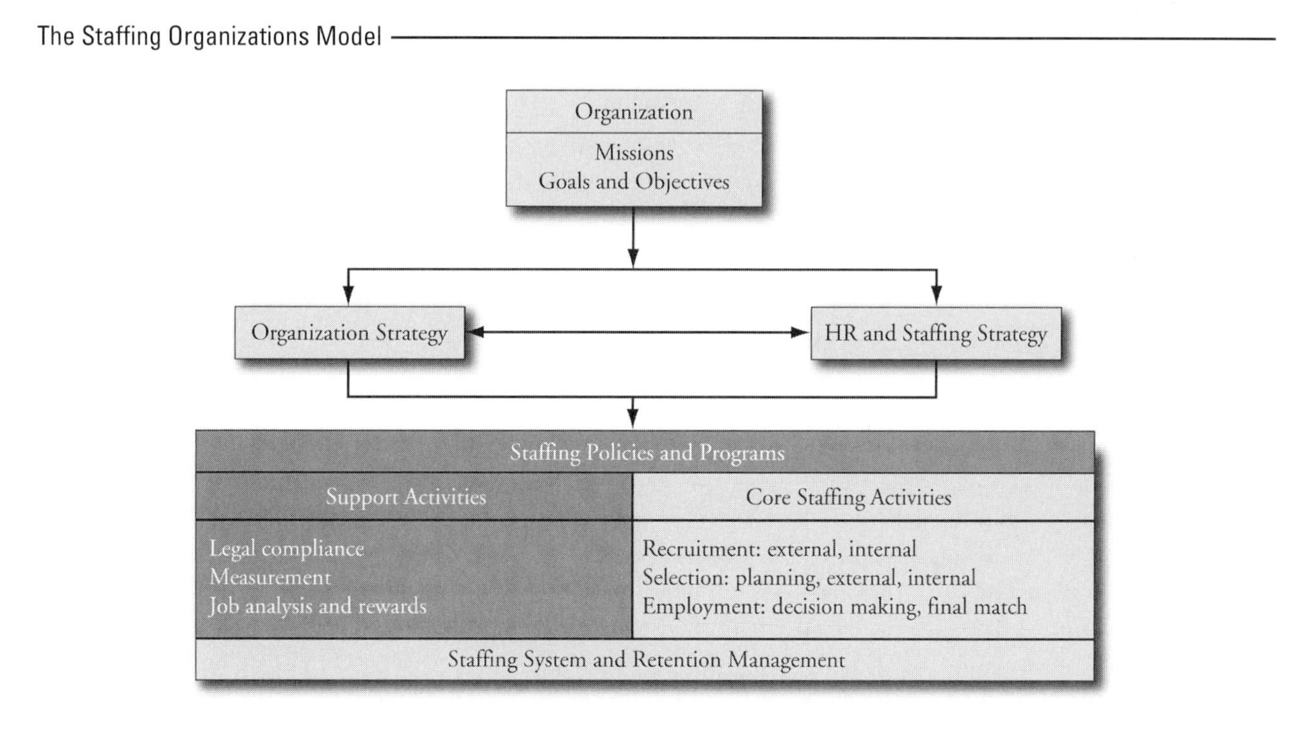

CHAPTER 2

LEGAL COMPLIANCE

LEARNING OBJECTIVES

After reading this chapter, you will be able to:

- Explain the legal implications of the employment relationship between employer-employee, employer-independent contractor, and employer-temporary employee
- Identify the laws and regulations that have an impact on and place constraints on the employment relationship
- Discuss the influence human rights and employment equity legislation have on staffing decisions
- Describe the other laws and regulations that have major impacts on staffing activities
- Use the chapter as a guide to develop staffing practices that are permissible and required

Laws and regulations have assumed an importance of major proportions in the process of staffing organizations. Virtually all aspects of staffing are subject to their influence. No organization can or should ignore provisions of the law; in this case, ignorance truly is not bliss. Every recruitment and selection decision pivots on aspects related to one or more laws discussed in this chapter. Comprehensive understanding of the Canadian legal landscape is a vital competency that staffing specialists need to develop to mitigate financial risk, negative publicity, and poor internal morale.

This chapter begins by discussing the formation of the employment relationships from a legal perspective. It first defines what an employer is, along with the rights and obligations of being an employer. The employer may acquire people to work for it in the form of employees, independent contractors, and temporary employees. Legal meanings and implications for each of these terms is provided.

For many reasons, the employment relationship has become increasingly regulated. Reasons for the myriad laws and regulations affecting the employment relationship and the major sources of laws and regulations controlling the employment relationship are discussed in-depth.

Equal employment opportunity and human rights laws and regulations have become paramount in the eyes of many who are concerned with staffing organizations. The general provisions of the Canadian human rights laws are summarized, along with information on how these laws

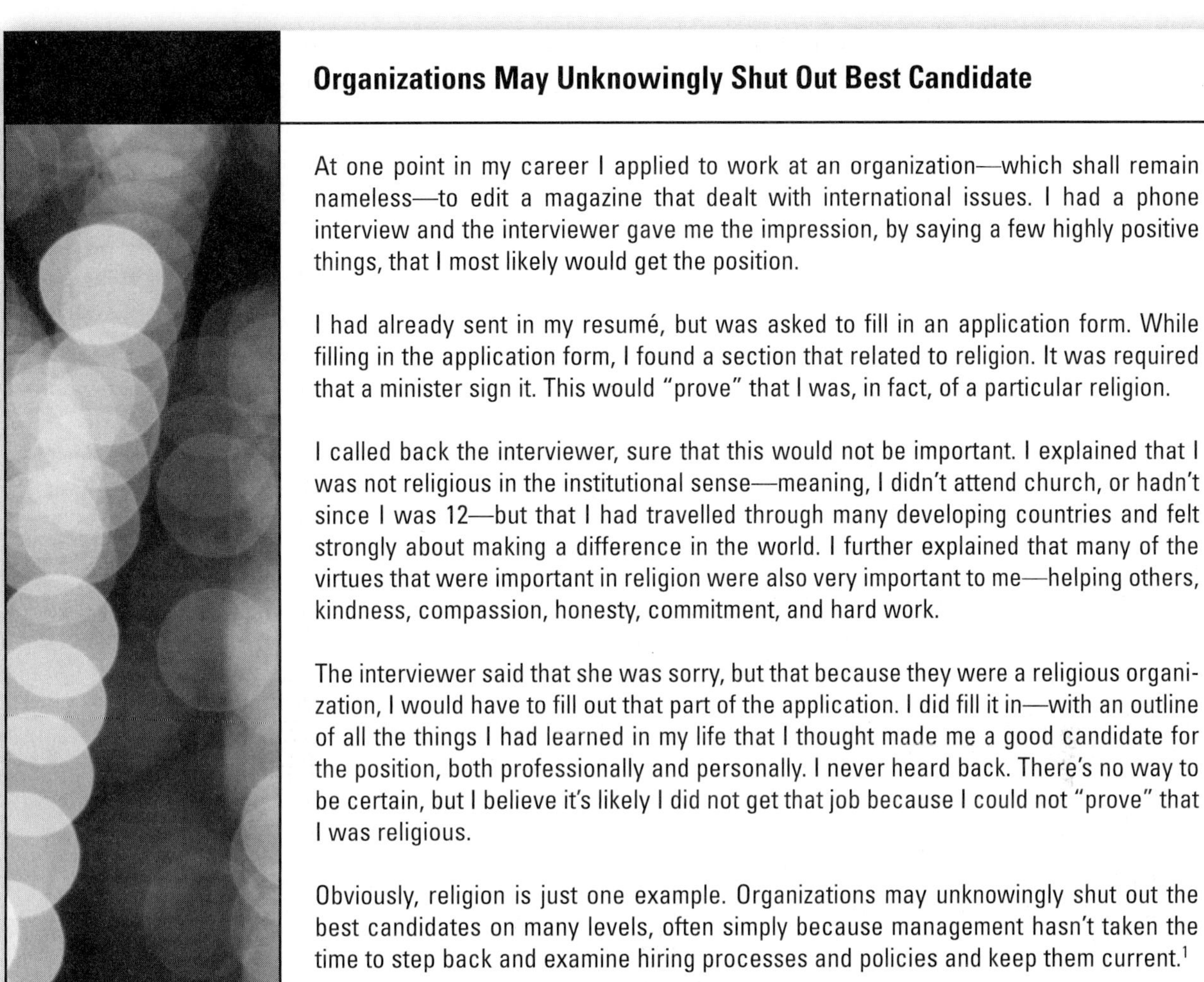

Organizations May Unknowingly Shut Out Best Candidate

At one point in my career I applied to work at an organization—which shall remain nameless—to edit a magazine that dealt with international issues. I had a phone interview and the interviewer gave me the impression, by saying a few highly positive things, that I most likely would get the position.

I had already sent in my resumé, but was asked to fill in an application form. While filling in the application form, I found a section that related to religion. It was required that a minister sign it. This would "prove" that I was, in fact, of a particular religion.

I called back the interviewer, sure that this would not be important. I explained that I was not religious in the institutional sense—meaning, I didn't attend church, or hadn't since I was 12—but that I had travelled through many developing countries and felt strongly about making a difference in the world. I further explained that many of the virtues that were important in religion were also very important to me—helping others, kindness, compassion, honesty, commitment, and hard work.

The interviewer said that she was sorry, but that because they were a religious organization, I would have to fill out that part of the application. I did fill it in—with an outline of all the things I had learned in my life that I thought made me a good candidate for the position, both professionally and personally. I never heard back. There's no way to be certain, but I believe it's likely I did not get that job because I could not "prove" that I was religious.

Obviously, religion is just one example. Organizations may unknowingly shut out the best candidates on many levels, often simply because management hasn't taken the time to step back and examine hiring processes and policies and keep them current.[1]

are administered and enforced. While volunteer compliance is preferred by the Canadian Human Rights Commission, if compliance fails litigation will follow.

For these same human rights laws, their specific (and numerous) provisions regarding staffing are then presented in detail. Within this presentation, the true scope, complexity, and impact of the laws regarding staffing become known.

Numerous information sources about human rights laws and regulations are then presented. Compliance with the various laws and regulations requires comprehensive and integrated human rights programs. Criteria for, and examples of, best practices by organizations in recruiting, hiring, promotion, and career advancement to achieve inclusion objectives are described.

Attention then turns to other staffing laws and regulations. These involve myriad federal laws, provincial and local laws, and public service laws and regulations. These laws, like federal human rights ones, have major impacts on staffing activities.

Finally, the chapter concludes with an indication that each of the chapters that follows has a separate section, "Legal Issues," at the end of it. In these sections, specific topics and applications of the law are presented. Their intent is to provide guidance and examples (not legal advice per se) regarding staffing practices that are permissible, impermissible, and required.

THE EMPLOYMENT RELATIONSHIP

From a legal perspective the term staffing refers to the formation of the employment relationship. That relationship involves several different types of arrangements between the organization and those who provide work for it. These arrangements have special and reasonably separate legal meaning. This section explores those arrangements: employer–employee, independent contractor, and temporary employee.[2]

Employer–Employee

By far the most prevalent form of the employment relationship is that of employer–employee. This arrangement is the result of the organization's usual staffing activities—a culmination of the person/job matching process. As shown in Exhibit 2.1, the employer and employee negotiate and agree on the terms and conditions that will define and govern their relationship. The formal agreement represents an employment contract, the terms and conditions of which represent the promises and expectations of the parties (job requirements and rewards, and KSAOs and motivation). Over time, the initial contract may be modified due to changes in requirements or rewards of the current job, or employee transfer or promotion. The contract may also be terminated by either party, thus ending the employment relationship.

Employment contracts come in a variety of styles. They may be written or oral (both types are legally enforceable), and their specificity may vary from extensive to bare bones. In some instances, where the contract is written, terms and conditions are described in great detail. Examples of such contracts are collective bargaining agreements and contracts for professional athletes, entertainers, and upper-level executives. At the other extreme, the contract may be little more than some simple oral promises about the job, such as promises about wages and hours, agreed to on the basis of a handshake.

EXHIBIT 2.1 Matching Process, Employment Contract, and Employment Relationships

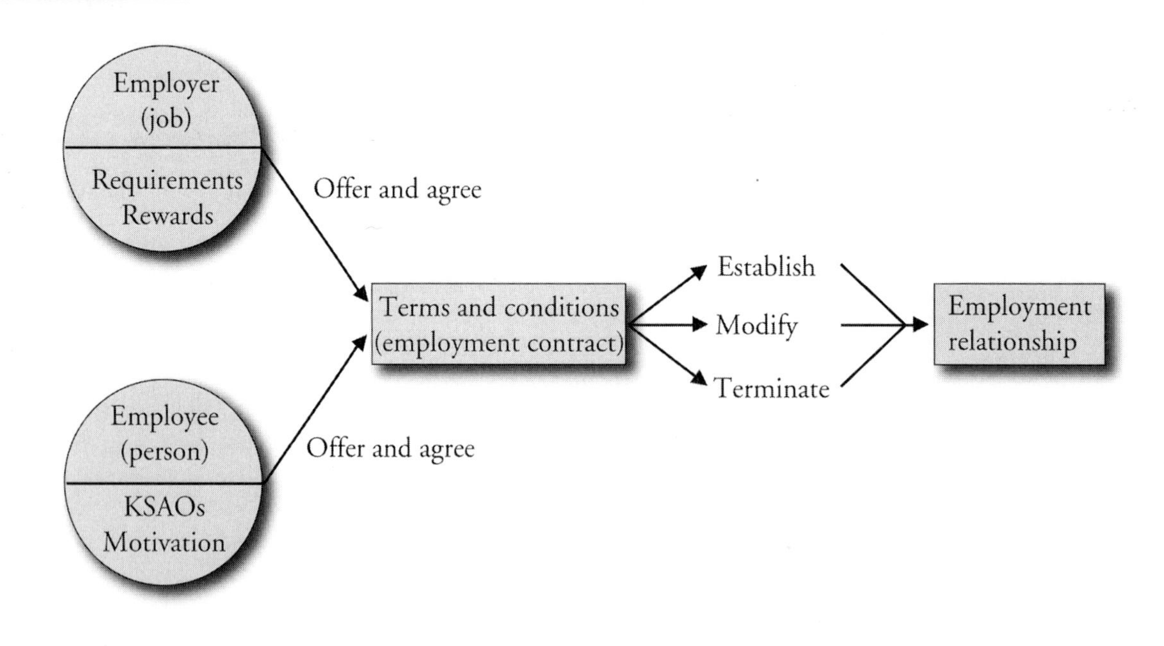

employer
An entity that employs others (employees or independent contractors) to do its work or work on its behalf

From a legal perspective, an **employer** is an entity that employs others (employees or independent contractors) to do its work or work on its behalf. When these "others" are employees, the employer has the right to specify both the work output (results) expected and the work methods to be followed by its employees. In exchange for this right to control employees, the employer incurs certain legal responsibilities and liabilities.

Specifically, the employer is required to:

- Withhold payroll deductions (income tax, Employment Insurance, and Canada Pension Plan)
- Pay taxes (Employment Insurance, Workers' Compensation, and Employer Health Tax)
- Abide by the myriad of laws and regulations governing the employment contract
- Be liable for the acts of its employees during employment

When and how the employment relationship may end is a matter of great importance to the employer and the employee. It is critical for the employer to ensure that proper legal procedures have been followed to reduce the likelihood of the employee successfully pursuing a claim for wrongful dismissal, which can be extremely costly.

Independent Contractors

independent contractor
A person or business who performs services under an expressed or implied contract

Hiring an **independent contractor** is a strategic organizational decision to minimize the highest cost for an employer—compensation and benefits. It gives employers the opportunity to practise "just-in-time" hiring when the flow of work warrants more workers. An independent contractor provides specific task and project assistance to the organization, such as maintenance, bookkeeping, advertising, programming, and consulting. The independent contractor can be a single individual (self-employed, freelancer) or an agency that specializes in hiring contract employees. Neither the independent contractor nor its employees are intended to be employees of the organization utilizing their services, and care should be taken to ensure that the independent contractor is not treated as an employee.

It is recommended that the independent contractor and the employer prepare and enter into a written agreement or contract between them. In general, the agreement should clarify the nature and scope of the project and contain language that reinforces the intent to have the independent contractor perform a specific function that is different from the functions of the organization's employees.

Thus the relationship between the independent contractor and company must be carefully defined to protect both parties. A common test for establishing the employment relationship between a independent contractor and company is the "four-in-one" test, which was summarized in the Federal Court of Appeals decision regarding *Wiebe Door Services Ltd. v. The Minister of National Revenue [1986] 3 F.C. 553* and was confirmed in the Supreme Court of Canada decision regarding *67112 Ontario Ltd. v. Sagaz Industries Canada Inc. [2001] S.C.R. 983.*[3]

The four tests most commonly used to define the contractor/employer relationship are:

1. **Control:** Determine how much control the employer has over the independent contractor related to the extent of the employer's involvement in traditional employee-related activities (e.g., performance management, coaching, disciplinary action, etc.)
2. **Ownership of tools:** Assess whether the tools used in the performance of the service are the property of the independent contractor or the employer
3. **Chance of profit or risk of loss:** Consider any income received by the independent contractor beyond contracted rate of pay to do the job, as well as any costs assumed if the job is not completed correctly
4. **Integration test:** Determine how integral the independent contractor's job is to the employer's overall business performance

EXHIBIT 2.2 Responsibilities in a Temporary Working Arrangement

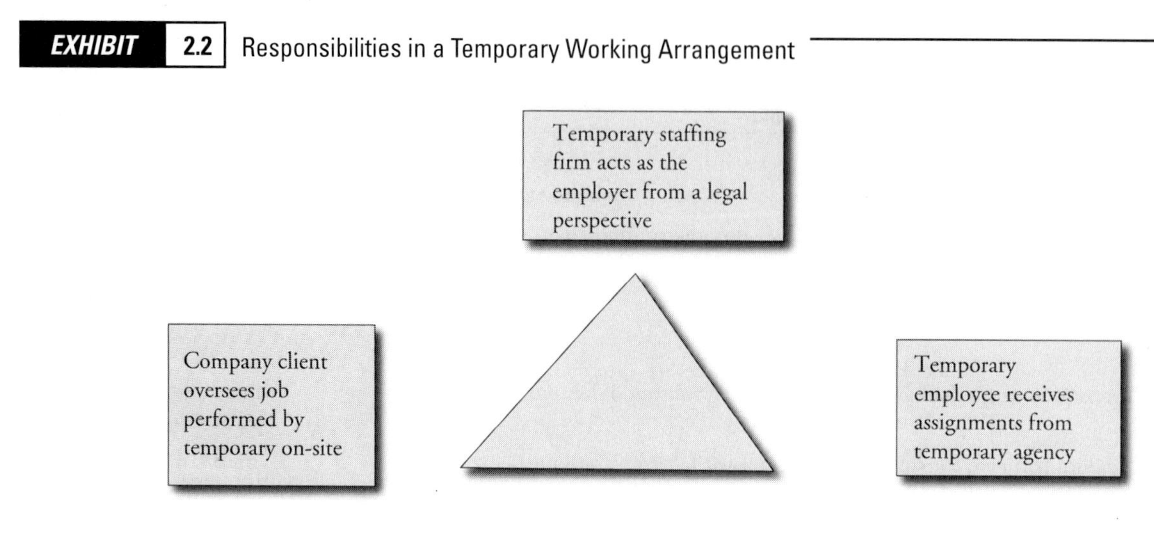

Temporary Employees

temporary or contingency worker
A supplemental worker who has a transitory employment relationship with an employer

Temporary or contingency workers are considered employees of temporary staffing agencies who use their own recruitment process to select suitable workers. Once the candidates pass the recruitment process, they are given job assignments with employers of the agency.

Contingency work is a "conditional and transitory employment relationship initiated by a need for labour—usually because a company has an increased demand for a particular service or product or technology, at a particular place, and at a specific time."[4]

As Exhibit 2.2 demonstrates, the relationship between the temporary employment agency, the employer, and the temporary worker is based on each party fulfilling specific obligations.[5]

During the assignment, the temporary employee remains on the payroll of the agency. Sixty percent of working Canadians are employed in jobs that fit the standard definition of permanent, full-time work. Forty percent have non-standard work, which would be temporary, part-time, or are self-employed, and the numbers are steadily increasing.[6]

Use of temporary employees often raises issues of co-employment, in which the client employer and the temporary agency share the traditional role of employer. Because both function as employers to an extent, there is a need to sort out their obligations and liabilities under various laws. Depending on the specific issue and law involved, both the client employer and agency may be legally considered the employer. It is important for an employer to work with an ethical firm whose practices are legally defensible. Exhibit 2.3 identifies factors that should be considered when choosing a staffing firm.[7]

The Canadian Human Rights Act and the provincial/territorial Employment Standards Acts, for example, apply to both the client employer and the agency. Thus, the usage of temporary employees by a client employer should be preceded by a thorough review of co-employment legal ramifications.

LAWS AND REGULATIONS

Establishment and maintenance of the employment relationship involves exercising discretion on the part of both the employer and the employee. Broadly speaking, laws affecting the employment relationship spring from a need to define the scope of permissible discretion and place limits on it. This chapter further explores the sources and specific factors that contribute to the need for **laws and regulations**.

EXHIBIT 2.3 Factors to Consider When Choosing a Staffing Firm

Factor	Issues
Agency and Its Reputation	How long in business; location; references from clients available
Types of Workers Provided	What occupation and KSAO levels; how many available
Planning and Leadtime	Does agency help client plan staffing levels and needs; how quickly can workers be provided
Services Provided	
Recruitment	What methods are used; how targeted and truthful is recruitment process
Selection	What selection techniques are used to assess KSAOs
Training	What types of training, if any, provided before workers placed with client
Wages and Benefits	How are wages determined; what benefits are provided
Orientation	How does the agency prepare workers for assignment with client; does agency have an employee handbook for its workers
Supervision	How does agency supervise its workers on site of client; does agency provide on-site manager
Temp-to-Perm	Does agency allow client to hire its temporary workers as permanent employees
Client Satisfaction	How does agency attempt to gauge client satisfaction with services, workers, costs
Worker Effectiveness	
Punctuality and Attendance	Does the agency monitor these; what is their record with previous clients
Job Performance	Is it evaluated; how are the results used
Retention	How long do workers remain on an assignment voluntarily; how are workers discharged by the agency
Cost	
Markup	What is the % over base wage charged to client (often it is 50% to cover benefits, overhead, profit margin)
For Special Services	What services cost extra beyond the markup (e.g., temp-to-perm), and what are those costs

Need for Laws and Regulations

laws and regulations
Laws and regulations in the employment relationship seek to limit the employer's discretion and power, provide guarantees of consistent treatment among employees, and provide guidance to employers on permissible and impermissible practices

Balance of Power Laws related to staffing are defined by the Constitution of Canada, which describes the balance of power in the employment relationship. The employer has something desirable to offer the employee (a job with certain requirements and rewards), and the employee has something to offer the employer (KSAOs and motivation). Usually, the employer has the upper hand in this power relationship because the employer has more to offer, and more control over what to offer, than does the employee.

It is the employer who controls:

- Creation of the jobs
- Definition of the jobs in terms of requirements and rewards
- Access to those jobs via staffing systems
- Movement of employees among jobs over time
- Retention or termination of employees

While employees participate in these processes and decisions to varying degrees, it is seldom as an equal or a partner of the employer. Employment laws and regulations thus exist, in part, to reduce or limit the employer's power in the employment relationship. Laws pertaining to wages, hours, equal employment opportunity, and so forth, all seek to limit employer discretion in the establishment of the terms and conditions of employment.

Protection of Employees Laws and regulations seek to provide specific protection to workers who may suffer discrimination in the labour market. These often are the most vulnerable workers who have lower skills or face constraints such as family responsibilities or the lack of financial resources to upgrade skills. Thus they are vulnerable when having to place themselves into the labour market.[8]

Laws and regulations provide guarantees for consistent treatment among employees. They constitute a constraint on the employer to treat employees equitably, and afford employees some measure of procedural justice, or fairness in the process whereby decisions are made about them.

Protection of Employers Employers also gain protection under laws and regulations. First, they provide guidance to employers as to what practices are permissible and impermissible. The Canadian Human Rights Act, for example, not only forbids certain types of discrimination (e.g., on the basis of race, colour, religion, etc.) but also specifically mentions permitted employment practices. One of those permitted practices is discriminating based on a Bona Fide Occupational Requirement.

Sources of Laws and Regulations

The laws and regulations that govern the employment relationship fall under the jurisdiction of either the federal government or the provinces and territories. Jurisdiction is defined as the "power or authority to pass laws."[9]

1.3

Federal Jurisdiction The federal government has the power to regulate businesses or agencies that fall under the legislative authority of the Parliament of Canada. The Parliament makes laws for Canada and outlines in the Constitution Act, 1987 Subsection 91(13), who must obey those laws. The following businesses/agencies fall under federal jurisdiction:[10]

- Transportation systems, including Canadian National Railway, highways, pipelines, canals, ferries, tunnels, and bridges
- Radio and television broadcasting, including the Canadian Broadcasting Corporation (CBC)
- First Nations communities and activities
- Federal Crown corporations, including Canada Mortgage and Housing and Canada Post Corporation

Provincial Jurisdiction The Constitution Act also gave the provinces and territories the sole jurisdiction regarding civil and property rights. The provinces and territories were given the power to pass laws defining the employment relationship.

Constitutional Law The British North America Act (1867) and the subsequent Constitution Act (1982) are examples of government legislation that have profound implications on staffing practices. They define the powers that different levels of government can exercise to monitor and regulate staffing activities. The American constitution was forged by revolution to win its independence. Canada's process was a peaceful one as our constitution was enacted by the British Parliament, which passed the British North America Act.

Canadian Charter of Rights and Freedoms

Guarantees every person freedom from discrimination based on race, national or ethnic origin, colour, sex, age, or mental or physical disability

The **Canadian Charter of Rights and Freedoms** emerged from the Constitution Act and it significantly contributed to diminishing discrimination. Section 15 of the Charter guarantees the following rights:

> "Every individual is equal before and under the law and has the right to the equal protection and equal benefit of the law without discrimination and, in particular, without discrimination based on race, national or ethnic origin, colour, religion, sex, age or mental or physical disability"

Many critics believe the Charter's language was too broad thus making it difficult to interpret. The difficulty in language interpretation was overshadowed by the opportunities the Charter created for new legislation to protect the fundamental rights of all Canadians. The Charter has "created a national consciousness of the need for equality—and it has compelled governments to build equality into every law right from the outset."[11]

The Charter directly applies to the government and its agencies, under federal jurisdiction, but also indirectly controls the actions of employers because the constitution is the Supreme Law of Canada as outlined in Section 52.

> "The Constitution of Canada is the supreme law of Canada, and any law that is inconsistent with the provisions of the Constitution is, to the extent of the inconsistency, of no force or effect."

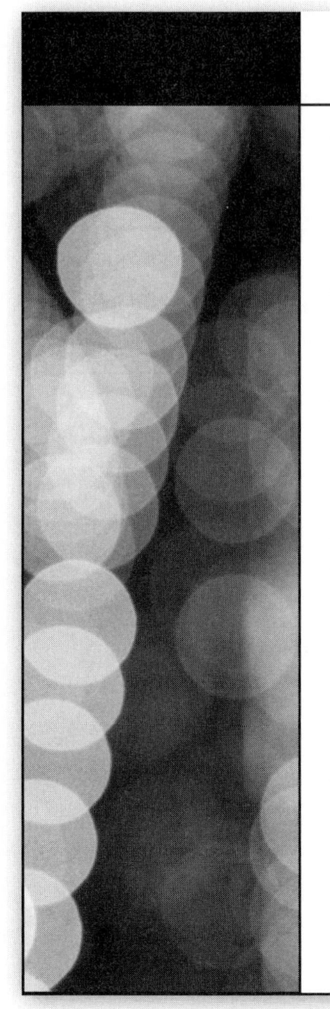

Constitution Act of 1982

WAS CANADA MEANT TO BE A DEMOCRACY?

Canadian law does not permit a province to secede unilaterally, even with the clearest mandate from the province's voters. That was the Supreme Court's conclusion in the Quebec Secession reference of 1998. In reply to a federal government query, posed in the wake of the 1995 sovereignty referendum, the court decided that Quebec's secession would amount to an amendment of the Canadian constitution and would therefore require the agreement of Ottawa and the other provinces.

The Canadian constitution says nothing about a province's right to secede, so the court had to base its decision on the fundamental principles of the constitution. But this was not as easy as you might think. What are those principles? Since its amendments in 1982, the constitution has declared that "Canada is founded upon the principles that recognize the supremacy of God and the rule of law." But it doesn't say outright what those principles are, though you can infer them from the Charter of Rights and Freedoms. That, though, is a modern document. Canada's original charter (the British North America Act, which some now call the Constitution Act, 1867) is even more reticent. It merely notes the desire of the colonies concerned to be "federally united ... with a constitution similar in principle to that of the United Kingdom."

Accordingly, the court based its decision on four unwritten constitutional principles, which it detected in the history of Canada and its founding. They were federalism, democracy, respect for minority rights, and, finally, "constitutionalism and the rule of law." Though unwritten, except for those vague allusions in the British North America Act, "it would be impossible to conceive our constitutional structure without them."

Excerpted with permission from "Was Canada Meant To Be A Democracy?" by Paul Romney, *The Beaver*, 80(2), April/May 2000.

Prohibited Grounds of Discrimination under the Canadian Human Rights Act

Race or ethnic origin	Disability
Colour	Marital Status
Sex	Family Status
Sexual Orientation	Conviction for which pardon has not been granted
Religion	
Age	

Source: Department of Justice, "Canadian Human Rights Act," Chapter H 6: Purpose of Act, R.S. 1985, **http://laws.justice.gc.ca/en/H-6/31435.html**.

HUMAN RIGHTS LAWS AND LEGISLATION

Canadian Human Rights Act

3.5

human rights legislation

Recognizes the dignity of all workers and encourages inclusion in the workplace

Canadian Human Rights Act

Gives all individuals equal opportunity to make for themselves the lives they wish without experiencing exclusion based on grounds of discrimination

Human rights legislation—including both federal and provincial laws and codes—provides equal rights and opportunities free from discrimination for members of "protected groups." **The Canadian Human Rights Act** of 1977 applies to all organizations under federal jurisdiction. The purpose of the Act is:

> "...that all individuals should have an opportunity equal with other individuals to make for themselves the lives that they are able and wish to have and to have their needs accommodated, consistent with their duties and obligations as members of society, without being hindered in or prevented from doing so by discriminatory practices..."[12]

The Act identifies the prohibited grounds of discrimination as shown in Exhibit 2.4. The provinces and territories followed by passing their own human rights laws and codes, with some variations. Before the Act there was no retribution for an employer asking marital status or age, for example.

Key concerns outlined in the Canadian Human Rights Act to limit discrimination in staffing policies and practices are:

- Employment applications and job advertisements
- Termination or limiting employment opportunities
- Equal wages
- Publication of discriminatory notices
- Hate messages
- Harassment and sexual harassment
- Accessibility standards for people with disabilities

Discrimination

discrimination

The act of treating people differently, negatively, or adversely and making a distinction between certain individuals or groups based on prohibited grounds of discrimination

The Canadian Human Rights Commission defines **discrimination** as "treating people differently, negatively or adversely ... and making a distinction between certain individuals or groups" based on prohibited grounds of discrimination.[13] Discrimination can take many forms. One would be an employer blatantly discriminating against a person from a "protected group." Another would be supporting a human resources practice that seems unbiased on the surface but has a damaging or adverse effect.

Exhibit 2.5 offers a comparative look at the prohibited grounds of discrimination as outlined in federal and provincial/territorial legislation and regulations.

EXHIBIT 2.5 Comparison of Grounds of Discrimination
(as outlined by federal and provincial/territorial Human Rights Commissions)

Prohibited Ground	Federal, Provinces/ Territories	Comments
Race or colour	All	Intended to get at the societal problem frequently referred to as racism
Religion	All	Yukon's Act reads: "religions or creed, or religious belief, religious association or religious activity"
Physical or mental disability	All	Quebec uses the phrase "handicap or use of any means to palliate a handicap"
Dependence on alcohol or drugs	All except Yukon and N.W.T.	Policy to accept complaints in B.C., Alberta, Saskatchewan, Manitoba, Ontario, New Brunswick, and P.E.I.; Quebec's language included in "handicap" ground; previous dependence only in New Brunswick and Nova Scotia
Age	All	Age is not defined under the Canadian Human Rights Act, however, the Act does state that a worker can be retired at the age that is "normal" for the kind of work involved; B.C. defines as 19 to 65; Alberta 18 and older; Saskatchewan 18 to 64; Ontario 18 to 65; Newfoundland 19 to 65; Quebec reads except as provided for by law
Sex (includes pregnancy and childbirth)	All	B.C. includes breast feeding; Alberta uses the term "gender"; Manitoba includes gender-determined characteristics; Ontario recognizes the protection of transgendered persons and accepts complaints related to "gender identity"; Ontario policy to accept complaints related to female genital mutilation
Marital status	All	Canadian Human Rights Act does not define marital status, however, the Canadian Human Rights Commission has issued publications that provide the Commission's view on what these prohibited grounds of discrimination mean; Quebec uses the term "civil status"
Family status	All except New Brunswick and Newfoundland	Saskatchewan defines as being in a parent-child relationship; Quebec uses the term "civil status"
Sexual orientation	All except N.W.T.	The Supreme Court of Canada read ground into the Alberta Human Rights, Citizenship and Multiculturalism Act in 1988
National or ethnic origin (including linguistic background)	All except B.C. and Alberta	Saskatchewan and N.W.T. use the term "nationality"; Ontario's code includes both "ethnic origin" and "citizenship"
Ancestry or place of origin	Yukon, B.C., Alberta, Saskatchewan, Manitoba, N.W.T., Ontario, and New Brunswick	
Language	Yukon, Ontario, and Quebec	Ontario accepts complaints under the grounds of ancestry, ethnic origin, place of origin, and race; although not an enumerated ground in New Brunswick, it will accept language-related complaints filed on the basis of ancestry
Social condition or origin	Quebec and Newfoundland	The definition of "social condition" is a person's standing in society as often determined by his/her occupation, income, education level, or family background.

Continued

EXHIBIT 2.5 *Continued*

Prohibited Ground	Federal, Provinces/ Territories	Comments
Source of income	Alberta, Saskatchewan, Manitoba, Quebec, P.E.I., and Nova Scotia	Defined as "receipt of public assistance" in Saskatchewan; in Quebec, included under social condition
Assignment, attachment, or seizure of pay	Newfoundland	In Quebec, included under social condition
Based on association	Yukon, Manitoba, Quebec, Nova Scotia, P.E.I., and Newfoundland	Newfoundland has prohibition basis on "political opinion"
Record of criminal conviction	Yukon, British Columbia, P.E.I., and Newfoundland	Yukon's Act reads: "criminal charges or criminal record"
Pardoned conviction	Federal, British Columbia, N.W.T., Ontario, and Quebec	Under the Canadian Human Rights Act, it is a discriminatory practice for a person against whom a complaint has been filed to retaliate or threaten retaliation against the individual who filed the complaint against the alleged victim

Source: Reproduced with the permission of the Minister of Public Works and Government Services of Canada and the Canadian Human Rights Commission, 2005.

direct discrimination
An illegal conscious act or practice to discriminate on a prohibited ground

Direct Discrimination **Direct discrimination** is a conscious act or practice to discriminate on a prohibited ground and it is illegal. When employers directly discriminate, they are consciously aware that their actions will exclude certain groups. For example, the purpose of a job posting on a Internet job board is to give prospective candidates information about the experience, skills, and educational requirement for the job. The wording of the ad should encourage all qualified candidates to apply. Exhibit 2.6 is an example of a job ad that could be construed to have the intent of dissuading older people from applying by using the word "young."

The ad specifically indicates an age preference and is discriminatory. Section 8 of the Canadian Human Rights Act states that "it is a discriminatory practice to use or circulate any form of application for employment, or in connection with employment or prospective employment, to publish any advertisement or to make any written or oral inquiry that expresses or implies any limitation, specification or preference based on a prohibited ground of discrimination."[14]

This form of direct discrimination is rarely seen today but it does occur in other areas of staffing and can often go undetected. Reviewing resumés is a prime example of where direct discrimination can occur. A recruiter can screen out applicants based on ethnic origin or religion if grounds are indicated on the resumé.

indirect, adverse affect, or constructive discrimination
An act that does not directly discriminate but results in excluding or restricting a group of persons who are identified by a prohibited ground

Indirect Discrimination **Indirect discrimination**, also called **adverse affect discrimination** or **constructive discrimination**, occurs when a policy or practice on its surface does not appear to discriminate on a prohibited ground but results in the exclusion or restriction of an employee who is identified by a prohibited ground of discrimination. It can also occur when preference is given to a specific group without the intent to discriminate directly but excludes females or people with a certain ethnic background, for example. Many leading cases on adverse affect discrimination involve discrimination against employees of minority religions.[15] Exhibit 2.7 demonstrates a situation where an employer indirectly discriminated based on religion.

EXHIBIT 2.6 Direct Discrimination in a Job Ad

Sales Representative

Suitable applicants should have 3 years direct selling experience with post-secondary education. Applicants must be young and energetic as this position requires high volume of cold calling.

In the situation described in Exhibit 2.7, it seemed a reasonable request to ask the employee to put out the poinsettia plants and there was no intent to discriminate. Although the action was not intentional, it adversely affected the employee's right to religious practice. Recognition of adverse effect discrimination represents a powerful and important breakthrough in human rights laws because "it identifies the adverse effect of apparently neutral policies, practices, and procedures on socially disadvantaged groups accorded protection against discrimination."[16]

systemic discrimination
An established practice or procedure that may appear neutral but that actually excludes employees in protected groups from jobs or opportunities

Systemic Discrimination **Systemic discrimination** is an established practice or procedure that may appear to be neutral and to apply equally to all employees but that actually excludes some persons from particular jobs or other opportunities. The "old boys network" is an example of systemic discrimination where favouritism was shown by promoting males instead of females into executive positions to maintain a comfortable status quo for male executives. In our fast-paced, ever-changing business environment, often policies and procedures are not kept up to date. Employment practices can operate for many years without being re-examined, and they may systematically be discriminatory because they are no longer valid and relevant to the performance of the job.[17]

discrimination based on association
An act that occurs because of relationships or associations with a person(s) protected by a prohibited ground

Discrimination Based on Association **Discrimination based on association** occurs because of a relationship or association with a person or persons who are protected by a prohibited ground of discrimination. An example is a group of people in an airport that are detained and searched excessively because one person in the group is of an ethnic background.

Bona Fide Occupational Requirement (BFOR)

Section 15(1) of the Canadian Human Rights Act outlines policies or practices that are not discriminatory practices, when a **bona fide occupational requirement** is established. The section states that a practice is not discriminator if "any refusal, exclusion, expulsion, suspension,

EXHIBIT 2.7 Indirect Discrimination

A British Columbia drug store employee, a Jehovah's Witness, had refused to put out six poinsettia plants on the grounds that his religion did not celebrate Christmas; that he, therefore, didn't want to promote it; and that, in his 16 years of employment with the company, he never had to do it before.

Because it took but 10 seconds for the supervisor to put out the plants and because the employee hadn't been asked to put out any Christmas decorations in the years before, the tribunal ruled that the drug store had to make accommodations that were short of undue hardship.

No matter that the controversial case was criticized as political correctness gone amok. People can moan all they want, but the Supreme Court of Canada and the other courts are making it very clear that they are not only moving in this direction, but also going even further than what people expect.

Policies need to be in place, and they need to be followed to the letter. It also means owners and managers need to become familiar with human rights legislation and be aware of what the courts are requiring.

Excerpted from "Take steps to avoid human rights disasters," by Marilyn Linton, *National Post*, March 16, 2005.

EXHIBIT 2.8 BFOR Established in a Nova Scotia Nursing Home

A Nova Scotia nursing home with strong ties to the Roman Catholic Church always employed at least one male orderly to assist male residents with toileting, bathing, dressing, and personal hygiene. The home customarily provided a "final home" to retired Catholic priests, who particularly objected to having intimate care delivered by a woman. In addition, some of the male residents exhibited "severe behavioural problems" with female staff, which improved when a male orderly took over their personal care.

In June 2002, the employer posted a vacancy for the orderly position, indicating that "the position requires a male staff person to provide intimate care to male residents." The Canadian Union of Public Employees, Local 1562, filed a grievance alleging that the posting violated Article 21.01 of the collective agreement, which stated: "The employer agrees that there shall be no discrimination ... with respect to any employee in the matter of hiring, wage rates, training, upgrading, promotion, transfer, layoff, recall, discipline, discharge or otherwise by reason of ... sex."

Arguments: The union took the position that the "no discrimination" clause in the collective agreement contained no provision allowing the employer to discriminate in employment based on a bona fide occupational requirement (BFOR), and the parties did not intend to include any such exception to the prohibition against discrimination. Consequently, the union submitted, it was not open to the employer to designate the position as male-only, regardless of whether gender was a BFOR.

The employer argued that gender was a bona fide occupational qualification for the orderly position, as provided for in s.6 of the Nova Scotia Human Rights Act, which states that the Act does not apply "where a denial, refusal or other form of alleged discrimination is...based upon a bona fide qualification." Emphasizing that historically the orderly position was always filled by a male applicant over more senior female applicants despite the long-time inclusion of the "no discrimination" clause in the collective agreement, the employer argued that the parties had negotiated a BFOR into the "no discrimination" clause.

Decision: Arbitrator Milton Veniot dismissed the grievance, ruling that being a man was a bona fide occupational requirement of the orderly.

Adapted with permission from "Nursing Home Residents' Rights Trump Gender Equity In Job Posting Case," Labour Arbitration, Lancaster Bi-weekly E-Bulletin, February 4, 2005, Issue No. 33.

bona fide occupational requirement
A practice that is established as an essential requirement of the job and is thus not discriminatory

limitation, specification or preference in relation to any employment is established by an employer to be based on a bona fide occupational requirement."

Exhibit 2.8 gives a synopsis of the findings for the case of the *Canadian Union of Public Employees, Local 1562 v. Ronald C. MacGillivray Guest Home Corporation* where a discriminatory practice was upheld as a BFOR.

The Meiorin Case The Supreme Court of Canada decision in *British Columbia (Public Service Employee Relations Commission) v. British Columbia Government and Service Employees' Union (B.C.G.S.E.U.)* was a milestone ruling because of its impact on staffing policies and practices. The case clarified the type of evidence that was required to apply for a BFOR.[18]

Tawney Meiorin had been employed as a forest fire fighter for three years. Her employer, the government of British Columbia, implemented a new series of fitness tests, including a running test designed to measure aerobic fitness. She failed the test and lost her job because she failed one aspect of a minimum fitness standard. Ms. Meiorin's union grieved that the aerobic standard discriminated against women in contravention of the British Columbia Human Rights Code, as women generally have lower aerobic capacity than men.

The union argued that Ms. Meioron should be accommodated and reinstated her fire fighting position, or relocated to another job within the ministry. The evidence was her positive work appraisals, experience in the job, and the fact that she met the required overall standard in the test.[19]

The government of British Columbia argued that the aerobic standard was a bona fide occupational requirement (BFOR) for a fire fighter to perform his or her duties. On appeal, the Supreme Court of Canada determined that the standard was not a BFOR. The Supreme Court first analyzed the case in the conventional view of discrimination attempting to determine whether it was direct or adverse effect discrimination. This approach was unsuitable because:

- There are cases where it is difficult to identify discrimination as clearly direct or adverse effect.
- The approach legitimized systemic discrimination as the testing seemed on the surface to apply equally to everyone but in fact women generally have lower aerobic capacity.
- The Charter of Rights and Freedom does not categorize discrimination as either direct or indirect. Its focus is on the harmful effects of a discriminatory practice or law.[20]

The Supreme Court rejected this traditional approach and proposed a unified test for BFOR defences of direct or adverse effect discrimination. Judge Beverley McLachlin set out a single test that puts the onus on the employer to justify a BFOR. For a practice or policy to become a bona fide occupational requirement it must answer the following questions, which constitute the unified test:[21]

1. Is this a policy or standard which discriminates either directly or by adverse effect based on a prohibited ground?
2. Did the employer adopt the policy or standard for a purpose rationally connected to the performance of the job?
3. Did the employer adopt the particular policy or standard in honest good faith that it was necessary to the fulfillment of the work-related purpose?
4. Is the policy or standard reasonably necessary to accomplish the essential duties of the job?

The employer is also expected to show that the policy or standard adopted is the least discriminatory way to fulfill the essential duties of the job. It includes the requirement of demonstrating that it is impossible to accommodate individual employees without imposing undue hardship on the employer.

accommodation
An employer's responsibility to eliminate rules, practices, or barriers that have an adverse impact on individuals with disabilities

duty to accommodate
An integral responsibility employers have to promote inclusion

Accommodation **Accommodation** is an employer's responsibility to eliminate rules, practices, or barriers that have an adverse impact on individuals with disabilities.[22] "Disabilities" is used as a broad category to include a range of physical, emotional, and mental conditions, which employers will need to consider as opportunities to accommodate. The Meiorin case gave credence to the employer's **duty to accommodate** to promote inclusion. Accommodation is an immense opportunity for disadvantaged groups because it mandates that workplaces be accessible for everyone. The duty to accommodate requires employers to identify and eliminate practices that prevent job equity for disadvantaged groups to the point of undue hardship. Section 15(2) of the Canadian Human Rights Act defines this point of undue hardship as:

> ...accommodation of the needs of an individual or a class of individuals affected would impose undue hardship on the person who would have to accommodate the needs, considering health, safety, and cost.

When the court considers undue hardship, the pertinent concerns are financial cost, misalignment with a collective bargaining agreement, problems of morale with other employees, and interchangeability of workforce and facilities.[23]

Examples of accommodation are increasing the spaces between cubicles in an open office concept to allow wheelchair access and providing specialized computer equipment, such as an ergonomic keyboard or mouse, to accommodate a repetitive strain injury.

reasonable accommodation
Can take many forms, such as modified job duties, altering a building to make it more accessible, finding an alternative job, or varying requirements to meet the work schedule

Reasonable Accommodation **Reasonable accommodation** can take many forms. Examples include modifying job duties, altering a building to make it more accessible, finding an alternate job (either a modified job description or a substitute job), or varying requirements to meet the work schedule. Two Supreme Court of Canada decisions, *O'Malley v. Simpson-Sears* (1985) and *Central Alberta Dairy Pool v. Alberta Human Rights Commission* (1990) were important cases in defining duty to accommodate and undue hardship.

The complainant in *O'Malley v. Simpson-Sears* worked as a full-time sales clerk for Simpson-Sears. A condition of employment with Simpson-Sears was that employees periodically had to work Friday evenings and Saturdays. She worked on the weekends, when required, for seven years until she became a member of the Seventh-day Adventist Church. Her new religion restricted her from working from sundown on Friday to sundown on Saturday as an observance of the Sabbath. Because she could no longer work on the weekends, she would lose her full-time position status and would have to work part-time.

She complained to the Ontario Human Rights Commission that she had been discriminated against because of her religious beliefs. The Supreme Court ruled that Simpson-Sears had the duty to take reasonable steps to accommodate the complainant short of undue hardship. The company could have changed her work schedule but it did not do so.[24]

In the *Central Alberta Dairy Pool v. Alberta Human Rights Commission* decision, the Supreme Court ruled against the Dairy Pool because it discriminated based on religion. The complainant worked in the milk processing plant and became a member of the Worldwide Church of God. The complainant's religion required he did not work on the Sabbath and holy days. He requested an unpaid leave for an Easter Monday to observe a holy day of the church. The leave was denied because Mondays were very busy days at the Dairy Pool. When he did not report to work, he was fired.

The company's intent was not to discrimination directly—Mondays were busy day—but its decision had an adverse effect on the complainant. The court specified that the Dairy Pool must meet its duty to accommodate the employee up to the point of undue hardship.[25]

Individual Accommodation Lifestyles are complicated with single-parent families, baby boomers who have children still living at home and ailing parents to look after, and employees suffering from stress and burnout as a result of downsizings and reorganizations. Employers are faced with more and more employees requesting individual accommodation, thus policies and practices require more flexibility to deal with requests related to the prohibited grounds of discrimination.

An excellent employee becomes a single mother and now needs to leave work at 4:30 p.m. instead of 5:00 p.m. because she does not have a support system. Today's convoluted lives require tolerance and understanding. Individual accommodation has forced employers to modernize their definition of inclusion.

Harassment

harassment
A discriminatory practice to harass an individual based on a prohibited ground of discrimination

Harassment stirs emotional outrage because of the damaging effects it has in the workplace. The laws that protect employees against harassment sometimes are seen as being politically correct. Actions that at one time would have been viewed as fun are now penalized as harassing someone. In the 1970s, for example, Polish jokes were rampant, without any thought of the psychological damage and the demeaning position they placed Polish people in. Today Polish jokes are classed as harassment, and policies are in place to eliminate them as racially discriminatory.

Section 14 of the Canadian Human Rights Act identifies harassment as a discriminatory practice to harass an individual on a prohibited ground of discrimination "in the provision of goods, services, facilities or accommodation customarily available to the general public. in the provision of commercial premises or residential accommodation, or in matters related to employment."[26]

Harassment as defined under the Canadian Human Rights Commission refers to comments or actions that are unwelcome or should be known to be unwelcome. Anti-harassment training focuses on changing attitudes, language, and actions with the purpose of protecting employees from demeaning, humiliating, or dangerous approaches. Exhibit 2.9 identifies specific areas that the Canadian Human Rights Commission defines as harassment.

EXHIBIT 2.9 Canadian Human Rights Commission—Forms of Harassment

Harassment is a form of discrimination. It can take many forms, including:

- Verbal abuse or threats
- Unwelcome remarks, jokes, innuendo, or sarcastic remarks about a person's body, attire, age, marital status, ethnic or national origin, religion, etc.
- Displaying of pornographic, racist, or other offensive or derogatory pictures
- Practical jokes that cause awkwardness or embarrassment
- Unwelcome invitations or requests, whether indirect or explicit, or intimidation
- Leering or other gestures
- Condescension or paternalism that undermines self-respect
- Unnecessary physical contact such as touching, patting, pinching, or punching
- Physical assault

Source: Canadian Human Rights Commission, "Discrimination and Harassment," **www.chrc-ccdp.ca/discrimination/what_is_it-en.asp.**

Protection against harassment is moving into other legal jurisdictions, signalling the importance placed on its elimination. In 2004, Quebec became the first North American jurisdiction to include protection of psychological harassment of employees in its Labour Standards Act. Employers are "facing new obligations and responsibilities in connection with the quality of work environments and workplace interactions."[27]

Sexual Harassment The Conference Board of Canada pointed out in a 2001 study that 48 percent of women executives cited inhospitable work environment as a reason for leaving a job.[28] The Canada Labour Code and the human rights codes for the provinces and territories provide protection against sexual harassment.

sexual harassment
Any conduct, comment, gesture, or contact of a sexual nature that is likely to cause offence or humiliation to any employee

The Canada Labour Code defines **sexual harassment** as "any conduct, comment, gesture, or contact of a sexual nature that is likely to cause offence or humiliation to any employee; or that might, on reasonable grounds, be perceived by that employee as placing a condition of a sexual nature on employment or on any opportunity for training or promotion."[29] Often when sexual harassment is alleged, the common argument used against the allegation is that the behaviour was not intended to be offensive. The courts look at how the behaviour affected the individual and do not accept lack of intent as a defence.

As Exhibit 2.10 shows, it is extremely important for organizations to develop and adopt a sexual harassment policy.

ENFORCEMENT

Canadian Human Rights Commission

Canadian Human Rights Commission
Body responsible for dealing with complaints regarding discrimination

The Canadian Human Rights Act established a **Canadian Human Rights Commission**, which is responsible for dealing with complaints regarding discrimination, educating the public on the Canadian Human Rights Act, sponsoring research related to the Act, and closely liaising with the provincial and territorial Human Rights Commissions to foster common policies and practices.

Since 2004, the Commission has gone through a significant period of change and growth to "improve the efficiency of processing and resolving human rights complaints, greater focus has been placed on the use of alternate dispute resolution, streamlining the investigation process, and

EXHIBIT 2.10 How Should an Employer Respond to an Allegation of Sexual Harassment?

Shortly after she began her employment in November 1998 as a health care worker with Thorvaldson Care Homes, Jeanette Budge began to experience unwelcome comments and physical contact from TS, a maintenance man at the workplace. She reported the problem to her supervisor early on, but nothing changed. In mid-December 1999, she had a phone conversation with Herman Thorvaldson, the president of the company, and explained the whole situation. Two days later, Budge found a Record of Employment in her pay envelope indicating that she had quit, although she had not.

On March 2000, Budge filed a formal human rights complaint against Thorvaldson, describing the ongoing course of sexual harassment by the maintenance man. Thorvaldson responded with a complete denial of the allegations. In his view, the complainant was being prodded by a group of "dissenters" who were intent on damaging his business. The maintenance man was not a villain; he was just joking around. Thorvaldson first said he was totally unaware of the unwanted touching of other employees and then revised his stance, asserting that the complainant had not said anything about it. Thorvaldson denied that management was unapproachable or that to complain was to put one's position in jeopardy. Those fired in the past had committed acts of misconduct, he maintained.

When the case was referred to the Human Rights Tribunal for a hearing, the Manitoba Human Rights Commission argued that Thorvaldson knew or ought to have known that a "climate of harassment" existed, and that he was "willfully blind" to the situation. Once an employer becomes aware of allegations of harassment, there is a duty to investigate, ascertain the nature of the problem, and take reasonable steps to stop any offending conduct, the Commission contended. Here, the employer did not do so.

As for remedy, Arne Peltz, the case's adjudicator, ordered Throvaldson "to prepare and adopt a harassment policy acceptable to the Commission, and to implement the policy in an expeditious manner." Since the maintenance man was still employed at Thorvaldson, a monitoring order was added, directing Thorvaldson to inform the Commission for two years whenever a female employee entered or left its employ. Peltz also ordered that Budge be compensated for her losses with 12 weeks' wages and benefits. Additionally, because of the severity and duration of the harassment, Thorvaldson was ordered to pay $4,000 in damages for injury to Budge's dignity, feelings, and self-respect.

Adapted with permission: "How Should an Employer Respond to an Allegation of Sexual Harassment?" Lancaster's Women/Pay Equity Employment Law News, July/August 2002, Jeffrey Sack, L.L.B., and Barbara Duckitt, L.L.B., editors, Lancaster House.

the overall management of complaints." In the Commission's 2004 Annual Report, it identified three issues the Commission will study:

- Repeal of Section 76 of the Canadian Human Rights Act, which restricts the ability of First Nations people living on the reserve to file a complaint against band councils or the federal government
- Telephone access for the deaf and hearing-impaired to foster equal access for all
- The Commission receives an increasing number of complaints under Section 13 of the Act, which prohibits transmitting hate messages through the Internet, and it will carry out a long-term strategy to deal with this issue.[30]

Exhibit 2.11 is a summary of the Commission's process for dealing with complaints.

Provincial/Territorial Human Rights Commissions

provincial and territorial human rights commissions
Bodies responsible for preventing discrimination before it occurs and for providing an effective, expeditious remedy through a fair process

The key responsibilities of the **provincial/territorial human rights commissions** are to correct persistent patterns of inequality, investigate discrimination against individuals, prevent discrimination before it occurs through education, provide effective solutions through a fair process, and continually research to identify emerging needs. Each of the provinces and territories has its own human rights code where federal jurisdiction does not apply. The provincial/territorial human rights commissions' complaint processes are broadly similar to the Canadian Human Rights Commission. Exhibit 2.12 gives information on the websites for the federal and provincial and territorial human rights commissions.

EXHIBIT 2.11 The Canadian Human Rights Commission's Complaints Procedure

When the commission receives an inquiry the following steps are taken:
- Information is provided on the Commission and the Canadian Human Rights Act
- An officer reviews the situation with the complainant and explains the complaint process
- If the complainant wishes to purse the matter, a complaint form is prepared

After the Commission accepts a complaint:
- Mediation may be offered as an option to both parties
- If the matter remains unresolved, an officer investigates the allegations and prepares a report for the Commissioners on the investigation findings
- The parties are given an opportunity to comment on the investigation report

When the commissioners make a decision, the commissioners can:
- Approve a settlement between the parties or appoint a conciliator to help the parties arrive at a settlement
- Refer the matter to the Canadian Human Rights Tribunal for further inquiry
- Dismiss the complaint on lack of evidence

If the matter is referred to the Canadian Human Rights Tribunal:
- On referral by the Commission, the Tribunal will conduct hearings into the complaint
- After weighing the evidence that is presented, the Tribunal will make a decision on the merits of the complaint and order an appropriate remedy

Federal Court of Canada
- The Federal Court can be asked by either party to review a decision of the Commission
- The Court can also review a decision or order of the Canadian Human Rights Tribunal

Adapted with permission from the Canadian Human Rights Commission: **www.chrc-ccdp.ca/publications/anti_discrimination_appendixa-en.asp?highlight=1**.

EXHIBIT 2.12 Federal, Provincial, and Territorial Human Rights Commissions

Canada: www.chrc-ccdp.ca
Alberta: www.albertahumanrights.ab.ca
British Columbia: www.bchrt.bc.ca
Manitoba: www.gov.mb.ca/hrc
New Brunswick: www.gnb.ca/hrc-cdp
Newfoundland and Labrador: www.justice.gov.nl.ca/hrc
Northwest Territories: www.nwthumanrights.ca
Nova Scotia: www.gov.ns.ca/humanrights
Nunavut: www.gov.nu.ca
Ontario: www.ohrc.on.ca
Prince Edward Island: www.gov.pe.ca/humanrights
Quebec: www.cdpdj.qc.ca/en
Saskatchewan: www.gov.sk.ca/shrc
Yukon Territory: www.yhrc.yk.ca

OTHER STAFFING LAWS

Employment Equity

The Canadian Human Rights Act paved the way for employment equity by outlining in Section 16(1) that it is not a discriminatory practice to adopt or carry out a special program designed to prevent disadvantages based on the prohibited grounds of discrimination. Employment equity is a term developed by Justice Rosalie Silberman Abella, commissioner of the Royal Commission on Equality in Employment (1984), to move policy decisions from ensuring "equal opportunity" to "employment equity" as a response to dealing with systemic discrimination.[31]

The history of employment equity started in the 1970s when women and minority groups brought increased pressure to establish special programs to improve their employment situation. In 1978, the federal government launched a voluntary affirmative action program aimed at the public sector. A pilot affirmative action program was established in three federal government departments: Canada Employment and Immigration Commission, Secretary of State, and Treasury Board Secretariat in 1980. The Royal Commission on Equality in Employment was established in 1983, with Justice Abella as the commissioner, and the Commission's mandate was to "explore the most efficient, effective and equitable means of promoting equality in employment."[32]

In 1986, the federal Employment Equity Act was passed to regulate organizations that came under federal jurisdiction. Its purpose is:

> "...to achieve equality in the workplace so that no person shall be denied employment opportunities or benefits for reasons unrelated to ability and, in the fulfilment of that goal, to correct the conditions of disadvantage in employment experienced by women, aboriginal peoples, persons with disabilities and members of visible minorities by giving effect to the principle that employment equity means more than treating persons in the same way but also requires special measures and the accommodation of differences."[33]

1.1

Employment Equity Act

Designed to achieve employment equity by eliminating employment barriers for people in the designated groups

The second **Employment Equity Act** was passed in 1995 and came into force on October 24, 1996. It focused on clarifying and enforcing obligations for employers within the federal jurisdiction. Approximately 400 employers are required to comply with the Act and an additional 900 employers are required to develop employment equity programs as a condition for receiving contracts from the federal government.[34]

The Act mandated that every employer under its jurisdiction implement employment equity by identifying and eliminating barriers to employment against persons in the designated groups, and instituting policies and practices that reasonably accommodate persons in the designated groups. The goal was to achieve a certain percentage of representation from the designated groups in each occupation group in the employers' workforce. The Act required an employment equity plan, which incorporated policies and practices for:

- Hiring, training, promoting, and retaining persons in the designated groups
- Providing reasonable accommodations to correct under-representation of persons in the designated groups
- Timetables for implementation and numerical goals for hiring and promotion of persons in the designated groups

The Royal Commission on Equality in Employment (1984) became responsible for enforcing the Act, and Employment Equity Tribunals were established to hear and make decisions on cases. Exhibit 2.13 is a summary of provincial employment equity structures.

A well-designed employment equity program can create an even playing field where people from the designated groups truly have an opportunity to create for themselves the life they wish to have as envisioned by the Canadian Human Rights Act. A well-designed employment equity program will clearly articulate that employment equity is part of an organization's strategic business direction. It outlines to the public and its employees the intent to be inclusive and to mirror society's demographics. Exhibit 2.14 is an example of an employment equity policy that includes the following policy statements:[35]

- A statement identifying the organization's commitment to employment equity
- A definition of employment equity as a human resource planning tool with the purpose of eliminating workplace barriers that prevent full participation of people from the designated groups
- A statement on how the organization proposes to monitor the implementation of the Act
- Identification that implementing fairness and avoiding bias are not new to the organization
- An outline of how the program will be administered, including the reporting relationship of the staff managing the program

EXHIBIT 2.13 Summary of Provincial Employment Equity Structures

Province	Employment Equity Policy in Place	Employment Equity Legislation in Place
Alberta	No	No
British Columbia	Yes	Yes
Manitoba	Yes	No
New Brunswick	Paper under discussion	No
Newfoundland	No	No
Nova Scotia	Yes; also a mandatory affirmative action program	No
Ontario	No; many departments include equity as part of their departmental mandate; official policy is equal opportunity	No; legislation has been repealed
Prince Edward Island	Yes	No
Quebec	There is a program of contract compliance (Programme d'Obligations Contractuelles)	No
Saskatchewan	Yes	No

Reprinted with permission from "Employment Equity Policy In Canada: An Interprovincial Comparison," by Abigail B. Bakan and Audrey Kobayashi, Queen's University, March 2000, Status of Women Canada, **www.swc-cfc.gc.ca/pubs/pubspr/0662281608/200003_0662281608_e.html**

EXHIBIT 2.14 CBC Radio One: Procedures on Employment Equity Policy

1. As outlined in the Employment Equity Act and the CBC Employment Equity Plan, all Supervisors and Managers are responsible for the establishment and implementation of actions which will ensure representation of designated group members reflected of their market availability.
2. Designated Groups are defined as women, aboriginal peoples, people with disabilities and members of visible minority groups.
3. Supervisors and Managers must establish training and development opportunities to increase the number of qualified eligible candidates for promotion and transfer opportunities.
4. External Recruitment processes must cast a wide net attracting qualified designated group members. All advertisement must contain the statement "The CBC is committed to equity in employment and programming."
5. The hiring manager must maintain a record, which contains information on designated group member interviews and reasons for non-selection. Whenever appropriate, i.e. presence of designated group candidates, selection committees must have designated group representation. Upon hiring, an employee is given the opportunity to self identify by completing an Employment Equity Survey Form.

Effective date: January 1, 2003

Reprinted by permission: Canadian Broadcasting Corporation, **http://cbc.radio-canada.ca/docs/policies/equity.shtml**.

Labour, Employment Standard, and Privacy Laws

Canada Labour Code
Protects employees' right to organize trade unions and to bargain collective agreements with employers

Staffing is indirectly affected by federal and provincial laws that outline employers' responsibilities in the areas of labour relations, employment rights and standards, and privacy. **The Canada Labour Code** protects the rights of employees who are under federal jurisdiction to organize trade unions and to bargain collective agreements with employers. The Labour Code and provincial labour relations acts designate Industrial Labour Boards to arbitrate complaints concerning unfair labour practices and to make decisions on the certification of trade unions as bargaining agents for bargaining units. The Code also provides minimum employment standards in a similar way to provincial laws and has applications beyond organized labour.

collective agreements
Vehicles used by unions/ employers to negotiate terms and conditions of employment

closed shop
a business where all employees must be union and new employees must be hired through the union

employment standard laws
Provincial and territorial regulations that set minimum standards and conditions for employment

Personal Information Protection and Electronic Documents Act (PIPEDA)
Law that protects the privacy of individuals with respect to information about themselves held by government institutions

Collective agreements are the vehicles used by unions and employers to negotiate terms and conditions of employment, for a specific period, for the employees within the bargaining unit. Some of the universal topics in a collective agreement are wages, grievance procedures, dismissal or suspension, arbitration, hours of work and overtime, holiday pay, seniority, notice of lay-off, lay-offs and recalls, transfers and promotions, vacations, and safety and health.[36] Unions are considered **closed shops**, and they determine how recruitment, selection, and promotion occur within the collective agreement.

The demographics of unions are changing in that unions at one time were predominately male, private sector, and blue collar. Now union membership is significantly female, public sector, and white collar. The female proportion of union members grew by 45 percent from 1962 to 1999, and the top ten unions now represent government employees.[37]

Provincial and territorial **employment standard laws** also define and regulate the employment relationship by setting minimum standards and conditions of employment. These laws regulate minimum wage, hours of work and overtime, minimum age of employment, rest periods and shift changes, statutory and general holidays, vacation with pay, maternity and parental leave, individual and group termination, and severance pay. The direct impact on staffing is ensuring that once the selection process is completed and when a candidate is hired, the employment agreement follows the relevant employment standards and conditions.

Protection of privacy is a relatively new issue with the enactment of the **Personal Information Protection and Electronic Documents Act (PIPEDA)** in 2001. The Act applies to the collection, use, and disclosure of personal information by organizations under federal jurisdiction. It also applies to non-federally regulated organizations that sell, use, or disclose personal information outside of the province it was gathered, and organizations that collect, use, or disclose personal information in connection with the operation of a federally regulated private sector business. The purpose of the Act is to "protect the privacy of individuals with respect to personal information about themselves held by government institutions and ... provide individuals with the right of access to that information.[38]

British Columbia, Alberta, and Quebec have their own privacy legislation; Ontario's is in draft form. Reference checking, for example, could be impacted by this legislation especially if the jurisdiction extends to the corporate world.[39]

LEGAL ISSUES

Strategic Implications of Legal Challenges

There are compelling reasons why employers need to staff organizations with a diverse workforce. As we move into an era of skill shortages caused by the exodus of the baby boomers, those companies who have solid practices and policies in place to promote inclusion will have the greatest opportunity for economic success.

Best Practice Criteria The rest of this book will discuss in further detail the following best practices in cultivating human rights in the workplace:

- Strategic direction for inclusion needs to be supported by the organization's executive team, both financially and in directing organizational policy.
- Practicing diversity becomes part of the mission statement and core values of the organization.
- A formalized process for staffing is in place, including organizational analysis, job analysis, recruitment planning, structuring the recruitment message, structuring the hiring process, and valid and measurable recruitment tools.
- Staffing policies clearly outline employee expectations.

- Employee training provided by management and union includes discussion of issues such as sexual and racial harassment.
- Responsive mediation, investigation, and reporting processes are clearly and consistently communicated within the organization.

Legal Issues in Remainder of Book

The laws and regulations applicable to staffing practices by organizations are multiple in number and complexity. The emphasis in this chapter has been on an understanding of the need for law, the sources of law, general provisions of the law, and a detailed presentation of specific provisions that pertain to staffing activities. Little has been said about practical implications and applications.

In the remaining chapters of the book, the focus shifts to the practical, with guidance and suggestions on how to align staffing practices with legal requirements. The last section of each remaining chapter is devoted to "Legal Issues" and discusses major issues from a compliance perspective. The issues so addressed, and the chapter in which they occur, are shown in Exhibit 2.15. Inspection of the exhibit should reinforce the importance accorded laws and regulations as an external influence on staffing activities.

It should be emphasized that there is a selective presentation of the issues in Exhibit 2.15. Only certain issues have been chosen for inclusion, and only a summary of their compliance implications is presented. It should also be emphasized that the discussion of these issues does not constitute professional legal advice.

EXHIBIT 2.15 Legal Issues Covered in Other Chapters

Chapter Title and Number	Topic
Measurement (3)	Representation statistics Standardization and validation
Job Analysis (4)	Job relatedness and court cases Essential job functions
External Recruitment (5)	Employment equity and diversity programs Human rights and temporary workers Electronic recruitment Job advertisements
Internal Recruitment (6)	Ceilings and sticky floors Barriers Overcoming barriers Employment equity programs
External Selection (7 and 8)	Screening procedures Drug testing Medical and health testing
Internal Selection (9)	Defensible selection procedures Glass ceiling
Decision Making (10)	Cut scores Hiring standards
Retention Management (11)	Separation laws and regulations Performance appraisal
Staffing System Management (12)	Record keeping, privacy, and reports Audits Training for managers and employees Dispute resolution

SUMMARY

Staffing involves the formation of the employment relationship. That relationship involves the employer acquiring individuals to perform work for it as employees, independent contractors, and temporary employees. The specific legal meanings and obligations associated with these various arrangements were provided.

Myriad laws and regulations have come forth from several sources to place constraints on the contractual relationship between employer and employee. These constraints seek to ensure a balance of power in the relationship, as well as provide protections to both the employee and employer.

The Constitution Act, 1987, and the subsequent Canadian Charter of Rights and Freedoms prohibited discrimination on the basis of race, sex, national or ethnic origin, colour, religion, age, or mental or physical disability. This prohibition applies to staffing practices intentionally used to discriminate (directly or indirectly). Human rights laws also contain specific provisions pertaining to staffing, which specify both prohibited and permissible practices. In both instances, the emphasis is on use of staffing practices that are job related, and the focus is on the person/job match.

A variety of information sources are available to help organizations conduct staffing practices that are in compliance with human rights laws and regulations. The Canadian Human Rights Commission and the provincial/territorial human rights commissions give practical guidance, as well as outline the provincial/territorial codes that must be adhered to.

Other laws and regulations also affect staffing practices. The mandate for employment equity, through the Employment Equity Act, is to eliminate employment barriers for women, aboriginal peoples, persons with disability, and visible minorities. The Act applies to corporations and agencies working under federal jurisdiction.

The right for employees to organize trade unions and to bargain collective agreements was enacted by the Canada Labour Code. The Code's intent is to support labour and management in their cooperative efforts to develop good relations and constructive collective agreements.

The federal and provincial Employment Standards Acts define and regulate the employment relationship related to minimum wage, hours of work and overtime, minimum age for employment, statutory and general holidays, vacation with pay, maternity and parental leave, individual and group termination, and severance pay.

With the dawn of the digital age, access to personal information became a critical concern. The Personal Information Protection and Electronic Documents Act (PIPEDA) protects the privacy of individuals with respect to personal information held by a government institution or collected during commerce activities.

Legal issues will continue to be addressed throughout the remainder of this book. The emphasis will be on explanation and application of the laws provisional to staffing practices. The issues will be discussed at the end of each chapter.

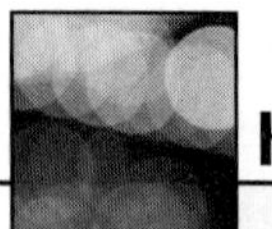

KEY TERMS

accommodation 43
bona fide occupational requirement 42
Canada Labour Code 49
Canadian Charter of Rights and Freedoms 37
Canadian Human Rights Act 38
Canadian Human Rights Commission 45
closed shop 50
collective agreements 50
direct discrimination 40
discrimination 38
discrimination based on association 41
duty to accommodate 43
employer 33
Employment Equity Act 48
employment standard laws 50
harassment 44

human rights legislation 38
independent contractor 33
indirect, adverse affect, or constructive discrimination 40
laws and regulations 35
Personal Information Protection and Electronic Documents Act (PIPEDA) 50
provincial and territorial human rights commission 46
reasonable accommodation 43
sexual harassment 45
systemic discrimination 41
temporary or contingency worker 34

RELEVANT WEB SITES

Canadian Council of Human Resources Association (CCHRA)
Lists Human Resources Associations for each province
www.cchra-ccarh.ca

Canadian Human Rights Act
http://laws.justice.gc.ca/en/H-6/31435.html

Employment Equity Act
http://laws.justice.gc.ca/en/E-5.401/50293.html

Ontario Ministry of Labour
Access to information on the Employment Standard, Occupational Health and Safety, and Labour Relations acts
www.labour.gov.on.ca

Conference Board of Canada
Offers a knowledge area on human resource management
www.conferenceboard.ca/humanresource/default.htm

Canadian National HR Reporter
www.hrreporter.com/default.asp

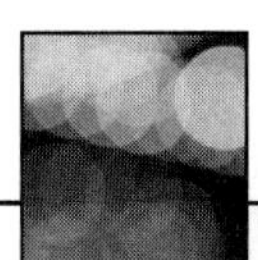

DISCUSSION QUESTIONS

1. Do you agree that "the employer usually has the upper hand" when it comes to establishing the employment relationship? When might the employee have maximum power over the employer?
2. What are the differences between staffing in the private and public sectors? Why would private employers probably resist adopting some of the laws that are mandated for the public sector?
3. Systemic discrimination is one of the more complex ways in which racial discrimination occurs. What would be some of the subtle policies and practices that would put employees at a disadvantage because of their race?
4. When the same-sex marriage bill was passed, Prime Minister Paul Martin said, "This same-sex bill is about the Charter of Rights" (*The Globe and Mail*, June 28, 2005). Would you agree or disagree and why?
5. A maximum security prison with mostly male inmates applies for a BFOR to the Canadian Human Rights Commission to be able to hire only male prison guards. The grounds for doing so are that male guards would ensure the safety, security, and privacy of inmates. How could this prison prove that this application is a business necessity?
6. What does an employer have to prove to change a claim of direct discrimination to adverse impact discrimination?

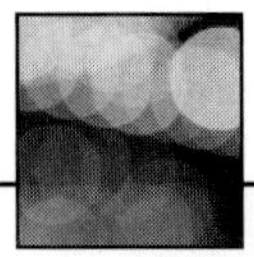

ETHICAL ISSUES

1. Assume that you're the staffing manager in an organization that informally, but strongly, discourages you and managers from hiring people with disabilities. The organization's rationale is that people with disabilities are unlikely to be high performers or long-term employees, and are costly to train, insure, and integrate into the work unit. What is your ethical assessment of the organization's stance? Do you have any ethical obligations to try to change the stance, and if so, how might you go about that?
2. Assume the organization you work for practices strict adherence to the law in its relationships with its employees and job applicants. The organization calls it "staffing by the book." But beyond that it feels that "anything goes" in terms of tolerated staffing practices. What is your assessment of this approach?

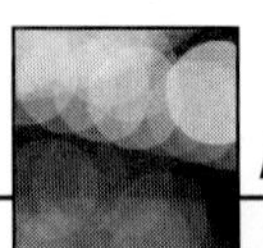

APPLICATIONS

Age Discrimination in a Promotion?

The Best Protection Insurance Company (BPIC) in Winnipeg, Manitoba, handled a massive volume of claims each year in the corporate claims function, as well as its four regional claims centres. The corporate claims department was headed by a senior vice president (SVPCC). She had two managers reporting to her—manager of corporate claims/life (MCC-L) and manager of corporate claims/residential (MCC-R)—and a highly skilled corporate claims specialist (CCS). Each regional office was headed by a regional centre manager (RCM); the RCM was responsible for both supervisors and claims specialists within the regional office. The RCMs reported to the vice president of regional claims (VPRC). Here is the structure before reorganization:

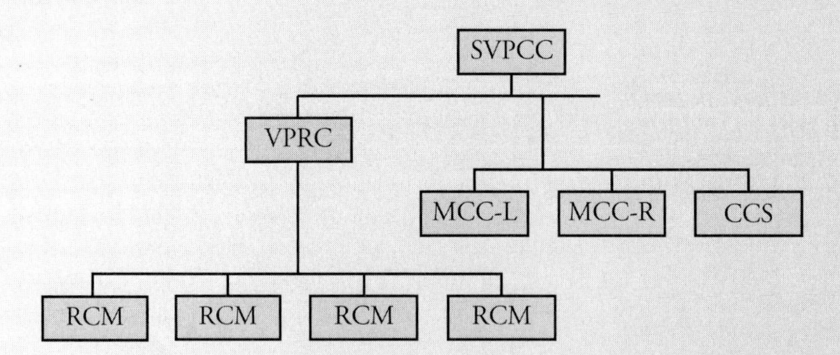

The company decided to reorganize its claims function by eliminating the four regional offices, thus eliminating the regional centre manager (RCM) positions. Those offices would be replaced with numerous small field offices throughout the country. The other part of the reorganization involved creating five new CCS positions. The CCS job itself was to be redesigned and upgraded in terms of knowledge and skills requirements. It was planned to staff these new CCS positions through internal promotions from within the claims department.

Gus Tavus, a 52-year-old RCM, was asked by the senior vice president to apply for one of the new CCS positions as his position was being eliminated. Other RCMs, all of whom were older than 40 years of age were also asked to apply. None of the RCMs, including Gus, was promoted to the new CCS positions. Other candidates were also bypassed, and some of them were also older than 40. The promotions went to five claims specialists and supervisors from within the former regional offices, all of whom were under 40 years of age. Two of these newly promoted employees had worked for and reported to Gus at one time.

Gus sought to determine why he was not promoted. The information he gathered led him to believe he had been discriminated against because of his age. He retained a lawyer, Bruce Davis, and Bruce met with the senior vice president to gather information about the promotion process and to find out why his client had not been promoted.

Bruce was told that there were a large number of candidates who were better qualified for the job than Gus because Gus lacked adequate technical and communications skills for the new CCS job. The senior vice president refused to reconsider Gus for the job and said all decisions were "etched in stone." Gus and Bruce then filed suit with the Manitoba Human Rights Commission claiming age discrimination. They also subpoenaed numerous BPIC documents, including the personnel files of all applicants for the CCS positions.

Based on these documents, and discussions with Gus, the following information emerged about the promotion process actually used by BPIC. The SVPCC and the two MCCs conducted the total process; they received no input from the VPRC or the company's human resources department. There was no formal, written job description for the new CCS position, nor was there a formal internal job posting as required by company policy. The SVPCC and the MCCs developed a list of employees they thought might be interested in the job, including Gus, and then met to consider the list of candidates. At that meeting, the personnel files and previous performance appraisals of the candidates were not consulted. After deciding on the five candidates who would be offered the promotion (all five accepted), the VPCC and MCCs did scan the personnel files and appraisals of these five (only) to check for any disconfirming information about the employees. None was found. Inspection of all the files by Bruce Davis revealed no written comments suggesting age bias in past performance appraisals for any of the candidates, including Gus. Also, there was no indication that Gus lacked technical and communication skills. All of Gus's previous appraisal ratings were above average, and there was no evidence of recent decline in the favourability of the ratings. Finally, an interview with the VPRC (Gus's boss) revealed that he had not been consulted at all during the promotion process, that he was "shocked beyond belief" that Gus had not been promoted, and that there was "no question" but that Gus was qualified in all respects for the CCS job.

1. Based on the above facts, prepare a written report that presents a convincing discrimination treatment claim that Gus had been intentionally discriminated against on the basis of his age.
2. Present a convincing rebuttal, from the viewpoint of BPIC, to this discrimination treatment claim.

Equal Treatment for People with Disabilities when Using Public Services

David Lepofsky, who is blind, argued before the Human Rights Tribunal of Ontario that the Toronto Transit Commission (TTC) should mandate its employees to announce subway stops consistently. He had lobbied the TTC directly for ten years, and the best result he had received was that subway employees announced the stops but the announcements were often inconsistent or incomprehensible. In 2005, the Tribunal ruled that the TTC had contravened David's right to equal treatment.[40] How has the TTC contravened David's rights and what will they have to do to ensure that blind people have equal treatment when riding the TTC?

Is Mandatory Retirement a Form of Discrimination?

Mandatory retirement has been banned in Manitoba, Quebec, Alberta, Prince Edward Island, Yukon, and North West Territories, and it soon will be banned in Ontario. Proponents of banning mandatory retirement state that mandating people to retire at 65 is age discrimination. Those supporting mandatory retirement feel that young people will lose opportunities to enter the workforce and be promoted if mandatory retirement is lifted. Others feel that lifting mandatory retirement will adversely impact older people because there are good reasons to believe they will suffer more injuries on the job. Based on the Canadian Human Rights Act, is mandatory retirement a form of age discrimination? How would you counter the arguments stated above?

ENDNOTES

1. Adapted from an editorial column by S. D. Phelps, *HR Professional*, April/May, 2005.
2. M. W. Bennett, D. J. Polden, and H. S. Rubin, *Employment Relationships: Law and Practice* (Frederick, MD: Aspen, 2004), pp. 1–1 to 3–50.
3. Federal Court of Appeal, *Wiebe Door Services Ltd. v. The Minister of National Revenue*, June 18, 1986, docket A-531-85, www.ei-ae.gc.ca/policy/appeals/Federal-Court/A053185e.html.
4. A. E. Polivka and T. Nardone, "On the definition of 'contingent work,'" *Monthly Labor Review*, 112(12), December 1989, p. 10.
5. L. F. Vosko, "Regulating Precariousness? The Temporary Employment Relationshop Under the NAFTA and the EC Treaty," *Industrial Relations*, 53(1), 1998, p. 6.
6. K. Costa and P. Tourigny, "Duration of non-standard employment," *Perspectives on Labour and Income*, 17(1), Spring 2005, p. 31.
7. R. J. Bohner, Jr., and E. R. Salasko, "Beware the Legal Risks of Hiring Temps," *Workforce*, Oct. 2003, pp. 50–57
8. R. P. Chaykowski, "Non-standard Work and Economic Vulnerability," *Canadian Policy Research Network Inc. (NPRN)*, March 2005, p. iii.
9. CCH Business, "Jurisdiction," *Ultimate HR Manual*, 2005, www.cchonline.ca.
10. CCH Business, "Jurisdiction," *Ultimate HR Manual*, 2005, www.cchonline.ca.
11. K. Makin, "Where's the guarantee?" *The Globe and Mail*, April 16, 2005, p. F2.
12. Department of Justice, "Canadian Human Rights Act," Chapter H 6: Purpose of Act, http://laws.justice.gc.ca/en/H-6/31435.html.
13. Canadian Human Rights Commission, "Discrimination and Harassment," www.chrc-ccdp.ca/discrimination/discrimination-en.asp.
14. Department of Justice, "Canadian Human Rights Act," Chapter H 6: Purpose of Act, http://laws.justice.gc.ca/en/H-6/31435.html.
15. C. Sheppard, "Of Forest Fires and Systemic Discrimination: A Review of British Columbia (Public Service Employee Relations Commission) v. B.C.G.S.E.U.," *McGill Law Journal*, 2001, Vol. 46, p. 544.
16. Sheppard, "Of Forest Fires and Systemic Discrimination," p. 542.
17. CCH Business, "Types of Discrimination", *Ultimate HR Manual*, 2005.
18. Canadian Human Rights Commission, "Bona Fide Occupational Requirements and Boan Fide Justifications under the Canadian Human Rights Act: The Implications of Meiorin and Grismer," www.chrc-ccdp.ca/discrimination/occupational-en.asp.
19. Sheppard, "Of Forest Fires and Systemic Discrimination," pp. 535–537.

20. Sheppard, "Of Forest Fires and Systemic Discrimination," pp. 541–544.
21. Canadian Human Rights Commission, "Bona Fide Occupational Requirements and Bona Fide Justifications under the Canadian Human Rights Act: The Implications of Meiorin and Grismer."
22. Canadian Human Rights Commission, "Practical Guide for Employment Accommodation for People with Disabilities," www.chrc-ccdp.ca/discrimination/barrier_free-en.asp.
23. H. F. Schwind, H. Das, and T. H. Wagar, *Canadian Human Resource Management* Toronto: McGraw-Hill Ryerson, 1999), p. 164.
24. LexUm in partnership with Supreme Court of Canada, *Ontario Human Rights Commission v. Simpsons-Sears*, 1985, http://scc.lexum.umontreal.ca/en/1985/1985rcs2-536/1985rcs2-536.html.
25. LexUM in partnership with Supreme Court of Canada, *Central Alberta Dairy Pool v. Alberta Human Rights Commission*, 1990, http://scc.lexum.umontreal.ca/en/1990/1990rcs2-489/1990rcs2-489.html.
26. Department of Justice, "Canadian Human Rights Act," Chapter H 6: Purpose of Act, http://laws.justice.gc.ca/en/H-6/31435.html.
27. P. A. Neena Gupta, "Quebec Legislation against Psychological Harassment Has Nation-Wide Implications." *Canadian Payroll and Employment Law*, December 2004, www.hrpao.org/HRPAO/LegalCentre/newscluster/Quebec+Legislation+Against+Psychological+Harassment+has+Nation-Wide+Implications.htm.
28. L. Sullivan, "Facing up to harassment," *Canadian HR Reporter*, 17(7), April 5, 2004.
29. Human Resources and Skills Development Canada, "Sexual Harassment," March 2004, www.hrsdc.gc.ca/asp/gateway.asp?hr=en/lp/lo/lswe/ls/publications/12.shtml&hs=lxn.
30. Minister of Public Works and Government Services, "Canadian Human Rights Commission Annual Report," 2005, www.chrc-ccdp.ca/pdf/AR_2004_RA_en.pdf.
31. Human Resources and Skills Development Canada, "What is Employment Equity?" September 2003, www.hrsdc.gc.ca/en/lp/lo/lswe/we/information/what.shtml.
32. Human Resources and Skills Development Canada, "History of Employment Equity," September 2003, www.hrsdc.gc.ca/en/lp/lo/lswe/we/information/history.shtml.
33. Department of Justice, "Employment Equity Act," 1995, c. 44, http://laws.justice.gc.ca/en/E-5.401/50293.html.
34. S. Modi, "About Staff: Employment Equity: An important piece in the human rights puzzle," *HR Professional*, April 2005.
35. Canadian Human Rights Commission, "Employment Equity: Importance of Positive Policies and Practices," www.chrc-ccdp.ca/publications/chapter_862_chapitre-en.asp.
36. F. Kehoe and M. Archer, *Canadian Industrial Relations* (Oakville, ON: Twentieth Century Labour Publications, 1999), pp. 294–295.
37. R. Ogmundson and M. Doyle, "The Rise and Decline of Canadian Labour/1960 to 2000: Elites, Power, Ethnicity and Gender," *Canadian Journal of Sociology*, 2002, Vol. 27, p. 413.
38. Department of Justice, Privacy Act, 2000, Chapter P-21, August 2004, http://laws.justice.gc.ca/en/p-21/95414.html.
39. CCH Business, "Current Privacy Provisions," *Ultimate HR Manual*, 2005.
40. O. Moore, "Blind Rider Celebrates Victory over TTC," *The Globe and Mail*, June 30, 2005, p. A15.

Visit the Online Learning Centre at
www.mcgrawhill.ca/olc/heneman

CHAPTER

3

MEASUREMENT

CHAPTER OBJECTIVES

After reading this chapter, you will be able to:

- Understand the types of measures that are used in selection procedures
- Recognize and interpret the important characteristics and statistics that provide information on the measures of selection
- Understand the guidelines and principles specified for the collection and use of selection measures
- Grasp the legal issues that apply to the use of selection measures

In staffing, measurement is a process used to gather and express information about persons and jobs in numerical form. A common example in which management employs measurement is to administer a test to job applicants and evaluate their responses to determine a test score for each of them. The first part of this chapter presents a view of the process of measurement in staffing decisions.

After showing the vital importance and uses of measurement in staffing activities, three key concepts are then discussed. The first concept is that of measurement itself, along with the issues raised by it—standardization of measurement, levels of measurement, and the difference between objective and subjective measures. The second concept is that of scoring and how to express scores in ways that help in their interpretation. The final concept is that of correlations between scores, particularly as expressed by the correlation coefficient and its significance. Calculating correlations between scores is a very useful way to learn even more about the meaning of scores.

What is the quality of the measures used in staffing? How sound an indicator of the attributes measured are they? Answers to these questions lie in the reliability and validity of the measures and the scores they yield. There are multiple ways of doing reliability and validity analysis; these are discussed in conjunction with numerous examples drawn from staffing situations. As these examples show, the quality of staffing decisions (e.g., who to hire or reject) depends heavily on the quality of measures and scores used as inputs to these decisions.

An important practical concern involved in the process of measurement is the collection of assessment data. There are various decisions about testing procedures (e.g., who is qualified to test applicants, what information should be disclosed to applicants, how to assess applicants with standardized procedures) that need to be made. The collection of assessment data also includes the acquisition of tests and test manuals. The collection of assessment data and the acquisition of tests and test manuals will vary depending on whether paper-and-pencil or computerized selection measures are utilized. Finally, in the collection of assessment data, organizations need to attend to professional standards that govern their proper use.

SCIENCE AND STAFFING

Often when science and staffing are mentioned together, students grimace in puzzlement as though the connection is unnecessary and contrived. However, a scientific perspective on staffing is as sensible and necessary as a scientific perspective is for other fields of human involvement. The application of a scientific perspective in staffing is used to develop and apply staffing methods and procedures to ensure that an organization attracts and retains people who are best suited for the job and fit well with the organization's work environment. This is obviously desirable from the organization's perspective, because the result is a workforce that contributes to the attainment of organizational objectives, but it is also beneficial to individual members of the organization because the demands of the work and organization match their capabilities and temperament.

An assumption of taking a scientific perspective to staffing is that our world is causal. The assumption of causality means that the outcomes and events that we observe have causes. A scientific approach is concerned with identifying the connection between causes and events. Applying this approach to staffing means that it is understood that how an individual performs his/her job, as an outcome, is determined by some causal characteristic(s) of the person. Determining the causes associated with specific jobs and then developing procedures for identifying the presence of these in job candidates is the focus of staffing.

A scientific perspective applies to staffing in the same way it applies to other aspects of the human condition. One of the goals of science is the acquisition of information and then to apply that information to engineer and control our environment. Often science is applied to understand and deal with problems that society encounters. For example, in the winter of 2003 Toronto was confronted with an outbreak of Severe Acute Respiratory Syndrome (SARS). The public health and medical community responded with procedures aimed at containing the infection and preventing its spread. The actions of the public health and medical community represented the application of knowledge of viral diseases developed through scientific inquiry. Similarly, there is undoubtedly an ongoing program of medical research with the goal of developing vaccines and drugs for preventing and treating SARS.

The SARS example outlines the framework that is applied for investigating staffing problems using a scientific approach. Organizations are faced with the ongoing challenge of finding people suitable for the job vacancies that develop. Without any guidelines for the selection process, organizations may find that a person they select is not well suited for a particular position. The problem may occur at any of the various stages of the selection process (e.g., resumé evaluation, testing, interviewing, assessing references). This is where science becomes involved. The difficulties that organizations encounter in identifying the best job candidate become the general topic of research for researchers concerned with recruitment and selection. These researchers usually investigate specific elements of the selection process (e.g., interviewing) with the objective of identifying the source(s) of the problem as well as the development of a prescription for more effective procedures. From a staffing practitioner's perspective, the procedures used in selection should be based on the findings of research that has been conducted using scientific methods. In the field of medicine, a patient expects that any treatment prescribed by a physician is supported by a scientific process that has provided evidence of the efficacy of the prescription. This same logic should apply to the prescriptions applied to staffing in order to select the best candidate for a job vacancy.

Although we have advocated that staffing programs and procedures should be based on a scientific method, we have not defined what this means. Next, with the goal of eliminating this confusion, the characteristics of a scientific method are described. The key characteristics of a scientific method include the following:[1]

- **Analytical:** The scientific method takes an approach to problems that is rational, detailed, and logical.
- **Objective:** An objective approach means that "the chips will fall where they may." Thus, the findings will speak for themselves and the investigators will have no preferences.
- **Systematic:** This method approaches a topic in an organized and planned manner in order to conduct a complete and thorough examination of the topic.
- **Empirical:** Problems are examined by using methods and techniques that allow the subject matter to be quantified and measured.

Using a scientific method with these characteristics to investigate organizational staffing issues produces knowledge that helps organizations develop procedures that provide the best staffing solution (i.e., human resources) for the problems faced.

Understanding the relevance of the scientific method to staffing is also enhanced by understanding the goals of science. The four goals of science are directly applicable to an organization's staffing goals. The goals of science are briefly outlined below.[2]

2.1

- **Describe:** At the most basic stage, a science has as its goal the description of the phenomena of the discipline. This most fundamental goal serves as the foundation for subsequent higher goals. Description equates with measurement; without accurate measurement, progress in a science is limited. In staffing, the goal is to develop accurate descriptions of the job tasks, standards of performance, and necessary KSAOs (knowledges, skills, abilities, and other characteristics) for a job.
- **Predict:** The second goal of a science is to use data describing the relationships between variables of investigation to predict what will occur. In staffing, the goal is to use data relating to factors that result in successful (versus unsuccessful) job performance to predict which of the potential job candidates has the greatest likelihood of success with an organization.
- **Explain:** The scientific goal of explanation is concerned with understanding cause-and-effect relationships. From a scientific perspective, explanation is often a central concern. However, in staffing, explanation may be of tangential interest. For instance, in selecting firefighters a fire department may evaluate candidates using a series of physically demanding simulation tests. Knowing that performance on the tests predicts subsequent job performance is sufficient for the fire department. The fact that test performance, in part, is explained by fast- and slow-twitch muscle fibres is not a concern.
- **Control:** The ultimate goal of any science—and staffing—is to use knowledge gathered from scientific research to engineer factors that bring about preferred outcomes. Thus, medical research uses research findings to prevent and treat disease and illness. In staffing, knowledge from the scientific investigation of staffing problems is used to engineer an organization's workforce.

In outlining the goals of science, it is clear that these are also the goals of staffing. It is important to note that the fundamental goal of science is description, or measurement. Without adequate measures of a discipline's variables, the discipline cannot attain the higher goals of prediction, explanation, or control. For this reason, all sciences are concerned with measures. This is also the case for staffing and provides the justification for a closer examination of the measurement issues in staffing.

IMPORTANCE AND USE OF MEASURES

Measurement is one of the key ingredients for, and tools of, staffing organizations. The process of staffing organizations is highly dependent on the availability and use of measures. Indeed, it is virtually impossible to have any type of systematic staffing process that does not use measures and an accompanying measurement process.

measures
Methods or techniques for describing and assessing attributes of objects

Measures are methods or techniques for describing and assessing attributes of objects that are of concern to us. Examples include tests of applicant KSAOs, evaluations of employees' job performance, and applicants' ratings of their preferences for various types of job rewards. These assessments of attributes are gathered through the measurement process. That process consists of the following:

1. Choosing an attribute of concern
2. Developing an operational definition of the attribute
3. Constructing a measure of the attribute (if no suitable measure is available) as it is operationally defined
4. Using the measure to actually gauge the attribute

Results of the measurement process are expressed as numbers or scores—for example, applicants' scores on an ability test, employees' performance evaluation rating scores, or applicants' ratings of rewards in terms of their importance. These scores become the indicators of the attribute. Through the measurement process, the initial attribute and its operational definition have been transformed into a numerical expression of the attribute.

KEY CONCEPTS

This section covers a series of key concepts in three major areas: measurement, scores, and correlation between scores.

Measurement

In the preceding discussion, the essence of measurement and its importance and use in staffing were described. It is now important to define the term measurement more formally and explore implications of that definition.

measurement
The process of assigning numbers to objects to represent quantities of an attribute of the objects

Definition **Measurement** may be defined as the process of assigning numbers to objects to represent quantities of an attribute of the objects.[3] Exhibit 3.1 contains a depiction of the general process of the use of measures in staffing, along with an example using the job of maintenance mechanic. Following from the description of the measurement process provided above, the first step in measurement is to choose and define an attribute (sometimes also called a construct) to be measured. In the example, this is knowledge of mechanical principles. Then a measure must be developed for the attribute, and at that point the attribute can physically be measured. In the example, a paper-and-pencil test may be developed to measure mechanical knowledge, and this test is then administered to applicants. Once the attribute is physically measured, numbers or scores are determined (e.g., in the example, the mechanical test is scored). At that point, scores are available on the applicants, so an evaluation can be made of the scores (which scores meet the job requirements) and a selection decision can be made (e.g., hire a maintenance mechanic).

Of course, in practice, this textbook process is often not followed explicitly. When this happens, selection errors are more likely. For example, if the methods used to determine scores on an attribute are not explicitly determined and evaluated, the scores themselves may be incorrectly determined. Similarly, if the evaluation of the scores is not systematic, each selection decision maker may put his or her own "spin" on the scores, thereby defeating the purpose of careful measurement. The best way to avoid these problems is for all of those involved in selection decisions to go through each step of the measurement process depicted in Exhibit 3.1, apply it to the job(s) in question, and reach agreement at each step of the way.

EXHIBIT 3.1 Use of Measures in Staffing

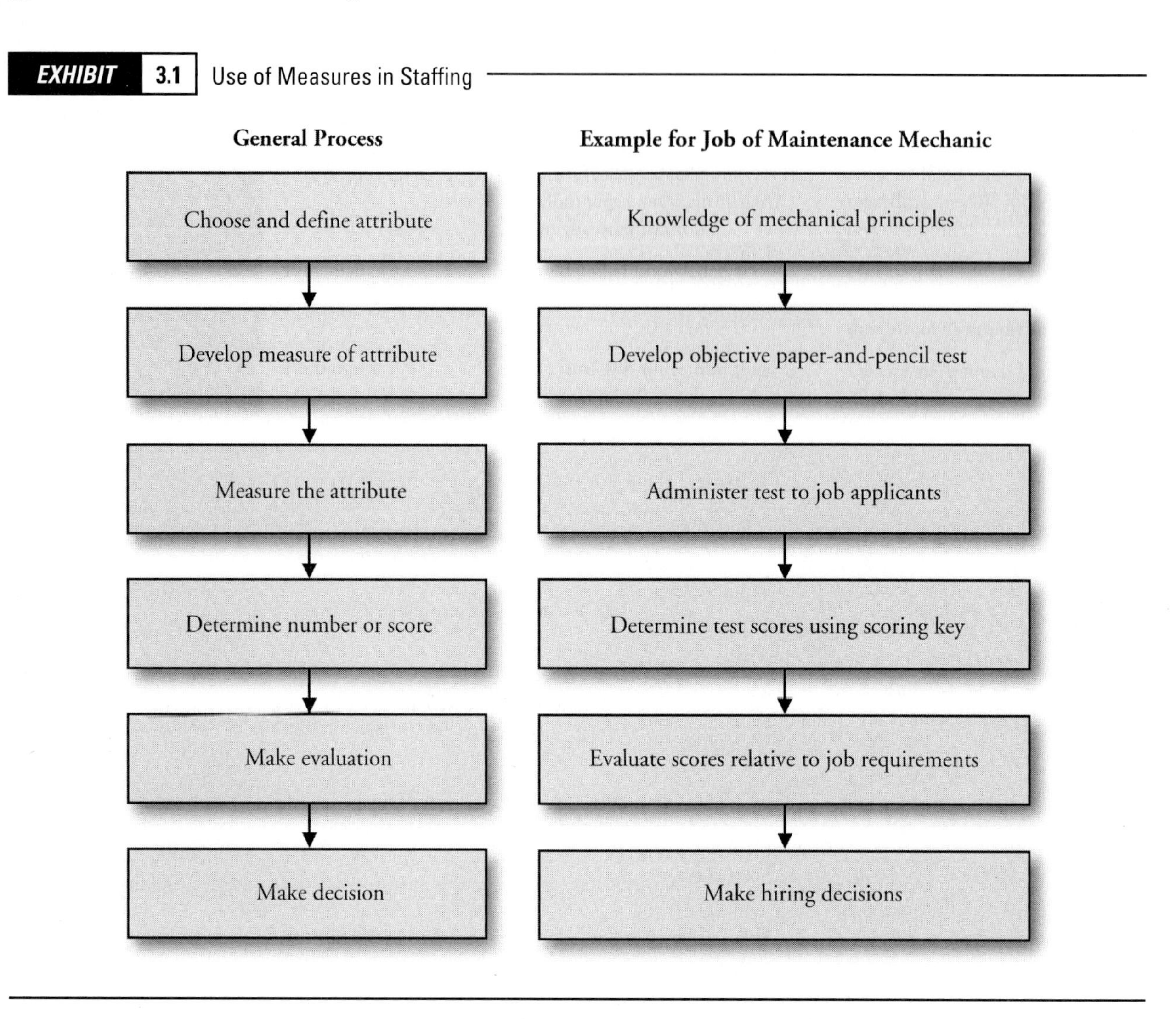

standardization
Means of controlling the influence of outside or extraneous factors on scores generated by a measure and ensuring that, as much as possible, the scores obtained are a reflection of the attribute measured

Standardization The hallmark of sound measurement practice is standardization.[4] **Standardization** is a means of controlling the influence of outside or extraneous factors on the scores generated by the measure and ensuring that, as much as possible, the scores obtained are a reflection of the attribute measured.

A standardized measure has three basic properties:

1. The content is identical for all objects measured (e.g., all job applicants take the same test).
2. The administration of the measure is identical for all objects (e.g., all job applicants have the same time limit on a test).
3. The rules for assigning numbers are clearly specified and agreed on in advance (e.g., a scoring key for the test is developed before it is administered).

These seemingly simple and straightforward characteristics of standardization of measures have substantial implications for the conduct of many staffing activities. These implications will become apparent throughout the remainder of this text. For example, assessment devices, such as the employment interview and letters of reference, often fail to meet the requirements for standardization, and organizations must undertake steps to make them more standardized.

Levels of Measurement There are varying degrees of precision in measuring attributes and in representing differences among objects in terms of attributes. Accordingly, there are different levels or scales of measurement.[5] It is common to classify any particular measure as falling into one of four levels of measurement: nominal, ordinal, interval, or ratio.

Nominal. With nominal scales, a given attribute is categorized, and numbers are assigned to the categories. With or without numbers, however, there is no order or level implied among the categories. The categories are merely different, and none is higher or lower than the other. For example, each job title could represent a different category, with a different number assigned to it: managers = 1, clericals = 2, sales = 3, and so forth. Clearly, the numbers do not imply any ordering among the categories.

Ordinal. With ordinal scales, objects are rank-ordered according to how much of the attribute they possess. Thus, objects may be ranked from "best" to "worst" or from "highest" to "lowest." For example, five job candidates, each of whom has been evaluated in terms of overall qualification for the job, might be rank-ordered from 1 to 5, or highest to lowest, according to their job qualifications.

Rank orderings only represent relative differences among objects, and they do not indicate the absolute levels of the attribute. Thus, the rank ordering of the five job candidates does not indicate exactly how qualified each of them is for the job, nor are the differences in their ranks necessarily equal to the differences in their qualifications. The difference in qualifications between applicants ranked 1 and 2 may not be the same as the difference between those ranked 4 and 5.

Interval. Like ordinal scales, interval scales allow us to rank-order objects. However, the differences between adjacent points on the measurement scale are now equal in terms of the attribute. If an interval scale is used to rank the order of the five job candidates, the difference in qualifications between those ranked 1 and 2 are equal to the difference between those ranked 4 and 5.

It should be pointed out that there are many instances in which the level of measurement falls somewhere between an ordinal and an interval scale. That is, objects can be clearly rank-ordered, but the differences between the ranks are not necessarily equal throughout the measurement scale. In the example of the five job candidates, the difference in qualifications between those ranked 1 and 2 might be slight compared with the difference between those ranked 4 and 5.

Unfortunately, this in-between level of measurement is characteristic of many of the measures used in staffing. Though it is not a major problem, it does signal the need for caution in interpreting the meaning of differences in scores among people.

Ratio. Ratio scales are like interval scales in that there are equal differences between scale points for the attribute being measured. In addition, however, ratio scales have a logical or absolute true zero point. Because of this, how much of the attribute each object possesses can be stated in absolute terms.

Normally, ratio scales are involved in counting or weighing things. There are many such examples of ratio scales in staffing. Assessing how much weight a candidate can carry over some distance for physically demanding jobs such as firefighting or general construction is an example of this. Perhaps the most common example is counting how much previous job experience (general or specific) job candidates have had.

Objective and Subjective Measures Frequently, staffing measures are described as being either "objective" or "subjective." Often, the term subjective is used in disparaging ways (e.g., "I can't believe how subjective that interview was; there's no way they can rate me fairly on the basis of it"). Exactly what is the difference between so-called objective and subjective measures?

The difference, in large part, pertains to the rules used to assign numbers to the attribute being assessed. With objective measures, the rules are predetermined and usually communicated and applied through some sort of scoring key or system. Most paper-and-pencil tests are considered objective. The scoring systems in subjective measures are more elusive and often involve a rater or judge who assigns the numbers. Many employment interviewers fall in this category, especially those with an idiosyncratic way of evaluating people's responses, one that is not known or shared by other interviewers.

In principle, any attribute can be measured objectively, subjectively, or both. Research shows that when an attribute is measured by both objective and subjective means, there is often relatively low agreement between scores from the two types of measures. A case in point pertains to the attribute of job performance. It may be measured objectively through quantity of output, and it may be measured subjectively through performance appraisal ratings. A review of the research shows that there is very low correlation between scores from the objective and subjective performance measures.[6] Undoubtedly, the raters' lack of sound scoring systems for rating job performance was a major contributor to the lack of obtained agreement.

It thus appears that whatever type of measure is being used to assess attributes in staffing, serious attention should be paid to the scoring system or key that is used. This requires nothing more, in a sense, than having a firm knowledge of exactly what the organization is trying to measure in the first place. This is true for both paper-and-pencil (objective) measures and judgmental (subjective) measures, such as the employment interview. It is simply another way of emphasizing the importance of standardization in measurement.

Scores

Measures yield numbers or scores to represent the amount of the attribute being assessed. Scores thus are the numerical indicator of the attribute. Once scores have been derived, they can be manipulated in various ways to give them even greater meaning, and to help better describe characteristics of the objects being scored.[7]

Central Tendency and Variability Assume that a group of job applicants was administered a test of the knowledge of mechanical principles. The test is scored using a scoring key, and each applicant receives a score on the test, known as a raw score. Their scores are shown in Exhibit 3.2.

Some features of this set of scores may be summarized through the calculation of summary statistics. These pertain to central tendency and variability in the scores and are also shown in Exhibit 3.2.

The indicators of central tendency are the mean, median, and mode. Since it was assumed that the data were interval level data, it is permissible to compute all three indicators of central tendency. Had the data been ordinal, the mean should not be computed. For nominal data, only the mode would be appropriate.

The variability indicators are the range and the standard deviation. The range shows lowest to highest actual score for the job applicants. The standard deviation shows, in essence, the average amount of deviation of individual scores from the average score. It summarizes the amount of spread in the scores. The larger the standard deviation, the greater the variability, or spread, in the data.

Percentiles A percentile score for an individual is the percentage of people scoring below the individual in a distribution of scores. Refer again to Exhibit 3.2, and consider applicant C. That applicant's percentile score is the 10th percentile ($2/20 \times 100$). Applicant S is in the 90th percentile ($18/20 \times 100$).

Standard Scores When interpreting scores, it is natural to compare individuals' raw scores to the mean, that is, to ask whether scores are above, at, or below the mean. But a true understanding of how well an individual did relative to the mean takes into account the amount of variability in scores around the mean (the standard deviation). That is, the calculation must be

EXHIBIT 3.2 Central Tendency and Variability: Summary Statistics

Data		Summary Statistics
Applicant	**Test Score (x)**	
A	10	A. Central tendency Mean ($\bar{\chi}$) = 338/20 = 16.9 Median = middle score = 17 Mode = most frequent score = 15 B. Variability Range = 10 to 24 Standard deviation (SD) = $\sqrt{\frac{\Sigma(\chi-\bar{\chi})^2}{N-1}} = 3.52$
B	12	
C	14	
D	14	
E	15	
F	15	
G	15	
H	15	
I	15	
J	17	
K	17	
L	17	
M	18	
N	18	
O	19	
P	19	
Q	19	
R	22	
S	23	
T	24	
	Total (Σ) = 338	
	N = 20	

"corrected" or controlled for the amount of variability in a score distribution to accurately present how well a person scored relative to the mean.

Calculation of the standard score for an individual is the way to accomplish this correction. The formula for calculation of the standard score, or Z, is as follows:

$$Z = \frac{X - \bar{X}}{SD}$$

Applicant S in Exhibit 3.2 had a raw score of 23 on the test; the mean was 16.9 and the standard deviation was 3.52. Substituting into the above formula, applicant S has a Z score of 1.7. Thus, applicant S scored about 1.7 standard deviations above the mean.

Standard scores are also useful for determining how a person performed, in a relative sense, on two or more tests. For example, assume the following data for a particular applicant:

	Test 1	**Test 2**
Raw score	50	48
Mean	48	46
SD	2.5	.80

On which test did the applicant do better? To answer that, simply calculate the applicant's standard scores on the two tests. The Z score on test 1 is .80, and the Z score on test 2 is 2.5. Thus, while the applicant got a higher raw score on test 1 than on test 2, the applicant got a higher Z score on test 2 than on test 1. Viewed in this way, it is apparent that the applicant did better on the second of the two tests.

Correlation between Scores

Frequently, in staffing there are scores on two or more measures for a group of individuals. One common occurrence is to have scores on two (or often, more than two) KSAO measures. For example, there could be a score on the test of knowledge of mechanical principles and also an overall rating of the applicant's probable job success based on the employment interview. In such instances, it is logical to ask whether there is some relation between the two sets of scores. Is there a tendency for an increase in knowledge test scores to be accompanied by an increase in interview ratings?

As another example, an organization may have scores on a particular KSAO measure (e.g., the knowledge test) and a measure of job performance (e.g., performance appraisal ratings) for a group of individuals. Is there a correlation between these two sets of scores? If there is, then this would provide some evidence about the probable validity of the knowledge test as a predictor of job performance. This evidence would help the organization decide whether to incorporate the use of the test into the selection process for job applicants.

Investigation of the relationship between two sets of scores proceeds through the plotting of scatter diagrams and through calculation of the correlation coefficient.

Scatter Diagrams Assume two sets of scores for a group of people: scores on a test and scores on a measure of job performance. A scatter diagram is simply the plot of the joint distribution of the two sets of scores. Inspection of the plot provides a visual representation of the type of relationship that exists between the two sets of scores. Exhibit 3.3 provides three different scatter diagrams for the two sets of scores. Each X represents a test score and job performance score combination for an individual.

Example A in Exhibit 3.3 suggests very little relationship between the two sets of scores. Example B shows a modest relationship between the scores, and example C shows a somewhat strong relationship between the two sets of scores.

Correlation Coefficient While scatter diagrams are a useful and important first step in determining the extent of the relationship between a set of scores, they also have obvious limitations. Scatter diagrams provide a picture of a relationship, but they do not provide precise information on the extent of the relationship between a set of scores. This information is provided by a **correlation coefficient**.

correlation coefficient
Provides precise information on the extent of the relationship between a set of scores

There are a number of different types of correlation coefficients that may be calculated for a set of score pairs; the appropriateness of a particular correlation is determined by the level of measurement involved (i.e., nominal, ordinal, interval, or ratio). For purpose of illustration here, the discussion will be limited to the Pearson product-moment correlation (as shown in Exhibit 3.4), which is used with an interval or ratio level of measurement.

The symbol for the correlation coefficient is *r*. Numerically, r values can range from r = − 1.0 to r = 1.0. The larger the absolute value of r, the stronger the relationship. When an r value is shown without the plus or minus sign, the value is assumed to be positive.

Naturally, the value of r bears a close resemblance to the scatter diagram. As a demonstration of this, Exhibit 3.3 also shows the approximate r value for each of the three scatter diagrams. In example A, a low r is indicated (r = .10). The r in example B is moderate (r = .25), and the r in example C is high (r = .60).

Actual calculation of the correlation coefficient is straightforward. An example of this calculation, and the formula for r, are shown in Exhibit 3.4. In the exhibit, there are two sets of scores for 20 people. The first set of scores is the set of test scores for the 20 individuals in Exhibit 3.2. The second set of scores is an overall job performance rating (on a 1–5 rating scale) for these people. As can be seen from the calculation, there is a correlation of r = .58 between the two sets of scores.

EXHIBIT 3.3 Scatter Diagrams and Corresponding Correlations

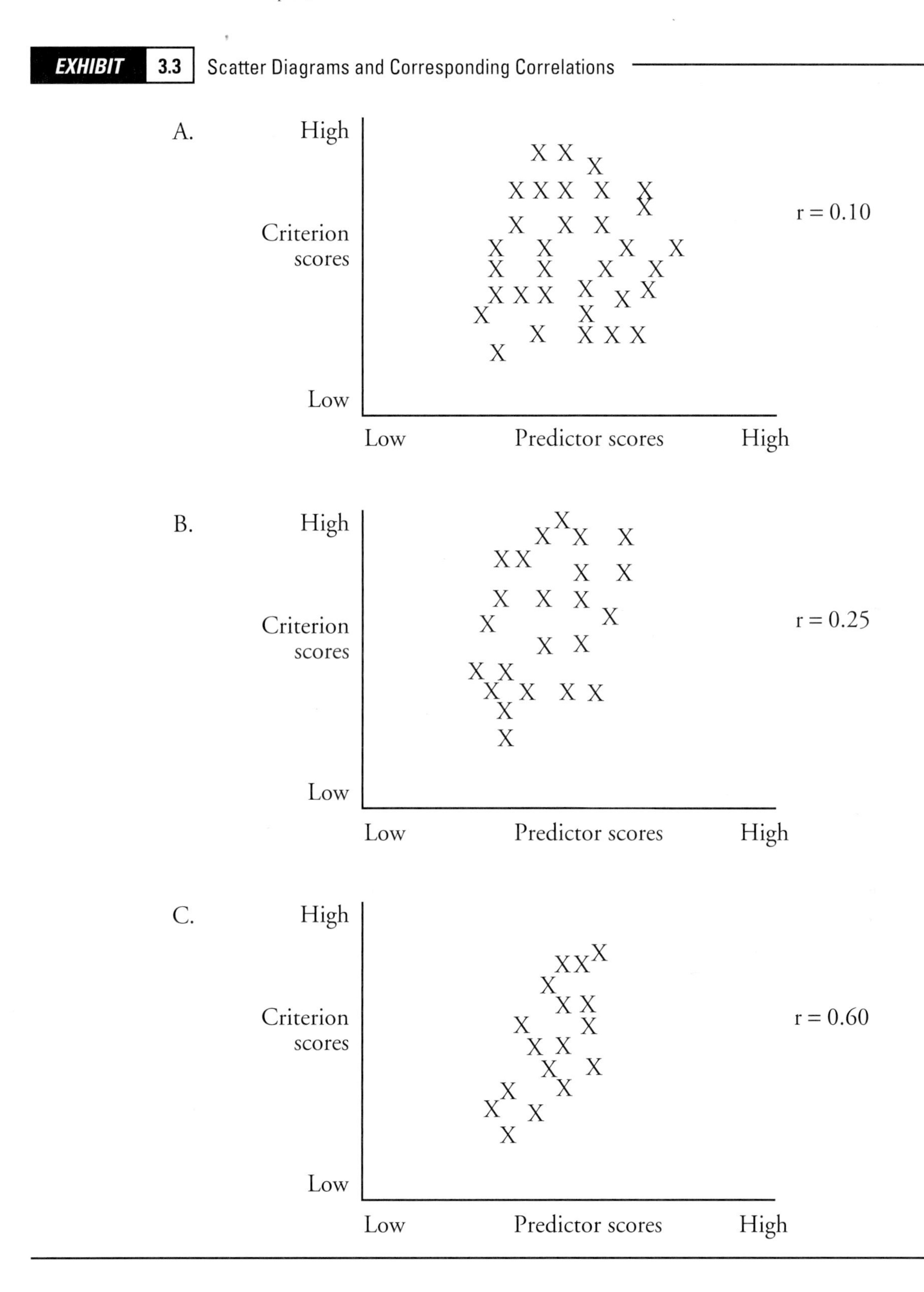

EXHIBIT 3.4 Calculation of Product-Moment Correlation Coefficient

Person	Test Score (X)	Performance Rating (Y)	(X^2)	(Y^2)	(XY)
A	10	2	100	4	20
B	12	1	144	1	12
C	14	2	196	4	28
D	14	1	196	1	14
E	15	3	225	9	45
F	15	4	225	16	60
G	15	3	225	9	45
H	15	4	225	16	60
I	15	4	225	16	60
J	17	3	289	9	51
K	17	4	289	16	68
L	17	3	289	9	51
M	18	2	324	4	36
N	18	4	324	16	72
O	19	3	361	9	57
P	19	3	361	9	57
Q	19	5	361	25	95
R	22	3	484	9	66
S	23	4	529	16	92
T	24	5	576	25	120
	$\Sigma X = 338$	$\Sigma Y = 63$	$\Sigma X^2 = 5948$	$\Sigma Y^2 = 223$	$\Sigma XY = 1109$

$$r = \frac{N\Sigma XY - (\Sigma X)(\Sigma Y)}{\sqrt{[N\Sigma X^2 - (\Sigma X)^2][N\Sigma Y^2 - (\Sigma Y)^2]}} = \frac{20(1109) - (338)(63)}{\sqrt{[20(5948) - (338)^2][20(223) - (63)^2]}} = .58$$

The correlation coefficient provides a statistic that summarizes the magnitude and direction of the relationship between a set of scores. However, the correlation coefficient in the form of the coefficient of determination provides further information on the nature of the relationship between the variables.

The coefficient of determination is obtained by simply squaring the correlation coefficient and multiplying the product by 100. If $r = .50$, then the coefficient of determination is 25 percent: $(.50)^2 \times 100 = 25$. While the calculation of the coefficient of determination is simple, the interpretation is often more difficult to grasp. To assist your understanding, a relevant illustration is provided below.

Consider the marks for students in your program at the university or college you attend. Student marks exist on a continuum that has a potential range of 0 to 100 percent, but for this example, let's assume that marks in your program range from 50 to 100 percent with an average of 75 percent. If your program is like most, this means that most students have marks around 75 percent while there are a few who are doing exceeding well (i.e., those with marks in the 90s) and a few who are not doing too well (i.e., those with marks in the 50s)—and if you wanted, you could use the equation from Exhibit 3.2 to determine the variance for the distribution of student marks. However, let us consider the question of why there is variability in student marks.

Although there are various factors that people identify as contributors to differences in marks, hours of study is a common candidate. In specifying hours of study as a factor that contributes to variability in marks, we are suggesting that students who study more get higher marks, those who study less get lower marks, and those who study an average amount attain average marks. Therefore we have suggested that there is a correlation between marks and studying.

Now, imagine what would occur if the dean of your program enjoyed some autocratic allowance and was able to dictate that all students in the program would study no more or less than the average number of hours of student study. The effect of this decree would be that those who normally study less would study more, and those who normally study more would study less. What would happen to the variability in marks? The logical answer to that question is that marks would become less variable; those who increased their studying would see their marks rise, those forced to study less would see their marks decrease, and the marks of the average students would remain the same.

The point of the example is to illustrate how the variance, or variability, in marks is, in part, explained by hours of study. The percentage of the variance in marks that is explained by hours of study depends on the magnitude of the correlation between the variables. This is what the coefficient of determination provides. This is an important statistic for staffing because it provides information on the factors (i.e., selection measures) that explain differences in organizational measures of performance (e.g., sales, accidents, attendance, productivity).

Assumptions and Limitations. The value of r is affected by how much variation there actually is in each set of scores. Other things being equal, the less variation there is in either or both sets of scores, the smaller the calculated value of r will be. At the extreme, if there is no variation in one of the sets of scores, the correlation will be r = .00. That is, for there to be a correlation there must be variation in both sets of scores. The lack of variation in scores is called the problem of restriction of range.

Also, the formula used to calculate the correlation in Exhibit 3.4 is based on the assumption that there is a linear relationship between the two sets of scores. This may not always be a good assumption; something other than a straight line may best capture the true nature of the relationship between scores. To the extent that two sets of scores are not related in a linear fashion, use of the formula for calculation of the correlation will yield a value of r that understates the actual strength of the relationship.

Finally, the correlation between two variables does not imply causation between them. A correlation simply says how two variables co-vary or correlate; it says nothing about one variable necessarily causing the other one.

Significance of the Correlation Coefficient Once the correlation coefficient is calculated, questions frequently arise as to the significance of the correlation. These questions may be addressed through consideration of a correlation's practical and statistical significance.

Practical Significance. The practical significance of the correlation refers to its size, regardless of its sign. The larger the r, the greater its practical significance.

This interpretation is very appealing. Recall that the correlation is really the amount of common or shared variation between two variables. The greater the degree of that co-variation, the more we can use one variable to help us understand or predict another variable.

Consider again the correlation between the knowledge of mechanical principles test and the job performance ratings. The greater the r between those two variables, the greater the certainty that knowledge of mechanical principles is a key underlying KSAO of job performance, and that scores on this test are useful in predicting the likely performance of individuals at the time they are job applicants. Indeed, prediction such as this is a major purpose of staffing systems. Calculation and use of correlations is thus an extremely important tool for staffing activities.

However, the practical significance of a correlation coefficient depends on whether the correlation provides an accurate estimate of the actual correlation. Information on this issue is provided by the statistical significance of the correlation.

Statistical Significance. The calculation of the correlation between a pair of variables is based on the data provided by the sample. For example, in a selection situation a correlation might be obtained for the relationship between test scores and job performance for a group of job applicants. The job applicants constitute a sample from the population of potential applicants. The correlation obtained from the sample data is an estimate of the relationship between the variables in the larger population of applicants.

Assessing the statistical significance of the sample correlation is a process that indicates whether the estimate provided by the obtained correlation is representative of the true correlation in the population. The logic of assessing the statistical significance of a correlation from a sample is based on the assumption that there is no correlation between the variables involved. If the true correlation is zero, and a large number of samples were obtained from the population and the correlation calculated for each sample, the correlations would cluster around zero. If the frequency of the occurrence of the various sample correlations is graphed, a sampling distribution is created. The statistical significance of a sample correlation is assessed within the context of the sampling distribution.

A hypothetical sampling distribution of sample correlations from a population where the actual correlation is zero is presented in Exhibit 3.5. In Exhibit 3.5, note that most of the sample correlations obtained cluster around a correlation of zero. However, you should also note that there are instances where moderate to large positive and negative sample correlations occur; the frequency distribution shows that these correlations have a low probability of occurrence. Denoting a correlation from a sample as significant occurs if the magnitude of the correlation is so large that it constitutes a rare event if the actual correlation in the population is zero. By convention, a correlation that would occur with a probability of .05 or less is termed significant, which means that, although it could be one of the rare events that occurs as a result of chance, it is considered to reflect the actual correlation in the population.

In consideration of the preceding documentation relating to selection (i.e., user guides, testing manuals, etc., that should provide correlation evidence to support the use of a selection device or the adoption of any other measurement instrument in selection), measures will state

EXHIBIT 3.5 Distribution of Sample Correlations

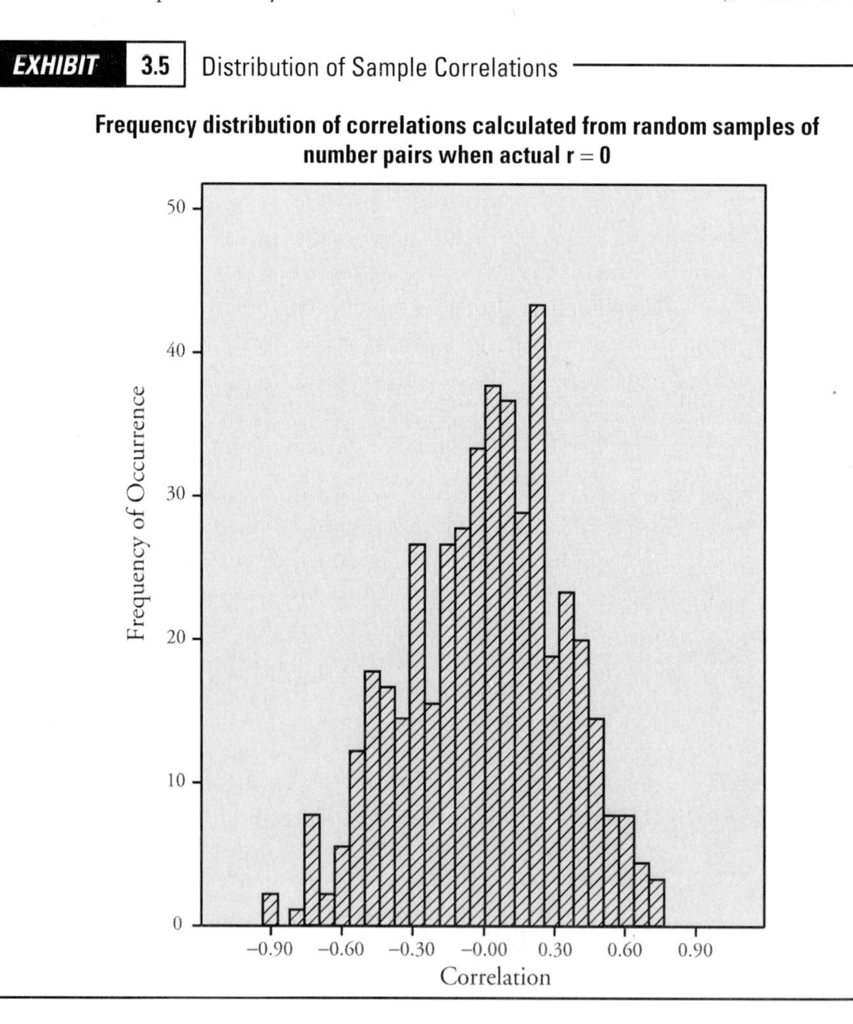

the correlation coefficient and its probability level (the probability level is indicated with the symbol *p*). In combination, this information indicates the nature of the correlation and whether it represents the true correlation between the pair of variables. For example, if a report assessing the correlation between a selection test and supervisor performance ratings finds that $r = .40$, $p < .05$ the correlation would be described as significant (i.e., the probability is less than .05) and the interpretation is that .40 is a reflection of the actual correlation. Conversely, if it was reported that $r = .40$, $p > .05$ the correlation would be described as not significant (note insignificant is not the term used) and the interpretation is that the correlation is what would be expected to occur if the actual correlation in the population is zero.

In the example above you might think that we have confused the situation by indicating that a correlation of .40 could be both significant and not significant. Instead of attempting to confuse the issue, the example will be used to describe the influence of sample size on significance. The relevance of sample size relates to the likelihood of rare events in large versus small samples. As an illustration, think about coin flips using a loonie. All things being equal, when flipping a loonie multiple times (e.g., 30 times), you would expect that heads and loonies will occur approximately equally often. If this is done repeatedly, all possible combinations of heads and loonies will occur. However, 30 heads, 30 loonies, and similar occurrences where one side of the coin comes up w th a higher frequency will occur rarely. Thus, with a large sample of 30 coin tosses, that true nature of the population of coin tosses (heads and loonies come up approximately equally) occurs most often and rare events (i.e., 30 heads or 30 loonies) have a low probability. Conversely, there is a much greater probability of obtaining all heads with a set of only two coin tosses (i.e., a small sample of coin tosses). In the same manner, there is a much greater probability of obtaining a large correlation (either positive or negative) using a small sample when in fact the actual correlation is zero. Thus, using a sample of 18, a correlation of .40 is not significant using a probability criteria of .05. With a sample of 18, a correlation must be .47 or larger before it is considered significant. Alternatively, with a sample of 32, a correlation of .40 is significant; in fact with this sample a correlation of .35 or greater is significant. An important issue related to correlation and sample size is that with very large samples rather small correlations will obtain significance. In these instances, the interpretation is that the correlation is a reflection of the actual correlation between the variables in the population.

Both the practical and statistical significance of the correlation are of concern in interpreting its significance. For example, if $r = .25$ and $p < .05$, the following kind of interpretation is made about significance. The correlation has moderate practical significance ($r^2 = .06$), and it meets a normal threshold for statistical significance. There is thus likely a relationship between the two variables in the population, based on what was found to be the relationship in this particular sample.

QUALITY OF MEASURES

Measures are developed and used to gauge attributes of objects. Results of measures are expressed in the form of scores, and various manipulations may be done to them. Such manipulations lead to better understanding and interpretation of the scores, and thus the attribute represented by the scores.

For practical reasons, in staffing the scores of individuals are treated as if they were, in fact, the attribute itself, rather than merely indicators of the attribute. For example, scores on a mental ability test are interpreted as being synonymous with how intelligent individuals are. Or individuals' job performance ratings from their supervisors are viewed as indicators of their true performance.

Treated in this way, scores become a major input to decision making about individuals. For example, scores on the mental ability test are used and weighted heavily to decide which job applicants will receive a job offer. Or performance ratings may serve as a key factor in deciding which individuals will be eligible for an internal staffing move, such as a promotion. In these and numerous other ways, management acts on the basis of scores to guide the conduct of staffing activities in the organization. This is illustrated through such phrases as "let the numbers do the talking," "we manage by the numbers," and "never measured, never managed."

The quality of the decisions and actions taken are unlikely to be any better than the quality of the measures on which they are based. Thus, there is a lot at stake in the quality of the measures used in staffing. Such concerns with the quality of measures are best viewed in terms of reliability and validity of measures.[8]

Measurement Error

In staffing, measures are used to characterize a person's status on characteristics relevant to how he/she will perform (i.e., predictors), or does perform (i.e., performance criteria), a job and how that person will fit, or does not fit, into an organization. However, because of the nature of the subject matter, the measurement devices contain measurement error. This type of error represents "noise" in the measure and measurement process. Its occurrence means that the measure did not yield perfectly consistent scores, or so-called true scores, for the attribute.

The scores actually obtained from the measure thus have two components to them, a true score and measurement error. That is,

actual score = true score + error

The error component of any actual score, or set of scores, represents unreliability of measurement. Unfortunately, unreliability is a fact of life for the types of measures used in staffing. To help understand why this is the case, the various types or sources of error that can occur in a staffing context must be explored. These errors may be grouped under the categories of deficiency and contamination error.[9]

Deficiency Error Deficiency error occurs when there is a failure to measure some portion or aspect of the attribute assessed. For example, if knowledge of mechanical principles involves gear ratios, among other things, and our test does not have any items (or an insufficient number of items) covering this aspect, then the test is deficient. As another example, if an attribute of job performance is "planning and setting work priorities," and the raters fail to rate people on that dimension during their performance appraisal, then the performance measure is deficient.

Deficiency error can occur in several related ways. First, there can be an inadequate definition of the attribute in the first place. Thus, the test of knowledge of mechanical principles may fail to get at familiarity with gear ratios because it was never included in the initial definition of mechanical principles. Or the performance measure may fail to require raters to rate their employees on "planning and setting work priorities" because this attribute was never considered an important dimension of their work.

A second way that deficiency error occurs is in the construction of measures used to assess the attribute. Here, the attribute may be well defined and understood, but there is a failure to construct a measure that adequately gets at the totality of the attribute. This is akin to poor measurement by oversight, which happens when measures are constructed in a hurried, ad hoc fashion.

Deficiency error also occurs when the organization opts to use whatever measures are available because of ease, cost considerations, sales pitches and promotional claims, and so forth. The measures so chosen may turn out to be deficient.

Contamination Error Contamination error represents the occurrence of unwanted or undesirable influences on the measure and on individuals for whom the measure is being used. These influences muddy the scores and make them difficult to interpret.

Sources of contamination abound, as do examples of them. Several of these sources and examples are shown in Exhibit 3.6, along with some suggestions for how they might be controlled. These examples show that contamination error is multifaceted, making it difficult to minimize and control.

EXHIBIT 3.6 Sources of Contamination Error and Suggestions for Control

Source of Contamination	Example	Suggestion for Control
Content domain	Irrelevant material on test	Define domain of test material to be covered
Standardization	Different time limits for same test	Have same time limits for everyone
Chance response tendencies	Guessing by test taker	Impossible to control in advance
Rater	Rater gives inflated ratings to people	Train rater in rating accuracy
Rating situation	Interviewees are asked different questions	Ask all interviewees same questions

Reliability of Measures

To interpret the measures obtained in selection, it is necessary to gain a sense of the measurement error associated with a given measurement device. This is provided through the determination of a measure's reliability.

Reliability of measurement refers to the consistency of measurement of an attribute. A measure is reliable to the extent that it provides a consistent set of scores to represent an attribute. Rarely is perfect reliability achieved because of the occurrence of measurement error. Reliability is thus a matter of degree.

There are several different types of reliability associated with selection measures. This may involve measures obtained to assess a candidate's standing on a relevant KSAO or performance measures collected from job incumbents, and may be assessed for measures that are objective, such as test scores, or measures that are subjective, such as interviewers' ratings of a candidate's suitability for a job. Each of the common types of reliability is described below.

Interrater Reliability. When raters serve as the measure, it is often convenient to talk about interrater reliability, or the amount of agreement among them. For example, if members of a group or panel interview independently rate a set of job applicants on a 1–5 scale, it is logical to ask how much they agreed with each other.

A simple way to determine this is to calculate the percentage of agreement among the raters. An example of this is shown in Exhibit 3.7.

There is no commonly accepted minimum level of interrater agreement that must be met in order to consider the raters sufficiently reliable. Normally, a fairly high level should be set—75 percent or higher. The more important the end use of the ratings, the greater the agreement required should be. Critical uses, such as hiring decisions, demand very high levels of reliability, well in excess of 75 percent agreement.

Interrater reliability may also be determined by calculating the correlation to determine the relationship between the ratings assigned by a pair of raters.

Test–Retest Reliability. To assess test–retest reliability, the test scores from two different time periods are correlated through calculation of the correlation coefficient (r). The r may be calculated on total test scores, or a separate r may be calculated for scores on each item. The resultant r provides an indication of the stability of measurement; the higher the r, the more stable the measure.

Interpretation of the r value is made difficult by the fact that the scores are gathered at two different points in time. Between those two time points, the attribute being measured has an opportunity to change. Interpretation of test–retest reliability thus requires some sense of how much the attribute may be expected to change, and what the appropriate time interval between tests is. Usually, for very short time intervals (hours or days), most attributes are quite stable, and a large test–retest r (r = .90 or higher) should be expected. Over longer time intervals, it is usual to expect much lower r values, depending on the attribute being measured. For example, over

EXHIBIT 3.7 Calculation of Percentage Agreement among Raters

Person (ratee)	Rater 1	Rater 2	Rater 3
A	5	5	2
B	3	3	5
C	5	4	4
D	1	1	5
E	2	2	4

$$\% \text{ Agreements} = \frac{\#\text{agreements}}{\#\text{ agreements} + \#\text{disagreements}} \times 100$$

% Agreement
Rater 1 and Rater 2 = 4/5 = 80%
Rater 1 and Rater 3 = 0/5 = 0%
Rater 2 and Rater 3 = 1/5 = 20%

six months or a year, individuals' knowledge of mechanical principles might change. If so, there will be lower test–retest reliabilities (e.g., $r = .50$).

Test–retest reliability may also be used to assess the reliability of ratings provided by a single rater. To calculate intrarater agreement, scores assigned to the same people by a rater in two different time periods are compared. The calculation could involve computing the correlation between the two sets of scores, or it could involve using the same formula as for interrater agreement (see Exhibit 3.7).

Interpretation of intrarater agreement is made difficult by the time factor. For short time intervals between measures, a fairly high relationship is expected (e.g., $r = .80$, or percentage agreement = 90%). For longer time intervals, the level of reliability may reasonably be expected to be lower.

Equivalent/Parallel Forms Reliability. Suppose companies involved in construction, logging, and other industries that have the potential for serious industrial accidents want to ensure that only qualified people work as industrial first aid attendants. To ensure that this occurs, safety representatives from the stakeholder industries develop a rigorous training program. At the end of the training, one of the evaluation requirements is to have candidates complete a written test. If the test standards for certification are difficult to attain, many candidates may have to write the certification exam more than once before they qualify. In such situations, it is necessary that different but equivalent forms, or parallel versions, of the certification test be developed. The different versions of the test should have similar average scores and similar variances. In addition, there should be consistency in the scores obtained by test takers completing different versions of the test. As an example, Exhibit 3.8 provides the possible results of the process of developing three versions of the industrial first aid written test using a sample of 100 already qualified industrial first aid attendants.

The results presented in Exhibit 3.8 show that the three tests produce very similar results (as indicated by the average scores and standard deviations). Similarly, there are significant (i.e., $p < .05$), positive correlations between the different versions of the test. The correlation results indicate the existence of reliability for the equivalent forms of the test.

Internal Consistency Reliability. A final form of reliability provides an index of the homogeneity that exists among a group of measures that have been designed to measure a common construct. For example, an organization may be interested in assessing potential managers' beliefs about appropriate methods of supervision in order to avoid hiring those with autocratic and domineering styles of management. To assess this tendency, a questionnaire is developed.

EXHIBIT 3.8 Industrial First Aid Attendant Parallel Forms Written Tests

Test Version	Mean Score	Standard Deviation
A	69.59	14.96
B	69.14	12.62
C	68.96	12.30
Test Pair	**r**	**p**
A-B	.78	.00
A-C	.82	.00
B-C	.75	.00

In the selection process, a measure of a candidate's management beliefs is obtained by having the candidate indicate the extent to which they agree with each of the five statements in the questionnaire and then creating an overall belief measure by averaging over the five items. However, before using the questionnaire, it is necessary to determine whether the five items are homogeneous measures that index a common construct. This involves assessing the internal consistency reliability of the set of items, and is accomplished using coefficient alpha.

Coefficient alpha is based on the average correlation among the items of a questionnaire. The formula for alpha is provided below:

$$\alpha = \frac{n(\bar{r})}{1+\bar{r}(n-1)}$$

In the formula α is coefficient alpha, $\bar{r}$ is the average correlation among the items and n is the number of items. For example, if there are five items (n = 5), and the average correlation among the five items is r = .80, then coefficient alpha is .94.

It can be seen from the formula and example that coefficient alpha depends on just two things—the number of items and the amount of the correlation between them. This suggests two basic strategies for increasing the internal consistency reliability of a measure-increase the number of items and increase the amount of agreement between the items. It is generally recommended that coefficient alpha be at least .80 for a measure to have an acceptable degree of reliability.

Implications of Reliability The degree of reliability of a measure has two implications. The first of these pertains to interpreting individuals' scores on the measure and the standard error of measurement. The second implication pertains to the effect that reliability has on the measure's validity.

Standard Error of Measurement. Measures yield scores, which, in turn, are used as critical inputs for decision making in staffing activities. For example, in Exhibit 3.1 a test of knowledge of mechanical principles was developed and administered to job applicants. The applicants' scores then were used as a basis for making hiring decisions.

The discussion of reliability suggests that measures and scores will usually have some amount of error in them. Hence, scores on the test of knowledge of mechanical principles most likely reflect both true knowledge and error. Since only a single score is obtained from each applicant, the critical issue is how accurate that particular score is as an indication of each applicant's true level of knowledge of mechanical principles alone.

The standard error of measurement addresses this issue. It provides a way to state, within limits, a person's likely score on a measure. The formula for the standard error of measurement (SEM) is

$$SEM = SD_x\sqrt{1-r_{xx}}$$

where SD_x is the standard deviation of scores on the measure and r_{xx} is an estimate of the measure's reliability. For example, if $SD_x = 10$, and $r_{xx} = .75$ (based on coefficient alpha), then SEM = 5.

With the SEM known, the range within which any individual's true score is likely to fall can be estimated. That range is known as a confidence interval or limit. There is a 95 percent chance that a person's true score lies within ±2 SEM of his or her actual score. Thus, if an applicant received a score of 22 on the test of knowledge of mechanical principles, the applicant's true score is most likely to be within the range of 22 ± 2(5), or between 12 and 32.

Recognition and use of the SEM allows for care in interpreting people's scores, as well as differences between them in terms of their scores. For example, using the preceding data, if the test score for applicant 1 = 22 and the score for applicant 2 = 19, what should be made of the difference between the two applicants? Is applicant 1 truly more knowledgeable of mechanical principles than applicant 2? The answer is probably not. This is because of the standard error of measurement and the large amount of overlap between the two applicants' intervals (12–32 for applicant 1, and 9–29 for applicant 2).

In short, there is not a one-to-one correspondence between actual scores and true scores. Most measures used in staffing are sufficiently unreliable that small differences in scores are probably due to error of measurement and should be ignored.

Relationship to Validity. The validity of a measure is defined as the degree to which it measures the attribute it is supposed to be measuring. For example, the validity of the test of knowledge of mechanical principles is the degree to which it measures that knowledge. There are specific ways to investigate validity; these are discussed in the next section. Here, it simply needs to be recognized that the reliability with which an attribute is measured has direct implications for the validity of the measure.

The relationship between the reliability and validity of a measure is

$$r_{xy} \leq \sqrt{r_{xx}}$$

where r_{xy} is the validity of a measure and r_{xx} is the reliability of the measure. For example, it had been assumed previously that the reliability of the test of knowledge of mechanical principles was $r = .75$. The validity of that test thus cannot exceed $\sqrt{.75} = .86$.

Thus, the reliability of a measure places an upper limit on the possible validity of a measure. It should be emphasized that this is only an upper limit. A highly reliable measure is not necessarily valid. Reliability does not guarantee validity; it only makes validity possible.

Validity of Measures

The validity of a measure is defined as the degree to which it measures the attribute it is intended to measure.[10] Refer back to Exhibit 3.1, which involved the development of a test of knowledge of mechanical principles that was then to be used for purposes of selecting job applicants. The validity of that test is the degree to which it truly measures the attribute or construct "knowledge of mechanical principles."

Judgments about the validity of a measure occur through the process of gathering data and evidence about the measure to assess how it was developed and whether accurate inferences can be made from scores on the measure. This process can be illustrated in terms of concepts pertaining to accuracy of measurement and accuracy of prediction. These concepts may then be used to demonstrate how validation of measures occurs in staffing.

Accuracy of Measurement How accurate is the test of knowledge of mechanical principles? This question asks for evidence about the accuracy with which the test portrays individuals' true levels of that knowledge. This is akin to asking about the degree of overlap between the attribute being measured and the actual measure of the attribute.

EXHIBIT 3.9 Accuracy of Measurement

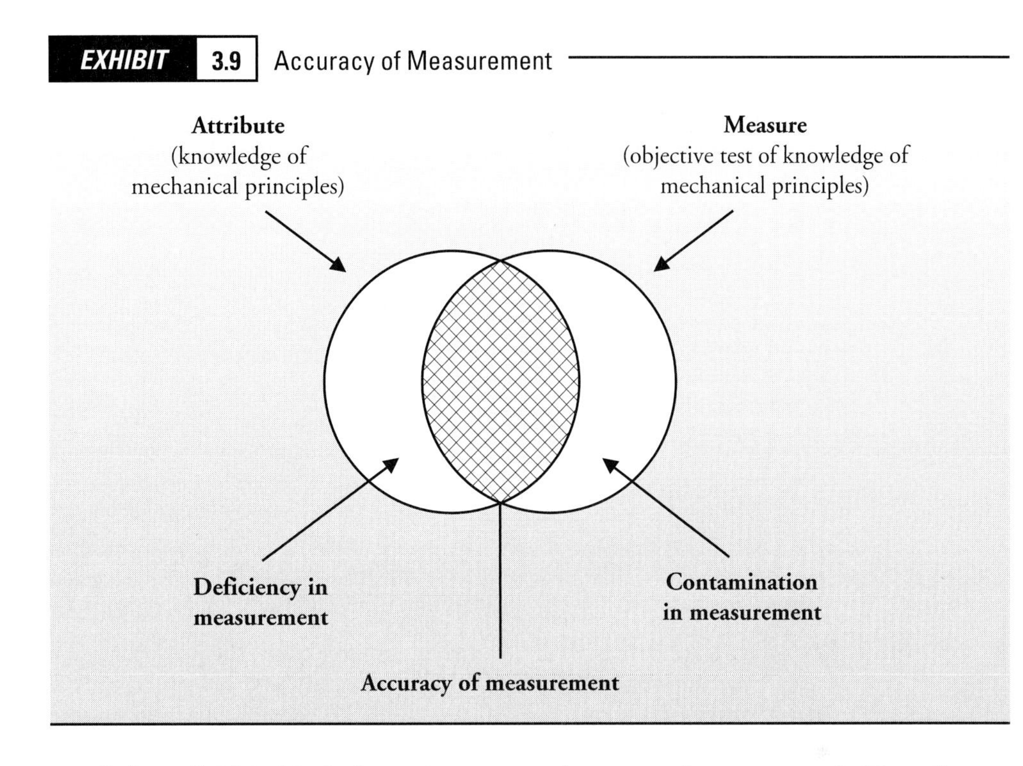

Refer to Exhibit 3.9. It shows the concept of accuracy of measurement in Venn diagram form. The circle on the left represents the construct "knowledge of mechanical principles," and the circle on the right represents the actual test of knowledge of mechanical principles. The overlap between the two circles represents the degree of accuracy of measurement for the test. The greater the overlap, the greater the accuracy of measurement.

Notice that perfect overlap is not shown in Exhibit 3.9. This signifies the occurrence of measurement error with the use of the test. These errors, as indicated in the exhibit, are the errors of deficiency and contamination previously discussed.

So how does accuracy of measurement differ from reliability of measurement, since both are concerned with deficiency and contamination? There is disagreement among people on this question. Generally, the difference may be thought of as follows: Reliability refers to consistency among the scores on the test, as determined by comparing scores as previously described. Accuracy of measurement goes beyond this to assess the extent to which the scores truly reflect the attribute being measured—the overlap shown in Exhibit 3.9. Accuracy requires reliability, but it also requires more by way of evidence. For example, accuracy requires knowing something about how the test was developed. Accuracy also requires some evidence concerning how test scores are influenced by other factors—for example, how do test scores change as a result of employees attending a training program devoted to providing instruction in mechanical principles? Accuracy thus demands greater evidence than reliability.

Accuracy of Prediction Measures are often developed because they provide information about people that can be used to make predictions about those people. In Exhibit 3.1, the knowledge test was to be used to help make hiring decisions, which are actually predictions about which people will be successful at a job. Knowing something about the accuracy with which a test predicts future job success requires examining the relationship between scores on the test and scores on some measure of job success for a group of people.

Accuracy of prediction is illustrated in the top half of Exhibit 3.10. Where there is an actual job success outcome (criterion) to predict, the test (predictor) will be used to predict the criterion. Each person is classified as high or low on the predictor and high or low on the criterion, based on

EXHIBIT 3.10 Accuracy of Prediction

A. General Illustration

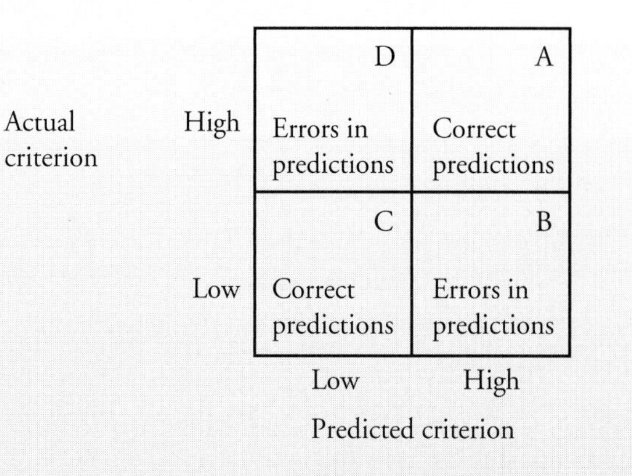

$$\text{Accuracy} = \frac{A+C}{A+B+C+D} \times 100$$

B. Selection Example (n = 100 job applicants)

Actual performance	Predicted performance (based on test scores): Low	Predicted performance (based on test scores): High
High	20	45
Low	25	10

$$\text{Accuracy} = \frac{45+25}{45+10+25+20} \times 100 = 70\%$$

predictor and criterion scores. Individuals falling into cells A and C represent correct predictions, and individuals falling into cells B and D represent errors in prediction. Accuracy of prediction is the percentage of total correct predictions. Accuracy can thus range from 0 to 100 percent.

The bottom of Exhibit 3.10 shows an example of the determination of accuracy of prediction using a selection example. The predictor is the test of knowledge of mechanical principles, and the criterion is an overall measure of job performance. Scores on the predictor and criterion measures are gathered for 100 job applicants and are dichotomized into high or low scores on each. Each individual is placed into one of the four cells. The accuracy of prediction for the test is 70 percent.

Validation of Measures in Staffing

In staffing, there is concern with the validity of predictors in terms of both accuracy of measurement and accuracy of prediction. It is important to have and use predictors that are accurate representations of the KSAOs to be measured, and those predictors need to be accurate in their predictions of job success. The validity of predictors is explored through the conduct of validation studies.

There are two types of validation studies typically conducted. The first of these is criterion-related validation, and the second is content validation. A third type of validation study, known as construct validation, involves components of reliability, criterion-related validation, and content validation. Each component is discussed separately in this book, and thus no further reference is made to construct validation.

Criterion-Related Validation Exhibit 3.11 shows the components of criterion-related validation and their usual sequencing.[11] The process begins with job analysis. Results of job analysis are then fed into criterion and predictor measures. Scores on the predictor and criterion are obtained for a sample of individuals; the relationship between the scores is then examined to make a judgment about the predictor's validity.

Job Analysis. Job analysis is undertaken to identify and define important tasks (and broader task dimensions) of the job. The KSAOs and motivation thought to be necessary for performance of these tasks are then inferred. Results of the process of identifying tasks and underlying KSAOs are expressed in the form of the job requirements matrix. The matrix is a "task × KSAO" matrix; it shows the tasks required, combined with the relevant KSAOs for each task.

EXHIBIT 3.11 Criterion-Related Validation

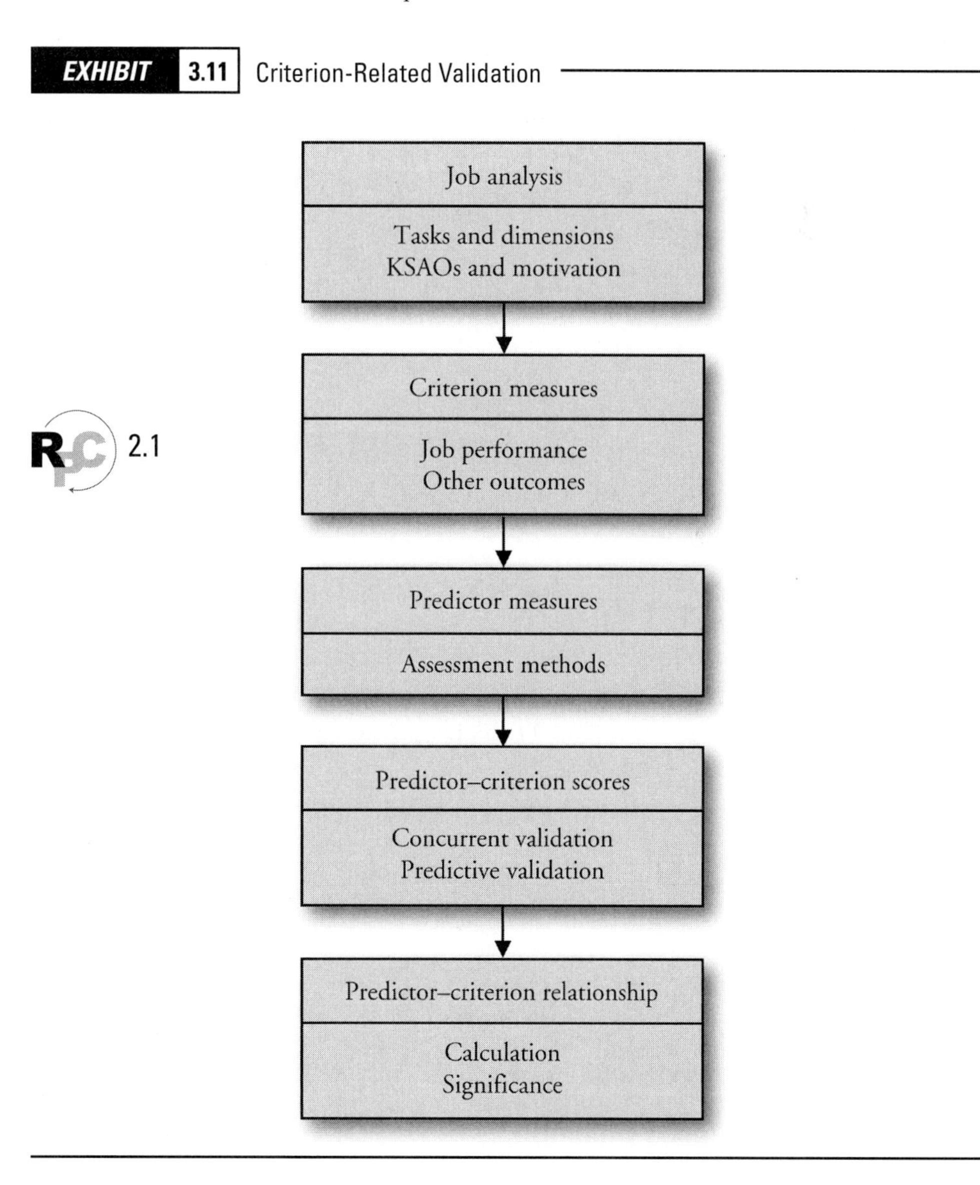

Criterion Measures. Measures of performance on tasks and task dimensions are needed. These may already be available as part of an ongoing performance appraisal system, or they may have to be developed. However gathered, the critical requirement is that the measures be as free from measurement error as possible.

Criterion measures need not be restricted to performance measures. Others may be used, such as measures of attendance, retention, safety, and customer service. As with performance-based criterion measures, these alternative criterion measures should also be as error-free as possible.

Predictor Measure. The predictor measure is the measure whose criterion-related validity is being investigated. Ideally, it taps into one or more of the KSAOs identified in job analysis. Also, it should be the type of measure most suitable to assess the KSAOs. Knowledge of mechanical principles, for example, is probably best assessed with some form of written, objective test.

Predictor–Criterion Scores. Predictor and criterion scores must be gathered from a sample of current employees or job applicants. If current employees are used, this involves use of a concurrent validation design. Alternately, if job applicants are used, a predictive validation design is used. The nature of these two designs is shown in Exhibit 3.12.

EXHIBIT 3.12 Concurrent and Predictive Validation Designs

Concurrent Validation Design

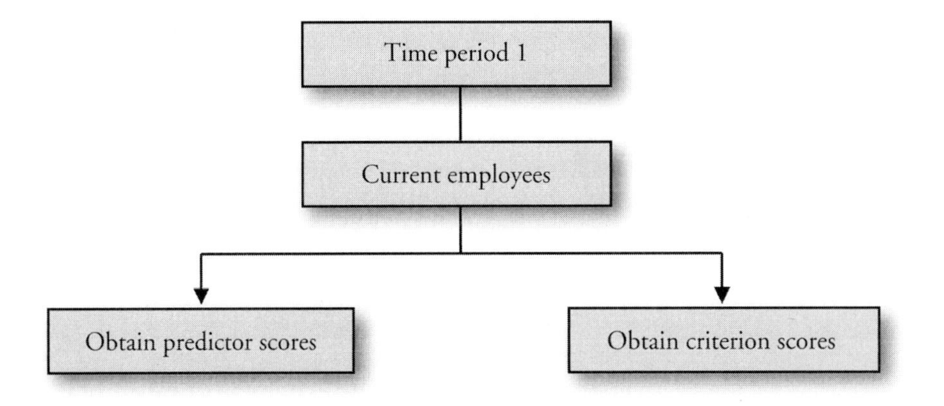

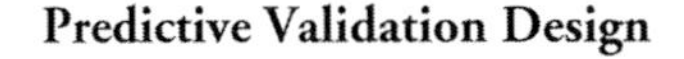

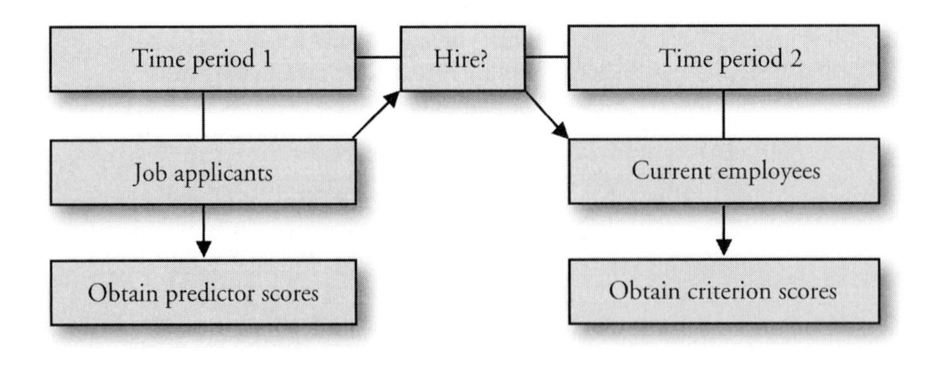

Concurrent validation definitely has some appeal. Administratively, it is convenient and can often be done quickly. Moreover, results of the validation study will be available soon after the predictor and criterion scores have been gathered.

Unfortunately, some serious problems can arise with use of a concurrent validation design. One problem is that if the predictor is a test, current employees may not be motivated in the same way that job applicants would be in terms of desire to perform well. Yet, it is future applicants for whom the test is intended to be used.

In a related vein, current employees may not be similar to, or representative of, future job applicants. Current employees may differ in terms of demographics such as age, race, sex, disability status, education level, and previous job experience. Hence, it is by no means certain that the results of the study will generalize to future job applicants. Also, some unsatisfactory employees will have been terminated, and some high performers may have been promoted. This leads to restriction of range on the criterion scores, which in turn will lower the correlation between the predictor and criterion scores.

Finally, current employees' predictor scores may be influenced by the amount of experience and/or success they have had on their current job. For example, scores on the test of knowledge of mechanical principles may reflect not only that knowledge but also how long people have been on the job and how well they have performed it. This is undesirable because one wants predictor scores to be predictive of the criterion, rather than a result of it.

Predictive validation overcomes the potential limitations of concurrent validation, since the predictor scores are obtained from job applicants. Applicants will be motivated to do well on the predictor, and they are more likely to be representative of future job applicants. And applicants' scores on the predictor cannot be influenced by success and/or experience on the job, because the scores were gathered prior to their being on the job.

Predictive validation is not without potential limitations, however. It is neither administratively easy nor quick. Moreover, results will not be available immediately, as some time must lapse before criterion scores can be obtained. Despite these limitations, predictive validation is considered the more sound of the two designs.

Predictor–Criterion Relationship. Once predictor and criterion scores have been obtained, the correlation r, or some variation of it, must be calculated. The value of the r is then referred to as the validity of the scores on the predictor. For example, if an r = .35 was found, the predictor would be referred to as having a validity of .35. Then, the practical and statistical significance of the r should be determined. Only if the r meets desired levels of practical and statistical significance should the predictor be considered "valid" and thus potentially usable in the selection system.

Illustrative Study. This study sought to identify predictors of job performance for clerical employees in a university system covering 20 different institutions. The clerical job existed within different schools (e.g., engineering, humanities) and nonacademic departments (e.g., payroll, data processing). The goal was to have a valid clerical test in two parallel forms that could be administered to job applicants in one hour.

The starting point was to conduct a job analysis, the results of which would be used as the basis for constructing the clerical tests (predictors) and the job performance ratings (criteria). Based on observation of the job and previous job descriptions, a task-based questionnaire was constructed by subject matter experts (SMEs) and administered to clerical incumbents and their supervisors throughout the system. Task statements were rated in terms of importance, frequency, and essentialness (whether it was essential for a newly hired employee to know how to do this task). Based on statistical analysis of the ratings' means and standard deviations, 25 of the 188 task statements were retained as critical task statements. These critical task statements were the key input to the identification of key KSAOs and the dimension of job performance.

Analysis of the 25 critical task statements indicated there were five KSAO components of the job: knowledge of computer hardware and software, ability to follow instructions and prioritize tasks, knowledge and skill in responding to telephone and reception scenarios, knowledge of the

English language, and ability to file items in alphabetical order. A test was constructed to measure these KSAOs as follows:

- Understanding computer hardware and software—17 questions
- Prioritizing tasks—18 questions
- Routing and transferring calls—14 questions
- Recording messages—20 questions
- Giving information on the phone—20 questions
- Correcting sentences with errors—22 questions
- Identifying errors in sentences—71 questions
- Filing—44 questions
- Typing—number of questions not reported

To develop the job performance (criterion) measure, a behavioural performance rating scale (1–7 rating) was constructed for each of the nine areas, ensuring a high content correspondence between the tests and the performance criteria they sought to predict. Scores on these nine scales were summed to yield an overall performance score.

The nine tests were administered to 108 current clerical employees to obtain predictor scores. A separate score on each of the nine tests was computed, along with a total test score for all tests. In addition, total scores on two short (50 question) forms of the total test were created (Form A and Form B).

Performance ratings of these 108 employees were obtained from their supervisors, who were unaware of their employees' test scores. The performance ratings were summed to form an overall performance rating. Scores on each of the nine tests, on the total test, and on Forms A and B of the test were correlated with the overall performance ratings.

Results of the concurrent validation study are shown in Exhibit 3.13. It can be seen that seven of the nine specific tests had statistically significant correlations with overall performance (filing and typing did not). Total test scores were significantly correlated with overall performance, as were scores on the two short forms of the total test. The sizes of the statistically significant correlations suggest favourable practical significance of the correlations as well.

EXHIBIT 3.13 Clerical Test Concurrent Validation Results

Test	Correlation with Overall Performance
Understanding computer software and hardware	.37**
Prioritizing tasks	.29*
Routing and transferring calls	.19*
Recording messages	.31**
Giving information on phone	.35**
Correcting sentences with errors	.32**
Identifying errors in sentences	.44**
Filing	.22
Typing	.10
Total test	45**
Form A	.55**
Form B	.49**

NOTE: *p < .05, **p < .01

Source: Adapted from J. E. Pynes, E. J. Harrick, and D. Schaefer, "A Concurrent Validation Study Applied to a Secretarial Position in a State University Civil Service System," *Journal of Business and Psychology*, 1997, 12, pp. 3–18.

EXHIBIT 3.14 Content Validation

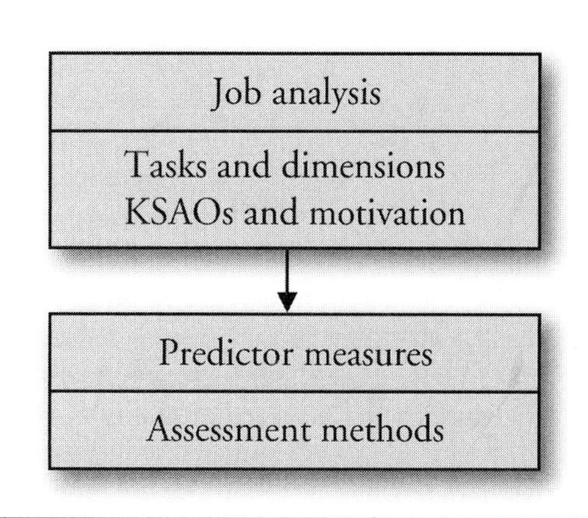

Content Validation Content validation differs from criterion-related validity in one important respect: there is no criterion measure used in content validation. Thus, predictor scores cannot be correlated with criterion scores as a way of gathering evidence about a predictor's validity. Rather, a judgment is made about the probable correlation, had there been a criterion measure. For this reason, content validation is frequently referred to as judgmental validation.[12]

Content validation is most appropriate, and most likely to be found, in two circumstances: when there are too few people to form a sample for purposes of criterion-related validation, and when criterion measures are not available, or they are available but are of highly questionable quality. At an absolute minimum, an n = 30 is necessary for criterion-related validation.

Exhibit 3.14 shows the two basic steps in content validation—conducting a job analysis and choosing or developing a predictor. These steps are commented on next. Comparing the steps in content validation with those in criterion-related validation (see Exhibit 3.11) shows that the steps in content validation are a part of criterion-related validation. Because of this, the two types of validation should be thought of as complementary, with content validation being a subset of criterion-related validation.

RPC 2.1

Job Analysis. As with criterion-related validation, content validation begins with job analysis, which, in both cases, is undertaken to identify and define tasks and task dimensions and to infer the necessary KSAOs and motivation for those tasks. Results are expressed in the job requirements matrix.

Predictor Measures. Sometimes the predictor will be one that has already been developed and is in use. An example here is a commercially available test, interviewing process, or biographical information questionnaire. Other times, there will not be such a measure available. This occurs frequently in the case of job knowledge, which is usually very specific to the particular job involved in the validation.

Lacking a readily available or modifiable predictor means that the organization will have to construct its own predictors. At this point, the organization has built predictor construction into the predictor validation process. Now, content validation and the predictor development processes occur simultaneously. The organization becomes engaged in test construction, a topic beyond the scope of this book.[13]

It should be emphasized that content validation procedures can be applied to any type of predictor or combination of predictors, as illustrated in a content validation study involving police emergency telephone operators.[14] A job analysis identified six critical KSAO requirements for the job (communication skills, emotional control, judgment, cooperativeness, memory, and clerical/technical skills). The predictors included

1. A spelling test in which applicants received 10 tape-recorded telephone calls and had to accurately record the pertinent information from each call on a form

2. A test in which applicants had to accurately record information received from monitoring police units
3. A typing test measuring both speed and accuracy
4. A situational interview in which applicants were asked how they would behave in a series of job-related situations
5. A role-playing exercise in which applicants assumed the role of police and telephone operators taking calls from complainants

This example makes clear that content validation is a flexible process for establishing task–KSAO–predictor linkages. At the same time that these linkages are being established administratively, validation evidence is emerging from a built-in process of content validation.

A final note about content validation emphasizes the importance of continually paying attention to the need for reliability of measurement and standardization of the measurement process. Though these are always matters of concern in any type of validation effort, they are of paramount importance in content validation. The reason for this is that without an empirical correlation between the predictor and criterion, only the likely r can be judged. It is important, in forming that judgment, to pay considerable attention to reliability and standardization.

Illustrative Study. A government department sought to develop a series of assessment methods for identifying supervisory potential among candidates for promotion to a first-level supervising position anywhere within the department. The content validation process and outputs are shown in Exhibit 3.15. As shown in the exhibit, job analysis was first conducted to identify and define a set of performance dimensions and then infer the KSAOs necessary for

EXHIBIT 3.15 Content Validation Study

Job Analysis: First-Level Supervisor—Ministry of Transportation

Seven performance dimensions and task statements:	Fourteen KSAOs and definitions:	
1. Organizing work	1. Organizing	8. Interpersonal skill
2. Assigning work	2. Analysis and decision making	9. Job knowledge
3. Monitoring work	3. Planning	10. Organizational knowledge
4. Managing consequences	4. Communication (oral and written)	11. Toughness
5. Counselling, efficiency reviews, and discipline	5. Delegation	12. Integrity
6. Setting an example	6. Work habits	13. Development of others
7. Employee development	7. Carefulness	14. Listening

Predictor Measures: Five Assessment Methods

1. Multiple-choice in-basket exercise (assume role of new supervisor and work through in-basket on desk)
2. Structured panel interview (predetermined questions about past experiences relevant to the KSAOs)
3. Presentation exercise (make presentation to a simulated work group about change in their work hours)
4. Writing sample (prepare a written reprimand for a fictitious employee)
5. Training and experience evaluation exercise (give examples of training and work achievements relevant to certain KSAOs)

Source: Adapted from M. A. Cooper, G. Kaufman, and W. Hughes, "Measuring Supervisory Potential," *IPMA News*, December, 1996, pp. 8–18. Reprinted with permission of *IPMA News*, published by the International Personnel Management Association (IPMA), 703-549-7100, **www.ipma-hr.org**.

successful performance in those dimensions. Several SMEs met to develop a tentative set of task dimensions and underlying KSAOs. The underlying KSAOs were in essence general competencies required of all first-level supervisors, regardless of work unit within the department. Their results were sent to a panel of experienced HR managers within the department for revision and finalization. Three assessment method specialists then set about developing a set of assessments that would (1) be efficiently administered, (2) be reliably scored, and (3) emphasize the interpersonal skills important for this job. As shown in Exhibit 3.15, five assessment methods were developed: multiple-choice in-basket exercise, structured interview panel, presentation exercise, writing sample, and training and experience evaluation exercise.

Candidates' performance on the exercises was to be evaluated by specially chosen assessors when the exercises were administered. To ensure that candidates' performance was skilfully observed and reliably evaluated by the assessors, an intensive training program was developed. The program provided both a written user's manual and specific skill training.

Validity Generalization

In the preceding discussions of validity and validation, an implicit premise is being made that validity is situation specific, and therefore validation of predictors must occur in each specific situation. All of the examples involve s pecific types of measures, jobs, individuals, and so forth. Nothing is said about generalizing validity across those jobs and individuals. For example, if a predictor is valid for a particular job in organization A, would it be valid for the same type of job in organization B? Or is validity specific to the particular job and organization?

The situation-specific premise is based on the following scenario, which, in turn, has its origins in findings from decades of previous research. Assume a large number of criterion-related validation studies have been conducted. Each study involves various predictor measures of a common KSAO attribute (e.g., general mental ability) and various criterion measures of a common outcome attribute (e.g., job performance). The predictor will be designated *X*, and the criterion will be designated *Y*. The studies are conducted in many different situations (types of jobs, types of organizations, and so on), and they involve many different samples (sample sizes, types of employees, and so on). In each study, r_{xy} is calculated. The results from all the studies reveal a wide range of r_{xy} values, though the average is $\bar{r}_{xy} = .25$. These results suggest that while on average there seems to be some validity to X, the validity varies substantially from situation to situation. Based on these findings, the best conclusion is that validity most likely is situation specific and thus cannot be generalized across the situations.

The concept of validity generalization questions this premise.[15] It says that much of the variation in the r_{xy} values is due to the occurrence of a number of methodological and statistical differences across the studies. If these differences were controlled for statistically, the variation in values would shrink and converge toward an estimate of the true validity of X. If that true r is significant (practically and statistically), one can indeed generalize validity of X across situations. Validity thus is not viewed as situation specific. The logic of this validity generalization premise is shown in Exhibit 3.16.

EXHIBIT 3.16 The Logic of Validity Generalization

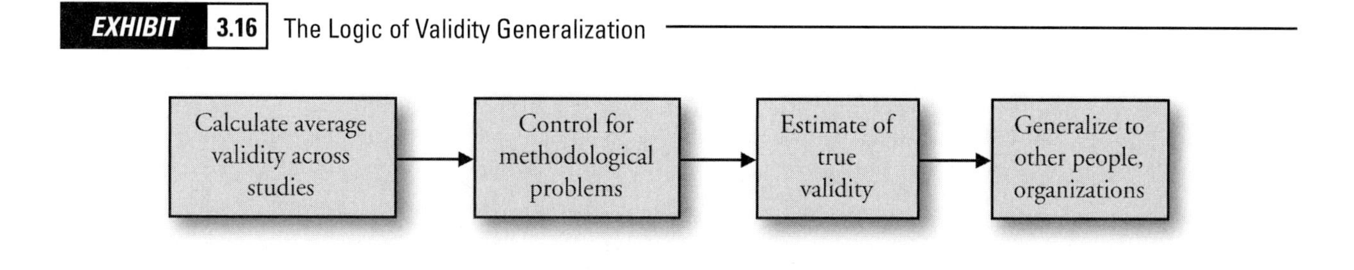

The distinction between situation-specific validity and validity generalization is important for two related reasons. First, from a scientific viewpoint, it is important to identify and make statements about X and Y relationships in general, without always having to say that everything depends on the sample, criterion measure, and so on. In this regard, validity generalization clearly allows greater latitude than does situation specificity. Second, from a practical standpoint, it would be convenient and less costly not to have to conduct a separate validation study for predictor X in every situation in which its use was a possibility. Validity generalization allows that to happen, whereas situation specificity does not.

Evidence is beginning to surface that is supportive of the validity generalization premise. For example, evidence suggests that tests of general mental ability have meaningful, practical validity for predicting job performance across a wide variety of types of employees and jobs. Until more is known about validity generalization, however, caution is called for in its use in either scientific or practical terms. In this light, the following recommendations are offered as guides to staffing practice:

1. At a minimum, all predictors should routinely be subject to content validation.
2. When feasible, criterion-related validation studies should be conducted unless there is sufficient validity generalization evidence available to support use of a predictor without prior validation.
3. Any claims of validity or validity generalization that are based on no criterion-related validity studies, or only a small number of them, should be suspect.
4. A predictor's validity is specific to the criterion against which it was validated (e.g., performance on a specific job), and the predictor's validity should not be extended to other criteria (e.g., performance on a different job, attendance) without validation evidence for those criteria.
5. Organizations should become involved in various cooperative arrangements devoted to validation research in order to explore the extent to which validity may be generalized.

A particular form of validity generalization that has proved useful is called meta-analysis. In meta-analysis the focus is on determining the average correlation between X and Y (i.e., $\bar{r}_{xy}$) noted above, such as between a particular selection technique (X) and job performance (Y) after controlling for methodological problems in the validation studies. For example, the average validity of general cognitive ability tests for predicting job performance is $\bar{r}_{xy} = .50$. This represents our best statement of the average degree of validity found for mental ability tests to date, as well as an expectation of the validity we would likely find for general mental ability tests in future validation studies. We can also compare this $\bar{r}_{xy}$ to the $\bar{r}_{xy}$ of another selection technique, such as the unstructured interview, as a way of indicating the relative validity of the two techniques. Meta-analysis results and comparisons for numerous selection techniques are presented in Chapters 7 and 8.

COLLECTION OF ASSESSMENT DATA

In staffing decisions, the process of measurement is put into practice by collecting assessment data on external or internal applicants. To this point in this chapter, we have discussed how selection measures can be evaluated. To be sure, thorough evaluation of selection measures is important. Selection decision makers must be knowledgeable about how to use the assessment data that have been collected; otherwise the potential value of the data will lie dormant. On the other hand, to put these somewhat theoretical concepts to use in practice, selection decision makers must know how to collect the assessment data. Otherwise, the decision maker may find himself in the unenviable "Big Hat, No Cattle" situation—knowing how to analyze and evaluate assessment data, but not knowing where to find the data in the first place. Thus, knowing how to evaluate selection measures goes hand in hand with knowing where to find good assessment data in the first place.

In collecting assessment data, if a predictor is purchased, support services are needed. Consulting firms and test publishers can provide support for scoring of tests. Also necessary is legal support to ensure compliance with laws and regulations. Validity studies are important to ensure the effectiveness of the measures. Training on how to administer the predictor also is needed.

Beyond these general principles, which apply no matter what assessment data are collected, there is other information that the selection decision maker must know about the tangible process of collecting assessment data. Collection of data with respect to testing procedures, tests and test manuals, and professional standards are discussed.

Testing Procedures

In the past, most data concerning selecting testing procedures were in reference to paper-and-pencil tests. With the growth of computerization and the Internet, however, more and more selection measures are available on the personal computer (PC) and Web. Accordingly, in the sections that follow, we separate our discussion of the collection of testing procedures data into paper-and-pencil measures and PC- or Web-based procedures.

Paper and Pencil Predictors cannot always be purchased by any firm that wants to use them; many test publishers require the purchaser to have certain expertise to use the test properly. For example, they may want the user to hold a Ph.D. in a field of study related to the test and its use. For smaller organizations, this means that they need to hire the consulting services of a specialist to use a particular test.

Care must be taken to ensure that correct answers for predictors are not shared with job applicants in advance of administration of the predictor. Any person who has access to the predictor answers should be fully trained and should sign a predictor security agreement. Also, a regular inventory procedure needs to be established to ensure that predictor materials are not inappropriately dispersed. Should a breach of security take place, use of the predictor should be abandoned and a new one should be used.

The predictor itself should be kept secure, but so should the results of the predictor in order to ensure the privacy of the individual. The results of the predictor should be used only for the intended purposes and by persons qualified to interpret them. Though feedback can be given to the candidate concerning the results, the individual should not be given a copy of the predictor or the scoring key.

Finally, it is imperative that all applicants be assessed with standardized procedures. This means that not only should the same or a psychometrically equivalent predictor be used, but individuals should take the test under the same circumstances. The purpose of the predictor should be explained to applicants, and they should be put at ease, held to the same time requirements to complete the predictor, and take the predictor in the same location.

PC- and Web-Based Many selection measures can now be administered on the PC. Some of these tools are used by organizations to make initial cuts among applicants, as is the case with resumé- and application-screening software. In these systems, applicants complete the requested information and then the software system, with input from the organization as to selection criteria and cut-offs, screens out unqualified applicants. Acclaim, for example, is an interactive program that tries to simulate the give-and-take of an initial screening interview. The software might pose a hypothetical situation (e.g., a rude customer) and ask the applicant for a response. In the United States, job applicants for hourly positions at Kmart, Albertson's, or the Sports Authority take an electronic assessment marketed by Unicru at in-store kiosks.

Other PC- and Web-based selection measures are formal tests. Many of the test publishers mentioned below offer selection decision makers the choice of paper-and-pencil or PC-based tests. For example, the *Wonderlic Personnel Test* has a version of the test that is administered and scored using a PC. It includes testing and scoring software and a user's manual. Typically, the cost of purchasing such tests is not much more than the paper-and-pencil version of the tests.

Still other programs are a hybrid of these two systems, where applicants first complete initial information and if they are deemed to be at least minimally qualified, they then take a formal test. For example, ePredix has applicants take a 15-minute initial screening test. Those who pass this hurdle are then asked to complete more detailed assessments. Although collecting assessment data in such a manner has the benefit of immediacy of results, organizations that choose to outsource pre-employment screening on the Web need to ensure that the data are legally compliant, valid, and secure. Additionally, applicants may be concerned over privacy issues or may lack familiarity with the Web or be uncomfortable with tests administered via the Web. Finally, there is a concern about faking, such as the case when an individual other than the applicant takes the test. If organizations are concerned about individuals other than the applicant taking the test, verification procedures can be implemented, including mandating that the applicant take the test at a site that allows verification of their identification.

In general, research suggests that Web-based tests work as well as paper-and-pencil tests, as long as they are validated in the same manner as other selection measures.

Acquisition of Tests and Test Manuals

The process of acquiring tests and test manuals requires some start-up costs in terms of the time and effort required to contact test publishers. Once one is on a mailing list, however, brochures from the publishers keep the selection decision maker updated on the latest developments and ordering information. In making decisions about which tests to acquire, a decision must be made not only about the particular type of test, but also the manner in which it will be administered and scored—paper and pencil versus PC-based.

Paper and Pencil Most paper-and-pencil tests are acquired by contacting the publisher of the tests. Some publishers of paper-and-pencil tests used in selection decisions are Wonderlic (www.wonderlic.com), CPP, Inc. (formerly Consulting Psychologists Press; www.cpp-db.com), Institute for Personality and Ability Testing (www.ipat.com), Psychological Assessment Resources (www.parinc.com), Pearson Assessments (www.pearsonassessments.com), Hogan Assessment Systems (www.hoganassessments.com), and Psychological Services, Inc. (www.psionline.com). All of these organizations have brochures that describe the products available for purchase. Most organizations will provide sample copies of the tests and a user's manual that selection decision makers may consult before purchasing the test. Costs of paper-and-pencil tests vary widely depending on the test and the number of copies ordered. One test that can be scored by the selection decision maker, for example, costs $100 for testing 25 applicants and $200 for testing 100 applicants. Another test that comes with a scoring system and interpretive report costs from $25 each for testing 5 applicants to $17 each for testing 100 applicants. Presumably, greater discounts are available for testing larger numbers of applicants.

Any test worth using will have a professional user's manual that accompanies it. This manual should describe the development and validation of the test, including validity evidence in selection contexts. A test manual also should include administration instructions, scoring instructions or information (many test marketers will score tests for organizations [for an additional fee]), interpretation information, and normative data. All of this information is crucial to make sure the test is an appropriate one and that it is used in an appropriate (valid, legal) manner. Avoid using a test that has no professional manual as it is unlikely to have been validated. Using a test without a proven track record is akin to hiring an applicant sight unseen. The *Wonderlic Personnel Test User's Manual* is an excellent example of a professional user's manual. It contains information about various forms of the *Wonderlic Personnel Test* (see Chapter 8), how to administer the test and interpret and use the scores, various norms by age, race, gender, and so on, and validity and fairness of the test.

PC- or Web-Based When selection measures are administered on the PC or Web, acquisition is simple since copies of the measures are contained in the software. Thus, once an organization decides to administer selection measures in this manner, the consulting firm or test publisher arranges for access to the tests. Generally, organizations are given special user names that applicants use to complete the measures (along with their own identifying information). In some cases, the user's manuals for PC- or Web-based tests are provided on the computer. In other cases, only hard copies of the manuals are available. Irrespective of how the tests were acquired or administered, organizations must make sure they validate the tests. Selection decision makers should not accept vague claims regarding the accuracy of selection measures, no matter how the tests were acquired and administered. The Society for Human Resource Management (SHRM) has launched the SHRM Assessment Center, whereby SHRM members can review and receive discounts on more than 200 Web-based tests.[16]

Professional Standards

Revised in 2003 by the Society for Industrial and Organizational Psychology (SIOP), and approved by the American Psychological Association, the *Principles for the Validation and Use of Personnel Selection Procedures* is a guidebook that provides testing standards for use in selection decisions. The *Principles* covers test choice, development, evaluation, and use of personnel selection procedures in employment settings. The specific topics covered in the *Principles* include the various ways selection measures should be validated, how to conduct validation studies, what sources can be used to determine validity, generalizing validation evidence from one source to another, test fairness and bias, how to understand worker requirements, data collection for validity studies, ways in which validity information can be analyzed, the appropriate uses of selection measures, and an administration guide.

The *Principles* was developed by many of the world's leading experts on selection, and therefore any selection decision maker would be well advised to consult this important document, which is written in practical, nontechnical language.

The *Principles*, which is free, can be ordered from SIOP by visiting their Web site (www.siop.org).

A related set of standards has been promulgated by the APA. Formulated by the Joint Committee on Testing Practices, *Rights and Responsibilities of Test Takers: Guidelines and Expectations* enumerates 10 rights and 10 responsibilities of test takers. One of the rights is for the applicant to be treated with courtesy, respect, and impartiality. Another right is to receive prior explanation for the purpose(s) of the testing. One responsibility is to follow the test instructions as given. In addition to enumerating test-taker rights and responsibilities, the document also provides guidelines for organizations administering the tests. For example, the standards stipulate that organizations should inform test takers about the purpose of the test. This document is available online at www.apa.org/science/ttrr.html. Organizations testing applicants should consult these guidelines to ensure, wherever possible, these rights are provided.

In Canada, the authority on testing standards is the Canadian Psychological Association (CPA). At the present time, the CPA testing guideline manual is under revision.

LEGAL ISSUES

Staffing laws and regulations, particularly those related to human rights and employment equity, place great reliance on the use of measurement concepts and processes. Here, measurement is an integral part of (1) judging an organization's compliance through the conduct of disparate impact analysis, and (2) requiring standardization and validation of measures.

Using staffing procedures that have demonstrated reliability and validity is an important goal for any organization. Procedures that have demonstrated validity for performance ensures that the measures used in decision making are relevant to the job. These issues also surface if the staffing procedures are challenged through human rights legislation. The relevance of these issues was emphasized in the Tawney Meiorin case described in Chapter 2.

In 1994, a B.C. coroner's inquest into the death of a wildland firefighter led to the recommendation that fitness testing be implemented because a lack of fitness had contributed to the death of the firefighter. As a result the B.C. government contracted exercise physiologists from the University of Victoria to develop a fitness test for selecting forest firefighters. The tests involved sit-ups, push-ups, chin-ups, and completing a 2.5km run in less than 11 minutes. Ms. Meiorin passed all but the run test, which after several tries, she could only complete in 11:49. Because of this, she was denied employment as a wildland firefighter, even though she had been employed as such during the preceding years.

The use of the 11-minute, 2.5km run was used as a proxy test for assessing VO_2 max, an index of a person's aerobic fitness. Research has demonstrated that the timed distance runs, as used to assess B.C. wildland firefighters correlates anywhere from .90 to .65 with VO_2 max.[17] So you might conclude that when she appealed the decision denying her employment she would be unsuccessful. But you would be wrong.

In hearing Ms. Meiorin's case, the Supreme Court, while implicitly acknowledging that the fitness run is an indicator of VO_2 fitness, judged that as a proxy measure the fitness run had not been demonstrated to be a bona fide occupational requirement (BFOR) for Ms. Meiorin as a wildland firefighter. So while the fitness run demonstrates validity as a predictor of VO_2 max, the court did not see this as equivalent to job performance.

Similarly, the Supreme Court took issue with scientific methodology used in setting the fitness standard cut-off at 11 minutes for the 2.5km run. Specifically, the court pointed out that the sample composition used in setting the standard was a primarily male sample that included few females. Because of this, the cut-off score was biased in favour of men and had the effect of discriminating against women firefighter candidates. The scientific aspects of Ms. Meiorin's case concerning validity played a prominent role in the decision in her favour that ordered her to be reinstated with back pay. Therefore, organizations need to be wise in the ways of science to ensure they are selecting the best job candidates. However, an understanding of the scientific and measurement issues in staffing is also a legal issue because these often become the focus in human rights and legal proceedings. For instance, data gathering and analysis play an important role in the human resource management systems of organizations operating within the context of federal employment equity guidelines.

Representation Statistics

Data collection and analysis is a cornerstone of recruitment and selection activities for organizations operating under federal employment equity legislation. This can involve a workforce analysis to compare the representation of designated groups within an organization's workforce in comparison to the external representation rate as it is relevant to a given job within the organization. The steps in this process are detailed in the Guideline 5: Workforce Analysis manual provided by the Human Resources and Social Development Canada.[18] The first step in this process is establishing internal representation by conducting a workforce survey. The survey is performed to determine the number of individuals from designated groups employed in the various jobs within an organization. Next, Ministry of Labour employment equity data are used to determine the number of designated group members available for specific jobs.

The internal representation rate is calculated by dividing the number of designated group members in a job by the total number of people performing the job within an organization. The internal representation rate is then compared to the external expected number using the external representation rate. As an example, if an organization employees 200 engineers and 40 are women, then the internal representation rate is 20 percent ($40 \div 200 = .2$ or 20%). If the national external representation of women engineers is 30 percent, the expected number of women engineers would be 60 (200 × .3). Thus, there would be a numerical gap of 20 (60 – 40), or 33.3 percent (20 ÷ 60).

The issue that confronts an employer is whether the gap between the internal workforce representation and the expected representation is significant. On this matter, at the federal level, a number of guidelines are provided. Using percentages, it is suggested that a gap of 20 percent or greater indicates significant under-representation and that a review of the employment system would be appropriate.

Employers are cautioned that under-representation may exist with percentage gaps that are lower than 20 percent. This relates to the size of the group examined. For instance, the gap's implications differ if the size of a workforce is 20 versus 200. An internal representation rate of 20 percent represents 4 women in the case of 20 job incumbents versus 40 women in the case of 200 job incumbents. With an external representation rate of 30 percent, these examples represent a gap of 2 women and 20 women respectively. In both instances, women are underrepresented, but the numerical differences are apparent. Using actual numbers, gaps of 30 to 50 persons in designated groups for a job indicate a significant under-representation.

The examples provided describe how important data collection and analysis are for meeting employment equity guidelines. For organizations operating under these guidelines, the collection, analysis, and reporting of the results are necessary and demanding undertakings.

Standardization and Validation

When it has been determined that an organization is in non-compliance with the law, such as through adverse impact statistics, the organization must take certain steps to move toward compliance. While the specific steps will obviously depend on the situation, measurement activities invariably will be actively involved in them. These activities will revolve around standardization and validation of measures.

Standardization A lack of consistency in the treatment of applicants is one of the major factors contributing to the occurrence of discrimination in staffing. This is partly due to a lack of standardization in measurement, in terms of both what is measured and how it is evaluated or scored.

Even if information is consistently gathered from all applicants, it may not be evaluated the same for all applicants. A male applicant who has a history of holding several different jobs may be viewed as a "career builder," while a female with the same history may be evaluated as an unstable "job hopper." In essence, different scoring keys are being used for men and women applicants.

Reducing, and hopefully eliminating, such inconsistency requires a straightforward application of the three properties of standardized measures discussed previously. Through standardization of measurement comes consistent treatment of applicants, and with it, the possibility of lessened adverse impact.

Validation Even with standardized measurement, adverse impact may occur. Under these circumstances, the question is whether adverse impact is still justified. Human rights legislation addresses this issue directly. When there is adverse impact, the organization must either eliminate it or justify it through the presentation of validity evidence regarding the measure(s) causing the adverse impact.

The types of validity evidence required under human rights legislation are precisely those presented in this chapter. The purpose of these requirements is to ensure that, if an organization's staffing system is causing adverse impact, it is for job-related reasons. Evidence of job relatedness thus becomes the employer's rebuttal to the plaintiff's charges of discrimination. In the absence of such validation evidence, the employer must take steps to eliminate the adverse impact. These steps will involve various recruitment, selection, and employment activities that will be discussed throughout the remainder of the book.

SUMMARY

Measurement, defined as the process of using rules to assign numbers to objects to represent quantities of an attribute of the objects, is an integral part of the foundation of staffing activities. Standardization of the measurement process is sought. This applies to each of the four levels of measurement: nominal, ordinal, interval, and ratio. Standardization is also sought for both objective and subjective measures.

Measures yield scores that represent the amount of the attribute being measured. Scores are manipulated in various ways to aid in their interpretation. Typical manipulations involve central tendency and variability, percentiles, and standard scores. Scores are also correlated to learn about the strength and direction of the relationship between two attributes. The significance of the resultant correlation coefficient is then judged in statistical and practical terms.

The quality of measures involves issues of reliability and validity. Reliability refers to consistency of measurement, both at a moment in time and between time periods. Various procedures are used to estimate reliability, including coefficient alpha, interrater and intrarater agreement, and test–retest. Reliability places an upper limit on the validity of a measure.

Validity refers to accuracy of measurement and accuracy of prediction, as reflected by the scores obtained from a measure. Criterion-related and content validation studies are conducted to help learn about the validity of a measure. In criterion-related validation, scores on a predictor (KSAO) measure are correlated with scores on a criterion (HR outcome) measure. In content validation, there is no criterion measure, so judgments are made about the content of a predictor relative to the HR outcome it is seeking to predict. Traditionally, results of validation studies were treated as situation specific, meaning that the organization ideally should conduct a new and separate validation study for any predictor in any situation in which the predictor is to be used. Recently, however, results from validity generalization studies have suggested that the validity of predictors may generalize across situations, meaning that the requirement of conducting costly and time-consuming validation studies in each specific situation could be relaxed.

Various practical aspects of the collection of assessment data were described. Decisions about testing procedures and the acquisition of tests and test manuals require the attention of organizational decision makers. The collection of assessment data and the acquisition of tests and test manuals vary depending on whether paper-and-pencil or computerized selection measures are utilized. Finally, organizations need to attend to professional standards that govern the proper use of the collection of assessment data.

Measurement is also said to be an integral part of an organization's legal compliance activities. When adverse impact is found, changes in measurement practices may be legally necessary. These changes will involve movement toward standardization of measurement and the conduct of validation studies.

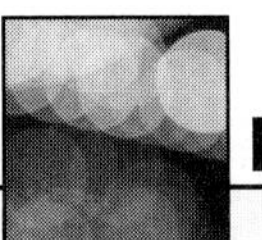

KEY TERMS

correlation coefficient 66
measurement 61
measures 61
standardization 62

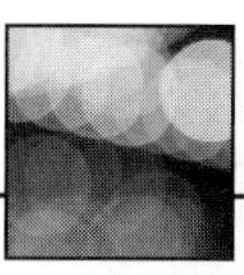

DISCUSSION QUESTIONS

1. Imagine and describe a staffing system for a job in which there are no measures used.
2. Describe how you might go about determining scores for applicants' responses to (a) interview questions, (b) letters of recommendation, and (c) questions about previous work experience.
3. Describe examples of when you would want the following for a written job knowledge test: (a) a low coefficient alpha (e.g., = .35), and (b) a low test–retest reliability.
4. Assume you gave a general ability test, measuring both verbal and computational skills, to a group of applicants for a specific job. Also assume that because of severe hiring pressures, you hired all of the applicants, regardless of their test scores. How would you investigate the criterion-related validity of the test?
5. Using the same example as in question #4 above, how would you go about investigating the content validity of the test?
6. What information does a selection decision maker need to collect in making staffing decisions? What are the ways in which this information can be collected?

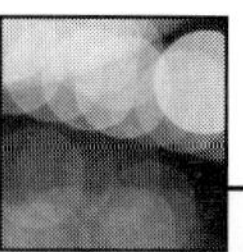

ETHICAL ISSUES

1. Do individuals making staffing decisions have an ethical responsibility to know measurement issues? Why or why not?
2. Is it unethical for an employer to use a selection measure that has high empirical validity but lacks content validity? Explain.

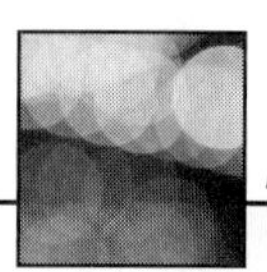

APPLICATIONS

Evaluation of Two New Assessment Methods for Selecting Telephone Customer Service Representatives

The Phonemin Company is a distributor of men's and women's casual clothing. It sells exclusively through its merchandise catalogue, which is published four times per year to coincide with seasonal changes in customers' apparel tastes. Customers may order merchandise from the catalogue via mail or over the phone. Currently, 70 percent of orders are phone orders, and the organization expects this to increase to 85 percent within the next few years.

The success of the organization is obviously very dependent on the success of the telephone ordering system and the customer service representatives (CSRs) who staff the system. There are currently 185 CSRs; that number should increase to about 225 CSRs to handle the anticipated growth in phone order sales. Though the CSRs are trained to use standardized methods and procedures for handling phone orders, there are still seemingly large differences among them in their job performance. A CSR's performance is routinely measured in terms of error rate, speed of order taking, and customer complaints. The highest 25 percent and lowest 25 percent of performers on each of these measures differ by a factor of at least three (i.e., the error rate of the lowest group is three times as high as that of the top group). Strategically, the organization knows that it could enhance CSR performance (and ultimately sales) substantially if it could improve its staffing "batting average" by more accurately identifying and hiring new CSRs who are likely to be top performers.

The current staffing system for CSRs is straightforward. Applicants are recruited through a combination of employee referrals and newspaper ads. Because turnover among CSRs is so high (50% annually), recruitment is a continual process at the organization. Applicants complete a standard application blank, which asks for information about education and previous work experience. The information is reviewed by the staffing specialist in the HR department. Only obvious misfits are rejected at this point; the others (95%) are asked to have an interview with the specialist. The interview lasts 20 to 30 minutes, and at the conclusion the applicant is either rejected or offered a job. Due to the tightness of the labour market and the constant presence of vacancies to be filled, 90 percent of the interviewees receive job offers. Most of those offers are accepted (95%), and the new hires then attend a one-week training program before being placed on the job.

The organization has decided to investigate fully the possibilities of increasing CSR effectiveness through sounder staffing practices. In particular, it is not pleased with its current methods of assessing job applicants; it feels that neither the interview nor the application blank provides the accurate and in-depth assessments of the KSAOs truly needed to be an effective CSR. Consequently, it has engaged the services of a consulting firm that offers various methods of KSAO assessment, along with validation and installation services. In cooperation with the HR staffing specialist, the consulting firm conducted the following study for the organization.

A special job analysis led to the identification of several specific KSAOs likely to be necessary for successful performance as a CSR. Three of these (clerical speed, clerical accuracy, and interpersonal skills) were singled out for further consideration because of their seemingly high impact on job performance. Two new methods of assessment, provided by the consulting firm, were chosen for experimentation. The first was a paper-and-pencil clerical test assessing clerical speed and accuracy. It is a 50-item test with a 30-minute time limit. The second was a brief work sample that could be administered as part of the interview process. In the work sample the applicant must respond to four different phone calls: from a customer irate about an out-of-stock item, from a customer wanting more product information about an item than was provided in the catalogue, from a customer who wants to change an order placed yesterday, and from a customer with a routine order to place. The applicant is rated by the interviewer (using a 1–5 rating scale) in terms of tactfulness (T) and in terms of concern for customers (C). The interviewer is provided with a rating manual containing examples of exceptional (5), average (3), and unacceptable (1) responses by the applicant.

A random sample of 50 current CSRs were chosen to participate in the study. At Time 1 they were administered the clerical test and the work sample; performance data were also gathered from company records for error rate (number of errors per 100 orders), speed (number of orders filled per hour), and customer complaints (number of complaints per week). At Time 2, one week later, the clerical test and the work sample were administered a second time to the CSRs. A member of the consulting firm sat in on all the interviews and served as a second rater of applicants' performance on the work sample at Time 1 and Time 2. It was expected that the clerical test and work sample would have positive correlations with speed and negative correlations with error rate and customer complaints.

Results for Clerical Test

	Time 1	**Time 2**
Mean score	31.61	31.22
Standard deviation	4.70	5.11
Coefficient alpha	.85	.86
Test-retest r		.92**
r with error rate	−.31**	−.37**
r with speed	.41**	.39**
r with complaints	−.11	−.08
r with work sample (T)	.21	.17
r with work sample (C)	.07	.15

Results for Work Sample (T)

	Time 1	Time 2
Mean score	3.15	3.11
Standard deviation	.93	1.01
% agreement (raters)	88%	79%
r with work sample (C)	.81**	.77**
r with error rate	–.13	–.12
r with speed	.11	.15
r with complaints	–.37**	–.35**

Results for Work Sample (C)

	Time 1	Time 2
Mean score	2.91	3.07
Standard deviation	.99	1.10
% agreement (raters)	80%	82%
r with work sample (T)	.81**	.77**
r with error rate	–.04	–.11
r with speed	.15	.14
r with complaints	–.40**	–.31**

(Note: ** means that r was significant at $p < .05$)

Based on the description of the study and results above, answer the following:

1. How do you interpret the reliability results for the clerical test and work sample? Are they favourable enough for Phonemin to consider using them "for keeps" in selecting new job applicants?
2. How do you interpret the validity results for the clerical test and work sample? Are they favourable enough for Phonemin to consider using them "for keeps" in selecting new job applicants?
3. What limitations in the above study should be kept in mind when interpreting the results and deciding whether or not to use the clerical test and work sample?

Conducting Empirical Validation and Adverse Impact Analysis

Yellow Blaze Candle Shops provides a full line of various types of candles and accessories such as candle holders. There are 150 shops located in shopping malls and strip malls throughout the country. More than 600 salespeople staff these stores, each of which has a full-time manager. Staffing the manager's position, by policy, must occur by promotion from within the sales ranks. The organization is interested in trying to improve its identification of salespeople most likely to be successful store managers. It has developed a special technique for assessing and rating the suitability of salespeople for the manager's job.

To experiment with this technique, the regional HR department representative met with the store managers in the region to review and rate the promotion suitability of each manager's salespeople. They reviewed sales results, customer service orientation, and knowledge of store operations for each salesperson, and then assigned a 1–3 promotion suitability rating (1 = not suitable, 2 = maybe suitable, 3 = definitely suitable) on each of these three factors. A total promotion suitability (PS) score, ranging from 3 to 9, was then computed for each salesperson.

The PS scores were gathered, but not formally used in promotion decisions, for all salespeople. Over the past year 30 salespeople have been promoted to store manager. Now it is time for the organization to conduct a preliminary investigation of the validity of the PS scores and to find out whether their use may lead to the occurrence of adverse impact against women or minorities. Each store manager's annual overall performance appraisal rating, ranging from 1 (low performance) to 5 (high performance), was used as the criterion measure in the validation study. The following data were available for analysis:

Employee ID	PS Score	Performance	Sex M/F	Designated Group Status (M = Minority NM = Nonminority)
11	9	5	M	NM
12	9	5	F	NM
13	9	1	F	NM
14	9	5	M	M
15	8	4	F	M
16	8	5	F	M
17	8	4	M	NM
18	8	5	M	NM
19	8	3	F	NM
20	8	4	M	NM
21	7	5	F	M
22	7	3	M	M
23	7	4	M	NM
24	7	3	F	NM
25	7	3	F	NM
26	7	4	M	NM
27	7	5	M	M
28	6	4	F	NM
29	6	4	M	NM
30	6	2	F	M
31	6	3	F	NM
32	6	3	M	NM
33	6	5	M	NM
34	6	5	F	NM
35	5	3	M	NM
36	5	3	F	M
37	5	2	M	M
38	4	2	F	NM
39	4	1	M	NM
40	3	4	F	NM

Based on the above data, calculate the following:

1. Average PS scores for the whole sample, males, females, nonminority, and minority.
2. The correlation between PS scores and performance ratings, and its statistical significance (an $r = .37$ or higher is needed for significance at $p < .05$).
3. Adverse impact (selection rate) statistics for males and females, and nonminorities and minorities. Use a PS score of 7 or higher as a hypothetical passing score (the score that may be used to determine who will or will not be promoted).

Using the data, results, and description of the study, answer the following questions:

1. Is the PS assessment a valid predictor of performance as a store manager? Would you recommend that the PS be used in the future to select salespeople for promotion to store manager?

2. With a cut score of 7 on the PS, would its use lead to adverse impact against women? Against minorities? If there is adverse impact, does the validity evidence justify use of the PS anyway?
3. What are limitations of this study?
4. Would you recommend that Yellow Blaze now actually use the PS for making promotion decisions? Why or why not?

TANGLEWOOD STORES CASE I

Identifying the methods that select the best employees for the job is indisputably one of the central features of the organizational staffing process. This chapter described statistical methods for assessing the relationship between organizational hiring practices and important outcomes. This case will help you see exactly how these data can be analyzed in an employment setting, and show how the process differs depending on the job being analyzed.

The Situation

Tanglewood has a history of very divergent staffing practices among stores, and they are looking to centralize their operations (see the Tanglewood case study in Chapter 5). For most stores, the only information collected from applicants is an application blank with education level and prior work experience. After a brief unstructured interview with representatives from the operations and HR department, store managers make a hiring decision. Many managers have complained that the result of this system is that many individuals are hired who have little understanding of Tanglewood's position in the retail industry and whose personalities are completely wrong for the company's culture. To improve their staffing system, Tanglewood has selected certain stores to serve as prototypes for an experimental selection system that includes a much more thorough assessment of applicant qualifications.

Your Tasks

The case considers concurrent validation evidence from the existing hiring system for store associates, as well as predictive validation evidence from the proposed hiring system. You will determine whether the proposed selection system represents a real improvement in the organization's ability to select associates who will perform well. Your willingness to generalize the results to other stores will also be assessed. An important ancillary activity in this case is ensuring that you communicate your statistical analyses in a way that is easy for a nonexpert to comprehend. Finally, you will determine if there are any other outcomes you would like to assess with the new staffing materials, such as the potential for adverse impact and the reactions of store managers to the new system. The background information for this case, and your specific assignment, can be found at www.mcgrawhill.ca/OLC/heneman.

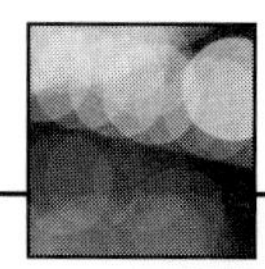

TANGLEWOOD STORES CASE II

Adverse Impact

One of the most significant equal employment opportunity concerns for any organization is when a large class of employees gathers together to propose that they have been discriminated against. In this case, you will assess a complaint of adverse impact proposed by designated-group employees of Tanglewood.

collected both within and from outside the organization. The focus should be on learning about employee reward preferences, and various ways to accomplish this are discussed.

Finally, two legal issues pertaining to job analysis are treated. Both issues involve the job requirements approach to job analysis as it applies to human rights under the Canadian Human Rights Act.

TYPES OF JOBS

jobs
The building blocks of an organization, in terms of both job content and the hierarchical relationships that emerge among them

Jobs are the building blocks of an organization, in terms of both job content and the hierarchical relationships that emerge among them.[3] They are explicitly designed and aligned in ways that enhance the production of the organization's goods and services. Job analysis naturally occurs within the broader framework of job design; it is through their design that jobs acquire their requirements and rewards in the first place. Several different types of jobs may be designed by the organization. These include traditional, evolving, flexible, idiosyncratic, team-based, and telework jobs.

Traditional

The traditional way of designing a job is to identify and define its elements and tasks precisely, and then incorporate them into a job description. The traditional approach can be viewed as a core task, which then includes virtually all tasks associated with the job. The result will be a natural flow of KSAOs. Thus defined, there are clear lines of demarcation between jobs in terms of both tasks and KSAOs, and there is little overlap between jobs on either basis. Each job also has its own set of extrinsic and intrinsic rewards. **Traditional job design** is marked by formal organization charts, clear and precise job descriptions and specifications, and well-defined relationships between jobs in terms of mobility (promotion and transfer) paths. Also, traditional jobs are very static, with little or no change occurring in tasks or KSAOs.

traditional job design
Identifies and defines its elements and tasks precisely, and then incorporates them into a job description

Certain terms are used frequently in discussions of traditional jobs. Definitions of some of the key terms, and examples of them, are provided in Exhibit 4.1. Note that the terms are presented in a logically descending hierarchy, starting with job category or family, and proceeding downward through job, position, task dimension, task, and element.

EXHIBIT 4.1 Terminology Commonly Used in Describing Jobs

Term	Example	Definition
Job family	Production, finance, human resources, marketing	A grouping of jobs, usually according to function
Job category	Managerial, sales, clerical, maintenance	A grouping of jobs according to generic job title or occupation
Job	Inside sales representative	A grouping of positions that are similar in their tasks and task dimensions
Position	Inside sales representative for computer software	A grouping of tasks/dimensions that constitute the total work assignment of a single employee, usually accounting for as many positions as there are employees
Task dimension	Resolving customer complaints	A grouping of similar types of tasks, sometimes called "duty," "area of responsibility," or "key results area"
Task	Telephone support	A grouping of elements that form an identifiable activity that is a logical and necessary step in the performance of the job
Element	Document customer complaints	The smallest unit into which work can be divided without analyzing separate motions, movements, and mental processes

Evolving

evolving job

A traditional job whose design or application may gradually change or evolve over time

Traditional jobs that gradually change or evolve their design or application may become an **evolving job**. These changes are not radical, are usually intentional, and are often due to technological and workload changes.

An excellent example of such an evolving job is that of "secretary."[4] Traditional or core tasks associated with the job include typing, filing, taking dictation, and answering phones. However, in many organizations the job has evolved to include new tasks such as word processing, managing multiple projects, creating spreadsheets, purchasing supplies and office technology, and gathering information on the Internet. These task changes lead to new KSAO requirements, such as planning and co-ordination skills and knowledge of spreadsheet software. Accompanying these changes is a change in job title to that of "administrative assistant."

It should be noted that jobs may evolve due to changing organization and technology requirements, as well as to employee-initiated changes through a process of job crafting.

Flexible

flexible jobs

Jobs that have frequently changing tasks and KSAO requirements

Flexible jobs have frequently changing task and KSAO requirements. These changes may be initiated by a new job incumbent, for example, one who constantly adds, drops, or passes off new assignments or projects as new opportunities present themselves. Other times the task changes may be dictated by changes in production schedules or client demands. Many small business owners, general managers of start-up strategic business units, and top management members perform such flexible jobs. These jobs are "loose cannon" ones, characterized by broad job titles (e.g., administrator, general manager, director, scientist) and job descriptions with only cursory statements about tasks and duties (e.g., "manages budget planning, human resources, and marketing processes"). Within this elastic job title–tasks combination, the employee is free to rattle and roll around.

Another example of flexible jobs is project jobs. Specific projects are undertaken (e.g., designing an advertising campaign) and when that project is completed new ones are assigned. As projects vary, task and KSAO flexibility is required by members of the project team.

Idiosyncratic

idiosyncratic jobs

Unique jobs created in response to the known or anticipated availability of a specific person with highly valued skills

Idiosyncratic jobs are unique and created in response to the known (or anticipated) availability of a specific person with highly valued skills.[5] The person may be a current employee or an outsider to the organization. The person for whom the position is created may in fact even be the instigator of its creation. He or she may approach the organization and explicitly communicate availability and the type of position (both requirements and rewards) desired. Former politicians and high-level government employees are often hired into such idiosyncratically designed jobs.

Team-Based

work team

An interdependent collection of employees who share responsibility for achieving a specific goal

Team-based jobs occur within work teams.[6] A **work team** is an interdependent collection of employees who share responsibility for achieving a specific goal. Examples of such goals include developing a product, delivering a service, winning a game, conducting a process, developing a plan, or making a joint decision.

Teams, and thus team-based jobs, occur in multiple forms. Classification of such forms includes the following:[7]

1. Advice/involvement teams, such as quality control circles, special committees, and advisory boards
2. Production/service teams, such as assembly, data processing, and client service teams

EXHIBIT 4.2 Example of Team Single-Job Performance

A product development team has mechanical engineers, computer-assisted design (CAD) specialists, product safety experts, and marketing specialists as team members. Each team member will likely perform only one of these jobs. Staffing these jobs will be a targeted approach toward job-specific KSAOs.

EXHIBIT 4.3 Example of Team Multiple-Job Performance

A team is responsible for the assembly of lawn mower engines. Different members on the team perform different jobs at any particular moment, and they are also required to be (or to become) proficient in all phases of engine assembly. Staffing this team will require selecting team members that have both job-specific and job-spanning KSAOs.

3. Project/development teams, such as research and development, project management, brand management, engineering, and task force teams
4. Action/negotiation teams, such as sports, collective bargaining, surgery, and flight crew teams

Each of these teams is composed of two or more employees, and there is an identifiable collection of tasks that the team is to perform. Usually, these tasks will be grouped into specific clusters and each cluster constitutes a position or job. A project management team, for example, may have separate jobs and job titles for budget specialists, technical specialists, coordinators, and field staff. Each of these jobs may be traditional, evolving, flexible, or idiosyncratic.

Another type of team, one that encompasses elements of all of the above team types, is the **global virtual team**.[8] Such a team is composed of members who are geographically dispersed, from multiple cultures, working in collaboration electronically. These teams are often assigned temporary, critical tasks such as globally developing new products, creating and implementing mergers and acquisitions, conducting global audits, and managing brands.

global virtual team
A work team composed of members who area geographically dispersed, from multiple cultures, working in collaboration electronically

While teams differ in many respects, two differences are very important in terms of their staffing implications. The first difference is in the extent to which each team member performs only one job, as opposed to multiple jobs. When members each perform only a single job, as shown in Exhibit 4.2, staffing each job requires a focus on recruitment and selection for only job-specific KSAOs. To the extent that members must perform multiple jobs, as shown in Exhibit 4.3, staffing must emphasize recruitment and selection for both job-specific KSAOs and job-spanning KSAOs. Another term used to connote job-spanning KSAOs is competencies. Many of these job-spanning KSAOs will involve flexibility, adaptability, and rapid learning skills that will facilitate performing, and switching between, multiple jobs.

The second important difference between teams regarding staffing is the degree of task interdependence among team members. The greater the task interdependence, the greater the importance of KSAOs pertaining to interpersonal qualities (e.g., communicating, collaborating, and resolving conflicts) and team self-management qualities (e.g., setting group goals, inspecting each other's work). Thus, task interdependence brings behaviourally oriented KSAOs to the forefront of job requirements for team-based jobs.

telework
A work arrangement in which the employee works away from the employer's work location using telecommunication technology to accomplish tasks

Telework

Telework is a work arrangement in which the employee works away from the employer's work location using telecommunications technology (e.g., personal computer, e-mail, fax, cellular phone) to accomplish tasks. It may be done from home, on the road, or at special satellite locations established by the employer. Also, telework may involve either full-time or part-time work, with either fixed or flexible work hours. Telework is applicable to many different functional work areas such as marketing, sales, technical writing, financial analysis, and programming.[9]

JOB REQUIREMENTS JOB ANALYSIS

Job analysis is the cornerstone for developing staffing strategies. Once a job can be comprehensively studied and defined, it provides the foundation for all staffing functions (e.g. recruitment, selection, compensation, training, and retention) that meet legal requirements and enhance individual and job/organizational fit. For example, identifying the KSAOs to be successful in a sales position by using a variety of job analysis techniques leads to the ability to profile the entire sales force and to identify skill gaps for which training programs can be developed. Also, structured situational and behavioural based questions can be developed to identify the best candidates for the sales position. Gathering job analysis information is "a demanding and time-consuming task. But failing to do it can result in irrelevant human resources activities, unfocused development efforts, lack of clear criteria for selection assessment and training programs, a general fuzziness of what current and future success criteria look like."[10]

job analysis
The process of studying jobs in order to gather, analyze, synthesize, and report information about job requirements

Job analysis may be defined as the process of studying jobs in order to gather, analyze, synthesize, and report information about job requirements. Note in this definition that job analysis is an overall process as opposed to a specific method or technique. The result of effective job analysis is richer and more accurate information for guiding staffing decisions that ultimately have real organizational impact.

Job analysis can also be referred to as strategic job modelling, where there is "an ongoing set of organizational activities that involve methodologically sound research procedures to systematically investigate, study, verify, and apply all relevant information to create a strategic description of the requisite components of success for a job or job group."[11]

job requirements job analysis
Seeks to identify and describe the specific tasks, KSAOs, and job context for a particular job

Job requirements job analysis seeks to identify and describe the specific tasks, KSAOs, and job context for a particular job. This type of job analysis is the most thoroughly developed and commonly used by organizations. A second type of job analysis, competency-based, attempts to identify and describe job requirements in the form of general KSAOs required across a range of jobs; task and work context requirements are of little concern. Interpersonal skills, for example, might be identified as a competency for sales and customer service jobs; leadership is a likely competency requirement for managerial jobs. Competency-based job analysis is more recent in origin, though it has some similarities to job requirements job analysis. It is discussed separately later in this chapter.

Job requirements job analysis yields information helpful in the recruitment, selection, and employment domains in such activities as:

- Communicating job requirements to job applicants
- Developing selection plans for KSAOs to focus on when staffing a job
- Identifying appropriate assessment methods to gauge applicants' KSAOs
- Establishing hiring qualifications
- Complying with relevant laws and regulations

Competency-based job analysis results will be helpful primarily in identifying a common set of general KSAOs in which all applicants must be proficient, regardless of the specific job for which they are applying.

Effective staffing definitely requires job requirements information, and possibly competency information, for each of the types of jobs described previously. Traditional and evolving jobs readily lend themselves to this. Their requirements are generally well known and unlikely to change except gradually. For idiosyncratic, flexible, team-based, and telework jobs, job analysis is more difficult and problematic. The requirements for these jobs may frequently be changing,

We now turn to a thorough discussion of each of the components of the job requirements matrix. These components are:

- Tasks
- Task dimensions and their importance
- KSAOs and their importance
- Job context
- Specific definitions, techniques, and classifications useful for successfully gathering and recording information
- Actual process of collecting job information and conducting job analysis

Task Statements Job analysis begins with the development of task statements, whose objective is to identify and record a set of tasks that both includes all of the job's major tasks and excludes nonrelevant or trivial tasks. The resultant task statements serve as the building blocks for the remainder of the job requirements job analysis.

task statements
Objectively written descriptions of the behaviours or work activities engaged by employees in order to perform a job

Identification and recording of tasks begins with the construction of **task statements**. These statements are objectively written descriptions of the behaviours or work activities engaged in by employees in order to perform a job. The statements are made in simple declarative sentences.

Ideally, each task statement will show several things. These are:

1. What the employee does, using a specific action verb at the start of the task statement
2. To whom or what the employee does what he or she does, stating the object of the verb
3. What is produced, indicating the expected output of the verb
4. What materials, tools, procedures, or equipment are used

Use of the sentence analysis technique is very helpful for writing task statements that conform to these four requirements. An example of the technique is shown in Exhibit 4.6 for several tasks from very different jobs.

In addition to meeting the preceding four requirements, the following are other suggestions for effective task statements:

1. Use specific action verbs that have only one meaning, such as analyze, plan, and evaluate. Examples of verbs that do not conform to this suggestion include support, assist, and handles.
2. Focus on recording tasks as opposed to specific elements that comprise a task. This requires use of considerable judgment because the distinction between task and element is relative and often fuzzy.
3. A useful rule to keep in mind is that most jobs can be adequately described within a range of 15 to 25 task statements. A task statement list exceeding this range is a warning that it may be too narrow in terms of activities defined.
4. Do not include minor or trivial activities in task statements; focus only on major tasks and activities. An exception to this recommendation occurs when a so-called minor task is judged to have great importance to the job (see the following discussion).
5. Take steps to ensure that the list of task statements is reliable.[13] The basic way to conform to this suggestion is to have two or more people ("analysts") independently evaluate the task statement list in terms of both inclusiveness and clarity. Close agreement between people signifies high reliability. Should disagreements between people be discovered, the nature of the disagreements can be discussed and appropriate modifications to the task statements made.
6. Have at least the manager and a job incumbent serve as the analysts providing the reliability checks. It is important to have the manager participate in this process in order to verify that the task statements are inclusive and accurate. For the job incumbent,

EXHIBIT 4.6 Use of the Sentence Analysis Technique for Task Statements

Sentence Analysis Technique

What does the worker do?		Why does the worker do it? What gets done?	What is the final result or technological objective?
Worker action		Purpose of the worker actions	Materials, products, subject matter, and/or services (MPSMS)
(Worker function)	(Work devices, people, or information)	(Work field)	(MPSMS)
Verb	Direct object	Infinitive phrase	
		Infinitive	Object of the infinitive
Sets up (*setting up*)	various types of metal-working machines (*work device*)	to machine (*machining*)	metal aircraft parts. (*material*)
Persuades (*persuading*)	customers (*people*)	to buy (*merchandising*)	automobiles. (*product*)
Interviews (*analyzing*)	clients (*people*)	to assess (*advising–counselling*)	skills and abilities. (*subject matter*)
Drives (*driving–operating*)	bus (*work device*)	to transport (*transporting*)	passengers. (*service*)

Source: Vocational Rehabilitation Institute, *A Guide to Job Analysis* (Menominee, WI: University of Wisconsin-Stout, 1982), p. 8.

the concern is not only that of verification but also acceptance of the task statements as adequate representations that will guide incumbents' performance of the job.

7. Ideally there should be multiple managers and job incumbents, along with a representative from the HR department, serving as analysts. This would expand the scope of input and allow for more precise reliability checks.
8. Recognize that the accuracy or validity of task statements cannot be evaluated against external criterion because there is no external criterion available to use.
9. Task descriptions are accurate and meaningful only to the extent that people agree on them. Because of this, the preceding recommendation regarding checks on content validity and reliability takes on added importance.

task dimensions
Groupings of task statements

Task Dimensions Task statement lists may be maintained in list form and subsequently incorporated into the job description. Often, however, it is useful to group sets of task statements into task dimensions, and then attach a name to each such dimension. Other terms for **task dimensions** are "duties," "accountability areas," "responsibilities," and "performance dimensions."

A useful way to facilitate the grouping process is to create a task dimension matrix. Each column in the matrix represents a potential task dimension, and a label is tentatively attached to it. Each row in the matrix represents a particular task statement. Cell entries in the matrix represent the assignment of task statements to task dimensions (the grouping of tasks). The goal is to have each task statement assigned to only one task dimension. The process is complicated by the fact that the dimensions and labels must be created prior to grouping; the dimensions and labels may have to be changed or rearranged to make task statements fit as one progresses through the assignment of task statements to dimensions.

Several things should be kept in mind about task dimensions. First, their creation is optional and should occur only if they will be useful. Second, there are many different grouping procedures, ranging from straightforward judgmental ones to highly sophisticated statistical ones.[14] For most purposes, a simple judgmental process is sufficient, such as having the people who participated in the creation of the task statements also create the groupings as part of the same exercise. As a rule, there should be four to eight dimensions, depending on the number of task statements, regardless of the specific grouping procedure used. Third, it is important that the grouping procedure yield a reliable set of task dimensions acceptable to managers, job incumbents, and other organizational members. Finally, as with task statements, it is not possible to empirically validate task dimensions against some external criterion; for both task statements and dimensions, their validity is in the eyes of the definers and beholders.

Importance of Tasks/Dimensions Rarely are all tasks/dimensions of a job thought to be of equal weight or importance. In some general sense, it is thus felt that these differences must be captured, expressed, and incorporated into job information, especially the job description. Normally, assessments of importance are made just for task dimensions, though it is certainly possible to make them for individual tasks as well.

Before actual weighting can occur, two decisions must be made. First, the specific attribute to be assessed in terms of importance must be decided (e.g., time spent on the task/dimension). Second, a decision is required regarding whether the attribute will be measured in categorical (e.g., essential or nonessential) or continuous (e.g., percent of time spent, 1–5 rating of importance) terms. Exhibit 4.7 shows examples of the results of these two decisions in terms of commonly used importance attributes and their measurement.

Once these decisions are made, it is possible to proceed with the actual process of assessing or weighting the tasks/dimensions in terms of importance. It should be noted here that if the

EXHIBIT 4.7 Examples of Ways to Assess Task/Dimension Importance

A. Relative Time Spent

For each task/dimension, rate the amount of time you spend on it, relative to all other tasks/dimensions of your job.

1	2	3	4	5
Very small amount		Average amount		Very large amount

B. Percentage (%) Time Spent

For each task/dimension, indicate the percentage (%) of time you spend on it (percentages must total to 100%).

Dimension ____________________ % Time spent ____________________

C. Importance to Overall Performance

For each task/dimension, rate its importance to your overall job performance.

1	2	3	4	5
Minor importance		Average importance		Major importance

D. Need for New Employee Training

Do new employees receive a standard, planned course of training for performance of this task, other than a customary job orientation?

_________ Yes

_________ No

tasks/dimensions are not explicitly assessed in such a manner, all tasks/dimensions end up being weighted equally by default.

If possible, it is desirable for the assessments to be done initially by independent analysts (e.g., incumbents and managers). In this way, it will be possible to check for the degree of reliability among raters. Where differences are found, they can be discussed and resolved. Just as it is desirable to have high reliability in the identification of tasks and dimensions, it is desirable to have high reliability in judgments of their importance.[15]

2.1

KSAOs KSAOs are inferred or derived from knowledge of the tasks and task dimensions themselves. The inference process requires that the analysts explicitly think in specific cause-and-effect terms. For each task or dimension, the analyst must in essence ask, "Exactly what KSAOs do I think will be necessary for (will cause) performance on this task or dimension?" Then the analyst should ask "Why do I think this?" in order to think through the soundness of the inferential logic. Discussions among analysts about these questions are encouraged.

knowledge
A body of information (conceptual, factual, or procedural) that can be applied directly to the performance of tasks

Knowledge. **Knowledge** is a body of information (conceptual, factual, procedural) that can be applied directly to the performance of tasks. It tends to be quite focused or specific in terms of job, organization, or occupation.

Analysts can get assistance in identifying and writing statements of knowledge requirements from National Occupational Classification 2001 (NOC 2001) Web site (www23.hrdc-drhc.gc.ca/2001/e/generic/welcome.shtml). The NOC 2001 provides a standardized methodology for organizing job classifications. The development of the job classifications is based on extensive occupational research across all spectrums of the Canadian labour market. There are occupational descriptions for 520 jobs.

The U.S. Department of Labor has developed an electronic database—Occupational Information Network, or O*NET (www.onetcenter.org). It provides definitions of 33 knowledges that are also transferable to analyzing Canadian occupations. Use of O*NET knowledges and their definitions is a helpful starting point in preparing knowledge statements. Exhibit 4.8 provides a listing of those knowledges. Definition of the knowledges are also provided by O*NET in print and online. For example, "sales and marketing" knowledge is defined as "knowledge of principles and methods involved in showing, promoting, and selling products or services; this includes marketing strategies and tactics, product demonstration and sales techniques, and sales control systems."[16]

As the knowledges are intended for general occupations, they will probably have to be supplemented with more job-specific statements crafted by the job analyst. When doing so, analysts should be particularly wary of using global or shorthand terms such as "knowledge of accounting principles." Here, it would be better to indicate which accounting principles are being utilized, and why each is necessary for task performance. It is important to keep in mind that job knowledge increases with experience on the job or with the task when the knowledge definition for a job is created.[17]

skill
An observable competence for working with or applying knowledge to perform a particular task or closely related set of tasks

Skill. **Skill** refers to an observable competence for working with or applying knowledge to perform a particular task or closely related set of tasks. A skill is not an enduring characteristic of the person; it depends on experience and practice. Skill requirements are directly inferred from observation or knowledge of tasks performed.

Considerable research has been devoted to identifying particular job-related skills and to organizing them into taxonomies. Job analysts should begin the skills inference process by referring to the results of this research.

An excellent example of such useful research is Employability Skills 2000+ developed by the Conference Board of Canada. Employability Skills 2000+ was developed in collaboration with more than 50 members of the Conference Board of Canada's Employability Skills Forum and Education Forum on Science, Technology, and Mathematics. The list of employability skills needed to participate in today's dynamic world of work can be found on the Conference Board of Canada Web site (www.conferenceboard.ca/education/learning-tools/pdfs/esp2000.pdf).

EXHIBIT 4.8 Knowledges Contained in O*NET

Knowledge Areas

- Business and management
  - Administration and management
  - Clerical
  - Economics and accounting
  - Sales and marketing
  - Customer and personal service
  - Personnel and human resources
- Manufacturing and production
  - Production and processing
  - Food production
- Engineering and technology
  - Computers and electronics
  - Engineering and technology
  - Design
  - Building and construction
  - Mechanical
- Mathematics and science
  - Mathematics
  - Physics
  - Chemistry
  - Biology
  - Psychology
  - Sociology and anthropology
  - Geography
- Health services
  - Medicine and dentistry
  - Therapy and counselling
- Education and training
  - Education and training
- Arts and humanities
  - English language
  - Foreign language
  - Fine arts
  - History and archaeology
  - Philosophy and theology
- Law and public safety
  - Public safety and security
  - Law, government, and jurisprudence
- Communications
  - Telecommunications
  - Communications and media
- Transportation
  - Transportation

Source: Adapted from N. G. Peterson, M. D. Mumford, W. C. Borman, P. R. Jeanneret, E. A. Fleishman, and K. Y. Levin, *O*NET Final Technical Report, Vol. 1* (Salt Lake City: Utah Department of Workforce Services, 1997), pp. 4–1 to 4–26. © Utah Department of Workforce Services on behalf of U.S. Department of Labor.

Another good example is found in the O*NET.[18] O*NET identifies and defines 46 skills applicable across the occupational spectrum. The first 10 of these are basic skills involving acquiring and conveying information; the remaining 36 are cross-functional skills used to facilitate task performance. Exhibit 4.9 provides a listing of all these skills. Definitions are also provided by O*NET, in print and online. For example, the basic skill "reading comprehension" is defined as "understanding written sentences and paragraphs in work-related documents," and the cross-functional skill "negotiation" is defined as "bringing others together and trying to reconcile differences." Reference to these 46 skills is a good starting point for the job analyst. More specific skills may need to be identified and described for the particular job being analyzed. An excellent example in this regard is computer-related skills such as use of spreadsheets and databases, use of software such as Microsoft® Word, and various type of programming.

ability
An underlying, enduring trait of the person useful for performing a range of different tasks

Ability. An **ability** is an underlying, enduring trait of the person useful for performing a range of different tasks. It differs from a skill in that it is less likely to change over time and is applicable across a wide set of tasks encountered on many different jobs. Four general categories of abilities are commonly recognized: cognitive, psychomotor, physical, and sensory abilities. O*NET contains a complete taxonomy of these four categories; they are shown in Exhibit 4.10. Definitions (not shown) accompany the abilities in print and online. The ability "oral expression," for example, is defined as "the ability to communicate information and ideas in speaking so others will understand." As another example, "dynamic flexibility" is "the ability to quickly and repeatedly bend, stretch, twist, or reach out with the body, arms and/or legs."[19]

EXHIBIT 4.9 Skills Contained in O*NET

Basic Skills

- Content
  - Reading comprehension
  - Active listening
  - Writing
  - Speaking
  - Mathematics
  - Science
- Process
  - Critical thinking
  - Active learning
  - Learning strategies
  - Monitoring

Cross-Functional Skills

- Social skills
  - Social perceptiveness
  - Coordination
  - Persuasion
  - Negotiation
  - Instructing
  - Service orientation
- Complex problem-solving skills
  - Problem identification
  - Information gathering
  - Information organization
  - Synthesis/reorganization
  - Idea generation
  - Idea evaluation
  - Implementation planning
  - Solution appraisal
- Resource management skills
  - Time management
  - Management of financial resources
  - Management of material resources
  - Management of personnel resources
- Technical skills
  - Operations analysis
  - Technology design
  - Equipment selection
  - Installation
  - Programming
  - Equipment maintenance
  - Troubleshooting
  - Repairing
  - Testing
  - Operation monitoring
  - Operation and control
  - Product inspection
- Systems skills
  - Visioning
  - Systems perception
  - Identification of downstream consequences
  - Identification of key causes
  - Judgment and decision making
  - Systems evaluation

Source: Adapted from N. G. Peterson, M. D. Mumford, W. C. Borman, P. R. Jeanneret, E. A. Fleishman, and K. Y. Levin, *O*NET Final Technical Report, Vol. 1* (Salt Lake City: Utah Department of Workforce Services, 1997), pp. 3–1 to 3–36. © Utah Department of Workforce Services on behalf of U.S. Department of Labor.

Other Characteristics. This is a catchall category for factors that do not fit neatly into the K (knowledge), S (skill), and A (ability) categories. Despite the catchall nature of these requirements, they are very important for even being able to enter the employment relationship (legal requirements), being present to perform the job (availability requirements), and having values consistent with organizational culture and values (character requirements). Numerous examples of these factors are shown in Exhibit 4.11. Care should be taken to ensure that these factors truly are job requirements, as opposed to whimsical and ill-defined preferences of the organization.

KSAO Importance As suggested in the job requirements matrix, the KSAOs of a job may differ in their weight or contribution to task performance. Hence, their relative importance must be explicitly considered, defined, and indicated. Failure to do so means that all KSAOs will be assumed to be of equal importance by default.

EXHIBIT 4.10 Abilities Contained in O*NET

Cognitive Abilities

- Verbal abilities
  - Oral comprehension
  - Written comprehension
  - Oral expression
  - Written expression
- Idea generation and reasoning abilities
  - Fluency of ideas
  - Originality
  - Problem sensitivity
  - Deductive reasoning
  - Inductive reasoning
  - Information ordering
  - Category flexibility
- Quantitative abilities
  - Mathematical reasoning
  - Number facility
- Memory
  - Memorization
- Perceptual abilities
  - Speed of closure
  - Flexibility of closure
  - Perceptual speed
- Spatial abilities
  - Spatial organization
  - Visualization
- Attentiveness
  - Selective attention
  - Time sharing

Psychomotor Abilities

- Fine manipulative abilities
  - Arm-hand steadiness
  - Manual dexterity
  - Finger dexterity
- Control movement abilities
  - Control precision
  - Multilimb coordination
  - Response orientation
  - Rate control
- Reaction time and speed abilities
  - Reaction time
  - Wrist-finger dexterity
  - Speed of limb movement

Physical Abilities

- Physical strength abilities
  - Static strength
  - Explosive strength
  - Dynamic strength
  - Trunk strength
- Endurance
  - Stamina
- Flexibility, balance, and coordination
  - Extent flexibility
  - Dynamic flexibility
  - Gross body coordination
  - Gross body equilibrium

Sensory Abilities

- Visual abilities
  - Near vision
  - Far vision
  - Visual colour discrimination
  - Night vision
  - Peripheral vision
  - Depth perception
  - Glare sensitivity
- Auditory and speech abilities
  - Hearing sensitivity
  - Auditory attention
  - Sound localization
  - Speech recognition
  - Speech clarity

Source: Adapted from N. G. Peterson, M. D. Mumford, W. C. Borman, P. R. Jeanneret, E. A. Fleishman, and K. Y. Levin, *O*NET Final Technical Report, Vol. 2* (Salt Lake City: Utah Department of Workforce Services, 1997), pp. 9–1 to 9–26.

As with task importance, deriving KSAO importance requires two decisions. First, what will be the specific attribute(s) on which importance is judged? Second, will the measurement of each attribute be categorical (e.g., required-preferred) or continuous (e.g., 1–5 rating scale)? Examples of formats for indicating KSAO importance are shown in Exhibit 4.12. The O*NET uses a 1–5 rating scale format and also provides actual importance ratings for many jobs.

EXHIBIT 4.11 Examples of Other Job Requirements

Legal Requirements
- Possession of licence (occupational, drivers, etc.)
- Citizen or permanent resident
- Geographic residency (e.g., within city limits for public employees)
- Security clearance

Availability Requirements
- Starting date
- Worksite locations
- Hours and days of week
- Travel
- Attendance and tardiness

Character Requirements
- Moral
- Work ethic
- Background
- Conscientiousness
- Honesty and integrity

EXHIBIT 4.12 Examples of Ways to Assess KSAO Importance

A. Importance to (acceptable) (superior) task performance
1 = minimal importance
2 = some importance
3 = average importance
4 = considerable importance
5 = extensive importance

B. Should the KSAO be assessed during recruitment/selection?
☐ Yes
☐ No

C. Is the KSAO required, preferred, or not required for recruitment/selection?
☐ Required
☐ Preferred
☐ Not required (obtain on job and/or in training)

Job Context As shown in the job requirements matrix, tasks and KSAOs occur within a broader job context. Job context and factors that are important in defining it should be considered when doing a job requirements job analysis. Exhibit 4.13 gives an example of a job analysis to specifically determine personal and contextual factors when determining creativity at work. Such consideration is necessary because these factors may have an influence on tasks and KSAOs; further, information about the factors may be used in the recruitment and selection of job applicants. For example, the information may be given to job applicants to provide them a realistic job preview during recruitment, and consideration of job context factors may be helpful in assessing likely person/organization fit during selection.

O*NET contains a wide array of job and work context factors useful for characterizing occupations.[20] The most relevant for specific job analysis purposes are the physical work conditions: setting, attire, body positioning, environmental conditions, and job hazards. Within each

EXHIBIT 4.13 Analysis of Personal and Contextual Factors When Determining Creativity at Work

Research was conducted in two manufacturing facilities that produced component parts for technical equipment. Each employee in the two facilities held one of 18 different jobs (e.g., design engineer, manufacturing engineer, design drafter, toolmaker, technician, etc.). Human resource managers for the two facilities were asked to identify individual work units within the facilities for possible participation for the research. All employees in the identified units were then contacted and asked to participate. A total of 171 employees participated.

The purpose of the research was to understand how organizational contexts contribute significantly to employees' creative performance at work. The two contexts that were analyzed were job complexity and supervisory style, and the three indicators of creativity in the organizational setting were patent disclosures written, contributions to organization suggestion program, and supervisory ratings of creativity.

Previous research suggested that the design of a job is an important contributor to employees' intrinsic motivation and creative performance at work. "Where jobs are complex and challenging, individuals are likely to be excited about their work activities and interested in completing these activities in the absence of external controls or constraints. The level of interest and excitement produced by a job's design is then expected to foster creative achievements at work."

The style of supervision, identified as an organizational context, is a significant contributor to employees' creativity at work. "Creative output was significantly related to the extent to which supervisors were empathetic and attempted to understand employees' feelings."

In general, the results of the research determined that "employees exhibited higher performance and lower intention to quit when their jobs were complex and when their supervisors were described as supportive and non-controlling."

The results were generally consistent with earlier approaches to understanding creativity and suggest that management should consider both personal and contextual factors to increase creativity in the workplace.

Source: Greg R. Oldman and Anne Cummings, "Employee creativity: personal and contextual factors at work," *Academy of Management Journal,* June 1996, 39(3), pp. 607–28.

of these categories are numerous specific facets; these are shown in Exhibit 4.14. The job analyst should use a listing such as this to identify the relevant job context factors and include them in the job requirements matrix.

The O*NET also contains work context factors pertaining to interpersonal relationships (communication, types of role relationships, responsibility for others, and conflictual contact with others) and to structural job characteristics (criticality of position, routine versus challenging work, pace and scheduling). These factors might also be considered in the job analysis.

Job Descriptions and Job Specifications

3.3

job description
A written statement listing the purpose, essential duties and responsibilities, level of work performed, qualifications, and context for a specific job or occupation

A **job description** is a written statement listing the purpose, essential duties and responsibilities, level of work performed, qualifications, and context for a specific job or occupations. A good job description is an excellent communication tool that can be used for a variety of staffing functions.

As mentioned earlier, the National Occupational Classification 2001 (NOC 2001) developed by Human Resources and Social Development Canada is an excellent resource in developing job descriptions. Occupations are classified in skill types and skill levels. Although descriptive tools such as NOC 2001 can be a guide, there are no standard formats or requirements for a job description. An example of a job description outlining job qualifications is shown in Exhibit 4.15.

EXHIBIT 4.14 Job Context (Physical Work Conditions) Contained in O*NET

Work Setting

- How frequently does this job require the worker to work:
  - Indoors, environmentally controlled
  - Indoors, not environmentally controlled
  - Outdoors, exposed to all weather conditions
  - Outdoors, under cover
  - In an open vehicle or operating open equipment
  - In an enclosed vehicle or operating enclosed equipment
- Privacy of work area
- Physical proximity

Work Attire

- How often does the worker wear:
  - Business clothes
  - A special uniform
  - Work clothing
  - Common protective or safety attire
  - Specialized protective or safety attire

Body Positioning

- How much time in a usual work period does the worker spend:
  - Sitting
  - Standing
  - Climbing ladders, scaffolds, poles, and so on
  - Walking or running
  - Kneeling, stooping, crouching, or crawling
  - Keeping or regaining balance
  - Using hands to handle, control, or feel objects, tools, or controls
  - Bending or twisting the body
  - Making repetitive motions

Environmental Conditions

- How often during a usual work period is the worker exposed to the following conditions:
  - Sounds and noise levels that are distracting and uncomfortable
  - Very hot or very cold temperatures
  - Extremely bright or inadequate lighting conditions
  - Contaminants
  - Cramped work space that requires getting into awkward positions
  - Whole body vibration

Job Hazards

- How often does this job require the worker to be exposed to the following hazards:
  - Radiation
  - Diseases/infections
  - High places
  - Hazardous conditions
  - Hazardous equipment
  - Hazardous situation involving likely cuts, bites, stings, or minor burns

Source: Adapted from N. G. Peterson, M. D. Mumford, W. C. Borman, P. R. Jeanneret, E. A. Fleishman, and K. Y. Levin, *O*NET Final Technical Report, Vol. 2* (Salt Lake City: Utah Department of Workforce Services, 1997), pp. 7–1 to 7–35. Utah Department of Workforce Services on behalf of U.S. Department of Labor.

Collecting Job Requirements Information

Job analysis involves not only consideration of the types of information (tasks, KSAOs, and job context) to be collected but also the methods, sources, and processes to be used for such collection. It is a methodical procedure to define successful performance and then develop criteria against which an employee's performance can be assessed.[21] These issues are discussed next, and as will be seen, there are many alternatives to choose from for purposes of developing an overall job analysis system for any particular situation. Potential inaccuracies and other limitations in the alternatives will also be pointed out.[22]

Methods Job analysis methods represent procedures or techniques for collecting job information related to tasks and/or worker attributes for a given job. Job analysis techniques can be classified as either work oriented or worker oriented. Work-oriented methods relate to describing various tasks performed on the job and the expected outcomes for those tasks.[23] For example, a receptionist's tasks may include answering a multi-line switchboard, opening and distributing mail; and greeting and directing visitors coming for appointments. The expected outcome for

EXHIBIT 4.15 Example of Job Description

FUNCTIONAL UNIT: CHILDREN'S REHABILITATION

JOB TITLE: REHABILITATION SPECIALIST

DATE: 12/5/05

JOB SUMMARY

Works with small children with disabilities and their families to identify developmental strengths and weaknesses, develop rehabilitation plans, deliver and coordinate rehabilitation activities, and evaluate effectiveness of those plans and activities.

MAJOR RESPONSIBILITIES AND DUTIES — **Time Spent (%)**

1. **Assessment** — **10%**

   Administer formal and informal motor screening and evaluation instruments to conduct assessments. Perform assessments to identify areas of strengths and need.

2. **Planning** — **25%**

   Collaborate with parents and other providers to directly develop the individualized family service plan. Use direct and consultative models of service in developing plans.

3. **Delivery** — **50%**

   Carry out individual and small group motor development activities with children and families. Provide service coordination to designated families. Work with family care and child care providers to provide total services. Collaborate with other staff members and professionals from community agencies to obtain resources and specialized assistance.

4. **Evaluation** — **15%**

   Observe, interpret, and report on client to monitor individual progress. Assist in collecting and reporting intervention data in order to prepare formal program evaluation reports. Write evaluation reports to assist in developing new treatment strategies and programs.

QUALIFICATIONS

1. **Licence:** Licence to practise physical therapy in the province
2. **Education:** BSc in physical or occupational therapy required; MSc preferred
3. **Experience:** Prefer (not required) one year experience working with children with disabilities and their families
4. **Skills:** Listening to and interacting with others (children, family members, co-workers); developing treatment plans; organizing and writing reports using Microsoft Word

JOB CONTEXT: indoors, office, business clothes, no environmental or job hazards.

those tasks would be efficiently answering the phone, distributing mail, and directing visitors to appropriate staff member.

Worker-oriented methods examine the broader human behaviours involved in completing the tasks (e.g. physical, sensory, interpersonal, and cognitive). For example, analysis of that same receptionist would include observing the number of calls answered in an hour and the length of time callers are left on hold, the demeanour with visitors, and the manner with which the phone is answered.

There have been many specific techniques and systems developed and named (e.g., Functional Job Analysis, Position Analysis Questionnaire). Rather than discuss each of the many techniques separately, we will concentrate on the major generic methods that underlie all specific techniques and applications. There are many excellent descriptions and discussions of the specific techniques available.[24]

prior information
Information about a job that is used as the starting point for a job analysis

Prior Information. For any job, there is usually some **prior information** available about it that could and should be consulted. Indeed, this information should routinely be searched for and used as a starting point for a job analysis.

There are many possible organizational sources of job information available, including current job descriptions and specifications, job-specific policies and procedures, training manuals, and performance appraisals. Externally, job information may be available from other employers, as well as trade and professional associations.

The O*NET, provided by the U.S. Department of Labor (www.onetcenter.org), contains extensive, research-based taxonomies in several categories: occupational tasks, knowledges, skills, abilities, education and experience/training, work context, organizational context, occupational interests and values, and work styles.[25] Additionally, O*NET contains ratings of the specific factors within each category for occupations; ratings for additional occupations are constantly being added. For example, occupational and importance ratings of the specific knowledges, skills, and abilities shown in Exhibits 4.8, 4.9, and 4.10 are provided. The job analyst could use these ratings as benchmarks against which to compare specific importance ratings the analyst determined for a specific job. For example, if the analyst was developing importance ratings for these knowledges, skills, and abilities for the job of registered nurse in a particular hospital, the compiled ratings could be compared to the ratings in O*NET for the same occupation. Reasonable similarity between the two sets of ratings would serve as a source of confirmation of the analyst's accuracy.

Some possible limitations to using only readily available prior job information are:

- There is the general issue of completeness. Usually, prior information will be deficient in some important areas of job requirements, as in evolving or non-traditional types of jobs. Sole reliance on prior information thus should be avoided.
- There will be little indication of exactly how the information was collected, and relatedly, how accurate it is.

Observation. Simply observing job incumbents performing the job is obviously an excellent way to learn about tasks, KSAOs, and context. It provides a thoroughness and richness of information unmatched by any other method. It is also the most direct form of gathering information because it does not rely on intermediary information sources, as would be the case with other methods (e.g., interviewing job incumbents and supervisors).

The following potential limitations to observation should be kept in mind:

- It is most appropriate for jobs with physical (as opposed to mental) components, as well as jobs with relatively short job cycles (i.e., amount of time required to complete job tasks before repeating them).
- The method may involve substantial time and cost.
- The ability of the observer to do a thorough and accurate analysis is open to question; it may be necessary to train observers prior to the job analysis.
- The method may require coordination with, and approval from, many people (e.g., supervisors and incumbents).
- The incumbents being observed may distort their behaviour during observation in self-serving ways, such as making tasks appear more difficult or time consuming than they really are.

interviews
Exercises that access job information from job incumbents and others, such as managers, employees who perform the job, and subject matter experts

Interviews. Conducting **interviews** with job incumbents and others, such as their managers, has many potential advantages. It respects the interviewee's vast source of information about the job. The interview format also allows the interviewer to explain the purpose of the job analysis, how the results will be used, and so forth, thus enhancing likely acceptance of the process by the interviewees. It can be structured in format to ensure standardization of collected information.

As with any job analysis method, the interview is not without potential limitations. It is time consuming and costly, and this may cause the organization to skimp on it in ways that jeopardize the reliability and content validity of the information gathered. The interview, not providing anonymity, may lead to suspicion and distrust on the part of interviewees. The quality of the information obtained, as well as interviewee acceptance, depends on the skill of the interviewer. Careful selection, and possible training, of interviewers should definitely be considered when the interview is the method chosen for collecting job information. Finally, the success of the interview also depends on the skill and abilities of the interviewee, such as verbal communication skills and ability to recall tasks performed.

Task Questionnaire. The task list is a critical deliverable because "it can be used as the foundation to create multiple derivative products, including curriculum design, behavioural interviewing guides, self-assessment tools, organizational assessments, job descriptions, and competency models."[26] A typical **task questionnaire** contains a lengthy list of task statements that cut across many different job titles and is administered to incumbents (all or samples of them) in these job titles. For each task statement, the respondent is asked to indicate (a) whether or not the task applies to the respondent's job (respondents should always be given a DNA—does not apply—option), and (b) task importance (e.g., a 1–5 scale rating difficulty or time spent).

task questionnaire
Tool used to develop a validated task list

The advantages of task questionnaires are numerous. They are standardized in content and format, thus yielding a standardized method of information gathering. They can obtain considerable information from large numbers of people. They are economical to administer and score, and the availability of scores creates the opportunity for subsequent statistical analysis. Finally, task questionnaires are (and should be) completed anonymously, thus enhancing respondent participation, honesty, and acceptance.

The advantages of task questionnaires are numerous. They are:

- Standardized in content and format, thus yield a standardized method of information gathering
- Useful in obtaining considerable information from large numbers of people
- Economical to administer and score, and the availability of scores creates the opportunity for subsequent statistical analysis
- Completed anonymously, thus enhancing respondent participation, honesty, and acceptance

A limitation of task questionnaires pertains to potential respondent reactions. Respondents may react negatively if they feel the questionnaire does not contain task statements covering important aspects of their jobs. Respondents may also find completion of the questionnaire to be tedious and boring; this may cause them to commit rating errors. Interpretation and understanding of the task statements may be problematic for some respondents who have reading and comprehension skill deficiencies.

Finally, it should be remembered that a typical task questionnaire focuses on tasks. Other job requirement components, particularly KSAOs and those related to job context, may be ignored or downplayed if the task questionnaire is relied on as the method of job information collection.

Committee or Task Force. Job analysis is often guided by an ad hoc committee or task force. Members of the committee or task force will typically include job experts—both managers and employees—as well as a representative from the human resources staff. These members may conduct a number of activities, including (1) reviewing existing information and gathering sample job descriptions; (2) interviewing job incumbents and managers; (3) overseeing the administration of job analysis surveys and analyzing the results; (4) writing task statements,

EXHIBIT 4.16 Criteria for Guiding Choice of Job Analysis Methods

1. Degree of suitability/versatility for use across different types of jobs
2. Degree of standardization in the process and in the reporting of results
3. Acceptability of process and results to those who will serve as sources and/or users
4. Degree to which method is operational and may be used "off the shelf" without modification, as opposed to method requiring tailor-made development and application
5. Amount of training required for sources and users of job information
6. Costs of the job analysis, in terms of both direct administrative costs and opportunity costs of time involvement by people
7. Quality of resultant information in terms of reliability and content validity
8. Usability of results in recruitment, selection, and employment activities

Source: Adapted from E. L. Levine, R. A. Ash, H. Hall, and F. Sistrunk, "Evaluation of Job Analysis Methods by Experienced Job Analysts," *Academy of Management Journal*, 1983, 26, pp. 339–348.

grouping them into task dimensions, and rating the importance of the task dimensions; and (5) identifying KSAOs and rating their importance. **Use of a committee or task force** brings considerable job analysis expertise to the process, facilitates reliability of judgment through conversation and consensus building, and enhances acceptance of the final results.

use of committee or task force
During job analysis, brings considerable expertise to the process, facilitates reliability of judgment, and enhances acceptance of the final results

Combined Methods. Only in rare instances does a job analysis involve use of only a single method. Much more likely is a hybrid, eclectic approach using multiple methods. This makes job analysis a more complicated process to design and administer than implied by a description of each of the methods alone.

Criteria for Choice of Methods. Some explicit choices regarding methods of job analysis need to be made. One set of choices involves decisions to use or not use a particular method of information collection. An organization must decide, for example, whether to use an "off-the-shelf" method or its own particular method that is suited to its own needs and circumstances. A second set of choices involves how to blend together a set of methods that will all be used, in varying ways and degrees, in the actual job analysis. Some criteria for guidance in such decisions are shown in Exhibit 4.16.

Sources to Be Used

Choosing sources of information involves considering who will be used to provide the information sought. While this matter is not entirely independent of job analysis methods (e.g., use of a task questionnaire normally requires use of job incumbents as the source), it is treated as such in the sections that follow.

job analyst
Conducts job analyses and guides the job analysis process

Job Analyst. A **job analyst** is someone who, by virtue of job title and training, is available and suited to conduct job analyses and to guide the job analysis process. The job analyst is also "out of the loop," being neither manager nor incumbent of the jobs analyzed. As such, the job analyst brings a combination of expertise and neutrality to the work.

Despite such advantages and appeals, reliance on a job analyst as the job information source is not without potential limitations. First, the analyst may be perceived as an outsider by incumbents and supervisors, a perception that may result in questioning the analyst's job knowledge and expertise, as well as trustworthiness. Second, the job analyst may, in fact, lack detailed knowledge of the jobs to be analyzed, especially in an organization with many different job titles. Lack of knowledge may cause the analyst to bring inaccurate job stereotypes to the analysis process. Finally, having specially designated job analysts (either employees or outside consultants) tends to be expensive.

job incumbents
During job analysis, sources of information related to a job's tasks, KSAOs, and job context

Job Incumbents. **Job incumbents** seem like a natural source of information to be used in job analysis, and indeed they are relied on in most job analysis systems. The major advantage to working with incumbents is their familiarity with tasks, KSAOs, and job context. In addition, job incumbents may become more accepting of the job analysis process and its results through their participation in it.

Some skepticism should be maintained about job incumbents as a source of workplace data, as is true for any source. They may lack the knowledge or insights necessary to provide inclusive information, especially if they are probationary or part-time employees. Some employees may also have difficulty in describing the tasks involved in their job or in being able to infer and articulate the underlying KSAOs necessary for the job. Another potential limitation of job incumbents as an information source pertains to their motivation to be a willing and accurate source. Feelings of distrust and suspicion may greatly hamper employees' willingness to function capably as sources. For example, incumbents may intentionally fail to report certain tasks as part of their job so that those tasks are not incorporated into the formal job description. Or, incumbents may deliberately inflate the importance ratings of tasks in order to make the job appear more difficult than it actually is.

supervisors
Not only supervise employees performing a job to be analyzed but also have played a major role in defining the job

Supervisors. **Supervisors** could and should be considered excellent sources for use in job analysis. They not only supervise employees performing the job to be analyzed but also have played a major role in defining it and later in adding/deleting job tasks (as in evolving and flexible jobs). Moreover, supervisors ultimately have to accept the resulting descriptions and specifications for jobs they supervise; inclusion of them as a source seems a way to ensure such acceptance.

subject matter experts (SMEs)
Bring particular expertise to the job analysis process, which is not available through standard sources

Subject Matter Experts. Often, the sources previously mentioned are called **subject matter experts (SMEs)**. Individuals other than those mentioned may also be used as SMEs. These people bring particular expertise to the job analysis process, an expertise thought not to be available through standard sources. Though the exact qualifications for being designated an SME are far from clear, examples of sources so designated are available. These include previous jobholders (e.g., recently promoted employees), private consultants, customer/clients, and citizens-at-large for some public sector jobs, such as superintendent of schools for a school district. Whatever the sources of SMEs, a common requirement for them is that they have recent, firsthand knowledge of the job being analyzed.[27]

Combined Sources. Combinations of sources, like combinations of methods, are most likely to be used in a typical job analysis. This is not only likely but also desirable. As noted previously, each source has some potentially unique insight to contribute to job analysis, as well as some limitations. Through a pooling of such sources and the information they provide, an accurate and acceptable job analysis is most likely to result.

Job Analysis Process Collecting job information through job analysis requires development and use of an overall process for doing so. Unfortunately, there is no set or best process to be followed; the process has to be tailor made to suit the specifics of the situation in which it occurs. There are, however, many key issues to be dealt with in the construction and operation of the process.[28] Each of these is briefly commented on next.

Purpose. The purpose(s) of job analysis should be clearly identified and agreed on. Since job analysis is a process designed to yield job information, the organization should ask exactly what job information is desired and why. Here, it is useful to refer back to the job requirements matrix to review the types of information that can be sought and obtained in a job requirements job analysis. Management must decide exactly what types of information are desired (task statements, task dimensions, and so forth) and in what format. Once the desired output and results of job analysis have been determined, the organization can then plan a process that will yield the desired results.

Scope. The issue of scope involves which job(s) to include in the job analysis. Decisions about actual scope should be based on consideration of (1) the importance of the job to the

EXHIBIT 4.17 Factors to Consider in Choosing Between Internal Staff or Consultants for Job Analysis

Internal Staff	Consultant
Cost of technical or procedural failure is low	Cost of technical or procedural failure is high
Project scope is limited	Project scope is comprehensive and/or large
Need for job data ongoing	Need for job data is a one-time, isolated event
There is a desire to develop internal staff skills in job analysis	There is a need for assured availability of each type and level of job analysis skill
Strong management controls are in place to control project costs	Predictability of project cost can depend on adhering to work plan
Knowledge of organization's norms, "culture," and jargon are critical	Technical innovativeness and quality are critical
Technical credibility of internal staff is high	Leverage of external "expert" status is needed to execute project
Process and products of the project are unlikely to be challenged	Process and products of the project are likely to be legally, technically, or politically scrutinized
Rational or narrative job analysis methods are desired	Commercial or proprietary job analysis methods are desired
Data collected are qualitative	Data collection methods are structured, standardized, and/or quantitative

Source: D. M. Van De Vort and B. V. Stalder, "Organizing for Job Analysis," in S. Gael (ed.), *The Job Analysis Handbook for Business, Industry and Government.* Copyright © 1988 by John Wiley & Sons, Inc. Reprinted by permission of John Wiley & Sons, Inc.

functioning of the organization, (2) the number of job applicants and incumbents, (3) whether the job is entry level and thus subject to constant staffing activity, (4) the frequency with which job requirements (both tasks and KSAOs) change, and (5) the amount of time lapsed since the previous job analysis.

Internal Staff or Consultant. The organization may conduct the job analysis using its own staff, or it may procure external consultants. This is a difficult decision to make because it involves not only the obvious consideration of cost but also many other considerations. Exhibit 4.17 highlights some of these concerns and the trade-offs involved.

Organization and Coordination. Any job analysis project, whether conducted by internal staff or external consultants, requires careful organization and coordination. There are two key steps to take to help ensure that this is achieved. First, an organizational member should be appointed to function as a project manager for the total process (if consultants are used, they should report to this project manager). The project manager should be assigned overall responsibility for the total project, including its organization and control. Second, the roles and relationships for the various people involved in the project—HR staff, project staff, line managers, and job incumbents—must be clearly established.

Communication. Clear and open communication with all concerned facilitates the job analysis process. Job analysis will be thought of by some employees as analogous to an invasive, exploratory surgical procedure, which, in turn, naturally raises questions in their minds about its purpose, process, and results. These questions and concerns need to be anticipated and addressed forthrightly.

Work Flow and Time Frame. Job analysis involves a mixture of people and paper in a process in which they can become entangled very quickly. The project manager should develop and adhere to a work flowchart that shows the sequential ordering of steps to be followed in the conduct of the job analysis. This should be accompanied by a time frame showing critical completion dates for project phases, as well as a final deadline.

EXHIBIT 4.18 Example of Job Requirements Job Analysis

1. Meet with manager of the job, discuss project →	2. Gather existing job information from O*NET, NOC 2001, current job description, observation of incumbents →	3. Prepare tentative set of task statements →
4. Review task statements with incumbents and managers; add, delete, rewrite statements →	5. Finalize task statements, get approval from incumbents and managers →	6. Formulate task dimensions, assign tasks to dimension, determine % time spent (importance) for each dimension →
7. Infer necessary KSAOs, develop tentative list →	8. Review KSAOs with incumbents and managers; add, delete, and rewrite KSAOs →	9. Finalize KSAOs, get approval from incumbents and manager →
10. Develop job requirements matrix and/or job description in usable format →	11. Provide matrix or job description to parties (e.g., incumbents, manager, HR department) →	12. Use matrix or job description in staffing activities, such as communicating with recruits and recruiters, developing the selection plan

Analysis, Synthesis, and Documentation. Once collected, job information must be analyzed and synthesized through use of various procedural and statistical means. These should be planned in advance and incorporated into the work-flow and time-frame requirements. Likewise, provisions need to be made for preparation of written documents, especially job descriptions and job specifications, and their incorporation into relevant policy and procedure manuals.

Maintenance of the System. Job analysis does not end with completion of the project. Rather, mechanisms must be developed and put into place to maintain the job analysis and information system over time. This is critical because the system will be exposed to numerous influences requiring response and adaptation. Examples of these influences include (1) changes in job tasks and KSAOs—additions, deletions, and modifications; (2) job redesign, restructuring, and realignment; and (3) creation of new jobs. In short, job analysis must be thought of and administered as an ongoing organizational process.

Example of Job Analysis Process. Because of the many factors involved, there is no best or required job analysis process. Rather, the process must be designed to fit each particular situation. Exhibit 4.18 shows an example of the job analysis process with a narrow scope, namely, for a single job—that of administrative assistant (secretary). This is a specially conducted job analysis that uses multiple methods (prior information, observation, interviews) and multiple sources (job analyst, job incumbents, supervisors). It was conducted by a previous holder of the job (subject matter expert), and it took the person about 20 hours over a 30-day period to conduct and prepare a written job description as the output of the process.

COMPETENCY-BASED JOB ANALYSIS

A recently emerging view of job requirements comes from the concepts of competency and competency models. These concepts are closely akin to KSAOs in some respects and are a substantial extension of KSAOs in other respects. They are an innovative and potentially fruitful approach to the identification, definition, and establishment of job requirements. Discussed below are the nature of competencies and the collection of competency information.

Nature of Competencies

competency
An underlying characteristic of an individual that contributes to the job or role performance and to organizational success

competency model
A combination of the several competencies deemed necessary for a particular job or role

A **competency** is an underlying characteristic of an individual that contributes to job or role performance and to organizational success.[29] Competencies specific to a particular job are the familiar KSAO requirements established through job requirements job analysis. Competency requirements may extend beyond job-specific ones to those of multiple jobs, general job categories, or the entire organization. These competencies are much more general or generic KSAOs, such as "technical expertise" or "adaptability." A **competency model** is a combination of the several competencies deemed necessary for a particular job or role. Usage of competencies and competency models in staffing reflects a desire to (1) connote job requirements in ways that extend beyond the specific job itself; (2) describe and measure the organization's workforce in more general, competency terms; and (3) design and implement staffing programs focused around competencies (rather than just specific jobs) as a way of increasing staffing flexibility in job assignments.

Despite the strong similarities between competencies and KSAOs, there are two notable differences. First, competencies may be job spanning, meaning that they contribute to success on multiple jobs. Members of a work team, for example, may each hold specific jobs within the team, but may be subject to job-spanning competency requirements, such as adaptability and teamwork orientation. Such requirements ensure that team members will interact successfully with each other and even perform portions or all of each others' jobs if necessary.

As another example, competency requirements may span jobs within the same category, such as sales jobs or managerial jobs. All sales jobs may have as a competency requirement "product knowledge," and all managerial jobs may require "planning and results orientation." Such requirements allow for greater flexibility in job placements and job assignments within the category.

Second, competencies can contribute not only to job performance but also to organizational success. These are very general competencies applicable to, and required for, all jobs. They serve to align requirements for all jobs with the mission and goals of the organization. A restaurant, for example, may have "customer focus" as a competency requirement for all jobs as a way of indicating that servicing the needs of its customers is a key component of all jobs.

Competency Example An illustration of the competency approach to job requirements is shown in Exhibit 4.19. The Green Care Corporation produces several lawn maintenance products: gas and electric lawn mowers, gas and electric "weed whackers," manual lawn edgers, and electric hedge trimmers. The company is in a highly competitive industry. To survive and grow, the company's core mission is product innovation and product reliability; its goals are to achieve annual 10 percent growth in revenues and 2 percent growth in market share. To help fulfill its mission and goals the company has established four general (strategic) workforce competencies—creativity/innovation, technical expertise, customer focus, and results orientation. These requirements are part of every job in the company.

At the business unit (gas lawn mowers) level, the company has also established job-specific and job-spanning requirements. Some jobs, such as design engineer, are traditional or slowly evolving jobs and as such have only job-specific KSAO or competency requirements. Because the products are assembled via team assembly processes, jobs within the assembly team (such as engine assembler, final assembler) have both job-specific and job-spanning competency requirements. The job-spanning competencies—team orientation, adaptability, communication—are general and behavioural. They are necessary because of task interdependence between engine and final assembly jobs and because employees may be shifted between the two jobs in order to cover sudden employee shortages due to unscheduled absences and to maintain smooth production flows. Each job in the business unit thus has four general competency requirements, multiple

EXHIBIT 4.19 Examples of Competencies

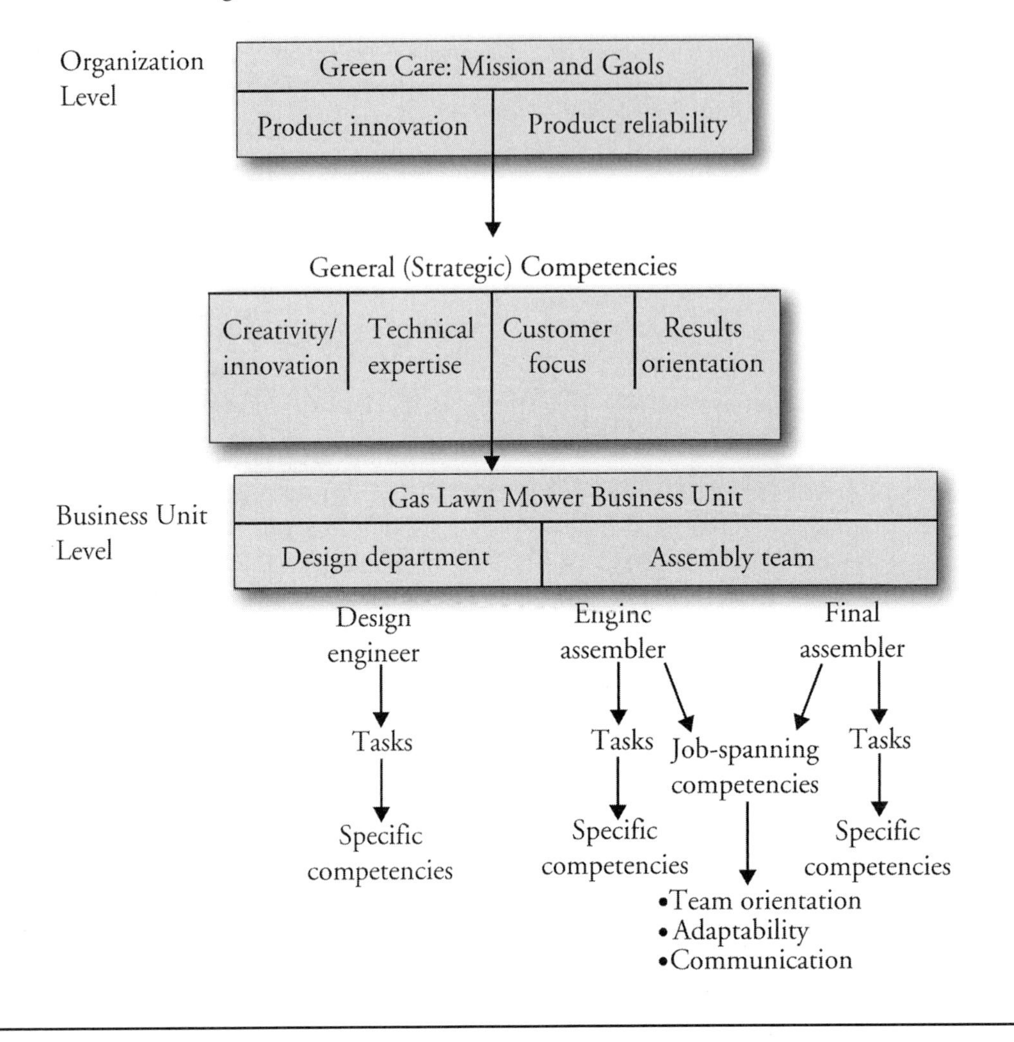

job-specific competency requirements, and, where appropriate, job-spanning competency requirements.

Organization Usage Organizations are beginning to experiment with the development of competencies and competency models and to use them as the underpinnings of several HR applications.[30] Research indicates that the experimentation is occurring in organizations of all sizes, but especially in large ones. The three key strategic HR reasons for doing competency modelling are to (1) create awareness and understanding of the need for change in business, (2) enhance the skill levels in the workforce, and (3) improve teamwork and coordination. Most of the emphasis has been on establishing general competencies such as:[31]

- Customer focus
- Communication
- Team orientation
- Technical expertise
- Results orientation
- Adaptability
- Innovation

Competency models are being used for many HR applications, especially staffing, career development, performance management, and compensation. Pertaining to staffing, one important application is in HR and staffing planning. Here, workforce requirements are specified in competency terms and compared to current workforce competency levels to identify competency gaps. Such comparisons may be particularly appropriate in replacement and succession planning.

Another important staffing application is in external and internal selection, where applicants are assessed not only for job-specific competencies but also for general competencies. For external hiring, competency-based interviews with applicants are conducted to gauge general competencies as a key factor in selection decisions and then in job placement decisions for those hired. For promotion decisions, competency-based interviews are used in conjunction with supervisory assessments of promotability.[32]

Despite their many potential applications to various staffing activities, adoption of competency models should be undertaken cautiously, since research has identified many potential barriers to success in their usage. Prominent among these barriers are (1) a lack of buy-in from top management, who may be unwilling to apply the competency model to themselves or may not see its usefulness; (2) the readiness of employees generally to accept the competency model and learn the new competency behaviours required by the model; (3) conflicts as to whether there should be separate models for separate units of the organization and the relative emphases to be placed on general job-spanning and job-specific competencies; and (4) the time and resources needed to implement the competency model, train employees in its usage, and maintain and update the model.[33]

Collecting Competency Information

Techniques and processes for collecting competency information are still in their infancy.[34] An exception, of course, is job requirements job analysis for job specific competencies. For more general competencies, much less is known about the best ways to identify and define competencies. General competencies at the organization (strategic) level are likely to be established by top management, with guidance from strategic HR managers.

At a minimum, effective establishment of general competency requirements would seem to demand the following:

- Established mission and goals prior to determination of competency requirements
- General competencies be truly important to all job levels
- General competencies should have specific behavioural definitions—not just labels—to provide meaning to all concerned

This will ensure that general competencies are derived from knowledge of mission and goals, much as job-specific competencies are derived from previous job tasks. Also, the usage of competencies as job requirements will focus and align all jobs with the organization's mission and goals. This principle also holds in the case where, instead of general competency requirements at the organization level, there are general competency requirements at the strategic business unit or sub-unit level.

EXHIBIT 4.20 Examples of HR Competencies

Professors Wayne Brockbank and Dave Yakonich developed a Human Resource Competency Toolkit, which is used by the Society of Human Resource Management (SHRM), of which the Canadian Council of Human Resources Association (CCHRA) is a member.

The Toolkit is based on the Human Resource Competency Study research project carried out over 15 years, and was sponsored by the Executive Education Center at the University of Michigan Business School. The purpose of the study was to assess the competencies that are necessary for HR professionals to maximize their contributions to organizational effectiveness.

The five HR competency domains are:

Domain	Factors
Strategic contribution	Strategic decision making, culture management, fast change, and market-driven connectivity
Personal credibility	Effective relationships, gets results, and personal communication
HR delivery	Development, structure and HR measurement, staffing, and performance management
Business knowledge	Understand their industry and organization they work for
HR technology	Use HR technology and Web-based channels to deliver services to employees

Professor Brockbank concludes, "In many companies, HR professionals have been more interested in developing other departments than they have been in developing themselves. This may have been partly because they were not entirely sure where to focus their developmental efforts. This Toolkit and the research on which it is based give a clear and compelling developmental agenda to enhance the competencies and contributions of HR professionals."

Source: SHRM Online, "A New Study Identifies Key Competencies Necessary for HR," June 22, 2003.

For job-spanning competencies, these definitions will necessarily be more task specific. To ensure effective identification and definition, several tasks should be undertaken. First, it is crucial to know the major tasks for which the competencies are to be established, meaning that some form of job analysis should occur first. For now, that process will have to be crafted by the organization, since we lack prototypes or best practice examples as guidance. Second, SMEs familiar with all the jobs or roles to which the competencies will apply should be part of the process. Third, careful definition of the competencies will be necessary. Acquiring definitions from other organizations, consultants, or O*NET will be useful steps here.

A final cautionary note is that the collection and usage of competencies beyond job-specific ones will occur in uncharted legal waters. Recalling the legal standard of job-relatedness for staffing practices that cause adverse impact, will staffing practices and decisions based on general competencies be construed as job related? Will it be a defensible argument to say that, although a particular competency requirement may not have a strong contribution to job success, it is necessary for organizational success? Such questions will inevitably arise; to be able to address them, the organization should conduct a thorough process for establishing competency requirements using the suggestions above as a starting point.

Exhibit 4.20 outlines the competencies required by HR professionals to maximize their contributions to organizational effectiveness.

JOB REWARDS

In the person/job match model, jobs are comprised of requirements and rewards. The focus so far in this chapter has been on job requirements vis-a-vis the discussion of job analysis. Attention now turns to job rewards. Providing and using rewards is a key staffing strategy for motivating several HR outcomes—applicant attraction, employee performance, and employee retention in particular. Successfully matching rewards provided with rewards desired will be critical in attaining the HR outcomes. Doing so first of all requires specification of the types of rewards potentially available and desired.

Types of Rewards

extrinsic rewards
tangible factors external to the job itself that are explicitly designed and granted to employees

intrinsic rewards
the "intangibles" that are more internal to the job itself and experienced by the employee as an outgrowth of actually doing the job

Organizations and jobs provide a wide variety of rewards. It is common to classify each reward as either extrinsic or intrinsic in nature. **Extrinsic rewards** are tangible factors external to the job itself that are explicitly designed and granted to employees by representatives of the organization. **Intrinsic rewards** are the "intangibles" that are more internal to the job itself and experienced by the employee as an outgrowth of actually doing the job and being a member of the organization.[35]

Exhibit 4.21 contains a listing of major types of extrinsic rewards. They fall into the major categories of direct pay (base and variable), indirect pay (benefits), hours of work, career advancement, and job security. Within each of these categories numerous examples are provided. The examples are by no means exhaustive of the total array of extrinsic rewards organizations have at their disposal. The sheer number of external rewards that might be provided means that the organization must be very careful in the choice of rewards that will actually be granted to employees.

Exhibit 4.22 displays a listing of the major intrinsic rewards associated with the job. The experiential nature of the rewards is evident, meaning that the organization cannot simply give them to the employee. Rather, the nature of the employee's job, and the relationship and communication with co-workers and management, create satisfying or dissatisfying experiences for the employee.

Employee Value Proposition

employee value proposition (EVP)
The package or bundle of rewards provided to employees and to which employees respond by joining, performing, and remaining with the organization

The totality of rewards, both extrinsic and intrinsic, associated with the job constitute the **employee value proposition (EVP)**.[36] The EVP is akin to the "package" or "bundle" of rewards provided to employees and to which employees respond by joining, performing, and remaining with the organization. It is the "deal" or " bargain" struck between the organization and employee, first as a promise to the prospective employee, later as a reality to the actual new employee, and later still as a new deal as the EVP changes due to reward improvements and/or internal job changes by the employee. The EVP thus functions like a glue that binds the employee and organization together, with the employee providing certain behaviours (attraction, performance, retention, and so forth) in exchange for the EVP.

The challenge to the organization is to create EVPs for various employee groups that on average are both attractive and affordable (how to create an individual EVP in the form of a formal job offer to a prospective employee is considered in Chapter 10). No reward, extrinsic or intrinsic, is costless, so the organization must figure out what it can afford as it creates its EVPs. Regardless of cost, however, the rewards must also be attractive to those for whom they are intended, so attraction and cost must be considered jointly when developing EVPs. The dual affordable-attractive requirements for EVPs creates some potential problems with EVPs: wrong magnitude, wrong mix, or not distinctive.[37]

wrong magnitude
A package of rewards that is either too small or too great monetarily

Wrong magnitude refers to a package of rewards that is either too small or too great monetarily. To the prospective or current employee, too small a package may be viewed as simply inadequate, non-competitive, or an insult, none of which are desirable perceptions to be creating. Such perceptions may arise very early in the applicant's job search, before the organization is even aware of the applicant, due to word-of-mouth information from others (e.g., former applicants or employees) or information obtained about the organization, such as through its print or electronic recruitment information. Alternatively, too small a package may not become

EXHIBIT 4.21 Extrinsic Rewards

Reward	Explanation
Direct Compensation—Base Pay	
Starting	Beginning wage or salary
Range	Minimum and maximum pay for job
Raises	Increases in base pay
Direct Compensation—Variable Pay	
Short-term incentives (one year or less)	Usually one-time cash bonus for performance to individual, team, or operating unit
Long-term incentives (more than one year)	Usually stock options, restricted stock plan, or performance plan tied to long-term performance growth or targets
Indirect Compensation—Benefits	
Health insurance	Employer-sponsored health care insurance
Retirement	Defined benefit, defined contribution, or cash balance plan for retirement pay
Work life	Examples include child care, parenting programs, lactation rooms, concierge services, financial services, employee assistance programs, home computer
Perks	Examples include cellphones, recreation facilities, subsidized cafeteria, free snacks, hair and manicure salon, car wash, student loan payoffs
Other	Examples include vacation, paid holidays, sick pay, life and disability insurance
Hours of Work	
Full or part time	Typical number of hours per week; more than 40 usually considered full time
Shift	Day, swing, or night work hours; premium pay above base pay for swing or night shift
Flextime	Nonstandard starting and ending daily times
Overtime	Hours beyond normal; voluntary or mandatory; premium pay above base pay
Career Advancement	
Training and development	Opportunities for KSAOs and competency improvement, mentoring
Job changes	Opportunities for promotion and transfer
Location changes	Opportunities or requirements for relocation
Job Security	
Job security enhancements	Fixed-term contracts Performance management Progressive discipline
Termination process	Procedures for terminating an employee
Severance package	Pay, benefits, and assistance provided to a terminated employee

an issue until fairly late in the job search process, as additional bits of reward package information become known to the applicant. Regardless of when the too-small perceptions emerge, they can be deal killers that lead to self-selection out of consideration for the job, job offer turndowns, or decisions to quit. While too-small packages may be unattractive, they often have the virtue of being affordable for the organization.

EXHIBIT 4.22 Intrinsic Rewards

Reward	Explanation
Skill variety	Use of complex skills to perform different tasks
Task identity	Complete a whole piece of work, rather than just a part of it
Task significance	Results of your work affect lives of others
Autonomy	Freedom to decide how to do your job
Feedback from job	Job itself gives you information about how well you are performing your job
Feedback from agents	Manager or co-workers give you information about how well you are performing your job
Dealing with others	Job requires you to work closely with others, such as co-workers or clients
Management relations	Communication from management; trust in management

Note: Based in part on the Job Diagnostic Survey.

Too large a package creates affordability problems for the organization. Those problems may not surface immediately, but long term they can threaten the organization's financial viability and possibly even survival. Affordability problems may be particularly acute in service-providing organizations, where employee compensation costs are a substantial percentage of total operating costs.

wrong mix
A situation in which the composition of the reward package is out of sync with the preferences of prospective or current employees

not distinctive
Individual reward packages that have no uniqueness or special appeal that would either win or retain employees

Wrong mix refers to a situation in which the composition of the reward package is out of sync with the preferences of prospective or current employees. A package that provides excellent retirement benefits and long-term performance incentives to a relatively young and mobile workforce, for example, is most likely a wrong mix one. Its attraction and retention power in all likelihood is minimal. It might also be relatively expensive to provide.

Not distinctive refers to individual rewards packages that are viewed as ho-hum in nature. They have no uniqueness or special appeal that would either win or retain employees. They do not signal anything distinctive about the organization or give the job seeker or employee any special reason to think the "deal" is one that simply cannot be passed up or given up.

In short, creating successful EVPs is a challenge, and the results can have important implications for workforce attraction, retention, and cost. To help create successful EVPs, the organization should seek to systematically collect job rewards information in order to learn about rewards that are important or unimportant to employees.

Collecting Job Rewards Information

Unlike job analysis as a mechanism for collecting job requirements information, mechanisms for collecting job rewards information are more fragmentary. Nonetheless, there are several things that can be done, all of which seek to provide data about the importance of rewards to employees—which rewards they most and least prefer. Armed with knowledge about employee preferences, the organization can begin to build EVPs that are of the right magnitude, mix, and distinctiveness. One approach for collecting job rewards information is to gauge the preferences of the organization's own employees. A different approach is to learn about employee preferences, and actual rewards provided, in other organizations.

Within the Organization To learn about employee reward preferences within the organization, interviews with employees, or more formal surveys of them, might be used.

Interviews with Employees. The interview approach requires decisions about who will guide the process, interview content, who will conduct the interviews, sampling confidentiality, data recording and analysis, and reporting of the results. The following are a few suggestions to guide each of those decisions. First, a person with special expertise in the employee interview process should guide the total process. This could be a person within the HR department, a person outside of HR with the expertise—such as in marketing research—or an outside consultant.

Second, the interviews should be structured, guided ones. The major content areas, and specific questions, should be decided in advance, tested on a small sample of employees as to their clarity and wording, and then placed in a formal interview protocol to be used by the interviewer. An example of potential questions is shown in Exhibit 4.23. Note that the major content areas covered in the interview are rewards offered, reward magnitude, reward mix, and reward distinctiveness.

Third, the interviews should be conducted by people who have sound employee interviewing skills and will be trusted by the employees interviewed. The person guiding the overall process might be one of the interviewers and should have a major say in the selection of other needed interviews. The interviewers should receive special training in the conduct of the interviews, including a "dry run" to ensure that the interview protocol is sound and that they are comfortable with it.

Fourth, employees from throughout the organization should be part of the sample. In small organizations, it might be possible to include all employees; in larger organizations, random samples of employees will be necessary. When sampling, it is important to include the sample employees from all job categories, organizational units, and organizational levels.

Fifth, it is strongly recommended that the interviews be treated as confidential, and that the responses of individuals only be seen by those recording and analyzing the data. At the same time, it would be useful to gather (with their permission) interviewees' demographic (e.g., age, gender) and organizational information (e.g., job title, organizational unit), since this will permit breakouts of responses during data analysis. Such breakouts will be very useful in decisions about whether to create separate EVPs for separate employee groups or organizational units.

EXHIBIT 4.23 Examples of Reward Preferences Interview Questions

Rewards to Offer

- Are there any rewards you wish the organization would provide now?
- Looking ahead, are there any rewards you hope the organization will provide?

Reward Magnitude

- Overall, do you think that the level of pay and benefits is too much, too little, or about right compared to other jobs like yours?
- Overall, do you think the reward intangibles are too much, too little, or about right compared to other jobs like yours?
- Would you be willing to start paying for the cost of certain rewards to ensure the organization continues to provide them?

Reward Mix

- Would you prefer the mix of pay and benefits shift more toward pay, benefits, or stay the same?
- What are the two most important rewards to you?
- What rewards are irrelevant to you?

Rewards Distinctiveness

- Which rewards that you receive are you most likely to tell others about?
- Which of our rewards really stand out to you? To job applicants?
- What rewards could we start offering that would be really unique?

Sixth, interviewees' responses should be recorded, rather than trusted to the memory of the interviewer. The preferred way to record responses is for the interviewer to take notes. Verbatim electronic recording of responses will likely threaten the interviewee's sense of confidentiality, plus require subsequent costly transcription. The response data will need to be analyzed with an eye toward capturing major "themes" in the data, such as the most and least important rewards, and the rewards that the employee could most do without. These findings can then be incorporated into a report that will be presented to organizational representatives.

Surveys of Employees. A survey of employees should proceed along the same lines, following many of the same recommendations, as for an employee interview process. The biggest difference will be the mechanism for gathering the data—namely a written set of questions with response scales, rather than a verbally administered set of questions with open-ended responses. To construct the survey, a listing of the rewards to be included on the survey must be developed. These could be chosen from a listing of the organization's current extrinsic rewards, plus some questions about intrinsic rewards. For response scales, it is common to use a 1 (very unimportant) to 5 (very important) rating format. An example of a partial employee reward preferences survey is shown in Exhibit 4.24.

As with interviews, it is recommended that a person with special expertise guide the project, the survey content be specially constructed (rather than canned), sampling include employees throughout the organization, employees be assured of confidentiality, thorough analysis of results be undertaken, and reports of findings be prepared for organizational representatives.

Which to Use? Should the organization opt for use of interviews, surveys, or both? The advantages of an interview are that it is of a personal nature; employees are allowed to respond in their own words; it is possible to create questions that probe preferences about reward magnitude, mix, and distinctiveness; and a very rich set of data are obtained that provide insights beyond mere rating scale responses. On the downside, interviews are costly to schedule and conduct, data analysis is messy and time consuming, and statistical summaries and analysis of the data are difficult. Surveys are easier to administer (especially online), and they permit statistical summaries and analyses that are very helpful in interpreting responses. The biggest downsides to surveys

EXHIBIT 4.24 Examples of Reward Preferences Survey Questions

Extrinsic Rewards	Very Unimportant		Neither Important nor Unimportant		Very Important
Base pay	1	2	3	4	5
Incentive pay	1	2	3	4	5
Overtime pay	1	2	3	4	5
Health insurance	1	2	3	4	5
Promotion opportunities	1	2	3	4	5
Job security	1	2	3	4	5
Intrinsic Rewards					
Using my skills	1	2	3	4	5
Doing significant tasks	1	2	3	4	5
Deciding how to do my job	1	2	3	4	5
Getting feedback from job	1	2	3	4	5
Trust in management	1	2	3	4	5
Communications from management	1	2	3	4	5

are the lack of richness of data, and that it is very difficult to construct questions that tap into employees' preferences about reward magnitude, mix, and distinctiveness.

Assuming adequate resources and expertise, a combined interview and survey approach would be best. This would allow the organization to capitalize on the unique strengths of each approach, as well as offset some of the weaknesses of each.

A final cautionary note is that both interviews and surveys of current employees miss out on two other groups from whom reward preference information would be useful. The first group is departing or departed employees, who may have left due to dissatisfaction with the EVP. In Chapter 11 we discuss the exit interview as a procedure for learning about this group. The second group is job applicants. Presumably the organization could conduct interviews and surveys with this group, but that could be administratively challenging (especially with Internet applicants) and also applicants might feel they are "tipping their hand" to the organization in terms of what they desire or would accept in a job offer. The more common way to learn about applicant reward preferences is from surveys of employees outside the organization, who might be representative of the types of applicants the organization will encounter.

Outside the Organization Data on the reward preferences of employees outside the organization are available from surveys of employees in other organizations. To the extent these employees are similar to the organization's own applicants and employees, the data will likely provide a useful barometer of preferences. An example is the Job Satisfaction survey conducted by the Society for Human Resource Management. It administered an online survey to a national random sample of $n = 604$ employees. The employees rated the importance of 21 extrinsic and intrinsic "rewards" to their own satisfaction on a 1–5 (very unimportant to very important) scale. The percentage of employees rating each reward as "very important" is shown in Exhibit 4.25. The data for 2004 are shown along with data from a similar survey in 2002.

It can be seen that extrinsic rewards, especially "benefits" and "compensation/pay," topped the reward preferences, followed by "feeling safe in the work environment," "job security" and "flexibility to balance work/life issues." For the most part, reward importance was very similar in the two time periods. An exception to this was a large increase in the importance of feeling safe in the work environment.

Not shown in Exhibit 4.25 were two other important findings. First, a sample of HR professionals was asked to predict the importance that employees attached to the rewards, and the HR professionals' predictions did not correspond all that closely to the actual employee ratings. For example, the two top rewards predicted by the HR professionals were "relationship with immediate supervisor" and "management recognition of employee job performance." The reward "feeling safe in the work environment" was the 13th most important reward as predicted by the HR professionals. A second finding was that there were some differences in reward importance as a function of employee age, tenure, gender, and industry; these differences, however, were relatively small.

Organizational Practices. A less direct way to assess the importance of rewards to employees is to examine the actual rewards that other organizations provide their employees. The assumption here is that these other organizations are attuned to their employees' preferences and try to provide rewards that are consistent with them. Since pay and benefits loom large in most employees' reward preferences, it is particularly important to become knowledgeable of other organizations' pay and benefit practices to assist in the developing of the EVP.

The best source of wage and salary information comes from the Statistics Canada study, "Earnings of Canadians, 2001 Census" (www.statcan.ca/bsolc/english/bsolc?catno=97F0019X). This information presents data on wages and salaries, net income from non-farm unincorporated businesses and/or professional practices, and net farm self-employment income of Canadians in 2000. The data also includes earnings by sex, age, and geographic area, as well as certain population groups (e.g., immigrants).

EXHIBIT 4.25 "Very Important" Aspects of Employee Job Satisfaction (Employees)

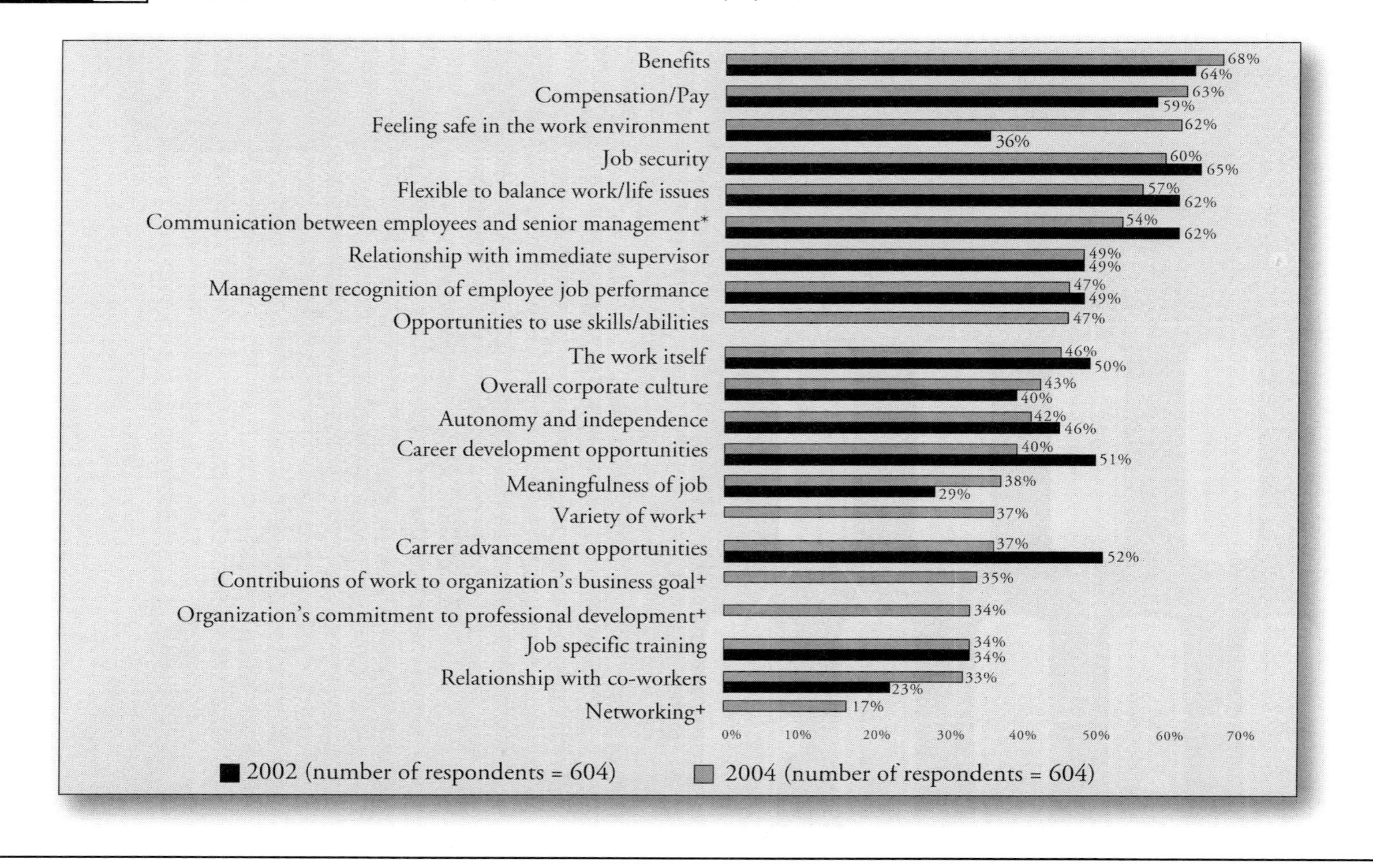

Note: Aspects are in order of importance by 2004 data.
*This question was modified in 2004 by specifying communication with "senior management" instead of "management."
+ This aspect was added in 2004. Therefore, no comparable data exists for 2002.

Source: E. Essen, Job Satisfaction Series (Alexandria, VA: Society for Human Resource Management, 2004), p. 156. Used with permission.

Human Resources and Social Development Canada also provides salary and wage information by province (access by visiting www.hrsdc.gc.ca and do a search for "salary"). In this report the salary information is divided into the following occupations: management; business, finance, and administration; natural and applied sciences; health; social, science, education, government service, and religion; art, culture, recreation, and sport; sales and service; trades, transport, and equipment operators; occupations unique to primary industry; and occupations unique to processing, manufacturing, and utilities.

LEGAL ISSUES

This chapter has emphasized the crucial role that job analysis plays in establishing the foundation for staffing activities. That crucial role continues from a legal perspective. Job analysis becomes intimately involved in court cases involving the job relatedness of staffing activities. The Canadian Human Rights Commission emphasizes the need to demonstrate the link between selection measures and the essential duties of a job, and courts in both the United States and Canada have consistently ruled that human resource systems must be supported by job analysis. It also occupies a prominent position in employment equity where federally regulated organizations are expected to determine essential functions for each job to ensure equal representation of all protected groups under the Canadian Human Rights Act, and job analysis can play a pivotal role in that process.[38]

Job Relatedness and Court Cases

In human rights court cases, the organization is confronted with the need to justify its challenged staffing practices as being job related. Common sense suggests that this requires first and foremost that the organization conduct some type of job analysis to identify job requirements. Recall that under the Canadian Human Rights Act an organization must not discriminate against a qualified person from one of the "protected" groups, who can perform the "essential function" of the job, without reasonable accommodation. This requirement raises three questions: What is an essential function? What is evidence of essential function? What is the role of job analysis? In addition, specific features or characteristics of the job analysis make a difference in the organization's defence. Specifically, an examination of court cases indicates that for purposes of legal defensibility the organization should conform to the following recommendations:

1. "Job analysis must be performed and must be for the job for which the selection instrument is to be utilized.
2. Analysis of the job should be in writing.
3. Job analysts should describe in detail the procedure used.
4. Job data should be collected from a variety of current sources by knowledgeable job analysts.
5. Sample size should be large and representative of the jobs for which the selection instrument is used.
6. Tasks, duties, and activities should be included in the analysis.
7. The most important tasks should be represented in the selection device.
8. Competency levels of job performance for entry-level jobs should be specified.
9. Knowledge, skills, and abilities should be specified, particularly if a content validation model is followed."[39]

These recommendations are very consistent with our more general discussion of job analysis as an important tool and basic foundation for staffing activities. Moreover, even though these recommendations were made several years ago, there is little reason to doubt or modify any of them on the basis of more recent court cases.

Essential Job Functions

What Are Essential Functions? In an employer's duty to accommodate, "job descriptions should be detailed, accurate and up to date, with essential and non-essential duties differentiated. Job redesign may be necessary; most job descriptions can be modified by looking at the expected outcomes of the job, and considering the needs of the applicant. Ensure that the postings are written in language that is easy to understand, are highly visible and easy to read, physically accessible and available in alternate formats."[40]

Essential job functions are fundamental job duties, and a job function may be considered essential for many reasons, including but not limited to the following:

- The function may be essential because the reason the position exists is to perform the function.
- The function may be essential because of the limited number of employees available to whom the performance of the job function can be distributed.
- The function may be highly specialized so that the incumbent in the position is hired for his or her expertise or ability to perform this particular function.

Evidence of Essential Functions The following are examples of what constitutes as evidence that any particular function is in fact an essential one. That evidence includes, but is not limited to:

- The employer's judgment as to which functions are essential
- Written job descriptions, prepared before advertising or interviewing applicants for the job
- The amount of time spent on the job performing the function
- The consequences of not requiring the incumbent to perform the function
- The terms of a collective bargaining agreement
- The work experience of past incumbents in the job
- The current work experience of incumbents in similar jobs

Roles of Job Analysis While job analysis is not required by law as a means of establishing essential functions of a job, it is strongly recommended. The job analysis should focus on tasks associated with the job. Where KSAOs are also studied or specific, they should be derived from an explicit consideration of their probable links to the essential tasks. With regard to tasks, the focus should be on the tasks themselves and the outcome or results of the tasks, rather than the methods by which they are performed. The job analysis should be useful in identifying potential reasonable accommodation.

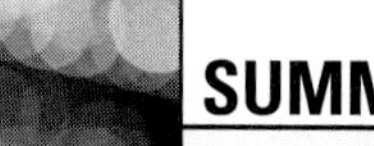

SUMMARY

Organizations design and use various types of jobs—traditional, evolving, flexible, idiosyncratic, team based, and telework. These design approaches all result in job content in the form of job requirements and rewards. Job analysis is described as the process used to gather, analyze, synthesize, and report information about job content. The job requirements approach to job analysis focuses on job-specific tasks, KSAOs, and job context. Competency-based job analysis seeks to identify more general KSAOs that apply across jobs and roles.

The job requirements approach is guided by the job requirements matrix. The matrix calls for information about tasks and task dimensions, as well as their importance. In a parallel fashion, it requires information about KSAOs required for the tasks, plus indications about the importance of those KSAOs. The final component of the matrix deals with numerous elements of the job context.

When gathering the information called for by the job requirements matrix, the organization is confronted with a multitude of choices. Those choices are shown to revolve around various job analysis methods, sources, and processes. The organization must pick and choose from among these; all have advantages and disadvantages associated with them. The choices should be guided by a concern for the accuracy and acceptability of the information that is being gathered.

A very new approach to identifying job requirements is competency-based job analysis. This form of job analysis seeks to identify general competencies (KSAOs) necessary for all jobs because the competencies support the organization's mission and goals. Within work units, other general competencies (job-spanning KSAOs) may also be established that cut across multiple jobs. Potential techniques and processes for collecting competency information are suggested.

Jobs offer a variety of rewards, both extrinsic and intrinsic. The totality or package of these rewards constitutes the employee value proposition. Difficulties in putting together the right EVP include providing the right magnitude and mix of rewards, along with having some of them be distinctive. To help form EVPs, it is necessary to collect job rewards information about employee reward preferences and rewards given to employees at other organizations. Numerous techniques for doing this are available.

From a legal perspective, job analysis is shown to assume major importance in creating staffing systems and practices that are in compliance with human rights laws and regulations. The employer must ensure (or be able to show) that its practices are job related. This requires not only having conducted a job requirements job analysis but also using a process that itself has defensible characteristics. Although job analysis is not required by law, the organization should strongly consider it as one of the tools to be used.

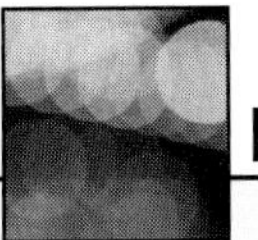

KEY TERMS

ability 112
competency 125
competency model 125
employee value proposition (EVP) 129
evolving job 103
extrinsic rewards 129
flexible jobs 103
global virtual team 104
idiosyncratic jobs 103
interviews 119
intrinsic rewards 129
job analysis 105
job analyst 121
job description 116
job incumbents 122
job requirements job analysis 105
jobs 102
knowledge 111
not distinctive 131
prior information 119
skill 111
subject matter experts (SMEs) 122
supervisors 122
task dimensions 109
task questionnaire 120
task statements 108
telework 104
traditional job design 102
use of committee or task force 121
work team 103
wrong magnitude 124
wrong mix 131

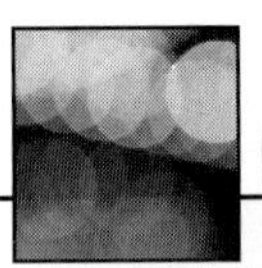

RELEVANT WEB SITES

NOC 2001
www23.hrdc-drhc.gc.ca/2001/e/generic/welcome.shtml

Employability Skills (The Conference Board of Canada)
www.conferenceboard.ca/education/learning-tools/pdfs/esp2000.pdf

How to Write a Job Description

www.pao.gov.ab.ca/class/forms/write-job-description/how-to-write-job-descr.htm
www.payequity.gov.on.ca/peo/english/pubs/guidejobinfo.html
www.payequity.gov.on.ca/peo/english/pubs/glossaryverbs.html
www.jobdescription.com

Society for Human Resource Management

www.shrm.org

O*NET

www.onetcenter.org

Essential Skills – Human Resources Skills Development Canada

www.hrsdc.gc.ca/en/hip/hrp/essential_skills/essential_skills_index.shtml

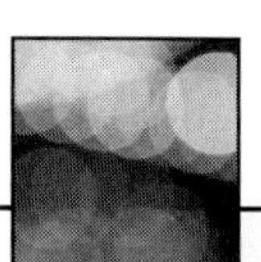

DISCUSSION QUESTIONS

1. Identify a team-based job situation. What are examples of job-spanning KSAOs required in that situation?
2. How should task statements be written, and what sorts of problems might you encounter in asking a job incumbent to write these statements?
3. Would it be better to first identify task dimensions and then create specific task statements for each dimension, or should task statements be identified first and then used to create task dimensions?
4. What would you consider when trying to decide what criteria (e.g., percent time spent) to use for gathering indications about task importance?
5. What are the advantages and disadvantages to using multiple methods of job analysis for a particular job? Multiple sources?
6. What are the advantages and disadvantages of identifying and using general competencies to guide staffing activities?
7. Why do you think HR professionals are not able to very accurately predict the importance of many rewards to employees? What are the implications for creating the employee value proposition?

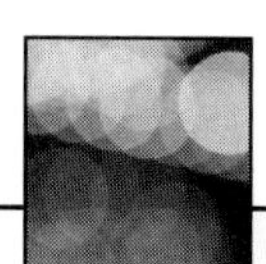

ETHICAL ISSUES

1. It has been suggested that "ethical conduct" be formally incorporated as a general competency requirement for any job within the organization. Discuss the pros and cons of this suggestion.
2. Assume you are assisting in conducting job analysis as an HR department representative. You have encountered several managers who want to delete certain tasks and KSAOs from the formal job description having to do with employee safety, even though they clearly are job requirements. How should you handle this situation?

APPLICATIONS

Conducting a Job Requirements or Job Rewards Job Analysis

Job analysis is defined as "the process of studying jobs in order to gather, synthesize, and report information about job content." Based on the person/job match model, job content consists of job requirements (tasks and KSAOs) and job rewards (extrinsic and intrinsic). The goal of a job requirements job analysis is to produce the job requirements matrix.

Your assignment is to conduct either a job requirements or job rewards job analysis. In this assignment you will choose a job you want to study, conduct either a job requirements or job rewards job analysis of that job, and prepare a written report of your project.

Your report should include the following sections:

1. **The job:** What job (job title) did you choose to study and why?
2. **The methods used:** What methods did you use (e.g., prior information, observation, interviews, task questionnaires, committee, and combinations of these), and exactly how did you use them?
3. **The sources used:** What sources did you use (e.g., job analyst, job incumbent, supervisor, subject matter experts, and combinations of these), and exactly how did you use them?
4. **The process used:** How did you go about gathering, synthesizing, and reporting the information? Refer back to Exhibit 4.18 for an example.
5. **The matrix:** Present the actual job requirements matrix.

Maintaining Job Descriptions

InAndOut, Inc. provides warehousing and fulfillment (order receiving and filling) services to small publishers of books with small print runs (number of copies of a book printed). After the books are printed and bound at a printing facility, they are shipped to InAndOut for handling. Books are received initially by handlers who unload the books off trucks, place them on pallets, and move them via forklifts and conveyors to their assigned storage space in the warehouse. The handlers also retrieve books and bring them to the shipping area when orders are received. The books are then packaged, placed in cartons, and loaded on delivery trucks (to take to air or ground transportation providers) by shippers. Book orders are taken by customer service representatives via written, phone, or electronic (e-mail, fax) forms. New accounts are generated by marketing representatives, who also service existing accounts. Order clerks handle all the internal paperwork. All of these employees report to either the supervisor of operations or the supervisor of customer service, who in turn report to the general manager.

The owner and president of InAndOut, Inc., Alta Fossom, is independently wealthy and delegates all day-to-day management matters to the general manager, Marvin Olson. Alta requires, however, that Marvin clear any new ideas or initiatives with her prior to taking action. The company is growing and changing rapidly. Many new accounts, often larger than the past norm, are opening. Publishers are demanding more services and faster order fulfillment. Information technology is constantly being upgraded, and new machinery (forklifts, computer-assisted conveyor system) is being utilized. And the workforce is growing in size to meet the business growth. There are now 37 employees, and Marvin expects to hire another 15 to 20 new employees within the next year.

Job descriptions for the company were originally written by a consultant about eight years ago. They have never been revised and are hopelessly outdated. The job of marketing representative has no job description at all because the job was created only five years ago. As general manager, Marvin is responsible for all HR management matters, but he has little time to devote to them. To help him get a better grip on his HR responsibilities, Marvin has hired you as a part-time HR intern. He has a "gut feeling" that the job descriptions need to be updated or written for the first time and has assigned you that project. Since Marvin has to clear new projects with Alta, he wants you to prepare a brief proposal that he can use to approach her for seeking approval. In that proposal he wants to be able to suggest to Alta the following:

1. Reasons why it is important to update and write new job descriptions
2. An outline of a process that could be followed for doing this that will yield a set of thorough and current job descriptions
3. A process to be used in the future for periodically reviewing and updating these new job descriptions

Marvin wants to meet with you and discuss each of these points. He wants very specific suggestions and ideas from you that he can use to prepare his proposal. What exactly would you suggest to Marvin?

ENDNOTES

1. Human Resources and Social Development Canada, "Essential Skills," 2005, www.hrsdc.gc.ca/en/hip/hrp/essential_skills/essential_skills_index.shtml.
2. Test of Workplace Essential Skills (TOWES), Bow Valley College, "Communication Folio: TOWES Validation Studies," March 2004, p. 6.
3. D. R. Ilgen and J. R. Hollenbeck, "The Structure of Work: Job Design and Roles," in M. D. Dunnette and L. M. Hough (eds.), *Handbook of Industrial and Organizational Psychology*, Vol. 2 (Palo Alto, CA: Consulting Psychologists Press, 1991), pp. 165–207.
4. E. R. Silverman, "You've Come a Long Way…," *Human Resource Executive*, Feb. 2000, pp. 64–68; A. Wrzesniewski and J. E. Dutton, "Crafting a Job: Revisioning Employees as Active Crafters of their Work," *Academy of Management Review*, 2001, 26, pp. 179–201.
5. A. S. Miner, "Idiosyncratic Jobs in Formalized Organizations," *Administrative Science Quarterly*, 1987, 32, pp. 327–351.
6. W. Bridges, "The End of the Job," *Fortune*, Sept. 19, 1994, pp. 62–74; B. Dumaine, "The Trouble with Teams," *Fortune*, Sept. 5, 1994, pp. 86–92; R. J. Klimoski and R. G. Jones, "staffing for Effective Group Decision Making: Key Issues in Matching People and Teams," in R. A. Guzzo, E. Salas, and Associates, *Team Effectiveness and Decision Making in Organizations* (San Francisco: Jossey-Bass, 1995), pp. 291–332; M. J. Stevens and M. A. Campion, "The Knowledge, Skill, and Ability Requirements for Teamwork: Implications for Human Resource Management," *Journal of Management*, 1994, 20, pp. 503–530; R. S. Wellins, W. C. Byham, and G. R. Dixon, *Inside Teams* (San Francisco: Jossey-Bass, 1994).
7. E. Sundstrom, K. P. DeMeuse, and D. Futrell, "Work Teams: Applications and Effectiveness," *American Psychologist*, 1990, 45, pp. 120–133.
8. M. Harvey, M. M. Novicevic, and G. Garrison, "Challenges to Staffing Global Virtual Teams" *Human Resource Management Review*, 2004, 14, pp. 275–294.
9. W. F. Cascio, "Managing a Virtual Workplace," *Academy of Management Executive*, 2000, 14(3), pp. 81–90; D. C. Feldman and T. W. Gainey, "Patterns of Telecommuting and Their Consequences: Framing the Research Agenda," *Human Resource Management Review*, 1997, 7, pp. 369–388; J. A. Segal, "Home Sweet Office," *HR Magazine*, Apr. 1998, pp. 119–129.
10. R. J. Mirabile, "The power of job analysis," *Training*, 27 (4), April 1990, pp. 70–74.

11. J. S. Schippman, *Strategic Job Modeling: Working at the Core of Integrated Human Resources* (Mahwah, NJ: Lawrence Erlbaum Associates Inc., 1999).
12. For excellent overviews and reviews, see M. T. Brannick and E. L Levine, *Job Analysis* (Thousand Oaks, CA: Sage, 2002); S. Gael (ed.), *The Job Analysis Handbook for Business, Industry and Government,* Vols. 1 and 2. (New York: Wiley, 1988); R. D. Gatewood and H. S. Feild, *Human Resource Selection,* fifth ed. (Orlando, FL: Harcourt, 2001), pp. 267–363; J. V. Ghorpade, *Job Analysis* (Englewood Cliffs, NJ: 1988); R. J. Harvey, "Job Analysis," in Dunnette and Hough, *Handbook of Industrial and Organizational Psychology,* pp. 71–163.
13. E. T. Cornelius III, "Practical Findings from Job Analysis Research," in Gael, *The Job Analysis Handbook for Business, Industry and Government,* Vol. 1, pp. 48–70.
14. C. J. Cranny and M. E. Doherty, "Importance Ratings in Job Analysis: Note on the Misinterpretation of Factor Analysis," *Journal of Applied Psychology,* 1988, 73, 320–322.
15. Gatewood and Feild, *Human Resource Selection,* pp. 295–298; Harvey, "Job Analysis," in Dunnette and Hough, pp. 75–79; M. A. Wilson, "The Validity of Task Coverage Ratings by Incumbents and Supervisors: Bad News," *Journal of Business and Psychology,* 1997, 12, pp. 85–95.
16. D. P. Costanza, E. A. Fleishman, and J. C. Marshall-Mies, "Knowledges: Evidence for the Reliability and Validity of the Measures" in N. G. Peterson, M. D. Mumford, W. C. Borman, P. R. Jeannerert, E. A. Fleishman, and K. Y. Levin, *O*NET Final Technical Report Vol. 1* (Salt Lake City: Utah Department of Workforce Services, 1997), pp. 4–1 to 4–26.
17. F. L. Schmidt and J. E. Hunter, "Tacit Knowledge, Practical Intelligence, General Mental Ability, and Job Knowledge," *Current Directions in Psychological Science,* Feb. 1993, 2(1), p. 8.
18. M. C. Mumford, N. G. Peterson, and R. A. Childs, "Basic and Cross-Functional Skills: Evidence for Reliability and Validity of the Measures" in Peterson et al., *O*NET Final Technical Report Vol. 1,* pp. 3–1 to 3–36.
19. E. A. Fleishman, D. P. Costanza, and J. C. Marshall-Mies, "Abilities: Evidence for the Reliability and Validity of the Measures" in Peterson, et al., *O*NET Final Technical Report Vol. 2,* pp. 9–1 to 9–26.
20. M. H. Strong, P. R. Jeanneret, S. M. McPhail, and B. R. Blakley, "Work Context: Evidence for the Reliability and Validity of the Measures," in Peterson, et al., *O*NET Final Technical Report Vol. 2,* pp. 7–1 to 7–35.
21. G. Latham and C. Sue-Chan, "Selecting Employees in the 21st Century: Predicting the Contribution of Industrial-Organizational Psychology to Canada," *Canadian Psychology,* Feb–May 1988.
22. F. P. Morgeson, K. Delaney-Klinger, M. S. Mayfield, P. Ferrara, and M. A. Campion, "Self- Presentations Processes in Job Analysis: A Field Experiment Investigating Inflation in Abilities Tasks, and Competencies," *Journal of Applied Psychology,* 2004, 89, pp. 674–686.
23. R. D. Gatewood and H. Field, *Human Resources Selection,* Third Ed. (Fort Worth, TX: Harcourt Brace, 1994).
24. For detailed treatments, see Brannick and Levine, *Job Analysis;* Gael, *The Job Analysis Handbook for Business, Industry and Government,* pp. 315–468; Gatewood and Feild, *Human Resource Selection,* pp. 267–363; Harvey, "Job Analysis," in Dunnette and Hough.
25. Peterson, et al., *O*NET Final Technical Report Vols. 1, 2, 3;* N. G. Peterson, M. D. Mumford, W. C. Borman, P. R. Jeanneret, E. A. Fleishman, K. Y. Levin, M. A. Campion, M. S. Mayfield, F. S. Morgeson, K. Pearlman, M. K. Gowing, A. R. Lancaster, M. B. Silver, and D. M. Dye, "Understanding Work Using the Occupational Information Network: Implications for Research and Practice," *Personnel Psychology,* 2001, 54, pp. 451–492.

26. D. E. Hartley, "Job Analysis at the Speed of Reality," *T+D,* Sept. 2004, 58(9), p. 20.
27. R. G. Jones, J. I. Sanchez, G. Parameswaran, J. Phelps, C. Shop-taugh, M. Williams, and S. White, "Selection or Training? A Two-fold Test of the Validity of Job-Analytic Ratings of Trainability," *Journal of Business and Psychology,* 2001, 15, pp. 363–389; F. J. Landy and J. Vasey, "Job Analysis: The Composition of SME Samples," *Personnel Psychology,* 1991, 44, pp. 27–50; D. M. Truxillo, M. E. Paronto, M. Collins, and J. L. Sulzer, "Effects of Subject Matter Expert Viewpoint on Job Analysis Results," *Public Personnel Management,* 2004 33(1), pp. 33–46.
28. See Brannick and Levine, Job Analysis, pp. 265–294; Gael, The Job Analysis Handbook for Business, Industry and Government, pp. 315–390; Gatewood and Feild, Human Resource Selection, pp. 267–363.
29. American Compensation Association, *Raising the Bar: Using Competencies to Enhance Employee Performance* (Scottsdale, AZ: author, 1996); M. Harris, "Competency Modeling: Viagraized Job Analysis or Impotent Imposter?" *The Industrial-Organizational Psychologist,* 1998, 36(2), pp. 37–41; R. L. Heneman and G. E. Ledford Jr., "Competency Pay for Professionals and Managers in Business: A Review and Implications for Teachers," *Journal of Personnel Evaluation in Education,* 1998, 12, pp. 103–122; J. S. Shipmann, R. A. Ash, M. Battista, L. Carr, L. D. Eyde, B. Hesketh, J. Kehoe, K. Pearlman, E. P. Prien, and J. I. Sanchez, "The Practice of Competency Modeling," *Personnel Psychology,* 2000, 53, pp. 703–740; L. M. Spenser and S. M. Spencer, *Competence at Work* (New York: Wiley, 1993).
30. American Compensation Association, *Raising the Bar,* pp. 7–15.
31. P. K. Zingheim, G. E. Ledford Jr., and J. R. Schuster, "Competencies and Competency Models: Does One Size Fit All?," *ACA Journal,* Spring 1996, pp. 56–65.
32. American Compensation Association, *Raising the Bar,* pp. 35–36.
33. D. Rahbar-Daniels, M. L. Erickson, and A. Dalik, "Here to Stay: Taking Competencies to the Next Level," *WorldatWork Journal,* 2001, First Quarter, pp. 70–77.
34. Shipman et.al., "The Practice of Competency Modeling."
35. F. H. Borgen, "Occupational Reinforcer Patterns," in Gael, *The Job Analysis Handbook for Business, Industry and Government,* Vol. 2, pp. 902–916; R. V. Dawis, "Person-Environment Fit and Job Satisfaction," in C. J. Cranny, P. C. Smith, and E. F. Stone (eds.), *Job Satisfaction* (New York: Lexington, 1992); C. T. Kulik and G. R. Oldham, "Job Diagnostic Survey," in Gael, *Handbook for Analyzing Jobs in Business, Industry and Government,* Vol. 2, pp. 936–959; G. Ledford, P. Mulvey, and P. LeBlanc, *The Rewards of Work* (Scottsdale, AZ: WorldatWork/Sibson, 2000).
36. E. E. Ledford and M. I. Lucy, *The Rewards of Work* (Los Angeles, CA: Sibson Consulting, 2003).
37. Ledford and Lucy, *The Rewards of Work,* p. 12.
38. Arieh Bonder, "A Blue-Print For The Future: Competency-Based Management In The Public Service Of Canada," *HRSDC,* May, 2002, www.hrma-agrh.gc.ca/hr-rh/tld-fap/ref_document/backandissues_e.asp.
39. D. E. Thompson and T. A. Thompson, "Court Standards for Job Analysis in Test Validation," *Personnel Psychology,* 1982, 35, pp. 865–874.
40. Canadian Human Rights Commission, "Practical Guide for Employment Accommodation for People with Disabilities," www.chrc-ccdp.ca/discrimination/barrier_free-en.asp.

Visit the Online Learning Centre at

www.mcgrawhill.ca/olc/heneman

PART 3

Staffing Activities: Recruitment

Chapter Five
External Recruitment

Chapter Six
Internal Recruitment

The Staffing Organizations Model

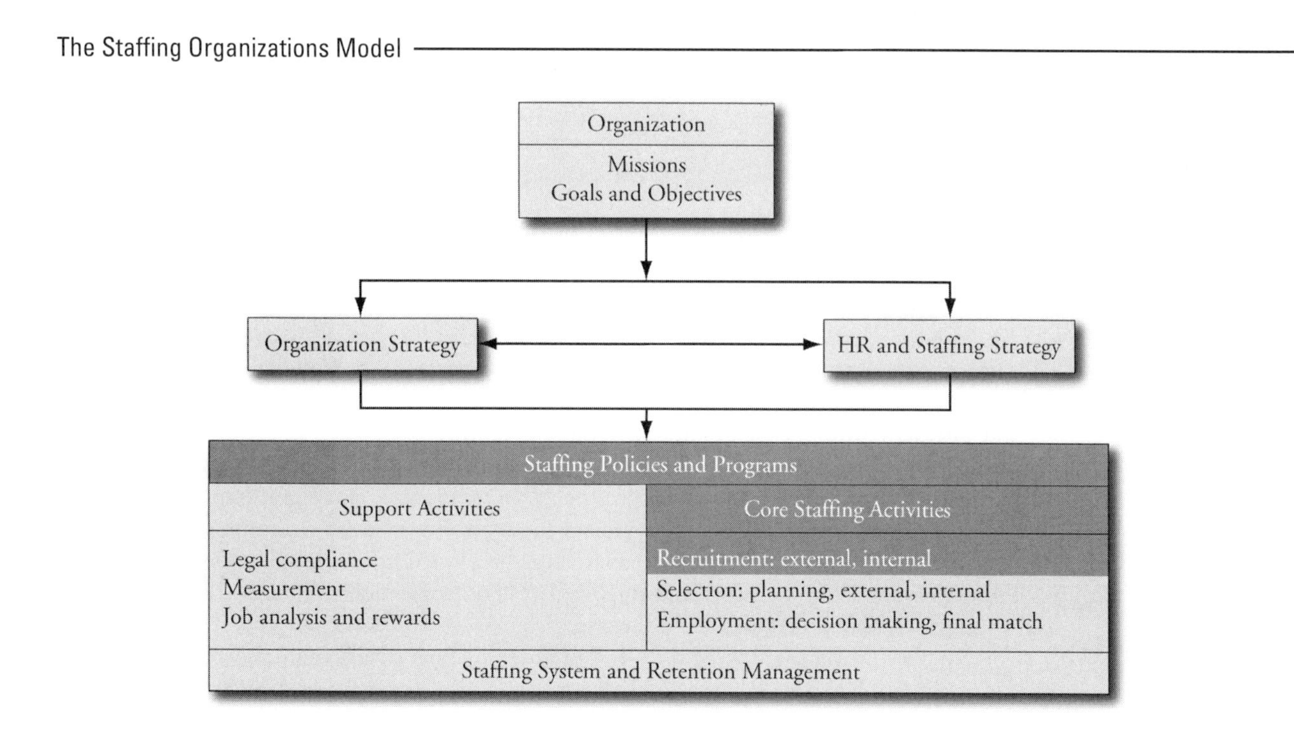

CHAPTER 5

External Recruitment

CHAPTER OBJECTIVES

After reading this chapter, you will be able to:

- Explain how external influences, organizational issues, and administrative issues impact external recruitment planning
- Analyze the advantages and disadvantages of using recruiters both from external and internal sources
- Develop a recruitment strategy to identify qualified applicants by understanding the recruitment sources available
- Discuss various communication media that can be used to attract job applicants and the pros and cons of each choice
- Understand the importance of legal compliance to limit exclusionary and deceptive practices

The objective of the external recruitment process is to identify and attract job applicants from outside the organization. From among these applicants, hiring decisions are made. The recruitment process begins with a planning phase during which external influences, organizational issues, and administrative issues, as well as those pertaining to recruiters, are addressed. External influences that impact recruitment decisions are economic conditions, labour markets, unions, and external and internal environmental scanning. Organizational issues that impact recruitment decisions include how the recruitment strategy fits with the overall staffing philosophy, strategic understanding of staffing planning, and selecting recruiters. Administrative issues that impact recruitment decisions include requisitions, timing, number and types of contacts, the recruitment budget, and development of a recruitment guide. Recruiters can be selected from a variety of sources, including HR professionals, line managers, and employees. The assessment of advantages and disadvantages of using each source identifies that quite often a variety of sources should be used.

Next, a recruitment strategy is formed in order to know where, and how, to look for qualified applicants. Knowing where to look requires an understanding of open and targeted recruitment strategies. Knowing how to look requires an understanding of recruitment sources and then deciding which ones to use.

Following the formation of strategy, the message to be communicated to job applicants is established. It is then decided which communication medium should be used to communicate the message.

Special consideration must be given to applicant reactions to recruiters and the recruitment process when undertaking each of these phases of the external recruitment process. Close attention must also be given to legal issues. This includes employment equity and diversity programs, human rights issues, temporary workers, electronic recruitment, and job advertisements.

EXTERNAL INFLUENCES

There are four major sources of external influence in HR and staffing planning that impact external recruitment. They are economic conditions, labour market, unions, and external and internal environmental scanning. Exhibit 5.1 provides specific examples of these influences, which are discussed next.

Economic Conditions

Numerous macro forces operate to determine the overall economic climate in which the organization functions. These include product and labour market competition (both national and global), inflation, interest rates, currency exchange rates, and government fiscal and monetary policy. Resulting from such forces is the degree of overall economic expansion or contraction.

economic conditions
Affect job growth, which governs the movement of people in and out of the organization

A direct derivative of the **economic conditions** that lead to these expansion and contraction forces is the amount of job creation and growth, both positive and negative. Positive job growth means expanding job opportunities for individuals, while slowdowns or contractions in job growth yield dwindling job opportunities. Organizations move people into (new hires), within (internal labour markets), and out of (turnover) the organization in varying rates, depending on the amount of job growth. Job growth thus functions like a spigot governing the movement of people.

Consider recruitment that occurs because of job expansion. When new jobs are created, new hire rates begin to increase for both entry-level and higher-level jobs. These new hires are either new entrants into the labour force (e.g., recent college graduates) or current members of the labour force, both unemployed and employed. There will also be increased movement within organizations' internal labour markets through the operation of their promotion and transfer systems. This movement causing current employees to leave the organization will create new jobs that could be filled internally or externally. Job vacancies will be created by employees leaving to take new job opportunities or leaving the organization due to retirement. Some, however, may be temporarily unemployed (while they look for new job opportunities), and others may leave the labour force entirely.

EXHIBIT 5.1 Examples of External Influences on Staffing

ECONOMIC CONDITIONS
- Economic expansion and contraction
- Job growth and job opportunities
- Internal labour market mobility
- Turnover rates

LABOUR MARKETS
- Labour demand: employment patterns, KSAOs sought
- Labour supply: labour force, demographic trends, KSAOs available
- Labour shortages and surpluses
- Employment arrangements

LABOUR UNIONS
- Negotiations
- Labour contracts: staffing levels, staffing quality, internal movement
- Grievance systems

EXTERNAL/INTERNAL ENVIRONMENTAL SCANS
- Data collection
- Trend reports
- Human resource management implications
- Workforce trends

With lesser rates of job growth or actual job contraction, the movement flows are lessened. Organizations will be hiring fewer people, and job seekers will have longer job searches and fewer job opportunities to choose from. Promotion and transfer opportunities for current employees will dry up, voluntary turnover rates will decrease, and many employees may even experience termination through involuntary layoff or a voluntary early retirement program.

Labour Markets

In and through labour markets, organizations express specific labour preferences and requirements (labour demand) and persons express their own job preferences and requirements (labour supply). Ultimately, person/job matches occur from the interaction of the demand and supply forces. Both labour demand and supply contain quantity and quality components, as described below. Labour shortages and surpluses, and a variety of possible employment arrangements are also discussed.

Labour Demand: Employment Patterns Labour demand is a derived demand, meaning it is a result of consumer demands for the organization's products and services. The organization acquires and deploys its workforce in ways that will allow it to be responsive to consumer demand in a competitive manner.

To learn about labour demand, national employment statistics are collected and analyzed. They provide data about employment patterns and projections for industries, occupations, and organization size.

Projections over the next five years suggest that approximately two million jobs will be created. The service sector will lead the growth by creating 75 percent of these new jobs in the areas of business services, communications, health, accommodations, food services, and personal services. The remaining 25 percent of new job openings will be in the goods-producing sector, primarily construction and manufacturing. Declines in job growth will be seen in the education sector, due to the age structure of the population; communication sector, primarily in the radio, television, and telecommunication industries; agriculture and mining sectors because of world commodity prices and automation; and fishing and forestry industries due to supply constraints, relatively weak world commodity prices, increased mechanization, and resource depletion.[1]

Labour Demand: KSAOs Sought KSAO requirements or preferences of employers are not widely measured, except for education requirements. Occupations requiring post-secondary training will grow significantly and will provide 70 percent of the newly created jobs. Occupations requiring a university degree accounted for 23.4 percent of new job creation from 1999 to 2004. Human Resources and Social Development Canada rates current labour market conditions as:

- Good for university graduates in the fields of business, natural and applied science, and health
- Fair for college or trade/vocational graduates
- Fair for university graduates in social science, arts, culture, and recreation
- Fair for those with high school diploma
- Limited for those with less than a high school diploma[2]

Statistics Canada's National Graduates Survey (NGS) provides information on the correlation between level of education and employment outcomes. In 1996, the NGS administered a survey to 43,040 graduates with high school, community college, and university diplomas. The results of the study suggested there was a strong relationship between graduates with postsecondary diplomas and their usefulness in the labour market.[3]

The "hot jobs" that will fuel employment growth are:

- Aircraft mechanics
- Computer systems analysts and engineers
- Health care professionals (doctors, dentists, chiropractors, optometrists, nurses)
- Human resources and business service professionals
- Medical technologists and technicians
- Paralegal and related occupations
- Physical science professionals
- Sales, marketing, and advertising managers
- University and college professors[4]

Surveys of employers regarding labour quality often reveal perceived deficiencies among job applicants. A Canadian Manufacturers & Exporters (CME) 2004 Management Issues Survey reveals that "23 percent of the respondent companies are having trouble finding entry-level employees with the necessary skill sets needed for further training. And one-third reported the basic skill sets of their employees were not up to snuff. Another 46 percent are having trouble finding people to fill shortages of more specialized skills."[5]

In manufacturing, for example, employers note many such deficiencies. They include a lack of skills in:

- Motivation
- Handling change
- Ability to take on new opportunities
- Ability to multi-task
- Team work
- Communication
- Problem solving
- Understanding instructions
- Literacy
- Numeracy[6]

A very thorough systematic source of information about KSAOs needed for jobs is the National Occupational Classification 2001 (NOC 2001) Web site (www23.hrdc-drhc.gc.ca/2001/e/generic/welcome.shtml). NOC 2001 provides a standardized methodology for organizing job classifications. The development of job classifications is based on extensive occupational research across all spectrums of the Canadian labour market. There are occupational descriptions for 520 jobs. At the managerial level, an interesting attempt was made to have experts forecast the most critical skills that managers will need for the future. The six identified skills are rapid response, sharp focus, stress busting, strategic empowerment, juggling, and team building.[7]

The above survey results show that employers have multiple general KSAO requirements that accompany their quantitative labour requirements. Naturally, the more specific requirements vary according to type of employer and type of job. It also appears that employers have identified general future KSAO needs for their workforces on the basis of skill gaps in their current workforces and, in the case of managers, what their projected critical KSAO requirements will be.

Labour Supply: The Labour Force and Its Trends Quantity of labour supplied is measured and reported periodically by Statistics Canada, which publishes a monthly Labour Force Survey (www.statcan.ca/english/Subjects/Labour/LFS/lfs-en.htm) updating employment changes in Canada. It identifies employment changes by provinces, industry sectors, adults, and youth. An example of basic results for July 2005 is given in Exhibit 5.2.

EXHIBIT 5.2 Labour Force Statistics

- Job gains totalled 110,000 (+7%) to date in 2005, slightly less than the 143.000 (+0.9%) over the same period a year ago.
- Unemployment rate was 6.8 percent—the lowest in almost three decades.
- The unemployment rate for adult men increased by 5.7 percent and decreased for adult women by 0.1 percent to 5.5 percent.
- The number of people working in retail and wholesale trade rose by 24,000, bringing gains so far this year to 67,000 (+2.7%).
- Employment increased by 18,000 in health care and social assistance.
- Employment rose by 16,000 in agriculture, bringing gains over the first seven months of 2005 to 42,000.
- Employment in manufacturing declined by 26,000 in July, with job losses mainly in Ontario and Quebec.
- Compared to a year ago, employment in manufacturing is down by 106,000 (–4.6%).
- Employment fell in construction by 21,000, with most of the decrease is in Ontario.
- Employment fell in professional, scientific, and technical services by 21,000, with losses spread across a number of provinces.

Source: Statistics Canada, excerpts from the "Latest release from the Labour Force Survey," July 2005.

Data reveal several labour force trends that have particular relevance for staffing organizations. Labour force growth is slowing, going from an annual growth rate of around 2 percent in the early 1990s to a projected rate of 1.1 percent by the year 2112. There are increasingly fewer new entrants to the labour force. This trend, coupled with the severe KSAO deficiencies that many of the new entrants will have, creates major adaptation problems for organizations.

Demographically, the labour force has become more diverse, and this trend will continue. If current demographic levels are extrapolated to the year 2012, the composition of the labour force will include:

- Fewer men and more women
- Fewer whites
- More Asians, Africans, Latin Americans, and people from the Middle East and Caribbean
- Fewer younger (16–24) workers
- More older (age 55+) workers[8]

Other, more subtle labour force trends are also under way. There has been a slight upward movement overall in the average number of hours that people work and a strong rise in the proportion of employees who work very long hours in certain occupations, such as managers and professionals. Indeed over the last 20 years, there has been a steady climb of a higher proportion of Canadians working more than 40 hours per week. Since 1976, the number of Canadians who work more than 50 hours per week has increased by 2.5 percent. For the average manager, the work week has grown by 15 percent from 1991 to 2000 from 38 hours to 43 hours plus working 32 hours of unpaid overtime a month.[9] There is also an increase in multiple job holding. According the 2001 census, the proportion of workers holding more than one job has risen from 2 to 5 percent over the last 20 years.[10]

Canada's population is becoming ever more diversified because of the growing number of immigrants. From 1991 to 1996, the immigration population has increased by 14.5 percent—more than triple the 4 percent expansion of the non-immigrant population.[11] In the manufacturing sector, the growth in the reliance on immigration increased by 166 percent from 1991 to 2001.[12] The Canadian government has set a target of increasing the number of immigrants coming into Canada by 300,000 new immigrants a year—about 1 percent of Canada's existing population. New Canadians make up about 70 percent of the growth in the labour market. It is forecasted that by 2011 they will account for all the growth in the workforce.[13]

Federal and provincial policies are increasingly pushing welfare recipients into the labour force, and they are mostly employed in low-wage jobs with low educational requirements. In British Columbia, 32,000 people on social assistance found work between 2002 and 2005 through Job Wave, a private company that provides a job-placement and a training-for-jobs program for the Ministry of Employment and Income Assistance.[14]

Labour Supply: KSAOs Available Data on KSAOs available in the labour force are very sparse. A labour force survey showed that about 32 percent of the population age 25 or older had attained a college degree or higher, whereas 10 percent had less than a high school diploma; the remainder had education attainment levels within this band.[15]

According to Statistics Canada, 47 percent of Canadian workers do not possess adequate literacy skills in reading text, document use, and numeracy.[16] Another study found 33 percent of new labour entrants fit into the bottom two categories of literacy levels. Here, literacy was measured in terms of prose, reading tables and charts, and quantitative data manipulation.[17] Data such as these reinforce the serious KSAO deficiencies reported by employees in at least some portions of the labour force.

Labour Shortages and Surpluses When labour demand exceeds labour supply for a given pay rate, the labour market is said to be "tight" and labour shortages are experienced by the organization. Shortages tend to be job or occupation specific. Low unemployment rates, surges in labour demand in certain occupations, and skill deficiencies all fuel both labour quantity and labour quality shortages for many organizations. The shortages cause numerous responses, such as:

- Increased pay and benefit packages
- Hiring bonuses and stock options
- Use of nontraditional labour (e.g., retirees, people with disabilities)
- Use of temporary employees
- Recruitment of immigrants
- Lower hiring standards
- Partnerships with high schools, technical schools, and colleges
- Increased mandatory overtime work
- Increased hours of operation

These types of responses are lessened or reversed when the labour market is "loose," meaning there are labour surpluses relative to labour demand.

Employment Arrangements Though labour market forces bring organizations and job seekers together, the specific nature of the employment arrangement can assume many forms. Data show that about 60 percent of people work in traditional full-time jobs, while 40 percent have part-time or temporary jobs or are self-employed. Non-traditional employment is a way of entering the workforce. Fifty-seven percent of unemployed people in 1999 found non-traditional jobs in 2000 or 2001.[18]

A second arrangement involves the issue of regular or shift work. Approximately 75 percent of employees work a regular schedule, while 25 percent perform shift work. Those who work shift work can have a variety in schedules, such as evening, night, split, and rotating.[19]

Two other types of arrangements, often considered in combination, are various "alternative" arrangements to the traditional employer–employee one, and the use of contingent employees. Alternative arrangements include the organization filling its staffing needs through use of independent contractors, on-call workers and day labourers, temporary help agency employees, and employees provided by a contract firm that provides a specific service (e.g., accounting). Contingent employees do not have an explicit or implicit contract for long-term employment; they expect their employment to be temporary rather than long term. Contingent employees may occur in combination with any of the four alternatives given above.

EXHIBIT 5.3 Usage of Alternative Employment Arrangements and Contingent Workers—1997 and 2003

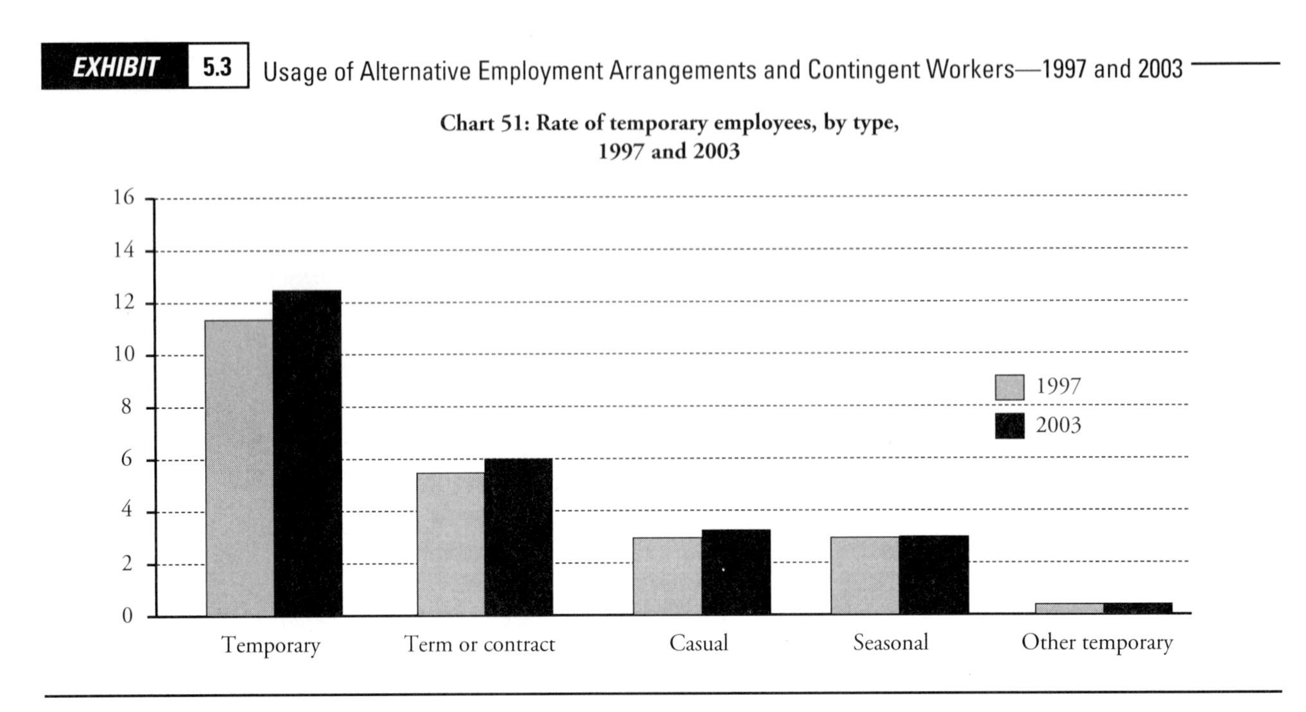

Source: Statistics Canada, Labour Force Survey, CANSIM table 282-0080.

National data on the use of alternative employment arrangements and contingent employees are shown in Exhibit 5.3. It can be seen that in 2003, approximately 88 percent of surveyed individuals worked in a traditional employer–employee arrangement.

Labour Unions

labour unions
Legally protected entities that organize employees and bargain with management to establish terms and conditions of employment via a labour contract

Labour unions are legally protected entities that organize employees and bargain with management to establish terms and conditions of employment via a labour contract. In 1997, approximately 37 percent of the private sector and 65.5 percent of the public sector were unionized.[20]

Labour and management are required to bargain in good faith to try to reach agreement on the contract. Many staffing issues may be bargained, including staffing levels, location of facilities, overtime and work schedules, job description and classifications, seniority provisions, promotion and transfers, layoffs and terminations, hiring pools, KSAO requirements, grievance procedures, alternative dispute resolution procedures, employment discrimination protections, and, very important, pay and benefits. Virtually all aspects of the staffing process are thus affected by negotiations and the resultant labour agreement.

Once a contract is agreed to, it standardizes the terms and conditions of employment, making them uniform for all covered employees. The contract cannot be replaced or supplemented by individual agreements with employees, as would be the case in a nonunion setting. Moreover, the terms in the contract are binding and cannot be unilaterally changed by management, thus "locking in" everything agreed to.

Labour unions thus have direct and powerful impacts on staffing and other HR systems. Even in nonunion situations the union influence can be felt through "spillover effects" in which management tries to emulate the pay and benefits, as well as staffing practices, found in unionized settings.

External and Internal Environmental Scanning

1.1

external environmental scan
A method of tracking workforce trends, developments, and migrations and studying their implications to various facets of staffing

External Scanning An **external environmental scan** is a method of tracking workforce trends, developments, and migrations and their implications to staffing in general. The discussion in this chapter focuses on the impact of environmental scans on recruitment strategy.

Many large corporations maintain fairly elaborate networks of line managers, technical specialists, and HR specialists, who monitor large numbers of publications, broadcast media, futurist think tanks, and conferences for relevant data. Periodically, these data are assembled and trend reports are prepared and made available. These reports usually include a summary of the major environmental trends and their implications for human resource management. Exhibit 5.4 shows an example of an environmental scan regarding the employment outlook.

Of the various areas monitored through external scanning, the labour market is most directly relevant to staffing planning. For a start-up organization in genetic engineering, for example, the future availability of geneticists, biologists, and other types of scientists and engineers is an important strategic contingency. If tight labour markets for these skills are expected, the organization must plan to put considerable time and money into attracting and retaining the needed talent (for example, by raising salaries or offering child care programs) or into developing alternative means of accomplishing its key research and development work (for instance, by using technicians wherever possible, thus reducing the need for scientists and engineers).

Clearly, then, an organization's grasp of impending developments in the outside world is very helpful to recruiters. It puts them in an excellent position to influence the nature of business plans (and thus the nature of future HR requirements) and to ensure that planned recruiting activities are both realistic and supportive of these business plans.

internal environmental scan
A method of observing and tracking from within an organization, using such tools as discussions with managers, employee attitude surveys, and employee performance statistics

Internal Scanning Also important is a firm grasp of an organization's internal environment. Thus, recruiters must be out and about taking an **internal environmental scan** of their organizations, taking advantage of opportunities to learn what is going on. Informal discussions with key managers can help, as can employee attitude surveys, special surveys, and the monitoring of key indicators such as employee performance, absenteeism, turnover, and accident rates. Of special interest is the identification of nagging personnel problems, as well as prevailing managerial attitudes concerning HR.

EXHIBIT 5.4 Example of Environmental Scan for Employment Outlook

- Health care costs will continue to rise; health care coverage will remain the most important benefit to applicants and employees.
- Lower HR staff-to-employee ratios are occurring, reflecting increased HR hiring relative to other employees.
- Employees demand more flexible work schedules to create better work/life balance.
- New ways of managing talent and measuring its impact on the bottom line are needed.
- Multiple employee privacy concerns are emerging as important—electronic monitoring, background checks, e-mail, identity theft.
- Attempts to link pay to performance will continue, but will be difficult.
- A growth in knowledge-based jobs may lead to more telecommuting.
- There is increased employee demand for work arrangements uniquely tailored to the individual and his or her specific job responsibilities.
- More paid time off will be demanded by employees.
- Rising health care costs could cause an employer backlash against providing health insurance benefits.

Nagging personnel problems refer to recurring difficulties that threaten to interfere with the attainment of future business plans or other important organizational goals. High turnover in a sales organization, for example, is likely to threaten the viability of a business plan that calls for increased sales quotas or the rapid introduction of several new products.

The values and attitudes of managers, especially top managers, toward HR are also important to developing a recruitment strategy. Trouble brews when these are inconsistent with the organization's business plans. For example, a mid-sized accounting firm may have formulated a business plan calling for very rapid growth through aggressive marketing and selected acquisitions of smaller firms, but existing management talent may be inadequate to the task of operating a larger, more complex organization. Moreover, there may be a prevailing attitude among the top management against investing much money in management development and against bringing in talent from outside the firm. This attitude conflicts with the business and recruitment plans, requiring a change in either the business plan or attitudes.

ORGANIZATIONAL ISSUES

The recruitment process in an organization can be organized in a variety of ways. It can be coordinated in-house or by an external recruitment agency. An organization can do its own recruiting or cooperate with other organizations in a recruitment alliance. Authority to recruit may be centralized or decentralized in the organization.

Staffing Philosophy

staffing philosophy
Help shapes the direction and character of an organization's staffing system and sends signals to applicants and employees about the organization as an employer

In conjunction with the staffing planning process to develop recruitment strategies, the organization's **staffing philosophy** should be reviewed. Weighed in conjunction with the organization's staffing strategies, results of this review help shape the direction and character of the specific staffing systems implemented. The review should focus on the following issues: internal versus external staffing, human rights practices, and applicant reactions.

The relative importance to the organization of external or internal staffing is a critical matter because it directly shapes the nature of the staffing system, as well as sends signals to applicants and employees alike about the organization as an employer. Exhibit 5.5 highlights the advantages and disadvantages of external and internal staffing. Clearly there are trade-offs

EXHIBIT 5.5 Staffing Philosophy: Internal versus External Staffing

RPC 1.4

	Advantages	Disadvantages
Internal	• Positive employee reactions to promotion from within • Quick method to identify job applicants • Less expensive • Less time required to reach full productivity	• No new KSAOs into the organization • May perpetuate current under-representation of minorities and women • Small labour market to recruit from • Employees may require more training time
External	• Brings employees in with new KSAOs • Larger number of minorities and women to draw from • Large labour market to draw from • Employees may require less training time	• Negative reaction by internal applicants • Time consuming to identify applicants • Expensive to search external labour market • More time required to reach full productivity

to consider in deciding the optimal internal-external staffing mix. The point regarding time to reach full productivity warrants special comment. Any new hire, either internal or external, will require time to learn the new job and reach a full productivity level. It is suggested that internal new hires have the advantage here. This reflects an assumption that internal new hires will require relatively little orientation time and may have received special training and development to prepare them for the new job. This specific advantage for internal new hires, however, needs to be weighed in tandem with the other advantages and disadvantages of each type of new hire.

In terms of human rights, the organization must be sure to consider or develop a sense of importance attached to being a human rights–conscious employer, as well as the commitment it is willing to make in incorporating human rights elements into all phases of the staffing system. Attitudes toward human rights can range all the way from outright hostility and disregard to benign neglect to aggressive commitment and support. As should be obvious, the stance that the organization adopts will have a major effect on its operational staffing system, as well as on job applicants and employees.

As a final point about staffing philosophy, recruiters must continue to bear in mind that staffing is an interaction involving both the organization and job applicants as participants. Just as organizations recruit and select applicants, so, too, do applicants recruit and select organizations (and job offers). Through their job search strategies and activities, applicants exert major influence on their own staffing destinies. Once the applicant has decided to opt into the organization's staffing process, the applicant is confronted with numerous decisions about whether to continue on in the staffing process or withdraw from further consideration. This process of self-selection is inherent to any staffing system. During staffing planning, those within the organization must constantly consider how the applicant will react to the staffing system and its components, and whether they want to encourage or discourage applicant self-selection.

Staffing Objectives

staffing objective
Derived from identified gaps between requirements and availabilities that respond to both shortages and surpluses in the workforce

Staffing objectives are derived from identified gaps between requirements and availabilities. As such, they involve objectives responding to both shortages and surpluses. They may require the establishment of quantitative and qualitative targets.

Quantitative targets should be expressed in head count for each job category/level and will be very close in magnitude to the identified gaps. Indeed, to the extent that the organization believes in the gaps as forecast, the objectives will be identical to the gap figures. A forecast shortage of 39 employees in A1, for example, should be transformed into a staffing objective of 39 accessions (or something close to it) to be achieved by the end of the forecasting time interval. Exhibit 5.6 provides an illustration of these points regarding quantitative staffing objectives.

EXHIBIT 5.6 Setting Numerical Staffing Objectives

Job Category and Level	Gap	Objectives					Total
		New Hires	Promotions	Transfers	Demotions	Exits	
A1	−39	For each cell, enter a positive number for head count additions and a negative number for head count subtractions.					+39
A2	+7						−7
B1	−110						+110
B2	−3						+3
Total							

Note: Assumes objective is to close each gap exactly.

Qualitative staffing objectives refer to the types or qualities of people in KSAO-type terms. For external staffing objectives, these may be stated in terms of averages, such as average education level for new hires and average scores on ability tests. Internal staffing objectives of a qualitative nature may also be established. These may reflect desired KSAOs in terms of seniority, performance appraisal record over a period of years, types of on- and off-the-job training, and so forth.

Generating Alternative Staffing Activities

With quantitative and, possibly, qualitative objectives established, it is necessary to begin identifying possible ways of achieving them. This requires an identification of the fullest possible range of alternative activities, which, if pursued, might lead to achievement of the objectives. At the beginning stages of generating alternatives, it is wise to not prematurely close the door on any alternatives. Exhibit 5.7 provides an excellent list of the full range of options available for initial consideration in dealing with employee shortages and surpluses.

Since the focus of this book is on acquisition of a workforce, our concern is with the employee shortage options. As shown in Exhibit 5.7, both short- and long-term options for shortages, involving a combination of staffing and workload management, are possible.

Short-term options include the following:

- Better utilization of current employees through more overtime, productivity increases, buybacks of vacation and holidays
- Outsourcing work to other organizations through subcontracts or transfer work out
- Acquiring additional employees on a short-term basis using temporary hires and assignments

Long-term options include the following:

- Staffing up with additional employees by recalling former employees, transferring in employees from other work units, or taking on new permanent hires
- Skill enhancement or retraining
- Pushing work on to other organizations by transferring work out

Assessing and Choosing Alternatives

As should be apparent, there is a veritable smorgasbord of alternative staffing activities available to address staffing gaps. Each of these alternatives needs to be assessed systematically to help decision makers choose from among the alternatives.

The goal of such assessment is to identify one or more preferred activities. A preferred activity is one offering the highest likelihood of attaining the staffing objective, within the time limit established, at the least cost or tolerable cost, and with the fewest negative side effects. There are no standard or agreed-on programs or formats for conducting these assessments. Thus, the organization will need to develop its own internal mechanisms for assessment. Whatever overall mechanism is developed, it should ensure that two things occur. First, a common set of assessment criteria (e.g., time for completion, cost, probability of success) should be identified and agreed on. Second, each alternative should be assessed according to each of these criteria. In this way, all alternatives will receive equal treatment, and tendencies to jump at an initial alternative will be minimized.

Once staffing objectives are set, the process is turned over to the recruiters. Selecting, training, and rewarding recruiters are critical responsibilities as they play a key role in whom the organization will hire. The use of in-house recruiters or external recruitment agencies is a strategic decision, which is determined by a number of factors including competency of in-house recruiters versus external recruiters, time, volume of vacancies, cost, and so on.

EXHIBIT 5.7 Staffing Alternatives to Deal with Employee Shortages and Surpluses

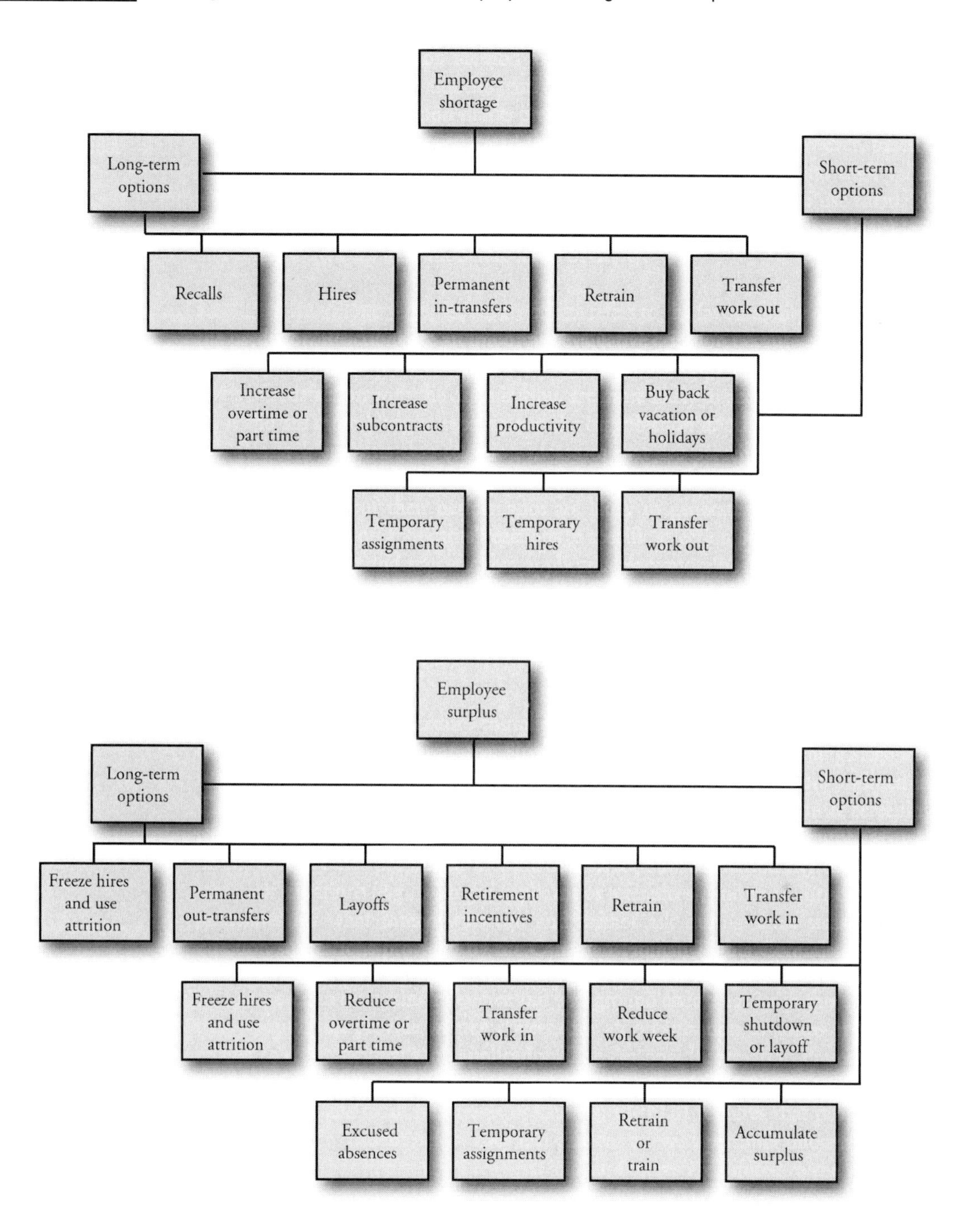

EXHIBIT 5.8 Comparison of Using Recruiters from Various Sources

Source	Advantages	Disadvantages
HR professionals	Very knowledgeable about career development issues; enthusiastic about the organization	Lack detailed knowledge regarding specific job responsibilities
Line managers	Have detailed knowledge about the company and jobs that they supervise	Not particularly knowledgeable about career development opportunities
Employees	Have in-depth understanding of their own jobs	Do not have much knowledge of the larger organization

Recruiters

Selecting Recruiters Many studies have been conducted to assess desirable characteristics of recruiters. Reviews of these studies indicate that an ideal recruiter would possess the following characteristics:

- Strong interpersonal skills
- Knowledge about jobs, career-related issues, and the organization
- Technology skills (e.g., knowing how to mine databases, Internet recruiting)
- Enthusiasm about the organization and job candidates
- These characteristics represent a start on developing a set of KSAOs to select recruiters.

Actual recruiters used by organizations come from a variety of sources, including HR professionals, line managers, and employees. As shown in Exhibit 5.8, each of these sources generally has some distinct advantages and disadvantages relative to the list of desirable characteristics for recruiters.

Training Recruiters Many recruiters who come from areas outside HR do not have any specialized training in HR. Hence, the training of recruiters is essential. Unfortunately, very few recruiters ever receive any training.

Based on current organizational practices, recruiters should receive training in the following areas:

Interviewing skills
Interpersonal aspects of recruiting
Forms and reports
Company and job characteristics
Marketing skills
Ethics
Job analysis
Laws and regulations
Recruitment targets
Technology skills
Working with other departments

First, in terms of technology skills, though access to large recruiting Web sites such as Monster.ca is to be expected, it must be recognized that many recruiters are mining these sites. Thus, recruiters must be instructed on accessing "niche" sites that specialize in a particular candidate cohort (e.g., CFO.com for finance executives), browsing for personal Web pages, or even infiltrating corporate Web sites.

When surfing the Internet, there are strategies to be learned.

- "Flipping": Finding resumés with links to a particular company
- "Peeling": Finding links to staff directories in URLs
- "X-raying": Identifying key employees by accessing those places on a company's Web site not directly accessible via links from the site's home page

Second, recruiters must be trained in marketing and sales techniques.[21] Some of these techniques are very simple, such as surfing resumé sites at night to get a leg up on the competition. Recruiters also need to be trained on how to be more creative in identifying candidates. For example, in tight labour markets, some recruiters are creative enough to stake out airports, temples and churches, and health clubs. One recruiter even flies from airport to airport just to "raid" the airport clubs for potential recruits. More generally, recruiters need instruction on how to sell their jobs to candidates. For example, recruiters can be trained on how to do market research, where job candidates are the market, and how to identify what they want. Related to developing their marketing skills, recruiters can be shown how to link up with other departments, such as marketing and public relations. For example, recruiters may be able to collaborate with marketing efforts to achieve a brand image that not only sells products to customers but sells the organization to prospective hires as well.

Finally, in their efforts to recruit more creatively, recruiters need training on ethical issues in recruitment. Is it ethical for a recruiter to recruit at a competitor's place of business? In parking lots? At weddings or funerals? Some recruiters will even lie to applicants in an effort to lure them. Some might even argue that the Internet strategies of "peeling," "flipping," and "x-raying" cross the ethical line. To ensure that recruiters behave ethically, standards should be developed and recruiters trained on these standards.[22]

Rewarding Recruiters To reinforce effective recruitment practices, it is essential that recruiter performance—both effective recruitment behaviours and end results—be monitored and rewarded. Measures of performance commonly used include being on time for appointments, favourable comments from students, meeting equity goals, and feedback from line managers. Unfortunately, very few organizations collect the data needed to make an objective assessment of these factors.

Rewards can be coupled with performance standards. For example, in one interesting study, it was shown that the efforts of U.S. Navy recruiters were substantially heightened when there was the promise of a monetary reward for meeting their recruitment quotas.[23] In addition to rewarding recruiters for the successful completion of results, rewards should also be provided for the demonstration of critical behaviours. For example, although good public relations activities may not result in more hires, they may result in more customer satisfaction, which is a major goal of most business organizations today. Accordingly, both the successful attraction of candidates and successful publicity concerning the organization should be rewarded.

In-House versus External Recruitment Agency Most organizational recruiting is done in-house. Smaller organizations may rely on external recruitment agencies rather than having an in-house function to coordinate their recruitment efforts, as smaller organizations may not have the staff or budget to run their own recruitment functions. Organizations with low turnover rates may also prefer to use external recruitment agencies because they recruit so infrequently that it would not make sense to have a recruitment function of their own. External recruitment agencies are growing in number. Some agencies, such as Robert Half International Inc., provide full-scale recruitment services ranging from identifying recruitment needs to advertising for applicants and checking references.

Large organizations and ones with frequent recruitment needs should have their own in-house recruitment function. An in-house function is needed to ensure that recruitment costs are minimized, recruitment searches are consistent from opening to opening, and the specific needs of the organization are being met.

ADMINISTRATIVE ISSUES

In the planning stage of recruitment, attention must be given to administrative as well as organizational issues.

Requisitions

requisition

A formal document that authorizes the filling of a job opening indicated by the signatures of top management

A **requisition** is a formal document that authorizes the filling of a job opening indicated by the signatures of top management. Supervisors are not given discretion to authorize the filling of job openings. Top managers, rather than supervisors, are more likely to be familiar with staffing planning information for the entire organization, and their approval is needed instead to ensure that recruitment activities are coordinated with staffing planning activities.

An example of a requisition is shown in Exhibit 5.9. A well-developed requisition will specify clearly both the quantity and the quality (KSAOs) of labour to be hired. Hence, each requisition will list the number of openings per job and the minimum qualifications an applicant must have. Qualifications should be based on the job requirements matrix.

Many smaller organizations do not have requisitions. They should, however, for two reasons. First, the procedure ensures that staffing activities are consistent with the business plan of the organization. Second, it ensures that the qualifications of the job are clearly detailed so that a good person/job match is made.

Timing

Two factors that drive the decision of when to look for job applicants are lead time concerns and time sequence concerns.

Lead Time Concerns Although managers would like to have each position filled immediately on approval of requisitions, this goal is not possible, as recruiters handle a large number of vacancies at any one time. It is possible, however, to minimize the delay in filling vacancies by planning for openings well in advance of their actual occurrence.

Effective planning requires that top management prioritize job openings so that they can be filled in the order that best meets the needs of the business. It also requires that recruiters be fully prepared to conduct the search. To do so, recruiters must be knowledgeable about print deadlines for the placement of ads in appropriate periodicals.

Also, recruiters should be knowledgeable about the availability of labour in the marketplace. With the growth of Internet recruiting, much recruiting is now continuous.[24] For example, log on to The Home Depot's Web site (www.homedepot.ca), and a list of job availabilities is continuously listed.

time-lapse statistics

Statistics that provide data on the average length of time that expires between various phases in the recruitment process

Time Sequence Concerns In a successful recruitment program, the steps involved in the process are clearly defined and sequenced in a logical order. A staffing flowchart should be used to organize all components of the recruitment process. The sequence of recruitment activities has a large bearing on the time that will be required to fill job vacancies.

A very useful set of indicators for time sequence concerns is known as **time-lapse statistics**. These statistics provide data on the average length of time that expires between various phases in the recruitment process. Organizations should routinely collect these data in order to assist managers in planning when vacancies are to be filled.

Number of Contacts

The pool of applicants to be selected almost always needs to be larger than the number of applicants that will be hired eventually. Some applicants who are contacted may not be interested in the position, and others may not be qualified.

It is very difficult to identify the exact number of contacts needed to fill a particular vacant position. However, historical data are very useful in establishing the targeted number of contacts. If careful records are kept, then yield ratios can be calculated to summarize the historical data and

EXHIBIT 5.9 Personnel Requisition

Position title	Division	Department	Department #
Salary/grade level	Work hours	Location	Reports to

Position eligible for the following incentive programs	Budgeted
☐ Sales commission ☐ Key contributor ☐ Production incentive ☐ Other (specify) ☐ Management incentive ☐ ________	☐ Yes ☐ No ☐ Replacement for: ________ Transfer/term date ________ ☐ Addition to staff

POSITION OVERVIEW

Instructions: (1) Complete Parts I, II, and III. (2) Attach position description questionnaire (if available) or complete reverse side.

I. POSITION PURPOSE: Briefly state in one or two sentences the primary purpose of this position.

II. POSITION QUALIFICATIONS: Lists the minimum education, formal training, and experience required to perform this position.

III. SPECIAL SKILLS: Lists the specialized clerical, administrative technical, or managerial skills needed to perform this position.

Do current or previous incumbents possess these qualifications and skills? If no, please describe the reason for these requirements when hiring for this position.

APPROVALS	FOR HUMAN RESOURCES USE ONLY
Party responsible for conducting second interview	Posting date ____ Advertising date ____
________ Hiring supervisor/manager Date	Req number ____ Job number ____
________ Next approval level Date	Acceptance date ____ Start date ____
________ Human resources approval Date	New employee ________
	Source ________

Source: Reprinted with pemission from United Health Care Corporation.

to guide decisions about the number of contacts to make. A yield ratio expresses the relationship of applicant inputs to outputs at various decision points. For example, if 90 people were contacted (as identified by the number of resumés submitted) to fill one position, then the yield ratio would be 90:1. To fill two identical positions, it would be necessary to contact 180 applicants, based on the historical yield ratio of 90:1.

Types of Contacts

The types of contacts to be made depend on two factors. First, it is essential that the qualifications needed to perform the job are clearly established. This is done through the process of job analysis, which results in the job requirements matrix. The more clearly these requirements are specified, the fewer the number of applicants who must be contacted to yield a successful candidate, and the narrower the recruitment search can be.

Second, consideration must be given to the job search and choice process used by applicants. That is, the organization must be aware of where likely applicants search for employment opportunities and what it will take to attract them to the organization. One consistent finding in the research is that job seekers are more likely to find out about jobs through friends and family than they are through employment agencies. Another consistent finding in the research is that job seekers rely heavily upon advertisements.

How proactive the organization should be in soliciting applicants is a policy issue that arises when deciding on the types of contacts the organization will make. Some organizations spend very few resources identifying contacts and actively soliciting applicants from these sources. For example, many times grocery stores simply post a job opening in their store window to fill a vacancy. Other organizations, however, are very proactive in making their presence known in the community. Many organizations are becoming involved with educational institutions through scholarships, adopt-a-school programs, mentorships, equipment grants, internships, and career planning services. NASA has programs to help educate teachers, students, and administrators on the application of science and math.[25] These approaches are likely to build goodwill toward an organization in the community and, as a result, foster greater informal contacts with job applicants.

Research has shown that greater employer involvement with prospective applicants is likely to improve the image of the organization. In turn, a better image of the organization is likely to result in prospective applicants pursuing contact with the organization.[26]

Recruitment Budget

The Conference Board of Canada calculates the estimated costs of turnover, including administrative, lost productivity, training, and other costs, is approximately $30,000 per employee.[27] When assessing the time spent by HR recruiters and departmental managers, advertising costs, equipment and supplies needed to set up a new employee, learning curve, training, loss in productivity, and so on, the hiring process can cost about 30 percent of a position's salary.[28] As a result of these high costs, many organizations are currently using cost containment programs in their recruitment efforts. Examples include the elimination of display advertising, greater reliance on government employment agencies, and the reduction of on-campus visits for college recruitment.[29] An example of a recruitment budget is shown in Exhibit 5.10.

The high costs of recruitment also point to the importance of establishing a well-developed recruitment budget. Two issues need to be addressed in establishing a recruitment budget. First, a top-down or a bottom-up procedure can be used to gather the information needed to formulate the budget. With a top-down approach, the budget for recruitment activities is set by top management on the basis of the business plan for the organization and on the basis of projected revenues. With a bottom-up approach, the budget for recruitment activities is set up on the basis of the specific needs of each business unit. The former approach works well when the emphasis is on controlling costs. The latter approach works better when commitment to the budget by business unit heads is the goal. A cumbersome, yet useful, method is to combine these two approaches into program-oriented budgeting in which there is heavy involvement in the budgeting process by both top management and business unit leaders.

A second issue that needs to be addressed in establishing a well-developed recruitment budget is to decide whether to charge recruitment costs to business unit users. That is, should

EXHIBIT 5.10 Example of a Recruitment Budget for 500 New Hires

Administrative Expenses	
Staff	32,000
Supplies	45,000
Equipment	10,000
	$87,000
Recruiter Expenses	
Salaries	240,000
Benefits	96,000
Expenses	150,000
	$486,000
Candidate Expenses	
Travel	320,000
Lodging	295,000
Fees	50,000
Relocation	150,000
	$815,000

Total Recruitment Expenses

87,000 + 486,000 + 815,000 = $1,388,000

Total Cost per Hire

$1,388,000/500 new hires = $2,776

recruitment expenses be charged to HR or to the business unit using HR services? Most organizations charge the HR department for the costs of recruitment rather than the business unit users of recruitment activities. Perhaps this is done to encourage each business unit to use the recruitment services of the HR group. However, it should be recognized that this practice of not charging the business unit may result in the business unit users not being concerned about minimizing recruitment costs.

Development of a Recruitment Guide

recruitment guide
A formal document that details the process to be followed to attract applicants to a job

A **recruitment guide** is a formal document that details the process to be followed to attract applicants to a job. It should be based on the organization's staffing flowcharts, if available. Included in the guide are details such as the time, money, and staff required to fill the job as well as the steps to be taken to do so. An example of a recruitment guide is shown in Exhibit 5.11.

Although a recruitment guide takes time to produce—time that may be difficult to find in the face of an urgent requisition to be filled—it is an essential document. It clarifies expectations for both the recruiter and the requesting department as to what will be accomplished, what the costs are, and who will be held accountable for the results. It also clarifies the steps that need to be taken to ensure that they are all followed in a consistent fashion and in accordance with organization policy as well as relevant laws and regulations. In short, a recruitment guide safeguards the interests of the employer, applicant, and recruiter.

Process Flow and Record Keeping

Prior to deciding where and how to look for applicants, it is essential that the organization prepare for the high volume of data that accompanies the filling of vacancies. This high volume of data results from the use of multiple sources to identify candidates (e.g., advertisements, walk-ins,

EXHIBIT 5.11 Recruitment Guide for Director of Claims

Position: Director, Claims Processing

Reports to: Senior Director, Claims Processing

Qualifications: 4-year degree in business;
8 years experience in health care, including 5 in claims, 3 of which should be in management

Relevant labour market: Atlantic Canada

Timeline: week of 1/17: Conduct interviews with qualified applicants
2/1/07: Targeted hire date

Activities to undertake to source well-qualified candidates:

Regional newspaper advertising

Post job opening on company Web site

Request employee referrals

Contact regional health and life insurance associations

Call HR departments of regional health and life insurance companies to see if any are outplacing any middle managers

Contact, if necessary, executive recruiter to further source candidates

Staff members involved:
HR Recruiting Manager
Sr. Director, Claims Processing
V.P. Human Resources
Potential peers and direct reports

Budget:
$3,000–$5,000

employment agencies), the need to circulate the applicant's credentials to multiple parties (e.g., hiring managers, human resources), and the need to communicate with candidates regarding the status of their application. If **process flow and record keeping** issues are not addressed before the recruitment search, then the organization may become overwhelmed with correspondence that is not dealt with in a timely and professional manner; in turn, the organization may lose well-qualified applicants.

process flow and record keeping
An effective information system that allows the candidate, hiring manager, and HR representative to know the status of the candidate's application file at any point in time

To manage the process flow and record keeping requirements, an information system must be created for recruitment efforts. An effective information system for recruitment purposes allows the candidate, hiring manager, and HR representatives to know the status of a candidate's application file at any point in time. The information system tracks the status of the applicant's file as it flows through the recruitment process in the organization. The information system can also periodically issue reports on the timeliness and accuracy with which applicant information is being processed.

The process of managing data and records has been transformed by online applications. Indeed, one might characterize it as a double-edged sword. On the one hand, data entry and record maintenance is facilitated in that applications are immediately transferred into a standardized database, which eliminates data entry and keeps everything in a standard form and a searchable database. On the other hand, using online applications generates much more data, including many applications from individuals who are poorly motivated to join the organization or obviously unqualified for the position, so there is much more data to wade through.

As the applicant progresses through the hiring process, additional record keeping is required. Information needs to be kept as to who has reviewed the file, how long each has had the file to be reviewed, what decision has been reached (e.g., reject, invite for a visit, conduct a second interview), and what step needs to be taken next (e.g., arrange for a flight and accommodations, schedule an interview). Throughout the process, communications with the applicant must also be tracked to ensure that applicants know when and if their credentials will receive further review and also to know what other steps, if any, they need to take to secure employment.

Even when an applicant is rejected for a position, there are record keeping responsibilities. The applicant's file should be stored in the event that another search arises that requires someone with the applicant's qualifications. Such storage should be for a maximum of one year.

STRATEGY DEVELOPMENT

Once the recruitment planning phase is complete, the next phase is the development of a strategy. In essence, strategy development helps assess those issues fundamental to the organization: open versus targeted recruitment, recruitment sources, choice of sources, and when to look. Each of these issues will be addressed in turn.

Open versus Targeted Recruitment

Once a requisition has been received, one of the most difficult aspects of recruitment is knowing where to look for applicants. In theory, the pool of potential job applicants is the eligible labour force (employed, unemployed, discouraged workers, new labour force entrants, and labour force re-entrants). In practice, the organization must narrow down this vast pool into segments or strata of workers believed to be the most desirable applicants for the organization. To do so, organizations can use open or targeted recruitment methods.

open recruitment
A passive recruiting approach where a wide net is cast and very little effort is made in segmenting the market into applicants with the most desirable KSAOs

Open Recruitment With an **open recruitment** approach, organizations cast a wide net to identify potential applicants for specific job openings. Very little effort is made in segmenting the market into applicants with the most desirable KSAOs. This approach is very passive in that anyone can apply for an opening. All who apply for a position are considered regardless of their qualifications. The advantage to an open recruitment method is that applicants often see it as being "fair" in that everyone has the opportunity to apply. Open recruitment helps ensure that a diverse set of applicants—including disabled, minority youth, former retirees, and often-overlooked employee groups are given a fair shot at being considered.[30] Another advantage of open recruitment is that it is useful—perhaps even essential—when large numbers of applicants must be hired. The disadvantage to this approach is that qualified applicants may be overlooked as no concerted effort is made to identify those markets with the most qualified applicants.

targeted recruitment
Recruiting approach where the organization identifies segments in the labour market where qualified candidates are likely to be

Targeted Recruitment A **targeted recruitment** approach is one whereby the organization identifies segments in the labour market where qualified candidates are likely to be. Often, this is done to find applicants with specific characteristics pertinent to the person/job or person/organization match.

What are some of the objects of targeted recruitment? Below is a list of targeted recruitment groups (of course these categories are not mutually exclusive):

- **Key KSAO shortages:** Here, the objective is to identify applicants with specific new areas of knowledge or "hot" skills.
- **Workforce diversity gaps:** Often, one must go beyond open recruitment to reach diverse groups and make special efforts (e.g., women managers).

- **Passive job seekers or noncandidates:** Sometimes excellent candidates can be found in "trailing spouses" or other dual-career couples.
- **Employment discouraged:** This category includes long-term unemployed, homemakers, welfare recipients, teenagers, and people with disabilities.
- **Reward seekers:** These candidates are attracted to the organization's employee value proposition, such as flexible work schedules or fully paid health care.
- **Former employees:** Consider those with good track records while they were employees.
- **Reluctant applicants:** Some individuals may have an interest in an organization, but are conflicted; research shows that flexible work arrangements may help attract such conflicted individuals.[31]

Making the Choice The choice between open and targeted recruitment is important as it dictates recruiting methods and sources. This is not to suggest that they necessarily achieve different goals. Targeted recruitment can achieve the same ends of inclusion as open recruitment, though by a different mechanism. Whereas open recruitment achieves inclusiveness by encouraging everyone to apply, targeted recruitment may actually seek out particular groups. In theory, open and targeted recruitment can be used in combination. For example, an organization may encourage all applications by posting jobs on its Web site and advertising broadly, while still making special efforts to reach certain populations. Of course, by seeking out one group, one may in a way exclude another from the same consideration. So, before targeted recruitment is undertaken, the organization needs to carefully consider the groups to target, as well as the job skills necessary to perform the job(s) in question. Similarly, before open recruitment is selected, the organization needs to decide whether they are prepared to handle and fairly consider the large number of applications that may flow in.

Recruitment Sources

1.2

recruitment sources

Institutions that act as intermediaries between the applicant and the employer to ensure that a match takes place

Fortunately for employers, when conducting a search for applicants, they do not have to identify each possible job applicant. Instead, there are institutions in our economy where job seekers congregate. Moreover, these institutions often act as intermediaries between the applicant and employer to ensure that a match takes place. These institutions are called **recruitment sources**, or methods in staffing. Some are very conventional and have been around for a long time. Others are more innovative and have less of a track record.

Unsolicited It is a common practice for employers to accept applications from job applicants who physically walk into the organization to apply for a job or who send in resumés. The usual point of contact for unsolicited walk-ins or resumé senders is the receptionist in smaller organizations and the employment office in larger organizations. When applications are accepted, a contact person who is responsible for processing such applicants needs to be assigned. Space needs to be created for walk-ins to complete application blanks and pre-employment tests. Hours need to be established when applicants can apply for jobs. Procedures must be in place to ensure that data from walk-ins and resumé senders are entered into the applicant process flow. If walk-ins or resumé senders are treated as being unexpected intruders, they may communicate a very negative image about the organization in the community.

Increasingly, unsolicited applications are received electronically. The primary transmission portal for electronic applications is via a company's Web site. When receiving electronic applications, organizations need to make sure that they don't get "lost in the system." They need to be regularly forwarded to recruiters or selection decision makers, and those who applied need to be contacted about the disposition of their application.

Employee Referrals Employees currently working for an employer are a valuable source for finding job applicants. The vast majority of organizations accept referrals, though only about half have formal programs. SRA International has recruited nearly half of its employees through referrals. The employees can refer people they know to their employer for consideration. In some organizations, a cash bonus is given to employees who refer job candidates who prove to be successful on the job for a given period of time. To ensure that there are adequate returns on bonuses for employee referrals, it is essential that there be a good performance appraisal system in place to measure the performance of the referred new hire. There also needs to be a good applicant tracking system to ensure that new hire performance is maintained over time before a bonus is offered. Other organizations use more creative incentives. Referral bonuses can range from $500 to $2,000 per employee hired. The organization can save significant costs by shortening the hiring cycle and not having to advertise or use external recruiter.[32]

Referral programs have many potential advantages, including low cost/hire, high-quality hires, decreased hiring time, and an opportunity to strengthen the bond with current employees. Employee referral programs sometimes fail to work because current employees lack the motivation or ability to make referrals. Employees sometimes don't realize the importance of recruitment to the organization. As a result, the organization may need to encourage employee participation by providing special rewards and public recognition along with bonuses for successful referrals. Employees may not be able to match people with jobs because they do not know about open vacancies or the requirements needed to fill them. Hence, communications regarding job vacancies and the requirements needed to fill these vacancies need to be constantly provided to employees.

Employee Networks Though not a formal referral program, many organizations use networks to identify potential hires. These networks can be one's own network of personal contacts, or they can be formal programs that keep an active database of professional contacts. The Human Resources Professional Association of Ontario has a career management centre, which provides members with access to human resource job postings and offers employers an opportunity to post their HR positions.

A relatively new way of finding applicants is through social networking, where friends or acquaintances are used to connect those looking for applicants to those looking for jobs. At Friendster.com, for example, you might sign up for the service by filling out a form and linking that form to all of your friends. When your friends do the same thing, Friendster.com claims that if 100 friends do this, you'll have 800,000 people with whom you can connect. Although it's unlikely that these networks will replace traditional networks, increasingly in an electronic age, it would seem to pay to be connected to others in this way.[33]

Advertisements A convenient way to attract job applicants is to write an ad that can be placed in newspapers, trade journals, and the like. Advertisements can also be recorded and placed on radio or television. Cable television channels, for example, sometimes have "job shows." Advertisements can be very costly and need to be monitored closely for yield. Advertisements in some periodicals may yield more and better qualified candidates than others. By carefully monitoring the results of each ad, the organization can then make a more informed decision as to which ads should be run next time a position is vacant. To track ads, each ad should be coded to assess the yield. Then, as resumés come into the organization in response to the ad, they can be recorded, and the yield for that ad can be calculated.

Coding an ad is a very straightforward process. For example, in advertising for a vice president of human resources, ads may be placed in a variety of HR periodicals, such as *Canadian HR Reporter,* and in national newspapers, such as *The Globe and Mail.* To track responses sent, applicants for the vacant position are asked to respond to the "Human Resource Department A" for *Canadian HR Reporter* and to the "Human Resource Department B" for *The Globe and Mail.* (The rest of the mailing address is, of course, the same for each publication.) As resumés arrive, those that are addressed to Department A are coded as responses from *Canadian HR Reporter,* and those addressed to Department B are coded as responses from *The Globe and Mail.*

Recruiting Online Recent surveys indicate that 85 percent of recruiters utilize the Internet to source job candidates and 91 percent of *Fortune*'s Global 500 have an online job page on their corporate Web sites. Likewise, most applicants for professional jobs now include the Internet in their job search repertoire. Millions of job seekers submit their resumés on the Web every year, and there are tens of thousands of job sites online. More than half of the resumés Microsoft receives are over the Internet. One difficulty in use of the Internet in recruiting is that many sites specifically designed for recruitment become defunct. Conversely, new recruitment Web sites come online on nearly a daily basis. Thus, one cannot assume that the recruiting sites used in the past will be the best ones in the future, or that they even will exist, and it is common for one site to poach resumés on another site. A growing problem for applicants is identity theft, where fake jobs are posted online in order to obtain vital information on a person, or to extract a fake fee.

There are four primary ways companies use the Web for recruiting: job postings on job boards, searching Web-based applicant databases, job postings on an organization's own Web site, and mining databases. Each of these is described below.

Job Postings on Internet Job Boards. One central means of recruiting on the Internet is through online job boards. For example, Monster.ca allows access both to applicants, who can search for positions by location and job category, and to recruiters, who can search among applicants by a wide array of search factors. Most of these boards are collection nodes for job postings, listing the jobs from many different companies that applicants can assess. Other systems focus on resumé screening and applicant management. Still other systems are a combination of the two. For example, Knighthunter.com allows organizations to search a private candidate pool as well as a large resumé database, create and approve job requisitions online, manage recruiting tasks, track the progress of open positions and candidates, and report on recruiting metrics (time-to-hire, cost per hire).

Organizations need to ensure that they not only post jobs on the large boards such as Monster.ca, but also smaller boards that may be targeted by occupation (there are job boards for jobs ranging from nurses to geologists to metal workers), by industry (sports, chemicals), or by location (cities, provinces, or regions often have their own sites). For example, the Engineering Institute of Canada (www.eic-ici.ca) is an engineering recruitment clearinghouse. Increasingly, job boards are targeting blue-collar jobs as well, including the Government of Canada's Job Bank (www.jobbank.gc.ca).

The job board business has become increasingly competitive. The two biggest companies—Workopolis (www.workopolis.ca) and Monster (www.monster.ca)—continue to slug it out. Workopolis is a unique and complementary partnership of three Canadian media companies—*The Globe and Mail* division of Bell Globemedia; Toronto Star Newspapers Ltd.; and Gesca Ltd., the newspaper publishing subsidiary of Power Corporation of Canada—allowing it to link to job ads in many newspapers. Yahoo! Hot Jobs (www.hotjobs.ca) is yet another competitor, with its advantage of being linked to the second-most popular Web browser. How this intense competition will affect companies and applicants is unclear, although since both parties are customers to job boards, one might expect better deals and better service.

Searching Web-Based Databases. As opposed to actively posting jobs online, another (but not mutually exclusive) means of recruiting on the Web is to search for applicants without ever having posted a position. Under this process, applicants submit their resumés online, which are then forwarded to employers when they meet the employer's criteria. Such systems allow searching the databases according to various search criteria, such as job skills, years of work experience, education, major, grade-point average, and so forth. It costs applicants anywhere from nothing to $200 or more to post their resumé or other information on the databases. For organizations, there is always a cost. The exact nature of the cost depends both on the database(s) to which the organization subscribes, and on the services requested. More databases allow organizations to search according to Boolean logic. For example, a recruiter interested in locating resumés of prospective human resource managers for a Calgary-based manufacturing facility might type "human resources + Calgary + manufacturing." One potential pitfall is that online job candidates are not a random sample of the population—the most common user is a young while male. So passive searching may not achieve a sufficiently diverse set of candidates.[34]

Exhibit 5.12 provides a listing of some Web-based systems that employers can use. Many of these combine the features of Internet job boards and Web-based databases so that employers can post jobs and search existing resumés at the same time. For example, though not listed in the exhibit, many Web browsers contain multipurpose databases. Yahoo! Hot Jobs (www.hotjobs.ca) maintains a career centre that contains more than 2.5 million resumés and allows employers to post jobs, which then are fed into a database of thousands of jobs posted weekly.

Job Postings on Organization's Web Site. Most large companies have a special section on their Web sites that describes employment opportunities in the organization and often provides formal job postings. Many of these Web sites allow applicants to apply online. Although surveys reveal that most employers believe their Web sites do a better job of attracting applicants than using job boards,[35] these Web sites do not live up to potential. They have been likened to little more than post office boxes where applicants can send their resumés. Many applicants receive no

EXHIBIT 5.12 List of Recruiting Web Sites

www.workpolis.ca
Assists employers in achieving their recruitment goals by maintaining a database of approximately 40,000 resumés. The Web site presents job posting, job distribution, resumé collection and management, and candidate searching and tracking. Applicants can post resumés and search for positions.

www.monster.ca
Allows job seekers to post their resumés and search a database of roughly 25,000 job postings. Applicants can find a job by field or by region on the site. It also contains a career centre that includes career advice that ranges from finding a new job to retaining one.

www.canjobs.com
Provides the opportunity for employers to list job openings regionally and for candidates to search for openings only in the cities and provinces in which they wish to work. The site also provides job searching advice for applicants.

www.jobboom.com
Offers services in both English and French and is Quebec's largest recruiting site. The site has more the 1,500 job postings in IT, engineering, accounting and finance, administrative support, sales, customer service, and multimedia. Employers can post openings on electronic billboards or send them directly via e-mail to selected applicants.

www.jobbank.gc.ca
Allows applicants to search thousands of job postings across Canada by job title, keyword, province, or region. Up to 2,000 new jobs are posted each day and up to 40,000 job postings can be accessed at a time. Employers can manage their own job advertisements to receive a list of qualified candidates.

www.hotjobs.ca
Offers to job seekers a place to post resumés, and to organizations a place to post job openings. Provides job tips and career advice. Includes Resumix Internet recruiter, which allows employers to post jobs that will be referred to job posting sites viewed by job seekers.

www.charityvillage.com
Presents approximately 3,000 new pages of jobs, information, and news for job seekers who are looking for opportunities in the non-profit secto. More than 6,000 organizations have advertised over 36,000 jobs at Charity Village.

www.cooljobscanada.com
Allows organizations to post job openings in the hospitality and retail sectors. Applicants can post resumés and search database by major resort centres.

more than an automated reply.[36] A study of the best practices of the Web sites of 140 high-profile organizations indicates seven features for high-impact Web sites:

1. A site layout that is easily navigated and provides information about the organization's culture
2. "Job cart" function that allows prospective applicants to search and apply for multiple positions within the organization
3. Resumé builders where applicants can easily submit their education, background, and experience
4. Detailed information on career opportunities
5. Clear graphics
6. Personal search engines that allow applicants to create profiles in the organization's database and update the data later
7. Self-assessment inventories to help steer college graduates toward appealing career paths

Some companies are turning to Web logs, or "blogs," as a more informal and personal method of hiring applicants. Such blogs may include photos of the company's softball team, employee reports on interview with a recent hire, and so forth. We have more to say on organizational Web sites in the "Communication Medium" section, later in this chapter.

Mining Databases. Though controversial, as noted earlier, many recruiters use various ploys (e.g., "flipping" and "peeling") to mine organizational and other databases to obtain intelligence on passive candidates. The power of this strategy is that it allows organizations to identify passive candidates who may be the best qualified but otherwise might not surface. The disadvantage is that many of these passive candidates may not be interested, and there are ethical issues to consider as well. (How would you feel about a competitor "x-raying" your Web site for information you never intended for them to have?)

Advantages and Disadvantages of Recruiting Online. Web-based recruiting offers many advantages to employers. There is no other method of reaching as many people with a job posting. This advantage is particularly important when filling large numbers of positions, when the labour market is national or international, or when the unique nature of the necessary qualifications requires casting a wide net. Furthermore, Web-based recruiting provides faster access to candidates. Most databases have resumés in their system within 24 hours of receipt (many nearly instantaneously), and these searchable databases facilitate access to candidates with desired qualifications. It is commonly argued that Internet recruiting presents cost advantages, and if one is comparing the cost of an ad in the *National Post* with the price for access to an online database, this is no doubt true. For a small organization seeking to hire a small number of applicants or for low-skilled positions, however, they likely can find a qualified applicant with less expense. Finally, there is administrative convenience where many individuals in the same organization can access the database. It also eliminates "paper pushing."

Some of the past limitations of Web-based recruiting—specifically, that the vast majority of applicants are in the technology area and that most Web users are white males—seem to be improving. On the other hand, recruiting on the Web is not a magical solution for matching applicants to employers. Despite some claims to the contrary, decision makers need to be involved in the process. In fact, some large organizations have created new positions for individuals to manage the Internet sites and databases. It is important to remember that no matter what lofty promises a system makes for screening out undesirable applicants, the system is only as good as the search criteria, which generally make fairly rough cuts (e.g., based on years of experience, educational background, broad areas of expertise). Like all sources, the Web must be evaluated against other alternatives to ensure that it is delivering on its considerable promise, and employers must remember that, for the time being, it is unlikely that the Web can be a sole source for recruiting applicants. The costs of Internet recruiting must be weighed against the benefits, including the number of qualified applicants, the relative quality of these applicants, and other criteria such as offer acceptance rates, turnover, and so forth.[37]

Colleges, Universities, and Placement Offices Colleges and universities are a source of people with specialized skills for professional positions. Most colleges and universities have a placement office or officer who is in charge of ensuring that a match is made between the employer's interests and the graduating student's interests.

In most cases, the placement office is the point of contact with colleges and universities. It should be noted, however, that not all students use the services of the placement office. Students sometimes avoid placement offices because they believe they will be competing against the very best students and will be unlikely to receive a job offer. Additional points of contact for students include individual professors, department heads, professional fraternities, honour societies, recognition societies, and national professional societies.

The first decision an employer needs to make is which colleges and universities are to be targeted for recruiting efforts. This choice often is a difficult one. Some companies, such as Shell, are narrowing their list of schools. Whereas Shell used to recruit at 84 colleges and universities, today they recruit at only 26. Why the change? Rather than cast a broad net, Shell is trying to focus its efforts on schools with the best return on investment (ROI), and invest in those programs more heavily. GE focuses its recruiting efforts on only 35 schools.

Other organizations, especially large organizations with relatively high turnover, find they need to cast a much broader net. In the end, the decision of breadth versus depth comes down to the number of individuals who need to be hired, the recruiting budget, and a strategic decision about whether to invest deeply in a few programs or more broadly in more programs.

The next decision to be made is which colleges and universities to target. Some factors to consider include the following:[38]

1. **History:** Past experiences with students at the school, including the quality of recent hires (measured in terms of performance and turnover), offer acceptance rates, and skills, experience, and training in the areas of applicants in areas where job openings exist, should all be factored in.
2. **Rankings of school quality:** *Maclean's, The Gorman Report,* and *Peterson's Guide* all offer comprehensive rankings of colleges and universities and various degree programs. *Business Week, The Wall Street Journal,* and *The Financial Times* provide rankings of business schools. Care must be exercised in judging these reports. Often, they are little more than beauty contests that reflect the prestige of the university. Applicants recruited from highly ranked programs almost always come at a premium, so organizations need to make sure they are getting a good return on their investment. If one wishes to recruit at Simon Fraser, York, or McGill, for example, competition is likely to be fierce, which usually leads to higher starting salaries and fewer offers being accepted.
3. **Costs:** Costs of recruiting at a particular school must be assessed. Colleges and universities that are nearby often mean substantially less resources expended on travel (both for recruiters traveling to the school and for bringing applicants in for interviews).

Employment Agencies A source of employees is employment agencies. These agencies contact, screen, and present applicants to employers for a fee. The fee is contingent on successful placement of a candidate with an employer and is a percentage (around 25%) of the candidate's starting salary. During difficult economic periods, employers cut back on the use of these agencies and/or attempt to negotiate lower fees in order to contain costs.

Care must be exercised in selecting an employment agency. It is a good idea to check the references of employment agencies with other organizations that have already used their services. Allegations abound regarding the shoddy practices of some of these agencies. They may, for example, flood the organization with resumés. Unfortunately, this flood may include both qualified and unqualified applicants. A good agency will screen out unqualified applicants and not attempt to dazzle the organization with a large volume of resumés.

Poor agencies may misrepresent the organization to the candidate and the candidate to the organization. Misrepresentation may take place when the agency is only concerned about a quick placement (and fee) without regard to the cost of poor future relationships with clients. A good agency will be in business for the long run and not misrepresent information and invite turnover. Poor agencies may pressure managers to make decisions when they are uncertain or do not want to do so. Also, they may "go around" the HR staff in the organization to negotiate "special deals" with individual managers. Special deals may result in paying higher fees than agreed on with HR and overlooking qualified minorities and women. A good agency will not pressure managers, make special deals, or avoid the HR staff. Finally, it is important to have a signed contract in place where mutual rights and responsibilities are laid out.

Executive Search Firms For higher-level professional positions or jobs with salaries of $100,000 and higher, executive search firms, or headhunters, may be used. Like employment agencies, these firms contact, screen, and present resumés to employers. The difference between employment agencies and search firms lies in two primary areas. First, search firms typically deal with higher-level positions than employment agencies. Second, search firms are more likely to operate on the basis of a retainer rather than a contingency. Search firms that operate on a retainer are paid regardless of whether a successful placement is made. The advantage of operating this way, from the hiring organization's standpoint, is that it aligns the interests of the search firm with those of the organization. Thus, search firms operating on retainer do not feel compelled to put forward candidates just so their contingency fee can be paid. Moreover, a search firm on retainer may be less likely to give up if the job is not filled in a few weeks.

Whether contracting with a search firm on a contingency or retainer basis, companies cannot take a completely hands-off approach to the recruitment process; they need to keep tabs on the progress of the search and, if necessary, "light a fire" under search firms. To expedite the search process, some companies are going online. Monster.ca's Web site has an area that caters to executives. Other executive-oriented Web sites where employers can post positions are 6figurejobs.com and ExecuNet.com. A disadvantage of most online databases is that they do not include passive candidates—executives who may be highly qualified for the position but who are not actively looking.

Professional Associations and Meetings Many technical and professional organizations have annual meetings around the country at least once a year. Many of these groups run a placement service for their members. There may be a fee to recruit at these meetings. This source represents a way to attract applicants with specialized skills or professional credentials. Also, some meetings represent a way to attract women and minorities. In addition to having placement activities at annual conventions, professional associations also may have a placement function throughout the year. For example, it is a common practice in professional association newsletters to advertise both positions available and interested applicants. Others may also have a computerized job and applicant bank.

Outplacement Services Some organizations retain an outplacement firm to provide assistance to employees who are losing their jobs. Outplacement firms usually offer job seekers assistance in the form of counselling and training to help facilitate a good person/job match. Most large outplacement firms have job banks, which are computerized listings of applicants and their qualifications. Registration by employers to use these job banks is usually free.

Larger organizations experiencing a downsizing may have their own internal outplacement function and perform the activities traditionally found in external outplacement agencies. They may also hold in-house job fairs. The reason for this in-house function is to save on the costs of using an external outplacement firm and to build the morale of those employees who remain with the organization and are likely to be affected by their friends' loss of jobs.

Community Agencies Some agencies in local communities may also provide outplacement assistance for the unemployed who cannot afford outplacement services. Community agencies may also offer counselling and training.

Job Fairs Professional associations, schools, employers, the military, and other interested organizations hold career or job fairs to attract job applicants. Typically, the sponsors of a job fair will meet in a central location with a large facility in order to provide information, collect resumés, and screen applicants. Often, there is a fee for employers to participate. Job fairs may provide both short- and long-term gains. In the short run, the organization may identify qualified applicants. In the long run, it may be able to enhance its visibility in the community, which, in turn, may improve its image and ability to attract applicants for jobs.

For a job fair to yield a large number of applicants, it must be advertised well in advance. Moreover, advertisements may need to be placed in specialized publications likely to attract minorities and women. In order for an organization to attract quality candidates from all of those in attendance, the organization must be able to differentiate itself from all the other organizations competing for applicants at the job fair. To do so, giveaway items such as mugs and key chains with company logos can be distributed to remind the applicants of employment opportunities at a particular organization. An even better promotion may be to provide attendees at the fair with assistance in developing their resumés and cover letters.

One strength of job fairs is also a weakness—although a job fair enables the organization to reach many people, the typical job fair has around 1,600 applicants vying for the attention of about 65 employers. Given the ratio of 25 applicants for every employer, the typical contact with an applicant is probably shallow. In response, some employers instead (or also) devote their resources to information sessions geared toward a smaller group of specially qualified candidates. During these sessions, the organization presents information about itself, including its culture, working environment, and career opportunities. Small gifts and brochures are also typically given out. One recent research study showed that applicants who were favourably impressed by an organization's information session were significantly more likely to pursue employment with the organization. Thus, both applicants and employers find information sessions a valuable alternative, or complement, to job fairs.[39]

Increasingly, job fairs are being held online. Most online job fairs have pre-established time parameters. One online recruiting site held a job fair that included 240 participating companies. In these virtual job fairs, recruiters link up with candidates through chat rooms.

Co-ops and Internships Students currently attending school are sometimes available for part-time work. Two part-time working arrangements are co-ops and internships. Under a co-op arrangement, the student works with one employer on an alternating quarter basis. In one quarter the student works full time, and the next quarter, attends school full time. Under an internship arrangement, the student has a continuous period of employment with an employer for a specified period of time. These approaches allow an organization to obtain services from a part-time employee for a short period of time, but they also allow the organization the opportunity to assess the person for a full-time position after graduation. One manager experienced in working with interns commented, "Working with them is one of the best talent-search opportunities available to managers."[40] In turn, interns have better employment opportunities as a result of their experiences.

Not only can the co-ops and interns themselves be a good source of candidates for full-time jobs but they can also be a good referral source. Those with a favourable experience with an employer are more likely to refer others from their schools for jobs. In order for this to occur, the students' experiences must be favourable. To ensure this happens, students should not be treated as cheap commodities. Care must be taken to provide them with meaningful job experiences and with the training necessary to do a good job.

Internships and co-op assignments can take a variety of different forms. One type of assignment is to have the student perform a part of the business that occurs on a periodic basis. For example, amusement parks that operate only in the summer may have a large number of employees who need to be hired and trained in the spring. A student with a background in HR could perform these hiring and training duties. Increasingly, colleges and universities are giving students college credit for, and even in some cases instituting a requirement for, working as a part of their professional degree.[41] A student in social work, for example, might be required to work in a social work setting. Occasionally, experience shows that some internships and co-op assignments do not provide these meaningful experiences that build on the qualifications of the student. Research shows that school-to-work programs often do not provide high utility to organizations in terms of benefit-cost ratios. Thus, organizations need to evaluate co-ops and internships not only in terms of the quality for the student but from a cost-benefit economic perspective as well.[42]

Meaningful experiences benefit both the organization and the student. The organization gains from the influence of new ideas that the student has been exposed to in his or her curriculum, and the student gains from having the experience of having to apply concepts while facing the realities of organizational constraints. For both parties to gain, it is important that a learning contract be developed and signed by the student, the student's advisor, and the corporate sponsor. The learning contract becomes, in essence, a job description to guide the student's activities. Also, it establishes the criteria by which the student's performance is assessed for purposes of grading by the academic advisor and for purposes of successful completion of the project for the organization. In the absence of a learning contract, internships can result in unrealistic expectations by the corporate sponsor, which, in turn, can result in disappointment when these unspoken expectations are not met.

To secure the services of students, organizations can contact the placement offices of high schools, colleges, universities, and vocational technology schools. Also, teachers, professors, and student chapters of professional associations can be contacted to obtain student assistance. Placement officials can provide the hiring organization with the policies that need to be followed for placements, while teachers and professors can give guidance on the types of skills students could bring to the organization and the organizational experiences the students would benefit from the most.

Innovative Sources Several innovative sources might also be experimented with, particularly for purposes of widening the search.

Religious Organizations. These organizations (e.g., churches) provide another source of labour that is often overlooked. Such institutions typically have many senior and teenage human resources. Organizations can attract members by sponsoring events such as socials and by making donations to charitable causes endorsed by them.

Interest Groups. There are many associations that help facilitate the interests of their members. One such group is the Canadian Association for Retired Persons (CARP). For example, Home Depot was partnered with CARP to help fill new positions the company anticipates.

Senior Networks. Many networks have been formed to advance the employment interests of older workers. These networks include Seniors Canada On-line, Retired Worker, Seniors Job Bank, workink.com, and Prime 50. These organizations provide many employment services, such as the training, counselling, and placement of older workers along with programs for employers on how to best utilize the talents of older workers.

Choice of Sources

There is no single best source for recruitment; each source has its strengths and weaknesses. The following criteria can be used to select which sources are most appropriate for each search:

1. **Sufficient quantity and quality:** Some sources, such as advertisements and company Web sites, produce a large number of applicants. Such sources are appropriate when the organization needs a large head count. If a premium is to be placed on high-quality candidates in the recruitment process, then some sources are better than others. If a very high level of KSAOs is required, an executive search firm is helpful. If certain skills are needed, schools that emphasize these skills may be better sources of employees.

2. **Cost.** Some sources, such as newspaper advertisements and search firms, are quite expensive. These methods may be worth the cost if the skill is in short supply or the job is crucial to the organization's success. On the other hand, some organizations simply do not have the resources to devote to expensive recruitment methods, and therefore must get by on relatively inexpensive methods such as networks and passive search strategies.
3. **Past experience with source:** Most organizations will be reluctant to abandon sources that have worked well in the past. Yet organizations also need to guard against inertia and avoid the justification, "Well, we use this source because we always have."
4. **Impact on HR outcomes:** A considerable amount of research has been conducted on the effectiveness of various recruitment sources and can be used as a starting point as to which sources are likely to be effective.[43] Research has defined effectiveness as the impact of recruitment sources on increased employee satisfaction, performance, and retention. The research suggests that overall, referrals, job postings, and rehiring of former employees are the most effective sources, whereas newspaper ads and employment agencies are the least effective.

Unfortunately, this research has focused on the effectiveness of only a few different sources; newer methods such as the Internet are virtually unstudied. Furthermore, as was noted earlier, effectiveness is likely to vary depending on the organization and context. Hence, organizations need to systematically collect their own data to gauge effectiveness and to guide their choice of recruitment sources. For example, organizations may need to code sources to ascertain which ones produce the greatest yield of qualified applicants.

SEARCHING

Once the recruitment planning and strategy development phases are completed, it is time to actively conduct the search. Searching for candidates first requires the development of a message and then the selection of a medium to communicate that message. Each of these phases is considered in turn.

Communication Message

RPC 1.3

Types of Messages To decide which kind of message works best for a candidate search, organizations may consider messages that are realistic, branded, or targeted.

Realistic Recruitment Message. A realistic recruitment message portrays the organization and job as they really are, rather than describing what the organization thinks job applicants want to hear. Organizations continue to describe their organizations in overly positive terms, overstating desired values to applicants such as risk taking, while understating undesirable values such as rules orientation. Some would argue this is not the best message to send applicants on either moral or practical grounds.

realistic job preview
Demonstrates the attributes of the job in specific terms, identifying both the positive and negative aspects of the job, and portraying the organization and the job as they really are

A very well-researched recruitment message is known as a **realistic job preview (RJP)**.[44] According to this practice, job applicants are given a "vaccination" by being told verbally, in writing, or on videotape what the actual job is like.[45] An example of the attributes that might be contained in an RJP is shown in Exhibit 5.13. It shows numerous attributes for the job of elementary school teacher. Note that the attributes are quite specific and that they are both positive and negative. Information like this "tells it like it is" to job applicants.

After receiving the information, job applicants can decide whether they want to work for the organization. The hope with the RJP is that job applicants will self-select into and out of the organization. By selecting into the organization, the applicant may be more committed to working there than they might otherwise have been. When an applicant self-selects out, the organization does not face the costs associated with recruiting, selecting, training, and compensating employees, only to then have them leave because the job did not meet their expectations.

EXHIBIT 5.13 Example of Job Attributes in an RJP for Elementary School Teachers

Positive Job Attributes

Comprehensive benefits are provided.

Innovative teaching strategies are encouraged.

A university is located nearby for taking classes.

There is a large support staff for teachers.

Negative Job Attributes

Salary growth has averaged only 2 percent in past three years.

Class sizes are large.

The length of the school day is long.

Interactions with community have not been favourable.

Increasingly, the Internet is an important source of organizational information that can provide a "realistic culture preview." For example, Coca-Cola's and PepsiCo's Web sites contain very different information about their heritage, culture, diversity, and benefits, as well as more specific job information (see www.coca-cola.com and www.pepsijobs.com).

A great deal of research has been conducted on the effectiveness of RJPs, which appear to lead to somewhat higher job satisfaction and lower turnover. This appears to be true because providing applicants with realistic expectations about future jobs helps them better cope with job demands once they are hired. RJPs also appear to foster the belief in employees that their employer is concerned about them and honest with them, which leads to higher levels of organizational commitment.

RJPs may lead applicants to withdraw from the recruitment process, although a recent review suggests that they have little effect on attrition from the recruitment process. This may appear to be great news to employers interested in using RJPs: providing applicants with realistic information provides employers with more satisfied and committed employees while still maintaining applicant interest in the position. Where the situation may become problematic is when one considers the type of applicant "scared away" by the realistic message. It appears plausible that the applicants most likely to be repelled by the realistic message are high-quality applicants, because they have more options. In fact, research suggests that the negative effects of RJPs on applicant attraction are particularly strong for high-quality applicants (those whose general qualifications are especially strong) and those with direct experience or familiarity with the job.

Although RJPs appear to have both weakly positive (slightly higher job satisfaction and lower turnover among new hires) and negative (slightly reduced ability to hire high-quality applicants) consequences, these outcomes have been found to be affected by a number of factors. A recent review of 40 studies on the effectiveness of RJPs suggested that RJPs had weak effects, but to some extent these effects were affected by a number of factors. The following recommendations can be gleaned from these findings:

- RJPs presented very early in the recruitment process are less effective in reducing post-hire turnover than those presented just before or just after hiring.
- Post-hire RJPs lead to higher post-hire levels of job performance than do RJPs presented before hiring.
- Verbal RJPs tend to reduce turnover more than written or videotaped RJPs.
- RJPs are less likely to lead to turnover when the organization "restricts" turnover for a period of time after the RJP (with contracts, above-market salaries, etc.).

In general, these findings suggest that RJPs should be given verbally (rather than in writing or by showing a videotape) and that it is probably best to reserve their use for later in the recruiting process (RJPs should not be part of the initial exposure of the organization to applicants).[46]

employment brand

A "good company tag" that places the image of "a great place to work" or "employer of choice" in the minds of job candidates

Employment Brand. Organizations wishing to portray an appealing message to potential applicants may develop an employment brand to attract applicants. An **employment brand** is a "good company tag" that places the image of "a great place to work" or "employer of choice" in the minds of job candidates. Under a branding strategy, the Canadian Armed Forces recruiting slogan, "No life like it," emphasizes the opportunities for travel and training as key advantages for enlisting.

One example of an employment brand is being named to *Maclean's* Top 100 Employers list. Being named to this list communicates to applicants that the organization treats its employees fairly, has employees who like their jobs, and offers good benefits. Obviously, this can be an enormous recruiting asset.

Beyond reputation, another employment brand may be value- or culture-based. For example, GE has long promoted its high performance expectations in order to attract achievement-oriented applicants seeking commensurate rewards.

There are several possible benefits to branding. Of course, establishing an attractive employment brand may help attract desired applicants to the organization. Moreover, having an established brand may help retain employees who were attracted to the brand to begin with. Research suggests that identifiable employment brands may breed organizational commitment on the part of newly hired employees.[47]

Research shows that having an employment brand can attract applicants to an organization, even beyond job and organizational attributes. Evidence also suggests that employers are most able to get their brand image out when companies engage in early recruitment activities such as advertising or generating publicity about the company.[48]

targeted messages

Developed to appeal to a particular audience as different audiences may be looking for different rewards from an employer

Targeted Messages. One way to improve upon matching people with jobs is with **targeted messages**. When targeting a recruitment message to a particular audience, organizations recognize that different audiences may be looking for different rewards from an employer. This would appear to be especially true of special applicant populations who may have special needs, such as teenagers, older workers, welfare recipients, people with disabilities, homeless individuals, veterans, and displaced homemakers. Older workers, for example, may be looking for employers who can meet their financial needs (e.g., supplement Canada Pension), security needs (e.g., retraining), and social needs (e.g., place to interact with people). College and university students appear to be attracted to organizations that provide rewards and promotions on the basis of individual rather than group performance. Also, students prefer to receive pay in the form of a salary rather than in the form of incentives.[49]

Choice of Messages The different types of messages—realistic, branded, and targeted—are not likely to be equally effective under the same conditions. Which message to convey depends on the labour market, vacancy characteristics, and applicant characteristics.

If the labour market is tight and applicants are difficult to come by, then realism may not be an effective message, because to the extent that applicants self-select out of the applicant pool, fewer are left for an employer to choose from during an already tight labour market. Hence, if the employment objective is simply to fill job slots in the short run and worry about turnover later, a realistic message will have counterproductive effects. Obviously then, when applicants are in abundance and turnover is an immediate problem, a realistic message is appropriate.

During a tight labour market, branded and targeted messages are likely to be more effective in attracting job applicants. Attraction is strengthened as there are inducements in applying for a job. In addition, individual needs are more likely to be perceived as met by a prospective employer. Hence, the applicant is more motivated to apply to organizations with an attractive or targeted message than those without. During loose economic times when applicants are plentiful, the branded or targeted approaches may be more costly than necessary to attract an adequate supply of labour. Also, they may set up false expectations concerning what life will be like on the job, and thus lead to turnover.

Job applicants have better knowledge about the actual characteristics of some jobs more than others. For example, service sector jobs, such as that of cashier, are highly visible to people. For these jobs, it may be redundant to give a realistic message. Other jobs, such as an outside sales position, are far less visible to people. They may seem very glamorous (e.g., sales commissions) to prospective applicants who fail to see the less glamorous aspects of the job (e.g., a lot of travel and paperwork).

Some jobs seem to be better suited to special applicant groups, and hence, a targeted approach may work well. For example, older employees may have social needs that can be met well by a job that requires a lot of public contact. Organizations, then, can take advantage of the special characteristics of jobs to attract applicants.

The value of the job to the organization also has a bearing on the selection of an appropriate recruitment message. Inducements for jobs of higher value or worth to the organization are easier to justify in a budgetary sense than jobs of lower worth. The job may be of such importance to the organization that it is willing to pay a premium through inducements to attract well-qualified candidates.

Some applicants are less likely than others to be influenced in their attitudes and behaviours by the recruitment message. In a recent study, for example, it was shown that a realistic message is less effective for those with considerable previous job experience.[50] A targeted message does not work very well if the source is seen as being not credible.[51] Inducements may not be particularly effective with applicants who do not have a family or have considerable wealth.

Communication Medium

Not only is the message itself an important part of the recruitment process, so, too, is the selection of a medium to communicate the message. The most common recruitment mediums are recruitment brochures, videos and videoconferencing, advertisements, voice messages, and online services.

Recruitment Brochures A recruitment brochure is usually sent or given directly to job applicants. Information in the brochure may be very detailed, and hence, the brochure may be lengthy. A brochure not only covers information about the job but also communicates information about the organization and its location. It may include pictures in addition to written narrative in order to illustrate various aspects of the job, such as the city in which the organization is located and actual co-workers.

The advantage of a brochure is that the organization controls who receives a copy. Also, it can be more lengthy than an advertisement. A disadvantage is that it can be quite costly to develop this medium.

Developing a brochure can be done inside the organization or by outside media professionals. By developing a brochure in-house, the organization may be able to keep the cost down. However, in-house capabilities may not be very technically advanced, so outside sources may be needed if technical advances are required.

A successful brochure possesses (1) a unique theme or point of view relative to other organizations in same industry and (2) a visual distinctiveness in terms of design and photographs. A good format for the brochure is to begin with a general description of the organization, including its history and its culture (values, goals, brand); include a description of the hiring process; provide a characterization of pay/benefits and performance reviews; and finally conclude with contact information.

Videos and Videoconferencing A video can be used along with the brochure but should not simply replicate the brochure. The brochure should be used to communicate basic facts and information. The video should be used to communicate the culture and climate of the organization. As part of the profile they can highlight characteristics of the city that the organization resides in, such as the climate, housing market, school systems, churches, performing arts, spectator sports, nightlife, and festivals. This profile can be communicated to job seekers via videocassette, diskette, CD-ROM, DVD-ROM, and the Internet.[52] Video diskettes can also be made interactive so that the job seeker can submit an application electronically, request additional information, or even arrange an interview.

A new form of communicating with job applicants is known as videoconferencing.[53] Rather than meeting in person with applicants, organizational representatives meet with applicants in separate locations, face to face on a television monitor. The actual image of the person in action appears on the screen, although the transmission appears to be in slow motion. The technology needed for videoconferencing is expensive, but the costs have decreased in recent years. Moreover, this technology makes it possible for the organization to screen applicants at multiple or remote locations without actually having to travel to these locations. Many college and university placement offices now have the equipment for videoconferencing. The equipment is also available at some FedEx Kinko's copy centres for applicants who do not have access to a placement office.

Advertisements Given the expense of advertising in business publications, ads are much shorter and to the point than are recruitment brochures. As a general rule, the greater the circulation of the publication, the greater the cost of advertising in it.

Ads appear in a variety of places other than business publications. Ads can be found in local, regional, and national newspapers; on television and radio; and in bargain shoppers, door hangers, direct mail, and welcome wagons. Advertisements can thus be used to reach a broad market segment. Although they are brief, there are many different types of ads:[54]

1. **Classified advertisements:** These ads appear in alphabetical order in the "Help Wanted" section of the newspaper. Typically, they allow for very limited type and style selection and are usually only one newspaper column in width. These ads are used most often for the purpose of quick resumé solicitation for low-level jobs at a low cost. Most large- and medium-sized newspapers now place their classified ads online, potentially reaching many more prospective job candidates.
2. **Classified display ads:** A classified display ad allows more discretion in the type that is used and its location in the paper. A classified display ad does not have to appear in alphabetical order and can appear in any section of the newspaper. The cost of these ads is moderate; they are often used as a way to announce openings for professional and managerial jobs. An example of a classified display ad is shown in Exhibit 5.14.
3. **Display ads:** These ads allow for freedom of design and placement in a publication. As such, they are very expensive and begin to resemble recruitment brochures. These ads are typically used when an employer is searching for a large number of applicants to fill multiple openings.
4. **Online ads:** More and more employers are choosing to place ads on the Internet. These ads can take several forms. One form is a clickable banner ad that appears on Web sites visited by likely prospects. Another form of advertising of sorts was reviewed earlier—posting positions using online Web sites such as Monster.ca.

Telephone Messages Though the telephone is hardly new, in times of tight labour markets, many employers resort to phoning prospective job candidates. These can be "cold calls" where the potential recruit's name was gleaned from a list (such as those "peeled" from an organization's Web site), "warm calls" where the prospective candidate was referred to the recruiter, formally or informally, or even "phon-a-thons" where a company advertises it will staff phone lines for a day to hire as many people as possible.

As a result of the latest advances in the telecommunications industry, a recent development in advertising is voice messages. With this approach, the applicant hears information over the

EXHIBIT 5.14 Classified Display Ad for Human Resource Generalist

HUMAN RESOURCE GENERALIST

ABC Health, a leader in the health care industry, currently has a position available for an experienced **Human Resource Generalist.**

As part of the human resources team, the successful candidate will serve as a business partner with our operational departments. Our team prides itself on developing and maintaining progressive and impactful human resources policies and programs.

Qualified candidates for this position will possess a bachelor's degree in business with an emphasis on human resource management, or a degree in a related field, such as industrial psychology. In addition, a minimum of three years of experience as a human resource generalist is required. This experience should include exposure to at least four of the following functional areas: compensation, employment, benefits, training, employee relations, and performance management.

In return for your contributions, we offer a competitive salary as well as comprehensive, flexible employee benefits. If you meet the qualifications and our opportunity is attractive to you, please forward your resumé and salary expectations to:

Human Resource Department
ABC Health
P.O. Box 123
Halifax, NS

An Equal Opportunity/Affirmative Action Employer

phone about job openings. Callers have access to each of the items on the menu by pressing keys on a keypad. If what they hear is of interest to them, they can leave a message in a voicemail box. All applicants receive a return call; if they seem to be qualified for a vacant position, they are invited for an interview.

Organizational Web Sites The Web is somewhat unique in that it may function as both a recruitment source and a recruitment medium. When a Web page only serves to communicate information about the job or organization to potential applicants, it serves as a recruitment medium. However, when a Web page attracts actual applicants, particularly when applicants are allowed to apply online, it also functions as a recruitment source.

It may not be an overstatement to conclude that organizational Web sites have become the single most important medium through which companies communicate with potential applicants. Nearly every large organization has a careers page on its Web site, and many small organizations have company and point-of-contact information for job seekers. Web sites are not only powerful means of communicating information about jobs, but they can also reach applicants who otherwise would not bother (or know how or where) to apply. Thus, care must be taken to ensure that the organizational Web site is appealing to potential job candidates.

The three core attributes driving the appeal of an organizational Web site are engagement, functionality, and content.

- **Engagement:** The Web site must be vivid and attractive to applicants. Some experts have noted that in recruiting Web sites, engagement often takes a back seat.
- **Functional:** The Web site must be functional, meaning that it is quick to load, easily navigated, and interactive. A Web site that is overly complex may be vivid, but it will only generate frustration if it is hard to decipher or slow to load.
- **Content:** An organizational Web site must convey the information prospective applicants would like to see, including current position openings, job requirements, and how to apply. It is important to remember that your communication with an applicant shouldn't end with his or her online application.

TD Bank Financial Group allows applicants to request automatic e-mails delivered when a job becomes available that matches their skills and interests. Kellogg's Canada also allows applicants to set up their own job alert by submitting an e-mail address through which applicants are notified about suitable job opportunities.[55]

One way to ensure that the Web site meets these requirements is to test it with "naïve" users—people who are not from the organization's IT department or recruiting staff. It is critical that the number of clicks is minimized, that the online application process is clear, and that animation and colour are used effectively to engage the prospective applicant. However, it's important not to overdo it. When Coach.com, a leather retailer, removed flash graphics from its Web site, page visits increased by 45 percent.[56]

Of course, there is more to designing an organizational Web site than just the three attributes discussed above. Exhibit 5.15 provides a thorough list of factors to keep in mind when designing a Web site for organizational recruitment.

Radio Another recruitment medium is radio. Companies that advertise on the radio purchase a 30- or 60-second time slot to advertise openings in specific job categories. Choice of radio stations often implicitly targets specific markets. For example, a classical music station is likely to reach a different audience than an alternative rock station. Organizations must take these market differences into account when choosing a statement. Radio stations generally have detailed demographic information available to potential advertisers. The advantage of radio ads is their reach; more people listen to radio than read newspapers.

Statistics Canada reported that the listening habits of Canadians changed significantly between 1995 and 2004, falling by 90 minutes a week on average. On average, Canadians spent 19.5 hours per week listening to radio in 2004. Provincially, Prince Edward Island residents spent the most time listening to the radio, with an average of 21.2 hours per week, followed by Newfoundland and Labrador, Quebec, Saskatchewan, and Alberta. Residents of British Columbia continued to report the lowest radio listening times in the country (17.8 hours per week).[57]

EXHIBIT 5.15 Factors to Keep in Mind in Designing Organizational Web Sites

1. **Keep it simple.** Surveys reveal that potential job candidates are overwhelmed by complex, difficult-to-navigate Web sites. Never sacrifice clarity for "jazziness"—remember that a good applicant is there for content of the Web site, not for the bells and whistles.
2. **Make access easy.** Web page and links should be easy to download. Studies reveal that individuals will not wait more than eight seconds for a page to download, so that four-colour page that looks great will backfire if it takes the user, working from a modem, time to download the page. Also make sure that the link to the recruiting site on the home page is prominently displayed.
3. **Provide an online application form.** Increasingly, potential candidates expect to be able to submit an application online. Online forms are not only desired by candidates, organizations can load them directly into searchable databases.
4. **Provide information about company culture.** Allow applicants to self-select out if their values clearly do not match those of your organization—you wouldn't want them anyway.
5. **Include selected links to relevant Web sites.** The words "selected" and "relevant" are key here; things to include might be a cost-of-living calculator and a career advice area.
6. **Make sure that necessary information is conveyed to avoid confusion.** Clearly specify job title, location, and so on. Make sure that applicants know the job for which they are applying and that, if there are several jobs, they don't apply for the wrong job.
7. **Keep information current.** Make sure that position information is updated regularly (e.g., weekly).
8. **Evaluate and track the results.** Periodically evaluate the performance of the Web site based on various criteria (number of hits, number of applications, application/hits ratio, quality of hires, cost of maintenance, user satisfaction, time to hire, etc.).

One company, for the cost of one ad in a Sunday newspaper, was able to run a 60-second commercial 73 times over three days. To some extent, the relative advantage of radio over newspapers depends on the job market. Help wanted ads are generally read by individuals who are less than perfectly happy with their present positions, or who are unemployed. Thus, in tight labour markets, radio ads are more likely to be heard by people with jobs, who are a likely source of applicants. One limitation with radio ads is that organizations cannot always buy ads when they want to run them if the time spots are already sold (whereas a help wanted section can simply add another page). Another drawback is that they are limited to a local market; thus, they are limited to jobs where the recruitment is confined to local labour markets.[58]

E-Mail It is tempting for organizations to initiate contact with prospective job candidates via e-mail. There is no direct cost, and support staff could send hundreds or even thousands of e-mail messages to prospective job candidates. In the age of spamming, however, it is important to remember that most individuals will regard mass e-mailings with even less enthusiasm than junk mail. To make the most out of e-mail recruitment, it is important to make the messages highly personal, reflecting some understanding of the candidate's unique qualifications.

One form of e-mail recruitment medium is an e-mail autoresponder. E-mail autoresponders are clickable e-mail addresses where prospective job candidates receive (usually within a few seconds) a text description of the position, organization, and so forth. The advantage of this hybrid of Web and e-mail communication is that applicants do not need to wait for the information to load on their computer (often slowly) and they can save the information for later reference. Furthermore, autoresponders can be used to send subsequent e-mails to the individuals who originally requested information, such as when related positions become available.

Some provinces have passed privacy legislation that prohibits businesses to collect, use, or disclose personal information without the knowledge and consent of individuals. Under this definition, an e-mail address is considered to be personal information. Marketers, for example, must obtain consent from individuals before sending them marketing e-mails. Thus companies need to cautious about using e-mail for recruiting purposes so they do not run afoul of the Privacy Act (PIPEDA).

APPLICANT REACTIONS

An important source of information in designing and implementing an effective recruitment system is applicant reactions to the system. Both attitudinal and behavioural reactions to components of the recruitment system are important. Components of this system that have been studied include the recruiter and the recruitment process.

Reactions to Recruiters

Considerable research has been conducted and carefully reviewed on the reactions of job applicants to the behaviour and characteristics of recruiters.[59] The data collected have been somewhat limited by the fact that they focus primarily on reactions to college and university recruiters rather than those outside the college and university environment. Despite this limitation, several key themes emerge in the literature.

First, though the recruiter does indeed influence job applicant reactions, he or she does not have as much influence on them as do actual characteristics of the job. This indicates that the recruiter cannot be viewed as a substitute for a well-defined and communicated recruitment message showing the actual characteristics of the job. It is not enough just to have good recruiters to attract applicants to the organization.

Second, the influence of the recruiter is more likely to be felt in the attitudes rather than the behaviours of the job applicant. That is, an applicant who has been exposed to a talented recruiter is more likely to walk away with a favourable impression of the recruiter than to accept a job on the basis of the interaction with a recruiter. This attitudinal effect is important, however, as it may lead to good publicity for the organization. In turn, good publicity may lead to a larger applicant pool to draw from in the future.

Third, demographic characteristics of the recruiter do not have much impact on applicant reactions, with one exception. Recruiters who are HR specialists do not fare as well in terms of applicant reactions as do line managers. Hence, the common practice of using line managers to recruit and HR people to coordinate recruitment activities appears to be appropriate.

Fourth, two behaviours of the recruiter seem to have the largest influence on applicant reactions. The first is the level of warmth that the recruiter shows toward the job applicant. Warmth can be expressed by being enthusiastic, personable, empathetic, and helpful in dealings with the candidate. The second behaviour is being knowledgeable about the job. This can be conveyed by being well versed with the job requirements matrix and the job rewards matrix. Finally, recruiters who show interest in the applicant are viewed more positively.

Reactions to the Recruitment Process

Only some administrative components of the recruitment process have been shown to have an impact on applicant reactions.[60] First, job applicants are more likely to have favourable reactions to the recruitment process when the screening devices that are used to narrow the applicant pool are seen as job related. That is, the process that is used should be closely related to the content of the job as spelled out in the job requirements matrix.

Second, delay times in the recruitment process do indeed have a negative effect on applicants' reactions. In particular, when long delays occur between the applicant's expression of interest and the organization's response, negative reactions are formed by the applicant. The negative impression formed is about the organization, rather than the applicant him- or herself. For example, with a long delay between an on-site visit and a job offer, an applicant is more likely to believe that something is wrong with the organization rather than with his or her personal qualifications. This is especially true of the better-qualified candidate, who is also likely to act on these feelings by accepting another job offer.

Third, simply throwing money at the recruitment process is unlikely to result in any return. There is no evidence that increased expenditures on the recruitment process result in more favourable attitudes or behaviours by job applicants. For expenditures to pay dividends, they need to be specifically targeted to effective recruitment practices, rather than indiscriminately directed to all practices.

Fourth, the influence of the recruiter on the applicant is more likely to occur in the initial rather than the latter stages of the recruitment process. In the latter stages, actual characteristics of the job carry more weight in the applicant's decision. At the initial screening interview, the recruiter may be the applicant's only contact with the organization. Later in the process, the applicant is more likely to have additional information about the job and company. Hence, the credibility of the recruiter is most critical on initial contact with applicants.

Finally, though little research is available, the increasing use of the Internet in recruitment, and that it is often the applicant's first exposure to an organization, suggests that applicants' reactions to an organization's Web site will increasingly drive their reactions to the organization's recruitment process. A survey revealed that 79 percent of college students and recent graduates indicated that the quality of a prospective employer's Web site was somewhat important (35%) or very important (44%) in their decision of whether or not to apply for a job.

Indeed, studies reveal that applicants are able to locate more relevant jobs on the Internet than in traditional sources such as print media. Moreover, applicants generally like the Internet, provided some provisos are kept in mind. As with general recruiting, perhaps the most important factor is the degree and speed of follow-up. Just as with other forms of recruiting, delays greatly harm the image of the recruiting organization, so organizations need to make sure that online applications are followed up. Also, research shows that job seekers are more satisfied with company Web sites when specific job information is provided and security provisions are taken to preserve the confidentiality of the information submitted. One key assurance is that the company will not share resumés with vendors who will spam applicants with various solicitations.[61]

LEGAL ISSUES

External recruitment practices are subject to considerable legal scrutiny and influence. Through external recruitment job applicants first establish contact with the organization and then become more knowledgeable about job requirements and rewards. During this process, there is ample room for the organization to exclude certain applicant groups (e.g., minorities, women, and people with disabilities), as well as deceive in its dealings with applicants. Various laws and regulations seek to place limits on these exclusionary and deceptive practices.

Legal issues regarding several of the practices are discussed in this section. These include employment equity and diversity programs, human rights and temporary workers, electronic recruiting, and job advertisements.

Employment Equity and Diversity Programs

Employment equity regulations are based on the Employment Equity Act and require organizations within federal jurisdictions to establish placement (hiring and promotion) goals for job groups in which there are disparities between the percentages of women and minorities actually employed and those available for employment. Although private organizations are not regulated by the Employment Equity Act, many private companies have implemented employment equity programs because they make good business sense. These **placement goals** are staffing objectives that should be incorporated into the organization's overall staffing planning. The regulations also require that the organization identify problem areas impeding equal employment opportunity and undertake action-oriented programs to correct these problem areas and achieve the placement goals. While recruitment is mentioned as one of those potential problem areas, the regulations say little else specifically about recruitment activities.

placement goals
Hiring and promotion objectives that should be incorporated into an organization's overall staffing planning

Some suggested actions for improvements to existing equity programs are the following:

- Update job descriptions and ensure their accuracy.
- Widely circulate approved job descriptions to hiring managers and recruitment sources.
- Carefully select and train all personnel included in staffing.
- Encourage woman and minority employees to refer job applicants.
- Include women and minorities on the HR department staff.
- Include minorities and women in recruitment brochures.
- Expand help wanted advertising to include women and minority news media.

Many of the above suggestions focus on developing very specific, targeted external recruitment programs. Examples of targeted recruitment occur within the context of larger human rights programs at employers such as McDonald's and Kentucky Fried Chicken (KFC). McDonald's started its McJobs program for hiring people with disabilities in 1981; it has hired more than 9,000 mentally and physically challenged people since then.

KFC's targeted recruitment program, called the Designates Program, is intended to identify and attract female and minority executives from other companies. It seeks to place or promote these recruits through the managerial ranks into senior-level management positions.

An augmented role for employment equity programs is to increase diversity within an organization's workforce in order to enhance its effectiveness. A successful program will have three main components: a workforce survey and analysis, an employment system review, and an employment equity plan.[62]

Much of staffing focuses on the initial acquisition of people and creation of the initial person/job match. Employment equity programs and, to an extent, organization diversity programs likewise share this emphasis. Once the initial match has occurred, however, the organization must be concerned about employee adaptation to the job, upward job mobility, and maintenance of the employment relationship over time.

Diversity programs arise out of a recognition that the labour force, and thus the organization's workforce, is becoming more demographically and culturally diverse. RBC Financial Group's ability to achieve overall corporate strategies is linked to leveraging diversity within the organization. The RBC value, "diversity for growth and innovation," is practised inclusively with employees, customers, and shareholders.[63] Another major focus of diversity programs is on the assimilation and adaptation of a diverse workforce once it has been acquired. Diversity programs thus may be viewed as a logical continuation of employment equity programs.

Diversity programs lack the legal basis and imperative given to employment equity programs. Instead, they rest on a foundation of a presumed strategic business imperative. The following illustrates that imperative:

> "The big topic these days is integrating diversity into the business .... This means recognizing that diversity is not just a recruitment, retention, and employee development issue, but that the benefits of diversity can extend to marketing, expanding market share, and improving customer loyalty. Companies have been pretty good about recruiting diverse talent, but now, once they get that talent in the door, they are looking for ways to really leverage that diversity. Diversity today has to be a comprehensive strategy. It has to include communication, education, recruitment, and vendor/supplier relationships; all of these need to be coordinated from the top. That comes from having a business sense that diversity is about business performance enhancement."[64]

Little research has been conducted on the effectiveness of diversity programs, but the little available evidence "casts doubt on the simple assertion that a diverse workforce inevitably improves business performance."[65] The looming skill shortage over the next ten years—and employers' ability to compete for highly skilled labour—will hinge on organizations having comprehensive diversity programs. The Government of Canada projects that all labour force growth by 2011 will be through immigration. The Conference Board of Canada estimates that by 2016, visible minorities will represent 20 percent of Canada's population, or 6.6 million people.[66]

Human Rights and Temporary Workers

The Canadian Human Rights Commission has provided guidance on coverage and responsibility requirements for temporary employment agencies (and other types of staffing firms) and their client organizations. When both the agency and the client exercise control over the temporary employee and both have the requisite number of employees, they are considered employers and jointly liable under the Canadian Human Rights Act. It should be noted that these laws also apply to individuals placed with organizations through welfare-to-work programs. The agency is obligated to make referrals and job assignments in a nondiscriminating manner, and the client may not set discriminatory job referral and job assignment criteria. The client must treat the temporary employees in a nondiscriminatory manner; if the agency knows this is not happening, the agency must take any corrective actions within its control. There are substantial penalties for noncompliance (e.g., back pay, front pay, compensatory damages) that may be obtained from either the agency or the client, or both.

Electronic Recruitment

Usage of electronic recruitment technologies has the possibility of creating artificial barriers to employment opportunities in two ways. First, online recruitment and application procedures assume that potential applicants have access to computers and the skills necessary to make online applications. Research suggests these may be poor assumptions, especially for some racial minorities and the economically disadvantaged. Whether such implicit denial of access to job application opportunities is illegal is an open question due to the newness of the issue. To guard against legal challenge and to ensure accessibility, there are several things the organization might do. One action is to supplement online recruitment with recruitment via other widely used sources, such as newspaper advertisements or other sources that organizational experience indicates are frequently used by women and minorities. Alternately, online recruitment and application could be restricted to certain jobs that have strong computer-related KSAO requirements, such as word processing, programming, spreadsheets, and Internet searches. Many managerial, professional, and technical jobs are likely to have such requirements; applicants in all likelihood will have easy access to computers and online recruitment, as well as the skills necessary to successfully navigate and complete the application. Another possibility would be to use the Internet simply as a recruitment tool, providing thorough, realistic information about available jobs and their associated KSAO requirements and rewards offered. Applicants could also be informed of the organization's application procedures, including the need to apply in writing, a requirement that dovetails nicely with our previous discussion of the definition of a job applicant.

A second potential legal issue is the use of recruitment software that conducts resumé searches within an applicant database using keyword search criteria. Organizational representatives, such as staffing specialists or hiring managers, often specify the search criteria to use, and they could select non-job-related criteria that cause adverse impact against women, minorities, or people with disabilities. Examples of such criteria include preferences for graduation from elite colleges or universities, age, and physical requirements. To guard against such a possibility, the organization should be certain that a job analysis has been done to ensure that every job vacancy lists current KSAO requirements, restrict the type of search criteria that may be used by organizational representatives, and train those representatives in the appropriate specification and usage of search criteria.[67]

Job Advertisements

Some of the earliest (and most blatant) examples of discrimination come from job advertisements. Newspaper employment ads were once listed under separate "Help Wanted—Male" and "Help Wanted—Female" sections, and the content of the ads contained statements like "Applicant must be young and energetic." Such types of ads obviously discouraged certain potential applicants from applying because of their gender or age.

The Canadian Human Rights Commission has issued policy statements regarding age- and sex-referent language in advertising. It bans the use of explicit age- or sex-based preferences. It also addresses more subtle situations in which ads contain implicit age- or sex-based preferences, such as "junior executive," "recent college graduate," "meter maid," and "patrolman." These are referred to in the policy statements as trigger words, and their use may deter certain individuals from becoming applicants. The statements make clear that trigger words, in and of themselves in an advertisement, are not illegal. However, the total context of the ad in which trigger words appear must not be discriminatory, or the trigger words will be a violation of the law.

An example of an advertisement with a trigger word: "Wanted: Individuals of all ages. Day and evening hours available. Full- and part-time positions. All inquiries welcomed. Excellent source of secondary income for retirees." Use of the trigger word "retiree" in this ad is considered permissible because the context of the ad makes it clear that applicants of all ages are welcome to apply.

SUMMARY

External forces shape the conduct and outcomes of recruitment planning. The key forces that emerge from them are economic conditions, labour markets, labour unions, and external and internal environmental scanning. Once these key forces are examined, the external recruitment process can commence.

The objective of the external recruitment process is to identify and attract qualified applicants. To meet this objective the organization must conduct recruitment planning. At this stage, attention must be given to both organizational issues (e.g., selecting recruiters) and administrative issues (e.g., budget size). Particular care needs to be taken in the selection, training, and rewards of recruiters.

The next stage in external recruitment is the development of a strategy. The strategy should consider open versus targeted recruitment, recruitment sources, and the choice of sources. Multiple sources should be used to identify specific applicant populations. There are trade-offs involved in using any source to identify applicants, which should be carefully reviewed prior to using it.

The next stage is to develop a message to give to the job applicants and to select a medium to convey that message. The message may be realistic, branded, or targeted. There is no one best message; it depends on the characteristics of the labour market, the job, and the applicants. The message can be communicated through brochures, videos, advertisements, voice messages, videoconferencing, online services, radio, or e-mail, each of which has different strengths and weaknesses.

Applicants are definitely influenced by characteristics of recruiters and the recruitment process. Through proper attention to these characteristics, the organization can help provide applicants with a favourable recruitment experience. That experience can be continued by carefully preparing applicants for the selection process.

Recruitment activities are highly visible and sensitive for employees. They raise a host of legal issues regarding potential exclusion of minority and female applicants. Employment equity programs are an extension and application of general HR and staffing planning. For enhanced representation of minorities and women in the applicant pool, targeted recruitment and possible changes in the use of conventional recruitment sources should be undertaken. Diversity programs are organizational initiatives to help effectively manage a diverse workforce. Such programs have the potential for successfully working in tandem with employment equity programs by contributing to the attraction and retention of visible minority groups. Consistent with this, electronic recruiting and job advertisements should not openly or implicitly express preferences for or against protected demographic characteristics of applicants.

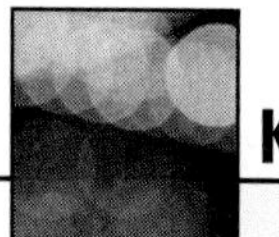

KEY TERMS

economic conditions 147
employment brand 177
external environmental scan 153
internal environmental scan 153
labour unions 152
open recruitment 165
placement goals 184
process flow and record keeping 164
realistic job preview 175
recruitment guide 163
recruitment sources 166
requisition 160
staffing objective 155
staffing philosophy 154
targeted messages 177
targeted recruitment 165
time-lapse statistics 160

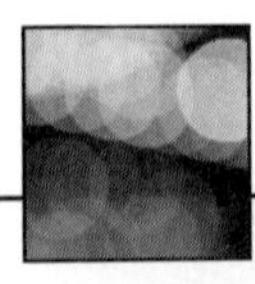

RELEVANT WEB SITES

Job Futures: Canada's National Career and Education Planning Tool

www.jobfutures.ca

Statistics Canada, "Labour Force Survey"

Updates on Canadian labour market status
www.statcan.ca/english/Subjects/Labour/LFS/lfs-en.htm

Canadian Labour and Business Centre

A national forum to research and develop information on Canadian labour market and skills issues
www.clbc.ca

Canadian HR Reporter

National news for the Canadian workplace
www.hrreporter.com

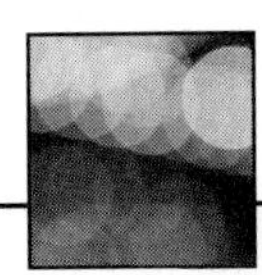

DISCUSSION QUESTIONS

1. List and briefly describe each of the administrative issues that needs to be addressed in the planning stage of external recruiting.
2. List ten sources of applicants that organizations turn to when recruiting. For each source, identify needs specific to the source, as well as pros and cons of using the source for recruitment.
3. In designing the communication message to be used in external recruiting, what kinds of information should be included?
4. What are the advantages of conveying a realistic recruitment message as opposed to portraying the job in a way that the organization thinks that job applicants want to hear?
5. What nontraditional inducements are some organizations offering so that they are seen as family-friendly organizations? What result does the organization hope to realize as a result of providing these inducements?

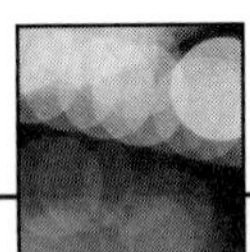

ETHICAL ISSUES

1. Many organizations adopt a targeted recruitment strategy. For example, some organizations have targeted workers 50 and older in their recruitment efforts, which includes advertising specifically in media outlets frequented by older individuals. Other organizations target recruitment messages at women, minorities, or those with desired skills. Do you think targeted recruitment systems are fair? Why or why not?
2. Most organizations have in place job boards on their Web page where applicants can apply for jobs online. What ethical obligations, if any, do you think organizations have to individuals who apply for jobs online?

APPLICATIONS

Improving a College Recruitment Program

The White Feather Corporation (WFC) is a rapidly growing consumer products company that specializes in the production and sales of specialty household items such as lawn furniture cleaners, spa (hot tub) accessories, mosquito and tick repellents, and stain-resistant garage floor paints. The company currently employs 400 salaried and 3,000 unionized employees, almost all of whom are full time. In addition to its corporate office in Winnipeg, Manitoba, the company has five plants and two distribution centres at various rural locations throughout the province.

Two years ago WFC created a corporate HR department to provide centralized direction and control for its key HR functions—planning, compensation, training, and staffing. In turn, the staffing function is headed by the senior manager of staffing, who has three managers as direct reports: the manager of unionized employment, the manager of salaried employment, and the manager of labour relations. The manager of salaried employment is Marianne Collins, who has been with WFC for ten years and has grown with the company through a series of sales and sales management positions. She was chosen for her current position as a result of the WFC's commitment to promotion from within, as well as her broad familiarity with the company's products and customers. When appointed, Marianne's key area of accountability was defined as college recruitment, with 50 percent of her time to be devoted to it.

In her first year, Marianne developed and implemented WFC's first-ever formal college recruitment program. Working with the HR planning person, they decided there was a need for 40 college graduate new hires by the end of the year. They were to be placed in the production, distribution, and marketing functions; specific job titles and descriptions were to be developed during the year. Armed with this forecast, Marianne began the process of recruitment planning and strategy development. The result was the following recruitment process.

Recruitment was to be conducted at 12 schools throughout the province. Marianne contacted the placement office(s) at each school and set up a one-day recruitment visit for each school. All visits were scheduled during the first week in May. The placement office at each school set up 30-minute interviews (16 at each school) and made sure that applicants completed and had on file a standard application form. To visit the schools and conduct the interviews, Marianne selected three young, up-and-coming managers (one each from production, distribution, and marketing) to be the recruiters. Each manager was assigned to four of the schools. Since none of the managers had any experience as a recruiter, Marianne conducted a recruitment briefing for them. During that briefing she reviewed the overall recruitment (hiring) goal, provided a brief rundown on each of the schools, and then explained the specific tasks the recruiters were to perform. Those tasks were to pick up the application materials of the interviewees at the placement office prior to the interviews, review the materials, conduct the interviews in a timely manner (they were told they could ask any questions they wanted to that pertained to qualifications for the job), and at the end of the day complete an evaluation form on each applicant. The form asked for a 1–7 rating of overall qualifications for the job, written comments about strengths and weaknesses, and a recommendation of whether or not to invite the person for a second interview in Winnipeg. These forms were to be returned to Marianne, who would review them and decide which people to invite for a second interview.

After the campus interviews were conducted by the managers, problems began to surface. Placement officials at some of the schools contacted Marianne and lodged several complaints. Among those complaints were that (1) one of the managers failed to pick up the application materials of the interviewees; (2) none of the managers were able to provide much information about the nature of the jobs they were recruiting for, especially jobs outside of their own functional area; (3) the interviewers got off schedule early on, so that applicants were kept waiting and others had shortened interviews as the managers tried to make up time; (4) none of the managers had any written information describing the company and its locations; (5) one of the managers asked female applicants very personal questions about marriage plans, use of drugs and alcohol, and willingness to travel with male co-workers; (6) one of the managers talked incessantly during the interviews, so that the interviewees had little opportunity to present themselves and their qualifications to the manager; and (7) all of the managers told interviewees they did not know when they would be contacted about decisions on invitations for second interviews. In addition to these complaints, Marianne had difficulty getting the managers to complete and turn in their evaluation forms (they claimed they were too busy, especially after being away from the job for a week). Based on the reports she did receive, Marianne extended invitations to 55 of the applicants for second interviews. Of these, 30 accepted the invitation. Ultimately, 25 of these were given job offers, and 15 of them accepted the offers.

To put it mildly, the first-ever college recruitment program was a disaster for WFC and Marianne. In addition to her embarrassment, Marianne was asked to meet with her boss and the president of WFC to explain what went wrong and to receive "guidance" from them as to their expectations for the next year's recruitment program. Marianne subsequently learned that she would receive no merit pay increase for the year and that the three managers all received above average merit increases.

To turn things around for the second year of college recruitment, Marianne realized that she needed to engage in a thorough process of recruitment planning and strategy development. As she began this undertaking, her analysis of past events led her to the conclusion that one of her key mistakes was to naively assume that the three managers would actually know how to be good recruiters and were motivated to do the job effectively. Marianne first decides to use 12 managers as recruiters, assigning one to each of the 12 campuses. She also decides that she cannot send them off to the campuses with just a recruitment "briefing." She determines that an intensive, one-day training program must be developed and given to the managers prior to the beginning of the recruitment "season."

You are a professional acquaintance of Marianne's, and you work in HR at another company in Winnipeg. Knowing that you have had some experience in both university recruiting and training, Marianne calls you for some advice. She asks you if you would be willing to meet and discuss the following questions:

1. What topics should be covered in the training program?
2. What materials and training aids will be needed for the program?
3. What skills should the trainees actually practice during the training?
4. Who should conduct the training?
5. What other changes might have to be made to ensure that the training has a strong impact on the managers and that during the recruitment process they are motivated to use what they learned in training?

Internet Recruiting

Selma Williams is a recruiter for Mervin/McCall-Hall (MMH), a large publisher of textbooks for education (K–12 and college). Fresh out of university, Selma's first big assignment at MMH is a tough one—to develop an Internet recruitment strategy for the entire company. Previously, MMH had relied on the traditional recruitment methods—college recruiting, word-of-mouth, newspaper advertisements, and search firms. As more and more of MMH's textbook business is connected to the Web, however, it became clear to Selma's boss, Jon Beerfly, that MMH needed to consider upgrading its recruitment process. Accordingly, after Selma had acclimated herself to MMH and worked on a few smaller recruitment projects (including doing a fair amount of recruiting at university campuses in the past three months), Jon described Selma's assignment to her, concluding, "Selma, I really don't know much about this. I'm going to leave it to you to come up with a set of recommendations about what we oughtta be doing. We just had a new intern come into the office for a stint in HR, and I'm going to assign this person to you to help on this assignment." Assume that you are the intern.

At your first meeting, you and Selma discuss many different issues and agree that regardless of what else is done, MMH must have a recruitment area on the MMH corporate Web site. After further discussion, Selma has given you several assignments toward this objective:

1. Look at three to five corporate Web sites that have a recruitment area and note their major features, strengths, and weaknesses (see Exhibit 5.15).
2. Interview three to five students who have used the recruitment area on a corporate Web site and ask them what they most liked and disliked about the recruitment areas.
3. Prepare a brief report that (a) summarizes your findings from assignments #1 and #2 and (b) recommends the design features that you and Selma will develop for inclusion in the MMH Web site.

TANGLEWOOD STORES CASE

You have just learned about many of the major methods that organizations use to encourage individuals to apply for vacancies. The recruiting case will provide an opportunity to see how staffing managers can use organizational data to resolve an internal dispute regarding which recruiting methods work best. In addition, the assignment will demonstrate how contextual factors can bring out different strengths of the various recruiting methods.

The Situation

Tanglewood is engaged in a process of centralization. Previously, most staffing decisions were made by each individual store, but the corporate offices would like to see more consistency. They also believe that there is a great deal the stores can learn by comparing their experiences across locations. You are provided data from Tanglewood's recruiting outcomes from four different geographic regions. These data are supplemented with narrative reports from the organization's managerial focus groups pertaining to the fit between applicants and the unique requirements of Tanglewood's culture.

Your Tasks

You will assess the information provided by the individual stores together with the narrative reports to develop a recruiting policy that can be used across the entire organization. This policy will include recommendations regarding which methods of recruiting are likely to be most successful, and also provide suggestions on whether the organization should use open or targeted recruiting. Once you have concluded what the best course of action will be, you will create a recruitment guide for the organization like the one presented in Exhibit 5.11. Finally, you will develop recruiting messages by considering the message and the medium by which information will be provided, along with varying levels of realism. The background information for this case, and your specific assignment, can be found at www.mcgrawhill.ca/OLC/heneman.

ENDNOTES

1. Going Global Career Guides, "Employment Trends and Opportunities," *Mobile*, 2004, pp. 15–16.
2. Going Global Career Guides, "Employment Trends and Opportunities," *Mobile*, 2004, pp. 16–17.
3. D. Walters, "The relationship between postsecondary education and skill: credentialism with human capital theory," *The Canadian Journal of Higher Education*, 2004, 34(2), p. 9.
4. Government of Canada, *Job Futures World of Work*, "Job futures: A Canadian guide for tomorrow's most promising jobs," www.jobfutures.ca/en/brochure/jobopportunities.html.
5. J. Terrett, "A promising approach to plugging the skill gap," *Plant*, June 13, 2005, 64(6), p. 7.
6. P. Beatty, "Preparing our young people for the future," *Plant*, July 14, 2003, 62(10), p. 26.
7. Society for Human Resource Management, "Management Skills for the Future," *Issues in HR*, March/April 1995, p. 5.
8. G.-E. Galabuzzi, "Factors Affecting the Social Economic Status of Canadians, *Canadian Issues*, Spring 2005, p. 53.
9. P. MacInnis, "Technology at the Heart of Longer Work Weeks," *Computing Canada*, June 17, 2005, 31(9), p. 9; and E. Opasini, "Working Harder? You're Not Alone," *Hardware & Home Magazine*, May 2005, 29(3), p. 3.
10. Correctional Services Canada, "A tough labour market for the young," 2004, www.csc-scc.gc.ca/text/pblct/forum/e08/e081a_e.shtml.
11. Human Resources and Social Development Canada, "Recent immigrants have experienced unusual economic difficulties," *Applied Research Bulletin*, Winter-Spring 2001, 7(1), p. 4, www.hrsdc.gc.ca/en/cs/sp/sdc/pkrf/publications/bulletins/2001-000004/page04.shtml.
12. Canadian Labour and Business Centre, "Workforce Profile of the Manufacturing Sector: March 2004, p. 7, www.cme-mec.ca/pdf/Manufacturing%20Workforce%20Profile%20May20.pdf.
13. A. Tomlinson, "More training critical in manufacturing: Study," *Canadian HR Reporter*, November 4, 2002, 15(19), p. 2.
14. R. Matas, "B.C. revamping welfare-to-work," *The Globe and Mail*, August 17, 2005, p. A8.
15. D. E. Hecker, "Occupational Employment Projects to 2012," *Monthly Labor Review*, 2004, 127(2), pp. 80–105.
16. S. Mingail, "Tackling Workplace Literacy a No-Brainer," *Canadian HR Reporter*, November 22, 2004, 17(20), p. 63; and Statistics Canada, "Latest release from the Labour Force Survey: workforce trends," August 5, 2005.
17. A. Packer, "Skill Deficiencies: Problems, Policies and Prospects," *Journal of Labor Research*, 1993, 14, pp. 227–247.
18. C. Kapsalis, P. Tourigny, "Duration of non-standard employment", *Perspectives on Labour and Income*, Spring 2005, 17(1), pg. 31.
19. Canadian Labour and Business Centre, "Changing Times, New Ways of Working: Alternative Working Arrangements and Changing in Working Time," 2003, www.clbc.ca/Research_and_Reports/Archive/archive04079701.asp.
20. H. Schwind, H. Das, and T. Wagar, *Canadian Human Resource Management* (Toronto: McGraw-Hill Ryerson, 1999).
21. J. Sullivan, "Becoming a Great Recruiter," in N. C. Burkholder, P. J. Edwards, and L. Sartain (eds.), *On Staffing* (Hoboken, NJ: Wiley, 2004), pp. 6–67.
22. C. Patton, "Recruiter Attack," *Human Resource Executive*, November 2000, pp. 106–109; E. Zimmerman, "Fight Dirty Hiring Tactics," *Workforce*, May 2001, pp. 30–34.

23. B. J. Asch, "Do Incentives Matter? The Case of Navy Recruiters," *Industrial and Labor Relations Review,* 43 (Special Issue), pp. 89–106.
24. "Cutting Corners to the Best Candidates," *Weddle's,* October 5, 2004, www.weddles.com.
25. I. J. Shaver, "Innovative Techniques Lure Quality Workers to NASA," *Personnel Journal,* August 1990, pp. 100–106.
26. R. D. Gatewood, M. A. Gowen, and G. Lautenschlager, "Corporate Image, Recruitment Image, and Initial Job Choice Decisions," *Academy of Management Journal,* 1993, 36(2), pp. 414–427.
27. D. McLean, "Workplaces That Work," The Conference Board of Canada: The Centre of Excellence for Women's Advancement, 2003, p. 10.
28. T. Williams, "The true cost of hiring," *Canadian HR Reporter,* July 14, 2003, 16(13).
29. Coopers and Lybrand, *Employment Policies, Turnover, and Cost-Per-Hire* (New York: Coopers and Lybrand Compensation Resources, 1992).
30. J. Barthold, "Waiting in the Wings," *HR Magazine,* April 2004, pp. 89–95; A. M. Chaker, "Luring Moms Back to Work," *New York Times,* December 30, 2003, pp. D1–D2.; B. McConnell, "Hiring Teens? Go Where They Are Hanging Out," *HR-News,* June 2002, p. 16; J. Mullich, "They Don't Retire Them They Hire Them," *Workforce Management,* December 2003, pp. 49–57; R. Rodriguez, "Tapping the Hispanic Labour Pool," *HR Magazine,* April 2004, pp. 73–79; " Sourcing Those Who Serve," *Weddle's,* May 2002 (www.weddles.com); C. Wilson, " Rehiring Annuitants," *IPMA—:HR News,* August 2003, pp. 1–6.
31. B. L. Rau and M. M. Hyland, "Role Conflict and Flexible Work Arrangements: The Effects on Applicant Attraction," *Personnel Psychology,* 2002, 55, pp. 111–136.
32. M. Laurie, "Employee referral programs: Highly qualified new hires who stick around," *Canadian HR Reporter,* June 4, 2001, 14(11), p. 21.
33. J. Borzo, "The Job Connection," *Wall Street Journal,* September 13, 2004, p. R14; "Can Social Networking Help Recruiters?" *Weddle's,* January 15, 2004 (www.weddles.com) A. Leung, " Different Ties for Different Needs: Recruitment Practices of Entrepreneurial Firms at Different Developmental Phases," *Human Resource Management,* 2003, 42, pp. 303–320; K. Maher, "Focus on Recruitment, Pay and Getting Ahead," *Wall Street Journal,* December 23, 2003, p. B6; D. Wolk, Workforce Management, August 2004, pp. 70–73.
34. E. Krell, "Recruiting Outlook: Creative HR for 2003," *Workforce,* December 2002, pp. 40–45.
35. R. T. Cobler, D. J. Brown, P. E. Levy, and J. H. Shalhoop, *HR Professionals' Attitudes Toward and Use of the Internet for Employee Recruitment,* Executive Report, University of Akron and Society for Human Resource Management Foundation, 2003.
36. K. Maher, "Online Job Hunting Is Tough. Just Ask Vinnie," *Wall Street Journal,* June 24, 2003, pp. B1, B10.
37. D. Graham, *Online Recruiting* (Palo Alto, CA: Davis-Black Publishing, 2000) "On-Line Recruiting," *IPMA News,* March 2001, pp. 12, 14; "Online Recruiting On-the-Rise," Weddle's, April 15, 2000, p. 1; T. Starner, "Getting It Right," Human Resource Executive, July 2001, p. 114.
38. J. Flato, "Key Success Factors for Managing Your Campus Recruiting Program: The Good Times and Bad," In Burkholder, Edwards, and Sartain (eds.), *On Staffing,* pp. 219–229; J. Floren, "Constructing a Campus Recruiting Network," *EMT,* Spring 2004, pp. 29–31; C. Joinson, "Red Hot College Recruiting," Employment Management Today, October 4, 2002 (www.shrm.org/emt); J. Mullich, "College Recruitment Goes for Niches," *Workforce Management,* February 2004 (www.workforce.com)
39. D. Aberman, "Smaller, Specialized Recruiting Events Pay Off in Big Ways," EMA Today, Winter 1996, pp. 8–10; T. A. Judge and D. M. Cable, "Role of Organizational

Information Sessions in Applicant Job Search Decisions," Working paper, Department of Management and Organizations, University of Iowa.

40. S. Armour, "Employers Court High School Teens," Arizona Republic, December 28, 1999, p. E5; C. Hymowitz, "Make a Careful Search to Fill Internships: They May Land a Star," Wall Street Journal, May 23, 2000, p. B1; "In a Tight Job Market, College Interns Wooed," IPMA News, November 2000, p. 22.
41. P. J. Franks, "Well-Integrated Learning Programs," in N. C. Burkholder, P. J. Edwards and L. Sartain (eds.), *On Staffing,* pp. 230–238.
42. L. J. Bassi and J. Ludwig, "School-to-Work Programs in the United States: A Multi-Firm Case Study of Training, Benefits, and Costs," *Industrial and Labour Relations Review,* 2000, 53, pp. 219–239.
43. "Search Tactics Poll," Society for Human Resource Management, April 2001; M. A. Zottoli and J. P. Wanous, "Recruitment Source Research: Current Status and Future Directions," Human Resource Management Review, 2000, 10, pp. 353–382.
44. S. L. Premack and J. P. Wanous, "A Meta-Analysis of Realistic Job Preview Experiments," *Journal of Applied Psychology,* 1985, 70, pp. 706–719.
45. J. P. Wanous, Recruitment, Selection, Orientation, and Socialization of Newcomers, second ed. (Reading, MA: Addison-Wesley, 1992).
46. R. D. Bretz Jr. and T. A. Judge, "Realistic Job Previews: A Test of the Adverse Self-Selection Hypothesis," *Journal of Applied Psychology,* 1998, 83, pp. 330–337; D. M. Cable, L. Aiman-Smith, P. W. Molvey, and J. R. Edwards, "The Sources and Accuracy of Job Applicants' Beliefs about Organizational Culture," *Academy of Management Journal,* in press; "The Fit Factor of Online Recruiting," *Weddle's,* July 2001, pp. 3–4; Y. Ganzach, A. Pazy, Y. Ohayun, and E. Brainin, "Social Exchange and Organizational Commitment: Decision-Making Training for Job Choice as an Alternative to Realistic Job Preview," *Personnel Psychology,* 2002, 55, pp. 613–637; P. W. Hom, R. W. Griffeth, L. E. Palich, and J. S. Bracker, "An Exploratory Investigation into Theoretical Mechanisms Underlying Realistic Job Previews," *Personnel Psychology,* 51, 1998, pp. 421–451; B. M. Meglino, E. C. Ravlin, and A. S. DeNisi, "A Meta-Analytic Examination of Realistic Job Preview Effectiveness: A Test of Three Counter-Intuitive Propositions," *Human Resource Management Review,* 2000, 10, pp. 407– 434; J. M. Phillips, "Effects of Realistic Job Previews on Multiple Organizational Outcomes: A Meta-Analysis," *Academy of Management Journal,* 1998, 41, pp. 673–690.
47. Corporate Leadership Council, *The Employment Brand: Building Competitive Advantage in the Labor Market* (Washington, DC: author, 1999); E. Silverman, "Making Your Mark," *Human Resource Executive,* October, 2004, pp. 32–36; M. Spitzmuüller, R. Hunington, W. Wyatt and A. Crozier, "Building a Company to Attract Talent," *Workspan,* July 2002, pp. 27–30.
48. C. J. Collins and C. K. Stevens, "The Relationship Between Early Recruitment-Related Activities and the Application Decisions of New Labour-Market Entrants: A Brand Equity Approach to Recruitment," *Journal of Applied Psychology,* 2002, 87, pp. 1121–1133; F. Lievens and S. Highhouse, "The Relation of Instrumental and Symbolic Attributes to a Company's Attractiveness as an Employer," *Personnel Psychology,* 56, 2003, pp. 75–102.
49. R. H. Bretz and T. A. Judge "The Role of Human Resource Systems in Job Applicant Decision Processes," *Journal of Management,* 1994, 20, pp. 531–551; D. Cable and T. Judge, "Pay Preferences and Job Search Decisions: A Person-Organization Fit Perspective," *Personnel Psychology,* 47, pp. 648–657; T. J. Thorsteinson, M. A. Billings, and M. C. Joyce, "Matching Recruitment Messages to Applicant Preferences," Poster presented at 16th annual conference of Society for Industrial and Organizational Psychology, San Diego, 2001.

50. R. J. Vandenberg and V. Scarpello, "The Matching Model: An Examination of the Processes Underlying Realistic Job Previews," *Journal of Applied Psychology,* 1990, 75(1), pp. 60–67.
51. D. R. Ilgen, C. D. Fisher, and M. S. Taylor, "Consequences of Individual Feedback on Behavior in Organizations," *Journal of Applied Psychology,* 1979, 64, pp. 349–371.
52. College Placement Council, College Relations and Recruitment Sourcebook; College Placement Council, "Technology," *Spotlight on Career Planning, Placement, and Recruitment,* 1995, 18(1), p. 2.
53. K. O. Magnusen and K. G. Kroeck, "Videoconferencing Maximizes Recruiting," HR Magazine, August 1995, pp. 70–72. B. Kelley, "High-Tech Hits Recruiting," Human Resource Executive, April 1994, pp. 43–45; College Placement Council, "Technology";
54. Wernimont, "Recruitment Policies and Practices."
55. R. T. Cober, D. J. Brown and P. E. Levy, "Form, Content, and Function: An Evaluative Methdology for Corporate Employment Web Sites," *Human Resource Management,* 2004, 43, pp. 201–218; R. T. Cober, D. J. Brown, P. E. Levy, A. B. Cobler and K. M.Keeping, "Organizational Web Sites: Web Site Content and Style as Determinants of Organizational Attraction," *International Journal of Selection and Assessment,* 11, 2003, pp. 158–169.
56. "A 'Shopper Friendly' Web Site," *Weddle's,* October 2002, p. 4; "KISS Your Web Site Visitors," *Weddles,* April 2002, p. 1.
57. Statistics Canada, "The Daily," July 8, 2005.
58. C. Johnson, "Turn Up the Radio Recruiting," *HR Magazine,* September 1998, pp. 64–70.
59 S. L. Rynes, "Recruitment, Job Choice, and Post-Hire Decisions," in M. D. Dunnette and L. M. Hough (eds.), *Handbook of Industrial and Organizational Psychology,* Vol. 2 (Palo Alto, CA: Consulting Psychologists Press, 1991), pp. 399–444; J. L. Scott, "Total Quality College Relations and Recruitment Programs: Students Benchmark Best Practices," *EMA Journal,* Winter 1995, pp. 2–5; J. P. Wanous, *Organizational Entry,* Second ed. (Reading, MA: Addison-Wesley, 1992).
60. W. R. Boswell, M. V. Roehling, M. A. Le Pine, and L. M. Moynihan, "Individual Job-Choice Decisions and the Impact of Job Attributes and Recruitment Practices: A Longitudinal Field Study," *Human Resource Management,* 2003, 42, pp. 23–37; A. M. Ryan, J. M. Sacco, L . A. McGarland, and S. D. Kriska, "Applicant Self Selection: Correlates of Withdrawal from a Multiple Hurdle Process," *Journal of Applied Psychology,* 2000, 85, pp. 163–179; S. L. Rynes, "Who's Selecting Whom? Effects of Selection Practices in Applicant Attitudes and Behaviors," in N. Schmitt, W. Borman, and Associates (eds.), *Personnel Selection in Organizations* (San Francisco: Jossey-Bass, 1993), pp. 240–276; S. L. Rynes, R. D. Bretz, and B. Gerhart, "The Importance of Recruitment and Job Choice: A Different Way of Looking," *Personnel Psychology,* 1991, 44, pp. 487–521; M. S. Taylor and T. J. Bergmann, "Organizational Recruitment Activities and Applicant Reactions to Different Stages of the Recruiting Process," *Personnel Psychology,* 1988, 40, pp. 261–285.
61. B. Dineen, S. R. Ash and r. A. Noe, " A Web of Applicant Attraction: Person-Organization Fit in the Context of Web-Based Recruitment," *Journal of Applied Psychology,* 87, 2002, pp. 723–734; D. C. Feldman and B. S. Klaas, "Internet Job Hunting: A Field Study of Applicant Experiences with On-Line Recruiting," *Human Resource Management,* 2002, 41, pp. 175–192; K. Maher, "The Jungle," *Wall Street Journal,* July 18, 2002, p. B10; D. L. Van Rooy, A. Alonso and Z. Fairchild, "In with the New, Out with the Old: Has the Technological Revolution Eliminated the Traditional Job Search Process?" *International Journal of Selection and Assessment,* 11, 2003, pp. 170–174.
62. S. Modi, "About Staff: Employment Equity: An important piece in the human rights puzzle," *HR Professional,* March 2005.

63. C. Coffey and N. Tombari, "The bottom-line for work/life leadership: Linking diversity and organizational culture, *Ivey Business Journal,* July/August, 2005, p. 1.
64. "Winning With Diversity" (no author). *Special Advertising Supplement to the New York Times Magazine,* March 28, 2004, p. 66.
65. M. E. A. Jayne and R. Dipboye, "Leveraging Diversity to Improve Business Performance: Research Findings and Recommendations for Organizations," *Human Resource Management,* 2004, 43, pp. 409–424.
66. D. Oliver (The Honourable), "Achieving results through diversity: A strategy for success," *Ivey Business Journal,* March/April 2005, p. 3.
67. Bureau of National Affairs, "Resume Scanning Tracking Software Raises new Discrimination Issues," *Daily Labor Report,* March 17, 1998, pp. C1–C2; C. Click, "Blend Established Practices with New Technologies," *HR Magazine,* November 1997, pp. 59-64; R. L. Hogler, C. Henie, and C. Bemus, "Internet Recruiting and Employment Discrimination" A Legal Perspective," *Human Resource Management Review,* 1998, 8, pp. 149–164; J. M. Stanton, "Validity and Related Issues in Web-Based Hiring," *The Industrial-Organizational Psychologist,* 1999, 36, pp. 69–77.

Visit the Online Learning Centre at

www.mcgrawhill.ca/olc/heneman

CHAPTER 6

INTERNAL RECRUITMENT

CHAPTER OBJECTIVES

After reading this chapter, you will be able to:

- Understand how recruitment can focus on filling positions with employees already employed in an organization
- Grasp the issues associated with internal recruitment
- Know the various methods of internal recruitment available to organizations and the criteria used in assessing those methods
- Understand the issues associated with internal recruitment and the job opportunities available to the members of designated groups such as women and visible minorities

internal recruitment process
Plan to identify and attract applicants from among current employees

The objective of the **internal recruitment process** is to identify and attract applicants from among individuals already holding jobs with the organization. The first step in this process is recruitment planning, which addresses both organizational and administrative issues. Organizational issues include mobility paths and mobility path policies. Administrative issues include requisitions, number and types of contacts, budgets, and the recruitment guide.

The second step in the internal recruitment process is strategy development. Attention is directed to where, when, and how to look for qualified internal applicants. Knowing where to look requires an understanding of open, closed, and targeted internal recruitment systems. Knowing how to look requires an understanding of job postings, skills inventories, nominations, employee referrals, and in-house temporary pools. Knowing when to look requires an understanding of lead time and time sequence concerns.

The third step in the process is searching for internal candidates. This step consists of the communication message and medium for notification of the job vacancy. The message can be realistic, branded, or targeted. The medium for delivery can be a job posting, other written documents, and potential supervisors and peers.

The fourth step in the process is developing a system to make the transition to selection for job applicants. Making a transition requires a well-developed job posting system and providing applicants with an understanding of the selection process and how to best prepare for it.

Finally, for some organizations it is necessary to consider the barriers that place limits on the opportunities of women and other designated groups. This will be directly relevant to organizations that have established an employment equity program. These organizations must take positive steps to address the problems of the glass ceiling that prevents women and others from realizing their full potential in their career pursuits.

RECRUITMENT PLANNING

Prior to identifying and attracting internal applicants to vacant jobs, attention must be directed to organizational and administrative issues that facilitate the effective matching of internal applicants with vacant jobs.

Organizational Issues

Just as the external labour market can be divided into segments or strata of workers believed to be desirable job applicants, so, too, can the internal labour market of an organization. This division is often done inside organizations on an informal basis. For example, managers might talk about the talented pool of managerial trainees this year and refer to some of them as "high-potential employees." As another example, people in the organization talk about their "techies," an internal collection of employees with the technical skills needed to run the business.

At a more formal level, organizations must create a structured set of jobs for their employees and paths of mobility for them to follow as they advance in their careers. To do this, organizations create internal labour markets. Each internal labour market has two components: mobility paths and mobility policies. Mobility paths depict the paths of mobility between jobs. Mobility policies cover the operational requirements needed to move people between jobs.

RPC 4.1

mobility path
Possible employee movements within the internal labour market structure

Mobility Paths A **mobility path** consists of possible employee movements within the internal labour market structure. Mobility paths are determined by many factors, including workforce, organization, labour union, and labour market characteristics. Mobility paths are of two types: traditional and innovative. Both types of mobility paths determine who is eligible for a new job in the organization.

Traditional Mobility Paths. Examples of traditional mobility paths are shown in Exhibit 6.1. As shown, the emphasis is primarily on upward mobility in the organization. Due to the upward nature of traditional mobility paths, they are often labelled promotion ladders. This label implies that each job is a step toward the top of the organization. Upward promotions in an organization are often seen by employees as prizes because of the promotions' desirable characteristics. Employees receive these prizes as they compete against one another for available vacancies. For

EXHIBIT 6.1 Traditional Mobility Paths

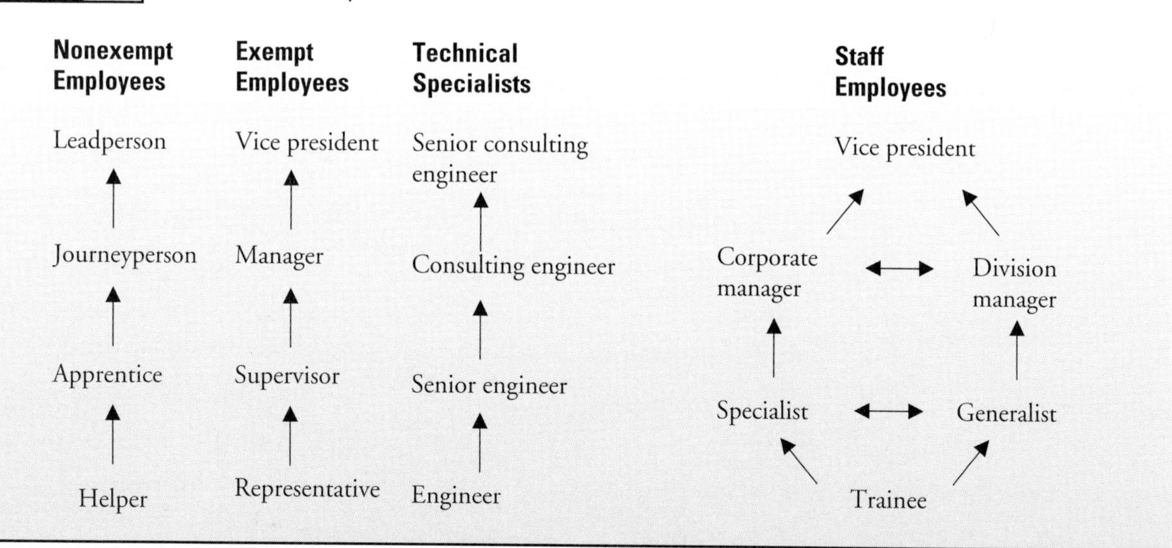

example, a promotion might lead to a higher rate of pay, and a transfer may result in a move to a better work location. Research has shown that these competitions may be contested, as opportunities for upward advancement are limited in most organizations.[1]

An exception to the primarily upward mobility in the promotion ladders in Exhibit 6.1 shows the lateral moves that sometimes occur for the staff member who has both generalist and specialist experiences as well as corporate and division experience. This staff member is considered more well-rounded and better able to work within the total organization. Experience as a specialist helps the person become familiar with technical issues that arise. Experience as a generalist gives the employee a breadth of knowledge about many matters in the staff function. Corporate experience provides a policy and planning perspective, whereas division experience provides greater insight on day-to-day operational matters.

Traditional mobility paths make it very easy, from an administrative vantage point, to identify where to look for applicants in the organization. For promotion, one looks at the next level down in the organizational hierarchy, and over, for transfer. Although such a system is straightforward to administer, it is not very flexible and may inhibit the matching of the best person for the job. For example, the best person for the job may be at two job levels down and in another division from the vacant job. It is very difficult to locate such a person under a traditional mobility path.

Innovative Mobility Paths. Examples of innovative mobility paths are shown in Exhibit 6.2. The emphasis here is no longer simply on upward mobility. Instead, movement in the organization may be in any direction, including up, down, and from side to side. Employee movement is emphasized to ensure continuous learning by employees such that each can make the greatest contribution to the organization. This is in direct contrast to the traditional promotion ladder, where the goal is for each person to achieve a position with ever-higher status. Many organizations have shifted to innovative mobility paths for two reasons: (1) There is the need to be flexible given global and technological changes, and (2) slower organizational growth has made it necessary to find alternative ways to utilize employees' talents. Parallel tracks allow for employees to specialize in technical work or management work and advance within either. Historically, technical specialists had to shift away from technical to managerial work if they wanted to receive higher-status job titles and pay. In other words, being a technical specialist was a dead-end job. Under a parallel track system, both job titles and salaries of technical specialists are elevated to be commensurate with their managerial counterparts.

EXHIBIT 6.2 Innovative Mobility Paths

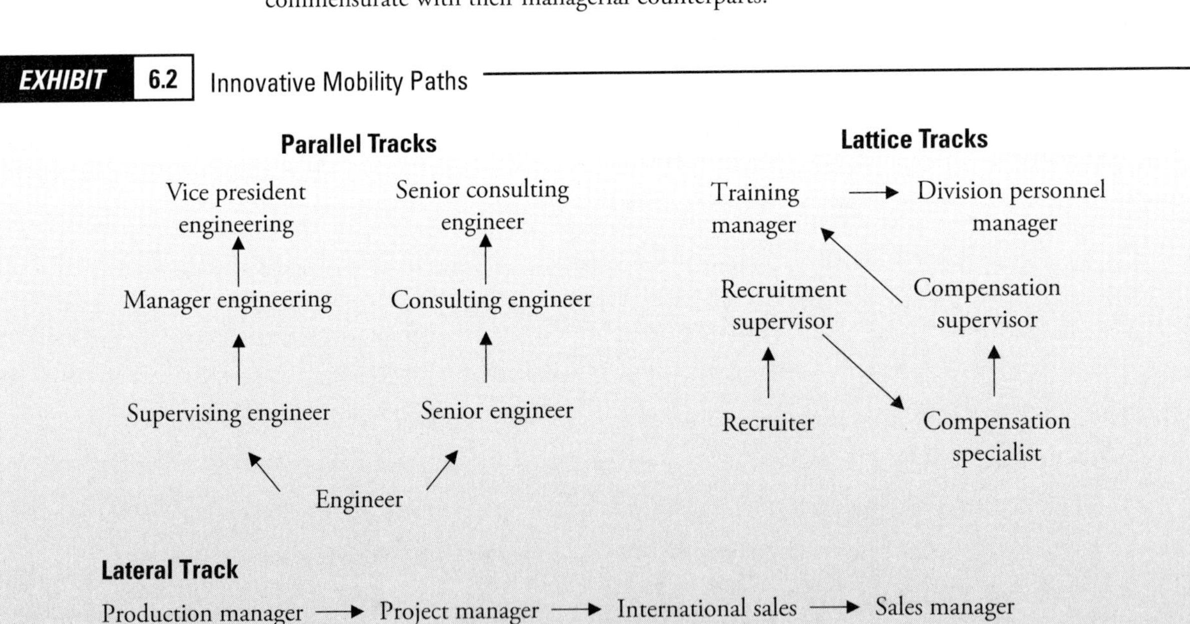

With a lateral track system, there may be no upward mobility at all. The individual's greatest contribution to the organization may be to stay at a certain level of the organization for an extended period of time while serving in a variety of capacities, as shown in Exhibit 6.2.

A lattice mobility path has upward, lateral, and even downward movement. For example, a recruiter may be promoted to a recruitment supervisor position, but to continue to contribute to the organization, the person may need to take a lateral step to become knowledgeable about all the technical details in compensation. After mastering these details, the person may then become a supervisor again, this time in the compensation area rather than recruitment. From a previous company, the person may have experience in training and be ready to take the next move to training manager without training experience internal to the organization. Finally, the person may take a lateral move to manage all the HR functions (e.g., recruitment, compensation, training) in a division as a division personnel manager.

Increasingly, some organizations have abandoned career structures altogether. In these team-based kinds of jobs, employees do not occupy traditional jobs but are "bonded" together with other employees, depending on the project. In this structure, employees are essentially entrepreneurial consultants, and the organization facilitates their activities. One example of such a cellular organization is TCG, based in Sydney, Australia. TCG partners with other organizations to provide computer assistance. TCG employees work on particular projects, depending on their expertise, and are rewarded based on the success of the project. These rewards may involve assignment to larger projects in the future, which is a form of promotion.[2]

The downside to innovative mobility paths, such as those discussed, is that they are very difficult to administer. Neat categories of where to look do not exist to the same degree as with traditional mobility paths. On the positive side, however, talented inside candidates who may not have been identified within a traditional system are identified because the system is flexible enough to do so.

When upward mobility is limited in an organization, as with many organizations using innovative mobility paths, special steps need to be taken to ensure that work remains meaningful to employees. If steps are not taken, the organization with limited promotional opportunities risks turnover of good employees. Examples of steps to make work more meaningful include the following:

1. **Alternative reward systems:** Rather than basing pay increases on promotions, pay increases can be based on knowledge and skill acquisition and contribution to the organization as a team member and individual. An example of a career system focused on skill development exists at Dupont Canada's research and development site in Kingston, Ontario. To ensure that scientists' competencies are current, Dupont developed the Career Pathways system, which rewards the development of strategic competencies. The system is linked to compensation whereby the mastery of competencies results in increases in employee compensation.[3]
2. **Team building:** Greater challenge and autonomy in the workplace can be created by having employees work in teams where they are responsible for all aspects of work involved in providing a service or product, including self-management.
3. **Counselling:** Workshops, self-directed workbooks, and individual advising can be used by organizations to ensure that employees have a well-reasoned plan for movement in the organization.
4. **Alternative employment:** Arrangements can be made for employee leaves of absence, sabbaticals, and consulting assignments to ensure that workers remain challenged and acquire new knowledge and skills.

mobility policies
Documents outlining the rules and eligibility criteria concerning employee movement between jobs in an organization

Mobility Policies Mobility paths show the relationship among jobs, but they do not show the rules by which people move between jobs. These rules are specified in written **mobility policies**, which must be developed and should specify eligibility criteria.

Development. A well-defined mobility path policy statement is needed for both traditional and innovative mobility paths and has the following characteristics:

1. The intent of the policy is clearly communicated.
2. The policy is consistent with the philosophy and values of top management.
3. The scope of the policy, such as coverage by geographic region, employee groups, and so forth, is clearly articulated.
4. Employees' responsibilities and opportunities for development are clearly defined.
5. Supervisors' responsibilities for employee development are clearly stated.
6. Procedures are clearly described, such as how employees will be notified of openings, time deadlines and data to be supplied by the employee, how requirements and qualifications will be communicated, how the selection process will work, and how job offers will be made.
7. Rules regarding compensation and advancement are included.
8. Rules regarding benefits and benefit changes as they relate to advancement are included.

A well-articulated and well-executed mobility path policy is likely to be seen by employees as fair. A poorly developed or nonexistent policy is likely to lead to employee claims of favouritism and discrimination.

Eligibility Criteria. An important component of an effective mobility policy is a listing of the criteria by which the organization will decide who is eligible to be considered for an open vacancy in a mobility path. In essence, these criteria restrict eligibility for recruitment to certain individuals. Usually these criteria are based on the amount of seniority, level of experience, KSAOs, or job duties required for the job. For example, to be considered for an international assignment, the applicant may be required to have been with the organization a certain length of time, have experience in a functional area in which there is a vacancy, be proficient in a foreign language, and be interested in performing new duties. These criteria need to be made very clear in the policy, otherwise unqualified people will apply and be disappointed when they are not considered. Also, the organization may be flooded with the paperwork and processing of applicants who are not eligible.

Of course, mobility policies may be too rigid and inflexible in organizations faced with tough competition for talented employees. For example, in his effort to retain talented managers at the Bank of Nova Scotia, CEO Rick Waugh broke the pattern of traditional career paths to promote three managers as co-heads of Scotia Capital. Mr. Waugh's actions broke the tradition of career bankers following well-worn career paths to assume these positions.[4]

Administrative Issues

Mobility paths and mobility policies must be established as part of the planning process, and so, too, must administrative matters. Those administrative matters include requisitions, coordination, budget, and recruitment guide.

Requisitions A requisition or authorization to fill a position by higher-level management is essential to the internal recruitment process. Without a formal requisition, it is far too easy for managers to make promises or "cut deals" with employees, contrary to organizational objectives. For example, managers may promote their employees into new job titles that have not been authorized by top management. In doing so, they may create perceptions of unfairness among those with similar backgrounds who were not promoted. This action thus runs contrary to the organizational goal of fair HR systems. Thus, formal requisitions should always be used in internal recruitment, just as they are in external recruitment.

Coordination Internal and external recruitment efforts need to be coordinated and synchronized via the organization's staffing philosophy (see Chapter 5). If this coordination is not done, disastrous results can occur. For example, if independent searches are conducted internally and externally, then two people may be hired for one open vacancy. If only an external recruitment search is conducted, the morale of existing employees may be reduced when they feel that they have been passed over for a promotion. If only an internal recruitment search is conducted, the person hired may not be as qualified as someone from the external market. Because of these possibilities, internal *and* external professionals must work together with the line manager to coordinate efforts before the search for candidates begins.

To coordinate activities, two steps should be taken. First, internal staffing specialist positions should be designated to ensure that internal candidates are considered in the recruitment process. External staffing specialists are called recruiters; internal staffing specialists are often known as placement or classification professionals, to acknowledge the fact that they are responsible for placing or classifying existing employees rather than bringing in or recruiting employees from outside the organization.

Second, policies need to be created that specify the number and types of candidates sought internally and the number and types of candidates sought externally.

Budget An organization's internal recruitment budgeting process should also closely mirror the budgeting process that occurs with external recruitment. The cost per hire may, however, differ between internal and external recruitment. The fact that internal recruitment targets candidates already working for the organization does not mean that the cost per hire is necessarily less than external recruitment. Sometimes internal recruitment can be more costly than external recruitment because some of the methods involved in internal recruitment can be quite expensive. For example, when internal candidates are considered for the job but not hired, they need to be counselled on what to do to further develop their careers to become competitive for the position the next time it is vacant. When a candidate is rejected with external recruiting, a simple and less costly rejection letter usually suffices.

recruitment guide
A formal document detailing the procedures for attracting applicants to a vacant job

Recruitment Guide As with external recruitment, internal recruitment activities involve the development of a **recruitment guide**, a formal document that details the process to be followed to attract applicants to a vacant job. Included in the plan are details such as the time, money, and staff activities required to fill the job, as well as the steps to be taken to fill the vacancy. An example of an internal recruitment guide is shown in Exhibit 6.3.

Timing

A final strategic consideration an organization must make is when to look for internal candidates. As with external recruitment, consideration involves calculation of lead time and time sequence concerns.

Lead Time Concerns A major difference between internal and external recruitment is that internal recruitment not only fills vacancies but also creates them. Each time a vacancy is filled with an internal candidate, a new vacancy is created in the spot vacated by the internal candidate.

As a result of this difference, it is incumbent on the organization to do HR planning along with internal recruitment. This planning involves elements of succession planning (see "Replacement and Succession Plans," later in this chapter). Such planning is essential for effective internal recruitment.

EXHIBIT 6.3 Internal Recruitment Guide

Position Reassignments into New Claims Processing Centre

Goal: Transfer all qualified claims processors and examiners from one company subsidiary to the newly developed claims processing centre. Terminate those who are not well qualified for the new positions and whose existing positions are being eliminated.

Assumptions: That all employees have been notified that their existing positions in company subsidiary ABC are being eliminated and they will be eligible to apply for positions in the new claims processing centre.

Hiring responsibility: Manager of claims processing and manager of claims examining

Other resources: Entire human resource department staff

Time frames:

Positions posted internally on April 2, 2007

Employees may apply until April 16, 2007

Interviews will be scheduled/coordinated during week of April 23, 2007

Interviews will occur during the week of April 30, 2007

Selections made and communicated by last week in May

Total number of available positions: 60

Positions available and corresponding qualification summaries:

6 claims supervisors: 4-year degree with 3 years of claims experience, including 1 year of supervisory experience

14 claims data entry operators: 6 months of data entry experience; knowledge of medical terminology helpful

8 physiotherapy claims examiners: 12 months of claims data entry/processing experience; knowledge of physiotherapy terminology necessary

8 drug claims examiners: 12 months of claims data entry/processing experience; knowledge of drug terminology necessary

8 dental claims examiners: 12 months of claims data entry/processing experience and 6 months of dental claims examining experience; knowledge of dental terminology necessary

8 mental health claims examiners: 12 months of claims data entry/processing experience and 6 months of mental health claims experience; knowledge of medical and mental health terminology necessary

8 substance abuse claims examiners: 12 months of claims data entry/processing experience and 6 months of substance abuse experience; knowledge of medical terminology necessary

Transfer request guidelines: Internal candidates must submit internal transfer requests and an accompanying cover page listing all positions for which they are applying, in order of preference.

Internal candidates may apply for no more than five positions.

Transfer requests must be complete and must be signed by the employee and the employee's supervisor.

Candidate qualification review process: Transfer requests from internal candidates will be reviewed on a daily basis. Those not qualified for any positions for which they applied will be notified by phone that day, due to the large volume of requests.

Continued

EXHIBIT 6.3 *Continued*

All transfer requests and accompanying cover pages will be filed by the position to which they refer. If internal candidates apply for more than one position, their transfer packet will be copied so that one copy is in each position folder.

Once all candidate qualifications have been received and reviewed, each candidate's transfer packet will be copied and transmitted to the managers for review and interview selection. Due to the large number of candidates, managers will be required to interview only those candidates with the best qualifications for the available positions. Managers will notify human resources with the candidates with whom they would like interviews scheduled. Whenever possible, the manager will interview the candidate during one meeting for all of the positions applied and qualified for.

Selection guidelines: Whenever possible, the best-qualified candidates will be selected for the available positions.

The corporation has committed to attempting to place all employees whose positions are being eliminated.

Managers reserve the right to not select employees currently on disciplinary probationary periods.

Employees should be slotted in a position with a salary grade comparable to their current salary grade. Employees' salaries shall not be reduced due to the involuntary nature of the job reassignment.

Notification of nonselection: Candidates not selected for a particular position will be notified by electronic message.

Selection notifications: Candidates selected for a position will be notified in person by the human resource staff and will be given a confirmation letter specifying starting date, position, reporting relationship, and salary.

Time Sequence Concerns As previously noted, it is essential that internal and external recruitment activities be coordinated properly. This proper coordination is especially true with the timing and sequencing of events that must be laid out carefully for both recruitment and placement personnel. Many organizations start with internal recruitment followed by external recruitment to fill a vacancy. Issues that need to be addressed include how long the internal search will take place, whether external recruitment can be done concurrently with internal recruitment, and who will be selected if both an internal and external candidate are identified with relatively equal KSAOs.

STRATEGY DEVELOPMENT

After organizational and administrative issues have been covered in the planning phase of internal recruitment, an organization must develop a strategy to locate viable internal job applicants. It must consider where to look, how to look, and when to look.

Closed, Open, and Targeted Recruitment

The strategy for where to look must be conducted within the constraints of the general eligibility criteria for mobility. Within these constraints it requires a knowledge of closed, open, and targeted systems.

EXHIBIT 6.4 Closed Internal Recruitment System

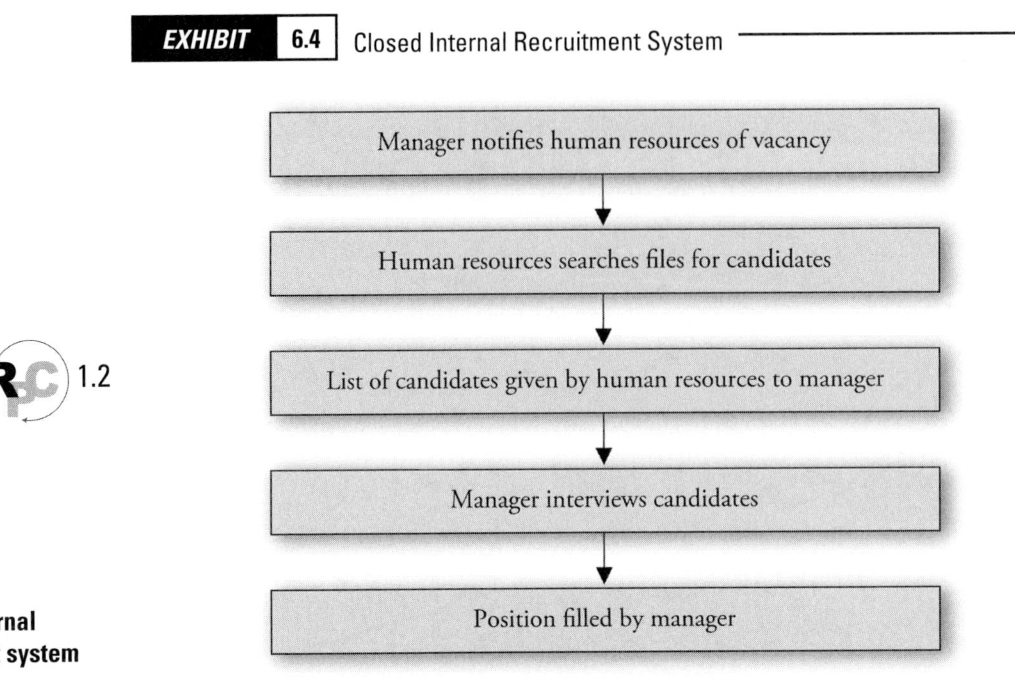

RPC 1.2

closed internal recruitment system
Internal recruitment process where the job vacancy is not posted, and viable internal candidates are identified by HR department and provided to line managers for assessment and selection

open internal recruitment system
A strategy to locate viable internal job applicants where employees are aware of job vacancies, usually through a job posting and bidding system

targeted internal recruitment system
A strategy to locate viable internal job applicants that includes elements of both open and closed internal recruitment system, allowing employees equal opportunity to apply and HR to uncover hidden talent

Closed Internal Recruitment System Under a **closed internal recruitment system**, employees are not made aware of job vacancies. The only people made aware of promotion or transfer opportunities are those who oversee placement in the HR department, line managers with vacancies, and contacted employees. The way a vacancy is typically filled under a closed system is shown in Exhibit 6.4.

A closed system is very efficient. There are only a few steps to follow, and the time and cost involved are minimal. However, a closed system is only as good as the files showing candidates' KSAOs. If inaccurate or out-of-date files are kept, qualified candidates may be overlooked.

Open Internal Recruitment System Under an **open internal recruitment system**, employees are made aware of job vacancies. Usually this is accomplished by a job posting and bidding system. The typical steps followed in filling a vacancy under an open internal recruitment system are shown in Exhibit 6.5.

An open system gives employees a chance to measure their qualifications against those required for advancement. It helps minimize the possibility of supervisors selecting only favourite employees for promotion or transfer. Hidden talent is often uncovered.

An open system may, however, create unwanted competition among employees for limited advancement opportunities. It is a very lengthy and time-consuming process to screen all candidates and provide them with feedback. Employee morale may be decreased among those who are not advanced.

Targeted Internal Recruitment System Under a **targeted internal recruitment system**, both open and closed steps are followed at the same time. Jobs are posted, and the HR department conducts a search outside the job posting system. Both systems are used to cast as wide a net as possible. The large applicant pool is then narrowed down by KSAOs, seniority eligibility, demographics, and availability of applicants.

A targeted system has three advantages: a thorough search is conducted, people have equal opportunity to apply for postings, and hidden talent is uncovered. The major disadvantage with a targeted system is that it entails a very time-consuming and costly process.

EXHIBIT 6.5 Open Internal Recruitment System

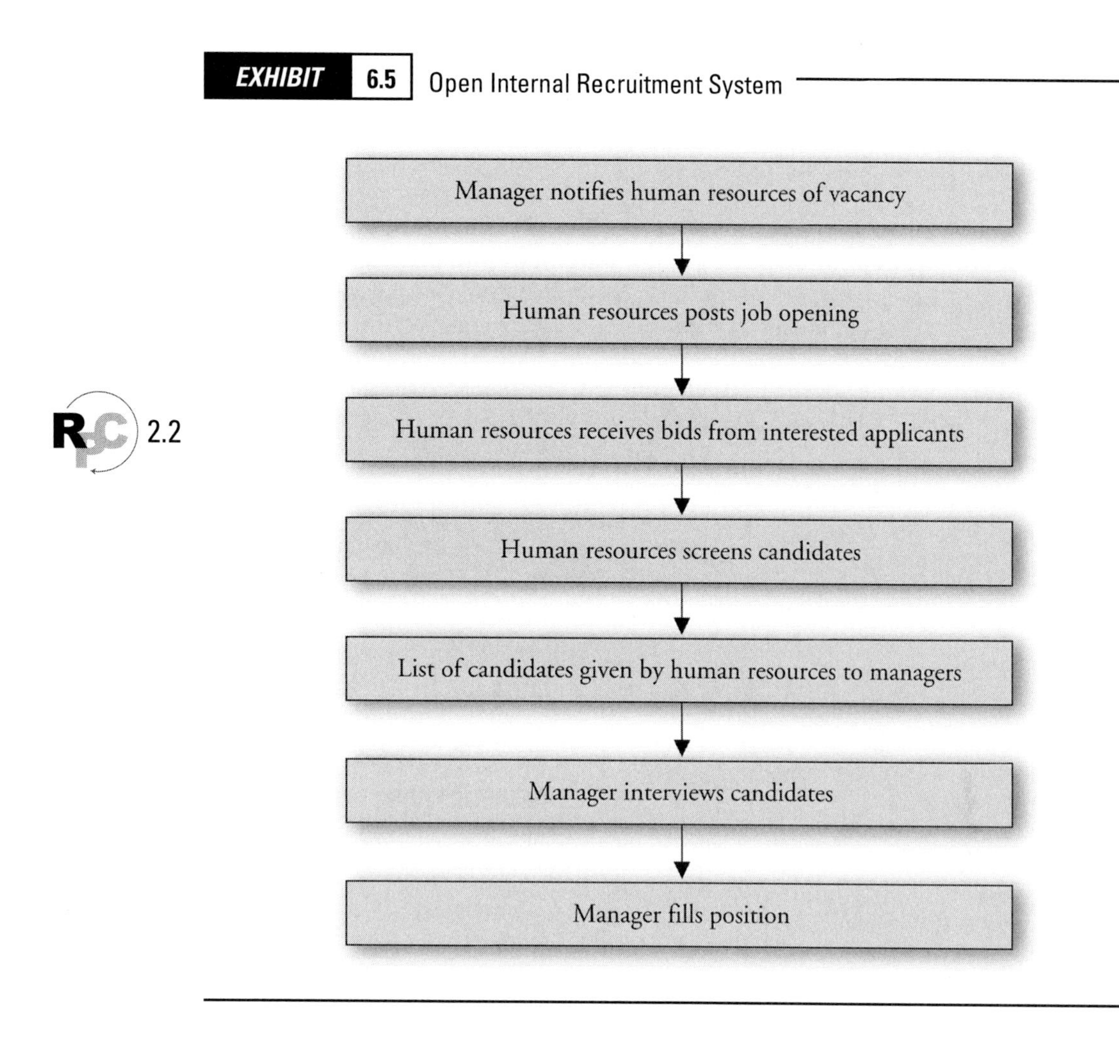

Criteria for Choice of System In an ideal world, with unlimited resources, one would choose a targeted system of internal recruitment. Resource constraints often make this choice impossible, so organizations must choose between open and closed systems. There are several criteria that need to be considered thoroughly before selecting an internal recruitment system:

1. A closed system is the least expensive in terms of search costs. However, it may lead to high legal costs if minorities and women do not have equal access to jobs. An open system is more costly; a targeted system costs the most.
2. Many managers want a person to start work immediately when they have a vacancy; a closed system offers the quickest response.
3. An open system is more likely than a closed system to identify more candidates, and hidden talent is less likely to be overlooked.
4. Some openings may require a very narrow and specialized KSAO set. A closed system may be able to identify these people quickly. An open system may be very cumbersome when only a select few meet the minimum qualifications needed to perform the job.
5. An open system may motivate migration of labour from jobs that are critical and difficult to fill. If so, then employees may create vacancies in critical areas, which in turn may create new recruitment problems.
6. A labour agreement or contract is a legally binding agreement. Whatever system is specified within must be followed.
7. An open system, where rules and regulations are known, enhances perception of fairness.

Although the choice between open and closed systems is important, with the advent of staffing software, bridges between these systems may be built so as to take advantage of the best features of each.

Recruitment Sources

1.2

Once it has been specified where and how in the organization individuals are likely to be found, there are several major methods that can be used to decide how to look for them: job postings, skills inventory, nominations, employee referral, and in-house temporary pool.

job posting
Spells out the duties and requirements of a job and shows how applicants can apply

Job Posting A **job posting** is very similar to the advertisement used in external recruitment. It spells out the duties and requirements of the job and shows how applicants can apply. Its content should be based on the job requirements matrix. A job posting begins when a job vacancy occurs. A position announcement is then posted. This posting may be through a bulletin board, newsletter, e-mail, or intranet (see the "Intranet and Intraplacement" section, later in this chapter). At this step, organizations must decide whether to first limit the posting or advertise it throughout the organization. If the first posting is limited to a department, location, or work area and if the job is not filled, then it should be posted more broadly. Applicants respond to job postings using a bid sheet like the one shown in Exhibit 6.6.

EXHIBIT 6.6 Example of Bidding Form

INTERNAL APPLICATION FORM COVER SHEET

To apply for a posted position, interested employees should:

1. Look at the job posting notebook(s) or postings posted on the bulletin boards and choose the job or jobs that you are qualified for and interested in applying for. (Check the Qualifications section of the posting.) Make note of the deadline for applying for this position, which is indicated on the posting.
2. Complete one Internal Application Form to apply for a position or positions. This form acts as a resumé/application form. Obtain your direct supervisor's signature before turning the form into human resources.
3. Indicate below the priority of the jobs for which you would like to be given consideration. (Priority: 1 = first choice, 2 = second choice, 3 = third choice)

Priority	Job Title
______	______
______	______
______	______
______	______
______	______

4. Attach this cover sheet to the UHC Internal Application Form and turn both in to Karen in human resources by the application deadline appearing on the job posting.
5. Sign and date below:

______________________ ______________
Employee Signature Date

Source: Reprinted with permission from United HealthCare Corporation and Physicians Health Plan of Ohio, Inc., Columbus, Ohio.

Major U.S. retailers Macy's, Home Depot, and Target have used kiosks to retain existing employees as well to attract new employees. Kiosks located in stores present job openings, sometimes featuring videos of the job. Those interested in a job can complete a brief set of screening questions that are automatically sent to a manager. Home Depot reported an 11 percent drop in employee turnover related to using the kiosks.[5]

Even advanced job posting systems may have some problems in administration. Examples of such difficulties include situations where employees believe that someone has been selected before the job was posted (a "bagged" job), cumbersome systems where managers and HR personnel are overwhelmed with resumés of unqualified candidates, and criticisms that the HR department is not doing an effective job of screening candidates for positions.

Some of these problems again point to the critical importance of the job requirements matrix. A good job posting system will clearly define the requisite KSAOs needed to perform the job. By having a job requirements matrix, employees, HR staff, and managers can do a more effective and efficient job of screening.

Another important issue with posting systems is feedback. Not only do employees need to know whether they receive the job or not, but those who do not receive the job need to be made aware of *why* they did not. Providing this feedback serves two purposes. First, it makes job posting part of the career development system of the organization. Second, it invites future bidding on postings by candidates. If employees are not given feedback, they may be less likely to bid for another job because they feel that their attempts to do so are futile.

An empirical study shows the characteristics of job posting systems that lead to high satisfaction by users.[6] Key characteristics include the adequacy of job descriptions, the adequacy of job notification procedures, the treatment received during the interview, the helpfulness of counselling, and the fairness of the job posting system. These characteristics should be treated as requirements of a good job posting policy.

As indicated, job posting can be done traditionally by physically posting job openings in a convenient location. Such an approach, however, can be very slow, inefficient, and create a large amount of paperwork. A faster and more efficient way to post jobs is to put them on personal computers, which also gives employees 24-hours-a-day access to job postings.

skills inventory
A file for each employee that includes KSAO strengths and weaknesses for possible advancement

Skills Inventory KSAOs that are used in making advancement decisions are stored in a **skills inventory**. The inventory consists of manual files or computer files for each employee. Examples of computer file screens for employees are shown in Exhibit 6.7. Unfortunately, many skills inventories are plagued by problems that make their usefulness suspect. One such problem is the very careful and tedious record keeping required to keep them up to date and useful. Maintenance of these files is critical. Qualified candidates may be bypassed if current files are not maintained. Another problem is that too much information is sometimes recorded. Variables having little relevance to advancement decisions are included, making them redundant with other files (e.g., payroll). Managers are often overwhelmed by the sheer volume in files and, as a result, may be resistant to using a skills inventory.

A final problem that must be confronted in maintaining a skills inventory is that files must be user friendly. Files must be understood and accepted by system users. Doing so requires the participation of users in deciding which variables are to be retained. A user-friendly database should also have the following attributes:

- Simplicity of format for data collection
- Easy method for updating basic information on a scheduled basis
- Reasonable and efficient techniques for extracting information from the database
- Provisions for varied formats for output
- Capability for statistical analysis using relational databases
- Confidentiality of information
- Representativeness of data provided
- Accuracy of data by audit and verification procedures

- Simplicity in querying data bank
- Inclusive but not unwieldy detail
- Integration with other HR files

nominations
Solicitations for names of internal candidates from potential supervisors and peers

Nominations **Nominations** for internal candidates to apply for open positions can be solicited from potential supervisors and peers. They may be an excellent source of names of internal candidates, as they have a great deal of familiarity with what is required to be successful in the

EXHIBIT 6.7 Sample Elements in Skills Inventory

Screen 1: Current employee data

Name:
SIN #:
Department:
Position:
Supervisor:
Date in position:
Date of hire:

Screen 2: Education data

	School Attended	Degree	Major	GPA	Year(s)
High school:					
Undergrad:					
Graduate:					
Doctorate:					

Additional course work:
Certifications/licences:
Additional training:
Company training:

Additional training recommended:

Screen 3: Company employment data

	Title	Date in Job	Performance Ratings/Dates
Present position:			
Previous positions:			

Positions in company qualified for:

Screen 4: Previous employment data

	Company	Title	From	To	Reference Quality
Prev. empl.					
Prev. empl.					
Prev. empl.					
Prev. empl.					

Screen 5: Express interests/goals

Areas of company:
Positions:
Additional training/education:

position. They can help establish the criteria for eligibility and then, through their contacts in the organization, search for eligible candidates. Self-nominations are also very useful in that they ensure that qualified candidates are not inadvertently overlooked using other applicant searching methods. Self-nomination is an especially important consideration in the internal recruitment of minorities and women.

employee referral
Using employees to refer potential hires to an organization

Employee Referral Using employees to refer potential hires to the organization is a common method of looking for candidates in external recruitment. Though not used extensively, some organizations have used internal as well as external recruitment to fill job vacancies. For example, using Web-based software, JOBTAG in the U.S. developed a talent referral network that can involve employees referring co-workers for job openings. Employees' willingness to use the system is increased by offering incentives for successful referrals.[7] Regardless of what system is used, as with external recruitment, **employee referral** programs used internally may need to rely on formal programs with recognition for participation to get employees actively participating in making referrals. Moreover, they need to be educated on eligibility requirements to ensure that qualified personnel are referred.

in-house temporary pools
Temporary staff that may become permanent staff when assessed as part of internal recruitment

In-House Temporary Pools **In-house temporary pools** are not only important to the temporary staffing of organizations as the temporary need for personnel arises periodically, but they are also an excellent source of permanent internal employment. From the perspective of the organization, they are a known commodity and require less orientation to the organization than would external hires. From the perspective of the applicant, in-house temporary employees are more likely to have realistic expectations regarding the organization and the job than external candidates. Internships are one source of temporary employees. For example, Electronic Arts, a video-game manufacturer based in Vancouver, B.C., offers internships to university students who work in designing video games. Electronic Arts identifies internship standouts and recruits them to become full-time employees after they have completed university. In addition to offering interns a job after university, Electronic Arts covers the costs of tuition and books for the final year of university.[8]

1.1

Replacement and Succession Plans A critical source of internal recruitment is provided by the results of replacement and succession planning. Replacement and succession planning focus on the identification of individual employees who will be considered promotion candidates, along with a thorough assessment of their current capabilities and deficiencies, coupled with training and development plans to erase any deficiencies. The focus is thus on both the quantity and quality of human resource availability. Through replacement and succession planning, the organization constructs internal talent pipelines that ensure steady and known flows of qualified employees to higher levels of responsibility and impact. Replacement planning precedes succession planning, and the organization may choose to stop at just replacement planning rather than proceeding into more complex succession planning.[9]

replacement charts
Plans for filling vacant positions internally as part of an organization's promote-from-within HR strategy

Most succession plans include **replacement charts**, which indicate positions and who is scheduled to fill those slots when they become vacant. Replacement charts, similar to the one shown in Exhibit 6.8, usually also indicate the time until the individual is ready for the assignment. Succession plans are organized by position and lists the skills needed for the prospective position (i.e., "for the employee to be ready for promotion into this position from her current position, these are the skills she needs to process or develop"). Dow Chemical's succession plan, for example, includes a list of "now ready" candidates; where there are jobs with similar competencies, it clusters roles and lists candidates for these roles as well. Dow has formal succession plans for 50 to 60 jobs that it has identified as critical corporate roles and also has plans for another 200 to 300 jobs that are identified as needing continuity.

It is critical that succession planning be future oriented, lest the organization plan be based on historical competencies that fail to meet new challenges. Software exists to assist companies with succession planning. Succession Plus is a succession planning package that interfaces with

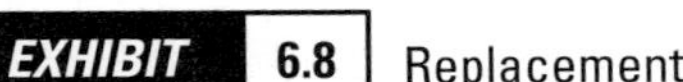

EXHIBIT 6.8 Replacement Chart Example

Organizational Unit: Merchandising—Soft Goods
Replacement for: Department Sales Manager (A2)
Pipelines for Replacement: Department Sales (A1)—preferred; External Hire—last resort
Minimum Eligibility Requirements: Two years full-time sale experience; overall performance rates of "exceeds expectation"; promotability rating of "ready now" or "ready in < 1 yr."

Department: Menswear
Store: Cloverdale

Incumbent Manager	**Years in Job**	**Overall Performance Rating**		
Seng Woo	7	X Exceeds expectations	___ Meets expectations	___ Below expectations

Promote to	**Promotability Rating**			
Group Sales Manager	X Ready now	___ Ready in < 1 yr.	___ Ready in 1–2 yrs.	___ Not promotable

Replacement	**Years in Job**	**Overall Performance Rating**		
Shantara Williams	8	X Exceeds expectations	___ Meets expectations	___ Below expectations

Promote to	**Promotability Rating**			
Sales Manager	X Ready now	___ Ready in < 1 yr.	___ Ready in 1–2 yrs.	___ Not promotable

Replacement	**Years in Job**	**Overall Performance Rating**		
Lars Stemke	2	X Exceeds expectations	___ Meets expectations	___ Below expectations

Promote to	**Promotability Rating**			
Sales Manager	___ Ready now	X Ready in < 1 yr.	___ Ready in 1–2 yrs.	___ Not promotable

a company's HR information system to provide replacement charts and "competency libraries" that allow an organization to identify developmental activities and assignments for individuals in the replacement charts. Many Fortune 500 companies use Succession Plus.

Succession planning is especially important as organizations begin to deal with the challenges of baby boomer retirements. For instance, in a 2004 survey of 142 Canadian companies, 24 percent of employees were ten years or fewer from retirement.[10] As large numbers of employees begin retiring, organizations need to prepare and develop succession plans. A key element in succession planning is the development and training of replacement managers. For example, Alliance Atlantis of Toronto develops its managerial talent base using work projects to increase managers' skills and knowledge base.[11] Similarly, Maple Leaf Foods in Ontario uses a grid that crosses manager accomplishments against corporate values for tracking managers' developments.[12] Unfortunately, succession planning activities such as these may be uncommon as a survey of 518 companies indicated that nearly half had not developed a succession plan.

intranet
A network similar to the Internet, except that it is confined to and accessible only to an organization

Intranet and Intraplacement An **intranet** is similar to the Internet, except that it is confined to the organization. This makes it ideal for internal recruitment because jobs can be quickly posted for all employees to see. Some companies have expanded their intranet to include an online career centre, where employees not only view job postings but also gain access to information about KSAOs needed for positions that might interest them; it may even include modules that will assist employees in acquiring these KSAOs.

Recently, Whirlpool set up an intranet system so that managers who have an opening can enter the criteria into the system, and employees can find a list of jobs that might match their skills and interests. Other companies such as BMW, Kellogg's, Hyatt, and Hewlett-Packard have followed suit. Some vendors, such as Recruitsoft, SAP, Oracle, and Authoria, have developed software specifically for this application.

Some tips for ensuring that companies make the best use of their intranet include impressing on managers the importance of competing for internal talent (so they will be motivated to use the system), encouraging employees to use the system and emphasizing that it is for them, and making sure the interested employees get personal attention (even if they are not selected).[13]

Choice of Sources

There is no single best source for recruitment; each source has its strengths and weaknesses. The following criteria can be used to select which sources are most appropriate for each search:

- **Sufficient quantity and quality:** Although precious few data are available on the subject, it seems likely that some methods, such as job postings and use of an intranet, will produce more internal applicants than other methods, such as nominations and referrals. Other methods, such as skills inventories and succession plans, only identify viable candidates. Thus, when these methods are used, they must be combined with other methods to generate actual interest on the part of internal applicants. As for quality, any of the methods of internal recruitment are capable of producing high-quality candidates. However, the quality of "open" sources (e.g., job postings), where literally anyone can apply, would seem to generate more candidates of variable quality. Thus, when high-quality applicants are paramount, sources such as succession plans and intraplacement should be used.
- **Cost:** Internal recruitment methods differ widely in their costs. Some methods, such as nominations and referrals, are virtually cost free. Other methods, such as using an intranet and succession plans, take a substantial commitment of resources to set up and maintain.
- **Past experience with source:** Organizations typically favour sources they have used in the past. Past experience can be valuable, as long as decision makers ensure they are objective about their sources and do not rely on inertia. Organizations that do so will neglect to take advantage of promising new developments such as an intranet. Moreover, although historically many unionized environments and government agencies have required that

jobs be formally posted, many of the newer methods, such as an intranet, benefit employees as much as employers, so unions may be more open to such innovations.

- **Impact on HR outcomes:** Because there is so little research on the effectiveness of internal recruitment sources, organizations will need to evaluate the methods themselves to ensure that they are using the most effective sources.

SEARCHING

Once the planning and strategy development phases are conducted, it is time to conduct the search. As with external recruitment, the search for internal recruits is activated with a requisition. Once the requisition has been approved, the message and medium must be developed to communicate the vacancy to applicants.

Communication Message

1.3

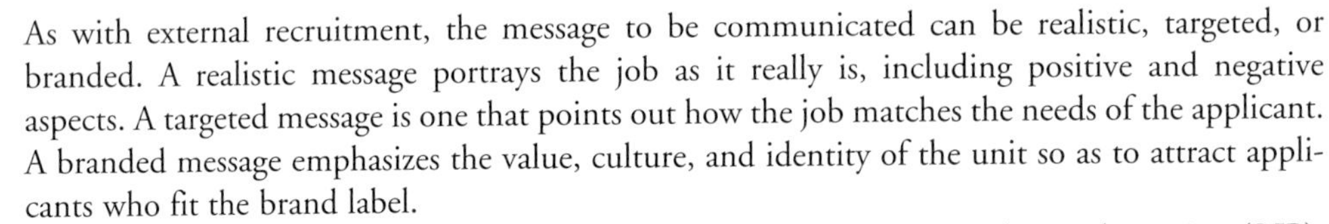

As with external recruitment, the message to be communicated can be realistic, targeted, or branded. A realistic message portrays the job as it really is, including positive and negative aspects. A targeted message is one that points out how the job matches the needs of the applicant. A branded message emphasizes the value, culture, and identity of the unit so as to attract applicants who fit the brand label.

Realistic messages can be communicated using a technique like a realistic job preview (RJP). This technique needs to be applied carefully for internal recruitment because applications, who are already members of the organization, may have an accurate picture of the job. Hence, an RJP may not be needed. It should not, however, be automatically assumed that all internal candidates have accurate information about the job and organization. Hence, RJPs are appropriate for internal applicants when they move to an unknown job, a newly created job, or a new geographic area, including an international assignment.

Targeted messages along with inducements are likely to attract experienced internal employees. Targeted messages about the desirability of a position and the actual rewards should come directly from the job rewards matrix. Clearly, the information in the job rewards matrix needs to be communicated by the hiring manager who hopes to catch an experienced employee, rather than offers of elaborate promises that the manager may not be able to keep.

Communication Medium

The actual method or medium used to communicate job openings internally may be a job posting, other written documents, potential supervisors and peers, and informal systems. In a job posting, the duties and requirements of the job should be clearly defined as should the eligibility requirements. To ensure consistency and fair treatment, job postings are usually coordinated by the HR department.

Other written documents used to communicate a vacancy may include a description of the organization and location as well as a description of the job. A brochure, videocassette, or CD- or DVD-ROM can be created to actually show and describe what the organization and the location of the organization is really like. This message may be of critical importance to the applicant who may, for example, be asked to relocate to a new geographic area or to accept an international assignment.

Potential supervisors and peers can be used to describe to the internal applicant how the position they are considering fits into the larger organizational picture. Supervisors will have knowledge about how the position fits with the strategic direction of the organization. Hence, they can communicate information regarding the expansion or contraction of the business unit within which the organization resides. Moreover, supervisors can convey the mobility paths and requirements for future movement by the applicants within the business unit, should they be hired. Peers can be used to supplement these supervisory observations to give candidates a realistic look at what actually happens by way of career development.

Informal systems exist in organizations where organizational members communicate with one another about job vacancies to be filled internally in the absence of verifiable information. The problem with "word of mouth," the "grapevine," and "hall talk" is that it can be a highly selective, inaccurate, and haphazard method of communicating information. It is selective because, by accident or design, not all employees hear about vacant jobs. Talented personnel, including minorities and women, may thus be overlooked. It is inaccurate because it relies on second- or thirdhand information; important details, such as actual job requirements and rewards, are omitted or distorted as they are passed from person to person. Informal methods are also haphazard in that there is no regular communication channel specifying set times for communicating job information. As a result of these problems, informal systems are not to be encouraged.

APPLICANT REACTIONS

A glaring omission in the research literature is a lack of attention paid to studying the reactions of applicants to the internal recruitment process. This lapse stands in stark contrast to the quantity of research conducted on reactions to the external recruitment process. One notable exception in the internal recruitment process is the study of perceived fairness. Given limited opportunities for promotion and transfer, issues of fairness often arise over mobility decisions within an organization. Issues of fairness can be broken down into the categories of distributive and procedural justice. Distributive justice refers to how fair the employee perceives the actual decision to be (e.g., promote or not promote). This particular aspect of fairness is very salient today because there are a large number of baby boomers competing for the few positions at the top of organizational hierarchies. At the same time, many organizations are eliminating middle management positions. Procedural justice refers to how fair the employee perceives the process (e.g., policies and procedures) that leads to the promotion or transfer decision to be. Reviews of the evidence suggest that procedures may be nearly as great a source of dissatisfaction to employees as decisions.[14] In some organizations, dissatisfaction arises as a result of the fact that there is no formal policy regarding promotion and transfer opportunities. In other organizations, there may be a formal policy, but it may not be closely followed. In yet other organizations, it may be who you know, rather than what you know, that serves as the criterion that determines advancement. Finally, in some organizations there is outright discrimination against women and minorities. All of these examples are violations of procedural justice and likely to be perceived as unfair.

TRANSITION TO SELECTION

As with external recruitment, once a job seeker has been identified and attracted to a new job, the organization needs to prepare the person for the selection process. It should not be assumed that just because job seekers come from inside the organization they will automatically know and understand the selection procedures. With the rapid advances being made in selection methods, the applicant may be unaware of new methods being used that are different from those used previously to hire the applicant to a previous job. Even if the same selection methods are being used, the applicant may need to be "refreshed" on the process, as a considerable period of time may have elapsed between the current and previous selection decisions.

LEGAL ISSUES

For some time, career advancement and development for women and members of other designated groups has been a topic of concern related to internal recruitment and selection practices. The concerns exist because of the career barriers and obstacles faced by the members of these groups.

Ceilings and Sticky Floors

glass ceiling
Strong but invisible barriers for women and minorities to promotion in an organization, particularly to its highest levels

concrete ceiling
Refers to upward mobility barrier faced by women of colour because they are the least represented in management jobs

sticky floor
Organizational situation that keeps people stuck in a job because of a lack of opportunities for development and advancement

"**Glass ceiling**" is a term used to characterize strong but invisible barriers for women and minorities to promotion in an organization, particularly to its highest levels. Evidence demonstrating the existence of the glass ceiling is substantial. In 2004, Catalyst Canada conducted a survey of the *Financial Post* 500 list, which describes the largest companies in Canada based on revenues. While women comprise approximately 47 percent of the Canadian workforce, only 19 of the companies on the *Financial Post* 500 list were led by a woman. Moving down the corporate hierarchy, women also only constituted 14.4 percent of corporate officers and 36.6 percent of management positions.[15]

The notion of an invisible barrier preventing the progression of women's careers using a glass ceiling metaphor suggests that the barrier is breakable. In contrast, the term "**concrete ceiling**" has been used to describe the barriers faced by women of colour. This concept is reinforced by data from Statistics Canada that show that visible minority women were the least likely to become managers when compared to other women, minority men, and non-minority men.[16]

Ceilings that limit advancement for designated group members are exacerbated by what has been deemed the "**sticky floor**." The existence of a sticky floor for designated group members is associated with the lack of opportunities made available for development and advancement.[17] Failing to provide opportunities for development keeps people stuck in their current position and makes breaking through any ceiling less likely.

Where these obstacles exist, there are important questions to ask. First, what are the reasons for the lack of upward mobility and representation for minorities and women at higher levels of the organization? Second, what changes need to be made, especially staffing-related ones, to help overcome the obstacles?

Barriers

An obvious conclusion to such data is that where there are barriers to mobility, many of them originate within the organization. In the United States, the Federal Glass Ceiling Commission conducted a four-year study of glass ceilings and barriers to mobility. It identified many barriers, including the following:[18]

- Lack of outreach recruitment practices, mentoring training in revenue-generating areas, and access to critical development assignments
- Initial selection for jobs in staff areas outside the upward pipeline to top jobs
- Biased performance ratings
- Little access to informal networks
- Harassment by colleagues

The barriers identified in the U.S. study are consistent with a Canadian study that examined the barriers encountered by women executives in Canada. The Canadian results expanded the list of barriers. The number one barrier cited by Canadian women executives was a lack of comfort by men in dealing with women on a professional level. Barriers related to this included the presence of gender stereotypes, a male-centric work culture, and exclusion from the "boys club." Organizational culture and policies were also singled out as barriers. Women further indicated that organizations failed to create an environment that facilitated the growth of women, did not value gender diversity, and did not have policies that prevented gender-based discrimination. Lastly, women also said that they experienced difficulties with conflict between work and family, had no organizational pioneers to make their careers easier by opening doors before them, and lacked role models and mentors to assist with the career progress.[19]

Understanding the nature of the barriers faced by women and members of other designated groups provides the foundation for removing and preventing the obstacles.

Overcoming Barriers

RPC 4.1

It is generally recognized that multiple actions, many of them beyond just staffing system changes, will be needed to overcome barriers to mobility, drawing upon the recommendations of the Glass Ceiling Commission in the United States, as well as the recommendations of Public Services Human Resources Management Agency of Canada.[20] Exhibit 6.9 provides a list of actions to take in addressing the career obstacles faced by women and members of other designated groups.

In terms of specific staffing practices that would help to eliminate the glass ceiling, we offer the following suggestions:

- **Barriers to upward mobility can be addressed and removed, at least in part, through internal recruitment activities.** Internal recruitment planning needs to involve the design and operation of internal labour markets that facilitate the identification and flow of people to jobs throughout the organization. This may very well conflict with seniority-based practices or seniority systems, both of which are likely well entrenched. Organizations simply have to make hard and clear choices about the role(s) that seniority will play in promotion systems.
- **In terms of recruitment strategy, where to look for employees looms as a major factor in potential change.** The organization must increase its scanning capabilities and horizons to identify candidates to promote throughout the organization. In particular, this requires looking across functions for candidates, rather than merely promoting within an area (from sales to sales manager to district manager, for example). Candidates should thus be recruited through both traditional and innovative career paths.
- **Recruitment sources have to be more open and accessible to far-ranging sets of candidates.** Informal, word-of-mouth, and "old boy club" sources do not suffice. Job posting and other recruitment strategies that encourage openness of vacancy notification and candidate application will become necessary.
- **Recruitment changes must be accompanied by many other changes.**[21] Top male managers need to understand fully that women executives differ from them and what they perceive to be the major barriers to advancement. Research suggests that women executives are more likely to see an exclusionary climate (e.g., male stereotyping and preconceptions of women, exclusion from informal networks, and inhospitable corporate culture) as a critical barrier, whereas top male managers are more likely to point to experience deficiencies (e.g., lack of significant general management and line experience, not being in the pipeline long enough) as the culprit. Hence, top management must take steps to not only create better experience-generating opportunities for women but also to develop and foster a more inclusive climate for women, such as through mentoring and providing access to informal networks. To encourage such changes and improve advancement results for women and minorities, managers must be held formally accountable for their occurrence. For example, at the Bank of Montreal the annual survey of employees includes a diversity index set of questions to assess whether employees feel that a manager's behaviours are consistent with the diversity values of the organization. These questions ask whether the manager ensures that employees have an equitable opportunity for advancement regardless of their gender, age, race, or disability, whereas another question asks whether the manager is committed to creating an equitable, diverse, and inclusive

work culture.[22] Responses to these questions indicate whether the work environment created by a manager is consistent with the employment equity values of the Bank of Montreal.

Research has shown that HR professionals think both women and minority employees could benefit from a set of changes that would help eliminate career-advancing barriers. The top

EXHIBIT 6.9 Ways to Improve Advancement for Women and Minorities

Examine the Organizational Culture

- Review HR policies and practices to determine if they are fair and inclusive.
- Examine the organization's informal culture: look at subtle behaviours, traditions, and norms that may work against women.
- Discover men's and women's perceptions about the organization's culture, their career expectations, and what drives their intentions to stay or leave.
- Identify the organization's best practices that support women's advancement.

Drive Change through Management Commitment

- Support top-management commitment to talent management, including women in senior positions.
- Ensure that diversity (including women in senior positions) is a key business measurement for success that is communicated to all employees by top management.
- Require line management accountability for advancement of women by incorporating it in performance goals.
- Train line managers to raise awareness and understand barriers to women's advancement.

Foster Inclusion

- Establish and lead a change-management diversity program for managers and employees.
- Affirm diversity inclusion in all employment brand communications.
- Develop a list of women for succession planning.
- Develop and implement retention programs for women.

Educate and Support Women in Career Development

- Emphasize the importance of women acquiring line management experience.
- Encourage mentoring via informal and formal programs.
- Acknowledge successful senior-level women as role models.
- Support the development and utilization of women's networks inside and outside the organization.
- Create and implement leadership development programs for women, including international assignments, if applicable.

Measure for Change

- Monitor the impact of recruiting strategies designed to attract women to senior levels of the organization.
- Track women's advancement in the organization (hiring, job rotation, transfers, international assignments, promotions).
- Determine who gets access to leadership and management training and development opportunities.
- Evaluate differences between salary of men and women at parallel levels within the organization.
- Measure women's turnover against men's.
- Explore reasons why women leave the organization.

Source: Adapted from N. Lockwood, *The Glass Ceiling* (Alexandria VA: Society for Human Resource Management, 2004), pp. 8–9. Used with permission.

five changes are (1) CEO support of women and minorities and professional senior roles, (2) dedicated effort to recruit and retain senior women and minority managers, (3) placement of women and minorities on boards of directors, (4) mentoring programs targeted to women and minorities, and (5) career development programs targeted toward women and minorities.[23]

Employment Equity Programs

For many organizations, the commitment to eliminating career obstacles for members of designated groups is a requirement of their operating environment. In the realm of the federal government, formal employment equity programs are required in organizations that are federally regulated with 100 or more employees. This includes banking, communications, and international and interprovincial transportation. All federal departments are also covered by the Legislated Employment Equity Program (LEEP). The other group of organizations required to establish formal employment equity programs are those that have obtained a federal goods or services contract of $200,000 or more and who employee 100 or more people. In this situation, the Federal Contractors Program (FCP) applies. In 2002, the FCP applied to nearly 900 organizations involving more than a million employees.[24]

When organizations embrace the goals and objectives of employment equity, it can produce dramatic results. Consider the Royal Bank of Canada. In 1987 visible minorities represented 7.8 percent of the workforce. As a result of its employment equity program, visible minorities represented 23.7 percent of the workforce by 2004.[25] Similarly, as a result of employment equity, women make up one-third of all managers at the Royal Bank.[26]

In summary, solutions to the glass ceiling problem require myriad points of attack. First, women and minorities must have visibility and support at top levels—from the board of directors, the CEO, and senior management. That support must include actions to eliminate prejudice and stereotypes. Second, women and minorities must be provided the job opportunities and assignments that will allow them to develop the depth and breadth of KSAOs needed for ascension to, and success in, top management positions. These developmental experiences include assignments in multiple functions, management of diverse businesses, line management experience with direct profit-loss and bottom-line accountability, diverse geographic assignments, and international experience. Naturally, the relative importance of these experiences will vary according to type and size of the organization. Third, the organization must provide continual support for women and minorities to help ensure positive person/job matches. Included here are mentoring, training, and flexible work hours systems. Fourth, the organization must gear up its internal recruitment to aggressively and openly track and recruit women and minority candidates for advancement. Finally, the organization must develop and use valid methods of assessing the qualifications of women and minority candidates.[27]

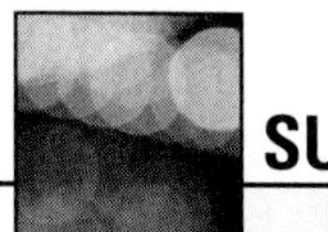

SUMMARY

The steps involved in the internal recruitment process closely parallel those in the external recruitment process. These steps include planning, strategy development, and communication. With internal recruitment, the search is conducted inside rather than outside the organization. Where both internal and external searches are conducted, they need to be coordinated with one another.

The planning stage requires that the applicant population be identified. Doing so requires an understanding of mobility paths in the organization and mobility path policies. To get access to the internal applicant population, attention must be devoted in advance of the search to requisitions, number and type of contacts, the budget, development of a recruitment guide, and timing.

In terms of strategy development, a closed, open, or targeted system can be used to decide where to look. How to look requires a knowledge of recruitment sources, such as job postings, skills inventories, nominations, employee referrals, in-house temporary pools, replacement and succession plans, and intranet and intraplacement. Just as with external recruitment, there are multiple criteria to be considered in choosing internal sources.

When searching for candidates, the message to be communicated can be realistic, targeted, or branded. Which approach is best to use depends on the applicants, job, and organization. The message is usually communicated with a job posting. It should, however, be supplemented with other media, including other written documents and potential peers' and supervisors' input. Informal communication methods with information that cannot be verified or with incomplete information are to be discouraged.

The organization needs to provide the applicant with assistance for the transition to selection. This assistance requires that the applicant be made fully aware of the selection process and how to best prepare for it. Taking this step, along with providing well-developed job postings and clearly articulated mobility paths and policies in the organization, should help applicants see the internal recruitment system as fair.

Internal recruitment activities have long been the object of close legal scrutiny. Past and current regulations make several suggestions regarding desirable promotion system features. The relevant laws permit bona fide seniority systems, as long as they are not intentionally used to discriminate. Seniority systems may have the effect of impeding promotions for women and members of other designated groups because these groups have not had the opportunity to accumulate an equivalent amount of seniority to that of white males. The glass ceiling refers to invisible barriers to upward advancement, especially to the top levels, for minorities and women. Studies of promotion systems indicate that internal recruitment practices contribute to this barrier. As a portion of an overall strategy to shatter the glass ceiling, changes are now being experimented with for opening up internal recruitment. These include actions to eliminate stereotypes and prejudices, training, and developmental experiences, mentoring, aggressive recruitment, and use of valid selection techniques.

KEY TERMS

closed internal recruitment system 206
concrete ceiling 216
employee referral 211
glass ceiling 216
in-house temporary pools 211
internal recruitment process 198
intranet 213
job posting 208
mobility path 199
mobility policies 201
nominations 210
open internal recruitment system 206
recruitment guide 203
replacement charts 211
skills inventory 209
sticky floor 216
targeted internal recruitment system 206

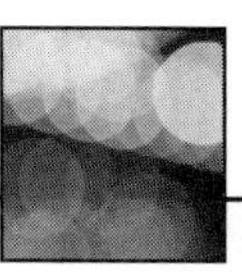

DISCUSSION QUESTIONS

1. Traditional career paths emphasize strict upward mobility within an organization. How does mobility differ in organizations with innovative career paths? List three innovative career paths discussed in this chapter, describing how mobility occurs in each.
2. A sound policy regarding promotion is important. List the characteristics necessary for an effective promotion policy.
3. Compare and contrast a closed internal recruitment system with an open internal recruitment system.
4. What information should be included in the targeted internal communication message?
5. Exhibit 6.9 contains many suggestions for improving the advancement of women and minorities. Choose the three suggestions you think are most important and explain why.

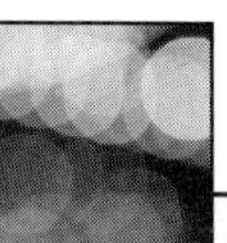

ETHICAL ISSUES

1. Let's say a company called MDN, Inc. is considering two employees for the job of senior manager. An internal candidate, Julie, has been with MDN for 12 years and received very good performance evaluations. The other candidate, Raoul, works for a competitor and has valuable experience in the product market into which MDN wishes to expand. Do you think MDN has an obligation to promote Julie? Why or why not?
2. Do organizations have an ethical obligation to have a succession plan in place? If no, why not? If so, what is the ethical obligation, and to whom is it owed?

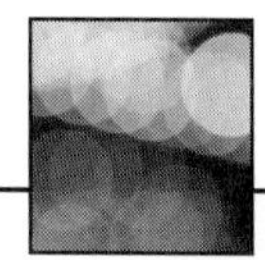

APPLICATIONS

Recruitment in a Changing Internal Labour Market

Mitchell Shipping Lines is a distributor of goods on the Great Lakes. Not only does it distribute goods but it also manufactures shipping containers used to store the goods while in transit. The name of the subsidiary that manufactures those containers is Mitchell-Cole Manufacturing, and the president and CEO is Zoe Brausch.

Brausch is in the middle of converting the manufacturing system from an assembly line to autonomous work teams. Each team will be responsible for producing a separate type of container, and each team will have different tools, machinery, and manufacturing routines for its particular type of container. Members of each team will have the job title "assembler," and each team will be headed by a permanent "leader." Brausch would like all leaders to come from the ranks of current employees, both in terms of the initial set of leaders and leaders in the future as vacancies arise. In addition, she wants employee movement across teams to be discouraged in order to build team identity and cohesion. The current internal labour market, however, presents a formidable potential obstacle to her internal staffing goals.

Based on a long history in the container manufacturing facility, employees are treated like union employees even though the facility is nonunion. Such treatment was desired many years ago as a strategy to remain nonunion. It was management's belief that if employees were treated like union employees, there should be no need for employees to vote for a union. A cornerstone of the strategy is use of what everyone in the facility calls the "blue book." The blue book looks like a typical labour contract, and it spells out all terms and conditions of employment. Many of those terms apply to internal staffing, and are very typical of traditional mobility systems found in unionized work settings. Specifically, internal transfer and promotions are governed by a facility-wide job posting system. A vacancy is posted throughout the facility and remains open for 30 days; an exception to this is identified entry-level jobs that are filled only externally. Any employee with two or more years of seniority is eligible to bid for any posted vacancy; employees with less seniority may also bid, but they are considered for positions only if no two-year-plus employees apply or are chosen. Internal applicants are assessed by the hiring manager and a representative from the HR department. They review applicants' seniority, relevant experience, past performance appraisals, and other special KSAOs. The blue book requires that the most senior employee who meets the desired qualifications should receive the transfer or promotion. Thus, seniority is weighted heavily in the decision.

Brausch is worried about this current internal labour market, especially for recruiting and choosing team leaders. These leaders will likely be required to have many KSAOs that are more important than seniority, and KSAOs likely to not even be positively related to seniority. For example, team leaders will need to have advanced computer, communication, and interpersonal skills. Brausch thinks these skills will be critical for team leaders to have and that they will more likely be found among junior rather than senior employees. Brausch is in a quandary. She asks for your responses to the following questions:

1. Should seniority be eliminated as an eligibility standard for bidding on jobs—meaning no longer giving the two-year-plus employees priority?
2. Should the job posting system simply be eliminated? If so, what should it be replaced with?
3. Should a strict promotion-from-within policy be maintained? Why or why not?
4. How could career mobility paths be developed that would allow across-team movement without threatening team identity and cohesion?
5. If a new internal labour market system is to be put in place, how should it be communicated to employees?

Succession Planning for a CEO

North Star Credit Union is based in the Northwest Territories. The president and CEO of North Star, Harry Ritter, has been with the company for 30 years, the last 12 in his current position as president and CEO. The last three years have been difficult for North Star, as earnings have been below average for the industry, and shareholders have grown increasingly impatient. Last month's quarterly earnings report was the proverbial last straw for the board. Particularly troublesome was Ritter's failure to invest enough of North Star's assets in higher-yielding investments. Though financial institutions are carefully regulated in terms of their investment strategies, Ritter's investment strategy was conservative even for a credit union.

In a meeting last week, the board decided to allow Ritter to serve out the last year of his contract and then replace him. An attractive severance package was hastily put together; when it was presented to Ritter, he agreed to its terms and conditions. Although the board feels it has made a positive step, it is unsure how to identify a successor. When they met with Ritter, he indicated that he thought the North Star's senior vice president of operations, Bob Bowers, would be an able successor. Some members of the board think they should follow Ritter's suggestion because he knows the inner workings of the credit union better than anyone on the board. Others are not sure what to do.

1. How should North Star go about finding a successor to Ritter? Should Bowers be recruited to be the next CEO?
2. How should other internal candidates be identified and recruited?
3. Does North Star need a succession plan for the CEO position? If so, how would you advise the board in setting up such a plan?
4. Should North Star have a succession plan in place for other individuals at the bank? If so, why and for whom?

ENDNOTES

1. W. T. Markham, S. L. Harlan, and E. J. Hackett, "Promotion Opportunity in Organizations: Causes and Consequences," in K. M. Rowland and G. R. Ferris (eds.), *Research in Personnel and Human Resources Management*, 1987, 5, pp. 223–287.
2. B. R. Allred, C. C. Snow, and R. E. Miles, "Characteristics of Managerial Careers in the 21st Century," *Academy of Management Executive*, 1998, 10, pp. 17–27.
3. M. Huselid, B. Becker, and R. Beatty, R., "Managing employees' careers allows for strategy execution," *Canadian HR Reporter*, June 6, 2005, 18(11), p. 22.
4. B. Crosariol, "CEOs focus on keeping the talent at home," *The Globe and Mail*, September 19, 2005, p. B12.
5. "Retailers use kiosks to screen applicants, retain staff," *Canadian HR Reporter*, April 23, 2001, 14(8).
6. L. W. Kleinman and K. J. Clark, "Users' Satisfaction with Job Posting," *Personnel Administrator*, 1984, 29(9), pp. 104–110.
7. C. S. Weinman, C.S., "JobTAG learned this trick on the schoolyard," *Philadelphia Business Journal*, October 30, 2000, p. 3.
8. T. Humber, "Playing the recruitment game," *Canadian HR Reporter*, May 19, 2003, 16(10), p. G3.
9. J. A. Conger and R. M. Fuller, "Developing Your Leadership Pipeline," *Harvard Business Review*, December 2003, pp. 76–84; International Public Management Association–Human Resources, *Succession Planning*, (Alexandria, VA: author, 2003); S. J. Wells, "Who's Next?" *HR Magazine*, November 2003, pp. 45–50.
10. A. Wahl and L. Bogomolny, "Leaders wanted," *Canadian Business*, March 2004, 77(5), pp. 1–8.
11. S. Singh, "Looking inside for leaders at CCL, Alliance Atlantis," *Canadian HR Reporter*, January 12, 2004, 17(1), p. 6.
12. D. Brown, "Banking on leadership development," *Canadian HR Reporter*, January 17, 2005, 18(1), pp. 7–8.
13. M. Frase-Blunt, "Intranet Fuels Internal Mobility," *EMT*, Spring 2004, pp. 16–21; L. G. Klaff, "New Internal Hiring Systems Reduce Cost and Boost Morale," *Workforce Management*, July 2004, pp. 17–20; C. Waxer, "Inside Jobs," *Human Resource Executive*, September 2004, pp. 36–41.
14. F. K. Foulkes, *Personnel Policies in Large Nonunion Companies* (Englewood Cliffs, NJ: Prentice-Hall, 1980); M. London and S. A. Stumpf, *Managing Careers* (Reading, MA: Addison Wesley, 1982); Markham, Harlan, and Hackett, "Promotion Opportunity in

Organizations: Causes and Consequences"; S. A. Stumpf and M. London, "Management Promotions: Individual and Organizational Factors Influencing the Decision Process," *Academy of Management Review*, 1981, 6(4), pp. 539–549.

15. Catalyst, "2005 Catalyst Census of Women Board Directors of the FP 500," 2005, www.catalystwomen.org/files/full/2005%20Canada%20WBD.pdf.
16. A. Tomlinson, "Concrete ceiling harder to break than glass for women of colour," *Canadian HR Reporter*, December 17, 2001, 14(22), pp. 7–8.
17. Conference Board of Canada, "Voices of visible minorities: Speaking out on breaking down barriers," www.conferenceboard.ca.
18. Federal Glass Ceiling Commission, "Good for Business: Making Full Use of the Nation's Human Capital," p. S19.
19. A. Marzolini, "Moving Forward 2002: Barriers & Opportunities for Executive Women in Canada," Women's Executive Network, 2002, www.wxnetwork.com/images/externalrpt_2002.pdf.
20. Public Services Human Resources Management Agency of Canada, "Employment Equity for Women … Still Matters," www.hrma-agrh.gc.ca/ee/publications/inclusive/eefw-eepf-4_e.asp.
21. P. Digh, "The Next Challenge: Holding People Accountable," *HR Magazine*, October 1998, pp. 63–69; B. R. Rugins, B. Townsend, and M. Mattis, "Gender Gap in the Executive Suite: CEOs and Female Executives Report on Breaking the Glass Ceiling," *Academy of Management Executive*, 1998, 12, pp. 28–42.
22. The Institute of Public Administration of Canada, "Diversity/Workplace Equity at Bank of Montreal," November 29, 2001, www.ipac.ca/manitoba/hogarth/hogarth.pdf.
23. Society for Human Resource Management, *Barriers to Advancement Survey* (Alexandria, VA: author, 2000).
24. Human Resources and Social Development Canada "What Is Employment Equity?" 2003, www.hrsdc.gc.ca/en/lp/lo/lswe/we/information/what.shtml.
25. Royal Bank of Canada, "2004 Employment Equity (EE) Narrative Report," www.rbc.com/uniquecareers/diversity/ee_report.html.
26. G. Nixon, "The Immigrant Imperative: View from an Employer," speech to Toronto Region Immigrant Employment Council (TRIEC), June 21, 2005, www.rbc.com/newsroom/20050621nixon.html.
27. K. L. Lyness and D. E. Thompson, "Climbing the Corporate Ladder: Do Male and Female Executives Follow the Same Route?" *Journal of Applied Psychology*, 2000, 85, pp. 86–101; S. J. Wells, "A Female Executive Is Hard to Find," *HR Magazine*, June 2001, pp. 40–49; S. J. Wells, "Smoothing the Way," *HR Magazine*, June 2001, pp. 52–58.

Online **Learning Centre**

Visit the Online Learning Centre at

www.mcgrawhill.ca/olc/heneman

PART 4

Staffing Activities: Selection

The Staffing Organizations Model

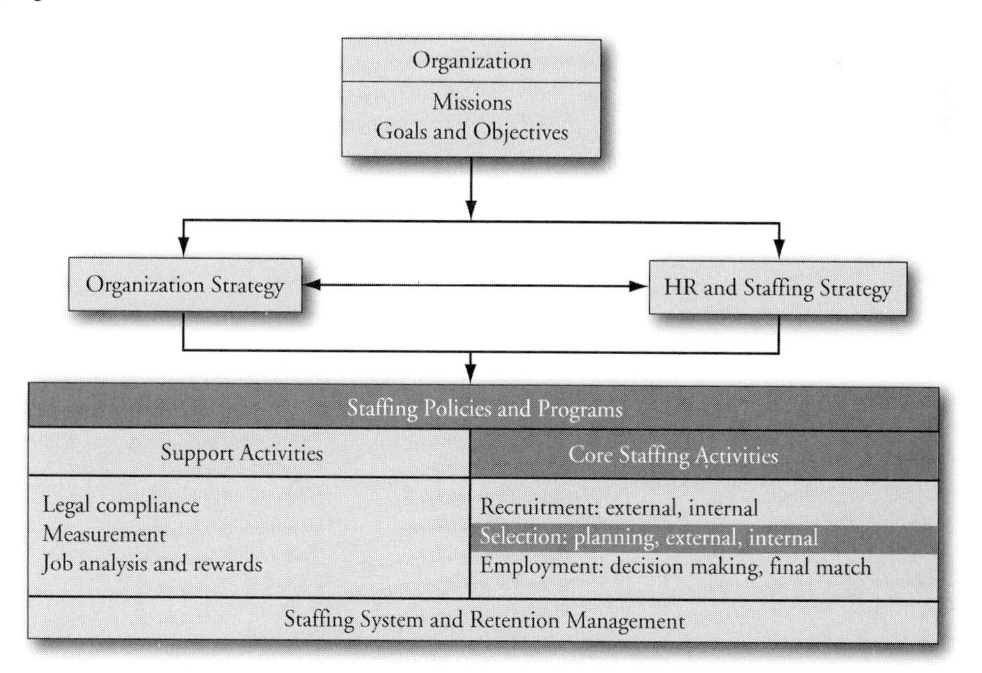

CHAPTER 7

External Selection: Screening

CHAPTER OBJECTIVES

After reading this chapter you will be able to:

- Discuss the pros and cons of using a variety of different assessment methods to evaluate external job applicants
- Define the preliminary issues that guide the use of various assessment methods
- Explain the effectiveness of various methods used to gather information on the job applicant's ability to meet the job requirements
- Discuss the factors that guide the choice of which initial assessment methods should be used
- Understand the importance of disclaimers that protect employer rights and legal issues that can arise from using reference and background checks and pre-employment inquiries

external selection
The assessment and evaluation of external job applicants

External selection refers to the assessment and evaluation of external job applicants. A variety of different assessment methods are used. Preliminary issues that guide the use of these assessment methods will be discussed. These issues include the logic of prediction, the nature of predictors, development of the selection plan, and the selection sequence.

A variety of assessment methods are used to select candidates from among the job applicants who initially apply for job openings. The initial assessment methods that will be reviewed are resumés and cover letters, application blanks, biographical information, letters of recommendation, reference and background checks, literacy testing, and screening interviews. The factors that should guide the choice of initial assessment methods will be reviewed. These factors are frequency of use, cost, reliability, validity, utility, and applicant reactions.

The use of assessment methods also requires a firm understanding of legal issues. One method of preventing legal difficulties—the use of disclaimers as a means of protecting employer rights—is described. Similar cautions are raised concerning preservation of the principles of the Personal Information Protection and Electronics Documents Act (PIPEDA) and the prohibitions that stem from human rights legislation.

PRELIMINARY ISSUES

Many times, selection is equated with one event, namely, the interview. Nothing could be further from the truth if the best possible person/job match is to be made. To ensure the best possible match, a series of well-thought-out activities needs to take place. Hence, selection is a process rather than an event. It is guided by a logic that determines the steps that need to be taken. The logic applies to all predictors that might be used, even though they differ in terms of several characteristics. Developing a selection plan is highly instrumental in the actual implementation of the logic of prediction. Implementation also requires creation of a selection sequence, which is an orderly flow of people through the stages of applicant, candidate, finalist, and offer receiver.

The Logic of Prediction

logic of prediction
Based on the theory that indicators of a person's degree of success in past situations should be predictive of how successful he or she will likely be in new situations

In Chapter 1, the selection component of staffing was defined as the process of assessing and evaluating people for purposes of determining the likely fit between the person and the job. This process is based on the **logic of prediction**, which holds that indicators of a person's degree of success in past situations should be predictive of how successful he or she will likely be in new situations. Application of this logic to selection is illustrated in Exhibit 7.1.

A person's KSAOs and motivation are the product of experiences of past job, current job, and nonjob situations. During selection, samples of these KSAOs and motivation are identified, assessed, and evaluated by the organization. The results constitute the person's overall qualifications for the new situation or job. These qualifications are then used to predict how successful the person is likely to be in that new situation or job regarding the HR outcomes. The logic of prediction works in practice if the organization accurately identifies and measures qualifications relative to job requirements, and if those qualifications remain stable over time so that they are carried over to the new job and used on it.

An example of how this logic can be followed in practice comes from a national communications organization with sales volume in the billions of dollars.[1] They were very interested in improving on the prediction of job success (sales volume) for their salespeople, whose sales figures had stagnated. To do so, they constructed what they labelled a "sales competency blueprint," or selection plan, to guide development of a new selection process. The blueprint depicted the KSAOs that needed to be sampled from previous jobs in order to predict sales success in a telemarketing sales job. The blueprint was established on the basis of a thorough job analysis in which subject matter experts identified the KSAOs thought necessary to be a successful telemarketer (e.g., knowledge of the product, how it was developed, and how it compared to the competitors' products). Then a structured interview was developed to sample the extent to which applicants for sales jobs in telemarketing had acquired the necessary KSAOs. In turn, the interview was used in selection to predict the likely success of applicants for the job.

The logic of prediction shown in Exhibit 7.1 demonstrates how critical it is to carefully scrutinize the applicant's past situation when making selection decisions. For example, in selecting someone for a police officer position, the success of the applicant in a previous security guard position might be considered a relevant predictor of the likelihood that the applicant will succeed

EXHIBIT 7.1 The Logic of Prediction

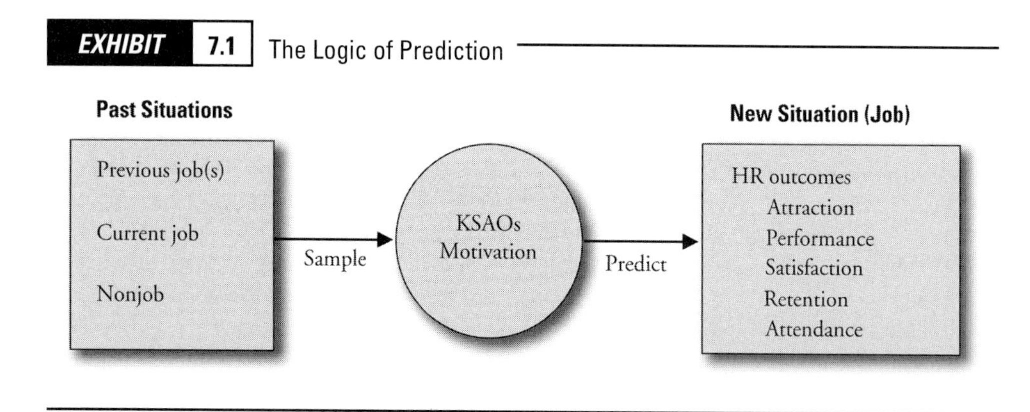

in the new police officer position. Alternatively, the fact that the person was previously successful as a homemaker might be viewed as totally irrelevant to the job of police officer. Surprisingly, considering the homemaker role to be irrelevant might well be an incorrect assessment. Research shows that there is a close correspondence between the homemaker and the police officer position. Specifically, thorough job analysis showed that both jobs rely heavily on troubleshooting and emergency handling skills. Hence, in the absence of a sound job analysis, many qualified applicants may inadvertently be overlooked even though they have some of the characteristics needed to perform the job. Nonjob experience in the home, in the community, and in other institutions may be as valuable as, or more valuable than, previous employment experiences.

Job titles, such as homemaker, are not nearly specific enough for making selection decisions. Similarly, the fact that someone has a certain number of years of experience usually does not provide sufficient detail to make selection decisions. What counts, and what is revealed through job analysis, are the specific types of experiences required and the level of success at each. Similarly, the fact that someone was paid or not paid for employment is not relevant. What counts is the quality of the experience as it relates to success on the new job. Thus, for example, someone who volunteered to serve as an arbitrator of disputes in the community may have more relevant experience for the position of labour relations representative than someone who was paid as a bookkeeper. In short, the logic of prediction indicates that a point-to-point comparison needs to be made between requirements of the job to be filled and the qualifications that applicants have acquired from a variety of past situations.

Not only is the logic of prediction important to selection, but it is important to recruitment as well. A recent study shows that applicant reactions to selection procedures are determined in part by the job relatedness of the selection procedure. If applicants see the selection process as job related, which should occur if the logic of prediction is used, then they are more likely to view the selection process as being fair.[2] It would be expected that applicants who view the selection procedure as fair are more likely to accept a job offer and/or encourage others to apply for a job in the organization.

The Nature of Predictors

As will be seen shortly, there is a wide variety of different types of predictors used in external selection, ranging from screening interviews to background checks. These types can be differentiated from one another in terms of content and form.

Content The substance or content of what is being assessed with a predictor varies considerably and may range from a sign to a sample to a criterion.[3] A sign is a predisposition of the person that is thought to relate to performance on the job. Personality as a predictor is a good example here. If personality is used as a predictor, the prediction is that someone with a certain personality (e.g., "abrasive") will demonstrate certain behaviours (e.g., "rude to customers") leading to certain results on the job (e.g., "failure to make a sale"). As can be seen, a sign is very distant from actual on-the-job results. A sample is closer than a sign to actual on-the-job results. Observing a set of interactions provides an example of a sample. The criterion is very close to the actual job performance, such as sales during a probationary period for a new employee.

speed test

A test that demonstrates a person's score on certain predictors based on the number of responses completed within a certain time frame

power test

A test that presents individuals with tasks of increasing difficulty and complexity to complete

Form The form or design of the predictor may vary along several different lines.

Speed versus Power. A person's score on some predictors is based on the number of responses completed within a certain time frame. One event in a physical abilities test may, for example, be the number of bench presses completed in a given period of time. This is known as a **speed test**. A **power test**, on the other hand, presents individuals with items of increasing difficulty. For example, a power test of numerical ability may begin with addition and subtraction, move on to multiplication and division, and conclude with complex problem-solving questions. A speed test is used when speed of work is an important part of the job, and a power test is used when the correctness of the response is essential to the job. Of course, some tests (see the ***Wonderlic Personnel Test*** in Chapter 8) can be both speed and power tests, in which case few individuals would finish.

Paper and Pencil versus Performance. Many predictors are of the paper-and-pencil variety; applicants are required to fill out a form, write an answer, or complete multiple choice items. Other predictors are **performance tests**, where the applicant is asked to manipulate an object or equipment. For example, NHL hockey players are tested using 150-pound bench press performed at a rate of 25 presses per minute until the player falls below the criterion rate. Paper-and-pencil tests are frequently used when psychological abilities are required to perform the job; performance tests are used when physical and social skills are required to perform the job.

performance test
A test where the applicant is asked to manipulate an object or equipment

Objective versus Essay. An **objective test** is a paper-and-pencil predictor that uses multiple choice questions or true/false questions. These tests should be used to measure specific knowledge in specific areas. Another form of a predictor is an essay, where a written answer is required of the respondent. **Essays** are best used to assess written communication, problem-solving, and analytical skills.[4]

objective test
A paper-and-pencil predictor that uses multiple choice or true/false questions

essay
A writing test that predicts written communication, problem-solving, and analytical skills

Oral versus Written versus Computer. Responses to predictor questions can be spoken, written, or entered into the computer. For example, when conducting interviews, some organizations listen to oral responses, read written responses, or read computer printouts of typed-in responses to assess applicants. As with all predictors, the appropriate form depends on the nature of the job. If the job requires a high level of verbal skill, then oral responses should be solicited. If the job requires a large amount of writing, then written responses should be required. If the job requires constant interaction with the computer, then applicants should enter their responses into the computer.[5]

Development of the Selection Plan

2.1

To translate the results of a job analysis into the actual predictors to be used for selection, a selection plan must be developed. A **selection plan** describes which predictor(s) will be used to assess the KSAOs required to perform the job. The recommended format for a selection plan, and an example of such a plan for the job of administrative assistant, is shown in Exhibit 7.2.

selection plan
Plan that describes which predictor(s) will be used to assess the KSAOs required to perform a job

In order to establish a selection plan, the following three steps are used:

1. A listing of KSAOs is written in the left-hand column. This list comes directly from the job requirement matrix.
2. For each KSAO, a "yes" or "no" is written to show whether this KSAO needs to be assessed in the selection process. Sometimes the answer is no because it is a KSAO that the applicant will acquire once on the job (e.g., knowledge of company policies and procedures).
3. Possible methods of assessment are listed for the required KSAOs, and the specific method to be used for each of these KSAOs is then indicated.

Although they are costly and time consuming to develop, organizations are increasingly finding that the benefits of developing a selection plan outweigh the costs. As a result, it is and should be a required step in the selection process. For example, as part of its selection plan, Hire Performance Inc. offers carrier companies in-depth screening related to criminal checks, federal bankruptcy search, and personal property registry search to ensure a higher level of security in cross-border shipping, particularly since the terrorist attacks on September 11, 2001. One of the screening steps is a personality profile assessment for managers, which "analyzes all character and talent traits as well as personality types that ultimately affect how well the person gets the job done according to the job requirements and the company's culture or management style."[6]

EXHIBIT 7.2 Selection Plan Format and Example for Administrative Assistant Position

Major KSAO Category	Necessary for Selection? (Y/N)	Method of Assessment								
		WP	CT	DB	LTR	TEF	ML	EM	TM	Interview
1. Ability to follow oral directions/listening skills	Y			X					X	
2. Ability to read and understand manuals/guidelines	Y	X	X	X	X	X	X	X		
3. Ability to perform basic arithmetic operations	Y			X		X				
4. Ability to organize	Y			X		X	X			
5. Judgments/priority setting/decision-making ability	Y			X						
6. Oral communication skills	Y									X
7. Written communication skills	Y		X		X			X	X	
8. Interpersonal skills	Y									X
9. Typing skills	Y	X	X		X					
10. Knowledge of word processing, graphics, database, and spreadsheet software	Y	X	X	X	X	X				
11. Knowledge of company policies and procedures	N									
12. Knowledge of basic personal computer operations	Y	X	X	X	X	X		X		
13. Knowledge of how to use basic office machines	N									
14. Flexibility in dealing with changing job demands	Y						X	X	X	
15. Ability to attend to detail and accuracy	Y	X	X	X	X	X	X	X	X	

WP-Word processing test, CT-Correction test, DB-Database exam, LTR-Letter, TEF-Travel expense form, ML-Mail log, EM-Electronic mail messages, and TM-Telephone messages.

Source: Adapted from N. Schmitt, S. Gilliland, R. S. Landis, and D. Devine, "Computer-Based Testing Applied to Selection of Secretarial Positions," *Personnel Psychology*, 1993, 46, pp. 149–165.

EXHIBIT 7.3 Assessment Methods by Applicant Flow Stage

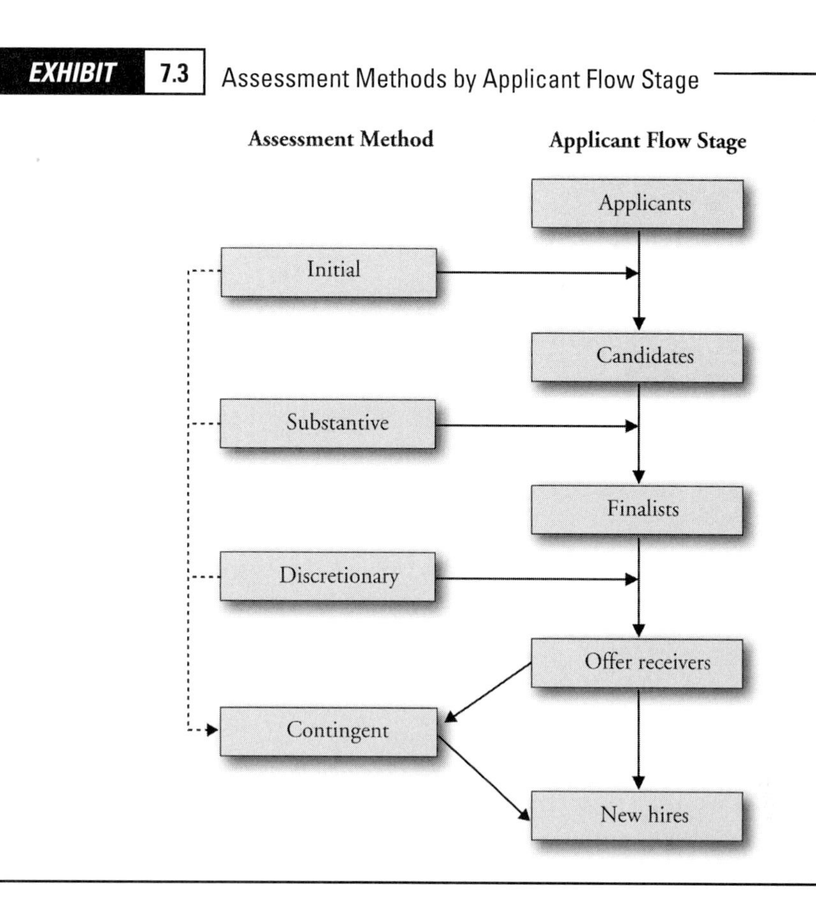

candidate
A job applicant who has not yet received an offer, but who possesses the minimum qualifications to be considered for further assessment

finalist
A job applicant who meets all the minimum qualifications and whom the organization considers fully qualified for the job

offer receivers
A finalist for a position to whom the organization extends an offer of employment

Selection Sequence

Usually, a series of decisions is made about job applicants before they are selected. These decisions are depicted in Exhibit 7.3. The first decision that is reached is whether initial applicants who have applied for the job become candidates or are rejected. A **candidate** is someone who has not yet received an offer, but who possesses the minimum qualifications to be considered for further assessment.

Initial assessment methods are used to screen out unsuitable applicants from applicants who become true candidates (these will be discussed later in this chapter). The second decision made is which candidates become finalists. A **finalist** is someone who meets all the minimum qualifications and whom the organization considers fully qualified for the job. Substantive assessment methods are used to select finalists. These methods will be discussed in the next chapter. The third decision made is which finalist receives the actual job offer. An **offer receiver** is a finalist to whom the organization extends an offer of employment. Discretionary methods are used to select finalists and also will be described in the next chapter. Contingent methods are sometimes used, meaning the job offer is subject to certain qualifications, such as passing a medical exam, before the offer receiver can become a new hire. Finally, some offer receivers become new hires when they decide to join the organization.

INITIAL ASSESSMENT METHODS

2.2

In this section, initial assessment methods are covered. These methods are also referred to as pre-employment inquiries and are used to minimize the costs associated with substantive assessment methods by reducing the number of people assessed. Predictors typically used to screen candidates from applicants include application blanks, biographical information, reference reports, literacy testing, and screening interviews. Each of these initial assessment methods will be described in turn. A general evaluation will be presented to help guide decisions about which initial assessment methods to use.

Resumés and Cover Letters

The first introduction of the applicant to the organization is often a cover letter and resumé. This introduction is controlled by the applicant as to the amount, type, and accuracy of information provided. As a result, resumés and cover letters always need to be verified with other predictors, such as application blanks, to ensure that there is accurate and complete data across all job applicants with which to make informed selection decisions.

One of the major issues with resumés as a selection tool depends on an organization's popularity and visibility, which could lead to a high volume of resumés to process. Online posting and resumé screening is becoming more popular; if used effectively, these processes can narrow down a list of candidates. Home Depot and Blockbuster use resumé-screening technology to process large numbers of candidates to produce a short list of candidates.[7] Employers that have online capability via their Web sites can be inundated with unqualified candidates. A Workopolis survey of 400 Canadian human resources professionals indicated that only 20 percent of resumés received are appropriate for the job posting because of ineffective use of the Internet for recruiting.[8]

It is very difficult for many organizations to store resumés for any extended period of time and read them accurately. Fortunately, technology has resolved this issue. For example, resumés from previous searches can be stored in databases so that when a new vacancy arises, a new recruitment search does not have to take place. Also, optical scanners now make it possible to machine-read resumés. Some resumé-tracking services even score applicant resumés and place a percentage next to an applicant's name reflecting the number of criteria each resumé meets. Hundreds of large companies currently use resumé-tracking software. For example, applicants for jobs with the city of Toronto have their resums electronically processed by Resumix. Resumix extracts information on the applicant's name, address, and phone number, as well as work history, experience, skills, and education (see www.toronto.ca/employment/resume_help.htm). Though such methods have powerful time-and cost-saving advantages, there are disadvantages, such as rejection of resumés that the software has trouble reading (e.g., those on coloured paper or with special formatting like bullets) and applicants who try to beat the system by loading their resumé with every conceivable skill or skills that appear in the advertisement. Despite these drawbacks, the efficiencies of such services make them particularly attractive for organizations facing large volumes of resumés.

The near universal use of e-mail in organizations has complicated the receipt and use of resumés. Examples include the following:

1. Most resumés are received via surface mail, but surveys reveal that most employers prefer to receive them via e-mail.
2. When many companies receive resumés, they are never read but instead are submitted to resumé-scanning software as described above.
3. Some consultants offer new formats for applicants to grab the attention of recruiters. These formats may include multimedia packages that include sound bites, photographs, and supporting documents. Some applicants even send employers CD-ROM resumés with sounds, photos, and animated graphics.
4. More and more resumés are submitted using online forms on the organization's Web site. Some online forms are very basic—asking the applicant to fill in standard information, others are online resumé builders.

Because of these changes, some have argued that the age of the traditional resumé is dead. The conclusion seems premature. Many recruiters still prefer the conventional resumés because they are short and easy to read. Other recruiters may be turned off by too many "bells and whistles."

The solution for applicants and for recruiters is to tailor the presentation of one's credentials to the situation. Applicants need to have multiple methods of presenting credentials at their disposal, including the traditional resumé. And they need to decide which presentation is best for each position or employer. Applicants would be well advised to follow the following pieces of advice in submitting their credentials to employers:

1. Applicants need to make sure their resumés are electronically scan-ready. This means applicants should avoid unusual fonts and formatting. With today's resumés, form definitely should follow function.
2. When submitting a resumé by e-mail, applicants should consider including it in the e-mail message itself rather attaching it as some have trouble reading attachments.
3. As opposed to the traditional emphasis on action verbs (e.g., "managed," "guided,"), applicants should use nouns to describe noteworthy aspects of their background (e.g., "nonprofit," "3.75 GPA," "environmental science experience") as nouns are more likely to be identified as keywords in scanning software. If the applicant believes his or her resumé is likely to be scanned, then the resumé needs to be built around such keywords that will be the focus of the scan.[9]
4. Do not include personal information on a resumé as it could be detrimental to the job seeker. In a survey conducted by ResumeDoctor.com where 100,000 resumés across a variety of industries were examined, one-third of applicants included irrelevant personal details on their resumés. An example would be listing hobbies or interests on the resumé. In a resumé submitted to a financial institution, an applicant stated that she participated in a beauty pageant. When the hiring manager interviewed the applicant, she "became concerned that the applicant had been coached on interview skills during her training for the contest, and ultimately decided she could not trust the results of the interview." This candidate was the best fit for the job but she did not get a job offer.[10]

One of the big problems with resumés is lying. Like the truth, resumés come in various degrees of accuracy, ranging from small unintentional mistakes to outright fabrication. Some degree of what we might call "fudging" is commonplace. For example, Ellie Strauss's two more recent full-time jobs lasted less than six months. Ellie represented these as freelance jobs with the heading "Senior Project Manager" to make them look like contract positions. Some might call this deception. Others might call it "creative marketing" or "tailoring." A study conducted by Christian & Timbers, a global search firm, where 7,000 IT resumés were reviewed, one-quarter of IT executives misrepresented information on their resumés. Misleading information included the number of years in a position, exaggerated responsibilities, and leaving out jobs altogether.[11]

According to a recent survey by ResumeDoctor.com, the most common misleading information put on resumés is the following:

- Inflated titles
- Inaccurate dates to cover up job-hopping or employment gaps
- Half-finished degrees, inflated education, or "purchased" degrees
- Inflated salaries
- Inflated accomplishments
- Outright lies with regard to role and responsibility

Employers have recourse if a candidate is subsequently hired and it is discovered that the employee lied on his or her resumé. The Supreme Court of Canada supports a termination with cause when "the misrepresentations are material and the employer has relied to its detriment upon the misrepresentation." In ***Bridgewater v. Lean's Manufacturing,*** an employee exaggerated his abilities and failed to disclose information about his past employment. The court concluded "that had there been disclosure of all relevant material in regard to his past employment, it is unlikely that he would have been hired for such a senior position with the company."[12]

Another common ruse is for people to claim they were downsized, or moved on to other opportunities, when in fact they were fired for cause. With the innovations in technology, some devious ploys are being hatched. For example, some job seekers will provide prospective bosses with toll-free numbers that are answered by Web site operators who "verify" the academic qualifications listed on the resumé. Some have even hacked into university Web sites to add their names to the list of graduates. The best way to combat resumé fraud or fudging is to conduct careful reference checks (see the "Reference Checks" section, later in this chapter). Also, applying a "smell" test to any suspicious information is wise policy.

Almost no research exists on resumés and cover letters. We do not know their validity or reliability. Nor is there information on their costs. This situation is unfortunate given their pervasive use in certain types of jobs, especially entry-level management, professional, and technical positions. Thus, organizations using resumés and cover letters in selection should carefully evaluate their effectiveness.

Application Blanks

application blank
A form filled out by an applicant that outlines the applicant's background in regard to education, training, and job experiences

Most **application blanks** request in written form the applicant's background in regard to educational experiences, training, and job experiences. This information is often on the resumé as well and may seem unnecessarily duplicated. An application blank can be used to verify the data presented on the resumé and also can be used to obtain data omitted on the resumé, such as whether the applicant is eligible to work in Canada or the type of business of previous employers. The information provided in an application blank can be used as a pre-screening tool to determine whether the applicants have the minimal qualifications that fit the job requirements. Another major advantage over resumés is that application blanks are standardized, thus saving recruiters a tremendous amount of time in the pre-screening process. Also, the organization rather than the applicant dictates what information is presented in an application blank versus the resumé. As a result, information critical to success on the job is less likely to be omitted by the applicant or overlooked by the reviewer of the resumé. The major issue with application blanks is to make sure that information requested is critical to job success, following the logic of prediction discussed earlier.

A sample application blank is provided in Exhibit 7.4. As with most application blanks, the major sections of the application are personal information, employment desired, educational background, work experience, and suggested references. The only information sought from the application blank should be KSAOs that can be demonstrated as relevant to the job. This not only avoids wasting the organization's and the applicant's time but also protects the employer from charges of unfair discrimination (see the "Legal Issues" section near the end of this chapter). It is important to take note of the statement at the bottom of the application blank, known as a disclaimer statement. It provides certain legal protections to the organization (discussed in the "Legal Issues" section near the end of this chapter). Asking applicants to sign a disclaimer also may decrease the incentive to distort or falsify information.

Educational Requirements Special care needs to be taken in wording items on an application blank when soliciting information about educational experiences and performance.[13] Several particularly important areas pertaining to educational requirement information on application blanks will now be discussed.

Level of Education. Level of education or educational performance can be used as an element to predict job performance. Often, level of education is measured by the attainment of a diploma or degree but these achievements should be assessed in conjunction with other educational requirements, such as proficiency in various computer software packages.

EXHIBIT 7.4 Sample Application Blank for Employment

PERSONAL INFORMATION

DATE: ____________________

NAME: ____
LAST FIRST MIDDLE

ADDRESS: ____
STREET APARTMENT NO.

____
CITY PROVINCE POSTAL CODE

HOME TELEPHONE NUMBER: ____________________

E-MAIL ADDRESS: ____________________

ARE YOU LEGALLY ELIGIBLE TO WORK IN CANADA? YES ☐ NO ☐

ARE YOU 18 YEARS OR OLDER, AND YOUNGER THAN 65 YEARS OF AGE? YES ☐ NO ☐

EMPLOYMENT DESIRED

POSITION APPLYING FOR: ____________________

DATE AVAILABLE TO WORK: ____________________

EDUCATION

SECONDARY SCHOOL ☐ GED ☐ COMMUNITY COLLEGE ☐

BUSINESS OR TRADE SCHOOL ☐ UNIVERSITY ☐ OTHER ☐ (SPECIFY) ____________________

HIGHEST GRADE OR LEVEL COMPLETED: ____________________

NAME OF PROGRAM: ____________________

LENGTH OF PROGRAM: ____________________

LICENCE/DIPLOMA/DEGREE AWARDED: YES ☐ NO ☐

OTHER COURSES, WORKSHOPS, SEMINARS: ____________________

COMPUTER SKILLS/SOFTWARE: ____________________

EMPLOYMENT HISTORY

1. NAME OF PRESENT/LAST EMPLOYER: ____________________

   POSITION: ____________________ NAME OF SUPERVISOR/MANAGER: ____________________

   DATE STARTED: ____________________ DATE FINISHED: ____________________

   MAIN DUTIES: ____________________

   ____

   REASON FOR LEAVING: ____________________

Continued

EXHIBIT 7.4 *Continued*

2. NAME OF PREVIOUS EMPLOYER: ______
   POSITION: ______ NAME OF SUPERVISOR/MANAGER: ______
   DATE STARTED: ______ DATE FINISHED: ______
   MAIN DUTIES: ______
   ______
   REASON FOR LEAVING: ______

REFERENCES

I GIVE PERMISSION TO CONTACT THE FOLLOWING REFERENCE:

PRESENT EMPLOYER YES ☐ NO ☐

PAST EMPLOYERS YES ☐ NO ☐

NAME AND CONTACT INFORMATION OF ADDITIONAL REFERENCES: ______

______

PLEASE READ THOROUGHLY AND SIGN BELOW:

"I certify that all the information submitted by me on this application is true and complete, and I understand that if any false information, omissions, or misrepresentations are discovered, my application may be rejected and, if I am employed, my employment may be terminated at any time. I give my permission to contact my present/past employers and the additional references indicated above."

DATE: ______ SIGNATURE: ______

Furthermore, a recent report indicates that the high school diploma may no longer be as good a predictor as it once was because the attainment of a GED (high school equivalency) is often used as a substitute for a diploma on an application form and does not predict as well.[14] Hence, in designing the application form, high school diploma and GED should be indicated as two separate items.

Even the meaning of a university degree or college diploma is changing. Currently, the number of students in online programs is in the millions and will only grow in the future. There are thousands of courses available online, and many universities and colleges are or will be offering online courses in the next few years. The quality of instruction and the amount of learning in these courses is mixed, and employers are often skeptical.[15] Some so-called online degrees are issued by "diploma mills" that simply sell degrees for cash. Two apparent examples are St. Regis University and Hamilton University.[16] Here again, employers need to do their homework and check "universities" out.

Grade Point Average. Classroom grades are measured using a grade point average (GPA). Care should be exercised in the interpretation of GPA information. For example, a GPA in one's major in university may be different (usually higher) than one's GPA for all classes. Grades also vary widely by field (e.g., grades in engineering tend to be lower than in other fields). Further, a GPA of 3.5 may be good at one school, but not at another. For example, GPAs are calculated on a 4-point scale at some schools, while they are calculated on a 5-point scale at other schools. Some schools do not report GPAs at all. Graduate students receive higher grades on average than do undergraduates. In short, GPA may be influenced by many factors in addition to the applicant's KSAOs and motivation. Research suggests that the validity of GPA in predicting job performance may be as high as the mid .30s. University grades are no more valid than high school grades, and grades are most valid in predicting early job performance. Although there is variability from employer to employer, evidence indicates that GPA does not play a large role in most recruiters' evaluations. GPAs do tend to have adverse impact against minorities, and, as with all selection measures with adverse impact, the validity evidence must be balanced against adverse impact implications.[17]

Quality of School. In recent times, much has been said and written about the quality of various educational programs. For example, the 2005 University Report Card survey, produced by ***The Globe and Mail*** in partnership with The Strategic Counsel, gave large, medium, and small universities grades in the following categories: education, accommodation, technology, reputation, finances, student services, and atmosphere. The education grade was based on teaching quality, class sizes, faculty-student interaction, and faculty availability outside classroom hours. The top three in the large university category were University of Western Ontario, University of Toronto, and York University; in the medium university category were University of Waterloo, McMaster University, and Queen's University; and in the small university category were Wilfred Laurier University, University of Winnipeg, and Trent University.[18]

Maclean's magazine also provides a yearly university ranking where schools are ranked in six broad groups—student body, classes, faculty, finances, library, and reputation—and divided into three categories.[19] The following are the 2005 top three universities in each of the categories:

- Undergraduate program: St. Francis Xavier, Mount Allison, Acadia
- Comprehensive (significant amount of research activity, wide range of undergraduate and graduate programs, and professional degrees): Waterloo, Victoria, and Guelph
- Medical/doctoral (broad range of PhD programs and research, as well as medical schools): McGill and Toronto (ranked first), Western, and UBC[20]

Increasingly, questions are being asked about the added value of educational degrees for employers. Organizations pay quite a premium for college-educated hires, so what may seem like a good return on investment to an undergraduate or graduate student may seem like an excessive premium to an employer.

Of particular focus are MBA degrees. Some educators argue that MBA degrees lack the depth of other graduate degrees. Others have blamed the MBA for the rash of corporate scandals. Although the validity of these claims is suspect, it is not unreasonable for an employer to ask whether hiring MBAs is worth the substantial pay premium they command. MBA graduates from Canada's top seven schools earned an average salary of $89,978 in 2004, 11 percent less than in 2001.[21]

High wage premiums for MBA degrees in particular, but also educational degrees in general, are commanded by graduates from prestigious universities. Sixty percent of corporate recruiters cite the reputation of the school as the top reason for recruiting at a particular university. As one article concluded, "It's not necessarily what you learn in an MBA program, but where you learn it."

Although the overwhelming majority of people who earn MBAs say it was worth it (89% in a recent survey), they generate mixed sentiments from employers. Some employers believe that universities are glorified placement services—merely a collection node for smart people. Roger Martin, dean of Rotman School of Management at the University of Toronto, talked about his previous job as a consultant where "given a choice of recruiting with the admission list or the graduation list from the Harvard Business School, it would take me seconds to decide—I'd go with the admissions list."[22]

Major Field of Study. The more specialized the knowledge requirements of a particular position, the more important an applicant's major field of study is likely to be as a predictor. An English major may do very well as an editor but may be unsuccessful as a physician. It should also be noted that choice of a major does not guarantee that a certain number or type of classes have been taken. The number and type of classes needed for a major or minor varies from school to school and needs to be carefully scrutinized to ensure comparability across majors. The relationship between field of study and job performance is very difficult to assess; therefore, no conclusive validity evidence is available.[23]

Training and Experience Requirements The application blank captures a variety of past experiences and training, which occurs after formal education that can predict future performance. In the selection decision, a great deal of weight is often put on work history and practical training based on the assumption that "actions speak louder than words." A natural assumption is that experienced surgeons tend to be more competent surgeons, for example. A study found that the mortality rate of procedures was about twice as high for inexperienced surgeons than for experienced ones.

The drawback of putting too much emphasis on previous work experience, however, is that the amount of experience or training an applicant has may be overstated. Also, applicants with high potential may be overlooked because they have not had the opportunity to gain the training or experience needed.

Various methods can be used to measure training and experience. Since training and experience information is not directly equivalent across applicants, all methods require the judgment of selection decision makers. These decision makers render judgments about how to classify and weight different levels of experience. An approach termed the "behavioural consistency method" has shown the highest degree of validity because it focuses on determining the quality of an applicant's previous training and experience. One of the means by which the behavioural consistency method determines quality is by asking applicants to complete a supplemental application wherein they describe their most significant accomplishments relative to a list of key job behaviours. Due to their involved nature, however, behavioural consistency ratings are time consuming and expensive to administer, and they require the applicant to possess some degree of analytical ability and writing skills. Thus, the choice of weighting methods rests on a trade-off between accuracy and ease and cost of administration.[24]

Licensing, Certification, and Job Knowledge Many professions and occupations require or encourage people to demonstrate mastery of a certain body of knowledge. A **licence** is required of people by law to perform an activity, whereas a certification is voluntarily acquired. The purpose of a licence is to protect the public interest, whereas the purpose of a **certification** is to identify those people who have met a minimum standard of proficiency. Licensing exams and certification exams are usually developed by subject matter experts in conjunction with testing specialists.

licence
Required of people by law to perform an activity and its purpose is to protect public interest

certification
Voluntarily acquired and its purpose is to identify those people who have met a minimum standard of proficiency

Many occupations are monitored by professional associations. In human resources, examples of certifications offered are the Human Resources Professional (CHRP), Employee Benefits Specialist (CBES), Compensation Professional (CCP), Benefits Professional (CBP), Global Remuneration Professional (GRP), Canadian Registered Safety Professional (CRSP), and Health and Safety Consultant (CHSC) designations.[25]

Certification helps guard against the misuse of job titles in HR selection. For example, anyone could adopt the title of safety consultant, but a certification from the Canadian Society of Safety Engineering guarantees that the person has mastered a certain amount of technical knowledge in the safety area.

As mentioned earlier, licensing and certification requirements can be used either as an initial or as a contingent assessment method. When used as an initial method, licensing and certification requirements are used to eliminate applicants who fail to possess these credentials. For example, a car repair shop electing to hire only certified mechanics might initially screen out individuals who fail to have the proper certification. When used as a contingent method, the selection process proceeds on the assumption that the applicant has the requisite credential (or will have it by the time of hire). This is then verified after an initial offer decision is made. For example, rather than verifying that each applicant for a nursing position possesses a nursing degree, a hospital may assess applicants based on the assumption they have a nursing degree and then verify this assumption after a tentative hiring decision has been made. Thus, the difference between using licensing and certification requirements as initial or contingent assessment methods depends on when the information is considered in the selection process.

Increasingly, organizations are using voluntary professional certifications as a method of verifying competence in various occupations. There are more than 1,000 professional certifications. Most of these voluntary certifications are issued on the basis of experience and education. The vast majority of certifications also require examinations. Over time, certifications may expand to most areas of management.[26]

Licensing and certification demonstrate mastery of a general body of knowledge applicable to a variety of organizations. There could be a need to assess a specific body of knowledge required within a particular organization. Job knowledge tests can assess the unique KSAOs that are a requirement of successful job performance. Job knowledge tests are usually used in the public sector as an initial screening device. In the private sector, they are used primarily for promotion purposes. Job knowledge tests are covered in more detail in Chapter 8.

weighted application blank
An application blank that uses a weighted scoring methodology to help differentiate between high and low performing individuals

Weighted Application Blanks Not all of the information contained on an application blank is of equal value to the organization in making selection decisions. Depending on the organization and job, some information predicts success on the job better than other information. Procedures have been developed that help weight application blank information by the degree to which the information differentiates between high- and low-performing individuals.[27] This scoring methodology is referred to as a weighted application blank and is useful not only in making selection decisions but also in developing application blanks as well. The statistical procedures involved help the organization discern which items should be retained for use in the application blank and which should be excluded, on the basis of how well they predict performance.

Evaluation of Weighted Application Blanks Evidence suggests that application blanks are not particularly valid predictors of job performance. This is not surprising given the rudimentary information that is collected. Another factor that may undermine the validity of application blanks is distortion. A study by the National Credential Verification Service found that about one-third of the investigations into the background of applicants suggested that misrepresentation occurred on the application blank. Subsequent studies have suggested that the most common questions that are misrepresented include education, tenure on previous jobs, and reasons for leaving previous jobs. One study revealed that 15 percent of previous employers documented by applicants on their application blanks indicated that the individual never worked for them. Thus, application information that is used in selection decisions should be verified.

Application blanks are very inexpensive means of collecting basic information on job applicants. Most organizations use application blanks only for initial screening decisions (to rule out applicants who are obviously unqualified for the job).

The validity for weighted application blanks is positive if they are well constructed. Items in the weighted application blank are scored and weighted based on their ability to predict job performance and are good predictors for work behaviours such as absenteeism, accidents, and turnover.[28] Thus, as long as ***some*** of the items are predictive, the scoring and weighting schemes embedded in the weighted application blank will ensure that the overall score is predictive. Because the process used to develop the weighted application blank is time consuming and expensive, more cost-benefit studies need to be conducted on the weighted application blank. Is the validity worth the cost? Unfortunately, there is little recent research on the weighted application blank, so answers to this question are difficult to attain.

biodata
Biographical information or personal history on an applicant's background and interests

Biographical Information

Biographical information, often called **biodata**, is personal history information on an applicant's background and interests. Basically, results from a biodata survey provide a general description of a person's life history. The principal assumption behind the use of biodata is the axiom "The best predictor of future behaviour is past behaviour." These past behaviours may reflect ability or motivation. Biodata inventories are thought to measure applicant motivation that can be inferred from past choices. However, research also suggests that many ability items are included in biodata inventories.[29]

Like application blanks, biographical information blanks ask applicants to report on their background. Responses to both of these questionnaires can provide useful information in making initial selection decisions about applicants. Unlike application blanks, however, biographical information can also be fruitfully used for substantive selection decisions. In fact, if scores on a biodata inventory are predictive of subsequent job performance (which, as we will see, is often the case), it may be somewhat limiting to use biodata scores only for initial assessment decisions. Thus, although biographical information is as much a substantive as an initial assessment method because it shares many similarities with application blanks, we have included it in this section. Nevertheless, it should also be considered in deliberations about which substantive assessment methods are to be used.

Biographical information also has similarities and differences with background checks (see the "Reference and Background Checks" section, later in this chapter). Biodata and background checks are similar in that both look into an applicant's past. However, the two types of selection methods differ in the following important ways:[30]

1. Background checks are used primarily when screening applicants for positions in which integrity and emotional adjustment are necessary (e.g., law enforcement, private security), whereas biodata inventories are used to screen applicants in many jobs.
2. Background information is obtained through interviews and conversations with references, while biodata information is usually collected by survey.
3. The criterion by which background information is validated is typically behavioural reliability (e.g., attendance, integrity), while performance is the principal criterion against which biodata scores are validated.

Thus, biodata inventories and background checks are distinct methods of selection that must be considered separately.

The type of biographical information collected varies a great deal from inventory to inventory and often depends on the job. For example, a biographical survey for executives might focus on career aspirations, accomplishments, and disappointments. A survey for blue-collar workers might focus on training and work experience. A biodata inventory for federal government workers might focus on school and educational experiences, work history, skills, and interpersonal relations. As can be seen from these examples, most biodata surveys consider individual accomplishments, group accomplishments, disappointing experiences, and stressful situations.[31] The domains in which these attributes are studied often vary from job to job, but can range from childhood experiences to educational or early work experiences to current hobbies or family relations.

Measures Typically, biographical information is collected in a questionnaire that applicants complete. Exhibit 7.5 provides example biodata items. As can been seen, the items are quite diverse. It is suggested that each biodata item can be classified according to the following ten criteria:

1. **History:** Does the item describe an event that has occurred in the past, or a future or hypothetical event?
2. **Externality:** Does the item address an observable event or an internal event such as values or judgments?
3. **Objectivity:** Does the item focus on reporting factual information or subjective interpretations?
4. **Firsthandedness:** Does the item seek information that is directly available to the applicant rather than an evaluation of the applicant's behaviour by others?
5. **Discreteness:** Does the item pertain to a single unique behaviour or a simple account of events instead of summary responses?

EXHIBIT 7.5 Examples of Biodata Items

1. In university, your grade point average was:
   a. I did not go to college or completed less than two years
   b. Less than 2.50
   c. 2.50 to 3.00
   d. 3.00 to 3.50
   e. 3.50 to 4.00
2. In the past five years, the number of different jobs you have held is:
   a. More than five
   b. Three to five
   c. Two
   d. One
   e. None
3. The kind of supervision you like best is:
   a. Very close supervision
   b. Fairly close supervision
   c. Moderate supervision
   d. Minimal supervision
   e. No supervision
4. When you are angry, which of the following behaviours most often describes your reaction:
   a. Reflect on the situation for a bit
   b. Talk to a friend or spouse
   c. Exercise or take a walk
   d. Physically release the anger on something
   e. Just try to forget about it
5. Over the past three years, how much have you enjoyed each of the following (use the scale at right below):

a.	______________	Reading	1 = Very much
b.	______________	Watching TV	2 = Some
c.	______________	Home improvements	3 = Very little
d.	______________	Music	4 = Not at all
e.	______________	Outdoor recreation	

6. In most ways is your life close to ideal?
   a. Yes
   b. No
   c. Undecided or neutral

6. **Verifiability:** Can the accuracy of the response to the item be confirmed?
7. **Controllability:** Does the item address an event that was under the control of the applicant?
8. **Equal accessibility:** Are the events or experiences expressed in the item equally accessible to all applicants?
9. **Job relevance:** Does the item solicit information closely tied to the job?
10. **Invasiveness:** Is the item sensitive to the applicant's right to privacy?

Exhibit 7.6 provides example items that fall into each of the categories above. This categorization has important implications for deciding how to construct biodata inventories, as will be discussed shortly.

Most selection tests simply score items in a predetermined manner and add the scores to arrive at a total score. These total scores then form the basis of selection decisions made about the applicants. With most biodata inventories, the process of making decisions on the basis of responses to items is considerably more complex.

Accomplishment Records A selection method that can be considered a form of a biographical information survey is the accomplishment record, sometimes termed an achievement history questionnaire or retrospective life essay.[32] Accomplishment records survey the past accomplishments of job candidates as they relate to dimensions of work that are part of performing effectively at a particular job. Information that is solicited from each candidate includes a written statement of the accomplishment, when it took place, any recognition for the accomplishment, and verification of the accomplishment. The emphasis is on achievements rather than just activities, and in this regard accomplishment records differ from application blanks that solicit data on activities.

EXHIBIT 7.6 A Taxonomy of Biodata Items

Historical
How old were you when you got your first paying job?

Future or hypothetical
What position do you think you will be holding in ten years?

External
Did you ever get fired from a job?

Internal
What is your attitude toward friends who smoke marijuana?

Objective
How many hours did you study for your real estate exam?

Subjective
Would you describe yourself as shy?

Firsthand
How punctual are you about coming to work?

Secondhand
How would your teachers describe your punctuality?

Discrete
At what age did you get your driver's licence?

Summative
How many hours do you study during an average week?

Verifiable
What was your grade point average in university?

Nonverifiable
How many fresh vegetables do you eat every day?

Controllable
How many tries did it take you to pass the CA exam?

Noncontrollable
How many brothers and sisters do you have?

Equal access
Were you ever class president?

Nonequal access
Were you captain of the football team?

Job relevant
How many units of cereal did you sell during the last calendar year?

Not job relevant
Are you proficient at crossword puzzles?

Noninvasive
Were you on the tennis team in high school?

Invasive
How many young children do you have at home?

Source: F. A. Mael, "A Conceptual Rationale for the Domain and Attributes of Biodata Items," *Personnel Psychology*, 1991, 44, pp. 763–792. Used with permission.

An example of an accomplishment record scoring key, developed to select attorneys, is shown in Exhibit 7.7. Specifically, it is used to evaluate the candidate's research and investigation skills. The scale is used to score the accomplishment record submitted by the candidate. Similar scales are used to score other aspects of the candidate's skills. The scale is anchored with behavioural benchmarks. These benchmarks are illustrative of what candidates would have to present in their essay to earn a certain score, which can range from 1 to 6. Research has suggested impressive validity for accomplishment records, although further study is needed.

Evaluation of Biodata Research that has been conducted on the reliability and validity of biodata is quite positive.[33] Responses tend to be reliable (test–retest coefficients range from .77 to .90). More important, past research suggests that biodata inventories are some of the most valid predictors of job performance.

EXHIBIT 7.7 Scoring Key Excerpt for an Accomplishment Record

Dimensions: Researching/Investigating

General Definition: Obtaining all information, facts, and materials that are important, relevant, or necessary for a case, project, or assignment; gathering accurate information from all possible sources (i.e., persons both within and outside, interviews, journals, publications, company records, etc.); being thorough and overcoming all obstacles in gathering the required information.

Guidelines for Ratings: In RESEARCHING/INVESTIGATING, accomplishments at the lower levels are characterized by projects which require a minimal amount of research or research that is mundane in nature, e.g., routine interviews or journal reviews. At progressively higher levels, the accomplishments describe information gathered from multiple sources or information that would require considerable expertise to collect. The research projects may be part of a case or procedure which is novel or of substantial import. The projects generally demand increasingly complex interpretation of the information gathered. At the highest levels of achievement, awards or commendations are likely.

Scale:

6 = I assumed major responsibility for conducting an industry-wide investigation of the industry and for preparation of a memorandum in support of complaints against the three largest members of the industry. A complaint was issued unanimously by the commission and a consent settlement was obtained subsequently from all three respondents. I obtained statistical data from every large and medium industry and from a selection of small ones. I obtained and negotiated subpoenas with, and obtained statistical information from numerous other members of the industry. I deposed *many* employees of manufacturers and renters. I received a Meritorious Service award.

5 = I obtained crucial evidence in Docket, which was used as the basis for obtaining consent orders against more than 25 companies. I personally conducted more than 30 investigational hearings by subpoena. I did much outside research and reading to become familiar with technology. I handled all investigational and research work. I obtained documentary material from many sources and obtained the files upon which the matter was finally based.

4 = As a lead attorney in a major investigation at the ________, I performed all of the tasks described in this category. I supervised the investigation and brought it to its ultimate conclusion, which was to recommend that the matter be closed with no official action. I interviewed witnesses, including interviews on official record, subpoenaed documents from target sources, and spoke with numerous experts about scientific and technical information related to the case.

3 = In the investigation, I helped develop and gather the evidence necessary to pursue litigation. I prepared several complex subpoenas and negotiated them with industry counsel from three major corporations. The subpoenas requested detailed information on activities of major ________.

2 = I interviewed potential witnesses and compiled evidence that was relevant to the case against Corporation. I analyzed documents submitted pursuant to subpoenas, interviewed witnesses, and wrote admission of fact.

1 = My research involved checking reference books, LEXIS, and telephone interviews with various people—individuals, government officials, etc.

Source: L. M. Hough, M. A. Keyes, and M. D. Dunnette, "An Evaluation of Three 'Alternative' Selection Procedures," *Personnel Psychology*, 1983, 36, p. 265. Used with permission.

Because biodata inventories are developed and scored on the basis of a particular job and sample, it has commonly been argued that the validity of a particular inventory in one organization is unlikely to generalize to another organization. However, one study demonstrated that biodata inventories can be constructed in a way that will lead to generalizing across organizations.[34] In this study, items to be included in the biodata inventory were selected based on two criteria: (1) their job relevance (based on job analysis data), and (2) their ability to generalize across organizations (whether the item was a valid predictor of job performance in at least four of the six organizations studied). Scores were computed for the retained items and then tested on a sample of other organizations. The cross-validation effort resulted in a validity coefficient of .33. These results were confirmed by the results from another study. Thus, this research suggests that biodata inventories can generalize across organizations when constructed in an appropriate manner.

One of the more important issues in evaluating the usefulness of biodata is the issue of falsification. Because responses to most biodata items are difficult if not impossible to verify (e.g., "Did you collect coins or stamps as a child?"), it is conceivable that applicants distort their responses to tell prospective employers what they want to hear. In fact, research clearly shows that such faking does occur. Research also suggests, though, that faking can be reduced in a couple of ways. First, use less "fakeable" items. Using the typology of biodata items in Exhibit 7.6, one study found that the least-fakeable items were more historical, objective, discrete, verifiable, external, and less job relevant.[35] Second, warn applicants against faking. One study found that warning applicants that faking could be detected and would reduce their score (even if faking could not actually be detected) reduced the faking of transparent items, that is, where the desirable response was clear (e.g., "I hate to see people suffer.").[36]

Another issue to consider is whether the items in the biodata are perceived as discriminatory or invading privacy. Individuals with highly desirable skill sets may form an unfavourable impression of the organization and decide to self-select out. In certain fields where there is a great deal of competition for available talent, it is prudent to fully explain to applicants the relevancy of gathering biodata information to assess the competencies and KSAOs of the job.

Reference and Background Checks

Background information about job applicants can come not only from the applicant but also from people familiar with the applicant in previous situations (e.g., employers, creditors, neighbours). Organizations often solicit this information on their own or use the services of agencies that specialize in investigating applicants. Background information solicited from others consists of letters of recommendation, reference checks, and background checks.

Letters of Recommendation A very common reference check in some settings (e.g., academic institutions) is to ask applicants to have letters of recommendation written for them. Two major problems with letters of reference are as follows:

1. These letters do little to help organizations discern more qualified from less qualified applicants because only very poor applicants are unable to arrange for positive letters about their accomplishments.
2. Most letters are not structured or standardized, so organizations receive data from letter writers that is not consistent across organizations. For example, a letter about one applicant may concern the applicant's educational qualifications, whereas a letter about another applicant may focus on work experience. Comparing the qualifications of applicants A and B under these circumstances is like comparing apples and oranges.

The problem with letters of recommendation is dramatically demonstrated in one study that showed there was a stronger correlation between two letters written by one person for two different applicants than between two different people writing letters for the same person.[37] This finding indicates that letters of recommendation have more to do with the letter writer than the person being written about. In fact, a recent study revealed that letter writers who had a dispositional tendency to be positive wrote consistently more favourable letters than letter writers with a tendency to be critical or negative.[38]

Such problems indicate that organizations should downplay the weight given to letters unless a great deal of credibility and accountability can be attached to the letter writer's comments. Also, a structured form should be provided so that each writer provides the same information about each applicant.

Another way to improve on letters of recommendation is to use a standardized scoring key. An example of one is shown in Exhibit 7.8. Using this method, categories of KSAOs are established and become the scoring key (shown at the bottom of Exhibit 7.8). Then the adjectives in the actual letter are underlined and classified into the appropriate category. The number of adjectives used in each category constitute the applicant's score.

reference check
A spot check usually conducted with the applicant's supervisor or the HR department of current or previous organizations for whom the applicant worked to verify the applicant's background

Reference Checks A **reference check** is a spot check usually conducted with the applicant's supervisor or the HR department of current or previous organizations for whom the applicant worked to verify the applicant's background. Reference checking is usually completed on candidates who have been successfully shortlisted through the interviewing process. The information gathered through referencing checking is a critical step in the selection plan as it verifies or discredits information gathered from a candidate's resumé, application blank, and interviews. Often a job offer

EXHIBIT 7.8 Scoring Letters of Recommendation

Dear Personnel Director:

Mr. John Anderson asked that I write this letter in support of his application as assistant manager and I am pleased to do so. I have known John for six years as he was my assistant in the accounting department.

John always had his work completed <u>accurately</u> and <u>promptly</u>. In his years here, he <u>never missed a deadline</u>. He is very <u>detail</u> oriented, <u>alert</u> in finding errors, and <u>methodical</u> in his problem-solving approach. Interpersonally, John is a very <u>friendly</u> and <u>helpful</u> person.

I have great confidence in John's ability. If you desire more information, please let me know.

MA 0 CC 2 DR 6 U 0 V 0

Dear Personnel Director:

Mr. John Anderson asked that I write this letter in support of his application as assistant manager and I am pleased to do so. I have known John for six years as he was my assistant in the accounting department.

John was one of the most <u>popular</u> employees in our agency as he is a <u>friendly</u>, <u>outgoing</u>, <u>sociable</u> individual. He has a great sense of <u>humour</u>, is <u>poised</u>, and is very <u>helpful</u>. In completing his work, he is <u>independent</u>, <u>energetic</u>, and <u>industrious</u>.

I have great confidence in John's ability. If you desire more information, please let me know.

MA 0 CC 2 DR 0 U 5 V 3

Key *MA = mental ability*
CC = consideration-cooperation
DR = dependability-reliability
U = urbanity
V = vigour

Source: M. G. Aumodt, D. A. Bryan, and A. J. Whitcomb, "Predicting Performance with Letters of Recommendation," *Public Personnel Management*, 1993, 22, pp. 81–90. Reprinted with permission of *Public Personnel Management*, published by the International Personnel Management Association.

hinges on the information gathered through reference checks. Surveys indicate that 96 percent of organizations conduct reference checks and the majority of checks are done by in-house HR staff versus third-party vendors. The most common information sought is "objective evidence of the applicant's knowledge, skills, experiences, preferences, values, and work habits in order to determine if he or she is qualified for the position and would be a good fit for the organization."[39]

It is recommended that a minimum of two to three reference checks be completed to gather a comprehensive snapshot of the candidate's past performance. In addition to asking questions to verify education, past employment, and job titles, using behavioural-based questions, which will be further discussed in Chapter 9, will verify whether the candidate is a fit for both the job and the organization. Exhibit 7.9 offers some sample questions that are typically asked when doing a reference check for a sales representative.

A significant concern is the reluctance of organizations to give out the requested information because they fear a lawsuit on grounds of invasion of privacy or defamation of character. To minimize legal ramifications, a statement should be included on the applicant blank, which is signed by the applicant, giving permission to contact the references stated on the application blank. Recall the survey results reported above indicating that 96 percent of employers always check references. The same survey indicated that 93 percent of employers refuse to provide reference information for fear of being sued. As one executive stated, "There's a dire need for better reference information but fear of litigation keeps employers from providing much more than name, rank, and serial number."[40] As a result of the reluctance to provide reference information, reference checkers claim to receive inadequate information roughly half of the time. To a large degree, this concern over providing even rudimentary reference information is excessive—less than 3 percent of employers have had legal problems with reference checks. It is important to remember that if every organization refused to provide useful reference information, a potentially important source of applicant information would lose any of its potential value.

EXHIBIT 7.9 A Sampling of Reference Questions for a Sales Representative

1. In what capacity did you work with _______________? How long?
2. Briefly describe _______________ main duties and responsibilities?
3. In the position of sales representative, _______________ will be responsible for a high volume of cold calling, demonstrating products, and attending trade shows. Why do you feel _______________ would be suitable for the position?
4. How would you compare _______________ to the other sales representatives within the organization?
5. In your opinion what motivates _______________?
6. Were there any issues with the following:

Attendance	Yes ☐	No ☐
Dependability	Yes ☐	No ☐
Ability to work under pressure	Yes ☐	No ☐
Ability to assume responsibility	Yes ☐	No ☐

7. How formalized were the computer reporting systems _______________ used?
8. How does _______________ function in a structured environment?
9. Our sales team is a small team where everyone has to work well together. How do you think _______________ would fit in and why?
10. How has _______________ been instrumental in growing the business?
11. If you had a suitable position would you rehire _______________?

It's still the case that most reference checking is done over the telephone. When properly structured, such checks can have a certain level of validity. As with all selection measures, it's critical that the questions be job related, and that the same information is asked about all applicants.

Background Checks How would you feel if you found out that the organization you had hoped to join was having your criminal or driving record checked. Ninety percent of HR practitioners polled by *Canadian HR Reporter* indicated that they conducted background checks; 92 percent checked previous employment history, 52 percent checked academic qualifications, 50 percent checked criminal record, and 10 percent conducted credit checks.[41]

Although it may seem to be a very invasive procedure, background investigations are routinely conducted to protect the public's interest. In 2005, Saskatchewan expanded its system of criminal checking to all employees who are responsible for taxpayer money or who have access to modifying government computer programs after two employees were fired over allegations of misspending funds. Previously, criminal checks were completed on civil servants who worked with vulnerable people, law enforcement, and the criminal justice system. The checks were re-done every five years.[42]

background checks
Solicitations about the reliability of an applicant's behaviour, integrity, and personal adjustment

At a general level, conducting **background checks** solicits the reliability of applicants' behaviour, integrity, and personal adjustment. These factors are often used as requirements for the selection of people in occupations such as law enforcement, private security, and nuclear power, and in positions requiring government-issued security clearances. Of course, background checking can be important for any position of importance. Increasingly, background checks are being used for non–security-related positions, partly due to public pressure over acts of violence and malfeasance in the workplace. In two separate incidents in South Carolina, Wal-Mart employees were accused of sexually assaulting young girls. Both of the accused employees had past criminal convictions for sexually related offences. In response, Wal-Mart instituted criminal background checks on all of its employees.

Some organizations do background testing on their own, while others employ agencies to do so. Background checks cost anywhere from $25 to $1,000 per hire, depending on the type of position and the information sought. One practical problem in background checking is that different information is contained in different databases. Various firms provide comprehensive background testing services, with fees depending on what databases are checked. Employers can check criminal record through local police or law enforcement agencies (e.g., RCMP). Employers must get a signed release from the applicant to obtain the following information: bond status, credit, employment verifications, educational histories, licence verification, and driving records. Extreme care needs to be taken in the use of such measures because of the limited validity reports available to date, as well as legal constraints on pre-employment inquiries (see the "Legal Issues" section near the end of this chapter).

Background checks do have limitations. First, the records can be wrong or can be misinterpreted. For example, sometimes peoples' identities are mixed up. Unless someone has a very unusual name, there are probably many others with the same name in the population. Also, sometimes the records are wrong or contain misleading information. Johnnie Ulrigg was denied a job in Missoula, Montana, because his background check turned up a list of probation violations. It turns out that several counties in the state list failure to pay a traffic ticket as a probation violation. It took Ulrigg two years to clear his record. Second, because background checks have become more commonplace, they can place a seemingly permanent bar on the reemployment of reformed criminals. Peter Demain was sentenced to six years for possessing 21 pounds of marijuana. While in prison, he was so adept in the prison kitchen that he quickly rose to head baker. Once out of prison, though, Demain was unable to find a job at bagel shops, coffee houses, grocery stores, and bakeries. Is it fair for reformed criminals, no matter how long ago or what the offence, to be banned from employment?[43] Such questions are difficult to answer.

Applicants can proactively respond to these problems by checking into their own credit and criminal histories. For example, Equifax Canada (www.equifax.com/EFX_Canada) and

TransUnion Canada (www.tuc.ca) are two services that enable applicants to perform their own credit checks and receive a free copy of a credit report once a year. Also one can receive a certified criminal record check through the RCMP Canadian Criminal Records Information Services (www.rcmp-grc.gc.ca/crimrec/finger_e.htm) for a nominal fee.

Evaluation of References Checks The empirical data that exists on the validity of reference checks are not all that positive. To some degree, the validity depends on who is providing the information. If it is co-workers or relatives, the information is not very valid. On the other hand, reference reports from supervisors and HR managers are somewhat more valid. The validity of HR managers may be less valid because they are less knowledgeable about the applicant's on-the-job performance; the reports of co-workers and relatives probably are less valid because these individuals are positively biased toward the applicant.

Although references do not have high validity, we need to take a cost-benefit approach. In general the quality of the information may be low, but in the few cases where reference information changes a decision, the payoff can be significant. Thus, since references are a relatively cheap method of collecting information on applicants, screening out the occasional unstable applicant or, in a few cases, learning something new and important about an applicant may make reference checks a good investment. As with unweighted application blanks, though, using reference checks requires employers to turn elsewhere to obtain suitable information for making final decisions about applicants.

Literacy Testing

Most jobs require that employees possess reading and writing skills. In some jobs, the need for these skills is obvious. In others, though the need is not obvious, these skills are nevertheless critical to successful on-the-job performance. A good example is the position of custodian. Reading skills at first do not seem important for this position, but the consequences could be harmful. For example, an illiterate night custodian that worked for a school district mistakenly used what he thought was a cleaning compound for toilets. The substance turned out to have a large amount of an acid compound, as identified by the hazardous information on the WHMIS (Workplace Hazardous Materials Information System) label on the bottle. He then used it to clean toilet seats. If someone had been hurt in this incident, the ramification for the school and the school board would have been significant. This incident emphasizes the importance of carefully identifying all relevant KSAOs when developing the job requirements matrix and selection plan.

More than 23,000 Canadians were tested on their literacy in prose, document, numeracy, and problem solving abilities in the 2003 International Adult Literacy and Skills Survey (IALSS). The results suggested that about 9 million adults, or 42 percent, scored below Level 3, which is considered the desired threshold, in prose literacy, and 55 percent scored below Level 3 in numeracy literacy.[44]

Historically, literacy was not a selection issue in industries where people's physical skills were much more important than their mental skills. Today, all that has changed. Ford, Chrysler, and General Motors claim to have invested nearly $100 million in literacy programs.[45] These dollars have gone toward providing training for presently employed workers who cannot read or write up to the standards required by new jobs in the auto industry.

Another way for employers to address the issue of literacy is to select in advance those people who already have the required reading and writing skills. A great deal of theory and research has gone into developing standardized reading tests.[46] In addition, organizations are developing their own tests. For example, the Construction Sector Council developed a comprehensive strategy to improve reading, writing, mathematics, and other essential skills among its workforce by "partnering with Bowe Valley College in Calgary to customize the college's widely respected Test of Workplace Essential Skills (TOWES) tool for three different groups in the industry to help construction employers assess their workforce."[47]

Screening Interview

The screening interview occurs very early in the initial assessment process and is often the applicant's first personal contact with the organization and its staffing system. At this point, applicants are relatively undifferentiated to the organization in terms of KSAOs. The screening interview will begin the process of necessary differentiation, a sort of "rough cut."

The purpose of the screening interview is, and should be, to screen out the most obvious cases of person/job mismatches. To do this, the interview should focus on an assessment of KSAOs that are absolute requirements for the applicant. Examples of such minimum levels of qualifications for the job include certification and licensure requirements and necessary (not just preferred) training and experience requirements.

These assessments may be made on the basis of information gathered from written means (e.g., application blank or resumé), as well as the interview per se. Care should be taken to ensure that the interviewer focuses only on this information as a basis for decision making. Evaluations of personal characteristics of the applicant (e.g., race, sex), as well as judgments about an applicant's personality (e.g., she seems so outgoing and "just right" for this job), are to be avoided. Indeed, to ensure that this focus happens, some organizations (e.g., civil service agencies) have basically eliminated the screening interview altogether and make the initial assessment only on the basis of written information provided by the applicant.

One of the limitations with the screening interview is that it is perhaps the most expensive method of initial assessment. One way to reduce costs is to use companies, such as Gallup, who conduct a screening interview via the telephone (applicants dial a toll-free number and answer a series of questions); the company then reports results back to the employer.

Video and Computer Interviews One means of reducing the costs of screening interviews is to use video interviews. Video interviews can take at least two forms. One form of the video interview is to link the applicant and recruiter via remote video access. This sort of video-conferencing allows the applicant and recruiter to see each other on a monitor and, in some cases, even exchange documents. The Rostie Group in Toronto experienced an increase in teleconference video employment interviews at the time of SARS. The link between SARS and travel made out-of-province employers wary of traveling to Toronto at the time.[48] A variant of this type of video interview is to hire a consulting firm to conduct the video interviews for the organization. Under this approach, the organization identifies the candidates (perhaps after screening their applications or resumés) and submits their names to the consulting firm. The firm then videotapes the interviews and submits the tapes to the organization. In general, one of the advantages of video-based interviews is that they can dramatically lower the cost of screening interviews. This is particularly true for employers who may wish to interview only a few applicants at a given location. Another advantage of these interviews is that they can be arranged on short notice (no travel and no schedule rearrangements). Of course, a disadvantage of these interviews is that they do not permit face-to-face contact. The effect of this limitation on validity and applicant reactions is unknown.

Another form of video interviews takes the process a step further. Computer-based interviews utilize software that asks applicants questions (e.g., "Why are you suitable for the position?") or presents realistic scenarios (e.g., presents an irate customer on the screen) while recording applicants' responses. These responses are then forwarded to selection decision makers for use in screening. The software can also be configured to inform applicants about job duties and requirements. It can even track how long it takes an applicant to answer each question. Retailers are beginning to use computerized interviews on-site, where applicants walk into a store, enter a kiosk, and submit information about their work habits and experiences. As with video interviews, computer-based interviews can offer dramatic costs savings (although start-up costs to customize such programs can be high). As before, though, the accuracy of these high-tech interviews as compared to the old standby, the person-to-person variety, is unclear. The same holds true for how applicants will react to these relatively impersonal methods.

Evaluation of Screening Interview Whether high-tech or traditional, the interview has benefits and limitations. Nearly all of the research evaluating the interview in selection has considered it a substantive method (see the "Structured Interview" section in Chapter 8). Thus, there is little evidence about the usefulness of the screening interview. However, organizations using the interview in selection are likely to find it more useful by following a few guidelines such as the following:

1. Ask questions that assess the most basic KSAOs identified by job analysis. This requires separating what is required from what is preferred.
2. Stick to basic, qualifying questions suitable for making rough cuts (e.g., "Have you completed the minimum certification requirements to qualify for this job?") rather than subtle, subjective questions more suitable for substantive decisions (e.g., "How would this job fit within your overall career goals?"). Remember that the purpose of the screening interview is closer to cutting with a saw than operating with a scalpel. Ask only the most fundamental questions now, and leave the fine-tuning for later.
3. Keep interviews brief. Most interviewers make up their minds quickly and, given the limited usefulness and the type of information collected, a long interview (45–60 minutes) is unlikely to add much over a shorter one (15–30 minutes).
4. As with all interviews, the same questions should be asked of all applicants, and human rights compliance must be monitored.

Choice of Initial Assessment Methods

1.4

As described, there is a wide range of initial assessment methods available to organizations to help reduce the applicant pool to bona fide candidates. A range of formats is available as well. Fortunately, with so many choices available to organizations, research results are available to help guide choices of methods to use. This research has been reviewed many times and is summarized in Exhibit 7.10, where each initial assessment method is rated according to several criteria. Each of these criteria will be discussed in turn.

use
In evaluation of assessment methods, refers to how frequently organizations use each predictor

Use Use refers to how frequently surveyed organizations use each predictor. Use is probably an overused criterion in deciding which selection measures to adopt. Benchmarking—basing HR decisions on what other companies are doing—is a predominant method of decision making in all areas of HR, including staffing. However, is this a good basis on which to make decisions about selection methods? Although it is always comforting to do what other organizations are doing, relying on information from other organizations assumes that they know what they are doing. When deciding on which selection measure to use, getting caught up in the wave of what other organizations have benchmarked as good predictors may not necessarily be a good choice for your organization. For example, a small organization adopting benchmarked predictors used by large organizations may mean shifting through a myriad of resumés of unqualified candidates. Circumstances differ from organization to organization. Perhaps more important, many organizational decision makers (and HR consultants) either lack knowledge about the latest findings in HR research or have decided that such findings are not applicable to their organization. It is also difficult to determine whether a successful organization that uses a particular selection method is successful because it uses this method or if there are other business drivers that determine its success. Thus, from a research standpoint, there may be real strategic advantage in relying on effectiveness criteria (e.g., validity and utility, discussed below) rather than worrying about the practices of other organizations.

Another reason to have a healthy degree of skepticism about the use criterion is that there is a severe lack of broad (i.e., coverage of many industries and regions in Canada) and timely surveys of selection practices. A 2001 survey of 141 organizations conducted by the Ivey School of Business identified that most selection decisions were based on "the 'warm body' approach

EXHIBIT 7.10 Evaluation of Initial Assessment Methods

Predictors	Use	Cost	Reliability	Validity	Utility	Reactions
Level of education	High	Low	Moderate	Low	Low	?
Grade point average	Moderate	Low	Moderate	Moderate	?	?
Quality of school	?	Low	Moderate	Low	?	?
Major field of study	?	Low	Moderate	Moderate	?	?
Training and experience	High	Low	High	Moderate	Moderate	?
Licensing and certification	Moderate	Low	?	?	?	?
Weighted application blanks	Low	Moderate	Moderate	Moderate	Moderate	?
Biographical data	Low	High	High	High	High	Negative
Letters of recommendation	Moderate	Low	?	Low	?	?
Reference checks	High	Moderate	Low	Low	Moderate	Mixed
Background checks	Low	High	?	?	?	Mixed
Resumés and cover letters	Moderate	Low	Moderate	?	?	Moderate
Screening interview	High	Moderate	Low	Low	?	Positive
Literacy testing	Low	Moderate	?	Low	?	?

because in a panic employers hire anyone who looks good at the time; the 'rituals' approach where traditional methods will suffice, regardless of rational evidence that suggests there are better approaches; and the 'gut feeling' approach where managers knowing their business use their intuition to make hiring decisions."[49] In providing conclusions about use of various selection methods in organizations, we are forced to make judgment calls concerning which survey to rely on. With other predictors, the use figures have shown a fair degree of volatility and change from year to year. Thus, in classifying the use of assessment methods, we rely on the most recent surveys that achieve some degree of breadth. For purposes of classifying the predictors, high use refers to use by more than two-thirds of organizations, moderate is use by one-third to two-thirds of organizations, and low use refers to use by less than one-third of organizations.

Having issued these caveats about the use criterion, Exhibit 7.10 reveals clear differences in the use of different methods of initial assessment. The most frequently used methods of initial assessment are education level, training and experience, reference checks, and screening interview. These methods are considered, to some degree, in selection decisions for most types of positions. Licensing and certification requirements, letters of recommendation, resumés, and cover letters have moderate levels of use. All three of these methods are widely used in filling some types of positions. The least widely used initial assessment methods are weighted application blanks, biographical information, background checks, and literacy testing. It is relatively unusual for organizations to use these methods for initial screening decisions. There are no reliable figures on the use of quality of school and major field of study in initial selection decisions; thus, their use could not be estimated.

cost
In evaluation of assessment methods, refers to expenses incurred in using the predictor

Cost **Cost** refers to expenses incurred in using the predictor. Although most of the initial assessment methods may seem relatively cost-free since the applicant provides the information on his or her own time, this is not entirely accurate. For most initial assessment methods, the major cost associated with each selection measure is administration. Consider an application blank. It is true that applicants complete application blanks on their own time, but someone must be present to hand out applications, answer inquiries in person and over the phone about possible openings, and collect, sort, and forward applications to the appropriate person. Then the selection decision maker must read each application, perhaps make notes and weed out the clearly unacceptable applicants, and then make decisions about candidates. Thus, even for the least expensive methods of initial assessment, costs associated with their use are far from trivial.

On the other hand, utility research has suggested that costs do not play a large part in evaluating the financial benefit of using particular selection methods. This becomes readily apparent when one considers the costs of hiring a poor performer. For example, an administrative assistant who performs one standard deviation below average (16th percentile, if performance is normally distributed) may cost the organization $8,000 in lost productivity per year. This person is likely to remain on the job for more than one year, multiplying the costs. Considered in this light, spending an extra few hundred dollars to accurately identify good administrative assistants is an excellent investment. Thus, although costs need to be considered in evaluating assessment methods, more consideration should be given to the fact that valid selection measures pay off handsomely and will return many times their cost.

As can be seen in Exhibit 7.10, the least costly initial assessment methods include information that can obtained from application blanks (level of education, grade point average, quality of school, major field of study, training and experience, licensing and certification) and other applicant-provided information (letters of recommendation, resumés, and cover letters). Initial assessment methods of moderate cost include weighted application blanks, reference checks, screening interviews, and literacy testing. Biographical information and background checks are relatively expensive assessment methods.

reliability
In evaluation of assessment methods, refers to consistency of measurement

Reliability **Reliability** refers to consistency of measurement. As we note in Chapter 13, reliability is a boundary for validity, so it would be very difficult for a predictor with low reliability to have high validity. By the same token, it is unlikely that a valid predictor would have low reliability. Unfortunately, the reliability information on many initial assessment methods is lacking in the literature. Some researchers have investigated distortion of applicant-reported information (application blanks and resumés). One study found that nearly half of the items on application blanks were distorted by 20 percent of the applicants. Other studies have suggested that one-third of application blanks contain some inaccuracies.[50] Thus, it is probably reasonable to infer that applicant-supplied information in application blanks and resumés is of moderate reliability. The reliability of reference checks appears to be relatively low. In terms of training and experience evaluations, while distortion can occur if the applicant supplies training and experience information, interrater agreement in evaluating this information is quite high.[51] Biographical information also generally has high reliability. The screening interview, like most unstructured interviews, probably has a relatively low level of reliability.

validity
In evaluation of assessment methods, refers to the strength of the relationship between the predictor and job performance

Validity **Validity** refers to the strength of the relationship between the predictor and job performance. Low validity refers to validity in the range of about .00 to .15. Moderate validity corresponds to validity in the range of about .16 to .30, and high validity is .31 and above. As might be expected, most initial assessment methods have moderate to low validity because they are used only for making "rough cuts" among applicants rather than for final decisions. Perhaps the two most valid initial assessment methods are biodata and training and experience requirements; their validity can range from moderate to high. Among the least valid initial methods is the screening interview.

utility
In evaluation of assessment methods, refers to the monetary return associated with using the predictor, relative to its cost

Utility **Utility** refers to the monetary return associated with using the predictor, relative to its cost. According to researchers and decision makers, when comparing the utility of selection methods, validity appears to be the most important consideration.[52] In short, it would be very unusual for a valid selection method to have low utility. Thus, as can be seen in Exhibit 7.10, high, moderate, and low validities tend to directly correspond to high, moderate, and low utility values, respectively. Question marks predominate this column in Exhibit 7.10 because relatively few studies have directly investigated the utility of these methods. However, based on the argument that validity should be directly related to utility, it is likely that high validity methods also will realize large financial benefits to organizations that choose to use them. Research does indicate that training and experience requirements have moderate (or even high) levels of utility, and reference checks have moderate levels of utility.

applicant reactions
In evaluation of assessment methods, refers to the favourability of applicants' reactions to the predictor

Applicant Reactions **Applicant reactions** refers to the favourability of applicants' reactions to the predictor. Reactions are an important evaluative criterion because research has indicated that applicants who feel positively about selection methods and the selection process report higher levels of satisfaction with the organization, are more likely to accept a position with the organization, and are more likely to recommend the organization to others.[53]

Research suggests that selection measures that are perceived as job related present applicants with an opportunity to perform, are administered consistently, and provide applicants with feedback about their performance are likely to generate favourable applicant reactions.[54] Although research on applicants' reactions to specific selection procedures is lacking, evidence has been accumulating and suggests that applicants react more positively to some initial assessment methods, such as interviews, resumés, and references.[55]

LEGAL ISSUES

Whether a screening procedure complies with relevant legal and human rights legislation is an obvious concern for organizations. First, it is essential that at the screening stage no information is collected, or requested, that is related to any of the prohibited factors outlined in Chapter 2. Thus, application blank questions, questions for references, nor any other screening procedure, should ask for information relating to religious affiliation, marital status, sexual orientation, or any of the other prohibited areas. These issues may be particularly difficult to deal with in interview situations (e.g., with the applicant or references), and most jurisdictions have provided guidelines for what interviewers can and cannot ask during these situations. The interview question suggestions provided by the Canadian Human Rights Commission are reproduced in Exhibit 7.11 for guidance.

As noted in discussing reference and background checks earlier in this chapter, it is necessary that an applicant provide written consent for an organization to access or request information related to the individual's job application. The Personal Information Protection and Electronics Documents Act (PIPEDA) applies in these situations. As of January 1, 2004, PIPEDA legislation became applicable to all businesses in Canada. PIPEDA requires that people provide organizations with their consent before they can disclose relevant personal information. It is important also to realize that information requests and disclosures are limited to the relevant uses; thus, it would be inappropriate to begin a process of "fishing" for information other than that which is relevant to the job application. It is worth noting that applicants should be informed of the information disclosed and that they have the right to challenge the accuracy of information if they consider it to be inaccurate.

The issues surrounding the disclosure of personal information creates clear difficulties in requesting references. Current or former employers of a job applicant may be reluctant to provide

EXHIBIT 7.11 Interview Guidelines

Subject: Name
Avoid asking:
- About name change, i.e., whether it was changed by court order, marriage, or other reason
- Maiden name

Comment:
- Ask after selection if needed to check on previously held jobs or educational credentials

Subject: Address
Avoid asking:
- For addresses outside Canada

Preferred:
- Ask place and duration of current or recent address

Subject: Age
Avoid asking:
- For birth certificates, baptismal records, or about age in general

Preferred:
- Ask applicants if they are eligible to work under Canadian laws regarding age restrictions

Comment:
- If precise age required for benefit plans or other legitimate purposes, it can be determined after selection

Subject: Sex
Avoid asking:
- Males or females to fill in different applications
- About pregnancy, child-bearing plans, or child care arrangements

Preferred:
- Ask applicant if the attendance requirements can be met

Comment:
- During the interview or after selection, the applicant, for purposes of courtesy, may be asked which of Dr., Mr., Mrs., Miss, or Ms. is preferred

Subject: Marital status
Avoid asking:
- Whether applicant is single, married, divorced, engaged, separated, widowed, or living common-law
- Whether an applicant's spouse may be transferred
- About the spouse's employment

Preferred:
- If transfer or travel is part of the job, the applicant can be asked whether he or she can meet these requirements
- Ask whether there are any circumstances that might prevent completion of a minimum service commitment

Comment:
- Information on dependents can be determined after selection if necessary

Subject: Family status
Avoid asking:
- Number of children or dependents
- About child care arrangements

Preferred:
- Ask if the applicant would be able to work the required hours and, where applicable, overtime

Comment:
- Contacts for emergencies and/or details on dependents can be determined after selection

Subject: National or ethnic origin
Avoid asking:
- About birthplace, nationality of ancestors, spouse, or other relatives
- Whether born in Canada
- For proof of citizenship

Preferred:
- Since those who are entitled to work in Canada must be citizens, permanent residents, or holders of valid work permits, applicants can be asked whether they are legally entitled to work in Canada

Comment:
- Documentation of eligibility to work (papers, visas, etc.) can be requested after selection

Subject: Military service
Avoid asking:
- About military service in other countries

Preferred:
- Inquire about Canadian military service where employment preference is given to veterans by law

Subject: Language
Avoid asking:
- Mother tongue
- Where language skills obtained

Preferred:
- Ask if applicant understands, reads, writes, or speaks languages required for the job

Continued

EXHIBIT 7.11 *Continued*

Comment:

- Testing or scoring applicants for language proficiency is not permitted unless job-related

Subject: Race or colour
Avoid asking:

- Any inquiry into race or colour, including colour of eyes, skin, or hair

Subject: Photographs
Avoid asking:

- For photo to be attached to applications or sent to interviewer before interview

Preferred:

- Photos for security passes or company files can be taken after selection

Subject: Religion
Avoid asking:

- Whether applicant will work a specific religious holiday
- About religious affiliation, church membership, frequency of church attendance
- For references from clergy or religious leader

Preferred:

- Explain the required work shift, asking whether such a schedule poses problems for the applicant

Comment:

- Reasonable accommodation of an employee's religious beliefs is the employer's duty

Subject: Height and weight
Comment:

- No inquiry unless there is evidence they are genuine occupational requirements

Subject: Disability
Avoid asking:

- For a list of all disabilities, limitations, or health problems
- Whether applicant drinks or uses drugs
- Whether applicant has ever received psychiatric care or been hospitalized for emotional problems
- Whether applicant has received worker's compensation

Comment:

- Disclose any information on medically-related requirements or standards early in the application process and then ask whether the applicant has any condition that could affect his or her ability to do the job, preferably during a pre-employment medical examination
- A disability is only relevant to job ability if it threatens the safety or property of others or prevents the applicant from safe and adequate job performance even when reasonable efforts are made to accommodate the disability

Subject: Medical information
Avoid asking:

- Whether the applicant is currently under a physician's care
- Name of family doctor
- Whether receiving counselling or therapy

Comment:

- Medical exams should be conducted after selection and only if an employee's condition is related to job duties
- Offers of employment can be made conditional on successful completion of a medical exam

Subject: Pardoned conviction
Avoid asking:

- Whether an applicant has ever been convicted
- Whether the applicant has ever been arrested
- Whether the applicant has a criminal record

Preferred:

- If bonding is a job requirement, ask whether the applicant is eligible

Comment:

- Inquiries about criminal record or convictions are discouraged unless related to job duties

Subject: Sexual orientation
Avoid asking:

- About the applicant's sexual orientation

Comment:

- Contacts for emergencies and/or details on dependents can be determined after selection

Subject: References
Comment:

- The same restrictions that apply to questions asked of applicants apply when asking for employment references

Source: Adapted from Canadian Human Rights Commission, "Guide to Screening and Selection in Employment," April 1999, **www.chrc-ccdp.ca/publications/screening_employment-en.asp**.

a reference (especially one with negative information about the applicant) because they fear the applicant may take legal action disputing the information. Hence, the organization may view requesting references to be somewhat fruitless. On the other hand, failure to conduct a reference check opens up the organization to the possibility of negligent hiring if an employee's behaviour results in some form of employment-related negative consequences. To deal with such problems and obtain thorough, accurate information, the following suggestions are offered:

1. Gather as much information as possible directly from the applicant, along with verification consent. In this way, use of reference providers and information demands on them are minimized.
2. Be sure to obtain written authorization from the applicant to check references. An applicant should sign a consent form for this purpose. Also, the organization could prepare a request-for-reference form that the applicant would give to the person(s) being asked to provide a reference. That form would authorize the person(s) to provide requested information, release the person from any liability for providing the information, and be signed by the applicant (see Exhibit 7.12).
3. Specify the type of information being requested and obtain the information in writing. That information should be specific, factual, and job related in content.
4. Limit access to reference information to those making selection decisions.

EXHIBIT 7.12 Sample Reference Request

TO BE COMPLETED BY APPLICANT

NAME (PRINT):

I have made application for employment at this company. I request and authorize you to release all information requested below concerning my employment record, reason for leaving your employ, or my education. I hereby release my personal references, my former employers and schools, and all individuals connected therewith, from all liability for any damage whatsoever for furnishing this information.

SIGNATURE ____________________ DATE ______________

SCHOOL REFERENCE

DATES ATTENDED

FROM: TO: GRADUATED? YES ☐ NO ☐

DEGREE AWARDED:

EMPLOYMENT REFERENCE

POSITION HELD: EMPLOYMENT DATES:

IMMEDIATE SUPERVISOR'S NAME

REASON FOR LEAVING DISCHARGED ☐ RESIGNED ☐ LAID OFF ☐

FORMER EMPLOYER OR SCHOOL—Please complete the following. Thank you.

IS THE ABOVE INFORMATION CORRECT? YES ☐ NO ☐

If not, give correct information: ______________________________________

____

Continued

EXHIBIT 7.12 *Continued*

PLEASE CHECK	EXCELLENT	GOOD	FAIR	POOR	COMMENTS:
ATTITUDE	______	______	______	______	
QUALITY OF WORK	______	______	______	______	
COOPERATION	______	______	______	______	
ATTENDANCE	______	______	______	______	

WOULD YOU RECOMMEND FOR EMPLOYMENT? YES ☐ NO ☐

ADDITIONAL COMMENTS

____

____

SIGNATURE OF EMPLOYER OR SCHOOL REPRESENTATIVE TITLE

The other legal issue that needs attention concerns an organization's attention to protecting itself. Two important notices that should be presented to a candidate at the screening stage involve the intent to verify information and the consequences of making false claims in the information provided to support an application. Although applicants deemed worth further investigation will be required to provide written authorization for reference or background checks as part of the application process, it is advisable to detail in writing a right to verify intent as part of an organizational disclaimer presented to applicants. Similarly, it is appropriate that the written disclaimer outline what actions will result if it is discovered that the applicant has falsified information concerning his/her application for employment. In presenting these policies to an applicant it is recommended that the applicant's signature be required to acknowledge that the information was reviewed and understood. Both of these issues are specified in the application form presented in Exhibit 7.4. Note also that the disclaimer may describe the process of terminating the employment relationship. This may be included at this phase of the selection process, although it is more logically presented as part of a job offer within an employment contract (note also that matters relating to the termination of employment may often be outline in detail as part of a collective agreement). By having an applicant accept the terms of the disclaimer at the screening phase incorporates these issues into the employment contract if a job offer is extended later.

SUMMARY

This chapter reviews the processes involved in external selection and focuses specifically on methods of initial assessment. Before candidates are assessed, it is important to base assessment methods on the logic of prediction and to use selection plans. The logic of prediction focuses on the requisite correspondence between elements in applicants' past situations and KSAOs critical to success on the job applied for. The selection plan involves the process of detailing the required KSAOs and indicating which selection methods will be used to assess each KSAO. The selection sequence is the means by which the selection process is used to narrow down the size of the initial applicant pool to candidates, then finalists, and, eventually, job offer receivers.

Initial assessment methods are used during the early stages of the selection sequence to reduce the applicant pool to candidates for further assessment. The methods of initial assessment were reviewed in some detail. The methods include resumés and cover letters, application blanks, biographical data, letters of recommendation, reference and background checks, literacy testing, and screening interviews. Initial assessment methods differ widely in their usefulness. The means by which these methods can be evaluated for potential use include frequency of use, cost, reliability, validity, utility, and applicant reactions.

Legal issues need to be considered in making initial assessments about applicants. The use of disclaimers as a protective mechanism is critical. Also, initial assessment requires that special attention be given to reference checking.

KEY TERMS

applicant reactions 253
application blank 234
background checks 247
biodata 239
candidate 231
certification 238
cost 251
essay 229
external selection 226
finalist 231
licence 238
logic of prediction 227
objective test 229
offer receivers 231
performance test 229
power test 228
reference check 245
reliability 252
selection plan 229
speed test 228
use 250
utility 253
validity 252
weighted application blank 239

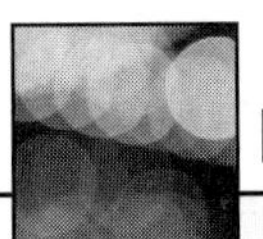

RELEVANT WEB SITES

Sample Application for Employment

www.ohrc.on.ca/english/publications/hr-at-work_10.shtml

Canadian Human Rights Commission Screening Interview Guideline

www.chrc-ccdp.ca/publications/screening_employment-en.asp

Human Resources and Social Development Canada Guideline to Employment Systems, Including Selection Methods

www.hrsdc.gc.ca/en/lp/lo/lswe/we/legislation/guidelines/gdln6.shtml

Service Canada: HR for Employers

http://hrmanagement.gc.ca/gol/hrmanagement/site.nsf/en/hr05221.html

Canadian Council of Human Resources Associations

www.cchra-ccarh.ca

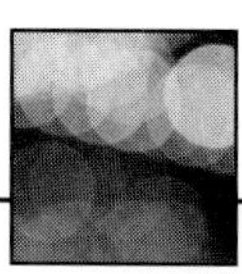

DISCUSSION QUESTIONS

1. A selection plan describes which predictor(s) will be used to assess the KSAOs required to perform the job. What are the three steps to follow in establishing a selection plan?
2. In what ways are the following three initial assessment methods similar and in what ways are they different: application blanks, biographical information, and reference and background checks?
3. Describe the criteria by which initial assessment methods are evaluated. Are some of these criteria more important than others?
4. Some methods of initial assessment appear to be more useful than others. If you were starting your own business, which initial assessment methods would you use and why?

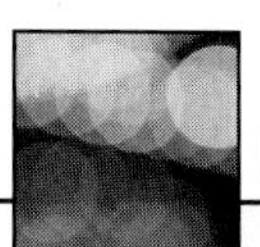

ETHICAL ISSUES

1. Is it wrong to "pad" one's resumé with information that, while not an outright lie, is an enhancement? For example, would it be wrong to term one's job "maintenance coordinator" when in fact one simply emptied garbage cans?
2. Do you think employers have a right to check into applicants' backgrounds? Even if there is no suspicion of misbehaviour? Even if the job poses no security or sensitivity risk? Even if the background check includes driving offences and credit histories?

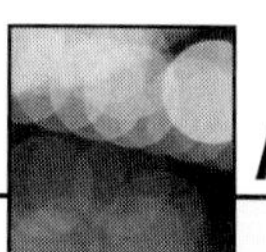

APPLICATIONS

Reference Reports and Initial Assessment in a Start-Up Company

Stanley Jausneister owns a small high-tech start-up company, called BioServer-Systems (BSS). Stanley's company specializes in selling Web server space to clients. The server space that Stanley markets runs from a network of personal computers. This networked configuration allows BSS to more efficiently manage its server space and provides greater flexibility to its customers, who often want weekly or even daily updates of their Web sites. The other innovation Stanley brought to BSS is special security encryption software protocols, which make the BSS server space nearly impossible for hackers to access. This flexibility is particularly attractive to organizations that need to manage large, security-protected databases with multiple points of access. Stanley even has been contacted by the government, which is interested in using BSS's systems for some of its classified intelligence.

Due to its niche, BSS has experienced rapid growth. In the past year, BSS has hired 12 programmers and 2 marketers, as well as a general manager, a human resources manager, and other support personnel. Before starting BSS, Stanley was a manager with a large pharmaceutical firm. Because of his industry connections, most of BSS's business has been with drug and chemical companies.

Yesterday, Stanley received a phone call from Lee Rogers, head of biotechnology for Mercelle-Poulet in Winnipeg, one of BSS's largest customers. Lee is an old friend, and he was one of BSS's first customers. When Lee called, he expressed concerned about BSS's security. One area of Mercelle-Poulet's biotech division is responsible for research and development on vaccines for various bioterrorist weapons such as anthrax and the plague. Because the research and development on these vaccines require the company to develop cultures of the biotech weapons themselves, Lee has used BSS to house information for this area. A great deal of sensitive information is housed on BSS's servers, including in some cases the formulas that are used in developing the cultures.

Despite the sensitivity of the information on BSS's servers, given BSS's advanced software, Stanley was very surprised to hear Lee's concern about security. "It's not your software that worries me," Lee commented, "It's the people running it." Lee explained that last week a Mercelle-Poulet researcher was arrested for attempting to sell certain cultures to an overseas client. It turns out that this individual had been dismissed from a previous pharmaceutical company for unethical behaviour, but this information did not surface during the individual's reference check. This incident not only caused Lee to re-examine Mercelle-Poulet's reference checks, but it also made him think of BSS, as certain BSS employees have access to Mercelle-Poulet's information.

Instantly after hearing Lee's concern, Stanley realized he had a problem. Like many small employers, BSS did not do thorough reference or background checks on its employees. They assumed that the information provided on the application was accurate and generally only called the applicant's previous employer (often with ineffective results). Stanley realized he needed to do more, not only to keep Lee's business but to protect his company and customers.

1. What sort of reference and background checking should BSS conduct on its applicants?
2. Is there any information BSS should avoid obtaining for legal or human rights checking reasons?
3. How can BSS know that its background checking programs are effective?
4. In the past, BSS has used the following initial assessment methods: application blank, interviews with Stanley and other BSS managers, and a follow-up with the applicant's former employer. Beyond changes to its background checking program, would you suggest any other alterations to BSS's initial assessment process?

Developing a Lawful Application Blank

The Consolidated Trucking Corporation, Inc. (CTCI) is a rapidly growing short-haul (local) firm within the greater Vancouver area. It has grown primarily through the acquisitions of numerous small, family-owned trucking companies. As of now it has a fleet of 150 trucks and over 250 full-time drivers. Most of the drivers were hired initially by the firms that CTCI acquired, and they accepted generous offers from CTCI to become members of the CTCI team. CTCI's expansion plans are very ambitious, but they will be fulfilled primarily from internal growth rather than additional acquisitions. Consequently, CTCI is now faced with the need to develop an external staffing system that will be geared up to hire 75 new truckers within the next two years.

Terry Tailgater is a former truck driver for CTCI who was promoted to truck maintenance supervisor, a position he has held for the past five years. Once CTCI's internal expansion plans become finalized, the firm's HR director (and sole member of the HR department) Harold Hornblower decided he needed a new person to handle staffing and employment law duties. Terry Tailgater was promoted by Harold to the job of staffing manager. One of Terry's major assignments was to develop a new staffing system for truck drivers.

One of the first projects Terry undertook was to develop a new, standardized application blank for the job of truck driver. To do this, Terry looked at the many different application blanks the current drivers had completed for their former companies. (These records were given to CTCI at the time of acquisition.) The application blanks showed that a large amount of information was requested, and that the specific information sought varied among the application forms. Terry scanned the various forms and made a list of all the questions the forms contained. He then decided to evaluate each question in terms of its probable lawfulness under federal and provincial law. Terry wanted to identify and use only lawful questions on the new form he is developing.

Shown below is the list of the questions Terry developed, along with columns labelled "probably lawful" and "probably unlawful." Assume that you are Terry and are deciding on the lawfulness of each question. Place a check mark in the appropriate column for each question. For each question, prepare a justification for its mark as "probably lawful" or "probably unlawful."

Questions Terry Is Considering Including on Application Blank

Question About	Probably Lawful	Probably Unlawful
Previous arrests	____	____
Previous felony convictions	____	____
Distance between work and residence	____	____
Ability to work long hours	____	____
Height	____	____
Weight	____	____
Previous work experience	____	____
Educational attainment	____	____
High school favourite subjects	____	____
Grade point average	____	____
Received workers' compensation in past	____	____
Currently receiving workers' compensation	____	____
Child care arrangements	____	____
Length of time on previous job	____	____
Reason for leaving previous job	____	____
Home ownership	____	____
Any current medical problems	____	____
History of mental illness	____	____
OK to seek references from previous employer?	____	____
Have you provided complete/truthful information?	____	____
Languages spoken	____	____
Willing to work on Easter and Christmas	____	____
Get recommendation from pastor/priest	____	____
Proof of clean abstract	____	____
Name of previous supervisor	____	____

ENDNOTES

1. G. J. Myszkowski and S. Sloan, "Hiring by Blueprint," *HR Magazine,* May 1991, pp. 55–58.
2. J. W. Smither, R. R. Reilly, R. E. Millsap, K. Pearlman, and R. Stoffey, "Applicant Reactions to Selection Procedures," *Personnel Psychology,* 1993, 46, pp. 49–76.
3. P. F. Wernimont and J. P. Campbell, "Signs, Samples, and Criteria," *Journal of Applied Psychology,* 1968, 52, pp. 372–376.
4. State of Wisconsin, Chapter 134, *Evaluating Job Content for Selection,* Undated.
5. State of Wisconsin, Evaluating Job Content for Selection.
6. B. Toews, "Matchmaking," *Motor Truck,* July/August 2003, 72(4), p. 32.
7. I. Kotlyar and K. Ades, "E-Selection: Advancement in Assessment Technology," *Canadian HR Reporter,* April 8, 2002, 15(7), p. 15.
8. D. Brown, "Unwanted online jobseekers swamp HR staff," *Canadian HR Reporter,* April 5, 2004, 17(7), pp. 1–2.
9. *Cover Letters and Resume Survey,* Society for Human Resource Management, May 2000; S. Greengard, "Don't Forget to Look Down Both Ends of the Resumé Pipe," *Workforce,* July 2000, pp. 78–79; E. R. Silverman, "Resumes Become Multimedia Productions," *Wall Street Journal,* February 1, 2000, p. B16; L. Stern, "Changing the Results of resumé Writing," *Kaplan/ Newsweek,* July 2000, pp. 22–23; K. B. Wheeler, "The End of the Resume," *Employment Management Today,* Fall 1999, pp. 7–8.
10. M. McQuigge, "Don't get personal on resume," *National Post,* November 9, 2005, FP Working, p. 3.
11. P. MacInnis, "Checking out references," *Computing Canada,* July 26, 2002, 15, p. 25.
12. N. C. MacDonald, "Lies, damned lies and resumes," *Canadian HR Reporter,* May 17, 2004, 17(10), pp. G3–G6.
13. A. Howard, "College Experiences and Managerial Performance," *Journal of Applied Psychology,* 1986, 71, pp. 530–552; R. Merritt-Halston and K. Wexley, "Educational Requirements: Legality and Validity," *Personnel Psychology,* 1983, 36, pp. 743–753.
14. K. W. Arenson, "More Youths Opt for G. E. O., Skirting High School Hurdle," *New York Times,* May 15, 2004, pp. A1, A12.
15. S. Caudron, "Evaluating E-Degrees," *Workforce,* February 2001, pp. 61–67; R. E. Silverman, "A Hire Degree?," *Wall Street Journal,* October 17, 2000, p. B16.
16. A. Trotter, "Educators Degrees Earned on Internet Raise Fraud Issues," *Education Week,* May 5, 2004, pp. 1–19.
17. A. E. McKinney, K. D. Carlson, R. L. Meachum, N. C. D'Angelo, and M. L. Connerly, "Recruiters' Use of GPA in Initial Screening Decisions: Higher GPAs Don't Always Make the Cut," *Personnel Psychology,* 2003, 56, pp. 823–845; P. L. Roth, C. A. BeVier, F. S. Switzer, and J. S. Schippmann, "Meta-Analyzing the Relationship Between Grades and Job Performance," *Journal of Applied Psychology,* 1996, 81, pp. 548–556; P. L. Roth and P. Bobko, "College Grade Point Average as a Personnel Selection Devise: Ethnic Group Differences and Potential Adverse Impact," *Journal of Applied Psychology,* 2000, 85, pp. 399–406.
18. "University Report Card," *The Globe and Mail,* April 21, 2005, pp. U1–U7.
19. A. D. Johnson and M. Dwyer, "University Ranking Methodology," *Maclean's.* November 6, 2005, www.macleans.ca/universities/article.jsp?content=20051114_115647_115647.
20. "2005 Overall Ranking Chart: Primarily Undergraduate Ranking," *MacLean's,* November 6, 2005, www.macleans.ca/universities/article.jsp?content=20051114_115122_115122.
21. J. Chow, "The MBA," *National Business Post,* March 2005, pp. 28–31.
22. J. Chow, "The MBA."

23. R. T. Schneider, The Rating of Experience and Training: A Review of the Literature and Recommendations on the Use of Alternative E & T Procedures (Alexandria, VA: International Personnel Management Association, 1994).
24. R. A. Ash, "A Comparative Study of Behavioral Consistency and Holistic Judgment Methods of Job Applicant Training and Work Experience Evaluation," *Public Personnel Management,* 1984, 13, pp. 157–172; M. A. McDaniel, F. L. Schmidt, and J. E. Hunter, "A Meta-Analysis of the Validity of Methods for Rating Training and Experience in Personnel Selection," *Personnel Psychology,* 1988, 41, pp. 283–314; R. Tomsho "Busy Surgeons Are Good for Patients," *Wall Street Journal,* November 28, 2003, p. B3.
25. University of Saskatchewan, College of Commerce Professional Designation Programs, www.commerce.usask.ca/programs/undergrad/hrm_designations.asp.
26. J. McKillip and J. Owens, "Voluntary Professional Certifications: Requirements and Validation Activities," *The Industrial-Organizational Psychologist,* July 2000, pp. 50–57; M. Schrage, "You're Nuts If You're Not Certified," *Fortune,* June 26, 2000, p. 338.
27. G. W. England, *Development and Use of Weighted Application Blanks* (Dubuque, IA: W. M. C. Brown, 1961).
28. V. M. Catano, W. H. Wiesner, R. D. Hackett and L. L. Methot, *Recruitment and Selection in Canada,* 3rd ed. (Toronto: Nelson, 2005).
29. B. K. Brown and M. A. Campion, "Biodata Phenomenology: Recruiters' Perceptions and Use of Biographical Information in Resume Screening," *Journal of Applied Psychology,* 1994, 79, pp. 897–908.
30. M. A. McDaniel, "Biographical Constructs for Predicting Employee Suitability," *Journal of Applied Psychology,* 1989, 74, pp. 964–970.
31. C. J. Russell, J. Mattson, S. E. Devlin, and D. Atwater, "Predictive Validity of Biodata Items Generated from Retrospective Life Experience Essays," *Journal of Applied Psychology,* 1990, 75, pp. 569–580.
32. L. M. Hough, M. A. Keyes, and M. D. Dunnette, "An Evaluation of Three 'Alternative' Selection Procedures," *Personnel Psychology,* 1983, 36, pp. 261–276; S. Landers, "PACE to be Replaced with Biographical Test," *APA Monitor,* 1989, 20(4), p. 14; Russell, Mattson, Devlin, and Atwater, "Predictive Validity of Biodata Items Generated from Retrospective Life Experience Essays."
33. See M. D. Mumford and G. S. Stokes, "Developmental Determinants of Individual Action: Theory and Practice in Applying Background Measures," in M. D. Dunnette and L. M. Hough (eds.), *Handbook of Industrial and Organizational Psychology,* second ed., vol. 3 (Palo Alto, CA: Consulting Psychologists Press, 1993), pp. 61–138.
34. K. D. Carlson, S. Sculten, F. L. Schmidt, H. Rothstein, and F. Erwin, "Generalizable Biographical Data Validity Can Be Achieved Without Multi-Organizational Development and Keying," *Personnel Psychology,* 1999, 52, pp. 731–755; H. P. Rothstein, F. L. Schmidt, F. W. Erwin, W. A. Owens, and C. P. Sparks, "Biographical Data in Employment Selection: Can Validities Be Made Generalizable?," *Journal of Applied Psychology,* 1990, 75, pp. 175–184.
35. T. E. Becker and A. L. Colquitt, "Potential versus Actual Faking of a Biodata Form: An Analysis Along Several Dimensions of Item Type," *Personnel Psychology,* 1992, 45, pp. 389–406.
36. A. N. Kluger and A. Colella, "Beyond the Mean Bias: The Effect of Warning Against Faking on Biodata Item Variances," *Personnel Psychology,* 1993, 46, pp. 763–780.
37. J. C. Baxter, B. Brock, P. C. Hill, and R. M. Rozelle, "Letters of Recommendation: A Question of Value," *Journal of Applied Psychology,* 1981, 66, pp. 296–301.

38. T. A. Judge and C. A. Higgins, "Affective Disposition and the Letter of Reference," *Organizational Behavior and Human Decision Processes,* 1998, 75, pp. 207–221.
39. C. Cohen, "Reference Checks," *CA Magazine,* November 2004, 137(9), pp. 41–42.
40. J. Click, "SJRM Survey Highlights Dilemmas of Reference Checks," *HR News,* July 1995, p. 13.
41. T. Humber, "Recruitment Isn't Getting Easier," *Canadian HR Reporter,* May 23, 2005, 18(10), p. R2.
42. "Government promises more background checks for employees," (Moose Jaw) *Times-Herald,* September 8, 2005, p. 1.
43. K. Maher, "The Jungle," *Wall Street Journal,* January 20, 2004, p. B8. A. Zimmerman, "Wal-Mart to Probe Job Applicants," *Wall Street Journal,* August 12, 2004, pp. A3, B6; A. Zimmerman and K. Stringer, "As Background Checks Proliferate, Ex-Cons Face Jobs Lock," *Wall Street Journal,* August 26, 2004, pp. B1, B3;
44. "International Adult Literacy and Skills Survey," Statistics Canada, *The Daily,* November 9, 2005, www.statcan.ca/Daily/English/051109/d051109a.htm.
45. K. Miller, "At GM, the Three R's Are the Big Three," *Wall Street Journal,* July 3, 1992, p. D1.
46. S. Schwartz (ed.), Measuring Reading Competence: A Theoretical Prescriptive Approach (New York: Praeger, 1985).
47. D. Brown, "Poor reading, math skills a drag on productivity, performance," *Canadian HR Reporter,* February 28, 2005, 18(4).
48. B. Simmons, "Screening candidates: Use of video interviews is on the rise; employers can recruit long-distance," *Toronto Star,* September 6, 2003, p. D10, www.rostie.com/torontostar.html.
49. L. Cassiani, "Employers gambling when it comes to hiring: survey", *Canadian HR Reporter,* March 26, 2001, 14(6).
50. I. L. Goldstein, "The Application Blank: How Honest Are the Responses?" *Journal of Applied Psychology,* 1974, 59, pp. 491–494; W. Keichel, "Lies on the Resume," *Fortune,* August 23, 1982, pp. 221–222, 224; J. N. Mosel and L. W. Cozan, "The Accuracy of Application Blank Work Histories," *Journal of Applied Psychology,* 1952, 36, pp. 365–369.
51. R. A. Ash and E. L. Levine, "Job Applicant Training and Work Experience Evaluation: An Empirical Comparison of Four Methods," *Journal of Applied Psychology,* 1985, 70, pp. 572–576.
52. G. P. Latham and G. Whyte, "The Futility of Utility Analysis," *Personnel Psychology,* 1994, 47, pp. 31–46.
53. Smither, Reilly, Millsap, Pearlman, and Stoffey, "Applicant Reactions to Selection Procedures."
54. S. W. Gilliland, "Fairness from the Applicant's Perspective: Reactions to Employee Selection Procedures," *International Journal of Selection and Assessment,* 1995, 3, pp. 11–19.
55. D. A. Kravitz, V. Stinson, and T. L. Chavez, "Evaluations of Tests Used for Making Selection and Promotion Decisions," *International Journal of Selection and Assessment,* 1996, 4, pp. 24–34; D. D. Steiner and S. W. Gilliland, "Fairness Reactions to Personnel Selection Techniques in France and the United States," *Journal of Applied Psychology,* 1996, 81, pp. 134–141.

Visit the Online Learning Centre at

www.mcgrawhill.ca/olc/heneman

CHAPTER 8

EXTERNAL SELECTION: TESTING

CHAPTER OBJECTIVES

After reading this chapter, you will be able to:

- Outline the differences between substantive, discretionary, and contingent testing methods
- Understand the constructs measured with the testing procedures reviewed
- Make test selection decisions based on the validity evidence
- Know the legal and human rights issues that apply when using selection tests

The previous chapter reviewed preliminary issues surrounding external staffing decisions made in organizations, including the use of initial assessment methods. This chapter continues the discussion of external selection by discussing in some detail substantive assessment methods. The use of discretionary and contingent assessment methods, collection of assessment data, and legal issues will also be considered.

Whereas initial assessment methods are used to reduce the applicant pool to candidates, substantive assessment methods are used to reduce the candidate pool to finalists for the job. Thus, the use of substantive methods is often more involved than using initial methods. Numerous substantive assessment methods will be discussed in depth, including various tests (e.g., personality, ability, job knowledge, performance and work samples, integrity); interest, values, and preference inventories; structured interviews; and clinical assessments. The average validity (i.e., $\bar{r}$) of each method and the criteria used to choose among methods will be reviewed.

Discretionary assessment methods are used in some circumstances to separate those who receive job offers from the list of finalists. The applicant characteristics that are assessed when using discretionary methods are sometimes very subjective. Several of the characteristics most commonly assessed by discretionary methods will be reviewed.

Contingent assessment methods are used to make sure that tentative offer recipients meet certain qualifications for the job. Although any assessment method can be used as a contingent method (e.g., licensing/certification requirements, background checks), perhaps the two most common contingent methods are drug tests and medical exams. These procedures will be reviewed.

All forms of assessment decisions require the collection of assessment data. The procedures used to make sure this process is properly conducted will be reviewed. In particular, several issues will be discussed, including support services, training requirements in using various predictors, maintenance of security and confidentiality, and the importance of standardized procedures.

Finally, many important legal issues surround the use of substantive, discretionary, and contingent methods of selection. The most important of these issues will be reviewed.

SUBSTANTIVE ASSESSMENT METHODS

substantive assessment methods

Assessment methods used after initial screening methods that involve more precise data concerning the match between a job candidate's KSAOs and the requirements of a job position

Organizations use initial assessment methods to make "rough cuts" among applicants—weeding out the obviously unqualified. Conversely, **substantive assessment methods** are used to make more precise decisions about applicants—among those who meet minimum qualifications for the job, which applicants are most likely to be high performers if hired? Because substantive methods are used to make fine distinctions among applicants, the nature of their use is somewhat more involved than initial assessment methods. As with initial assessment methods, however, substantive assessment methods are developed using the logic of prediction outlined in Exhibit 7.1 and the selection plan shown in Exhibit 7.2. Predictors typically used to select finalists from the candidate pool include personality tests; ability tests; job knowledge tests; performance tests and work samples; interest, values, and preference inventories; structured interviews; and clinical assessments. Each of these predictors is described next in some detail.

Personality Tests

2.2

Until recently, personality tests were not perceived as a valid selection method. Historically, most studies estimated the validity of personality tests to be between .10 and .15, which would rank them among the poorest predictors of job performance—only marginally better than a coin toss.[1] Starting with the publication of an influential review in the 1960s, personality tests were not viewed favourably, nor were they widely used.[2]

personality tests

Survey, or other, measurement that provides information indicating a job candidate's behavioural tendencies that have been determined to be relevant to the requirements of a job or fit with an organization's environment

Recent advances, however, have suggested much more positive conclusions about the role of **personality tests** in predicting job performance. Mainly, this is due to the widespread acceptance of a major taxonomy of personality, often called the Big Five. The Big Five is used to describe behavioural (as opposed to emotional or cognitive) traits that may capture up to 75 percent of an individual's personality. The Big Five factors are *emotional stability* (disposition to be calm, optimistic, and well adjusted), *extraversion* (tendency to be sociable, assertive, active, upbeat, and talkative), *openness to experience* (tendency to be imaginative, attentive to inner feelings, have intellectual curiosity and independence of judgment), *agreeableness* (tendency to be altruistic, trusting, sympathetic, and cooperative), and *conscientiousness* (tendency to be purposeful, determined, dependable, and attentive to detail). The Big Five are a reduced set of many more specific traits. The Big Five are very stable over time, and there is even research to suggest a strong genetic basis of the Big Five traits (roughly 50% of the variance in the Big Five traits appears to be inherited).[3] Because job performance is a broad concept that comprises many specific behaviours, it will be best predicted by broad dispositions such as the Big Five. In fact, some research evidence supports this proposition.[4]

Measures of Personality Measures of personality traits can be surveys, projective techniques, or interviews. Most personality measures used in personnel selection are surveys. There are several survey measures of the Big Five traits that are used in selection. The *Personal Characteristics Inventory* (PCI) is a self-report measure of the Big Five that asks applicants to report their agreement or disagreement (using a "strongly disagree" to "strongly agree" scale) with 150 sentences.[5] The measure takes about 30 minutes to complete and has a grade 5 to grade 6 reading level. Exhibit 8.1 provides sample items from the PCI. Another commonly used measure of the Big Five is the *NEO Personality Inventory* (NEO), of which there are several versions that have been translated into numerous languages.[6] A third alternative is the *Hogan Personality Inventory* (HPI), which also is based on the Big Five typology. Responses to the HPI can be scored to yield measures of employee reliability and service orientation.[7] All three of these measures have shown validity in predicting job performance in various occupations.

EXHIBIT 8.1 Sample Items for Personal Characteristics Inventory

Conscientiousness
I can always be counted on to get the job done.
I am a very persistent worker.
I almost always plan things in advance of work.

Extraversion
Meeting new people is enjoyable to me.
I like to stir up excitement if things get boring.
I am a "take-charge" type of person.

Agreeableness
I like to help others who are down on their luck.
I usually see the good side of people.
I forgive others easily.

Emotional Stability
I can become annoyed at people quite easily (reverse-scored).
At times I don't care about much of anything (reverse-scored).
My feelings tend to be easily hurt (reverse-scored).

Openness to Experience
I like to work with difficult concepts and ideas.
I enjoy trying new and different things.
I tend to enjoy art, music, or literature.

Source: M. K. Mount and M. R. Barrick, *Manual for Personal Characteristics Inventory* (December, 1995). Reprinted with permission of the Wonderlic Personnel Test, Inc.

Although surveys are the most common means of assessing personality, other methods have been used, such as projective tests and interviews. However, with few exceptions (e.g., the *Miner Sentence Completion Scale* has shown validity in predicting managerial performance[8]), the reliability and validity of projective tests and interviews as methods of personality assessment are questionable at best. Thus, survey measures in general, and the Big Five measures in particular, are the most reliable and valid means of personality testing for selection decisions.

Evaluation of Personality Tests Many comprehensive reviews of the validity of personality tests have been published. Nearly all of the recent reviews focus on the validity of the Big Five. Although there has been a debate over inconsistencies in these studies, the largest-scale study revealed the following:

1. Conscientiousness predicts performance across all occupational groupings.[9]
2. Emotional stability predicts performance in most occupations, especially sales, management, and teaching.[10]
3. Extraversion predicts performance of salespeople.[11]
4. In a meta-analysis of studies in Europe, conscientiousness and emotional stability emerged as significant predictors of performance.[12]

More recent evidence further supports the validity of conscientiousness in predicting job performance. A recent update to the original findings suggested that the validity of conscientiousness in predicting overall job performance is $\bar{r} = .31$, and it seems to predict many specific facets of performance (training proficiency, reliability, quality of work, administration).[13] The conclusion that conscientiousness is a valid predictor of job performance across all types of jobs and organizations studied is significant. Previously, researchers believed that personality was valid only for *some* jobs

Possible Factors Explaining the Importance of Conscientiousness in Predicting Job Performance

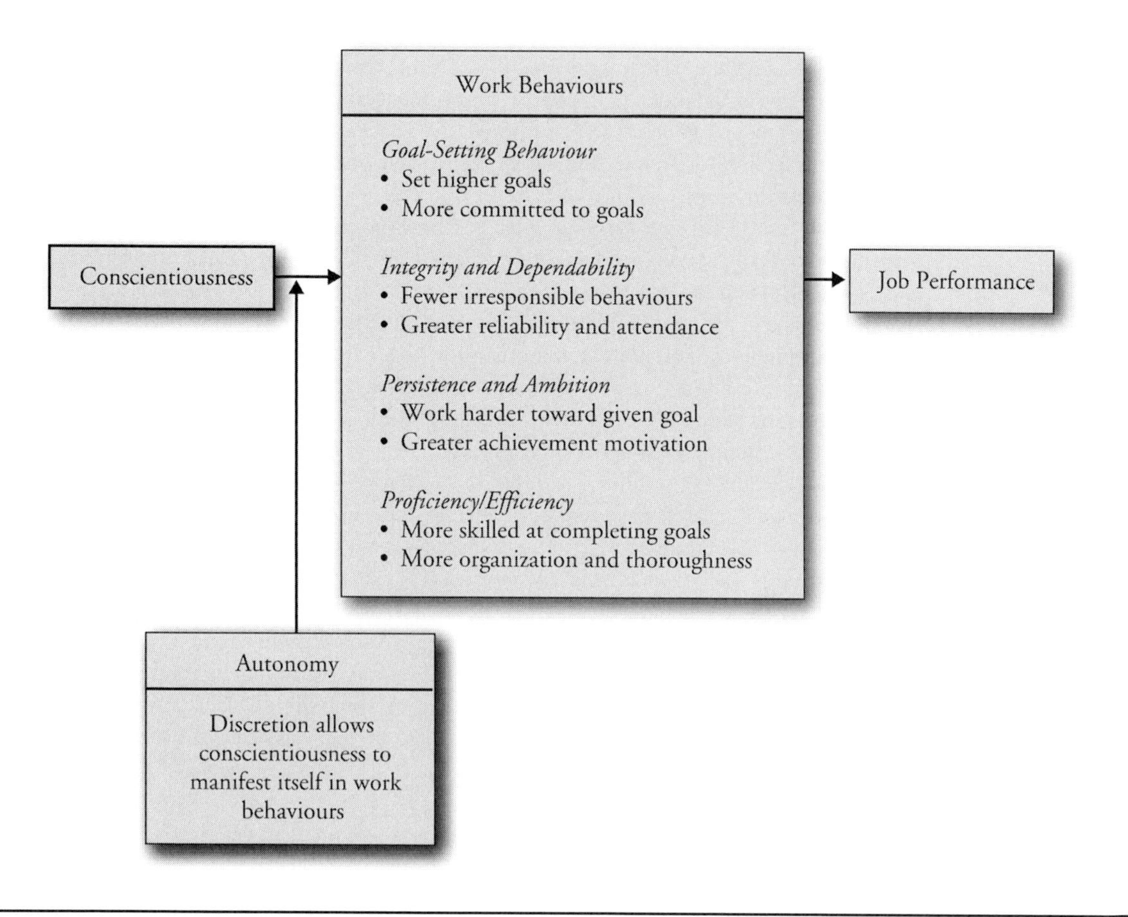

in *some* situations. These results suggest that conscientiousness is important to job performance whether the job is working on an assembly line or selling automotive parts or driving trucks.

Why is conscientiousness predictive of performance? Exhibit 8.2 provides some possible answers.[14] When employees have autonomy, research shows that conscientious employees set higher work goals for themselves and are more committed to achieving the goals they set. Also, conscientiousness is an integral part of integrity, and two of the key components of conscientiousness—achievement and dependability—are related to reduced levels of irresponsible job behaviours (e.g., absenteeism, insubordination, use of drugs on job). Conscientiousness also predicts work effort and is associated with ambition. Further, conscientious individuals are more technically proficient in their jobs and more organized and thorough. Thus, conscientiousness predicts job performance well because it is associated with a range of attitudes and behaviours that are important to job success.

Beyond conscientiousness, is there a role for the other Big Five traits in selection? Except for emotional stability, the other traits do not predict job performance. In considering the validity of other elements of the Big Five, it is possible that they are too broad and that to predict specific work behaviours, more fine-grained traits are necessary.[15] When predicting criteria more specific than overall job performance, this is undoubtedly true. For example, measures of compliance, trust, and dutifulness (all are subfacets of the NEO) might do a better job of predicting attendance than any of the five general traits. Similarly, the tendency to fantasize or be original or be creative may better predict creative work behaviours than the general openness to experience factor. Furthermore, even among the Big Five, each of the traits is probably predictive of performance in certain types of jobs. For example, agreeableness may be an important trait in predicting the performance of customer service representatives, but the same level of agreeableness might actually be a liability for a bill collector! Openness to experience might be important for artists, inventors, or those in advertising, while it has been argued that conscientiousness is a liability for jobs requiring creativity.[16] Thus, the key is to match traits, both in terms of type and level of generality, to the criteria that are being predicted. Research indicates that such strategies make personality tests valid methods of selection.[17]

With respect to emotional stability, evidence indicates that this trait is a much more valid predictor of job performance when it is assessed broadly. Most measures of emotional stability substantially assess anxiety, stress-proneness, and susceptibility to psychological disorders. Such items may be appropriate screens for certain situations, such as public-safety or security-sensitive positions. However, for many occupations, the aspect of emotional stability that may be more relevant to job performance is positive self-concept, or the degree to which individuals feel positively about themselves and their capabilities. Indeed, research suggests that traits that reflect positive self-concept, such as self-esteem, are better predictors of job performance than typical measures of emotional stability.

Researchers have argued that for measures of emotional stability to be as useful as they might, emotional stability needs to be assessed broadly, and specifically needs to include assessment of individuals' beliefs in their worthiness, capabilities, and competence. One measure that assesses these characteristics is the *Core Self-Evaluations Scale.* This measure is shown in Exhibit 8.3. Research indicates that core self-evaluations are predictive of job performance, and the Core Self-Evaluations Scale appears to have validity equivalent to that of conscientiousness. Thus, organizations that wish to use personality testing should consider supplementing their measures of emotional stability with the Core Self- Evaluations Scale. A further advantage of this measure is that it is nonproprietary (free).[18]

EXHIBIT 8.3 The Core Self-Evaluations Scale

Instructions: Below are several statements about you with which you may agree or disagree. Using the response scale below, indicate your agreement or disagreement with each item by placing the appropriate number on the line preceding that item.

1	2	3	4	5
Strongly Disagree	Disagree	Neutral	Agree	Strongly Agree

1. ——I am confident I get the success I deserve in life.
2. ——Sometimes I feel depressed. (r)
3. ——When I try, I generally succeed.
4. ——Sometimes when I fail, I feel worthless. (r)
5. ——I complete tasks successfully.
6. ——Sometimes I do not feel in control of my work. (r)
7. ——Overall, I am satisfied with myself.
8. ——I am filled with doubts about my compentence. (r)
9. ——I determine what will happen in my life.
10. ——I do not feel in control of my success in my career. (r)
11. ——I am capable of coping with most of my problems.
12. ——There are times when things look pretty bleak and hopeless to me. (r)

Note: r = reverse-scored (for these items, 5 is scored 1, 4 is scored 2, 2 is scored 4, and 1 is scored 5).

Source: T. A. Judge, A. Erez, J. E. Bono, and C. J. Thoresen, "The Core Self-Evaluations Scale: Development of a Measure," *Personnel Psychology,* 2003, 56, pp. 303–331.

It's clear that personality testing is in much better standing in selection research, and the use of it is on the rise. However, some limitations need to be kept in mind. First, there is some concern that applicants may distort their responses. This concern is apparent when one considers the items (see Exhibit 8.1) and the nature of the traits. Few individuals would want to describe themselves as disagreeable, neurotic, closed to new experiences, and unconscientious. Furthermore, since answers to these questions are nearly impossible to verify (e.g., imagine trying to verify whether an applicant prefers reading a book to watching television), the possibility of "faking good" is quite real. In fact, research suggests that applicants can enhance or even fake their responses if they are motivated to do so. Given that a job is on the line when applicants complete a personality test, the tendency to enhance is undeniable. Although applicants do try to look good by enhancing their responses to personality tests, it seems clear that such enhancement does not significantly detract from the validity of the tests. Why might this be the case? Evidence suggests that socially desirable responding, or presenting oneself in a favourable light, doesn't end once someone takes a job. So, the same tendencies that cause someone to present themselves in a somewhat favourable light on a personality test also help them do better on the job.[19]

Second, remember that although personality tests have a certain level of validity, the validity is far from perfect. No reasonable person would recommend that applicants be hired solely on the basis of scores on a personality test. They may be a useful tool, but they are not meant as "stand-alone" hiring tools.[20]

Third, remember that even though personality tests generalize across jobs, it doesn't mean they will work in every case. And sometimes when they work and when they don't is counter-intuitive. For example, evidence suggests that conscientiousness and positive self-concept work well in predicting player success in professional sports leagues, but not so well in predicting the performance of police officers.[21] Organizations need to perform their own validation studies to ensure that the tests are working as hoped.

Finally, it is important to evaluate personality tests not only in terms of their validity but also from the applicant's perspective. From an applicant's standpoint, the subjective and personal nature of the questions asked in these tests may cause questions about their validity and concerns about invasiveness. In fact, the available evidence concerning applicants' perceptions of personality tests suggests that they are viewed negatively. One study reported that 46 percent of applicants had no idea how a personality test could be interpreted by organizations, and 31 percent could not imagine how qualifications could be assessed with a personality inventory.[22] Similarly, another study found that newly hired managers perceived personality tests as the 13th least-valid predictor of job performance of 14 selection tools.[23] Other studies suggest that applicants believe personality tests are invasive and unnecessary for companies to make accurate selection decisions.[24] Thus, while personality tests—when used properly—do have validity, this validity does not seem to translate into favourable applicant perceptions. More research is needed into the ways that these tests could be made more acceptable to applicants.

Ability Tests

2.2

ability tests
Measures that assess an individual's capacity to function in a certain way

Ability tests are measures that assess an individual's capacity to function in a certain way. There are two major types of ability tests: aptitude and achievement. Aptitude tests look at a person's innate capacity to function, whereas achievement tests assess a person's learned capacity to function. In practice, these types of abilities are often difficult to separate. Thus, it is not clear this is a productive, practical distinction for ability tests used in selection.

Surveys reveal that between 15 and 20 percent of organizations use some sort of ability test in selection decisions.[25] Organizations that use ability tests do so because they assume the tests assess a key determinant of employee performance. Without a certain level of ability, innate or learned, performance is unlikely to be acceptable, regardless of motivation. Someone may try extremely hard to do well in a very difficult class (e.g., calculus), but will not succeed unless they have the ability to do so (e.g., mathematical aptitude).

There are four major classes of ability tests: cognitive, psychomotor, physical, and sensory/perceptual.[26] As these ability tests are quite distinct, each will be considered separately below. Because most of the research attention—and public controversy—has focused on cognitive ability tests, they are discussed below in considerable detail.

cognitive ability tests
Measures that provide an indication of a person's capacity in relation to the construct(s) tested (i.e., verbal ability, mathematical ability, etc.) and considered relevant to job performance

Cognitive Ability Tests **Cognitive ability tests** refer to measures that assess abilities involved in thinking, including perception, memory, reasoning, verbal and mathematical abilities, and the expression of ideas. Is cognitive ability a general construct or does it have a number of specific aspects? Research shows that measures of specific cognitive abilities, such as verbal, quantitative, reasoning, and so on, appear to reflect general intelligence (sometimes referred to as IQ or "g").[27] One of the facts that best illustrates this finding is the relatively high correlations between scores on measures of specific facets of intelligence. Someone who scores well on a measure of one specific ability is more likely to score well on measures of other specific abilities. In other words, general intelligence causes individuals to have similar scores on measures of specific abilities.

Measures of Cognitive Ability. There are many cognitive ability tests that measure both specific cognitive abilities and general mental ability. Many test publishers offer an array of tests. For example, Harcourt Educational Measurement (formerly The Psychological Corporation) sells the *Employee Aptitude Survey,* a test of ten specific cognitive abilities (e.g., verbal comprehension, numerical ability, numerical and verbal reasoning, word fluency). Each of these specific tests is sold separately and each takes no more than five minutes to administer to applicants. Harcourt (www.harcourtassessment.com) also sells the *Wonderlic Personnel Test,* perhaps the most widely used test of general mental ability for selection decisions. The Wonderlic is a 12-minute, 50-item test. Items range in type from spatial relations to numerical problems to analogies. Exhibit 8.4 provides examples of items from one of the forms of the Wonderlic. In addition to being a speed (timed) test, the Wonderlic is also a power test—the items get harder as the test progresses (very few individuals complete all 50 items). Although cognitive ability tests are not entirely costless, they are among the least expensive of any substantive assessment method.

EXHIBIT 8.4 Sample Cognitive Ability Test Items

Look at the row of numbers below. What number should come next?

8 4 2 1 1/2 1/4 ?

Assume the first 2 statements are true. Is the final one: (1) true, (2) false, (3) not certain?

The boy plays baseball. All baseball players wear hats. The boy wears a hat.

One of the numbered figures in the following drawing is most different from the others. What is the number in that drawing?

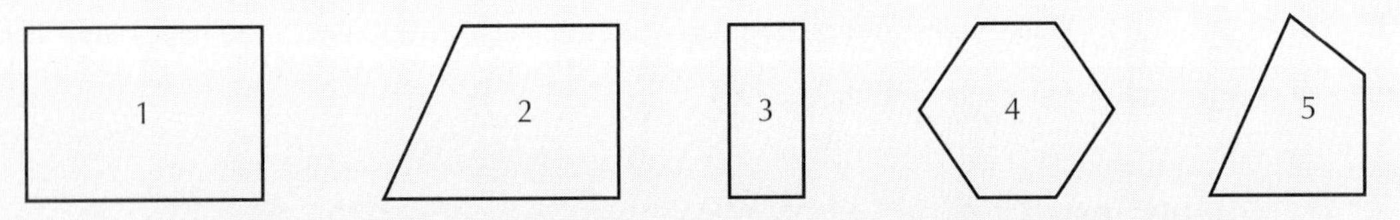

A train travels 20 feet in 1/5 second. At this same speed, how many feet will it travel in three seconds?

How many of the six pairs of items listed below are exact duplicates?

3421	1243
21212	21212
558956	558956
10120210	10120210
612986896	612986896
356471201	356571201

The hours of daylight and darkness in SEPTEMBER are nearest equal to the hours of daylight and darkness in

(1) June (2) March (3) May (4) November

Source: Reprinted with permission from C. F. Wonderlic Personnel Test, Inc., *1992 Catalog: Employment Tests, Forms, and Procedures* (Libertyville, IL: author—Charles F. Wonderlic, 1992).

There are many other tests and test publishers in addition to those reviewed above. Before deciding which test to use, organizations should seek out a reputable testing firm. An association of test publishers has been formed with bylaws to help ensure this process.[28] It is also advisable to seek out the advice of researchers or testing specialists. The Canadian Psychological Association has outlined the relevant testing and assessment principles in its *Guidelines for Educational and Psychological Testing*. However, at this time the document is unavailable and is awaiting updating. As an alternative the same titled document of the American Psychological Association is recommended.[29]

Evaluation of Cognitive Ability Tests The findings regarding general intelligence have had profound implications for personnel selection. A number of meta-analyses have been conducted on the validity of cognitive ability tests. Although the validities found in these studies have fluctuated to some extent, the most comprehensive reviews have estimated the "true" validity of measures of general cognitive ability to be roughly $\bar{r} = .50$.[30] The conclusions from these meta-analyses are dramatic:

1. Cognitive ability tests are among the most valid, if not *the* most valid, methods of selection.
2. Cognitive ability tests appear to generalize across all organizations, all job types, and all types of applicants; thus, they are likely to be valid in virtually any selection context.
3. Cognitive ability tests appear to generalize across cultures, with validities at least as high in Europe as in Canada and the United States.
4. Organizations using cognitive ability tests in selection enjoy large economic gains compared to organizations that do not use them.

These conclusions are not simply esoteric speculations from the ivory tower. They are based on hundreds of studies of hundreds of organizations employing hundreds of thousands of workers. Thus, whether an organization is selecting engineers, customer service representatives, or meat cutters, general mental ability is likely the single most valid method of selecting among applicants. A large-scale quantitative review of the literature suggested relatively high average validities for many occupational groups, such as the following:[31]

- Manager, $\bar{r} = .53$
- Clerk, $\bar{r} = .54$
- Salesperson, $\bar{r} = .61$
- Protective professional, $\bar{r} = .42$
- Service worker, $\bar{r} = .48$
- Trades and crafts, $\bar{r} = .46$
- Elementary industrial worker, $\bar{r} = .37$
- Vehicle operator, $\bar{r} = .28$
- Sales clerk, $\bar{r} = .27$

These results show that cognitive ability tests have some degree of validity for all types of jobs. The validity is particularly high for complex jobs (i.e., manager, engineer), but even for simple jobs the validity is positive. The same review also revealed that cognitive ability tests have very high degrees of validity in predicting training success $\bar{r} = .37$ for vehicle operators to $\bar{r} = .87$ for protective professionals. This is due to the substantial learning component of training and the obvious fact that smart people learn more.[32]

Whereas cognitive ability tests are more valid for jobs of medium (e.g., police officers, salespersons) and high (e.g., computer programmers, pilots) complexity, they are valid even for jobs of relatively low complexity (e.g., bus driver, factory worker). Why are cognitive ability tests predictive even for relatively simple jobs where intelligence would not appear to be an important attribute? The fact is that some degree of intelligence is important for *any* type of job. The validity of cognitive ability tests even seems to generalize to performance on and off athletic teams

EXHIBIT 8.5 Cognitive Ability Testing in the National Football League

Lest you think cognitive ability testing is used only to select applicants for unimportant jobs such as rocket scientists or nuclear engineers, completing the *Wonderlic Personnel Test* is an important part of the selection process in the National Football League (NFL). The NFL uses the Wonderlic as one component in its physical and mental screening of potential draft picks. Most teams rely on Wonderlic scores, to varying degrees, in making draft decisions. The major justification for use of these tests is a belief that players need intelligence to understand the increasingly complex NFL playbooks. NFL officials believe this to be particularly true for positions that rely heavily on the playbook, namely, quarterback and offensive lineman.

The average NFL draftee score is 20 compared to 21 for the population as a whole. Quarterbacks and centres score the highest of players in all positions. Offensive players tend to do better than defensive players. Some teams even have cutoff scores for different positions. For example, one team used to require quarterbacks to score 25 on the Wonderlic compared to a cutoff of only 12 for wide receivers. Cutoffs seem to be highest for quarterbacks and offensive linemen.

Of course, like all selection methods, cognitive ability tests have their limits. George Young, general manager of the New York Giants, was the individual responsible for convincing the NFL to use the Wonderlic. He recalls a game where a defensive lineman with an IQ of 90 went up against an offensive lineman with a 150 IQ. According to Young, "The defensive lineman told the offensive lineman, 'Don't worry. After I hit you a few times, you'll be just as dumb as I am.'"

Source: Adopted from R. Hofer, "Get Smart," *Sports Illustrated*, September 5, 1994; B. Plaschke and E. Almond, "Has the NFL Become a Thinking Man's Game?" *Los Angeles Times*, April 21, 1995.

(see Exhibit 8.5). In addition to performance as a professional football player, one study also found that college basketball teams high in cognitive ability performed better than teams low in cognitive ability.[33] Thus, cognitive ability may be unimportant to performance in some jobs, but, if this is true, we have yet to find them.

Why do cognitive ability tests work so well in predicting job performance? Research has shown that most of the effect of cognitive ability tests is due to the fact that intelligent employees have greater job knowledge.[34] Another important issue in understanding the validity of cognitive ability tests is the nature of specific versus general abilities. As was noted earlier, measures of specific abilities are available and continue to be used in selection. These specific measures will likely have some validity in predicting job performance, but this is simply because these tests measure general mental ability. Research has suggested rather conclusively that specific abilities do not explain additional variance in job performance over and above that explained by measures of general cognitive ability.[35] One recent study found that the average validity of general mental abilities tests, for various types of jobs, was $\bar{r} = .46$. The average incremental validity of a composite of specific abilities (i.e., controlling for general mental ability) was only .02.[36] In fact, in many cases, the validity of a combination of specific cognitive abilities is lower than that for general ability.[37] Thus, in most cases, organizations would be better served by using a measure of general cognitive ability than measures of specific abilities.

Some researchers have argued that cognitive ability tests measure only academic knowledge and that although such tests may be somewhat predictive of job performance, other types of intellectual abilities may be relevant as well. In particular, it has been argued that common sense (termed tacit knowledge or practical intelligence) can be an important predictor of job performance because practical knowledge is important to the performance of any job.[38] It is argued, for example, that a carpenter or nurse or lawyer can have all the intelligence in the world, but without common sense, these people will not be able to adequately perform their jobs. Accordingly, measures of tacit knowledge have been developed. An example is provided in Exhibit 8.6 for a sales manager. In this example, examinees rate the quality of each piece of advice on a 1 (low) to 9 (high) scale. Research suggests that the correlation between scores on a tacit knowledge measure and job performance ranges from .3 to .4. Such measures have modest relations with intelligence, but it has been argued that such measures simply reflect job knowledge.[39] If this is true, the importance of distinguishing common sense from general intelligence is called into question.

EXHIBIT 8.6 Sample Measure of Tacit Knowledge

You have just learned that detailed weekly reports of sales-related activities will be required of employees in your department. You have not received a rationale for the reports. The new reporting procedure appears cumbersome and it will probably be resisted strongly by your group. Neither you nor your employees had input into the decision to require the report, nor in decisions about its format. You are planning a meeting of your employees to introduce them to the new reporting procedures. Rate the quality of the following things you might do:

- Emphasize that you had nothing to do with the new procedure.
- Have a group discussion about the value of the new procedure and then put its adoption to a vote.
- Promise to make your group's concerns known to the supervisors, but only after the group has made a good faith effort by trying the new procedure for six weeks.
- Since the new procedure will probably get an unpleasant response anyway, use the meeting for something else and inform them about it in a memo.
- Postpone the meeting until you find out the rationale for the new procedure.

Source: R. J. Sternberg, "Tacit Knowledge and Job Success," in N. Anderson and P. Herriot (eds.), *Assessment and Selection in Organizations* (Chichester, England: Wiley, 1994), pp. 27–39.

(We will have more to say about the utility of job knowledge tests in the next section.) In short, arguing that practical intelligence is anything other than job knowledge, without further data, could be likened to "putting old wine in a new bottle."[40]

Potential Limitations If cognitive ability tests are so valid and cheap, one might wonder why more organizations aren't using them. One of the main reasons is concern over the racial differences and fairness of these tests. Regardless of the type of measure used, cognitive ability tests have demonstrated the existence of racial differences that raises the spectre of adverse impact when used in selection. Specifically, although there is considerable overlap between distributions, the results of cognitive ability tests comparing different racial groups' averages has found that Asians score about .4 of a standard deviation higher than Whites, Hispanics average score is approximately .7 of a standard deviation below Whites, and Blacks average score is .3 of a standard deviation lower than Hispanics.[41] In the United States, these differences have led to close scrutiny—and sometimes rejection—of cognitive ability tests in the legal courts.

The issue of fairness of cognitive ability tests has been a source of debate and has generated a great deal of research. One way to think of fairness is in terms of the accuracy of prediction of a test. If a test predicts job performance with equal accuracy for different groups, then many people would say the test is "fair." The difficulty is that even though the test is equally accurate for the groups, the average test scores may be different between groups. When this occurs, use of the test will disadvantage groups with lower averages. This causes a dilemma: Should the organization use the test because it is an accurate and unbiased predictor of job performance, or should the use of the test be abandoned because it adversely impacts members of a designated group? The research shows that cognitive ability tests are equally accurate predictors of job performance for various racial and ethnic groups. But the research also shows that there are average score differences among groups. Thus the dilemma noted above is a real one for the organization. It must decide whether to (1) use cognitive ability tests because they accurately predict performance; (2) not use cognitive ability tests to avoid adverse impact, and substitute an alternative measure that does not demonstrate adverse impact; or (3) use cognitive ability tests in conjunction with other predictors that do not involve adverse impact, thus lessening the adverse impact overall.

Another aspect of using cognitive ability tests in selection is concern over applicant reactions. Research on how applicants react to cognitive ability tests is scant and somewhat mixed. One study suggested that 88 percent of applicants for managerial positions perceived the Wonderlic as job related.[42] Another study, however, demonstrated that applicants thought companies had little need for information obtained from a cognitive ability test.[43] Perhaps one explanation for these conflicting findings is the nature of the test. One study characterized eight cognitive ability tests as either concrete (vocabulary, mathematical word problems) or abstract (letter sets, quantitative comparisons) and found that concrete cognitive ability test items were viewed as job related while abstract test items were not.[44] Thus, while applicants may have mixed reactions to cognitive ability tests, concrete items are less likely to be objectionable. In general, applicants perceive cognitive ability tests to be more valid than personality tests, but less valid than interviews or work samples.[45]

Conclusion In sum, cognitive ability tests are one of the most valid selection measures across jobs; they also positively predict learning and training success, and negatively predict turnover.[46] But they also have some troubling "side effects," notably that applicants aren't wild about the tests, and the tests have substantial adverse impact against minorities.[47]

A recent survey of 703 members of the main professional association in which cognitive ability tests are used generated some interesting findings. Among the experts, there were several areas of consensus:[48]

1. Cognitive ability is measured reasonably well by standardized tests.
2. General cognitive ability will become increasingly important in selection as jobs become more complex.
3. The predictive validity of cognitive ability tests depends on how performance is defined and measured.
4. The complex nature of job performance means that cognitive ability tests need to be supplemented with other selection measures.
5. There is more to intelligence than what is measured by a standard cognitive ability test.

Notwithstanding the potential merits of cognitive ability tests for employee selection, it seems likely that the use of these tests could be problematic in Canada given the Supreme Court of Canada's rulings in the Tawney Meiorin case. To begin, as noted in Chapter 2, in deciding the Meiorin case the court determined that it was inappropriate to draw a distinction between direct discrimination and adverse impact discrimination in dealing with claims disputing the use of some standard or test result as a bona fide occupational requirement (BFOR). Related to the court's ruling, an organization using a cognitive ability test for selection would have to defend the practice in light of the principles laid out by the court in its decision. In particular, it would seem plausible for an organization to claim that a cognitive ability test was used because it was a rational predictor of job performance and that the test was used in the good faith belief that it was necessary for the achievement of work purposes. However, organizations might encounter greater difficulties in defending the claim that a specific cut-off score on a cognitive ability tests is necessary to accomplish job-related work purposes. This last standard laid out in the Meiorin ruling requires the organization to demonstrate that the selection device is the least discriminatory possibility and that there is no other device available that might be used to accommodate a job candidate.

psychomotor ability tests
Measures that provide information describing a person's mind-movement interactions as reflected by indicators such as hand-eye coordination and finger dexterity

Other Types of Ability Tests In the following sections we consider tests that measure other types of abilities. Following the earlier classification of abilities into cognitive, psychomotor, physical, and sensory/perceptual, and having just reviewed cognitive ability tests, we now consider the other types of ability tests: psychomotor, physical, and sensory/perceptual.

Psychomotor Ability Tests. **Psychomotor ability tests** measure the correlation of thought with bodily movement. Involved here are processes such as reaction time, arm-hand steadiness, control precision, and manual and digit dexterity. As an example, the York University fitness protocol for assessing applicants for firefighter positions requires that candidates demonstrate their psychomotor abilities by coupling and uncoupling a hose while perched at the top of a 40-foot ladder.[49] Some tests of mechanical ability are psychomotor tests. For example, the *MacQuarrie*

Test for Mechanical Ability is a 30-minute test that measures manual dexterity. Seven subtests require tracing, tapping, dotting, copying, and so on.

physical abilities tests

Tests that measure muscular strength, cardiovascular endurance, and movement quality

Physical Abilities Tests. **Physical abilities tests** measure muscular strength, cardiovascular endurance, and movement quality.[50] An example of a test that requires all three comes from the city of Vancouver. The test mimics the tasks required in firefighting and includes carrying a 40-pound equipment bag up four flights of stairs, using a rope to hoist a 40-pound hose to a height of 40 feet, using an 8-pound sledgehammer to drive a 167-pound steel beam a distance of 5 feet on the ground, dragging a 2.5-inch hose 100 feet, and then dragging a 175-pound dummy 100 feet.[51] Some have argued that such tests are the single most effective means of reducing workplace injuries.[52]

Another reason to use physical abilities tests for appropriate jobs is to avoid injuries on the job. Well-designed tests will screen out applicants who have applied for positions that are poorly suited to their physical abilities. Thus, fewer injuries should result. In fact, one study found, using a concurrent validation approach on a sample of railroad workers, that 57 percent of all injury costs were due to the 26 percent of current employees who failed the physical abilities test.[53]

When carefully conducted for appropriate jobs, physical abilities tests can be highly valid. One comprehensive study reported average validities of $\bar{r} = .39$ for warehouse workers to $\bar{r} = .87$ for enlisted army men in the United States.[54] Applicant reactions to these sorts of tests are unknown.

sensory/perceptual abilities tests

Tests that assess the ability to detect and recognize environmental stimuli

Sensory/Perceptual Abilities Tests. **Sensory/perceptual abilities tests** assess the ability to detect and recognize environmental stimuli. An example of a sensory/perceptual ability test is a flight simulator used as part of the assessment process for airline pilots. Some tests of mechanical and clerical ability can be considered measures of sensory/perceptual ability, although they take on characteristics of cognitive ability tests. For example, the most commonly used mechanical ability test is the *Bennett Mechanical Comprehension Test,* which contains 68 items that measure an applicant's knowledge of the relationship between physical forces and mechanical objects (e.g., how a pulley operates, how gears function, etc.). In terms of clerical tests, the most widely known is the *Minnesota Clerical Test.* This timed test consists of 200 items in which the applicant is asked to compare names or numbers to identify matching elements. For example, an applicant might be asked (needing to work under time constraints) to indicate which of the following pair of number series is the same:

109485	________	104985
456836	________	456836
356823	________	536823
890940	________	890904
205837	________	205834

These tests of mechanical and clerical ability and others like them have reliability and validity data available that suggests they are valid predictors of performance within their specific area.[55] The degree to which these tests add validity over general intelligence, however, is not known.

RC 2.2

Job Knowledge Tests

job knowledge tests

Measures that directly test an applicant's knowledge of information necessary to performing a job

Job knowledge tests attempt to directly assess an applicant's comprehension of job requirements. Job knowledge tests can be one of two kinds. One type asks questions that directly assess knowledge of the duties involved in a particular job. For example, an item from a job knowledge test for an oncology nurse might be, "Describe the five oncological emergencies in cancer patients." The other type of job knowledge test focuses on the level of experience with, and corresponding knowledge about, critical job tasks and tools/processes necessary to perform the job. For example, one organization uses an *Objective Inventory Questionnaire* (OIQ) to evaluate applicants on the

EXHIBIT 8.7 An Example of an Objective Inventory Questionnaire

For each of the following tasks, indicate your level of proficiency using the following codes. Use the one code that best describes your proficiency.

A = I have not performed the task or activity.
B = I have not performed the task independently, but have assisted others in performing it.
C = I have performed the task independently, without assistance, and am fully proficient.
D = I have led or trained others in performing this task.

_____ compiled database (DB2) tables in production
_____ rebuilt a master catalogue
_____ installed a tape input system

Source: *Developing Wisconsin State Civil Service Examinations and Assessment Procedures* (Madison, WI: Wisconsin Department of Employment Relations, 1994).

basis of their experience with tasks, duties, tools, technologies, and equipment that are relevant to a particular job.[56] OIQs ask applicants to evaluate their knowledge about and experience using skills, tasks, tools, and so forth by means of a checklist of specific job statements. Applicants can rate their level of knowledge on a scale ranging from "have never performed the task" to "have trained others and evaluated their performance on the task." An example of an OIQ is provided in Exhibit 8.7. An advantage of OIQs is that they are fast and easy to process and can provide broad content coverage. A disadvantage of an OIQ is that applicants can easily falsify information. Thus, if job knowledge is an important prerequisite for a position, it is necessary to verify this information independently.

There has been less research on the validity of job knowledge tests than most other selection measures. A recent study, however, provided relatively strong support for the validity of job knowledge tests. A meta-analytic review of 502 studies indicated that the "true" validity of job knowledge tests in predicting job performance is .45. These validities were found to be higher for complex jobs and when job and test content was similar.[57]

Performance Tests and Work Samples

RC 2.2

performance test
Procedure for assessing a job candidate's ability to perform the work by requiring the person to actually do the job (e.g., as an intern)

work sample
A test designed to capture parts of the job, for example, a drill press test for machine operators and a programming test for computer programmers

These tests are mechanisms to assess actual performance rather than underlying capacity or disposition. As such, they are more akin to samples rather than signs of work performance. For example, at Domino's Pizza Distribution, job candidates for the positions of dough maker, truck driver, and warehouse worker are given performance tests to ensure that they can safely perform the job.[58] Exhibit 8.8 provides examples of performance tests and work samples for a variety of jobs. As can be seen in the exhibit, the potential uses of these selection measures are quite broad in terms of job content and skill level.

Types of Tests

Performance Test versus Work Sample. A **performance test** measures what the person actually does on the job. The best examples of performance tests are internships, job tryouts, and probationary periods. Although probationary periods have their uses when one cannot be completely confident in an applicant's ability to perform a job, they are no substitute for a valid prehire selection process. Discharging and finding a replacement for a probationary employee is expensive and can precipitate a legal response.[59] A **work sample** is designed to capture parts of the job, for example, a drill press test for machine operators and a programming test for computer programmers.[60] A performance test is more costly to develop than a work sample, but it is usually a better predictor of job performance.

EXHIBIT 8.8 Examples of Performance Tests and Work Samples

Professor
- Teaching a class while on a campus interview
- Reading samples of applicant's research

Mechanic
- Repairing a particular problem on a car
- Reading a blueprint

Clerical
- Typing test
- Proofreading

Cashier
- Operating cash register
- Counting money and totalling balance sheet

Manager
- Performing a group problem-solving exercise
- Reacting to memos and letters

Airline Pilot
- Pilot simulator
- Rudder control test

Taxi Cab Driver
- Driving test
- Street knowledge test

TV Repair Person
- Repairing broken television
- Finger and tweezer dexterity test

Police Officer
- Check police reports for errors
- Shooting accuracy test

Computer Programmer
- Programming and debugging test
- Hardware replacement test

motor work sample test
A work sample test that requires the completion of tasks involving physcially manipulating as the focus

verbal work sample test
A work sample test that focuses on verbal skills and interpersonal interactions

high-fidelity test
Test that uses very realistic equipment and scenarios to simulate the actual tasks of the job, thus eliciting actual responses encountered in performing the task

Motor versus Verbal Work Samples. A **motor work sample test** involves the physical manipulation of things. Examples include a driving test and a clothes-making test. A **verbal work sample test** involves a problem situation requiring language skills and interaction with people. Examples include role-playing tests that simulate contacts with customers, and an English test for foreign teaching assistants.

High- versus Low-Fidelity Tests. A **high-fidelity test** uses very realistic equipment and scenarios to simulate the actual tasks of the job. As such, they elicit actual responses encountered in performing the task.[61] A good example of a high-fidelity test is one being developed to select truck drivers in the petroleum industry. The test is on the computer and mimics all the steps taken to load and unload fuel from a tanker to a fuel reservoir at a service station.[62] It is not a test of perfect high fidelity, because fuel is not actually unloaded. It is, however, a much safer test because the dangerous process of fuel transfer is simulated rather than performed. Most of Station Casinos' applicants (more than 800 per week) are customers, so the casino starts off with a very short high-fidelity test (five minutes behind a bank-type counter); applicants pass through successive simulations, such as assembling a jigsaw puzzle in a group to assess teamwork skills.[63]

low-fidelity test

Test that simulates the task in a written or verbal description and elicits a written or verbal response rather than an actual response

A **low-fidelity test** is one that simulates the task in a written or verbal description and elicits a written or verbal response rather than an actual response. An example of a low-fidelity test is describing a work situation to job applicants and asking them what they would do in that particular situation. This was done in writing in a study by seven companies in the telecommunications industry for the position of manager.[64] Low-fidelity work samples bear many similarities to some types of structured interviews, and in some cases they may be indistinguishable (see the "Structured Interview" section, later in this chapter).

Work sample tests are becoming more innovative. Increasingly, work sample tests are being used for customer service positions. For example, Aon Consulting has developed a Web-based simulation called "REPeValuator" in which applicants assume the role of a customer service specialist. In the simulation, the applicant takes simulated phone calls, participates in Internet "chat," and responds to e-mails. The test takes 30 minutes to complete and costs $20 per applicant. The test provides scores on rapport, problem solving, communication, empathy, and listening skills.[65] Another interesting work sample resembles a job tryout, except that the applicant is not hired or compensated. For example, one small business actually took a promising applicant on a sales call. In this case, although the applicant looked perfect on paper, the sales call revealed troubling aspects to the applicant's behaviour, and she wasn't hired.[66] Finally, some technology companies are hosting "coding competitions" at colleges and universities, where in return for a hefty prize (first-place awards can be as high as US$50,000) and a job offer, students can try to develop software or solve a programming problem. The company gets a chance to spread its brand name and a crack at hiring high-quality applicants who have just proven themselves.[67]

Computer Interaction Performance Tests versus Paper-and-Pencil Tests. As with ability testing, the computer has made it possible to measure aspects of work not possible to measure with a paper-and-pencil test. The computer can capture the complex and dynamic nature of work. This is especially true in work where perceptual and motor performance is required.

An example of how the computer can be used to capture the dynamic nature of service work comes from Connecticut General Life Insurance Company. Fact-based scenarios, such as processing claims, are presented to candidates on the computer. The candidates' reactions to the scenarios, both mental (e.g., comprehension, coding, calculation) and motor (e.g., typing speed and accuracy), are assessed.[68]

The computer can also be used to capture the complex and dynamic nature of management work. On videotape, Accu Vision shows the candidate actual job situations likely to be encountered on the job. In turn, the candidate selects a behavioural option in response in each situation. The response is entered in the computer and scored according to what it demonstrates of the skills needed to successfully perform as a manager.[69]

situational judgment tests

Tests that place applicants in hypothetical, job-related situations, and then ask applicants to choose a course of action among several alternatives

Situational Judgment Tests. A hybrid selection procedure that takes on some of the characteristics of job knowledge tests as well as some of the types of work samples reviewed above is a situational judgment test. **Situational judgment tests** are tests that place applicants in hypothetical, job-related situations. Applicants are then asked to choose a course of action among several alternatives. For example, 911 operators may listen to a series of phone calls and be asked to choose the best response from a series of multiple-choice alternatives. Or, an applicant for a retail sales position may see a clip showing an angry customer and then is asked to choose from various options about how he or she would respond to the situation.

As one can see, there are similarities between situational judgment tests and job knowledge tests and work samples. A job knowledge test more explicitly taps the content of the job (areas that applicants are expected to know immediately upon hire), whereas situational judgment tests are more likely to deal with future hypothetical job situations. Furthermore, job knowledge tests are less "holistic" than situational judgment tests in that the latter are more likely to include video clips and other more realistic material. Situational judgment tests differ from work samples in that the former present applicants with multiple-choice responses to the scenarios, whereas in the latter applicants actually engage in behaviour that is observed by others. Despite our distinctions here, the differences among these procedures are subtle, and it is possible what one may term a situational judgment test by one individual may be labelled a job knowledge test or work sample by another.

A recent meta-analysis of the validity of situational judgment tests indicated that such tests were reasonably valid predictors of job performance ($\bar{r} = .34$). Such tests were significantly correlated with cognitive ability ($\bar{r} = .46$). Research does suggest that situational judgment tests have less (but not zero) adverse impact against minorities. Furthermore, video-based situational judgment tests appear to generate positive applicant reactions. Given these advantages, and the correlation between situational judgment and cognitive ability tests, one might be tempted to use situational judgment tests in place of cognitive ability tests. Indeed, it does appear that situational judgment tests add validity controlling for cognitive ability test scores. On the other hand, just because situational judgment tests add beyond cognitive ability tests does not mean that cognitive ability tests do not also add beyond situational judgment tests.[70]

Evaluation Research indicates that performance or work sample tests have a high degree of validity in predicting job performance. One meta-analysis of a large number of studies suggested that the average validity was $\bar{r} = .54$ in predicting job performance.[71] Because performance tests measure the entire job and work samples measure a part of the job, they also have a high degree of content validity. Thus, when one considers the high degree of empirical and content validity, work samples are perhaps the most valid method of selection for many types of jobs.

Performance tests and work samples have other advantages as well. Research indicates that these measures are widely accepted by applicants as being job related. One study found that no applicants complained about performance tests when 10 to 20 percent complained about other selection procedures.[72] Another study of North American workers in a Japanese automotive plant concluded that work sample tests are best able to accommodate cross-cultural values and therefore are well suited for selecting applicants in international joint ventures.[73] Another important advantage of performance tests and work samples is that they have low degrees of adverse impact.

Work samples do have several limitations. The costs of the realism embedded in work samples are high. The closer a predictor comes to simulating actual job performance, the more expensive it becomes to use it. Actually having people perform the job, as with an internship, may require paying a wage. Using videotapes and computers adds cost as well. As a result, performance tests and work samples are among the most expensive means of selecting workers. The costs of performance tests and work samples are amplified when one considers the lack of generalizability of such measures. Probably more than any other selection method, performance tests and work samples are tied to the specific job at hand. This means that a different test, based on a thorough analysis of the job, will need to be developed for each job. While their validity may well be worth the cost, in some circumstances the costs of work samples may be prohibitive. One means of mitigating the administrative expense associated with performance tests or work samples is to use a two-stage selection process whereby the full set of applicants is reduced using relatively inexpensive tests. Once the initial cut is made, then performance tests or work samples can be administered to the smaller group of applicants who demonstrated minimum competency levels on the first-round tests.[74]

The importance of safety must also be considered as more realism is used in the selection procedure. If actual work is performed, care must be taken so that the candidate's and employer's safety are ensured. When working with dangerous objects or procedures, the candidate must have the knowledge to follow the proper procedures. For example, in selecting nurse's aides for a long-term health care facility, it would not be wise to have candidates actually move residents in and out of their beds. Both the untrained candidate and resident may suffer physical harm if proper procedures are not followed.

Finally, most performance tests and work samples assume that the applicant already possesses the KSAOs necessary to do the job. If substantial training is involved, applicants will not be able to perform the work sample effectively, even though they could be high performers with adequate training. Thus, if substantial on-the-job training is involved and some or many of the applicants would require this training, work samples simply will not be feasible.

Integrity Tests

2.2

integrity tests
Tests that attempt to assess an applicant's honesty and moral character

Integrity tests attempt to assess an applicant's honesty and moral character. There are two major types of integrity tests: clear purpose (sometimes called overt) and general purpose (sometimes called veiled purpose). Exhibit 8.9 provides examples of items from both types of measures. In the exhibit, the clear purpose test questions directly assess employee attitudes toward theft. Such tests often consist of two sections: (1) questions of antitheft attitudes (see items 1–5 in Exhibit 8.9), and (2) questions about the frequency and degree of involvement in theft or other counterproductive activities (see items 6–10 in Exhibit 8.9).[75] The general or veiled purpose integrity test questions in the exhibit assess employee personality with the idea that personality influences dishonest behaviour (see items 11–20 in Exhibit 8.9). Many integrity tests are commercially available. A report issued by the American Psychological Association (APA) has issued guidelines for using integrity tests.[76] Organizations considering adopting such tests must consider the validity evidence offered for the measure. The APA report identified 46 publishers of integrity tests, only 30 of which complied with the task force's request.[77] Thus, it cannot be assumed that all tests being marketed are in good scientific standing.

EXHIBIT 8.9 Sample Integrity Test Questions

Clear Purpose or Overt Test Questions

1. Do you think most people would cheat if they thought they could get away with it?
2. Do you believe a person has a right to steal from an employer if he or she is unfairly treated?
3. What percentage of people take more than $5 per week (in cash or supplies) from their employer?
4. Do you think most people think much about stealing?
5. Are most people too honest to steal?
6. Do you ever gamble?
7. Did you ever write a cheque knowing there was not enough money in the bank?
8. Did you make a false insurance claim for personal gain?
9. Have you ever been in serious indebtedness?
10. Have you ever stolen anything?

Veiled Purpose or Personality-Based Test Questions

11. Would you rather go to a party than read a newspaper?
12. How often do you blush?
13. Do you almost always make your bed?
14. Do you like to create excitement?
15. Do you like to take chances?
16. Do you work hard and steady at everything you do?
17. Do you ever talk to authority figures?
18. Are you more sensible than adventurous?
19. Do you think taking chances makes life more interesting?
20. Would you rather "go with the flow" than "rock the boat" ?

The use of integrity tests in selection decisions has grown dramatically in the past decade. Estimates are that several million integrity tests are administered to applicants each year.[78] There are numerous reasons why employers are interested in testing applicants for integrity, but perhaps the biggest factor is the high cost of employee theft in organizations. The Retail Council of Canada reports that Canadian retailers lose $8 million per day to inventory shrinkage, which costs nearly 2 percent of sales and equates with 30 percent of profits lost. Importantly, the council also notes that 40 percent of the shrinkage is attributed to internal employee theft.[79] In a like manner, in the United States, one-third of all employees have admitted to stealing something from their employers.[80] Thus, the major justification for integrity tests is to select employees who are less likely to steal or engage in other undesirable behaviours at work. Integrity tests are most often used for clerks, tellers, cashiers, security guards, police officers, and high-security jobs.

The construct of integrity is still not well understood. Presumably, the traits that these tests attempt to assess include reliability, conscientiousness, adjustment, and sociability. In fact, some recent evidence indicates that several of the Big Five personality traits are related to integrity test scores, particularly conscientiousness.[81] One study found that conscientiousness correlated significantly with scores on two integrity tests.[82] It appears that applicants who score high on integrity tests also tend to score high on conscientiousness, low on neuroticism, and high on agreeableness.[83] It has been suggested that integrity tests might measure a construct even more broad than those represented by the Big Five traits.[84] More work on this important issue is needed, particularly the degree to which integrity is related to, but distinct from, more established measures of personality.

Measures The most common method of measuring employee integrity is paper-and-pencil measures. Some employers had previously used polygraph (lie detector) tests, but for most employers these tests are now prohibited by law. Another approach has been to try to detect dishonesty in the interview. However, research tends to suggest that the interview is a very poor means of detecting lying. In fact, in a study of U.S.-based interviewers who should be experts at detecting lying (members of the Secret Service, CIA, FBI, National Security Agency, Drug Enforcement Agency, California police detectives, and psychiatrists), only the Secret Service performed significantly better than chance.[85] Thus, paper-and-pencil measures are the most feasible for assessing integrity for selection decisions.

Evaluation Until recently, the validity of integrity tests was poorly studied. However, a recent meta-analysis of more than 500,000 people and more than 650 individual studies was recently published.[86] The principal findings from this study are the following:

1. Both clear and general purpose integrity tests are valid predictors of counterproductive behaviours (actual and admitted theft, dismissals for theft, illegal activities, absenteeism, tardiness, workplace violence). The average validity for clear purpose measures ($\bar{r} = .55$) was higher than for general purpose ($\bar{r} = .32$).
2. Both clear and general purpose tests were valid predictors of job performance ($\bar{r} = .33$ and $\bar{r} = .35$, respectively).
3. Limiting the analysis to estimates using a predictive validation design and actual detection of theft lowers the validity to $\bar{r} = .13$.
4. Integrity test scores are related to several Big Five measures, especially conscientiousness, agreeableness, and emotional stability.[87]
5. Integrity tests have no adverse impact against women or minorities and are relatively uncorrelated with intelligence. Thus, integrity tests demonstrate incremental validity over cognitive ability tests and reduce the adverse impact of cognitive ability tests.

Results from this comprehensive study suggest that organizations would benefit from using integrity tests for a wide array of jobs. Since most of the individual studies included in the meta-analysis were conducted by test publishers (who have an interest in finding good results), however, organizations using integrity tests should consider conducting their own validation studies.

One of the most significant concerns with the use of integrity tests is obviously the possibility that applicants might fake their responses. Consider answering the questions in Exhibit 8.9. Now consider answering these questions in the context of applying for a job that you desire. It seems more than plausible that applicants might distort their responses in such a context (particularly given that most of the answers would be impossible to verify). This possibility becomes a real concern when one considers the prospect that the individuals most likely to "fake good" (people behaving dishonestly) are exactly the type of applicants organizations would want to weed out.

Only recently has the issue of faking been investigated in research literature. One study found that subjects who were asked to respond as if they were applying for a job had 8 percent more favourable scores than those who were instructed to respond truthfully. Subjects who were specifically instructed to "fake good" had 24 percent more favourable scores than those who were told to respond truthfully.[88] A more recent study found some enhancement in completing an integrity test, but the degree of distortion was relatively small and did not undermine the validity of the test.[89] These results are consistent with the meta-analysis results reported earlier in the sense that if faking were pervasive, integrity test scores would either have no validity in predicting performance from applicant scores, or the validity would be *negative* (honest applicants reporting worse scores than dishonest applicants). The fact that validity was positive for applicant samples suggests that if faking does occur, it does not severely impair the predictive validity of integrity tests. It has been suggested that dishonest applicants do not fake more than honest applicants because they believe that everyone is dishonest and therefore they are reporting only what everyone else already does.

Objections to Integrity Tests and Applicant Reactions Integrity tests have proven controversial. There are many reasons for this. Perhaps the most fundamental concern is misclassification of truly honest applicants as being dishonest. For example, the results of one study that was influential in a government report on integrity testing is presented in Exhibit 8.10. In this study, it has been claimed that 93.3 percent of individuals who failed the test were misclassified because no thefts were detected among 222 of the 238 individuals who failed the test. However, this ignores the strong possibility that some of the 222 individuals who failed the test and for whom no theft was detected may have stolen without being caught. In fact, the misclassification rate is unknown and, most likely, unknowable. (After all, if all thefts were detected there would be no demand for integrity tests!) Also, all selection procedures involve misclassification of individuals because all selection methods are imperfect (have validities less than 1.0). Perhaps a more valid concern is the stigmatization of applicants who are thought to be dishonest based on their test scores,[90] but these problems can be avoided with proper procedures for maintaining the confidentiality of test scores.

There has been little research on how applicants react to integrity tests. Research suggests that applicants view integrity tests less favourably than most selection practices; they also perceive them as more invasive.[91] Thus, although the evidence is scant, it appears that applicants do not view integrity tests favourably. Whether these negative views affect their willingness to join an organization, however, is unknown.

EXHIBIT 8.10 Integrity Test Results and Theft Detections

Theft Category	Failed Test	Passed Test	Total
No theft detected	222	240	462
Theft detected	16	1	17
Total	238	241	479

Source: U.S. Congress, Office of Technology Assessment, *The Use of Integrity Tests for Preemployment Screening*, OTA-SET-442 (Washington, D.C.: U.S. Government Printing Office, 1990).

Interest, Values, and Preference Inventories

2.2

interest, values, and preference inventories

Measures that attempt to assess the activities an individual prefers to do both on and off the job

Interest, values, and preference inventories attempt to assess the activities individuals prefer to do both on and off the job. This is in comparison with predictors that measure whether the person can do the job. However, just because a person can do a job does not guarantee success on the job. If the person does not want to do the job, that individual will fail regardless of ability. Although interests seem important, they have not been used very much in HR selection.

Standardized tests of interests, values, and preferences are available. Many of these measure vocational interests (e.g., the type of career that would motivate and satisfy someone) rather than organizational interests (e.g., the type of job or organization that would motivate and satisfy someone). The two most widely used interest inventories are the *Strong Vocational Interest Blank* (SVIB) and the *Myers–Briggs Type Inventory* (MBTI). Rather than classify individuals along continuous dimensions (e.g., someone is more or less conscientious than another), both the SVIB and MBTI classify individuals into distinct categories based on their responses to the survey. With the MBTI, individuals are classified in 16 types that have been found to be related to the Big Five personality characteristics discussed earlier.[92] Example interest inventory items are provided in Exhibit 8.11. The SVIB classifies individuals into six categories (realistic, investigative, artistic, social, enterprising, and clerical) that match jobs that are characterized in a corresponding manner. Both of these inventories are used extensively in career counselling in high school, university, and trade schools.

EXHIBIT 8.11 Sample Items from Interest Inventory

1. Are you usually:
   (a) A person who loves parties?
   (b) A person who prefers to curl up with a good book?
2. Would you prefer to:
   (a) Run for an elective office?
   (b) Fix a car?
3. Is it a higher compliment to be called:
   (a) A compassionate person?
   (b) A responsible person?
4. Would you rather be considered:
   (a) Someone with much intuition?
   (b) Someone guided by logic and reason?
5. Do you more often:
   (a) Do things on the "spur of the moment"?
   (b) Plan out all activities carefully in advance?
6. Do you usually get along better with:
   (a) Artistic people?
   (b) Realistic people?
7. With which statement do you most agree?
   (a) Learn what you are, and be such.
   (b) Ah, but a man's reach should exceed his grasp, or what's a heaven for?
8. At parties and social gatherings, do you more often:
   (a) Introduce others?
   (b) Get introduced?

Past research has suggested that interest inventories are not valid predictors of job performance. The average validity of interest inventories in predicting job performance appears to be roughly $\bar{r} = .10$.[93] This does not mean that interest inventories are invalid for all purposes. Research clearly suggests that when individuals' interests match those of their occupation, they are happier with their jobs and are more likely to remain in their chosen occupation.[94] Thus, although interest inventories fail to predict job performance, they do predict occupational choices and job satisfaction levels. Undoubtedly, one of the reasons why vocational interests are poorly related to job performance is because the interests are tied to the occupation rather than the organization or the job.

Research suggests that while interest inventories play an important role in vocational choice, their role in organizational selection decisions is limited. However, a more promising way of considering the role of interests and values in the staffing process is to focus on person/organization fit.[95] As was discussed in Chapter 1, person/organization fit argues that it is not the applicants' characteristics alone that influence performance but rather the interaction between the applicants' characteristics and those of the organization. For example, an individual with a strong interest in social relations at work may perform well in an organization that emphasizes cooperation and teamwork, but the same individual might do poorly in an organization whose culture is characterized by independence or rugged individualism. Thus, interest and value inventories may be more valid when they consider the match between applicant values and organizational values (person/organization fit).[96] Research has shown that congruence between applicant values and those emphasized within the organization predicts applicant job choice decisions and organizational selection decisions. Employee–organizational values congruence is predictive of employee satisfaction, commitment, and turnover decisions. Although not often studied, values congruence also may predict job performance.[97] Thus, in considering the relationship of interests, values, and preferences with job performance, it seems necessary to also consider how well those characteristics match the culture of the organization.

Structured Interview

2.2

structured interview

Standardized, interview assessment that is constructed using information directly relevant to a job as revealed through job and organizational analysis

The **structured interview** is a very standardized, job-related method of assessment. It requires careful and thorough construction, as described in the sections that follow. It is instructive to compare the structured job interview with an unstructured or psychological interview. This comparison will serve to highlight the difference between the two.

A typical unstructured interview has the following sorts of characteristics:

- It is relatively unplanned (e.g., just sit down and "wing it" with the candidate) and often "quick and dirty" (e.g., 10–15 minutes).
- Rather than being based on the requirements of the job, questions are based on interviewer "hunches" or "pet questions" in order to psychologically diagnose applicant suitability.
- It consists of casual, open-ended, or subjective questioning (e.g., "Tell me a little bit about yourself").
- It has obtuse questions (e.g., "What type of animal would you most like to be, and why?").
- It has highly speculative questions (e.g., "Where do you see yourself ten years from now?").
- The interviewer is unprepared (e.g., forgot to review job description and specification before the interview).
- The interviewer makes a quick, and final, evaluation of the candidate (e.g., often in the first couple of minutes).

Interviews are the most commonly used selection practice, and the unstructured interview is the most common form of interview in actual interview practice.[98] Research shows that organizations clearly pay a price for the use of the unstructured interview, namely, lower reliability and validity.[99] Interviewers using the unstructured interview (1) are unable to agree among themselves in their evaluation of job candidates, and (2) cannot predict the job success of candidates with any degree of consistent accuracy.

Fortunately, research has begun to unravel the reasons why the unstructured interview works so poorly and what factors need to be changed to improve reliability and validity. Sources of error or bias in the unstructured interview include the following:

- Reliability of the unstructured interview is relatively low. Interviewers base their evaluations on different factors, have different hiring standards, and differ in the degree to which their actual selection criteria match their intended criteria.[100]
- Applicant appearance, including facial attractiveness, cosmetics, and attire, has consistently been shown to predict interviewer evaluations. In fact, attractiveness is so important to interviewer evaluations that one review of the literature stated, "Physical attractiveness is always an asset for individuals." Moreover, it doesn't seem that presenting selection decision makers with more job-relevant information helps eliminate the bias.[101]
- Nonverbal cues (e.g., eye contact, smiling, etc.) have been found to be related to interview ratings.[102]
- Negative information receives more weight than positive in the interview. Research suggests it takes more than twice as much positive as negative information to change an interviewer's initial impression of an applicant. As a result, the unstructured interview has been labelled a "search for negative evidence."[103]
- There are primacy effects, where information obtained prior to the interview or during its early stages, dominates interviewer judgments. An early study suggested that on average, interviewers reached final decisions about applicants after only *four* minutes of a half-hour interview. These first impressions are particularly influential because interviewers engage in hypothesis confirmation strategies that are designed to confirm their initial impressions.[104]
- Similarity effects, where applicants who are similar to the interviewer with respect to race, gender, or other characteristics receive higher ratings, also seem to exist.[105]
- Poor recall by interviewers often plagues unstructured interviews. One study demonstrated this by giving managers an exam based on factual information after watching a 20-minute videotaped interview. Some managers got all 20 questions correct, but the average manager only got half right.[106]

Thus, the unstructured interview is not very valid, and research has identified the reasons why this is so. The structured interview is an attempt to eliminate the biases inherent in unstructured formats by standardizing the process.

situational interviews
Structured interview used with less experienced applicants that asks them what they would do if they encountered various hypothetical situations critical to job performance

experienced-based interviews
Structured interviews used with experienced applicants that asks them what they did when they encountered situations critical to job performance

Characteristics of Structured Interviews There are numerous hallmarks of structured interviews. Some of the more prominent characteristics are the following:[107]

1. Questions are based on job analysis.
2. The same questions are asked of each candidate.
3. The response to each question is numerically evaluated.
4. Detailed anchored rating scales are used to score each response.
5. Detailed notes are taken, particularly focusing on interviewees' behaviours.

There are two principal types of structured interviews: situational and experience-based. **Situational interviews** assess an applicant's ability to project what his or her behaviour would be in future, hypothetical situations.[108] The assumption behind the use of the situational interview is that the goals or intentions individuals set for themselves are good predictors of what they will do in the future.

Experienced-based interviews, also called job-related interviews, assess past behaviours that are linked to the prospective job. The assumption behind the use of experienced-based interviews is the same as that for the use of biodata—past behaviour is a good predictor of future behaviour. It is assumed that applicants who are likely to succeed have demonstrated success with past job experiences similar to the experiences they would encounter in the prospective job. An example of an experienced-based interview is the *Patterned Behaviour Description Interview,* which collects four types of experiential information during the interview: (1) *credentials* (objective verifiable information about past experiences and accomplishments); (2) *experience descriptions* (descriptions of applicants' normal job duties, capabilities, and responsibilities); (3) *opinions* (applicants' thoughts about their strengths, weaknesses, and self-perceptions); (4) *behaviour descriptions* (detailed accounts of actual events from the applicants' job and life experiences).[109]

Situational and experienced-based interviews have many similarities. Generally, both are based on the critical incidents approach to job analysis where job behaviours especially important to (as opposed to typically descriptive of) job performance are considered. Also, both approaches attempt to assess applicant *behaviours* rather than feelings, motives, values, or other psychological states. Finally, both methods have substantial reliability and validity evidence in their favour.

On the other hand, situational and experienced-based interviews have important differences. The most obvious difference is that situational interviews are future oriented ("what *would* you do if?"), whereas experienced-based interviews are past oriented ("what *did* you do when?"). Also, situational interviews are more standardized in that they ask the same questions of all applicants, while many experienced-based interviews place an emphasis on discretionary probing based on responses to particular questions. Presently, there is little basis to guide decisions about which of these two types of structured interviews should be adopted. However, one factor to consider is that experienced-based interviews may only be relevant for individuals who have had significant job experience. It does not make much sense to ask applicants what they did in a particular situation if they have never been in that situation. Another relevant factor is complexity of the job. Situational interviews fare worse than experience-based interviews when the job is complex. This may be because it is hard to simulate the nature of complex jobs.

Evaluation Traditionally, the employment interview was thought to have a low degree of validity. Recently, however, evidence for the validity of structured (and even unstructured) interviews has been much more positive. A recent meta-analysis suggested the following conclusions:[110]

1. The average validity of interviews was found to be $\bar{r} = .37$. This figure increased to $\bar{r} = .37$ when estimates were corrected for range restriction, which is not without controversy.[111] To be conservative, the estimates reported here are those uncorrected for range restriction.
2. Structured interviews were more valid ($\bar{r} = .31$) than unstructured interviews ($\bar{r} = .23$).
3. Situational interviews were more valid ($\bar{r} = .35$) than experienced-based interviews ($\bar{r} = .28$).
4. Panel interviews were *less* valid ($\bar{r} = .22$) than individual interviews ($\bar{r} = .31$).

It is safe to say that these values are higher than researchers had previously thought. Even unstructured interviews were found to have moderate degrees of validity. One of the reasons the validity may have been higher than previously thought is because in order to validate unstructured interviews, each interview must be given a numerical score. Assigning numerical scores to an interview imposes some degree of structure (interviewees are rated using the same scale), so it might be best to think of the unstructured interviews included in this analysis as semistructured rather than purely unstructured. Therefore, the estimated validity for "unstructured" interviews included in the meta-analysis is probably higher than that of the typical unstructured interview.

Still, in practice, unstructured interviews are much more widely used than structured interviews. Given their advantages, the lack of use of structured interviews is perplexing. As one review concluded, "Structured interviews are infrequently used in practice." Like all of us, selection decision makers show considerable inertia and continue to use the unstructured interview because they always have, and because others in their organization continue to do so. Thus, a cycle of past practice generating continued use needs to be broken by changing the climate. The best way to do this is to educate decision makers about the benefits of structured interviews.[112]

Another important factor to consider in evaluating the employment interview is that it serves other goals besides identifying the best candidates for the job. One of the most important uses of the interview is recruitment. The interview is the central means through which applicants learn about important aspects of the job and the organization. This information can be very useful to applicants for making decisions about organizations. A recent study suggested that the goals of recruitment and selection in the interview are not complementary. Interviews that are focused solely on recruitment lead applicants to learn more about the job and the organization than interviews that are dual purpose (recruitment and selection).[113] The more information applicants acquire during an interview, the more likely they are to think highly of an organization and thus accept an offer from them.

In fact, applicants tend to react very favourably to the interview. Research suggests that most applicants believe the interview is an essential component of the selection process, and most view the interview as the most suitable measure of relevant abilities.[114] As a result, the interview has been rated by applicants as more job related than any other selection procedure.[115] Why do applicants react so favourably to the interview? One model of applicant reactions to selection procedures suggested that selection methods that are perceived as controllable by the candidate, obvious in purpose, providing task-relevant information, and offering a means of feedback are considered the most socially valid or acceptable.[116] The interview would appear to offer all of these components. As a result, applicants may perceive the interview as a mutual exchange of relevant information predictive of future performance and therefore job related. Thus, the interview generates very positive applicant reactions and can serve an important role in recruitment.

Regardless of what information the interview is structured around, the process of structuring an interview requires that organizations follow a systematic and standardized process. Next, the process of constructing a structured interview is described. For purposes of illustration, we describe development of a situational interview.

Constructing a Structured Interview

The structured interview, by design and conduct, standardizes and controls for sources of influence on the interview process and the interviewer. The goal is to improve interview reliability and validity beyond that of the unstructured interview. Research shows that this goal can be achieved. Doing so requires following each of these steps, which are elaborated on in the upcoming sections:

1. Consult the job requirements matrix.
2. Develop the selection plan.
3. Develop the structured interview plan.
4. Select and train interviewers
5. Evaluate effectiveness.

The Job Requirements Matrix The starting point for the structured interview is the job requirements matrix. It identifies the tasks and KSAOs that define the job requirements around which the structured interview is constructed and conducted.

The Selection Plan As previously described, the selection plan flows from the KSAOs identified in the job requirements matrix. The selection plan addresses which KSAOs are necessary to assess during selection, and whether the structured interview is the preferred method of assessing them.

Is the KSAO Necessary? Some KSAOs must be brought to the job by the candidate, and others can be acquired on the job (through training and/or job experience). The bring-it/acquire-it decision must be made for each KSAO. This decision should be guided by the importance indicator(s) for the KSAOs in the job requirements matrix.

EXHIBIT 8.12 Partial Selection Plan for Job of Retail Store Sales Associate

Task Dimension: Customer Service

KSAO	Necessary for Selection?	Method of Assessment
1. Ability to make customer feel welcome	Yes	Interview
2. Knowledge of merchandise to be sold	Yes	Written test
3. Knowledge of location of merchandise in store	No	none
4. Skill in being cordial with customers	Yes	Interview
5. Ability to create and convey ideas to customers	Yes	Interview

Is the Structured Interview the Preferred Method? It must be decided if the structured interview is the preferred method of assessing each KSAO necessary for selection. Several factors should be considered when making this decision. First, job knowledge is usually best assessed through other methods, such as a written ability or job knowledge test or specific training and experience requirements. The structured interview thus should focus more on skills and abilities. Second, many alternative methods are available for assessing these skills and abilities, as discussed throughout this chapter. Third, the structured interview is probably best suited for assessing only some of these skills and abilities, such as verbal, interpersonal, adaptability, and flexibility skills and abilities.

An example of a selection plan for the job of sales associate in a retail clothing store is shown in Exhibit 8.12. While there were five task dimensions for the job in the job requirements matrix (customer service, use of machines, use of customer service outlets, sales and departmental procedures, cleaning and maintenance), the selection plan is shown only for the dimension customer service.

Note in the exhibit that the customer service dimension has several required KSAOs. However, only some of these will be assessed during selection, and only some of those will be assessed by the structured interview. The method of assessment is thus carefully targeted to the KSAO to be assessed.

The Structured Interview Plan Development of the structured interview plan proceeds along three sequential steps:

1. Construction of interview questions
2. Construction of benchmark responses for the questions
3. Weighting of the importance of the questions

The output of this process for the sales associate job is shown in Exhibit 8.13 and is referred to in the discussion that follows.

Constructing Question. One or more questions must be constructed for each KSAO targeted for assessment by the structured interview. Many different types of questions have been experimented with and researched, including situational interviewing, behaviour description interviewing, job content interviewing, and structured behavioural interviewing. Despite differences, there is a major underlying characteristic common to all.

That characteristic is sampling of the candidate's behaviour, as revealed by past situations and what the candidate reports would be his or her behaviour in future situations. The questions ask in essence, "What have you done in this situation?" and "What would you do if you were in this situation?"

The key to constructing both types of questions is to create a scenario relevant to the KSAO in question and to ask the candidate to respond to it by way of answering a question. Situations

EXHIBIT 8.13 Structured Interview Questions, Benchmark Responses, Rating Scale, and Question Weights

Job: Sales Associate
Task Dimension: Customer Service

	Rating Scale					Rating	X	Weight	=	Score
	1	2	3	4	5					
Question No. One (KSAO 1) A customer walks into the store. No other salespeople are around to help the person, and you are busy arranging merchandise. What would you do if you were in this situation?	Keep on arranging merchandise		Keep working, but greet the customer		Stop working, greet customer, and offer to provide assistance	5		1		5
Question No. Two (KSAO 4) A customer is in the fitting room and asks you to bring her some shirts to try on. You do so, but by accident bring the wrong size. The customer becomes irate and starts shouting at you. What would you do if you were in this situation?	Tell customer to"keep her cool"		Go get correct size		Apologize, go get correct size	3		1		3
Question No. Three (KSAO 5) A customer is shopping for the "right" shirt for her 17-year-old granddaughter. She asks you to show her shirts that you think would be "right" for her. You do this, but the customer doesn't like any of them. What would you do if you were in this situation?	Tell customer to go look elsewhere		Explain why you think your choices are good ones		Explain your choices, suggest gift certificate as alternative	5		2		10
										18

may be drawn from past job experiences as well as nonjob experiences. Inclusion of nonjob experiences is important for applicants who have not had similar previous job experience or have not had any previous job experience at all.

The "what would you do if" questions should be constructed around important scenarios or events that the person is likely to encounter on the job. The candidate may draw on both previous job and nonjob situations, as well as more general behavioural intentions, in fashioning a response.

Exhibit 8.13 shows three questions for the KSAOs to be assessed by the interview, as determined by the initial selection plan for the job of sales associate in a retail store. As can be seen, all three questions present very specific situations that a sales associate is likely to encounter. The content of all three questions is clearly job relevant, a logical outgrowth of the process that began with the development of the job requirements matrix.

Benchmark Responses and Rating Scales. The interviewer must somehow evaluate or judge the quality of the candidates' response to the interview questions. Prior development of benchmark responses and corresponding rating scales is the method for providing firm guidance to the interviewer in doing this task. Benchmark responses represent qualitative examples of the types of candidate response that the interviewer may encounter. They are located on a rating scale (usually 1–5 or 1–7 rating scale points) to represent the level or "goodness" of the response.

Exhibit 8.13 contains benchmark responses, positioned on 1–5 rating scales, for each of the three interview questions. Note that all the responses are quite specific, and they clearly suggest that some answers are better than others. These responses represent judgments on the part of the organization as to the desirability of behaviours its employees could engage in.

Weighting Responses. Each candidate will receive a total score for the structured interview. It thus must be decided whether each question is of equal importance in contributing to the total score. If so, the candidate's total interview score is simply the sum of the scores on the individual rating scales.

If some questions are more important than others in assessing candidates, then those questions receive greater weight. The more important the question, the greater its weight relative to the other questions.

Exhibit 8.13 shows the weighting decided on for the three interview questions. As can be seen, the first two questions receive a weight of 1, and the third question receives a weight of 2. The candidate's assigned ratings are multiplied by their weights and then summed to determine a total score for this particular task dimension. In the exhibit, the candidate receives a score of 18 (5 + 3 + 10 = 18) for customer service. The candidate's total interview score would be the sum of the scores on all the dimensions.

Selection and Training of Interviewers Some interviewers are more accurate in their judgments than others. In fact, several studies have found significant differences in interviewer validity.[117] Thus, rather than asking, "How valid is the interview?" it might be more appropriate to ask, "Who is a valid interviewer?" Answering this question requires selecting interviewers based on characteristics that will enable them to make accurate decisions about applicants. Little research is available regarding the factors that should guide selection of interviewers. Perhaps not surprisingly, cognitive ability has been linked to accuracy in evaluating others. It also would be possible to design an interview simulation where prospective interviewers are asked to analyze jobs to determine applicant KSAOs, preview applications, conduct hypothetical interviews, and evaluate the applicants. Thus, selecting interviewers who are intelligent and who demonstrate effective interviewing skills in interview simulations likely will improve the validity of the interviewing process.

Training interviewers is another means of increasing the validity of structured interviews. Interviewers will probably need training in the structured interview process. The process is probably quite different from what they have encountered and/or used, and training becomes a way of introducing them to the process. Logical program content areas to be covered as part of the training are:

- Problems with the unstructured interview
- Advantages of the structured interview
- Development of the structured interview
- Use of probe questions and note taking
- Elimination of rating errors
- Actual practice in conducting the structured interview

Though research suggests that interviewers are generally receptive to training attempts, it is not clear that such efforts are successful. As one review concluded, the evidence regarding the ability of training programs to reduce rating errors showed that these programs "have achieved at best mixed results."[118] This makes it even more important to accurately select effective interviewers as a means of making the interview process more accurate.

Finally, whether used for initial or substantive assessment, applicants need to realize that first impressions are lasting ones in the interview. Exhibit 8.14 provides some insights into the factors that create first impressions in the interview.

EXHIBIT 8.14 The Importance of First Impressions in the Interview

A firm handshake is one of the common recommendations in the employment interview to create a positive first impression on interviewers. However, there has been no empirical data to verify whether this is good advice for job seekers. Empirical research has revealed insights into both who gives good handshakes and how handshakes are perceived by others. In collecting the data, the researchers analyzed the handshakes of 112 individuals by having each individual shake the hand of four testers. Handshakes were coded along eight characteristics such as strength, vigour, dryness, completeness of grip, and duration. The study found that individuals who scored high on extraversion and emotional stability gave firmer handshakes. Additionally, men had firmer handshakes than did women. Consistent with that hoary advice, firm handshakes did generate more positive impressions on the part of the testers.

What are the implications of this study? First, a dry, firm, vigorous handshake does create a positive first impression on the part of interviewers. And we know from previous interview research that first impressions are lasting ones in the interview. Second, certain individuals who are predisposed to give less than exemplary handshakes need to work on their technique. Specifically, job seekers who are introverted and lack confidence, as well as female interviewees, need to ensure that their handshakes are firm, dry (dry those sweaty palms!), and vigorous and strong.

Additionally, a recent survey of employers revealed that they place heavy weight on candidate grooming in forming first impressions of interviewees. Handshakes also were important to their initial evaluations of interviewees. Though not as important as a handshake in this survey, other aspects of candidate appearance did receive at least some weight from employers, including nontraditional hair colour, obvious tattoos, and body piercing.

Source: W. F. Chaplin, J. B. Phillips, J. D. Brown, and J. L. Stein, "Handshaking, Gender, Personality and First Impressions," *Journal of Personality and Social Psychology*, 2000, 79, pp. 110–117; "Employers Frown on Poor Appearance, Wacky Interview Attire, and Limp Handshakes," *IPMA News*, June 2001, p. 3.

Evaluating Effectiveness As with any assessment device, there is a constant need to learn more about the reliability, validity, and utility of the structured interview. This is particularly so because of the complexity of the interview process. Thus, evaluation of the structured interview's effectiveness should be built directly into the process itself.[119]

Clinical Assessments

clinical assessment
A mechanism whereby a trained psychologist makes a judgment about the suitability of a candidate for a job

A **clinical assessment** is a mechanism whereby a trained psychologist makes a judgment about the suitability of a candidate for a job. Typically, such assessments are used for selecting people for middle- and upper-level management positions. A typical assessment takes about half a day. Judgments are formed on the basis of an interview, personal history form, ability tests, and personality tests. Feedback to the organization usually includes a narrative description of the candidate, with or without a stated recommendation.[120]

Scott Paper Company has taken this approach in an effort to improve its selection for 50 management positions in the manufacturing operations of the company. In particular, Scott was very interested in shifting the orientation of its management staff away from an autocratic, hierarchical system of decision making to one in which the participation and the development of subordinates was emphasized. To do so, selection of individuals with this management style was emphasized as opposed to the training of managers to acquire this style. Clinical assessments were made to ensure that this selection procedure worked.[121] This example nicely demonstrates the role that clinical assessments can play in the selection process. They can be useful when making decisions about criteria in the job requirements matrix that are difficult to quantify. In the case of many companies, as with Scott, management style is one such KSAO. Clinical assessments have the limitation of being unstandardized, however, and very little validity evidence is available.

Choice of Substantive Assessment Methods

2.3

As with the choice of initial assessment methods, there has been a large amount of research conducted on substantive assessment methods that can help guide organizations on the appropriate methods to use. Reviews of this research, using the same criteria that were used to evaluate initial assessment methods, are shown in Exhibit 8.15. Specifically, the criteria are use, cost, reliability, validity, utility, and applicant reactions.

Use As can be seen in Exhibit 8.15, there are no widely used (at least two-thirds of all organizations) substantive assessment methods. Job knowledge tests, structured interviews, and performance tests and work samples have moderate degrees of use. The other substantive methods are only occasionally or infrequently used by organizations.

Cost The costs of substantive assessment methods vary widely. Some methods can be purchased from vendors quite inexpensively (personality tests; ability tests; interest, value, and preference inventories; integrity tests). (Of course, the costs of administering and scoring the tests must be factored in.) Some methods, such as job knowledge tests, can vary in price depending on whether the organization develops the measure itself or purchases it from a vendor. Other methods, such as structured interviews, performance tests and work samples, and clinical assessments, generally require extensive time and resources to develop; thus, these measures are the most expensive substantive assessment methods.

Reliability The reliability of all substantive assessment methods is moderate or high. Generally, this is true because many of these methods have undergone extensive development efforts by vendors. However, whether an organization purchases an assessment tool from a vendor or develops it independently, the reliability of the method must be investigated. Just because a vendor claims a method is reliable does not necessarily mean it will be so within a particular organization.

Validity Like cost, the validity of substantive assessment methods varies a great deal. Some methods, such as interest, value, and preference inventories and clinical assessments, have demonstrated little validity in past research. However, steps can be taken to increase their validity. Some methods, such as personality tests and structured interviews, have at least moderate levels of validity. Some structured interviews have high levels of validity, but the degree to which they add validity beyond cognitive ability tests remains in question. Finally, ability tests, performance tests

EXHIBIT 8.15 Evaluation of Substantive Assessment Methods

Predictors	Use	Cost	Reliability	Validity	Utility	Reactions
Personality tests	Low	Low	High	Moderate	?	Negative
Ability tests	Low	Low	High	High	High	Negative
Performance tests and work samples	Moderate	High	High	High	High	Positive
Interest, value, and preference inventories	Low	Low	High	Low	?	?
Structured interviews	Moderate	High	Moderate	High	?	Positive
Clinical assessments	Low	High	Moderate	Low	?	?
Job knowledge tests	Moderate	Moderate	High	High	?	Neutral
Integrity tests	Low	Low	High	High	High	Negative

and work samples, job knowledge tests, and integrity tests have high levels of validity. As with many structured interviews, while the validity of job knowledge tests is high, the degree to which job knowledge is important in predicting job performance beyond cognitive ability is suspect. Integrity tests are moderate to high predictors of job performance; their validity in predicting other important job behaviours (counterproductive work behaviours) appears to be quite high.

Utility As with initial assessment methods, the utility of most substantive assessment methods is unknown. A great deal of research has shown that the utility of ability tests (in particular, cognitive ability tests) is quite high. Performance tests and work samples and integrity tests also appear to have high levels of utility.

Applicant Reactions Research is just beginning to emerge concerning applicant reactions to substantive assessment methods. From the limited research that has been conducted, however, applicants' reactions to substantive assessment methods appear to depend on the particular method. Relatively abstract methods that require an applicant to answer questions not directly tied to the job (i.e., questions on personality tests, most ability tests, and integrity tests) seem to generate negative reactions from applicants. Thus, research tends to suggest that personality, ability, and integrity tests are viewed unfavourably by applicants. Methods that are manifestly related to the job for which applicants are applying appear to generate positive reactions. Thus, research suggests that applicants view performance tests and work samples and structured interviews favourably. Job knowledge tests, perhaps because they are neither wholly abstract nor totally experiential, appear to generate neutral reactions.

A comparison of Exhibits 7.10 and 8.15 is instructive. In general, both the validity and the cost of substantive assessment procedures are higher than those of initial assessment procedures. As with the initial assessment procedures, the economic and social impact of substantive assessment procedures is not well understood. Many initial assessment methods are widely used, whereas most substantive assessment methods have moderate or low degrees of use. Thus, many organizations rely on initial assessment methods to make substantive assessment decisions. This is unfortunate, because, with the exception of biographical data, the validity of substantive assessment methods is higher. This is especially true of the initial interview relative to the structured interview. At a minimum, organizations need to supplement the initial interview with structured interviews. Better yet, organizations should strongly consider using ability, performance, personality, and work sample tests along with either interview.

DISCRETIONARY ASSESSMENT METHODS

discretionary assessment methods
Typically subjective and intuitive assessment methods used to separate those who receive job offers from the list of finalists

organizational citizenship behaviour
Actions outside a job's requirements that benefit an organization, such as doing extra work, helping others at work, and covering for a co-worker

Discretionary assessment methods are used to separate those who receive job offers from the list of finalists. Sometimes discretionary methods are not used because all finalists may receive job offers. When used, discretionary assessment methods are typically very subjective and rely heavily on the intuition of the decision maker. Thus, factors other than KSAOs may be assessed. Organizations intent on maintaining strong cultures may wish to consider assessing the person/organization match at this stage of the selection process.

Another interesting method of discretionary assessment that focuses on person/organization match is the selection of people on the basis of likely **organizational citizenship behaviour**.[122] With this approach, finalists not only must fulfill all of the requirements of the job but also are expected to fulfill some roles outside the requirements of the job, called organizational citizenship behaviours. These behaviours include things like doing extra work, helping others at work, covering for a sick co-worker, and being courteous.

Discretionary assessments should involve use of the organization's staffing philosophy regarding employment equity commitments. Here, the commitment may be to enhance the representation of minorities and women in the organization's workforce, either voluntarily or as part of an organization's employment equity policy. At this point in the selection process, the demographic characteristics of the finalists may be given weight in the decision about to whom the job offer will be extended. Regardless of how the organization chooses to make its discretionary assessments, they should never be used without being preceded by initial and substantive methods.

CONTINGENT ASSESSMENT METHODS

contingent assessment methods
Typically involve decisions about whether applicants meet certain objective requirements for the job, such as possessing a licence or passing a drug test

As was shown in Exhibit 7.3, **contingent assessment methods** are not always used, depending on the nature of the job and legal mandates. Virtually any selection method can be used as a contingent method. For example, a health clinic may verify that an applicant for a nursing position possesses a valid licence after a tentative offer has been made. Similarly, a security firm may perform a security clearance check on applicants once initial, substantive, and discretionary methods have been exhausted. While these methods may be used as initial or contingent methods, depending on the preferences of the organization, two selection methods, drug testing and medical exams, should be used exclusively as contingent assessment methods for legal compliance.

Drug Testing

In the United States it has been estimated that drug and alcohol abuse costs $60 billion per year.[123] For example, a U.S. National Transportation Safety Board study found that 31 percent of all fatal truck accidents were due to alcohol or drugs.[124] Additionally, substance abuse has been associated with higher utilization of benefits, such as sick time and health care. Focusing on this issue, a study of drug abuse at work found that the average drug user was 3.6 times more likely to be involved in an accident, received 3 times the average level of sick benefits, was 5 times more likely to file a workers' compensation claim, and missed 10 times as many work days as nonusers.[125] The cost of substance abuse is also linked to higher absenteeism, as well as psychological (e.g., day dreaming), physical (e.g., longer break periods, falling asleep at work), and other work withdrawal behaviours.[126] As a result of these findings, drug testing is used by 67 percent of major U.S. corporations in an attempt to prevent and curtail dysfunctional behaviours attributable to substance abuse.[127]

In Canada, the direct costs of alcohol and drug abuse in the workplace has been estimated at $20.1 million per year.[128] However, in Canadian jurisdictions drug and alcohol testing as part of the employment process is almost illegal and allowed only in a limited number of specific situations. For example, within their jurisdictions, the Canadian Human Rights Commission (CHRC) notes that because drug and alcohol tests do not represent bona fide occupational requirements (BFORs), organizations may not establish any of the following:[129]

- Pre-employment drug testing
- Pre-employment alcohol testing
- Random drug testing
- Random alcohol testing of employees in non-safety sensitive positions

Canadian Employee Selection and Drug Testing The restrictions specified by the CHRC and provincial human rights commissions have made employment-related drug and alcohol testing a difficult proposition for Canadian organizations. The difficulties are reflected in human rights and court case decisions that have dealt with the issues. As an example, the Toronto Dominion (TD) Bank sought to establish a drug testing program as a condition of employment for prospective and returning employees. Eventually, after a human rights tribunal had initially upheld the policy, TD Bank's program came before the Federal Court of Appeals. In its decision, the court concluded that the drug testing policy as a condition of employment constituted adverse impact discrimination because those with a drug dependency would be denied employment as a consequence of their disability. In addition, the court focused on the failure to establish a link between drug testing and job performance as required within the context of justified discrimination based on a legitimate BFOR.[130]

In another case (*Entrop v. Imperial Oil Ltd.*), the rulings of an Ontario Human Rights Board of Inquiry went to judicial review on appeal by Imperial Oil. These hearings developed when Imperial Oil sought to establish a drug and alcohol testing program related to safety-sensitive jobs. As a part of the process, the company required employees to disclose any past substance abuse difficulties. When Martin Entrop provided information on his past alcohol abuse, he was reassigned and became the subject of enhanced monitoring and evaluation. In considering the case, the court upheld the Board of Inquiry's ruling that a policy of pre-employment testing was against the law because the company failed to demonstrate that a positive test result was related to impairment. Similarly, it was noted that Imperial Oil had failed to prove that screening was reasonably necessary to deter alcohol impairment on the job. The court also reiterated that issues of substance abuse and drug dependency relate to a personal disability and represent a prohibited ground for discrimination.[131]

Safety Issues Alcohol and drug testing may be acceptable only within certain circumstances. Random alcohol testing may be performed in safety-sensitive job situations because of the potential for accidents due to impairment. However, drug testing is not permitted because it does not indicate that a person is impaired, only that drugs were used at some time. However, drug or alcohol testing may be performed in collecting evidence after an accident has occurred, but only if there is reasonable justification that drug or alcohol impairment was a contributor to the accident. Some form of periodic drug or alcohol testing may also be allowed if it is an element of a rehabilitation program that includes support and monitoring.

Accommodation If permissible testing does indicate drug or alcohol use by an employee, the organization must accommodate the employee to the point of undue hardship. The CHRC prescribes individualized accommodation that takes into account the specifics of the employee's circumstances and advocates that sanctions, including dismissal, should be avoided. The process of providing support and accommodation can only be abandoned if the accommodation costs begin to threaten the viability of the organization (i.e., undue hardship), or if the act of accommodation contributes to the existence of ongoing serious safety problems in the workplace.

Testing Methods Although testing for substance abuse is limited, it is appropriate to acquire an understanding of the basic testing possibilities. To test for alcohol, a Breathalyzer test is used. The Breathalyzer requires a sample of a person's breath, which is obtained by the person blowing into the testing device. The Breathalyzer test is based on a chemical reaction that provides a reading on the percentage of blood-alcohol concentration. The chemical reaction uses potassium dichromate, which is a yellow-orange substance. When potassium dichromate interacts with alcohol vapour in a person's breath, it changes to green and the degree of the colour change is correlated with the level of alcohol present.

Drug tests may involve performance tests, papillary reaction testing, hair samples, or the analysis of body fluids (i.e., saliva, blood, or urine).[132] Different technologies exist for performing these tests. For example, urine samples can be measured using the enzyme-multiplied immunoassay technique or the gas chromatography/spectrometry technique. The latest innovation in drug testing allows companies to test applicants and receive results on the spot, using a strip that is dipped into a urine sample, similar to a home pregnancy test.

A new drug testing product is being marketed to employers in Canada. DrugWipe uses wipes that detect the presence of drugs on surfaces. Wiping surfaces such as steering wheels, keyboards, or computer mice can detect minute traces of amphetamines, cocaine, marijuana, or opiates. The use of wipes to detect whether someone who has been in contact with drugs has been using equipment owned by a company creates a unique situation because it does not involve testing employees or potential employees directly.[133]

Indirect testing concerning drug use may also be accomplished using integrity tests. Integrity tests commonly include a section that asks applicants about drug use. The section on substance abuse often includes 20 or so items that inquire about past and present drug use (e.g., "I only drink at work when things get real stressful") as well as attitudes toward drug use (e.g., "How often do you think the average employee smokes marijuana on the job?").[134] Interestingly, responses to substance abuse questions as part of integrity tests have demonstrated validity in regard to some personnel measures. In particular, it was found that 77 percent of job applicants not recommended for employment based on their integrity test scores were subsequently disciplined for excessive absenteeism, whereas the discipline rate for other applicants was 41 percent. Similarly, in assessing the convergent validity of drug questions from a paper-and-pencil test, it was found that test scores were in agreement with medical drug test results for 84 percent of applicants.[135]

Administration If performed, drug and alcohol testing programs must be carried out with appropriate attention to established testing protocol. To ensure this, it is advised that drug and alcohol testing be performed by trained professionals. Aside from their qualifications concerning sample collecting and adhering to accepted procedures in test administration, professionals will also be aware of issues such as cross-reactions and adulterants. Cross-reactions can occur when common products (e.g., poppy seeds in baked goods) interact with antibodies and identify a person as a substance abuser. Similarly, some prescription medications may also affect drug test results. Adulterants are compounds that test takers use to mask the presence of a drug to avoid detection.

In spite of the HR restrictions on drug and alcohol testing in Canada, there is pressure from employers to allow testing. In Alberta, for example, a task force considering drug testing, created by the Canadian Association of Petroleum Producers, has indicated that its goal is a safe workplace for all employees and that drug and alcohol testing is part of this. Similarly, the Construction Owners Association of Alberta deems acceptable drug testing to include post-accident as well as pre-employment testing.[136] And in a survey conducted by *Canadian Occupational Safety* magazine, 76 percent of respondents indicated that they felt Canada's approach to substance abuse in the workplace was inconsistent with workplace safety requirements.[137]

Medical and Health Testing

Medical or other physical condition testing may occur as part of the general selection process. For example, as part of the assessment of police officer candidates, the Ontario Association of Chiefs of Police requires hearing and sight testing. Similarly, candidates must complete the Physical Readiness Evaluation for Police Constable (PREP) test. The PREP involves an aerobic shuttle run as well as a pursuit and physical restraint circuit.[138] In other situations, medical or physical testing is requested subsequent to a job offer. In these situations, a candidate has passed all other assessments and his/her employment is contingent on the medical or physical assessment results.

Medical Testing Medical testing for job candidates is used to determine whether a candidate has any physical incapacities that may prevent that person from handling the demands of a job. For example, in the transportation industry in Canada, a commercial motor vehicle driver must be physically qualified to drive and must obtain a medical examination certificate to verify this. The certificate indicates that there are no health problems with myocardial infarction, angina pectoris, and other cardiac dysfunctions. Similarly, because of a reciprocity agreement reached between the United States and Canada in 1999, drivers who have epilepsy, hearing impairments, or use insulin to treat diabetes are not allowed to drive commercial vehicles in the United States. Therefore, in the transportation industry, medical conditions may be used as a BFOR in screening out individuals who would otherwise be considered disabled. However, in keeping with the principle of accommodation, it is incumbent on a trucking and transportation company to find driving assignments for a driver prohibited from driving across the Canada–U.S. border.[139]

HIV Testing AIDS is a health condition that would most often fall within the realm of a disability and be prohibited as a criteria in denying employment. However, in three areas, the CHRC has deemed it appropriate to use a positive HIV test as a BFOR in selection. Situations where a candidate's HIV or AIDS status may be used in selection are listed below:

- May be applicable in situations involving travel to countries that restrict entrance to people who are HIV-positive or who have developed AIDS.
- May be an employment consideration in health care work environments where there is a risk of infecting the recipients of health care treatments.

- May be considered in jobs that are safety sensitive, where the work involves the public, and where a worker performs his/her duties alone. The issue in these situations is AIDS-related dementia, which may compromise a worker's cognitive functioning, although it needs to be recognized that this occurs in the late stages of the disease and should not present a problem before this situation develops.[140]

Genetic Testing One of the developments accompanying advancements in understanding human genetics has been the development of genetic tests to identify people with a predisposition for certain genetic diseases. For example, through the 1990s, researchers were able to identify genes associated with the development of Huntington's disease, hereditary colorectal cancer, and hereditary breast cancer. In advance of these discoveries, the genetics of sickle cell anemia had been identified within people with an African heritage. The issue that has developed from these discoveries is whether employers should have the opportunity to screen for genetic conditions.

One argument posited in favour of genetic screening is that it would allow employers to better ensure a safe workplace for employees. Thus, employees would be prevented from working in situations that would expose them to activities or materials that might be deleterious given their genetic condition. Another related consideration is that the screening would avoid economic costs stemming from absenteeism and health insurance claims. The counter argument is that employers should exercise their diligence in ensuring occupational safety for employees to minimize the influence of factors that might agitate genetic diseases. A further counter to genetic testing is the fact that the information obtained through testing is considered private and confidential and raises the issue of personal privacy.[141]

SUMMARY

This chapter continues discussion of proper methods and processes to be used in external selection. Specifically, substantive, discretionary, and contingent assessment methods are discussed, as well as collection of assessment data and pertinent legal issues.

Most of the chapter discusses various substantive methods, which are used to separate out finalists from candidates. As with use of initial assessment methods, use of substantive assessment methods should always be based on the logic of prediction and the use of selection plans. The substantive methods that are reviewed include personality tests; ability tests; job knowledge tests; performance tests and work samples; integrity tests; interest, values, and preference inventories; structured interviews; and clinical assessments. As with initial assessment methods, the criteria used to evaluate the effectiveness of substantive assessment methods are frequency of use, cost, reliability, validity, utility, and applicant reactions. In general, substantive assessment methods show a marked improvement in reliability and validity over initial assessment methods. This is probably due to the stronger relationship between the sampling of the applicant's previous situations with the requirements for success on the job.

Discretionary selection methods are somewhat less formal and more subjective than other selection methods. When discretionary methods are used, two judgments are most important: Will the applicant be a good organizational citizen, and do the values and goals of this applicant match those of the organization?

Though discretionary methods are subjective, contingent assessment methods typically involve decisions about whether applicants meet certain objective requirements for the job. The two most common contingent methods are drug testing and medical exams. Particularly in the case of drug testing, the use of contingent methods is relatively complex from an administrative and legal standpoint.

Regardless of predictor type, attention must be given to the proper collection and use of predictor information. In particular, support services need to be established, administrators with the appropriate credentials need to be hired, data need to be kept private and confidential, and administration procedures must be standardized.

Along with administrative issues, legal issues need to be considered as well. Particular attention must be paid to regulations that govern permissible activities by organizations.

KEY TERMS

ability tests 271
clinical assessment 293
cognitive ability tests 272
contingent assessment methods 296
discretionary assessment methods 295
experienced-based interviews 287
high-fidelity test 279
integrity tests 282
interest, values, and preference inventories 285
job knowledge tests 277
low-fidelity test 280
motor work sample test 279
organizational citizenship behaviour 295
performance test 278
personality tests 267
physical abilities tests 277
psychomotor ability tests 276
sensory/perceptual abilities tests 277
situational interviews 287
situational judgment tests 280
structured interview 286
substantive assessment methods 267
verbal work sample test 279
work sample 278

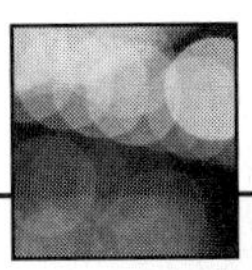

DISCUSSION QUESTIONS

1. Describe the similarities and differences between personality tests and integrity tests. When is each warranted in the selection process?
2. How would you advise an organization considering adopting a cognitive ability test for selection?
3. Describe the structured interview. What are the characteristics of structured interviews that improve on the shortcomings of unstructured interviews?
4. What are the most common discretionary and contingent assessment methods? What are the similarities and differences between the use of these two methods?

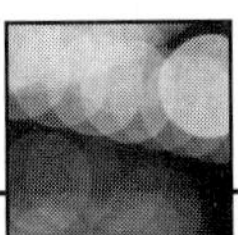

ETHICAL ISSUES

1. Do you think it's ethical for employers to select applicants on the basis of preferences such as, "Dislike loud music" and "Enjoy wild flights of fantasy," even if the scales that measure such items have been shown the predict job performance? Explain.
2. Cognitive ability tests are one of the best predictors of job performance, yet they have substantial adverse impact. Do you think it's fair to use such tests? Why or why not?

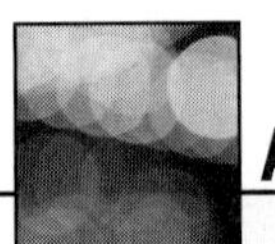

APPLICATIONS

Assessment Methods for the Job of Human Resources Director

Nairduwel, Inoalot, and Imslo (NII) is a law firm specializing in business law. Among other areas, the firm deals in employment equity law, business litigation, and workplace torts. The firm has more than 50 partners and approximately 120 employees. The firm does business in three provinces and has law offices in two major metropolitan areas. The firm has no federal contracts.

NII has plans to expand into two additional provinces with two major metropolitan areas. One of the primary challenges accompanying this ambitious expansion plan is how to staff, train, and compensate individuals who will fill the positions in the new offices. Accordingly, the firm wishes to hire an HR director to oversee the recruitment, selection, training, performance appraisal, and compensation activities accompanying the business expansion, as well as supervise the HR activities in the existing NII offices. The newly created job description for the HR director is listed in the accompanying exhibit.

The firm wishes to design and then use a selection system for assessing applicants that will achieve two objectives: (1) create a valid and useful system that will do a good job of matching applicant KSAOs to job requirements, and (2) be in compliance with all relevant human rights and employment law.

The firm is considering numerous selection techniques for possible use. For each method listed below, decide whether you would probably use it or not in the selection process, and state why.

1. Job knowledge test specifically designed for HR professionals that focuses on an applicant's general knowledge of HR management
2. Drug test and medical examination at the beginning of the selection process in order to determine whether applicants are drug free and able to cope with the high level of stress and frequent travel requirements of the job
3. Paper-and-pencil integrity test
4. A structured, behavioural interview that will be specially designed for use in filling only this job
5. General cognitive ability test
6. Personal Characteristics Inventory
7. A set of interview questions that the firm typically uses for filling any position:
   a. Tell me about a problem you solved on a previous job.
   b. Do you have any physical impairments that would make it difficult for you to travel on business?
   c. Have you ever been tested for AIDS?
   d. Are you currently unemployed, and if so, why?
   e. This position requires fresh ideas and energy. Do you think you have those qualities?
   f. What is your definition of success?
   g. What kind of sports do you like?
   h. How well do you work under pressure? Give me some examples.

EXHIBIT

Job Description for Human Resources Director

Job Summary

Performs responsible administrative work managing personnel activities. Work involves responsibility for the planning and administration of HRM programs, including recruitment, selection, evaluation, appointment, promotion, compensation, and recommended change of status of employees, and a system of communication for disseminating information to workers. Works under general supervision, exercising initiative and independent judgment in the performance of assigned tasks.

Tasks

1. Participates in overall planning and policy making to provide effective and uniform personnel services.
2. Communicates policy through organization levels by bulletin, meetings, and personal contact.

(Continued)

EXHIBIT *(Continued)*

3. Supervises recruitment and screening of job applicants to fill vacancies. Supervises interviewing of applicants, evaluation of qualifications, and classification of applications.
4. Supervises administration of tests to applicants.
5. Confers with supervisors on personnel matters, including placement problems, retention or release of probationary employees, transfers, demotions, and dismissals of permanent employees.
6. Initiates personnel training activities and coordinates these activities with work of officials and supervisors.
7. Establishes effective service rating system. Trains unit supervisors in making employee evaluations.
8. Supervises maintenance of employee personnel files.
9. Supervises a group of employees directly and through subordinates.
10. Performs related work as assigned.

Job Specifications

1. **Experience and training:** Should have considerable experience (6 years minimum) in area of HRM administration
2. **Education:** Graduation from a four-year college or university, with major work in human resources, business administration, or industrial psychology; master's degree in one of these areas is preferable
3. **Knowledge, skills, and abilities:** Considerable knowledge of principles and practices of HRM, including staffing, compensation, training, and performance evaluation
4. **Responsibility:** Ability to supervise the human resource activities of six office managers, one clerk, and one assistant

Choosing Among Finalists for the Job of Human Resources Director

Assume that Nairduwel, Inoalot, and Imslo (NII), after weighing their options, decided to use the following selection methods to assess applicants for the HR director job: resumé evaluation, cognitive ability test, job knowledge test, structured interview, and questions (f) and (g) from the list of generic interview questions in the preceding section.

NII advertised for the position extensively, and out of a pool of 23 initial applicants, they came up with a list of three finalists. Shown in the accompanying exhibit are the results from the assessment of the three finalists using these selection methods. In addition, information from an earlier resumé screen is included for possible consideration. For each finalist, you are to decide whether you would be willing to hire the person and why.

EXHIBIT

Results of Assessment of Finalists for Human Resource Director Position

Selection Method	Finalist 1—Lola Vega	Finalist 2—Sam Fein	Finalist 3—Shawanda Jackson
Resumé	GPA 3.9/University of New Brunswick	GPA 2.8/University of Prince Edward Island	GPA 3.2/Memorial University
	BBA Human Resource Management	BBA Finance	BBA Business and English
	5 years' experience in HRM	20 years' experience in HRM	8 years' experience in HRM
	• 4 years in recruiting	• Numerous HR assignments	• 3 years HR generalist • 4 years compensation analyst

(Continued)

EXHIBIT *(Continued)*

Selection Method	Finalist 1—Lola Vega	Finalist 2—Sam Fein	Finalist 3—Shawanda Jackson
	No supervisory experience	15 years' supervisory experience	5 years' supervisory experience
Cognitive ability test	90% correct	78% correct	84% correct
Knowledge test	94% correct	98% correct	91% correct
Structured interview (out of 100 pts.)	85	68	75
Question (f)	Ability to influence others	To do things you want to do	Promotions and earnings
Question (g)	Golf, shuffleboard	Spectator sports	Basketball, tennis

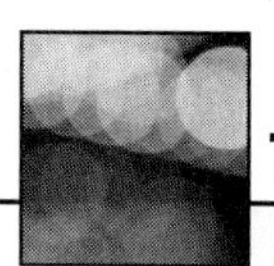

TANGLEWOOD STORES CASE

In our second chapter on external selection, you read how structured interviews are developed. However, following these steps is more complex than you might think. By using the procedures described in the chapter, you will better understand the challenges posed by developing a good structured interview. You will also be able to see the advantages of using a structured protocol.

The Situation

Tanglewood is looking to revise their method for selecting department managers. Currently, external candidates are assessed by an application blank and unstructured interview. Neither of these methods is satisfactory to the organization, and they would like to use your knowledge of structured interviews to help them design a more reliable, valid selection procedure.

Your Tasks

First, you should carefully examine the job description for the position in Appendix A and then create a selection plan as shown in Exhibit 8.12. Then, you will write situational and experience-based interview questions designed to assess candidates' knowledge, skills, and abilities for the department manager position like those in Exhibit 8.13. After writing up these initial questions and behavioural rating scales, you will try them out on a friend to see how they react to the questions as either an applicant or interviewer. Based on the comments of your "test subjects," you will revise the content of the questions and make recommendations on the process to be followed in conducting the interview. The background information for this case, and your specific assignment, can be found at www.mcgrawhill.ca/OLC/heneman.

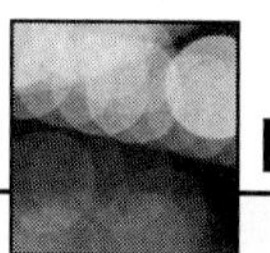

ENDNOTES

1. L. M. Hough, "The 'Big Five' Personality Variables—Construct Confusion: Description versus Prediction," *Human Performance,* 1992, 5, 139–155.
2. R. M. Guion and R. F. Gottier, "Validity of Personality Measures in Personnel Selection," *Personnel Psychology,* 1965, 18, pp. 135–164.
3. P. T. Costa Jr. and R. R. McCrae, "Four Ways Five Factors Are Basic," *Personality and Individual Differences,* 1992, 13, pp. 653–665.

4. D. S. Ones and C. Viswesvaran, "Bandwidth-Fidelity Dilemma in Personality Measurement for Personnel Selection," *Journal of Organizational Behavior,* 1996, 17, pp. 609–626.
5. M. K. Mount and M. R. Barrick, *Manual for the Personal Characteristics Inventory* (Iowa City, IA: author, 1995).
6. P. T. Costa Jr. and R. R. McCrae, *Revised NEO Personality Inventory (NEO-PI-R) and NEO Five- Factor (NEO-FFI) Inventory Professional Manual* (Odessa, FL: Psychological Assessment Resources, 1992).
7. J. Hogan and R. Hogan, "How to Measure Employee Reliability," *Journal of Applied Psychology,* 1989, 74, pp. 273–279.
8. J. B. Miner, "The Miner Sentence Completion Scale: A Reappraisal," *Academy of Management Journal,* 1978, 21, pp. 283–294.
9. M. R. Barrick and M. K. Mount, "The Big Five Personality Dimensions and Job Performance: A Meta-Analysis," *Personnel Psychology,* 1991, 44, pp. 1–26; G. M. Hurtz and J. J. Donovan, "Personality and Job Performance: The Big Five Revisited," *Journal of Applied Psychology,* 2000, 85, pp. 869–879.
10. T. A. Judge and J. E. Bono, "Relationship of Core Self-Evaluations to Job Satisfaction and Job Performance: A Meta-Analysis," 1998, Working paper, University of Iowa.
11. A. J. Vinchur, J. S. Schippmann, F. A. Switzer, and P. L. Roth, "A Meta-Analysis of the Predictors of Job Performance for Salespeople," *Journal of Applied Psychology,* 1998, 83, pp. 586–597.
12. J. F. Salgado, "The Five-Factor Model of Personality and Job Performance in the European Community," *Journal of Applied Psychology,* 1997, 82, pp. 30–43.
13. M. K. Mount and M. R. Barrick, "The Big Five Personality Dimensions: Implications for Research and Practice in Human Resources Management," in G. R. Ferris (ed.), *Research in Personnel and Human Resources Management,* vol. 13 (Greenwich, CT: JAI Press), pp. 153–200.
14. M. R. Barrick and M. K. Mount, "Autonomy as a Moderator of the Relationships Between the Big Five Personality Dimensions and Job Performance," *Journal of Applied Psychology,* 1993, 78, pp. 111–118; M. R. Barrick, M. K. Mount, and J. P. Strauss, "Conscientiousness and Performance of Sales Representatives: Test of the Mediating Effects of Goal Setting," *Journal of Applied Psychology,* 1993, 78, pp. 715–722; I. R. Gellatly, "Conscientiousness and Task Performance: Test of a Cognitive Process Model," *Journal of Applied Psychology,* 1996, 81, pp. 474–482; K. R. Murphy and S. L. Lee, "Personality Variables Related to Integrity Test Scores: The Role of Conscientiousness," *Journal of Business and Psychology,* 1994, 9, pp. 413–424.
15. Hough, "The 'Big Five' Personality Variables—Construct Confusion: Description Versus Prediction"; R. P. Tett, "Is Conscientiousness ALWAYS Positively Related to Job Performance?" *The Industrial-Organizational Psychologist,* 1998, pp. 24–29.
16. B. Azar, "Which Traits Predict Job Performance?" *APA Monitor,* July 1995, pp. 30–31.
17. I. T. Robertson, "Personality Assessment and Personnel Selection," *European Review of Applied Psychology,* 1993, 43, pp. 187–194; R. P. Tett, D. N. Jackson, and M. Rothstein, "Personality Measures as Predictors of Job Performance: A Meta-Analytic Review," *Personnel Psychology,* 1991, 44, pp. 703–742.
18. A. Erez and T. A. Judge, "Relationship of Core Self-Evaluations to Goal Setting, Motivation, and Performance," *Journal of Applied Psychology,* 2001, 8, pp. 1270–1279; T. A. Judge and J. E. Bono, "Relationship of Core Self-Evaluations Traits—Self-Esteem, Generalized Self-Efficacy, Locus of Control, and Emotional Stability—with Job Satisfaction and Job Performance: A Meta-Analysis," *Journal of Applied Psychology,* 2001, 86, pp. 80–92; T. A. Judge, A. Erez, J. E. Bono, and C. J. Thoresen, "The Core Self-Evaluations Scale: Development of a Measure," *Personnel Psychology,* 2003, 56,

pp. 303–331. 2001; T. A. Judge, C. J. Thoresen, V. Pucik, and T. M. Welbourne, "Managerial Coping with Organizational Change: A Dispositional Perspective," *Journal of Applied Psychology,* 1999, 84, pp. 107–122.

19. J. E. Ellingson, D. B. Smith, and P. R. Sackett, "Investigating the Influence of Social Desirability on Personality Factor Structure," *Journal of Applied Psychology,* 2001, 86, pp. 122–133; D. B. Smith and J. E. Ellingson, "Substance versus Style: A New Look at Social Desirability in Motivating Contexts," *Journal of Applied Psychology,* 2002, 87, pp. 211–219;
20. H. Wessel, "Personality Tests Grow Popular," *Seattle Times,* August 3, 2003, pp. G1, G3.
21. G. V. Barrett, R. F. Miguel, J. M. Hurd, S. B. Lueke, and J. A. Tan, "Practical Issues in the Use of Personality Tests in Police Selection," *Public Personnel Management,* 2003, 32, pp. 497–517; V. M. Mallozzi, "This Expert in Scouting Athletes Doesn't Need to See Them Play," *New York Times,* April 25, 2004, pp. SP3, SP7.
22. H. Schuler, "Social Validity of Selection Situations: A Concept and Some Empirical Results," in H. Schuler, J. L. Farr and M. Smith (eds.), *Personnel Selection and Assessment: Individual and Organizational Perspectives* (Hillsdale, NJ: Erlbaum, 1993), pp. 11–26.
23. J. W. Smither, R. R. Reilly, R. E. Millsap, K. Pearlman, and R. W. Stoffey, "Applicant Reactions to Selection Procedures," *Personnel Psychology,* 1993, 46, pp. 49–76.
24. J. G. Rosse, J. L. Miller, and M. D. Stecher, "A Field Study of Job Applicants' Reactions to Personality and Cognitive Ability Testing," *Journal of Applied Psychology,* 1994, 79, pp. 987–992; S. L. Rynes and M. L. Connerley, "Applicant Reactions to Alternative Selection Procedures," *Journal of Business and Psychology,* 1993, 7, pp. 261–277; D. D. Steiner and S. W. Gilliland, "Fairness Reactions to Personnel Selection Techniques in France and the United States," *Journal of Applied Psychology,* 1996, 81, pp. 134–141.
25. P. M. Rowe, M. C. Williams, and A. L. Day, "Selection Procedures in North America," *International Journal of Selection and Assessment,* 1994, 2, pp. 74–79.
26. E. A. Fleishman and M. E. Reilly, *Handbook of Human Abilities* (Palo Alto, CA: Consulting Psychologists Press, 1992).
27. M. J. Ree and J. A. Earles, "The Stability of Convergent Estimates of g," *Intelligence,* 1991, 15, pp. 271–278.
28. F. Wonderlic Jr., "Test Publishers Form Association," *Human Resource Measurements* (Supplement to the January 1993 Personnel Journal), p. 3.
29. B. Azar, "Could 'Policing' Test Use Improve Assessments?" *APA Monitor,* June 1994, p. 16.
30. L. S. Gottfredson, "Societal Consequences of the g Factor in Employment," *Journal of Vocational Behavior,* 1986, 29, pp. 379–410; J. F. Salgado, N. Anderson, S. Moscoso, C. Bertua, F. de Fruyt, and J. P. Rolland, "A Meta-Analytic Study of General Mental Ability Validity for Different Occupation in the European Community,"*Journal of Applied Psychology*. 2003, 88, pp. 1068–1081.
31. J. E. Hunter, "Cognitive Ability, Cognitive Aptitudes, Job Knowledge, and Job Performance," *Journal of Vocational Behavior,* 1986, 29, pp. 340–362.
32. M. J. Ree and J. A. Earles, "Predicting Training Success: Not Much More Than g," *Personnel Psychology,* 1991, 44, pp. 321–332.
33. P. M. Wright, G. McMahan, and D. Smart, "Team Cognitive Ability as a Predictor of Performance: An Examination of the Role of SAT Scores in Determining NCAA Basketball Team Performance," Working paper, Department of Management, Texas A&M University.
34. Hunter, "Cognitive Ability, Cognitive Aptitudes, Job Knowledge, and Job Performance"; F. L. Schmidt and J. E. Hunter, "Development of a Causal Model of Processes

Determining Job Performance," *Current Directions in Psychological Science,* 1992, 1, pp. 89–92.

35. J. J. McHenry, L. M. Hough, J. L. Toquam, M. A. Hanson, and S. Ashworth, "Project A Validity Results: The Relationship Between Predictor and Criterion Domains," *Personnel Psychology,* 1990, 43, pp. 335–354.
36. M. J. Ree, J. A. Earles, and M. S. Teachout, "Predicting Job Performance: Not Much More than g," *Journal of Applied Psychology,* 1994, 79, pp. 518–524.
37. Hunter, "Cognitive Ability, Cognitive Aptitudes, Job Knowledge, and Job Performance."
38. R. J. Sternberg, R. K. Wagner, W. M. Williams, and J. A. Horvath, "Testing Common Sense," *American Psychologist,* 1995, 50, pp. 912–927; R. J. Sternberg, "Tacit Knowledge and Job Success," in N. Anderson and P. Herriot (eds.), *Assessment and Selection in Organizations* (Chichester, England: Wiley, 1994), pp. 27–39.
39. F. L. Schmidt and J. E. Hunter, "Tacit Knowledge, Practical Intelligence, General Mental Ability, and Job Knowledge," *Current Directions in Psychological Science,* 1992, 1, pp. 8–9.
40. F. J. Landy and L. J. Shankster, "Personnel Selection and Placement," *Annual Review of Psychology,* 1994, 45, pp. 261–296.
41. J. P. Rushton and A. R. Jensen, "Thirty years of research on race differences in cognitive ability," *Psychology, Public Policy, and Law,* 2005, 11(2), pp. 235–294.
42. T. A. Judge, D. Blancero, D. M. Cable, and D. E. Johnson, "Effects of Selection Systems on Job Search Decisions." Paper presented at the Tenth Annual Conference of the Society for Industrial and Organizational Psychology, 1995, Orlando, FL.
43. Rynes and Connerley, "Applicant Reactions to Alternative Selection Procedures."
44. Smither et al., "Applicant Reactions to Selection Procedures."
45. J. P. Hausknecht, D. V. Day, and S. C. Thomas, "Applicant Reactions to Selection Procedures: An Updated Model and Meta-Analysis," *Personal Psychology,* 2004, 57, pp. 639–683.
46. S. M. Gully, S. C. Payne, K. L. K. Koles, "The Impact of Error Training and Individual Differences on Training Outcomes: An Attribute-Treatment Interaction Perspective," *Journal of Applied Psychology,* 2002, 87, pp. 143–155; J. P. Hausknecht, C. O. Trevor, and J. L. Farr, "Retaking Ability Tests in a Selection Setting: Implications for Practice Effects, Training Performance, and Turnover," *Journal of Applied Psychology,* 2002, 87, pp. 243–254; J. F. Salgado, N. Anderson, and S. Moscoso, "International Validity Generalization of GMA and Cognitive Abilities: A European Community Meta-Analysis," *Personnel Psychology,* 2003, 56, pp. 573– 605.
47. J. L. Duttz, "The Role of Cognitive Ability Tests in Employment Selection," *Human Performance,* 2002, 15, pp. 161–172; K. R. Murphy, "Can Conflicting Perspectives on the Role of g in Personnel Selection be Resolved?" *Human Performance,* 2002, 15, pp. 173–186; R. E. Ployhart and M. G. Ehrhart, "Modeling the Practical Effects of Applicant Reactions: Subgroup Differences in Test-Taking Motivation, Test Performance, and Selection Rates," *International Journal of Selection and Assessment,* 2002, 10, pp. 258–270;
48. K. R. Murphy, B. E. Cronin, and A. P. Tam, "Controversy and Consensus Regarding Use of Cognitive Ability Testing in Organizations," *Journal of Applied Psychology,* 2003, 88, pp. 660–671.
49. Firefighter fitness assessment: York University protocol, www.recruitfirefighter.com/page0017.htm.
50. J. Hogan, "Physical Abilities," in M. D. Dunnette and L. M. Hough (eds.), *Handbook of Industrial and Organizational Psychology,* vol. 2 (Palo Alto, CA: Consulting Psychologists Press, 1991), pp. 753–831.

51. "Vancouver Fire and Rescue Services: Guide for applicants," August 2005, www.city.vancouver.bc.ca/FIRE/about/recruit/pdf/VFRS_application_guide.pdf.
52. G. Carmean, "Strength Testing for Public Employees: A Means of Reducing Injuries caused by Over Exertion," *IPMA News,* April 2002, pp. 12–13.
53. T. A. Baker, "The Utility of a Physical Test in Reducing Injury Costs," paper presented at the Ninth Annual Meeting of the Society for Industrial and Organizational Psychology, Nashville, TN, 1995.
54. B. R. Blakley, M. A. Quinones, M. S. Crawford, and I. A. Jago, "The Validity of Isometric Strength Tests," *Personnel Psychology,* 1994, 47, pp. 247–274.
55. E. E. Ghiselli, "The Validity of Aptitude Tests in Personnel Selection," *Personnel Psychology,* 1973, 61, pp. 461–467.
56. Wisconsin Department of Employment Relations, *Developing Wisconsin State Civil Service Examinations and Assessment Procedures* (Madison, WI: author, 1994).
57. D. M. Dye, M. Reck, and M. A. McDaniel, "The Validity of Job Knowledge Measures," *International Journal of Selection and Assessment,* 1993, 1, pp. 153–157.
58. L. McGinley, "Fitness Exams Help to Measure Worker Activity," *Wall Street Journal,* April 21, 1992, p. B1.
59. R. Miller, "The Legal Minefield of Employment Probation," *Benefits and Compensation Solutions,* 1998, 21, pp. 40–43.
60. J. J. Asher and J. A. Sciarrino, "Realistic Work Sample Tests: A Review," *Personnel Psychology,* 1974, 27, pp. 519–533.
61. S. J. Motowidlo, M. D. Dunnette, and G. Carter, "An Alternative Selection Procedure: A Low-Fidelity Simulation," *Journal of Applied Psychology,* 1990, 75, pp. 640–647.
62. W. Arthur Jr., G. V. Barrett, and D. Doverspike, "Validation of an Information Processing-Based Test Battery Among Petroleum-Product Transport Drivers," *Journal of Applied Psychology,* 1990, 75, pp. 621–628.
63. J. Cook, "Sure Bet," *Human Resource Executive,* January 1997, pp. 32–34.
64. Motowidlo, et al., "An Alternative Selection Procedure: A Low-Fidelity Simulation."
65. "Making a Difference in Customer Service," *IPMA News,* May 2002, pp. 8–9.
66. P. Thomas, "Not Sure of a New Hire? Put Her to a Road Test," *Wall Street Journal,* January 2003, p. B7.
67. S. Greengard, "Cracking the Hiring Code," *Workforce Management,* June 2004.
68. S. Sillup, "Applicant Screening Cuts Turnover Costs," *Personnel Journal,* May 1992, pp. 115–116.
69. Electronic Selection Systems Corporation, *Accu Vision: Assessment Technology for Today, Tomorrow, and Beyond* (Maitland, FL: author, 1992).
70. D. Chan and N. Schmitt, "Video-Based versus Paper-and-Pencil Method of Assessment in Situational Judgment Tests: Subgroup Differences in Test Performance and Face Validity Perceptions," *Journal of Applied Psychology,* 1997, 82, pp. 143–159; J. Clevenger, G. M. Pereira, D. Wiechmann, N. Schmitt, and V. S. Harvey, "Incremental Validity of Situational Judgment Tests," *Journal of Applied Psychology,* 2001, 86, pp. 410–417; M. A. McDaniel, F. P. Morgeson, E. B. Finnegan, M. A. Campion, and E. P. Braverman, "Use of Situational Judgment Tests of Predict Job Performance: A Clarification of the Literature," *Journal of Applied Psychology,* 2001, 86, pp. 730–740; N. Schmitt and A. E. Mills, "Traditional Tests and Job Simulations: Minority and Majority Performance and Test Validities," *Journal of Applied Psychology,* 2001, 86, pp. 451–458; J. A. Weekley and C. Jones, "Further Studies of Situational Tests," *Personnel Psychology,* 1999, 52, pp. 679–700.
71. J. E. Hunter and R. F. Hunter, "Validity and Utility of Alternative Predictors of Job Performance," *Psychological Bulletin,* 1984, 96, pp. 72–98.
72. W. Cascio and W. Phillips, "Performance Testing: A Rose Among Thorns?," *Personnel Psychology,* 1979, 32, pp. 751–766.

73. K. G. Love, R. C. Bishop, D. A. Heinisch, and M. S. Montei, "Selection Across Two Cultures: Adapting the Selection of American Assemblers to Meet Japanese Job Performance Dimensions," *Personnel Psychology,* 1994, 47, pp. 837–846.
74. K. A. Hanisch and C. L. Hulin, "Two-Stage Sequential Selection Procedures Using Ability and Training Performance: Incremental Validity of Behavioral Consistency Measures," *Personnel Psychology,* 1994, 47, pp. 767–785.
75. P. R. Sackett and J. E. Wanek, "New Developments in the Use of Measures of Honesty, Integrity, Conscientiousness, Dependability, Trustworthiness, and Reliability for Personnel Selection," *Personnel Psychology,* 1996, 49, pp. 787–829.
76. L. R. Goldberg, J. R. Grenier, R. M. Guion, L. B. Sechrest, and H. Wing, *Questionnaires Used in the Prediction of Trustworthiness in Pre-Employment Selection Decisions: An APA Task Force Report* (Washington, DC: American Psychological Association, 1991).
77. W. J. Camera and D. L. Schneider, "Integrity Tests: Facts and Unresolved Issues," *American Psychologist,* 1994, 49, pp. 112–119.
78. P. R. Sackett, "Integrity Testing for Personnel Selection," *Current Directions in Psychological Science,* 1994, 3, pp. 73–76.
79. Retail Council of Canada, "2003 Canadian Retail Security Report Executive Summary," September 23, 2003.
80. R. C. Hollinger and J. P. Clark, *Theft by Employees* (Lexington, MA: Lexington Books, 1983).
81. D. S. Ones, "The Construct Validity of Integrity Tests," unpublished doctoral dissertation, University of Iowa, Iowa City, Iowa, 1993.
82. K. R. Murphy and S. L. Lee, "Personality Variables Related to Integrity Test Scores: The Role of Conscientiousness," *Journal of Business and Psychology,* 1994, 9, pp. 413–424.
83. D. S. Ones, C. Viswesvaran, F. L. Schmidt, and A. D. Reiss, "The Validity of Honesty and Violence Scales of Integrity Tests in Predicting Violence at Work," paper presented at the Academy of Management Annual Meeting, Dallas, TX, August 1994.
84. D. S. Ones, F. L. Schmidt, and C. Viswesvaran, "Do Broader Personality Variables Predict Job Performance with Higher Validity?" paper presented at the annual meeting of the Society for Industrial and Organizational Psychology, Nashville, TN, 1994; D. S. Ones, C. Viswesvaran, and F. L. Schmidt, "Integrity Tests: Overlooked Facts, Resolved Issues, and Remaining Questions," *American Psychologist,* 1995, 50, pp. 456–460.
85. P. Ekman and M. O'Sullivan, "Who Can Catch a Liar?" *American Psychologist,* 1991, 46, pp. 913–920.
86. D. S. Ones, C. Viswesvaran, and F. L. Schmidt, "Comprehensive Meta-Analysis of Integrity Test Validities: Findings and Implications for Personnel Selection and Theories of Job Performance," *Journal of Applied Psychology* (monograph), 1993, 78, pp. 531–537.
87. J. Hogan and K. Brinkenmeyer, "Bridging the Gap Between Overt and Personality-Based Integrity Tests," *Personnel Psychology,* 1997, 50, pp. 587–599; Ones, "The Construct Validity of Integrity Tests"; D. S. Ones and C. Viswesvaran, "Gender, Age and Race Differences on Overt Integrity Tests: Results Across Four Large-Scale Job Applicant Data Sets," *Journal of Applied Psychology,* 1998, 83, pp. 35–42.
88. A. M. Ryan and P. R. Sackett, "Preemployment Honesty Testing: Fakability, Reactions of Test Takers, and Company Image," *Journal of Business and Psychology,* 1987, 1, pp. 248–256.
89. M. R. Cunningham, D. T. Wong, and A. P. Barbee, "Self-Presentation Dynamics on Overt Integrity Tests: Experimental Studies of the Reid Report," *Journal of Applied Psychology,* 1994, 79, pp. 643–658.
90. S. O. Lilienfeld, G. Alliger, and K. Mitchell, "Why Integrity Testing Remains Controversial," *American Psychologist,* 1995, 50, pp. 457–458; M. L. Rieke and

S. J. Guastello, "Unresolved Issues in Honesty and Integrity Testing," *American Psychologist,* 1995, 50, pp. 458–459.

91. S. W. Gilliland, "Fairness from the Applicant's Perspective: Reactions to Employee Selection Procedures," *International Journal of Selection and Assessment,* 1995, 3, pp. 11–19; D. A. Kravitz, V. Stinson, and T. L. Chavez, "Evaluations of Tests Used for Making Selection and Promotion Decisions," *International Journal of Selection and Assessment,* 1996, 4, pp. 24–34.
92. R. R. McCrae and P. T. Costa Jr., "Reinterpreting the Myers-Briggs Type Indicator from the Perspective of the Five-Factor Model of Personality," *Journal of Personality,* 1989, 57, pp. 17–40.
93. Hough, "The 'Big Five' Personality Variables—Construct Confusion: Description Versus Prediction."
94. M. Assouline and E. I. Meir, "Meta-Analysis of the Relationship Between Congruence and Well-Being Measures," *Journal of Vocational Behavior,* 1987, 31, pp. 319–332.
95. See B. Schneider, H. W. Goldstein, and D. B. Smith, "The ASA Framework: An Update," *Personnel Psychology,* 1995, 48, pp. 747–773.
96. D. M. Cable, "The Role of Person-Organization Fit in Organizational Entry," unpublished doctoral dissertation, Cornell University, Ithaca, New York, 1995.
97. D. F. Caldwell and C. A. O'Reilly III, "Measuring Person-Job Fit with a Profile Comparison Process," *Journal of Applied Psychology,* 1990, 75, pp. 648–657; J. A. Chatman, "Matching People to Organizations: Selection and Socialization in Public Accounting Firms," *Administrative Science Quarterly,* 1989, 36, pp. 459–484; C. A. O'Reilly III, J. Chatman, and D. F. Caldwell, "People and Organizational Culture: A Profile Comparison Approach to Assessing Person-Organization Fit," *Academy of Management Journal,* 1991, 34, pp. 487–516.
98. A. M. Ryan and P. R. Sackett, "A Survey of Individual Assessment Practices by I/O Psychologists," *Personnel Psychology,* 1987, 40, pp. 455–488.
99. R. L. Dipboye, *Selection Interviews: Process Perspectives* (Cincinnati, OH: South-Western, 1992), pp. 150–180; R. W. Eder and M. Harris (eds.), *The Employment Interview Handbook* (Thousand Oaks, CA: Sage, 1999).
100. L. M. Graves and R. J. Karren, "The Employee Selection Interview: A Fresh Look at an Old Problem," *Human Resource Management,* 1996, 35, pp. 163–180.
101. M. Hosoda, E. F. Stone-Romero, and G. Coats, "The Effects of Physical Attractiveness on Job- Related Outcomes: A Meta-Analysis of Experimental Studies," *Personnel Psychology,* 2003, 56, pp. 431–462.
102. J. R. Burnett and S. J. Motowidlo, "Relation Between Different Sources of Information in the Structured Selection Interview," *Personnel Psychology,* 1998, 51, pp. 963–980.
103. P. M. Rowe, "Unfavorable Information and Interview Decisions," in R. W. Eder and G. R. Ferris (eds.), *The Employment Interview: Theory, Research, and Practice* (Newbury Park, CA: Sage, 1989), pp. 77–89.
104. T. W. Dougherty, D. B. Turban, and J. C. Callender, "Confirming First Impressions in the Employment Interview: A Field Study of Interviewer Behavior," *Journal of Applied Psychology,* 1994, 79, pp. 659–665.
105. A. J. Prewett-Livingston, H. S. Feild, J. G. Veres, and P. M. Lewis, "Effects of Race on Interview Ratings in a Situational Panel Interview," *Journal of Applied Psychology,* 1996, 81, pp. 178–186.
106. R. E. Carlson, P. W. Thayer, E. C. Mayfield, and D. A. Peterson, "Improvements in the Selection Interview," *Personnel Journal,* 1971, 50, pp. 268–275.
107. J. R. Burnett, C. Fan, S. J. Motowidlo, and T. DeGroot, "Interview Notes and Validity," *Personnel Psychology,* 1998, 51, pp. 375–396; M. A. Campion, D. K. Palmer, and

J. E. Campion, "A Review of Structure in the Selection Interview," *Personnel Psychology,* 1997, 50, pp. 655– 702.

108. G. P. Latham, L. M. Saari, E. D. Pursell, and M. A. Campion, "The Situational Interview," *Journal of Applied Psychology,* 1980, 65, pp. 422–427; S. D. Maurer, "The Potential of the Situational Interview: Existing Research and Unresolved Issues," *Human Resource Management Review,* 1997, 7, pp. 185–201.
109. A. I. Huffcutt, J. N. Conurey, P. L. Roth, and U. Klehe, "The Impact of Job Complexity and Study Design on Situational and Behavior Description Interview Validity," *International Journal of Selection and Assessment,* 2004, 12, pp. 262–273; T. Janz, "The Patterned Behavior Description Interview: The Best Prophet of the Future Is the Past," in R. W. Eder and G. R. Ferris (eds.), *The Employment Interview: Theory, Research, and Practice* (Newbury Park, CA: Sage, 1989), pp. 158–168.
110. M. A. McDaniel, D. L. Whetzel, F. L. Schmidt, and S. D. Maurer, "The Validity of Employment Interviews: A Comprehensive Review and Meta-Analysis," *Journal of Applied Psychology,* 1994, 79, pp. 599–616.
111. L. R. James, R. G. Demaree, S. A. Mulaik, and R. T. Ladd, "Validity Generalization in the Context of Situational Models, *Journal of Applied Psychology,* 1992, 77, pp. 3–14.
112. K. I. van der Zee, A. B. Bakker, and P. Bakker, "Why Are Structured Interviews So Rarely Used in Personnel Selection?" *Journal of Applied Psychology,* 2002, 87, pp. 176–184.
113. A. E. Barber, J. R. Hollenbeck, S. L. Tower, and J. M. Phillips, "The Effects of Interview Focus on Recruitment Effectiveness: A Field Experiment," *Journal of Applied Psychology,* 1994, 79, pp. 886–896.
114. T. N. Bauer, D. M. Truxillo, M. E. Paronto, J. A. Weekley, and M. A. Campion, "Applicant Reactions to Different Selection Technology: Face-to-Face, Interactive Voice Responses, and Computer-Assisted Telephone Screening Interviews," *International Journal of Selection and Assessment,* 2004, 12, pp. 135–148; D. S. Chapman, K. L. Uggerslev, and J. Webster, "Applicant Reactions to Face-to-Face and Technology-Mediated Interviews: A Field Investigation," *Journal of Applied Psychology,* 2003, 88, pp. 944–953; G. N. Powell, "Applicant Reactions to the Initial Employment Interview: Exploring Theoretical and Methodological Issues," *Personnel Psychology,* 1991, 44, pp. 67–83; S. Rynes and B. Gerhart, "Interviewer Assessments of Applicant "Fit": An Exploratory Investigation" *Personnel Psychology,* 1990, 43, pp. 13–22; Schuler, "Social Validity of Selection Situations: A Concept and Some Empirical Results."
115. Rynes and Connerley, "Applicant Reactions to Alternative Selection Procedures"; Smither, et al., "Applicant Reactions to Selection Procedures."
116. Schuler, "Social Validity of Selection Situations: A Concept and Some Empirical Results."
117. Dougherty, Turban, and Callender, "Confirming First Impressions in the Employment Interview: A Field Study of Interviewer Behavior"; G. F. Dreher, R. A. Ash, and P. Hancock, "The Role of the Traditional Research Design in Underestimating the Validity of the Employment Interview," *Personnel Psychology,* 1988, 41, pp. 315–327; L. M. Graves and R. J. Karren, "Interviewer Decision Processes and Effectiveness: An Experimental Policy Capturing Investigation," *Personnel Psychology,* 1992, 45, pp. 313–340; A. J. Kinicki, C. A. Lockwood, P. W. Hom, and R. W. Griffeth, "Interviewer Predictions of Applicant Qualifications and Interviewer Validity: Aggregate and Individual Analyses," *Journal of Applied Psychology,* 1990, 75, pp. 477–486; E. D. Pulakos, N. Schmitt, D. Whitney, and N. Smith, "Individual Differences in Interviewer Ratings: The Impact of Standardization, Consensus Discussion, and Sampling Error on the Validity of a Structured Interview," *Personnel Psychology,* 1996, 49, pp. 85–102.
118. Dipboye, *Selection Interviews: Process Perspectives;* see also M. Harris, "Reconsidering the Employment Interview: A Review of Recent Literature and Suggestions for Future Research," *Personnel Psychology,* 1989, 42, pp. 691–726.

119. Dipboye, Selection Interviews: Process Perspectives, pp. 150–179.
120. Ryan and Sackett, "A Survey of Industrial Assessment Practices by I/O Psychologists."
121. R. J. Stahl, "Succession Planning Drives Plant Turnaround," *Personnel Journal,* September 1992, pp. 67–70.
122. W. C. Borman and S. J. Motowidlo, "Expanding the Criterion Domain to Include Elements of Contextual Performance," in N. Schmitt, W. Borman, and Associates (eds.), *Personnel Selection in Organizations* (San Francisco: Jossey-Bass, 1993), pp. 71–98.
123. S. Dentzer, B. Cohn, G. Raine, G. Carroll, and V. Quade, "Can You Pass This Job Test?," *Newsweek,* May 5, 1986, pp. 46–53.
124. Smithers Institute, "Drug Testing: Cost and Effect," *Cornell/Smithers Report* (Ithaca, NY: Cornell University, 1992), 1, pp. 1–5.
125. Smithers Institute, "Drug Testing: Cost and Effect."
126. W. E. K. Lehman and D. D. Simpson, "Employee Substance Abuse and On-the-Job Behaviors," *Journal of Applied Psychology,* 1992, 77, pp. 309–321.
127. A. Freedman, "Tests of Choice," *Human Resource Executive,* June 2, 2004, pp. 48–50; A. Meister, "Negative Results," *Workforce Management,* October 2002, pp. 35–40.
128. E. Single, L. Robson, X. Xie, et al., *The costs of substance abuse in Canada: a cost estimation study* (Ottawa: Canadian Centre on Substance Abuse, 1996).
129. "Canadian Human Rights Commission Policy on Alcohol and Drug Testing," June 2002, www.caw.ca/whatwedo/substanceabuse/pdf/CHRCPolicyonAlcoholDrugTesting.pdf.
130. *Toronto-Dominion Bank v. Canadian Human Rights Commission and Canadian Civil Liberties Association,* 1998, http://reports.fja.gc.ca/en/1998/1998fc22873.html/1998fc22873.html.html.
131. S. Rudner, "Keep drugs, alcohol out of workplace without violating human rights," *Canadian HR Reporter,* February 2004, 17(3).
132. J. A. Segal, "To Test or Not to Test," *HR Magazine,* April 1992, pp. 40–43.
133. N. Underwood, "Touched by drugs," *Maclean's* magazine, January 16, 2006, p. 46.
134. S. L. Martin and D. J. DeGrange, "How Effective Are Physical and Psychological Drug Tests?" *EMA Journal,* Fall 1993, pp. 18–22.
135. J. Michaelis, "Waging War," *Human Resource Executive,* October 1993, pp. 39–42.
136. Rudner, "Keep drugs, alcohol out of workplace without violating human rights."
137. "Reader panel – Employee drug testing," *Canadian Occupational Safety,* July 14, 2004, www.cos-mag.com/index.php?option=com_content&task=view&id=793&Itemid=23.
138. "What It Means to Be a Police Constable," Ontario Association of Chiefs of Police, no date, www.oacp.on.ca/content/programs/constable_selection.html.
139. Federal Motor Carrier Safety Administration, "Qualifications of Drivers and Longer Combination Vehicle (LCV) Driver Instructors," October 2000, www.fmcsa.dot.gov/rules-regulations/administration/fmcsr/fmcsrruletext.asp?section=391.41#SubpartE.
140. R. Jurgen and M. Palles, "Mandatory or Compulsory HIV Testing – Part 2," *HIV Testing and Confidentiality: Final Report,* Canadian HIV/AIDS Legal Network and Canadian AIDS Society, March 1997.
141. D. Jones, "Selected Legal Issues in Genetic Testing: Guidance from Human Rights," Health Canada, August 2005, www.hc-sc.gc.ca/sr-sr/pubs/hpr-rpms/wp-dt/2001-0104-genet-legal-jur/intro_e.html.

CHAPTER 9

INTERNAL SELECTION

CHAPTER OBJECTIVES

After reading this chapter, you will be able to:

- Describe the primary assessment methods used in evaluating internal job candidates
- Describe and understand the principal substantive assessment methods used in differentiating among internal job candidates

Internal selection refers to the assessment and evaluation of employees from within the organization as they move from job to job via transfer and promotion systems. Many different assessment methods are used to make internal selection decisions. Preliminary issues we will discuss to guide the use of these assessment methods include the logic of prediction, the nature of predictors, and the development of a selection plan.

Initial assessment methods are used to select internal candidates from among the internal applicants. Initial assessment methods that will be reviewed include skills inventories, peer and self-assessments, managerial sponsorship, and informal discussions and recommendations. The criteria that should be used to choose among these methods will be discussed.

Substantive assessment methods are used to select internal finalists from among internal candidates. Various methods will be reviewed, including seniority and experience, job knowledge tests, performance appraisal, promotability ratings, assessment centres, interview simulations, and promotion panels and review boards. The criteria used to choose among the substantive assessment methods will also be discussed.

Discretionary assessment methods are used to select offer recipients from among the finalists. The factors on which these decisions are based, such as employment equity concerns, whether the finalist had previously been a finalist, and second opinions about the finalist by others in the organization, will be considered.

All of these assessment methods require the collection of a large amount of data. Accordingly, attention must be given to support services; the required expertise needed to administer and interpret predictors; security, privacy and confidentiality; and the standardization of procedures.

The use of internal selection methods requires a clear understanding of legal issues. In particular, defending internal selection procedures and the glass ceiling are reviewed.

PRELIMINARY ISSUES

The Logic of Prediction

RPC 1.4

The logic of prediction described in Chapter 7 is equally relevant to the case of internal selection. Specifically, indicators of internal applicants' degree of success in past situations should be predictive of their likely success in new situations. Past situations importantly include previous jobs, as well as the current one, held by the applicant with the organization. The new situation is the internal vacancy the applicant is seeking via the organization's transfer or promotion system.

There also may be similarities between internal and external selection in terms of the effectiveness of selection methods. As you may recall from Chapters 7 and 8, three of the most valid external selection measures are biographical data, cognitive ability tests, and work samples. These methods also have validity in internal selection decisions. Biographical information has been found to be a valid predictor in selecting top corporate leaders. Research indicates that cognitive ability is strongly predictive of long-term job performance and advancement. Finally, work samples are valid predictors of advancement.[1] In this chapter we focus on processes and methods of selection that are unique to promotion and transfer decisions. However, in considering these methods and processes, it should be kept in mind that many of the techniques of external selection may be relevant as well.

Although the logic of prediction and the likely effectiveness of selection methods are similar for external and internal selection, in practice there are several potential advantages of internal over external selection. In particular, the data collected on internal applicants in their previous jobs often provide greater depth, relevance, and verifiability than the data collected on external applicants. This is because organizations usually have much more detailed and in-depth information about internal candidates' previous job experiences. In this age of computers, where organizations can store large amounts of data on employees' job experiences, this is especially true. It is far more difficult to access data in a reliable manner when external candidates are used. As indicated in Chapter 7, previous employers are often hesitant to release data on previous employees due to legal concerns, such as potential invasion of privacy. As a result, employers often have to rely on reports by external candidates of their previous experiences, and the candidates may not always present the whole picture or an accurate picture of their past experiences.

In terms of the relevance of past experiences, organizations may also have better data with which to make selection decisions on internal than external candidates. The experiences of insiders may more closely mirror the experiences likely to be encountered on the new job than the experiences of outsiders. For example, organizations often worry about whether some candidate will be willing to live in a certain geographic area. The answer may be obvious with an internal candidate who already lives in that location. As another example, organizations often wonder about the transferability of skills learned in another organization to their own. Hence, when a new CEO is brought to a computer company from a manufacturing company, many will comment on whether he or she will do well in this new environment.

Along with depth and relevance, another positive aspect of the nature of predictors for internal selection is verifiability. Rather than simply relying on the opinion of one person as to the suitability of an internal candidate for the job, multiple assessments may be solicited. Opinions about the suitability of the candidate also can be solicited from other supervisors and peers. By pooling opinions, it is possible to get a more complete and accurate picture of a candidate's qualifications.

Types of Predictors

The distinctions made between types of predictors used in external selection are also applicable to types of internal predictors. One important difference to note between internal and external predictors pertains to content. There is usually greater depth and relevance to the data available on internal candidates. That is, the organization can go to their own files or to managers to get reports on the applicants' previous experiences.

Selection Plan

Often it seems that internal selection is done on the basis of "who you know" rather than relevant KSAOs. Managers tend to rely heavily on the subjective opinions of previous managers who supervised the internal candidate. When asked why they rely on these subjective assessments, the answer is often, "Because the candidate has worked here for a long time, and I trust his supervisor's feel for the candidate."

Decision errors often occur when relying on subjective feelings for internal selection decisions. For example, in selecting managers to oversee engineering and scientific personnel in organizations, it is sometimes felt that those internal job candidates with the best technical skills will be the best managers. This is not always the case. Some technical wizards are poor managers and vice versa. Sound internal selection procedures need to be followed to guard against this error. A sound job analysis will show that both technical and managerial skills need to be assessed with well-crafted predictors.

Feel, hunch, gut instinct, intuition, and the like do not substitute for well-developed predictors. Relying solely on others' "feelings" about the job applicant may result in lowering hiring standards for some employees, discrimination against protected-class employees, and decisions with low validity. As a result, it is imperative that a selection plan be used for internal as well as external selection. As described in Chapter 7, a selection plan lists the predictors to be used for assessment of each KSAO.

INITIAL ASSESSMENT METHODS

The internal recruitment process may generate a large number of applications for vacant positions. This is especially true when an open rather than closed recruitment system is used—where jobs are posted for employees to apply. Given the time and cost of rigorous selection procedures, organizations use initial assessment methods to screen out applicants who do not meet the minimum qualifications needed to become a candidate. Initial assessment methods for internal recruitment typically include the following predictors: skills inventories, peer evaluations, self-assessments, managerial sponsorship, and informal discussions and recommendations. Each of these predictors will be discussed in turn, followed by a general evaluation of them all.

Skills Inventory

2.2

traditional skills inventory
A listing of KSAOs held by each employee in the organization, usually recording such skills as education, experience, and supervisory training received

An immediate screening device in applicant assessment is to rely on existing data on employee skills. These data can be found in personnel files, which are usually on the computer in larger organizations and in file drawers in smaller organizations. The level of sophistication of the data kept by organizations varies considerably, depending on the method used. Methods include traditional skills inventories, upgraded skills inventories, and customized skills assessments.

Traditional Skills Inventory A **traditional skills inventory** is a listing of the KSAOs held by each employee in the organization. Usually, the system records a small number of skills listed in generic categories, such as education, experience, and supervisory training received. A sound traditional system should be systematically updated on a periodic basis by the HR group. Unfortunately, the maintenance of the database is often a low-priority project; as a result, traditional skills inventories often do not reflect current skills held by employees.

EXHIBIT 9.1 Customized Skill Inventory

Name: ______________________ **Skills Required for Future Position**

KSAO Dimension	Associate	Team Leader	Manager
Technical knowledge	1. ______ 2. ______ 3. ______	1. ______ 2. ______ 3. ______	1. ______ 2. ______ 3. ______
Coaching, counselling, teamwork		1. ______ 2. ______ 3. ______	1. ______ 2. ______ 3. ______
Strategic management			1. ______ 2. ______ 3. ______

upgraded skills inventory
A listing of new KSAOs acquired by employees through job assignments, training, and other developmental activities

Upgraded Skills Inventory In an **upgraded skills inventory**, managers systematically enter the latest skills acquired by employees into the database as soon as they are developed. The system may also include a listing of the skill sets held by external job candidates who were not hired. Members of the HR group systematically record and enter the skills of people whose resumés they receive. Thus, even though some individuals were not hired for an initial position, their resumés can be drawn on for future positions where they match the qualifications. In essence, HR is enlarging the existing internal applicant pool with external applicants' files.

customized skills assessment
An assessment of KSAOs that are directly relevant to specific jobs

Customized Skill Assessment Both the traditional and upgraded skills inventory rely on broadly defined skill categories. As has been indicated repeatedly throughout this book, the more specific the KSAOs required for the job, the more likely is a good person/job match. A **customized skills assessment** (CSA) moves in this direction. With a CSA, specific skill sets are recorded for specific jobs. Skills are not included simply because they are relevant to all jobs or because they happen to match a particular computer software package. Instead, subject matter experts (e.g., managers and experienced job incumbents) identify skills that are critical to job success.

An example of a customized skills inventory is shown in Exhibit 9.1. As can be seen, each job requires increasing numbers of KSAOs. The associate position requires technical skills only. The team leader position requires technical skills plus coaching, counselling, and teamwork skills. The manager position requires all of these skills plus strategic management skills. An inventory like this is kept for each employee. As the person gains skills, they are entered into the appropriate boxes. Once a column of boxes is completed, the person then becomes eligible for the appropriate position when a vacancy exists.

Peer Assessments

2.2

Assessments by peers or co-workers can be used to evaluate the promotability of an internal applicant. A variety of methods can be used, including peer ratings, peer nominations, and peer rankings.2 Examples of all three are shown in Exhibit 9.2.

As can be seen in Exhibit 9.2, whereas peers are used to make promotion decisions in all three methods of peer assessments, the format of each is different. With peer ratings, readiness to be promoted is assessed for each peer using a rating scale. The person with the highest ratings

EXHIBIT 9.2 Peer Assessments Methods

Peer Rating

Please consider each of the following employees and rate them using the following scale for the position of manager described in the job requirements matrix:

	Not Promotable 1	2	Promotable in One Year 3	4	Promotable Now 5
Jean	1	2	3	4	5
John	1	2	3	4	5
Andy	1	2	3	4	5
Herb	1	2	3	4	5

Peer Nominations

Please consider each of the following employees and mark an X for the one employee who is most promotable to the position of manager as described in the job requirements matrix:

Joe __________
Nishant __________
Carlos __________
Suraphon __________
Renee __________

Peer Ranking

Please rank order the following employees from the most promotable (1) to the least promotable (5) for the position of manager as described in the job requirements matrix:

Ila __________
Karen __________
Phillip __________
Yi-Chan __________
Kimlang __________

is deemed most promotable. On the other hand, peer nominations rely on voting for the most promotable candidates. Peers receiving the greatest number of votes are the most promotable. Finally, peer rankings rely on a rank ordering of peers. Those peers with the highest rankings are the most promotable.

Peer assessments have been used extensively in the military over the years and to a lesser degree in industry. A virtue of peer assessments is that they rely on raters who presumably are very knowledgeable of the applicants' KSAOs due to their day-to-day contact with them. A possible downside to peer assessments, however, is that they may encourage friendship bias. Also, they may undermine morale in a work group by fostering a competitive environment.

Another possible problem with peer assessment is that the criteria by which assessments are made are not always made clear. For peer assessments to work, care should be taken in advance to carefully spell out the KSAOs needed for successful performance in the position the peer is being considered for. To do so, a job requirements matrix should be used.

A probable virtue of peer assessments is that peers are more likely to feel that the decisions reached are fair, because they had an input into the decision. The decision is thus not seen as a "behind the backs" manoeuvre by management. As such, peer assessments are used more often with open rather than closed systems of internal recruitment.

2.2

EXHIBIT 9.3 Self-Assessment Form Used for Application in Job Posting System

Supplemental Questionnaire

This supplemental questionnaire will be the principal basis for determining whether you are highly qualified for this position. You may add information not identified in your SF-171 or expand on that which is identified. You should consider appropriate work experience, outside activities, awards, training, and education for each of the items listed below.

1. Knowledge of the Department of Indian and Northern Affairs Canada's mission, organization, structure, policies, and functions, as they relate to land claims.
2. Knowledge of technical administrative requirements to provide technical guidance in administrative areas such as personnel regulations, travel regulations, time and attendance requirements, budget documents, PIPEDA, FOIPOP, etc.
3. Ability to work with program directors and administrative staff, to apply problem-solving techniques and management concepts, and to analyze facts and problems and develop alternatives.
4. Ability to operate various computer programs and methodology in the analysis and design of automated methods for meeting the information and reporting requirements for the division.
5. Knowledge of the bureau budget process and statistical profile of all field operations that impact the land claims program.

On a separate sheet of paper, address the above items in narrative form. Identify the vacancy announcement number across the top. Sign and date your supplemental questionnaire.

Source: Adapted from the Department of the Interior, Bureau of Indian Affairs. Form BIA-4450 (4/22/92).

Self-Assessments

Job incumbents can be asked to evaluate their own skills as a basis for determining promotability. This procedure is sometimes used with open recruitment systems.

An example of this approach is shown in Exhibit 9.3. Caution must be exercised in using this process for selection, as it may raise the expectations of those rating themselves that they will be selected. Also, this approach should be coupled with other internal selection procedures as employees may have a tendency to overrate themselves.

Managerial Sponsorship

Increasingly, organizations are relying on higher-ups in the organization to identify and develop the KSAOs of those at lower levels in the organization. Historically, the higher-up has been the person's immediate supervisor. Today, however, the higher-up may be a person at a higher level of the organization who does not have direct responsibility for the person being rated. Higher-ups are sometimes labelled coaches, sponsors, or mentors, and their roles are defined in Exhibit 9.4. In some organizations, there are formal mentorship programs where employees are assigned coaches, sponsors, and mentors. In other organizations, these matches may naturally occur, often progressing from coach to sponsor to mentor as the relationship matures. Regardless of the formality of the relationship, these individuals are often given considerable influence in promotion decisions. Their weight is due to their high organizational level and in-depth knowledge of the employee's KSAOs. Not only is the judgment of these advocates important but so, too, are their behaviours. Mentors, for example, are likely to put employees in situations where they receive high visibility. That visibility may increase the applicants' chances of promotion.

EXHIBIT 9.4 Employee Advocates

Coach

- Provides day-to-day feedback
- Diagnoses and resolves performance problems
- Creates opportunities for employees using existing training programs and career development programs

Sponsor

- Actively promotes person for advancement opportunities
- Guides person's career rather than simply informing them of opportunities
- Creates opportunities for people in decision-making capacities to see the skills of the employee (e.g., lead a task force)

Mentor

- Becomes personally responsible for the success of the person
- Available to person on and off the job
- Lets person in on "insider" information
- Solicits and values person's input

Source: Reprinted with permission from Dr. Janina Latack, PhD, Nelson O'Connor & Associates/Outplacement International, Phoenix/Tucson.

Informal Discussions and Recommendations

Not all promotion decisions are made on the basis of formal HR policy and procedures. Much of the decision process occurs outside normal channels, through informal discussions and recommendations. These discussions are difficult to characterize because some are simply idle hall talk, while others are directly job related. For example, a lawyer who is expected to be a rainmaker (someone who brings in clients and possible revenue) may be assessed by his contacts in the community. An assessment of the person's qualifications for rainmaking may be done by an informal conversation between a senior partner and a previous client of the supposed rainmaker at a board meeting. Unfortunately, many informal discussions are suspect in terms of their relevance to actual job performance.

Choice of Initial Assessment Methods

As was discussed, several formal and informal methods of initial assessment are available to screen internal applicants to produce a list of candidates. Research has been conducted on the effectiveness of each method, which will now be presented to help determine which initial assessment methods should be used. The reviews of this research are summarized in Exhibit 9.5.

In Exhibit 9.5, the same criteria are applied to evaluating the effectiveness of these predictors as were used to evaluate the effectiveness of predictors for external selection (see Exhibit 8.15). Cost refers to expenses incurred in using the predictor. Reliability refers to the consistency of measurement. Validity refers to the strength of the relationship between the predictor and job performance. Low validity refers to validity in the range of about .00 to .15, moderate validity corresponds to validity in the range of about .16 to .30, and high validity is .31 and above. Utility refers to the monetary return, minus costs, associated with using the predictor. Finally, reactions refer to the likely impact on applicants.

Two points should be made about the effectiveness of initial internal selection methods. First, skills inventories and informal methods are used extensively. This suggests that many organizations continue to rely on closed rather than open internal recruitment systems. Certainly this is a positive procedure when administrative ease is of importance. However, it must be noted that

EXHIBIT 9.5 Evaluation of Initial Assessment Methods

Predictors	Use	Cost	Reliability	Validity	Utility	Reactions
Self-nominations	Low	Low	Moderate	Moderate	?	Mixed
Skills inventories	High	High	Moderate	Moderate	?	?
Peer assessments	Low	Low	High	High	?	Negative
Managerial sponsorship	Low	Moderate	?	?	?	Positive
Informal methods	High	Low	?	?	?	Mixed

these approaches may result in overlooking talented applicants. Also, there may be a discriminatory impact on designated group members such as women and visible minorities.

The second point to be made is that peer assessment methods are very promising in terms of reliability and validity. They are not frequently used, but need to be given more consideration by organizations as a screening device. Perhaps this will take place as organizations continue to decentralize decision making and empower employees to make business decisions historically made only by the supervisor.

SUBSTANTIVE ASSESSMENT METHODS

The internal applicant pool is narrowed down to candidates using the initial assessment methods. A decision as to which internal candidates will become finalists is usually made using the following substantive assessment methods: seniority and experience, job knowledge tests, performance appraisal, promotability ratings, assessment centres, interview simulations, and review boards. After each of these methods is discussed, an evaluation is made.

Seniority and Experience

RPC 2.2

seniority
Length of service or tenure with the organization, department, or job

experience
Related to seniority but includes the different types of jobs, tasks, and activities that an employee has performed during his/her tenure

At first blush the concepts of seniority and experience may seem the same. In reality, they may be quite different. **Seniority** typically refers to length of service or tenure with the organization, department, or job. For example, company seniority is measured as length of continuous employment in an organization and is operationalized as the difference between the present date of employment and the date of hire. Thus, seniority is a purely quantitative measure that has nothing to do with the type or quality of job experiences.

Conversely, **experience** generally has a broader meaning. While seniority may be one aspect of experience, experience also reflects *type* of experience. Two employees working in the same company for 20 years may have the same level of seniority, but very different levels of experience if one employee has performed a number of different jobs, worked in different areas of the organization, enrolled in various training programs, and so on. Thus, experience includes not only length of service in the organization or in various positions in the organization but also the kinds of activities employees have undertaken in those positions. Thus, although seniority and experience are often considered synonymous, they are quite different, and—as we will see in the following discussion—these differences have real implications for internal selection decisions.

Use and Evaluation Seniority and experience are among the most prevalent methods of internal selection. In most unionized companies, heavy reliance is placed on seniority over other KSAOs for advancement.[3] In policy, nonunion organizations claim to place less weight on seniority than other factors in making advancement decisions. In practice, however, at least one study showed that regardless of the wording in policy statements, heavy emphasis is still placed on seniority in nonunion settings.[4] Research has shown that seniority is more likely to be used for promotions in small, unionized, and capital-intensive companies.[5] Although few data are available, there is reason to believe that experience also is frequently considered in internal selection decisions.

There are various reasons why seniority and experience are so widely used as methods of internal selection decisions. First, organizations believe that direct experience in a job content area reflects an accumulated stock of KSAOs necessary to perform the job. In short, experience may be content valid because it reflects on-the-job experience. Second, seniority and experience information is easily and cheaply obtained. Furthermore, unions believe that reliance on objective measures such as seniority and experience protects the employee from capricious treatment and favouritism. Finally, promoting experienced or senior individuals is socially acceptable because it is seen as rewarding loyalty. In fact, it has been found that most decision makers feel that negative repercussions would result if a more junior employee is promoted over a more senior employee.

In evaluating seniority and experience as methods of internal selection, it is important to return to our earlier distinction between the two concepts. Several studies have found that seniority is unrelated to job performance.[6] In fact, one study of unionized plants found that 97 percent of the promotions went to the most senior employee, yet in nearly half the cases this person was not the highest performer. Thus, seniority does not seem to be a particularly valid method of internal selection. In fact, the "Big Three" automakers cite abandoning seniority for promotions as a reason for their improved performance in the mid-1990s.[7]

As compared to seniority, evidence for the validity of experience is more positive. A large-scale review of the literature has shown that experience is moderately related to job performance.[8] Research suggests that experience is predictive of job performance in the short run, but is followed by a plateau during which experience loses its ability to predict job performance. It appears that most of the effect of experience on performance is due to the fact that experienced employees have greater job knowledge. However, while experience may result in increased performance due to greater job knowledge, it does not remedy performance difficulties due to low ability; initial performance deficits of low-ability employees are not remedied by increased experience over time.[9] Thus, while experience is more likely to be related to job performance than seniority, neither ranks among the most valid predictors for internal selection decisions.

Based on the research evidence, several conclusions about the use of seniority and experience in internal selection decisions seem appropriate:

1. Experience is a more valid method of internal selection than seniority (although unionized employers may have little choice but to use seniority).
2. Experience is better suited to predict short-term rather than long-term potential.
3. Experience is more likely to be content valid if the past or present jobs are similar to the future job.
4. Employees seem to expect that promotions will go to the most senior or experienced employee, so using seniority or experience for promotions may yield positive reactions from employees.
5. Experience is unlikely to remedy initial performance difficulties of low-ability employees.

Job Knowledge Tests

Job knowledge measures one's mastery of the concepts needed to perform certain work. Job knowledge is a complex concept that includes elements of both ability (capacity to learn) and seniority (opportunity to learn). It is usually measured with a paper-and-pencil test. To develop a paper-and-pencil test to assess job knowledge, the content domain from which test questions will be constructed must be clearly identified. For example, a job knowledge test used to select sales managers from among salespeople must identify the specific knowledge necessary for being a successful sales manager.

An innovative video-based job knowledge test to be used as part of the promotion system was developed by Federal Express.[10] Federal Express developed the interactive video test to assess employees' ability to deal with customers. The test is based on job analysis data derived from the critical tasks necessary to deliver high levels of customer service. The test, termed QUEST (Quality Using Electronic Systems Training), presents employees with a menu of modules on CD-ROM (e.g., delivering packages, defensive driving, etc.). A 90 percent competency level on the test is established as the expectation for minimum performance—and subsequent promotability. This suggests that such assessments could fruitfully be used in internal selection decisions when promoting employees into customer-sensitive positions. The greater the portfolio of customer skills employees have, the better able they should be to help Federal Express meet its customer service goals.

Although job knowledge is not a well-researched method of either internal or external employee selection, it holds great promise as a predictor of job performance. This is because it reflects an assessment of previous experiences of an applicant and an important KSAO, namely, cognitive ability.[11]

Performance Appraisal

One possible predictor of future job performance is past job performance. This assumes, of course, that elements of the future job are similar to the past job. Data on employees' previous performance are routinely collected as a part of the performance appraisal process and thus available for use in internal selection.

One advantage of performance appraisals over other internal assessment methods is that they are readily available in many organizations. Another desirable feature of performance appraisals is that they probably capture both ability and motivation. Hence, they offer a very complete look at the person's qualifications for the job. Care must still be taken in using performance appraisals because there is not always a direct correspondence between the requirements of the current job and the requirements of the position applied for. Performance appraisals should only be used as predictors when job analysis indicates a close relationship between the current job and the position applied for.

For example, performance in a highly technical position (e.g., scientist, engineer) may require certain skills (e.g., quantitative skills) that are required in both junior- and senior-level positions. As a result, using the results of the performance appraisal of the junior position is appropriate in predicting the performance in the senior position. It is not, however, appropriate to use the results of the performance appraisal for the junior-level technical job to predict performance in a job, such as manager, requiring a different set of skills (e.g., planning, organizing, staffing).

Although there are some advantages to using performance appraisal results for internal selection, they are far from perfect predictors. They are subject to many influences that have nothing to do with the likelihood of success in a future job.[12]

The well-known "Peter Principle"—that individuals rise to their lowest level of incompetence—illustrates another limitation with using performance appraisal as a method of internal staffing decisions.[13] The argument behind the Peter Principle is that if organizations promote individuals on the basis of their past performance, the only time that people stop being promoted is when they are poor performers at the job into which they were last promoted. Thus, over time, organizations will have internally staffed positions with individuals who are incompetent. In fact, the authors have data from a Fortune 100 company showing that less than one-fifth of the variance in an employee's current performance rating can be explained by their previous three year's performance ratings. Thus, although past performance may have some validity in predicting future performance, the relationship may not be overly strong.

This is not to suggest that organizations should abandon using performance ratings as a factor in internal staffing decisions. Rather, the validity of using performance appraisal as an internal selection method may depend on a number of considerations. Exhibit 9.6 provides several questions that should be used in deciding how much weight to place on performance appraisal as a means of making internal selection decisions. Affirmative answers to these questions suggest that past performance may be validly used in making internal selection decisions.

EXHIBIT 9.6 Questions to Ask in Using Performance Appraisal as a Method of Internal Staffing Decisions

- Is the performance appraisal process reliable and unbiased?
- Is present job content representative of future job content?
- Have the KSAOs required for performance in the future job(s) been acquired and demonstrated in the previous job(s)?
- Is the organizational or job environment stable such that what led to past job success will lead to future job success?

An advance over simple use of performance ratings is to review past performance records more thoroughly, including an evaluation of various dimensions of performance that are particularly relevant to job performance (where the dimensions are based on job analysis results). For example, a study of police promotions used a pool of six supervisors to score officers on four job-relevant police officer performance dimensions—supervisory-related education and experience, disciplined behaviour, commendatory behaviour, and reliability—with the goal of predicting future performance. Results of the study indicated that ratings of past performance records was an effective method of promoting officers.[14] Such a method might be adapted to other positions and provide a useful means of incorporating past performance data into a more valid prediction of future potential.

Promotability Ratings

In many organizations, an assessment of promotability (assessment of potential for higher-level job) is made at the same time that performance appraisals are conducted. Replacement and succession planning frequently use both types of assessments (see Chapter 6). An example of a form to be used is shown in Exhibit 9.7.

promotability ratings
Method of assessing employees' potential for higher-level jobs

Promotability ratings are useful not only from a selection perspective but also from a recruitment perspective. By discussing what is needed to be promotable, employee development may be encouraged as well as coupled with organizational sponsorship of the opportunities needed to develop. In turn, the development of new skills in employees increases the internal recruitment pool for promotions.

Caution must be exercised in using promotability ratings as well. If employees receive separate evaluations for purposes of performance appraisal, promotability, and pay, the possibility exists of mixed messages going out to employees that may be difficult for them to interpret. For example, it is difficult to understand why one receives an excellent performance rating and a solid pay raise, but at the same time is rated as not promotable. Care must be taken to show employees the relevant judgments that are being made in each assessment. In the example presented, it must be clearly indicated that promotion is based not only on past performance but also on skill acquisition and opportunities for advancement.

Assessment Centres

assessment centre
Internal, in-depth, and multiple-method of assessment used to identify employees—most often high-level managers—who possess the attributes associated with successful performance

An elaborate method of employee selection, primarily used internally, is known as an assessment centre. An **assessment centre** is a collection of predictors used to forecast success, primarily in higher-level jobs. It is used for higher-level jobs because of the high costs involved in conducting the centre. The assessment centre can be used to select employees for lower-level jobs as well, though this is rarely done.

The theory behind assessment centres is relatively straightforward. Concern is with the prediction of an individual's behaviour and effectiveness in critical roles, usually managerial. Since these roles require complex behaviour, multiple KSAOs will predict those behaviours. Hence,

EXHIBIT 9.7 Promotability Rating Form

Form INAC-4450
(4/22/92)

DEPARTMENT OF INDIAN AND NORTHERN AFFAIRS CANADA

44 INAC 335
Illustration 4
Page 1 of 2

SUPERVISORY APPRAISAL OF DEMONSTRATED PERFORMANCE OF POTENTIAL

ANNOUNCEMENT NO. CO-92-125

PLEASE HAVE THIS APPRAISAL COMPLETED BY YOUR SUPERVISOR AND SUBMIT WITH YOUR APPLICATION. SF-171 (If the appraisal is submitted directly by the supervisor, the applicant will be permitted to review and/or obtain a copy of the appraisal upon request.)

Name of Applicant: ______________________ Position: Program Specialist

Basis of Appraisal								
Check One					Level of Performance			
Outside Activities	On-the-job Performance	Formal Training	Unable to Appraise	RANKING FACTORS (Knowledge, Skills, Abilities, and Personal Characteristics)	Check as appropriate: 4 – Exceptional 3 – Above average 2 – Average/Satisfactory 1 – Rarely Satisfactory			
					4	3	2	1
				1. Knowledge of the department's mission, organization, structure, policies, and functions, as they relate to land claims.				
				2. Knowledge of technical administrative requirements to provide technical guidance in administrative areas, such as personnel regulations, travel regulations, time and attendance requirements, budget documents, PIPEDA, and FOIPOP, etc.				
				3. Ability to work with program directors and administrative staff and ability to apply problem-solving techniques and management concepts; ability to analyze facts and problems and develop alternatives.				
				4. Ability to operate various computer programs and methodology in the analysis and design of automated methods for meeting the information and reporting requirements for the division.				
				5. Knowledge of the department's budget process and statistical profile of all field operations that impact land claims.				

44 INAC, 335, REL. 127, 4/22/92

Continued

EXHIBIT 9.7 *Continued*

Form INAC-4450
(4/22/92)

DEPARTMENT OF INDIAN AND NORTHERN
AFFAIRS CANADA

44 INAC 335
Illustration 4
Page 2 of 2

SUPERVISORY APPRAISAL OF DEMONSTRATED
PERFORMANCE OF POTENTIAL

ANNOUNCEMENT NO. CO-92-125

NARRATIVE: BRIEFLY EVALUATE THE CANDIDATE'S OVERALL ABILITY TO PERFORM THE DUTIES AND RESPONSIBILITIES OF THE POSITION. NARRATIVE COMMENTS ARE REQUIRED FOR ALL EVALUATIONS.

IN WHAT CAPACITY ARE YOU MAKING THIS APPRAISAL? (Please ✓ as appropriate)

( ) Present Immediate Supervisor

( ) Former Immediate Supervisor

( ) Present 2nd Level Supervisor

( ) Former 2nd Level Supervisor

( ) Other
(specify)

Period during which you supervised the applicant:
From: To:

Appraiser:

(Signature) (Date) (Phone No.)

Source: Adapted from Department of the Interior, Bureau of Indian Affairs, Form BIA-4450 (4/22/92).

EXHIBIT 9.8 Selection Plan for an Assessment Centre

KSAO	Writing Exercise	Speech Exercise	Analysis Problem	In-Basket		Leadership Group Discussion	
				Tent.	Final	Management Problems	City Council
Oral communications					X	X	X
Oral presentation		X				X	
Written communications	X		X	X	X		
Stress tolerance				X	X	X	X
Leadership					X	X	
Sensitivity			X	X	X	X	X
Tenacity				X	X	X	
Risk taking			X	X	X	X	X
Initiative			X	X	X	X	X
Planning and organization			X	X	X	X	X
Management control			X	X	X		
Delegation				X	X		
Problem analysis			X	X	X	X	X
Decision making			X	X	X	X	X
Decisiveness			X	X	X	X	X
Responsiveness			X	X	X	X	X

Source: Department of Employment Relations, State of Wisconsin.

there is a need to carefully identify and assess those KSAOs. This will require multiple methods of assessing the KSAOs, as well as multiple assessors. The result should be higher validity than could be obtained from a single assessment method or assessor.

As with any sound selection procedure, the assessment centre predictors are based on job analysis to identify KSAOs and aid in the construction of content valid methods of assessment for those KSAOs. As a result, a selection plan must be developed when using assessment centres. An example of such a selection plan is shown in Exhibit 9.8.

Characteristics of Assessment Centres Whereas specific characteristics vary from situation to situation, assessment centres generally have some common characteristics. Job candidates usually participate in an assessment centre for a period of days rather than hours. Most assessment centres last two to three days, but some may be as long as five days. Exhibit 9.9 is an example of a three-day assessment centre (exercises are defined below). Participants take part in a series of simulations and work sample tests known as exercises. The participants may also be assessed with other devices, such as interviews, personality and ability tests, and biographical information blanks. As they participate in the exercises, trained assessors evaluate participants' performance. Assessors are usually line managers, but sometimes psychologists are used as well. The average ratio of assessors to assessees ranges from 1:1 to 4:1.

EXHIBIT 9.9 Assessment Centre Program Schedule

Sunday	P.M.	Candidates arrive for social hour, orientation, meeting, and discussion.
Monday	A.M.	Leaderless group discussion. The candidates were divided into two groups of five to discuss a possible business investment. Each group was observed by three assessors who took notes on the total activity and the individual participants.
	P.M.	1. Individual interview with clinical psychologist. 2. Psychological testing with candidates for assessment information and research purposes.
Tuesday	A.M.	Individual exercise (in-basket).
	P.M.	1. Interview regarding in-basket performance. 2. Additional testing. 3. Group exercise.
Wednesday	A.M.	Case analysis.
	P.M.	1. Assessors write two- to three-page narrative reports based on observation of participants. 2. Candidates are notified of their overall assessment.

The participants in the centre are usually managers who are being assessed for higher-level managerial jobs. Normally, they are chosen to participate by other organization members, such as their supervisor. Often selection is based on an employee's current level of job performance.

At the conclusion of the assessment centre, the participants are evaluated by the assessors. Typically, this involves the assessor examining all the information gathered about each participant. The information is then translated into a series of ratings on several dimensions of managerial jobs. Typical dimensions assessed include communications (written and oral), leadership and human relations, planning, problem solving, and decision making. In evaluating these dimensions, assessors are trained to look for critical behaviours that represent highly effective or ineffective responses to the exercise situations in which participants are placed. There may also be an overall assessment rating that represents the bottom-line evaluation for each participant. Assessment centre dimensions are relatively highly correlated with one another, though evidence suggests that the dimensions do add to the prediction of performance beyond the overall score.[15] Exhibit 9.10 provides a sample rating form.

A variety of different exercises are used at a centre. Experts argue that the simulation is the key to an assessment centre, though exactly how future performance is simulated varies from assessment centre to assessment centre.[16] The most frequently used exercises are the in-basket exercise, leaderless group discussions, and case analysis. Each of these exercises will be briefly described.

In-Basket Exercise. An element common to most higher-level positions is an in-basket. The in-basket usually contains memoranda, reports, phone calls, and letters that require a response. In an assessment centre, a simulated in-basket is presented to the candidate. The candidate is asked to respond to the paperwork in the in-basket by prioritizing items, drafting memos, scheduling meetings, and so forth. It is a timed exercise, and usually the candidate has two to three hours to respond. Even when used alone, the in-basket exercise seems to forecast ascendancy, one of the key criteria of assessment centres. The in-basket is the most often used exercise; a study of assessment centres indicated that the in-basket was used in 82 percent of assessment centres.[17]

Leaderless Group Discussion. In a leaderless group discussion, a small group of candidates is given a problem to work on. The problem is one they would likely encounter in the higher-level position for which they are applying. As a group, they are asked to resolve the problem. As they work on the problem, assessors sit around the perimeter of the group and evaluate how each candidate behaves in an unstructured setting. They look for skills such as leadership and communication. Roughly 60 percent of assessment centres include a leaderless group discussion.

Case Analysis. Cases of actual business situations can also be presented to the candidates. Each candidate is asked to provide a written analysis of the case, describing the nature of the problem, likely causes, and recommended solutions. Not only are the written results evaluated

EXHIBIT 9.10 Sample Assessment Centre Rating Form

Participant Name: ______________________

Personal Qualities:

1. Energy ______
2. Risk taking ______
3. Tolerance for ambiguity ______
4. Objectivity ______
5. Reliability ______

Communication Skills:

6. Oral ______
7. Written ______
8. Persuasion ______

Human Relations:

9. Teamwork ______
10. Flexibility ______
11. Awareness of social environment ______

Leadership Skills:

12. Impact ______
13. Autonomy ______

Decision-Making Skills:

14. Decisiveness ______
15. Organizing ______
16. Planning ______

Problem-Solving Skills:

17. Fact finding ______
18. Interpreting information ______

Overall Assessment Rating:

Indication of potential to perform effectively at the next level is:

Excellent ______

Good ______

Moderate ______

Low ______

but the candidate's oral report is scored as well. The candidates may be asked to give an oral presentation to a panel of managers and to respond to their questions, comments, and concerns. Case analyses are used in roughly half of all assessment centres.

Validity and Effective Practices In a study of 50 different assessment centres, their average validity was very favourable $\bar{r} = .37$. This study showed that the validity of the assessment centre was higher when multiple predictors were used, when assessors were psychologists rather than managers, and when peer evaluations as well as assessor evaluations were used. The latter results call into question the common practice of using only managers as assessors. The finding suggests that multiple assessors be used, including psychologists and peers as well as managers. Such usage provides a different perspective on participants' performance, one that may be overlooked by managers.[18] Assessment centres have incremental validity in predicting performance and promotability beyond personality traits and cognitive ability tests, though the incremental validity may be relatively small because assessment centre scores are substantially correlated with cognitive ability.[19]

There are some problems with past assessment centre research.[20] One of the most commonly cited problems is the "crown prince or princess" syndrome. Here, it is alleged, decision makers may know how people did on the assessment centre and therefore promote those who did well versus those who did not do well. Thus, assessment centres could be a self-fulfilling prophecy—they are valid only because decision makers think they are. However, research indicates that assessment centres are valid even when the results of the assessment centre are "blind" to decision makers. Thus, due to the validity of assessment centres, they should be seriously considered in making promotion decisions—if they can be afforded.

One of the biggest limitations with assessment centres is their cost. The nature of the individualized assessment and the requirement of multiple assessors make them cost prohibitive for many organizations. One way some organizations are mitigating the costs of assessment centres is through other, related assessments. Some organizations videotape assessees' performance, so that assessors can evaluate their performance when convenient. This saves coordination and travel costs. A practice that results in even greater cost savings is to use situational judgment tests, where assessees are given various exercises in written, video, or computerized form. A recent analysis of 102 studies suggested that the validity of situational judgment tests is about as high $\bar{r} = .34$ as assessment centres.[21]

There is little research that has examined participant reactions to assessment centres. However, it is commonly noted that although assessment centres are stressful to participants, they generate positive reactions for assessors and assessees. This probably is partly due to the fact that they are seen as valid by participants. Furthermore, they may result in increased self-confidence for participants, even for those who are not promoted as a result of the assessment centre. The positive effects of assessment centres on employee attitudes and self-confidence may be relatively fleeting, however, as one study of British managers found. Thus, it is possible that the positive impact of assessment centres on assessees wanes over time. The International Task Force on Assessment Centre Guidelines has published a set of guidelines for the development and use of assessment centres. They are a useful tool for those wishing to ensure that an assessment centre is conducted in a valid, fair, and effective manner. Another group of experts has discussed common pitfalls in using assessment centres, and has provided recommendations to avoid these problems.[22]

Assessment for Global Assignments When assessment centres were developed, little thought was given to the prospect of using assessment data to forecast job success in a foreign environment. As globalization continues, however, organizations increasingly are promoting individuals into positions overseas. A survey indicated that 80 percent of midsize and large companies send professionals abroad and many plan on increasing this percentage. Because overseas assignments present additional demands on an employee beyond the typical skills and motivations required to perform a job in the host country, staffing overseas positions presents special challenges for employers. Indeed, one study revealed that cultural factors were much more important to success in an overseas assignment than were technical skills factors. Although many competencies are important to expatriate success, such as family stability/support and language skills, the most important competency is cultural adaptability and flexibility.

One means of predicting success in overseas assignments is a personality test. For example, employees who respond positively to items such as "It is easy for me to strike up conversations with people I do not know" or "I find it easy to put myself in other people's position." Personnel Decisions International has developed a personality test designed to assess whether employees will be successful in overseas assignments. The company reports a positive relationship between scores on the test and success in overseas assignments. Another tool is simulations or interviews designed to simulate conditions overseas or typical challenges that arise.[23] As one can see, bringing these methods together may make the assessment process for global assignments closely resemble an assessment centre.

Interview Simulations

interview simulation
Exercises such as role-play, fact-finding interview, and oral presentation that simulate oral communication required on the job

An **interview simulation** simulates the oral communication required on the job. It is sometimes used in an assessment centre, but less frequently than in-baskets, leaderless group discussions, and case analysis. It is also used as a predictor separate from the assessment centre. There are several different forms of interview simulations.[24]

Role-Play With a role-play, the job candidate is placed in a simulated situation where he or she must interact with a person at work, such as the boss, a subordinate, or a customer. The interviewer or someone else plays one role, and the job candidate plays the role of the person in the position applied for. So, for example, in selecting someone to be promoted to a supervisory level, the job candidate may be asked to role-play dealing with a difficult employee.

Fact-Finding Interview In a fact-finding interview, the job candidate is presented with a case or problem with incomplete information. It is the job of the candidate to solicit from the interviewer or a resource person the additional facts needed to resolve the case. If one was hiring someone to be an employment equity specialist, one might present him or her with a case where adverse impact is suggested, and then evaluate the candidate according to what data he or she solicits to confirm or disconfirm adverse impact.

Oral Presentations In many jobs, presentations need to be made to customers, clients, or even boards of directors. To select someone to perform this role, an oral presentation can be required. This approach would be useful, for example, to see what sort of sales pitch a consultant might make or to see how an executive would present his or her proposed strategic plan to a board of directors.

Given the importance of interpersonal skills in many jobs, it is unfortunate that not many organizations use interview simulations. This is especially true with internal selection where the organization knows if the person has the right credentials (e.g., company experiences, education, training), but may not know if the person has the right interpersonal "chemistry" to fit in with the work group. Interview simulations allow for a systematic assessment of this chemistry rather than relying on the instinct of the interviewer. To be effective, these interviews need to be structured and evaluated according to observable behaviours identified in the job analysis as necessary for successful performance.

Promotion Panels and Review Boards

In some sectors, it is a common practice to use a panel or board of people to review the qualifications of candidates. Frequently, a combination of both internal and external candidates is assessed. Typically, the panel or board consists of job experts, HR professionals, and representatives from constituencies in the community that the board represents. Having a hiring board offers two advantages. First, as with assessment centres, multiple assessors ensure a complete and accurate assessment of the candidate's qualifications. Second, by participating in the selection process, constituents are likely to be more committed to the decision reached. This "buy-in" is particularly important for community representatives with whom the job candidate will interact. It is hoped that by having a say in the process, they will be less likely to voice objections once the candidate is hired.

Choice of Substantive Assessment Methods

Along with research on initial assessment methods, there has also been research conducted on substantive assessment methods. The reviews of this research are summarized in Exhibit 9.11. The same criteria are applied to evaluating the effectiveness of these predictors as were used to evaluate the effectiveness of initial assessment methods.

EXHIBIT 9.11 Evaluation of Substantive Assessment Methods

Predictors	Use	Cost	Reliability	Validity	Utility	Reactions
Seniority	High	Low	High	Low	?	?
Experience	High	Low	High	Moderate	High	Positive
Job knowledge tests	Low	Moderate	High	High	?	?
Performance appraisal	Moderate	Moderate	?	Moderate	?	?
Promotability ratings	Low	Low	High	High	?	?
Assessment centre	Low	High	High	High	High	?
In-basket exercise	Low	Moderate	Moderate	Moderate	High	Mixed
Leaderless group discussion	Low	Low	Moderate	Moderate	?	?
Case analysis	Low	Low	?	Moderate	?	?
Global assignments	High	Moderate	?	?	?	?
Interview simulations	Low	Low	?	?	?	?
Panels and review boards	Low	?	?	?	?	?

An examination of Exhibit 9.11 indicates that there is no single best method of narrowing down the candidate list to finalists. What is suggested, however, is that some predictors are more likely to be effective than others. In particular, job knowledge, promotability ratings, and assessment centres have a strong record in terms of reliability and validity in choosing candidates. A very promising development for internal selection is use of job knowledge tests. The validity of these tests appears to be substantial, but, unfortunately, few organizations use them for internal selection purposes.

The effectiveness of several internal selection predictors (case analysis, interview simulations, panels and review boards) is not known at this stage. Interview simulations appear to be a promising technique for jobs requiring public contact skills. All of them need additional research. Other areas in need of additional research are the utility and reactions associated with all substantive assessment methods.

DISCRETIONARY ASSESSMENT METHODS

Discretionary methods are used to narrow down the list of finalists to those who will receive job offers. Sometimes all finalists will receive offers, but at other times, there may not be enough positions to fill for each finalist to receive an offer. As with external selection, discretionary assessments are sometimes made on the basis of organizational citizenship behaviour and staffing philosophy regarding employment equity.

Two areas of discretionary assessment differ from external selection and need to be considered in deciding job offers. First, previous finalists who do not receive job offers do not simply disappear. They may remain with the organization in hopes of securing an offer the next time the position is open. At the margin, this may be a factor in decision making because being bypassed a second time may create a disgruntled employee. As a result, a previous finalist may be given an offer over a first-time finalist, all other things being equal.

Second, multiple assessors are generally used with internal selection. That is, not only can the hiring manager's opinion be used to select who will receive a job offer but so can the opinions of others (e.g., previous manager, top management) who are knowledgeable about the candidate's profile and the requirements of the current position. As a result, in deciding which candidates will receive job offers, evaluations by people other than the hiring manager may be accorded substantial weight in the decision-making process.

LEGAL ISSUES

From a legal perspective, methods and processes of internal selection are to be viewed in the same ways as external selection ones. The laws and regulations make no major distinctions between them. Consequently, most of the legal influences on internal selection have already been treated in Chapters 7 and 8. There are, however, some brief comments to be made about internal selection legal influences. The concerns are with the defensibility of the selection procedures and the glass ceiling.

Defensible Selection Procedures

When evidence of adverse impact in promotions exists, a organization may entertain the option of defending the procedure using validity evidence. This may involve conducting criterion-related studies to demonstrate that the procedure(s) are valid. However, logistically conducting criterion-related validity studies would create administrative and research challenges for most organizations. As an alternative it may be more appropriate to focus on content validity as way of defending promotion procedures.

Many of the assessment methods used in internal selection attempt to gauge KSAOs and behaviours directly associated with a current job that are felt to be related to success in higher-level jobs. Examples include seniority, performance appraisals, and promotability ratings, all of which are based on current, as well as past, job content. Validation of these methods, if legally necessary, likely occurs along content validation lines. Still, it is important to recognize that in defending procedures that evidence shows discriminates against members of a designated group, an organization will likely be required to defend its procedures against the three steps outlined in the Tawney Meiorin decision (see Chapter 2). The most important of these steps requires an organization to show that a standard is reasonably necessary for the effective accomplishment for a given work purpose and that it is impossible to accommodate an individual applicant without suffering undue hardship.

The Glass Ceiling

In Chapter 6, the nature of the glass ceiling was discussed, as well as staffing steps to remove it from organizational promotion systems. Most of that discussion centred on internal recruitment and supporting activities that could be undertaken. Surprisingly, selection methods used for promotion assessment are rarely mentioned in literature on the glass ceiling.

This is a major oversight. Whereas the internal recruitment practices recommended may enhance the identification and attraction of designated group members as candidates for promotion, effectively matching them to their new jobs requires application of internal selection processes and methods. What might this require of an organization committed to shattering the glass ceiling?

The first possibility is for greater use of selection plans. As discussed in Chapter 7, these plans lay out the KSAOs required for a job, which KSAOs are necessary to bring to the job (as opposed to being acquired on the job), and of those necessary, the most appropriate method of assessment for each. Such a plan forces an organization to conduct job analysis, construct career ladders or KSAO lattices, and consider alternatives to many of the traditional methods of assessment used in promotion systems.

A second suggestion is for the organization to back away from use of these traditional methods of assessment as much as possible, in ways consistent with the selection plan. This means a move away from casual, subjective methods, such as supervisory recommendation, typical promotability ratings, quick reviews of personnel files, and informal recommendations. In their place should come more formal, standardized, and job-related assessment methods. Examples here include assessment centres, promotion review boards or panels, and interview simulations.

A final suggestion is for the organization to pay close attention to the types of KSAOs necessary for advancement, and undertake programs to impart these KSAOs to aspiring employees. These developmental actions might include key job and committee assignments, participation in conferences and other networking opportunities, mentoring and coaching programs, and skill acquisition in formal training programs. Internal selection methods would then be used to assess proficiency on these newly acquired KSAOs, in accordance with the selection plan.

SUMMARY

The selection of internal candidates follows a process very similar to the selection of external candidates. The logic of prediction is applied, and a selection plan is developed and implemented.

One important area where internal and external selection methods differ is in the nature of the predictor. Predictors used for internal selection tend to have greater depth and more relevance and are better suited for verification. As a result, there are often different types of predictors used for internal than for external selection decisions.

Initial assessment methods are used to narrow down the applicant pool to a qualified set of candidates. Approaches used are skills inventories, peer assessments, self-assessments, managerial sponsorship, informal discussions and recommendations, and career concepts. Of these approaches, no single approach is particularly strong in predicting future performance. Hence, consideration should be given to using multiple predictors to verify the accuracy of any one method. These results also point to the need to use substantive as well as initial assessment methods in making internal selection decisions.

Substantive assessment methods are used to select finalists from the list of candidates. Predictors used to make these decisions include seniority and experience, job knowledge tests, performance appraisals, promotability ratings, assessment centres, interview simulations, and panels and review boards. Of this set of predictors, ones that work well are job knowledge tests, promotability ratings, and assessment centres. Organizations need to give greater consideration to the latter three predictors to supplement traditional seniority and experience.

Although very costly, the assessment centre seems to be very effective. It is so effective because it is grounded in behavioural science theory and the logic of prediction. In particular, samples of behaviour are analyzed, multiple assessors and predictors are used, and predictors are developed on the basis of job analysis.

Internal job applicants have the potential for far greater access to selection data than do external job applicants due to their physical proximity to the data. As a result, procedures must be implemented to ensure that manual and computer files with sensitive data are kept private and confidential.

Two areas of concern for internal selection decisions are the defensibility of the selection procedure and the glass ceiling. In terms of defending a selection procedure, particular care must be taken to ensure that internal selection methods are valid if adverse impact is occurring. To minimize glass ceiling effects, organizations should make greater use of selection plans and more objective internal assessment methods, as well as help impart the KSAOs necessary for advancement.

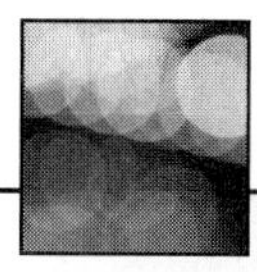

KEY TERMS

assessment centre 322
customized skills assessment 315
experience 319
interview simulation 329
promotability ratings 322
seniority 319
traditional skills inventory 314
upgraded skills inventory 315

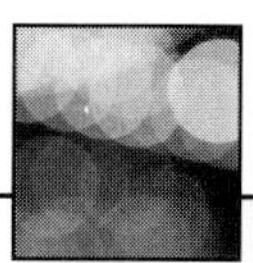

DISCUSSION QUESTIONS

1. Explain how internal selection decisions differ from external selection decisions.
2. What are the differences between peer ratings, peer nominations, and peer rankings?
3. Explain the theory behind assessment centres.
4. Describe the three different types of interview simulations.
5. Evaluate the effectiveness of seniority, assessment centres, and job knowledge as substantive internal selection procedures.
6. What steps should be taken by an organization that is committed to shattering the glass ceiling?

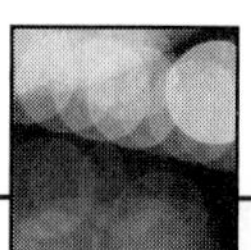

ETHICAL ISSUES

1. Given that seniority is not a particularly valid predictor of job performance, do you think it's unethical for a company to use it as a basis for promotion? Why or why not?
2. Vincent and Peter are both sales associates, and are up for promotion to sales manager. In the last five years, on a 1 = poor to 5 = excellent scale, Vincent's average performance rating was 4.7 and Peter's was 4.2. In an assessment centre that was meant to simulate the job of sales manager, on a 1 = very poor to 10 = outstanding scale, Vincent's average score was 8.2 and Peter's was 9.2. Other things being equal, who should be promoted? Why?

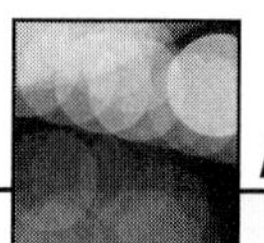

APPLICATIONS

Changing a Promotion System

Bioglass Inc. specializes in sales of a wide array of glass products. One area of the company, the commercial sales division (CSD), specializes in selling high-tech mirrors and microscope and photographic lenses. Sales associates in CSD are responsible for selling the glass products to corporate clients. CSD has four levels of sales associates, ranging in pay from $28,000 to $76,000 per year. CSD also has four levels of managerial positions; those positions range in pay from $76,000 to $110,000 per year (the latter amount is what the division president makes).

Tom Caldwell has been a very effective sales associate. He has consistently demonstrated good sales techniques in his 17 years with Bioglass and has a large and loyal client base. Over the years, Tom has risen from the lowest level of sales associate to the highest. He has proven himself successful at each stage. An entry- (first-) level management position in CSD opened up last year, and Tom was the natural candidate. Although several other candidates were given consideration, Tom was the clear choice for the position.

However, once in the position, Tom had a great deal of difficulty being a manager. He was not accustomed to delegating and rarely provided feedback or guidance to the people he supervised. Although he set goals for himself, he never set performance goals for his workers. Morale in Tom's group was low, and group performance suffered. The company felt that demoting Tom back to sales would be disastrous for him and present the wrong image to other employees; firing such a loyal employee was considered unacceptable. Therefore, Bioglass decided to keep Tom where he was, but never promote him again. They were also considering enrolling Tom in some expensive managerial development programs to enhance his management skills.

Meanwhile, Tom's replacement, although successful at the lower three levels of sales associate positions, was having a great deal of difficulty with the large corporate contracts that the highest-level sales associates must service. Two of Tom's biggest clients had recently left Bioglass for a competitor. CSD was confused about how such a disastrous situation had developed when they seemed to make all the right decisions.

Based on this application and your reading of this chapter, answer the following questions:

1. What is the likely cause of CSD's problems?
2. How might CSD, and Bioglass more generally, make better promotion decisions in the future? Be specific.
3. In general, what role should performance appraisals play in internal selection decisions? Are there some cases in which they are more relevant than others? Explain.

Promotion from within at Delta Farms

Lori Cheug is the director of human resources for Delta Farms, a produce and flower farm enterprise located in Richmond, B.C. Delta Farms supplies fruit and vegetables to grocery stores, local convenience stores, and restaurants in B.C. and Alberta, and supplies flowers to florists across the country. Delta Farms has been growing rapidly, and a constant feature of Lori's job for the last number of years has been worry about how to hire and promote enough qualified individuals to staff the ever-expanding array of positions within the company.

One way Lori has been able to staff positions internally is by contracting with Staffing Systems West (SSW), a management consulting firm located in West Vancouver. When positions open up at Delta Farms that are appropriate to staff internally, Lori sends a group of candidates to SSW to participate in their assessment centre. The candidates return from SSW three days later, and a few days after that, SSW sends Lori the results of the assessment centre with a recommendation. Though Lori has never formally evaluated the accuracy of the promotions, it was her feeling the evaluation process was pretty accurate. Of course, for $5,500 per candidate Lori thought that it should be accurate.

A few days ago, Lori was hosting a celebration for the Chinese New Year. Her brother-in-law Felix Chen was at the celebration. Felix is completing his doctoral degree in human resource management in the business school at the nearby Coastal International University. After dinner, while Lori, Felix, and the rest of the family were relaxing, Lori talked with Felix about her difficulties promoting from within and the cost of SSW's assessment process. Felix realized that SSW was using an assessment centre process. He was also aware of research suggesting that once one takes account an applicant's personality and cognitive ability, assessment centre scores may contribute little additional validity. Given the cost of the assessment centres, he reasoned, one must consider whether they incremental validity (i.e., the validity the assessment centre contributes beyond the validity provided by personality and cognitive ability tests) would prove cost effective. After Felix conveyed these impressions to Lori, she felt that she needed to re-examine Delta Farm's internal selection process.

Based on this application and your reading of this chapter, answer the following questions:

1. Drawing from concepts presented in Chapter 3, how could Lori more formally evaluate SSW's assessment process, as well as the alternative presented to her by Felix?
2. Construct a scenario in which you think Lori should continue her business relationship with SSW. On the other hand, if Lori decides on an alternative assessment process, what would that process be? How would she evaluate whether that process was effective?
3. Delta Farms has considered expanding its operations into Asia. One of Lori's concerns is how to staff such positions. If Delta Farms does expand its operations to different cultures, how should Lori go about staffing such positions? Be specific.

ENDNOTES

1. A. Howard and D. W. Bray, "Predictions of Managerial Success over Long Periods of Time: Lessons from the Management Progress Study," in K. E. Clark and M. B. Clark (eds.), *Measures of Leadership* (West Orange, NJ: Leadership Library of America, 1990), pp. 113–130; C. J. Russell, "Selecting Top Corporate Leaders: An Example of Biographical Information," *Journal of Management,* 1990, 16, pp. 73–86; J. S. Schippman and E. P. Prien, "An Assessment of the Contributions of General Mental Ability and Personality Characteristics to Management Success," *Journal of Business and Psychology,* 1989, 3, pp. 423–437.
2. J. J. Kane and E. E. Lawler, "Methods of Peer Assessment," *Psychological Bulletin,* 1978, 85, pp. 555–586.
3. Bureau of National Affairs, *Basic Patterns in Union Contracts* (Washington, DC: author, 1995).
4. F. K. Folkes, *Personnel Policies in Large Non-Union Companies* (Englewood Cliffs, NJ: Prentice-Hall, 1985).
5. C. Ichniowski, J. T. Delaney, and D. Lewin, "The New Resource Management in US Workplaces: Is It Really New and Is It Only Nonunion?" *Industrial Relations,* 1989, 44, pp. 97–119.
6. K. G. Abraham and J. L. Medoff, "Length of Service and Promotions in Union and Nonunion Work Groups," *Industrial and Labor Relations Review,* 1985, 38, pp. 408–420; M. E. Gordon and W. J. Fitzgibbons, "An Empirical Test of the Validity of Seniority as a Factor in Staffing Decisions," *Journal of Applied Psychology,* 1982, 67, pp. 311–319.
7. A. Lienert, "From Rust to Riches," *Management Review,* 1994, 83, pp. 10–14.
8. M. A. Quinones, J. K. Ford, and M. S. Teachout, "The Relationship Between Work Experience and Job Performance: A Conceptual and Meta-Analytic Review," *Personnel Psychology,* 1995, 48, pp. 887–910; P. E. Tesluk and R. R. Jacobs, "Toward an Integrated Model of Work Experience," *Personnel Psychology,* 1998, 51, pp. 321–355.
9. F. L. Schmidt, J. E. Hunter, and A. N. Outerbridge, "Joint Relation of Experience and Ability with Job Performance: Test of Three Hypotheses," *Journal of Applied Psychology,* 1988, 73, pp. 46–57.

10. W. Wilson, "Video Training and Testing Supports Customer Service Goals," *Personnel Journal,* 1994, 73, pp. 47–51.
11. F. L. Schmidt and J. E. Hunter, "Development of a Causal Model of Processes Determining Job Performance," *Current Directions in Psychological Science,* 1992, 1, pp. 89–92.
12. K. R. Murphy and J. M. Cleveland, *Performance Appraisal: An Organizational Perspective* (Boston: Allyn and Bacon, 1991).
13. L. J. Peter and R. Hull, *The Peter Principle* (New York: William Morrow, 1969).
14. G. C. Thornton III and D. M. Morris, "The Application of Assessment Center Technology to the Evaluation of Personnel Records," *Public Personnel Management,* 2001, 30, pp. 55–66.
15. W. Arthur, Jr., E. A Day, T. L. McNelly, and P. S Edens, "A Meta-Analysis of the Criterion- Related Validity of Assessment Center Dimensions," *Personnel Psychology,"* 2003, 56, pp. 125–154.
16. D. A. Joiner, "Assessment Center: What's New?" *Public Personnel Management,* 2003, 31, pp. 179–185.
17. A. C. Spychalski, M. A. Quinones, B. B. Gaugler, and K. Pohley, "A Survey of Assessment Center Practices in Organizations in the United States," *Personnel Psychology,* 1997, 50, pp. 71–90.
18. B. B. Gaugler, D. B. Rosenthal, G. C. Thornton III, and C. Bentson, "Meta-Analysis of Assessment Center Validity," *Journal of Applied Psychology,* 1987, 72, pp. 493–511.
19. K. Dayan, R. Kasten, and S. Fox, "Entry-Level Police Candidate Assessment Center: An Efficient Tool or a Hammer to Kill a Fly?" *Personnel Psychology,* 2002, 55, pp. 827–849; R. D. Goffin, M. G. Rothstein, and N. G. Johnson, "Personality Testing and the Assessment Center: Incremental Validity for Managerial Selection," *Journal of Applied Psychology,* 1996, 81, pp. 746–756; H. W. Goldstein, K. P. Yusko, E. P. Brauerman, D. B. Smith, and B. Chung, "The Role of Cognitive Ability in Subgroup Differences and Incremental Validity of Assessment Center Exercises," *Personnel Psychology,* 1998, 51, pp. 357–374; F. L. Schmidt and J. E. Hunter, "The Validity and Utility of Selection Methods in Personnel Psychology: Practical and Theoretical Implications of 85 Years of Research Findings," *Psychological Bulletin,* 1998, 124, pp. 262–274.
20. Gaugler et al., "Meta-Analysis of Assessment Center Validity"; A. Howard, "An Assessment of Assessment Centers," *Academy of Management Journal,* 1974, 17, pp. 115–134; R. Klimoski and M. Brickner, "Why Do Assessment Centers Work? The Puzzle of Assessment Center Validity," *Personnel Psychology,* 1987, 40, pp. 243–260; P. R. Sackett, "A Critical Look at Some Common Beliefs About Assessment Centers," *Public Personnel Management,* 1988, 11, pp. 140–146.
21. M. A. McDaniel and N. T. Nguyen, "Situational Judgment Tests: A Review of Practice and Constructs Assessed," *International Journal of Selection and Assessment,* 2001, 9, pp. 103–113.
22. C. Fletcher, "Candidates' Reactions to Assessment Centres and Their Outcomes: A Longitudinal Study," *Journal of Occupational Psychology,* 1991, 64, pp. 117–127; "Guidelines and Ethical Considerations for Assessment Center Operations," *Public Personnel Management,* 2000, 29, pp. 315–331; C. Cladwell, G. C THornton III, and M. L. Gruys, "Ten Classic Assessment Center Erroes," *Public Personnel Management,* 2003, 32, pp 73–78.

23. J. E. Abueva, "Return of the Native Executive," *New York Times,* May 17, 2000, pp. B1, B8; P. Caligiuri and W. F. Cascio, "Sending Women on Global Assignments," *WorldatWork,* Second Quarter 2001, pp. 34–41; J. A. Hauser, "Filling the Candidate Pool: Developing Qualities in Potential International Assignees," *WorldatWork,* Second Quarter 2000, pp. 26–33; M. Mukuda, "Global Leaders Wanted . . . ApplyWithin," *Workspan,* April 2001, pp. 36–41; C. Patton, "Match Game," *Human Resource Executive,* June 2000, pp. 36–41.
24. G. C. Thornton, *Assessment Centers in Human Resource Management* (Reading, MA: Addison-Wesley, 1992).

Online **LearningCentre**

Visit the Online Learning Centre at
www.mcgrawhill.ca/olc/heneman

CHAPTER

10

Decision Making

CHAPTER OBJECTIVES

After reading this chapter, you will be able to:

- Understand the process of setting cut scores for selection as well as the outcomes of setting cut scores
- Understand and use the methods available for decision making for employee selection
- Be conversant with the essential terms and conditions normally set out in an offer of employment

Individuals flow through the staffing process, passing through several stages: applicant, candidate, finalist, offer receiver, and new hire. To implement and manage this flow, key decisions that must be made in several areas will be discussed. First, the factors that determine the choice of assessment methods to be used will be reviewed. Discussion will focus on the important considerations of validity, the correlation of one assessment method with other methods, likely adverse impact, and the utility of the method.

Once assessment data have been collected from applicants, decisions must be made about how to determine assessment scores. The process of translating predictor scores into assessment scores will be discussed for using single predictors and multiple predictors. In the case of multiple predictors, methods to combine predictor scores will be considered. Methods that will be reviewed are a compensatory model, multiple hurdles, and a combined approach. Each has distinct strengths and weaknesses.

Hiring standards and cut scores must be established to determine passing levels for the assessment scores. The process used to determine cut scores will be described, as well as the consequences of cut scores and methods to determine cut scores. Methods that will be covered are minimum competency, top-down, and banding. Professional guidelines for determining cut scores also will be reviewed.

Methods of final choice must be considered to determine who from among the finalists will receive a job offer. Methods of final choice that will be reviewed include random selection, ranking, and grouping. Each method may be advantageous, depending on one's objectives.

For all the preceding decisions, consideration must be given to who should be involved in the decision process. The role of various potential decision makers will be discussed, including HR professionals, line managers, and employees. In general, decisions about the staffing procedures to be followed are determined by HR professionals. Actual hiring decisions are usually made by managers. Increasingly, employees are being involved in both decisions.

A final match occurs when the offer receiver and the organization have determined that the probable overlap between the person's KSAOs/motivation and the job's requirements/rewards is sufficient to warrant entering into the employment relationship. Once this decision has been made, the organization and the individual seek to become legally bound to each other through mutual agreement on the terms and conditions of employment. They thus enter into an employment contract, and each expects the other to abide by the terms of the contract.

The formation of, and agreement on, the employment contract occurs in both external and internal staffing. Any time the matching process is set in motion, either through external or internal staffing, the goal is establishment of a new employment relationship.

Knowledge of employment contract concepts and principles is central to understanding the final match. This chapter includes an overview of such material, emphasizing the essential requirements for establishing a legally binding employment contract, as well as some of the nuances in doing so. A strategic approach to job offers is then presented, followed by a discussion of the major components of a job offer, and points to address in it. As is apparent, staffing organizations effectively demands great skill and care by the employer as it enters into employment contracts. The employer and offer receiver are accorded great freedom in the establishment of terms and conditions of employment; both parties have much to decide and agree on pertaining to job offer content.

Finally, legal issues should also guide the decision making. Particular consideration will be given to the role of diversity considerations in hiring decisions.

The chapter concludes with a discussion of specific legal issues that pertain not only to the establishment of the employment contract but also to potential long-term consequences of that contract that must be considered at the time it is established.

CHOICE OF ASSESSMENT METHOD

In our discussions of external and internal selection methods (Chapters 7–9), we listed multiple criteria to consider when deciding which method(s) to use (e.g., validity, utility). Some of these criteria require more amplification, specifically correlation with other predictors (newly discussed here), adverse impact, and utility.

Correlation with Other Predictors

If a predictor is to be considered useful, it must add value to the prediction of job success. To add value, it must add to the prediction of success above and beyond the forecasting powers of current predictors. In general, a predictor is more useful the smaller the correlation it has with other predictors and the higher the correlation it has with the criterion.

In order to assess whether the predictor adds anything new to forecasting, a matrix showing all the correlations between the predictors and the criteria should always be generated. If the correlations between the new predictor and existing predictors are higher than the correlations between the new predictor and criterion, then the new predictor is not adding much that is new. There are also relatively straightforward techniques, such as multiple regression, that take the correlation among predictors into account.[1]

Predictors are likely to be highly correlated with one another when their domain of content is similar. For example, both biodata and application blanks may focus on previous training received. Thus, using both biodata and application blanks as predictors may be redundant, and neither one may augment the other much in predicting job success.

Adverse Impact

3.5 A predictor discriminates between people in terms of the likelihood of their success on the job. A predictor may also discriminate by screening out a disproportionate number of designated group members. To the extent that this happens, the predictor has adverse impact, and it may result in legal problems. As a result, when the validity of alternative predictors is the same, and one predictor has less adverse impact than the other predictor, then the predictor with less adverse impact should be used.

A very difficult judgment call arises when one predictor has high validity and high adverse impact while another predictor has low validity and low adverse impact. From the perspective of accurately predicting job performance, the former predictor should be used. From a human rights standpoint, the latter predictor is preferable. Balancing the trade-offs is difficult and requires use of the organization's staffing philosophy regarding human rights and employment equity. One of the suggested solutions to this trade-off is banding, discussed later in this chapter.

Utility

Utility refers to the expected gains to be derived from using a predictor. Expected gains are of two types: hiring success and economic.

Hiring Success Gain Hiring success refers to the proportion of new hires who turn out to be successful on the job. Hiring success gain refers to the increase in the proportion of successful new hires that is expected to occur as a result of adding a new predictor to the selection system. If the current staffing system yields a success rate of 75 percent for new hires, how much of a gain in this success rate will occur by adding a new predictor to the system? The greater the expected gain, the greater the utility of the new predictor. This gain is influenced not only by the validity of the new predictor (as already discussed) but also by the selection ratio and base rate.

Selection Ratio. The selection ratio is simply the number of people hired divided by the number of applicants (sr = number hired/number of applicants). The lower the selection ratio, the more useful the predictor. When the selection ratio is low, the organization is more likely to be selecting successful employees.

If the selection ratio is low, then the denominator is large or the numerator is small. Both conditions are desirable. A large denominator means that the organization is reviewing a large number of applicants for the job. The chances of identifying a successful candidate are much better in this situation than when an organization hires the first available person or only reviews a few applicants. A small numerator indicates that the organization is being very stringent with its hiring standards. The organization is hiring people likely to be successful rather than hiring anyone who meets the most basic requirements for the job; it is using high standards to ensure that the very best people are selected.

Base Rate. The base rate is defined as the proportion of current employees who are successful on some criterion or HR outcome (br = number of successful employees/number of employees). A high base rate is desired for obvious reasons. A high base rate may come about from the organization's staffing system alone or in combination with other HR programs, such as training and compensation.

When considering possible use of a new predictor, one issue is whether the proportion of successful employees (i.e., the base rate) will increase as a result of using the new predictor in the staffing system. This is the matter of hiring success gain. Dealing with it requires simultaneous consideration of the organization's current base rate and selection ratio, as well as the validity of the new predictor.

The Taylor-Russell tables provide the necessary assistance for addressing this issue. An excerpt from the Taylor-Russell tables is shown in Exhibit 10.1.

The Taylor-Russell table shows in each of its cells the percentage of new hires who will turn out to be successful. This is determined by a combination of the validity coefficient for the new predictor, the selection ratio, and the base rate. The top matrix (A) shows the percentage of successful new hires when the base rate is low (.30), the validity coefficient is low (.20) or high (.60), and the selection ratio is low (.10) or high (.70). The bottom matrix (B) shows the percentage of successful

EXHIBIT 10.1 Excerpts from the Taylor-Russell Tables

A.

	Base Rate = .30 Selection Ratio	
Validity	**.10**	**.70**
.20	43%	33%
.60	77%	40%

B.

	Base Rate = .80 Selection Ratio	
Validity	**.10**	**.70**
.20	89%	83%
.60	99%	90%

Source: H. C. Taylor and J. T. Russell, "The Relationship of Validity Coefficients to the Practical Effectiveness of Tests in Selection," *Journal of Applied Psychology,* 1939, 23, pp. 565–578.

new hires when the base rate is high (.80), the validity coefficient is low (.20) or high (.60), and the selection ratio is low (.10) or high (.70). Two illustrations show how these tables may be used.

The first illustration has to do with the decision whether to use a new test to select computer programmers. Assume that the current test used to select programmers has a validity coefficient of .20. Also assume that a consulting firm has approached the organization with a new test that has a validity coefficient of .60. Should the organization purchase and use the new test?

At first blush, the answer might seem to be affirmative, because the new test has a substantially higher level of validity. This initial reaction, however, must be gauged in the context of the selection ratio and the current base rate. If the current base rate is .80 and the current selection ratio is .70, then, as can be seen in the lower matrix (B) of Exhibit 10.1, the new selection procedure will only result in a hiring success gain from 83 percent to 90 percent. The organization may already have a very high base rate due to other facets of HR management it does quite well (e.g., training, rewards). Hence, even though it has validity of .20, the base rate of its current predictor is already .80.

On the other hand, if the existing base rate of the organization is .30 and the existing selection ratio is .10, then it should strongly consider use of the new test. As shown in the top matrix (A) in Exhibit 10.1, the hiring success gain will go from 43 percent to 77 percent with the addition of the new test.

The point of this example is to show that when confronted with the decision of whether to use a new predictor, the decision depends on the validity coefficient, base rate, and selection ratio. They should not be considered independent of one another. HR professionals should carefully record and monitor base rates and selection ratios. Then, when asked by management whether they should be using a new predictor, they can respond appropriately. Fortunately, the Taylor-Russell tables are for any combination of validity coefficient, base rate, and selection ratio values. The values shown in Exhibit 10.1 are excerpts for illustration only. When other values need to be considered, then the original tables should be consulted to provide the appropriate answers.

Economic Gain Economic gain refers to the bottom line or monetary impact of a predictor on the organization. A predictor is more useful the greater the economic gain it produces. Considerable work has been done over the years on assessing the economic gain associated with predictors. The basic utility formula used to estimate economic gain is shown in Exhibit 10.2.

EXHIBIT 10.2 Economic Gain Formula

$\Delta U = (T \times N_n \times r_{xy} \times SD_y \times \bar{Z}_s) - (N_a \times C_y)$

Where:

ΔU = expected dollar value increase to the organization using the predictor versus random selection

T = average tenure of employees in position

N_n = number of people hired

r_{xy} = correlation between predictor and job performance

SD_y = dollar value of job performance

$\bar{Z}_s$ = average standard predictor score of selected group

N_a = number of applicants

C_y = cost per applicant

Adapted from: C. Handler and S. Hunt, "Estimating the Financial Value of Staffing Assessment Tools," *Workforce Management*, Mar. 2003 (***www.workforce.com***).

At a general level, the economic gain formula shown in Exhibit 10.2 works as follows. Economic gains derived from using a valid predictor versus random selection (the left-hand side of the equation) depend on two factors (the right-hand side of the equation). The first factor (the entry before the subtraction sign) is the revenue generated by hiring productive employees using the new predictor. The second factor (the entry after the subtraction sign) is the costs associated with using the new predictor. Positive economic gains are achieved when revenues are maximized and costs are minimized. Revenues are maximized by using the most valid selection procedures. Costs are minimized by using the predictors with the least costs. To estimate actual economic gain, values are entered into the equation for each of the variables shown. Values are usually generated by experts in HR research relying on the judgments of experienced line managers.

Several variations on the economic gain (utility) formula shown in Exhibit 10.2 have been developed. For the most part, these variations require consideration of additional factors, such as assumptions about tax rates and applicant flows. In all of these models, the most difficult factor to estimate is the dollar value of job performance, which represents the difference between productive and nonproductive employees in dollar value terms. A variety of methods have been proposed, ranging from manager estimates of employee value to percentages of compensation (usually 40% of base pay).[2] Despite this difficulty, economic gain formulas represent a significant way of estimating the economic gains that may be anticipated with the use of a new (and valid) predictor.

Limitations with Utility Analysis Although utility analysis can be a powerful method to communicate the bottom-line implications of using valid selection measures, it is not without its limitations. Perhaps the most fundamental concern among researchers and practitioners is that utility estimates lack realism because of the following:

1. Virtually every organization uses multiple selection measures, yet existing utility models assume that the decision is whether to use a single selection measure rather than selecting applicants by chance alone.[3]
2. There are many important variables missing from the model, such as human rights concerns (e.g., employment equity) and applicant reactions.[4]
3. The utility formula is based on many assumptions that are probably overly simplistic, including that validity does not vary over time;[5] that nonperformance criteria such as attendance, trainability, applicant reactions, and fit are irrelevant;[6] and that applicants are selected in a top-down manner and all job offers are accepted.[7]

Perhaps as a result of these limitations, several factors indicate that utility analysis may have a limited effect on managers' decisions about selection measures. For example, a survey of managers who have discontinued use of utility analysis found that 40 percent did so because they felt that utility analysis was too complicated, whereas 32 percent discontinued use because they believed that the results were not credible.[8] Other studies have found that managers' acceptance of utility analysis is low; one study found that reporting simple validity coefficients was more likely to persuade HR decision makers to adopt a particular selection method than was reporting utility analysis results.[9]

These criticisms should not be taken as arguments that organizations should ignore utility analysis when evaluating selection decisions. However, decision makers are much less likely to become disillusioned with utility analysis if they are informed consumers and realize some of the limitations inherent in such analyses. Researchers have the responsibility of better embedding utility analysis in the strategic context in which staffing decisions are made, while HR decision makers have the responsibility to use the most rigorous methods possible to evaluate their decisions.[10] By being realistic about what utility analysis can and cannot accomplish, the potential to fruitfully inform staffing decisions will increase.

DETERMINING ASSESSMENT SCORES

Single Predictor

Using a single predictor in selection decisions makes the process of determining scores easy. In fact, scores on the single predictor are the final assessment scores. Thus, concerns over how to combine assessment scores are not relevant when a single predictor is used in selection decisions. Although using a single predictor has the advantage of simplicity, there are some obvious drawbacks. First, few employers would feel comfortable hiring applicants on the basis of a single attribute. In fact, almost all employers use multiple methods in selection decisions. A second and related reason for using multiple predictors is that utility increases as the number of valid predictors used in selection decisions increases. In most cases, using two valid selection methods will result in more effective selection decisions than using a sole predictor. For these reasons, although basing selection decisions on a single predictor is a simple way to make decisions, it is rarely the best one.

Multiple Predictors

Given the less-than-perfect validities of predictors, most organizations use multiple predictors in making selection decisions. With multiple predictors, decisions must be made about combining the resultant scores. These decisions can be addressed through consideration of compensatory, multiple hurdles, and combined approaches.

Compensatory Model With a compensatory model, scores on one predictor are simply added to scores on another predictor to yield a total score. What this means is that high scores on one predictor can compensate for low scores on another. For example, if an employer is using an interview and grade point average (GPA) to select a person, an applicant with a low GPA who does well in the interview may still get the job.

The advantage of a compensatory model is that it recognizes that people have multiple talents and that many different constellations of talents may produce success on the job. The disadvantage to a compensatory model is that, at least for some jobs, level of proficiency for specific talents cannot be compensated for by other proficiencies. For example, a firefighter requires a certain level of strength that cannot be compensated for by intelligence.

In terms of making actual decisions using the compensatory model, there are four procedures that may be followed: clinical prediction, unit weighting, rational weighting, and multiple regression. The four methods differ from one another in terms of the manner in which predictor scores (raw or standardized) are weighted before being added together for a total or composite score.

EXHIBIT 10.3 Four Compensatory Model Procedures for Three Predictors

A. Models

Clinical Prediction

$P_1 \rightarrow P_2 \rightarrow P_3 \rightarrow$ Total Score

Unit Weighting

$P_1 + P_2 + P_3 =$ Total Score

Rational Weighting

$w_1 P_1 + w_2 P_2 + w_3 P_3 =$ Total Score

Multiple Regression

$a + b_1 P_1 + b_2 P_2 + b_3 P_3 =$ Total Score

Where: P = predictor score
w = rational weight
a = intercept
b = statistical weight

B. Raw Scores for Applicant on Three Predictors

	Predictors		
Applicant	**Interview**	**Application Blank**	**Recommendation**
A	3	5	2
B	4	3	4
C	5	4	3

The following example will be used to illustrate these procedures. In all four, raw scores are used to determine a total score. Standard scores (see Chapter 3) may need to be used rather than raw scores if each predictor variable uses a different method of measurement or is measured under different conditions. Differences in weighting methods are shown in Part A of Exhibit 10.3. In Part B of Exhibit 10.3, there is a selection system consisting of interviews, application blanks, and recommendations. For simplicity, assume that scores on each predictor range from 1 to 5. Scores on these three predictors are shown for three applicants.

Clinical Prediction. Returning to Exhibit 10.3, note that with a clinical prediction, managers use their expert judgment to arrive at a total score for each applicant. That final score may or may not be a simple addition of the three predictor scores shown in Exhibit 10.3. Hence, applicant A may be given a higher total score than applicant B even though simple addition shows that applicant B had one point more (4 + 3 + 4 = 11) than A (3 + 5 + 2 = 10).

Frequently, clinical prediction is done by initial screening interviewers or hiring managers. These decision makers may or may not have "scores" per se, but they have multiple pieces of information on each applicant, and they make a decision on the applicant by "taking everything into account." In initial screening decisions, this summary decision is whether the applicant gets over the initial hurdle and passes on to the next level of assessment. For example, a manager at a fast food restaurant might make an initial screening decision on an applicant by subjectively combining his or her impressions of various bits of information about the applicant on the application form. A hiring manager for a professional position might focus on a finalist's resumé and answers to the manager's interview questions to decide whether to extend an offer to the finalist.

The advantage to the clinical prediction approach is that it draws on the expertise of managers to weight and combine predictor scores. In turn, managers may be more likely to accept the selection decisions than if a mechanical scoring rule (e.g., add up the points) were used.

The problem with this approach is that the reasons for the weightings are known only to the manager. Also, clinical predictions have generally been shown to be less accurate than mechanical decisions, although there are times when using intuition and a nuanced approach is necessary or the only option.[11]

Unit Weighting. With unit weighting, each predictor is weighted the same at a value of 1.00. What this means is shown in Exhibit 10.3 (Part A): the predictor scores are simply added together to get a total score. So, in Exhibit 10.3 (Part B), the total scores for applicants A, B, and C are 10, 11, and 12, respectively. The advantage to unit weighting is that it is a simple and straightforward process to follow and makes the importance of each predictor explicit to decision makers. The problem with this approach is that it assumes that each predictor contributes equally to the prediction of job success, which often will not be the case.

Rational Weighting. With rational weighting, each predictor receives a differential rather than equal weighting. Managers and other subject matter experts establish the weights for each predictor according to degree to which each is believed to predict job success. These weights (w) are then multiplied times each raw score (P) to yield a total score as shown in Exhibit 10.3 (Part A).

For example, the predictors in Exhibit 10.3 (Part B) may be weighted .5, .3, and .2 for the interview, application blank, and recommendation. Each applicant's raw score in Exhibit 10.3 (Part B) is multiplied times the appropriate weight to yield a total score. For example, the total score for applicant A is $(.5)3 + (.3)5 + (.2)2 = 3.4$.

The advantage to this approach is that it considers the relative importance of each predictor and makes this assessment explicit. The downside, however, is that it is an elaborate procedure that requires managers and subject matter experts to agree on the differential weights to be applied.

Multiple Regression. Multiple regression is similar to rational weighting in that the predictors receive different weights. With multiple regression, however, the weights are established on the basis of statistical procedures rather than on the basis of judgments by managers or other subject matter experts. The statistical weights are developed on the basis of (1) the correlation of each predictor with the criterion, and (2) the correlations among the predictors. As a result, regression weights provide optimal weights in the sense that the weights are those that will yield the highest total validity.

The calculations result in a multiple regression formula like the one shown in Exhibit 10.3 (Part A). A total score for each applicant is obtained by multiplying the statistical weight (b) for each predictor by the predictor (P) score and summing these along with the intercept value (a). As an example, assume the statistical weights are .9, .6, and .2 for the interview, application blank, and recommendation, respectively, and that the intercept is .09. Using these values, the total score for applicant A is $.09 + (.9)3 + (.6)5 + (.2)2 = 6.19$.

Multiple regression offers the possibility of a much higher degree of precision in the prediction of criterion scores than do the other methods of weighting. Unfortunately, this level of precision is realized only under a certain set of circumstances. In particular, for multiple regression to be more precise than unit weighting, there must be a small number of predictors, low correlations between predictor variables, and a large sample.[12] Many selection settings do not meet these criteria, so in these cases consideration should be given to unit or rational weighting instead. In situations where these conditions are met, however, multiple regression weights can produce higher validity and utility than the other weighting schemes.

Choice among Weighting Schemes. The choice from among different weighting schemes is important because how various predictor combinations are weighted is critical in determining the usefulness of the selection process. To illustrate, Exhibit 10.4 provides the changes in validity and utility that occur when supplementing the most empirically valid method of selection (cognitive ability tests) with another selection method. The first column shows that change in validity by unit weighting scores on the cognitive ability test with the specified selection measure. For example, the validity of a cognitive ability test, when used by itself to predict job performance, has been estimated to be .50. Past research suggests that the validity of an integrity

EXHIBIT 10.4 Effects of Unit Weighting and Multiple Regression Weighting on the Validity and Utility of Cognitive Ability Tests

Additional Selection Method	Unit-Weighted Composite	Regression-Weighted Composite
Integrity test	27.6%	28.2%
Structured interview	27.0%	27.1%
Work sample	23.9%	24.1%
Conscientiousness	13.7%	17.1%
Job knowledge test	12.8%	12.9%
Unstructured interview	10.8%	12.8%
Reference check	6.8%	12.2%
Assessment centre	−1.5%	2.8%
Biodata	−2.6%	2.4%
Job experience	−4.3%	6.1%
Interest inventory	−15.4%	2.0%
Handwriting analysis	−26.5%	0.0%

Columns show the change in validity and utility by adding specified selection method to cognitive ability tests (general mental ability test) in predicting job performance.

Source: Adapted from D. S. Ones, F. L. Schmidt, and K. Yoon, "Validity of an Equally-Weighted Composite of General Mental Ability and a Second Predictor" and "Predictive Validity of General Mental Ability Combined with a Second Predictor Based on Standardized Multiple Regression." Working papers (University of Iowa, Iowa City: author, 1996). Used with permission.

test, when used by itself to predict job performance, is .41. When scores on the cognitive ability and integrity test are combined by weighting them equally, the total validity increases to .65, an increase of 27.6 percent over the validity of the cognitive ability test alone. When scores are weighted according to multiple regression, however, the increase in validity becomes 28.2 percent. In fact, the exhibit shows that when supplementing cognitive ability tests with additional selection procedures, using multiple regression to establish weights always yields higher validity than unit weighting. Furthermore, when using selection methods that have moderate or low levels of validity in conjunction with cognitive ability tests, unit-weighted combinations often provide lower levels of validity than using only cognitive ability tests.

These results do not prove that multiple regression weighting is a superior method in all circumstances. In fact, limitations of regression-based weighting schemes were noted above. What this example does help illustrate, though, is that the choice of the best weighting scheme is consequential, and likely depends on answers to the most important questions about clinical, unit, rational, and multiple regression schemes (in that order):

- Do selection decision makers have considerable experience and insight into selection decisions, and is managerial acceptance of the selection process important?
- Is there reason to believe that each predictor contributes relatively equally to job success?
- Are there adequate resources to use relatively involved weighting schemes such as rational weights or multiple regression?
- Are the conditions under which multiple regression is superior (relatively small number of predictors, low correlations among predictors, large sample) satisfied?

Answers to these questions—and the importance of the questions themselves—will go a long way toward deciding which weighting scheme to use. We also should note that while statistical weighting is more valid than clinical weighting, the combination of both methods may yield the highest validity. One study indicated that regression-weighted predictors were more valid than clinical judgments, but clinical judgments contributed uniquely to performance controlling for regression-weighted predictors. This suggests that both statistical and clinical weighting might be used. Thus, the weighting schemes are not necessarily mutually exclusive.[13]

Multiple Hurdles Model With a multiple hurdles approach, an applicant must earn a passing score on each predictor before advancing in the selection process. Such an approach is taken when each requirement measured by a predictor is critical to job success. Passing scores are set using the methods to determine cut scores discussed in the next section. With multiple hurdles, unlike the compensatory model, a high score on one predictor cannot compensate for a low score on another predictor.

Multiple hurdles are used to prevent false-positive errors. They are costly and time consuming to set up. As a result, they are used to select people for jobs where the occupational hazards are great (e.g., firefighters) or the consequences of poor performance have a great impact on the public at large (e.g., police officers).

Combined Model For jobs where some but not all requirements are critical to job success, a combined method may be used in which the compensatory and multiple hurdles models are combined together. The process starts with the multiple hurdles and ends with the compensatory method.

An example of the combined approach for the position of recruitment manager is shown in Exhibit 10.5. The selection process for recruitment manager starts with two hurdles that must be passed, in succession, by the applicant. These are the application blank and the job knowledge test. Failure to clear either hurdle results in rejection. Having passed them, applicants take an interview and have their references checked. Information from the interview and the references is combined in a compensatory manner. Those who pass are offered the job, and those who do not pass are rejected.

EXHIBIT 10.5 Combined Model for Recruitment Manager

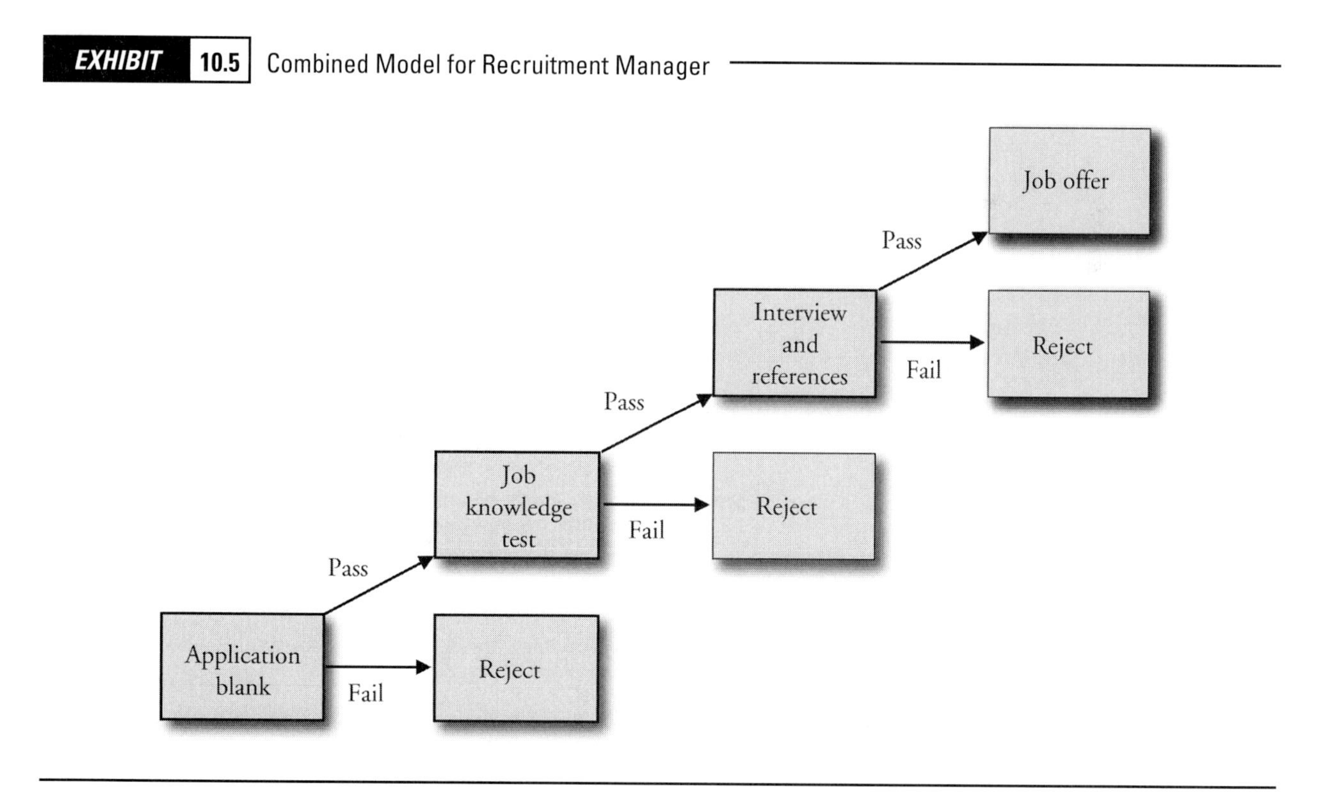

HIRING STANDARDS AND CUT SCORES

Hiring standards or cut scores address the issue of what constitutes a passing score. The score may be a single score from a single predictor, or a total score from multiple predictors. To address this, a description of the process and the consequences of cut scores are presented. Then, methods that may be used to establish the actual cut score are described.

Description of the Process

Once one or more predictors have been chosen for use, a decision must be made as to who advances further in the selection process. This decision requires that one or more cut scores be established. A cut score is the score that separates those who advance further in the process (e.g., applicants who become candidates) from those who are rejected. For example, assume a test is used on which scores may range from 0 to 100 points. A cut score of 70 would mean that those applicants with a 70 or more would advance, while all others would be rejected for employment purposes.

Consequences of Cut Scores

Setting a cut score is a very important process, as it has consequences for the organization and the applicant. The consequences of cut scores can be shown using Exhibit 10.6, which contains a summary of a scatter diagram of predictor and criterion scores. The horizontal line shows the criterion score at which the organization has determined whether an employee is successful or unsuccessful—for example, a 3 on a 5-point performance appraisal scale where 1 is the low performance and 5 is the high performance. The vertical line is the cut score for the predictor—for example, a 3 on a 5-point interview rating scale where 1 reveals no chance of success and 5 a high chance of success.

The consequences of setting the cut score at a particular level are shown in each of the quadrants. Quadrants A and C represent correct decisions, which have positive consequences for the organization. Quadrant A applicants are called true positives because they were assessed as having a high chance of success using the predictor and would have succeeded if hired. Quadrant C applicants are called true negatives because they were assessed as having little chance for success and, indeed, would not be successful if hired.

EXHIBIT 10.6 Consequences of Cut Scores

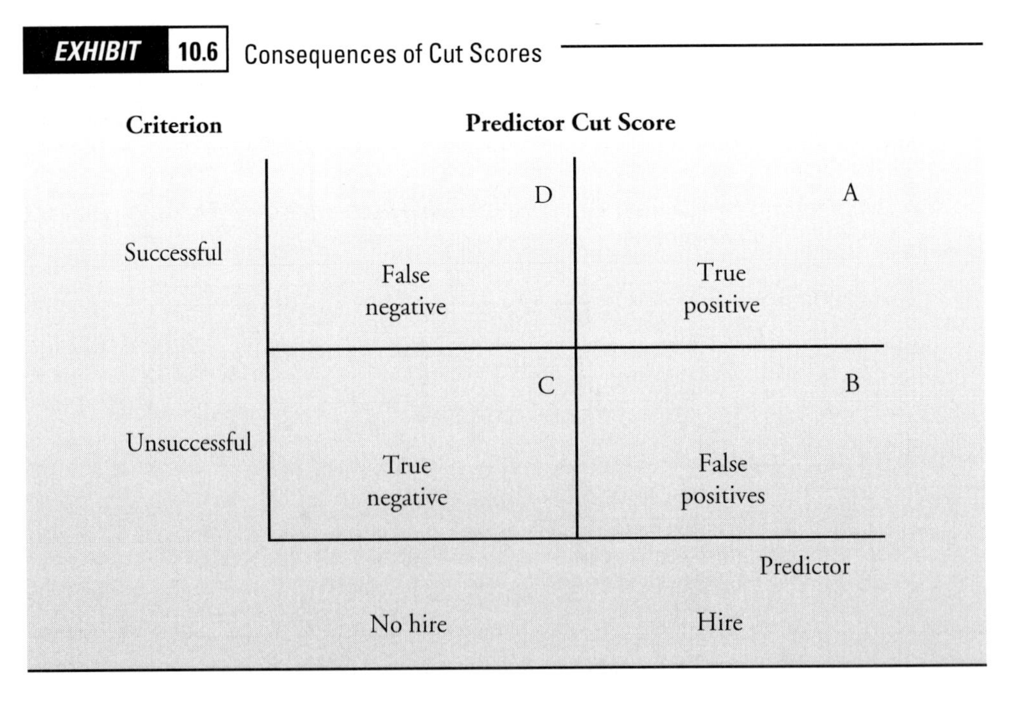

Quadrants D and B represent incorrect decisions, which have negative consequences to the organization and affected applicants. Quadrant D applicants are called false negatives because they were assessed as not being likely to succeed, but had they been hired, they would have been successful. Not only was an incorrect decision reached but also a person who would have done well was not hired. Quadrant B applicants are called false positives. They were assessed as being likely to succeed, but would have ended up being unsuccessful performers. Eventually, these people would need to receive remedial training, be transferred to a new job, or even be terminated.

How high or low a cut score is set has a large impact on the consequences shown in Exhibit 10.6, and trade-offs are always involved. Compared with the moderate cut score in Exhibit 10.6, a high cut score results in fewer false positives, but a larger number of false negatives. Is this a good, bad, or inconsequential set of outcomes for the organization? The answer depends on the job open for selection and the costs involved. If the job is an airplane pilot, then it is essential that there be no false positives. The cost of a false positive may be the loss of human life.

Now consider the consequences of a low cut score, relative to the one shown in Exhibit 10.6. There are fewer false negatives and more true positives, but more false positives are hired. In organizations that gain competitive advantage in their industry by hiring the very best, this set of consequences may be unacceptable.

In short, when setting a cut score, attention must be given to the consequences. As indicated, these consequences can be very serious. As a result, different methods of setting cut scores have been developed to guide decision makers. These will now be reviewed.[14]

Methods to Determine Cut Scores

Three different methods may be used to determine cut scores: minimum competency, top-down, and banding. Each of these is described below along with professional guidelines for setting cut scores.

minimum competency
Cut scores that reflect the necessary minimum qualification(s) required to perform a job

Minimum Competency Using the **minimum competency** method, the cut score is set on the basis of the minimum qualifications deemed necessary to perform the job. Subject matter experts are usually used to establish a minimum competency score. This approach is often needed in situations where the first step in the hiring process is the demonstration of minimum skill requirements. Exhibit 10.7 provides an illustration of the use of cut scores in selection. The exhibit lists the scores of 25 applicants on a particular test. Using the minimum competency method, the cut score is set at the level at which applicants who score below the line are deemed unqualified for the job. In this case, a score of 75 was determined to be the minimum competency level necessary. Thus, all applicants who scored below 75 are deemed unqualified and rejected, and all applicants who scored 75 or above are deemed at least minimally qualified. Finalists and ultimately offer receivers can then be chosen among these qualified applicants on the basis of other criteria.

A variation of the minimum competency approach is hiring the first acceptable candidate. It is often used when candidates come to the attention of the hiring person sequentially, one at a time, rather than having a total pool of candidates to choose from in order to get some finalists. It also is used when the organization is desperate for "warm bodies" and willing to hire anyone who meets some threshold. Although at times a rush to hire is understandable, the consequences can be most unfortunate. For example, due to the difficulty in finding telemarketers, a home mortgage call centre had a policy of hiring the first acceptable candidate. The hiring manager at this call centre overhead a newly hired employee telling a customer, "If I had a rate as high as yours, I'd slit my wrists, then climb to the top of the highest building and jump off." It turned out this employee had recently chipped his front tooth from his favourite experiment—seeing how close he could get to a fast-moving train.[15] So, while hiring the first acceptable candidate may seem necessary, it is far from an ideal hiring strategy and the costs may not be revealed until it is too late—as in the above example of the newly hired telemarketer.

EXHIBIT 10.7 Use of Cut Scores in Selection Decisions

Rank	Test Scores	Minimum Competency			Top-Down*	Banding*
1.	100	100		100	1st choice	100
2.	98	98		98	2nd choice	98
3.	97	97		97	3rd choice	97
4.	96	96		96	4th choice	96
T5.	93	93		95	5th choice	93
T5.	93	93		95	5th choice	93
7.	91	91		91	"	91
T8.	90	90		90	"	90
T8.	90	90		90	"	90
10.	88	88	Qualified	88	"	88
11.	87	87		87	"	87
T12.	85	85		85	"	85
T12.	85	85		85	"	85
14.	83	83		83	"	83
15.	81	81		81	"	81
16.	79	79		79	"	79
T17.	77	77		77	"	77
T17.	77	77		77	"	77
19.	76	76		76	"	76
20.	75	75	Minimum competency	75	"	75
21.	74	74		74	21st choice	74
22.	71	71		71	22nd choice	71
23.	70	70	Unqualified	70	23rd choice	70
24.	69	69		69	24th choice	69
25.	65	65		65	25th choice	65

*All scores within brackets treated as equal; choice of applicants within brackets (if necessary) can be made on the basis of other factors, such as human rights considerations.

Another variant on the minimum competency approach is to impose a sort of *maximum* competency on "overqualified" applicants. The assumption here is that the job will not be sufficiently rewarding, and the overqualified employee will quickly quit. Care needs to be taken per se selecting out seemingly overqualified applicants. We are aware of no scientific evidence that employees can be too smart or too conscientious or too positive for a job. It is possible that some seemingly overqualified applicants are not serious about a job. But this hypothesis needs to be tested directly, rather than assuming that a well-qualified applicant is not serious. Sometimes people are interested in a job for reasons that the hiring manager does not know (without asking). There are also legal dangers as many apparently overqualified applicants are over 40. As one manager said, "I think it's a huge mistake not to take a second look at overqualified candidates. Certainly there are valid reasons to reject some candidates, but it shouldn't be a blanket response."[16]

top-down
Selecting applicants by starting with the most qualified—based on predictor scores—and then progressing down through the applicant distribution until the required number of applicants have been selected; the cut score is the score of the last applicant selected

Top-Down Another method of determining at what level the cut score should be set is to simply examine the distribution of predictor scores for applicants and set the cut score at the level that best meets the demands of the organization. This **top-down** method of setting cut scores is illustrated in Exhibit 10.7. As the exhibit shows, under top-down hiring, cut scores are established by the number of applicants that need to be hired. Once that number has been determined, applicants are selected from the top based on the order of their scores until the number desired is reached. The advantage of this approach is that it is a system that is easy to administer. It also minimizes judgment required because the cut score is determined on the basis of the demand for labour. The big drawback to this approach is that validity has often not been established prior to the use of the predictor. Also, there may be over-reliance on the use of a single predictor and cut score, while other potentially useful predictors are ignored.

A well-known example of a top-down method is the Angoff method.[17] According to this approach, subject matter experts are used to set the minimum cut scores needed to proceed in the selection process. These experts go through the content of the predictor (e.g., test items) and determine which items the minimally qualified person should be able to pass. Usually seven to ten subject matter experts (e.g., job incumbents, managers) are used who must agree on the items to be passed. The cut score is the sum of the number of items that must be answered correctly.

There are several problems with this particular approach and subsequent modifications to it. First, it is a time-consuming procedure. Second, the results are dependent on the subject matter experts. It is a very difficult matter to get members of the organization to agree on who are "the" subject matter experts. Which subject matter experts are selected may have a bearing on the actual cut scores developed. Finally, it is unclear how much agreement there must be among subject matter experts when they evaluate test items. There also may be judgmental errors and biases in how cut scores are set.[18]

Banding The traditional selection cut score method is the top-down approach. For both external hiring and internal promotions, the top-down method will yield the highest validity and utility. This method has been criticized, however, for ignoring the possibility that small differences between scores are due to measurement error. The top-down method also has been criticized for its ability to yield socially undesirable outcomes. Particularly in the area of cognitive ability testing, top-down decisions are likely to exclude substantial numbers of minorities. As a result, the selection measures are likely to have adverse impact against minorities. The magnitude of the adverse impact is such that, on a standard cognitive ability test, if half the white applicants are hired, only 16 percent of the black applicants would be expected to be hired.[19]

One suggestion that has been made for reducing the adverse impact of top-down hiring is using different norms for minority and majority groups; thus, hiring decisions are based on normatively defined (rather than absolute) scores. For example, a black employee who achieved a score of 75 on a test where the mean of all black applicants was 50 could be considered to have the same normative score as a white applicant who scored a 90 on a test where the mean for white applicants was 60. However, this "race-norming" of test scores, while not prohibited in Canada, is controversial.

banding

Method of determining cut score whereby applicants who score within a certain score range or band are considered to have scored equivalently

Banding refers to the procedure whereby applicants who score within a certain score range or band are considered to have scored equivalently. A simple banding procedure is provided in Exhibit 10.7. In this example, using a 100-point test, all applicants who score within the band of 10-point increments are considered to have scored equally. For example, all applicants who score 91 and above could be assigned a score of 9, those who score 81–90 are given a score of 8, and so on. (In essence, this is what is done when letter grades are assigned based on exam scores.) Hiring within bands then could be done at random or, more typically, based on race or sex in conjunction with other factors (e.g., seniority, experience, etc.). Banding might reduce the adverse impact of selection tests because such a procedure tends to reduce differences between higher- and lower-scoring groups (as is the case with white and minority applicants on cognitive ability tests). In practice, band widths are usually calculated on the basis of the standard error of measurement.

Research suggests that banding procedures result in substantial decreases in the adverse impact of cognitive ability tests while, under certain conditions, the losses in terms of utility are relatively small.[20] Various methods of banding have been proposed, but the differences between these methods are relatively unimportant.[21]

Although banding does have considerable social appeal in terms of increasing diversity and reducing the adverse impact of selection processes,[22] numerous limitations are evident. One limitation is that decreases in validity and utility resulting from banding become significant when even moderately reliable tests are used. Because the standard error of the difference between test scores is partly a function of the reliability of the test, when test reliability is low, band widths are wider than when the reliability of the test is high. For example, if the reliability of a test is .80, at a reasonable level of confidence, nearly half the scores on a test can be considered equivalent.[23] Obviously, taking scores on a 100-point test and lumping applicants into only two groups wastes a great deal of important information on applicants (it is very unlikely that an applicant who scores a 51 on a valid test will perform the same on the job as an applicant who scores 99). Therefore, if the reliability of a test is even moderately high, the validity and utility decrements that result from banding become quite severe.

Another limitation of banding is that although it will always be expected to yield lower utility, using banding and random selection within bands may not reduce the adverse impact of cognitive ability tests.[24] Given the adverse impact of cognitive ability tests, too few minorities may be placed into the upper bands. Thus, even if selection from the upper bands is done at random, there may not be enough minorities in these bands to prevent adverse impact. As a result, banding may require more drastic modifications to ensure that the desired result (less adverse impact) is achieved. Finally, it appears that when banding is associated with employment equity goals, applicants react negatively.[25]

The scientific merit of test banding is hotly debated.[26] It is unlikely that we could resolve here the myriad ethical and technical issues underlying their use. Organizations considering the use of banding in personnel selection decisions must weigh the pros and cons carefully. However, it should be noted that, when using cognitive ability tests in selection, the goals of validity and diversity may not be complementary. If organizations decide to use banding as a means of promoting diversity, they do so at some potential cost to the validity and utility of their selection process. Given that banding often can be expected to result in validity and utility losses, perhaps a better solution to the sometimes conflicting goals of utility and diversity is to supplement cognitive ability tests with other valid selection methods that have less (or no) adverse impact. Research suggests that the adverse impact of a selection process that uses cognitive ability tests can be reduced, and overall validity increased, by supplementing ability tests with other selection procedures, such as biodata inventories, personality tests, and structured interviews. On the other hand, it is unlikely that using such tests will eliminate adverse impact altogether. In short, there is a trade-off between validity and diversity given that the most valid single selection measure (cognitive ability tests) also has the highest adverse impact. Researchers have developed various frameworks that will help organizations better balance the dual goals of validity and diversity.[27]

Unfortunately, as a recent review concluded, though "there is extensive evidence supporting the validity" of cognitive tests, "adverse impact is unlikely to be eliminated as long as one assesses" cognitive abilities in the selection process.[28] There are some methods to reduce adverse impact when cognitive tests are used, such as test-taking coaching programs, use of more generous time limits, and removal of culturally biased items. However, as the review cited above indicates, these programs have a relatively small effect on adverse impact. Some research suggests that increased weighting on noncognitive aspects of performance, such as helping behaviours in the workplace, reduces the adverse impact of cognitive ability tests.[29] Whether increasing the weight placed on noncognitive aspects of performance (e.g., helping or citizenship behaviours), relative to core task performance, is justified from a cost-benefit perspective is open to question.

Guidelines

Much more research is needed on systematic procedures that are effective in setting optimal cut scores. In the meantime, a sound set of guidelines for setting cut scores is shown in Exhibit 10.8.

EXHIBIT 10.8 Guidelines for Setting Cut-off Scores

1. It is unrealistic to expect that there is a single "best" method of setting cut-off scores for all situations.
2. The process of setting a cut-off score (or a critical score) should begin with a job analysis that identifies relative levels of proficiency on critical knowledge, skills, abilities, or other characteristics.
3. The validity and job relatedness of the assessment procedure are crucial considerations.
4. How a test is used (criterion-referenced or norm-referenced) affects the selection and meaning of a cut-off score.
5. When possible, data on the actual relation of test scores to outcome measures of job performance should be considered carefully.
6. Cut-off scores or critical scores should be set high enough to ensure that minimum standards of job performance are met.
7. Cut-off scores should be consistent with normal expectations of acceptable proficiency within the workforce.

Source: W. F. Cascio, R. A. Alexander, and G. V. Barrett, "Setting Cutoff Scores: Legal, Psychometric, and Professional Issues and Guidelines," *Personnel Psychology*, 1988, 41, pp. 21–22. Used with permission.

METHODS OF FINAL CHOICE

The discussion thus far has been on decision rules that can be used to narrow down the list of people to successively smaller groups who advance in the selection process from applicant to candidate to finalist. How can the organization now choose from among the finalists to decide which of them will receive job offers? Discretionary assessments about the finalists must be converted into final choice decisions. The methods of final choice are the mechanisms by which discretionary assessments are translated into job offer decisions.

Methods of final choice include random selection, ranking, and grouping. Examples of each of these methods of final choice are shown in Exhibit 10.9 and are discussed here.

Random Selection

With random selection, each finalist has an equal chance of being selected. The only rationale for the selection of a person is the "luck of the draw." For example, the six names from Exhibit 10.9 could be put in a hat and the finalist drawn out. The one drawn out would be the person selected and tendered a job offer. This approach has the advantage of being quick. Also, with random selection, one cannot be accused of favouritism because everyone has an equal chance of being selected. The disadvantage to this approach is that discretionary assessments are simply ignored.

Ranking

With ranking, finalists are ordered from the most desirable to the least desirable based on results of discretionary assessments. As shown in Exhibit 10.9, the person ranked 1 (Keisha) is the most desirable, and the person ranked 6 (Luis) is the least desirable. It is important to note that desirability should be viewed in the context of the entire selection process. When this is done, persons with lower levels of desirability (e.g., ranks of 3, 4, 5) should not be viewed necessarily as failures. Job offers are extended to people on the basis of their rank ordering, with the person ranked 1 receiving the first offer. Should that person turn down the job offer or suddenly withdraw from the selection process, then the finalist ranked 2 receives the offer, and so on.

EXHIBIT 10.9 Methods of Final Choice

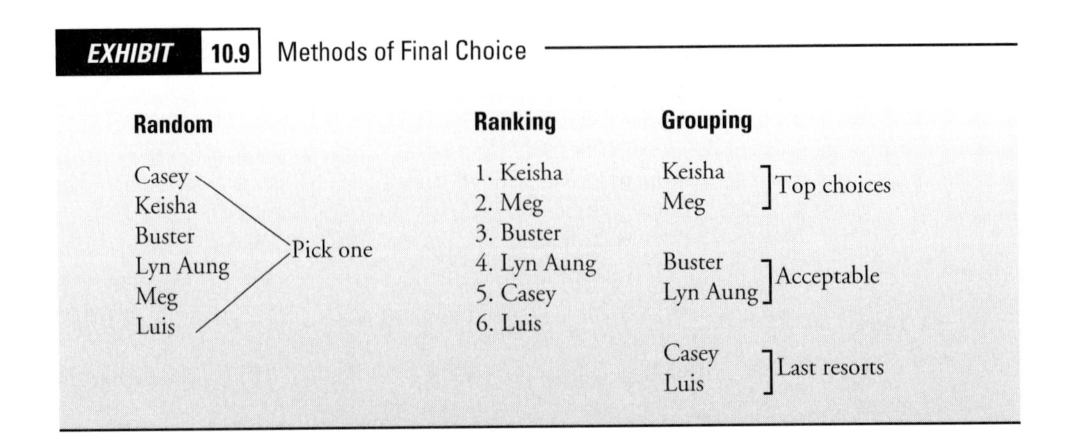

The advantage to ranking is that it provides an indication of the relative worth of each finalist for the job. It also provides a set of backups should one or more of the finalists withdraw from the process.

It should be remembered that backup finalists may decide to withdraw from the process to take a position elsewhere. Although ranking does give the organization a cushion if the top choices withdraw from the process, it does not mean that the process of job offers can proceed at a leisurely pace. Immediate action needs to be taken with the top choices in case they decide to withdraw and there is a need to go to backups. This is especially true in tight labour markets where there is a strong demand for the services of people on the ranking list.

Grouping

With the grouping method, finalists are banded together into rank-ordered categories. For example, in Exhibit 10.9, the finalists are grouped according to whether they are top choices, acceptable, or last resorts. The advantage of this method is that it permits ties among finalists, thus avoiding the need to assign a different rank to each person. The disadvantage is that choices still have to be made from among the top choices. These might be made on the basis of factors such as probability of each person accepting the offer.

EMPLOYMENT CONTRACTS

Covered next are some very basic, yet subtle, issues associated with employment contracts. It is crucial to understand the elements that comprise a legally enforceable contract, and the form of the contract (e.g., written, oral), disclaimers, fulfillment of other conditions, reneging on an offer or acceptance, and other sources (e.g., employee handbooks) that may also constitute a portion of the total employment contract.

Requirements for an Enforceable Contract

There are three basic elements required for a contract to be legally binding and enforceable: offer, acceptance, and consideration.[30] If any one of these is missing, there is no binding contract.

Offer The offer is usually made by the employer. It is composed of the terms and conditions of employment desired and proposed by the employer. The terms must be clear and specific enough to be acted on by the offer receiver. Vague statements and offers are unacceptable (e.g., "Come to work for me right now; we'll work out the details later"). The contents of newspaper ads for the job and general written employer material, such as a brochure describing the organization, probably are also too vague to be considered offers. Both the employer and the offer receiver should have a definite understanding of the specific terms being proposed.

Acceptance To constitute a contract, the offer must be accepted on the terms as offered. Thus, if the employer offers a salary of $35,000 per year, the offer receiver must either accept or reject that term. Acceptance of an offer on a contingency basis does not constitute an acceptance. If the offer receiver responds to the salary offer of $35,000 by saying, "Pay me $37,500, and I'll come to work for you," this is not an acceptance. Rather, it is a counteroffer, and the employer must now either formally accept or reject it.

The offer receiver must also accept the offer in the manner specified in the offer. If the offer requires acceptance in writing, for example, the offer receiver must accept it in writing. Or, if the offer requires acceptance by a certain date, it must be accepted by that date.

Consideration Consideration entails the exchange of something of value between the parties to the contract. Usually, it involves an exchange of promises. The employer offers or promises to provide compensation to the offer receiver in exchange for labour, and the offer receiver promises to provide labour to the employer in exchange for compensation. The exchange of promises must be firm and of value, which is usually quite straightforward. Occasionally, consideration can become an issue. For example, if the employer makes an offer to a person that requires a response by a certain date, and then does not hear from the person, there is no contract, even though the employer thought that they "had a deal."

Form of the Contract

Employment contracts may be written, oral, or even a combination of the two.[31] All may be legally binding and enforceable. Within this broad parameter, however, are numerous caveats and considerations.

Written Contracts A written contract may take many forms, and all may be legally enforceable. Examples of a written document that may be construed as a contract include a letter of offer and acceptance (the usual example), a statement on a job application blank (such as an applicant voucher to the truthfulness of information provided), internal job posting notices, and statements in employee handbooks or other personnel manuals. The more specific the information and statements in such documents, the more likely they are to be considered employment contracts.

Unintended problems may arise with these documents. They may become interpreted as enforceable contracts even though that was not their intent (perhaps the intent was merely informational). Or, statements on a given term or condition of employment may contradict each other in various documents.

Care must thus be taken to ensure that all written documents accurately convey only the intended meanings regarding terms and conditions of employment. To this end, the following suggestions should be heeded:[32]

- Before putting anything in writing, ask, "Does the company mean to be held to this?"
- Choose words carefully; where appropriate, avoid using words that imply binding commitment.
- Make sure all related documents are consistent with each other.
- Always have a second person review what another has written.
- Form the habit of looking at the entire hiring procedure and consider any writings within that context.

Oral Contracts While oral contracts may be every bit as binding as written contracts, in the absence of written statements to the contrary, oral statements may indeed be enforceable. For example, if the letter of appointment was silent on the issue of weekend work, then the oral promise of no weekend work might well be enforceable.

More generally, oral statements are more likely to be enforceable as employment contract terms under the following conditions:[33]

- When there is no written statement regarding the term (e.g., weekend work) in question
- When the term is quite certain ("You will not have to work on weekends," as opposed to, "Occasionally, we work weekends around here")
- When the person making the oral statement is in a position of authority to do so (e.g., the hiring manager as opposed to a co-worker)
- The more formal the circumstances in which the statement was made (the manager's office as opposed to around the bar or dinner table as part of a recruiting trip), and
- The more specific the promise ("You will work every other Saturday from 8 a.m. to 5 p.m.," as opposed to, "You may have to work from 8 a.m. to the middle of the afternoon on the weekends, but we'll try to hold that to a minimum")

As this discussion makes clear, from a legal perspective, oral statements are a potential minefield in establishing employment contracts. They obviously cannot be avoided (employer and applicant have to speak to each other), and they may serve other legitimate and desired outcomes, such as providing realistic recruitment information to job applicants. Nonetheless, the organization should use oral statements with extreme caution and alert all members to its policies regarding their use. As further protection, the organization should include in its written offer that, by accepting the offer, the employee agrees the organization has made no other promises than those contained in the written offer.

Disclaimers

A disclaimer is a statement (oral or written) that explicitly limits an employee right and reserves that right for the employer.[34] Disclaimers are often used in letters of appointment, job application blanks, and employee handbooks.

For example, the employer explicitly makes no promise of any job security and reserves the right to terminate the employment relationship. The following is an example of such a disclaimer that survived legal challenge:

> In consideration of my employment, I agree to conform to the rules and regulations of [Acme Company], and recognize that employment and compensation can be terminated, with or without cause, and with or without notice, at any time, at the option of either the company or myself. I understand that no store manager or representative of [Acme Company], other than the president or vice-president of the company, has any authority to enter into any agreement for employment for any specified period of time, or to make any agreement contrary to the foregoing.[35]

An employment disclaimer should appear in the job offer letter. It should also appear on the application blank, along with two other disclaimers (see Chapter 7). First, there should be a statement of consent by the applicant for the organization to check provided references, along with a waiver of the right to make claims against them for anything they said. Second, there should be a so-called false statement warning, indicating that any false statement, misleading statement, or material omission may be grounds for dismissal.

Disclaimers are generally enforceable. They can thus serve as an important component of employment contracts. Their use should be guided by the following set of recommendations:[36]

1. They should be clearly stated and conspicuously placed in appropriate documents.
2. The employee should acknowledge receipt and review of the document and the disclaimer.

3. The disclaimer should state that it may be modified only in writing and by whom.
4. The terms and conditions of employment, including the disclaimer, as well as limits on their enforceability, should be reviewed with offer receivers and employees.

It would be wise to obtain legal counsel for drafting language for all disclaimers.

Contingencies

Often, the employer may wish to make a job offer that is contingent on certain other conditions being fulfilled by the offer receiver.[37] Examples of such contingencies include (1) passage of a particular test, such as a licensure exam (e.g., CPA or bar exam); (2) passage of a medical exam; (3) satisfactory background and reference checks; and (4) proof of employability.

Though contingencies to a contract are generally enforceable, contingencies to an employment contract (especially those involving any of the preceding examples) are exceedingly complex and may be made only within defined limits. For this reason, contingencies should not be used in employment contracts without prior legal counsel.

JOB OFFERS

A job offer is an attempt by the organization to induce the offer receiver into the establishment of an employment relationship. Assuming that the offer is accepted and that consideration is met, the organization and offer receiver will have established their relationship in the form of a legally binding employment contract. That contract is the culmination of the staffing process. The contract also signifies that the person/job match process has concluded and that the person/job match is now about to become a reality. That reality, in turn, becomes the start of, and foundation for, subsequent employee effectiveness on the various HR outcomes. For these reasons, the content and extension of the job offer become critical final parts of the overall staffing process.

This section discusses the actual content of job offers, along with some of the complexities associated with that.

Job Offer Content

The organization has considerable latitude in the terms and conditions of employment that it may offer to people. That latitude, of course, should be exercised within the organization's particular applicant attraction strategy, as well as the rewards generally available and shown in the job rewards matrix.

With some degree of latitude in terms and conditions offered for almost any job, it is apparent that job offers should be carefully constructed. There are definite rewards that can, and for the most part should, be addressed in any job offer. Moreover, the precise terms or content of the offer to any given finalist requires careful forethought. What follows is a discussion of the types of rewards to address, as well as some of their subtleties and complexities.

Starting Date Normally, the organization desires to control when the employment relationship begins. To do so, it must provide a definite starting date in its offer. If it does not, acceptance and consideration of the offer occurs at the time the new hire actually begins work. Normally, the starting date is one that allows the offer receiver at least two weeks to provide notification of resignation to a current employer.

Duration of Contract Employment contracts may be of a fixed term (i.e., have a definite ending date) or indeterminate term (i.e., have no definite ending date).

A fixed-term contract provides certainty to both the new hire and organization regarding the length of the employment relationship. Both parties decide to and must abide by an agreed-on term of employment. The organization can then terminate the contract prior to its expiration date for "just cause" only. Determination and demonstration of just cause can be a complicated legal problem for the organization.

A compromise between a fixed-term and indefinite-term provision is to have a contract provision that states it is for an indefinite term, that the employer may terminate the agreement at any time for good cause, and that either the employer or the employee may terminate the contract on 30 days' (or some other time period) written notice. Such a provision provides protection to the employee against arbitrary, immediate termination, and to the employer against a sudden and unanticipated loss of an employee.[38]

Compensation Compensation is the most important reward that the organization has to offer in its attraction strategy. It is a multifaceted reward that may be presented to the offer receiver in many forms. Sometimes that may consist of a standard pay rate and benefits package, which must be simply accepted or rejected. Other times the offer may be more tailor made, often negotiated in advance.

Benefits Normally there is a fixed benefits package for a job, and it is offered as such to all offer receivers. Examples include health insurance and retirement and work/life plans. When a fixed or standard benefits package is offered, the offer letter should not spell out all of the specific benefit provisions. Rather, it should state that the employee will be eligible to participate in the benefit plans maintained by the organization, as provided in written descriptions of these plans. In this way, the job offer letter does not inadvertently make statements or promises that contradict or go beyond the organization's actual benefits plan.

Hours Statements regarding hours of work should be carefully thought out and worded. For the organization, such statements will affect staffing flexibility and cost. In terms of flexibility, a statement such as, "Hours of work will be as needed and scheduled," provides maximum flexibility. Designation of work as part time, as opposed to full time, may affect cost because the organization may provide restricted, if any, benefits to part-time employees.

Factors other than just number of hours may also need to be addressed in the job offer. If there are to be any special, tailor-made hours of work arrangements, these need to be clearly spelled out. Examples include "Weekend work will not be required of you," and "Your hours of work will be from 7:30 to 11:30 a.m. and 1:30 to 5:30 p.m." Overtime hours requirements and overtime pay, if applicable, could also be addressed.

Special Hiring Inducements At times, the organization may want or need to offer special inducements to enhance the distinctiveness of the employee value proposition (EVP) to increase the likelihood that an offer will be accepted. Examples of these inducements are hiring bonuses, relocation assistance, and severance packages.

Hiring Bonuses. Hiring, signing, or "up-front" bonuses are one-time payments offered and subsequently paid on acceptance of the offer. Typically, the bonus is in the form of an outright cash grant; the bonus may also be in the form of a cash advance against future expected earnings.

One example of hiring bonuses is that employed by brokerage firms, who have long used them as a way of luring applicants away from competitors. Bonuses up to $100,000 are not uncommon. The bonus is usually a combination of cash grant and cash advance against future sales commissions.[39]

Generally, as labour markets tighten and employee shortages increase, hiring bonuses become more prevalent and of larger size. This happens at all job levels, including nondegree jobs such as fast food workers, butchers, bartenders, hairstylists, and pizza cooks.[40] The converse is also true, with looser labour markets and employee surpluses leading to lesser or disappearing hiring bonuses.

In addition to simply helping attract highly desired individuals (monetary flattery), hiring bonuses can provide an offset for something the offer receiver may give up by changing jobs, such as a pending pay raise or a promotion. Also, hiring bonuses might be a useful way to lure people to rural areas or to offset relocation costs or higher cost of living. Finally, use of a hiring bonus might help in avoiding a permanent elevation in base pay, thus holding down labour costs.

Offers of hiring bonuses should be used judiciously, or they will lose their particular distinctiveness as part of the EVP, as well as lead to other problems. For example, while it is desirable to maintain a policy of flexibility as to the use and amount of hiring bonuses, it is necessary to carefully monitor them so that they do not get out of control. Also, it is important to avoid getting into overly spirited hiring bonus bidding wars with competitors—the other rewards of the job need to be emphasized in addition to the bonus. Another danger is that hiring bonuses might give rise to feelings of jealousy and inequity, necessitating the need for retention bonuses if existing employees get wind of the bonuses being given to new hires. To avoid this possibility, hiring bonuses should be considered confidential.[41] Another potential problem is that bonus recipients may be tempted to "take the money and run," and their performance motivation may be lessened because their bonus money is not contingent on their job performance.

To address these problems, the organization may place restrictions on the bonus payment, paying half up front and the other half after some designated time period, such as 6 or 12 months; another option is to make payment of a portion or all of the bonus contingent on meeting certain performance goals within a designated time period. Such payment arrangements should help other employees see the hiring bonus as not a total "freebie" and should encourage only serious and committed offer receivers to actually accept the offer.[42]

Relocation Assistance. Acceptance of the offer may require a geographic move and entail relocation costs for the offer receiver. The organization may want to provide assistance to conduct the move, as well as totally or partially defray moving costs. Thus, a relocation package may include assistance with house hunting, guaranteed purchase of the applicant's home, a mortgage subsidy, actual moving cost reimbursement and a cost-of-living adjustment if the move is to a higher-cost area. To simplify things, a lump-sum relocation allowance may be provided, thus reducing record keeping and other paperwork.[43]

Severance Packages. Terms and conditions that the organization states the employee is entitled to upon departure from the organization constitute a severance package. Content of the package typically includes one or two weeks of pay for every year of service, earned vacation and holiday pay, extended health insurance coverage and premium payment, and outplacement assistance in finding a new job.[44] What is the organization willing to provide?

Restrictions on Employees In some situations, the organization may want to place certain restrictions on employees to protect its own interests. These restrictions should be known, and agreed to, by the new employee at the time of hire. As such, they should be incorporated into the job offer and resultant employment contract.

One form of restriction involves so-called confidentiality clauses that prohibit current or departing employees from the unauthorized use or disclosure of confidential information during or after employment. Confidential information is any information not made public and that gives the organization an advantage over its competitors. Examples of such information include trade secrets, customer lists, secret formulas, manufacturing processes, marketing and pricing plans, and business forecasts. It will be necessary to spell out, in some degree, exactly what information the organization considers confidential, as well as the time period after employment for which confidentiality must be maintained.

Another restriction, known as a noncompete agreement, seeks to keep departed employees from competing against the organization. Such agreements cannot keep departed employees from practicing their trade or profession completely or indefinitely, for this would in essence restrict the person from earning a living in a chosen field. Accordingly, the noncompete agreement must be crafted carefully in order to be enforceable. The agreement should probably not be a blanket statement that applies to all employees, but only to employees who truly could turn into competitors, such as high-level managers, scientists, and technical staff. Also, the agreement must be limited in time and geography.

Acceptance Terms The job offer should specify terms of acceptance required of the offer receiver. For reasons previously noted regarding oral contracts, acceptances should normally be required in writing only. The receiver should be required to accept or reject the offer in total, without revision. Any other form of acceptance is not an acceptance, merely a counteroffer. Finally, the offer should specify the date, if any, by which it will lapse. A lapse date is recommended so that certainty and closure are brought to the offer process.

Job Offer Letter A job offer letter should be read and analyzed for purposes of becoming familiar with job offer letters, as well as gaining an appreciation for the many points that need to be addressed in such a letter. Remember that normally, whatever is put in the job offer letter, once accepted by the receiver, becomes a binding employment contract. Examples of more complex job offer letters, more relevant to executives, might also be consulted.

LEGAL ISSUES

The legal issue of major importance in decision making is that of cut scores or hiring standards. These scores or standards regulate the flow of individuals from applicant to candidate to finalist. Throughout this flow, adverse impact may occur.

If there is no adverse impact in decision making, the discretion being exercised by the organization as it makes its selection decisions is thus unconstrained legally. If there is adverse impact occurring, however, then human rights concerns exist.

Recall that under the conditions set out in the Tawney Meiorin decision (see Chapter 2) that organizations are directed to show that a standard is reasonably necessary for the effective accomplishment for a given work purpose. This is particularly relevant to setting cut scores. In the Meiorin case, the cut score for the 12-minute run, aside from being based on a male-biased sample, was not defensible as a standard that was reasonably necessary in order to work effectively as a forest firefighter. Thus, even with a valid predictor, an organization needs to be cautious that its hiring standards are not set so high that they discriminate against designated group members and fail as a justifiable bona fide occupational requirement (BFOR). The other issue that an organization must consider is that it may be necessary to accommodate job candidates by using alternative selection procedures that present fewer difficulties in regard to adverse impact for designated group members.

SUMMARY

The selection component of a staffing system requires that decisions be made in several areas. The critical concerns are deciding which predictors (assessment methods) to use, determining assessment scores and setting cut scores, making final decisions about applicants, considering who within the organization should help make selection decisions, and complying with legal guidance.

In deciding which assessment methods to use, consideration should be given to the validity coefficient and its correlation with other predictors, adverse impact, utility, and applicant reactions. Ideally, a predictor would have a validity coefficient with large magnitude and significance, low correlations with other predictors, little adverse impact, and high utility. In practice, this ideal situation is hard to achieve, so decisions about trade-offs are necessary.

How assessment scores are determined depends on whether a single predictor or multiple predictors are used. In the case of a single predictor, assessment scores are simply the scores on the predictor. With multiple predictors, a compensatory, multiple hurdles, or combined model must be used. A compensatory model allows a person to compensate for a low score on one predictor with a high score on another predictor. A multiple hurdles model requires that a person achieve a passing score on each successive predictor. A combined model uses elements of both the compensatory and multiple hurdles models.

In deciding who earns a passing score on a predictor or combination of predictors, cut scores must be set. When doing so the consequences of setting different levels of cut scores should be considered, especially those of assessing some applicants as false positives and false negatives. Approaches to determining cut scores include minimum competency, top-down, and banding methods. Guidelines are reviewed on how best to set cut scores.

Methods of final choice involve determining, from among those who have passed the initial hurdles, who will receive job offers. Several methods of making these decisions are reviewed, including random selection, ranking, and grouping. Each has advantages and disadvantages.

A basic concern is how to set cut scores in ways that help minimize adverse impact. Finally, after making a decision on the prospective job candidates an employment contract is drafted for the prospective employee's consideration. The contract must provide sufficient detail on the terms and conditions of work so that individuals can make an informed decision on whether the offer is acceptable.

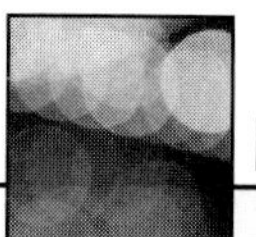

KEY TERMS

banding 351 minimum competency 349 top-down 350

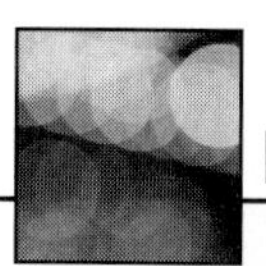

DISCUSSION QUESTIONS

1. Your boss is considering using a new predictor. The base rate is high, the selection ratio is low, and the validity coefficient is high for the current predictor. What would you advise your boss and why?
2. What are the positive consequences associated with a high predictor cut score? What are the negative consequences?
3. Under what circumstances should a compensatory model be used? When should a multiple hurdles model be used?
4. What are the advantages of ranking as a method of final choice over random selection?
5. What roles should HR professionals play in staffing decisions? Why?

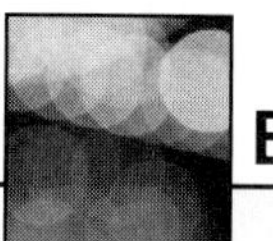

ETHICAL ISSUES

1. Do you think companies should use banding in selection decisions? Defend your position.
2. Is clinical prediction the fairest way to combine assessment information about job applicants, or are the other methods (unit weighting, rational weighting, multiple regression) fairer? Why?

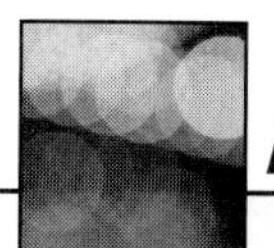

APPLICATIONS

Utility Concerns in Choosing an Assessment Method

Randy May is a 32-year-old airplane mechanic for a small airline based in Ontario's Muskoka region. Recently, Randy won $2 million in the lottery. Because Randy is relatively young, he decided to invest his winnings in a business to create a future stream of earnings. After weighing many investment decisions, Randy opted to open up a chain of ice cream shops in several towns in the Muskoka area. Based on his own budgeting, Randy figured he had enough cash to open shops in four towns. Randy contracted with a local builder and the construction/renovation of the four shops is well under way.

The task that is occupying Randy's attention now is how to staff the shops. Two weeks ago, he placed advertisements in three area newspapers. So far, he has received 100 applications. Randy has done some informal HR planning and figures he needs to hire 50 employees to staff the four shops. Being a novice at this, Randy is unsure how to select the 50 people he needs to hire. Randy consulted his friend, Mary, who owns the lunch counter at the airport. Mary advised Randy that she used the interview to get "the most knowledgeable people possible," and recommended it to Randy because her people had "generally worked out well." While Randy greatly respected Mary's advice, on reflection several questions came to mind. Does Mary's use of the interview mean that it meets Randy's requirements? How could Randy determine whether his chosen method of selecting employees was effective or ineffective?

Confused, Randy also sought the advice of Professor Ray Higgins, from whom Randy took an HR management course while getting his business degree. After learning of the situation and offering his consulting services, Professor Higgins suggested that Randy choose between one of two selection methods (after paying Professor Higgins' consulting fees, he cannot afford to use both methods). The two methods Professor Higgins recommended are, like Mary, the interview and also a work sample test that entails scooping ice cream and serving it to the customer. Randy estimates that it would cost $100 to interview an applicant and $150 per applicant to administer the work sample. Professor Higgins has told Randy that the validity of the interview is r = .30 while the validity of the work sample is r = .50. Professor Higgins also informed Randy that if the selection ratio is .50, the average score on the selection measure of those applicants selected is z = .80 (.80 standard deviations above the mean). Randy plans to offer employees a wage of $7.75 per hour. (Over the course of a year, this would amount to a full-time salary of $15,500.)

Based on the information presented above, Randy would really appreciate it if you could help him answer the following questions:

1. How much money would Randy save using each selection method?
2. If Randy can use only one method, which should he use?
3. If the number of applicants increases to 200 (more applications are coming in every day), how would your answers to questions 1 and 2 change?
4. What limitations are inherent in the estimates you have made?

Choosing Entrants into a Management Training Program

Come As You Are, a convenience store chain headquartered in Lethbridge, Alberta, has developed an assessment program to promote employees into its management training program. The minimum entrance requirements into the program are five years of company experience, a university degree from an accredited university, and a minimum acceptable job performance rating (3 or higher on their 1–5 scale). Any interested applicant into the program can enrol in the half-day assessment program, where the following assessments are made:

1. Cognitive ability test
2. Handwriting test
3. Integrity test
4. Signed permission for background test
5. Brief (30-minute) interview by various members of the management team

At the Fort MacLeod store, 11 applicants have applied for openings in the management training program. The selection information on the candidates is provided in the nearby exhibit. (The scoring key is provided at the bottom of the exhibit.) It is estimated that there are three slots in the program available for qualified candidates from the Fort MacLeod location. Given this information and what you know about external and internal selection, as well as staffing decision making, answer the following questions:

1. How would you go about the process of making decisions about whom to select for the openings? In other words, without providing your decisions for the individual candidates, describe how you would weigh the various selection information to reach a decision.
2. Using the decision-making process from the previous question, which applicant would you select into the training program? Explain your decisions.
3. Although the data provided in the exhibit reveals that all selection measures were given to all 11 candidates, would you advise Come As You Are to continue to administer all the predictors at one time during the half-day assessment program? Or, should the predictors be given in a sequence so that a multiple hurdles or combined approach could be used? Explain your recommendation.

EXHIBIT

Predictor Scores for Eleven Applicants to Management Training Program

Name	Company Experience	University Degree	Performance Rating	Cognitive Ability Test	Handwriting Test	Integrity Test	Background Test	Interview Rating
Radhu	4	Yes	4	9	3	6	OK	6
Merv	12	Yes	3	3	9	6	OK	8
Marianne	9	Yes	4	8	1	5	Arrest '95	4
Helmut	5	Yes	4	5	4	5	OK	4
Siobhan	14	Yes	5	7	6	8	OK	8
Galina	7	No	3	3	7	4	OK	6
Raul	6	Yes	4	7	7	8	OK	2
Frank	9	Yes	5	2	10	5	OK	7
Osvaldo	10	Yes	4	10	3	9	OK	3
Byron	18	Yes	3	3	8	7	OK	6
Aletha	11	Yes	4	7	4	6	OK	5
Scale	*Years*	*Yes–No*	*1–5*	*1–10*	*1–10*	*1–10*	*OK–Other*	*1–10*

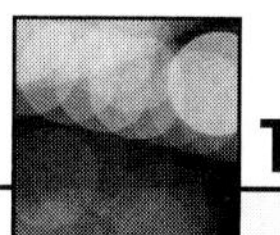

TANGLEWOOD STORES CASE

The cases you have considered up to this point have involved making aggregated decisions about a large number of applicants. After gathering relevant information, there are still the important tasks of determining how to combine this information to arrive at a set of candidates. This case combines several concepts from the chapters on selection and decision making.

The Situation

Tanglewood is faced with a situation in which eleven qualified applicants have advanced to the candidate stage for the job of store manager. These individuals have submitted resumés, completed several standardized tests similar to those described in the case on measurement, and engaged in initial interviews. There is considerable debate among the regional management staff that is responsible for selecting store managers about which of these candidates are best qualified to make it to the finalist stage, and they have asked you to help them reach a more informed decision.

Your Tasks

You will select the top candidates for the finalist pool by using various combinations of the predictors. The methods for combining predictors will include clinical prediction, unit weighting, rational weighting, and a multiple hurdle model. In your answers you will provide detailed descriptions of how you made decisions and also assess how comfortable you are with the results. You will also describe what you think are appropriate minimal cut scores for each of the predictors. The background information for this case, and your specific assignment, can be found at www.mcgrawhill.ca/OLC/heneman.

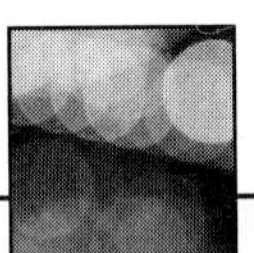

ENDNOTES

1. L. G. Grimm and P. R. Yarnold, *Reading and Understanding Multivariate Statistics* (Washington, DC: American Psychological Association, 1995).
2. C. Handler and S. Hunt, "Estimating the Financial Value of Staffing-Assessment Tools," *Workforce Management,* March 2003, (www.workforce.com); J. Sullivan, "The True Value of Hiring and Retaining Top Performers," *Workforce Management,* Aug. 2002 (www.workforce.com).
3. M. C. Sturman and T. A. Judge, "Utility Analysis for Multiple Selection Devices and Multiple Outcomes," Working paper, Cornell University, 1994.
4. J. Hersch, "Equal Employment Opportunity Law and Firm Profitability," *Journal of Human Resources,* 1991, 26, pp. 139–153.
5. G. V. Barrett, R. A. Alexander, and D. Doverspike, "The Implications for Personnel Selection of Apparent Declines in Predictive Validities over Time: A Critique of Hulin, Henry, and Noon," *Personnel Psychology,* 1992, 45, pp. 601–617; C. L. Hulin, R. A. Henry, and S. L. Noon, "Adding a Dimension: Time as a Factor in Predictive Relationships," *Psychological Bulletin,* 1990, 107, pp. 328–340; C. T. Keil and J. M. Cortina, "Degradation of Validity over Time: A Test and Extension of Ackerman's Model," *Psychological Bulletin,* 2001, 127, pp. 673–697.
6. J. W. Boudreau, M. C. Sturman, and T. A. Judge, "Utility Analysis: What Are the Black Boxes, and Do They Affect Decisions?," in N. Anderson and P. Herriot (eds.), *Assessment and Selection in Organizations* (Chichester, England: Wiley, 1994), pp. 77–96.
7. K. M. Murphy, "When Your Top Choice Turns You Down," *Psychological Bulletin,* 1986, 99, pp. 133–138; F. L. Schmidt, M. J. Mack, and J. E. Hunter, "Selection Utility in the Occupation of US Park Ranger for Three Modes of Test Use," *Journal of Applied Psychology,* 1984, 69, pp. 490–497.
8. T. H. Macan and S. Highhouse, "Communicating the Utility of Human Resource Activities: A Survey of I/O and HR Professionals," *Journal of Business and Psychology,* 1994, 8, pp. 425–436.
9. K. C. Carson, J. S. Becker, and J. A. Henderson, "Is Utility Really Futile? A Failure to Replicate and an Extension," *Journal of Applied Psychology,* 1998, 83, pp. 84–96; J. T. Hazer and S. Highhouse, "Factors Influencing Managers' Reactions to Utility Analysis: Effects of SDy Method, Information Frame, and Focal Intervention," *Journal of Applied Psychology,* 1997, 82, pp. 104–112; G. P. Latham and G. Whyte, "The Futility of Utility Analysis," *Personnel Psychology,* 1994, 47, pp. 31–46; G. Whyte and G. Latham, "The Futility of Utility Analysis Revisited: When Even an Expert Fails," *Personnel Psychology,* 1997, 50, pp. 601–610.

10. C. J. Russell, A. Colella, and P. Bobko, "Expanding the Context of Utility: The Strategic Impact of Personnel Selection," *Personnel Psychology,* 1993, 46, pp. 781–801.
11. J. Sawyer, "Measurement and Predictions, Clinical and Statistical," *Psychological Bulletin,* 1966, 66, pp. 178–200; D. Westen and J. Weinberger, "When Clinical Description Becomes Statistical Prediction," *American Psychologist,* 2004, 59, pp. 595–613.
12. F. L. Schmidt, "The Relative Efficiency of Regression and Sample Unit Predictor Weights in Applied Differential Psychology," *Educational and Psychological Measurement,* 1971, 31, pp. 699–714.
13. Y. Ganzach, A. N. Kluger, and N. Klayman, "Making Decisions from an Interview: Expert Measurement and Mechanical Combination," *Personnel Psychology,* 2000, 53, pp. 1–20.
14. W. F. Cascio, R. A. Alexander, and G. V. Barrett, "Setting Cutoff Scores: Legal, Psychometric, and Professional Issues and Guidelines," *Personnel Psychology,* 1988, 41, pp. 1–24.
15. J. Bennett, "Scientific Hiring Strategies are Raising Productivity While Reducing Turnover," *Wall Street Journal,* February 10, 2004, p. B7.
16. S. J. Wells, "Too Good to Hire?" *HR Magazine,* October 2004, pp. 48–54.
17. W. H. Angoff, "Scales, Norms, and Equivalent Scores," in R. L. Thorndike (ed.), *Educational Measurement* (Washington, DC: American Council on Education, 1971), pp. 508–600; R. E. Biddle, "How to Set Cutoff Scores for Knowledge Tests Used in Promotion, Training, Certification, and Licensing," *Public Personnel Management,* 1993, 22, pp. 63–79.
18. J. P. Hudson, Jr., and J. E. Campion, "Hindsight Bias in an Application of the Angoff Method for Setting Cutoff Scores," *Journal of Applied Psychology,* 1994, 79, pp. 860–865.
19. P. R. Sackett and S. L. Wilk, "Within-Group Norming and Other Forms of Score Adjustment in Preemployment Testing," *American Psychologist,* 1994, 49, pp. 929–954.
20. W. F. Cascio, J. Duttz, S. Zedeck, and I. L. Goldstein, "Statistical Implications of Six Methods of Test Score Use in Personnel Selection," *Human Performance,* 1991, 4, pp. 233–264; P. R. Sackett and L. Roth, "A Monte Carlo Examination of Banding and Rank Order Selection Methods of Test Score Use in Personnel Selection," *Human Performance,* 1991, 4, pp. 279–296.
21. K. R. Murphy, K. Osten, and B. Myors, "Modeling the Effects of Banding in Personnel Selection," *Personnel Psychology,* 1995, 48, pp. 61–84.
22. R. M. Guion, "Banding Background and General Management Purpose," in H. Aguinis (ed.), *Test-Score Banding in Human Resource Selection* (Westport, CT: Praeger, 2004), pp. 49–69.
23. K. R. Murphy, "Potential Effects of Banding as a Function of Test Reliability," *Personnel Psychology,* 1994, 47, pp. 477–495.
24. Sackett and Wilk, "Within-Group Norming and Other Forms of Score Adjustment in Preemployment Testing."
25. D. M. Truxillo and T. N. Bauer, "Applicant Reactions to Test Score Banding in Entry-Level and Promotional Contexts," *Journal of Applied Psychology,* 1999, 84, pp. 322–339.
26. M. A. Campion, J. L. Duttz, S. Zedeck, F. L. Schmidt, J. F. Kehoe, K. R. Murphy, and R. M. Guion, "The Controversy over Banding in Personnel Selection: Answers to 10 Key Questions," *Personnel Psychology,* 2001, 54, 149–185; W. F. Cascio, I. L. Goldstein, J. buttz, and S. Zedeck, "Social and Technical Issues in Staffing Decisions," in H. Aguinis (ed.), *Test-Score Banding in Human Resource Selection,* pp. 7–28.
27. W. Arthur, D. Doverspike, and G. V. Barrett, "Development of a Job Analysis-Based Procedure for Weighting and Combining Content-Related Tests into a Single

Test Battery Score," *Personnel Psychology,* 1996, 49, pp. 971–985; P. R. Sackett and J. E. Ellingson, "The Effects of Forming Multi-Predictor Composites on Group Differences and Adverse Impact," *Personnel Psychology,* 1997, 50, pp. 707–721; P. R. Sackett and L. Roth, "Multi-Stage Selection Strategies: A Monte Carlo Investigation of Effects on Performance and Minority Hiring," *Personnel Psychology,* 1996, 49, pp. 549–572; N. Schmitt, D. Chan, L. Sheppard, and D. Jennings, "Adverse Impact and Predictive Efficiency of Various Predictor Combinations," *Journal of Applied Psychology,* 82, pp. 719–730.

28. P. R. Sackett, N. Schmitt, J. E. Ellingson, and M. B. Kabin, "High-Stakes Testing in Employment, Credentialing, and Higher Education," *American Psychologist,* 2001, 56, pp. 302–318.
29. W. De Corte, "Weighing Job Performance Predictors to Both Maximize the Quality of the Selected Workforce and Control the Level of Adverse Impact," *Journal of Applied Psychology,* 1999, 84, pp. 695–702; K. Hattrup, J. Rock, and C. Scalia, "The Effects of Varying Conceptualizations of Job Performance on Adverse Impact, Minority Hiring, and Predictor Performance," *Journal of Applied Psychology,* 1997, 82, pp. 656–664.
30. M. W. Bennett, D. J. Polden, and H. J. Rubin, *Employment Relationships: Law and Practice* (New York: Aspen, 2004), pp. 3–3 to 3–4; A. G. Feliu, *Primer on Individual Employee Rights,* second ed. (Washington, DC: Bureau of National Affairs, 1996), pp. 7–29; G. P. Panaro, *Employment Law Manual* (Boston, MA: Warren, Gorham and Lamont, 1993), pp. 4–2 to 4–4.
31. Bennett, Polden, and Rubin, *Employment Relationships: Law and Practice,* pp. 3–22 to 3–23; Panaro, *Employment Law Manual,* pp. 4–5 to 4–60.
32. Panaro, *Employment Law Manual,* pp. 4–18 to 4–19.
33. Feliu, *Primer on Individual Employee Rights,* pp. 48–51.
34. Bennett, Polden, and Rubin, *Employment Relationships: Law and Practice,* pp. 3–30 to 3–32; Feliu, *Primer on Individual Employee Rights,* pp. 22–25.
35. Feliu, *Primer on Individual Employee Rights,* p. 24.
36. Feliu, *Primer on Individual Employee Rights,* p. 26.
37. Panaro, *Employment Law Manual,* pp. 4–66 to 4–136.
38. D. S. Fortney and B. Nuterangelo, "Written Employment Contracts: When?, How?, Why?" *Legal Report,* Society for Human Resource Management, Spring 1998, pp. 5–8.
39. W. Power and M. Siconolfi, "Wall Street Sours on Up-Front Bonuses," *Wall Street Journal,* June 13, 1991, p. C1.
40. J. S. Lublin, "Now Butchers, Engineers Get Signing Bonuses," *Wall Street Journal,* June 2, 1997, p. B1.
41. M. E. Medland, "When to Pay Signing Bonuses," *HR Magazine,* December 2003, pp. 99–102.
42. J. R. Bratkovich and J. Ragusa, "The Perils of the Signing Bonus," *Employment Management Today,* Spring 1998, pp. 22–25.
43. L. G. Klaff, "Tough Sell," *Workforce Management,* November 2003, pp. 47–50; J. S. Lublin, "The Going Rate," *Wall Street Journal,* January 11, 2000, p. B14.
44. J. S. Lublin, "You Should Negotiate a Severence Package—Even Before the Job Starts," *Wall Street Journal,* May 1, 2001, p. B1.

Online **LearningCentre**

Visit the Online Learning Centre at
www.mcgrawhill.ca/olc/heneman

PART 5

Retention and Staffing System Management

The Staffing Organizations Model

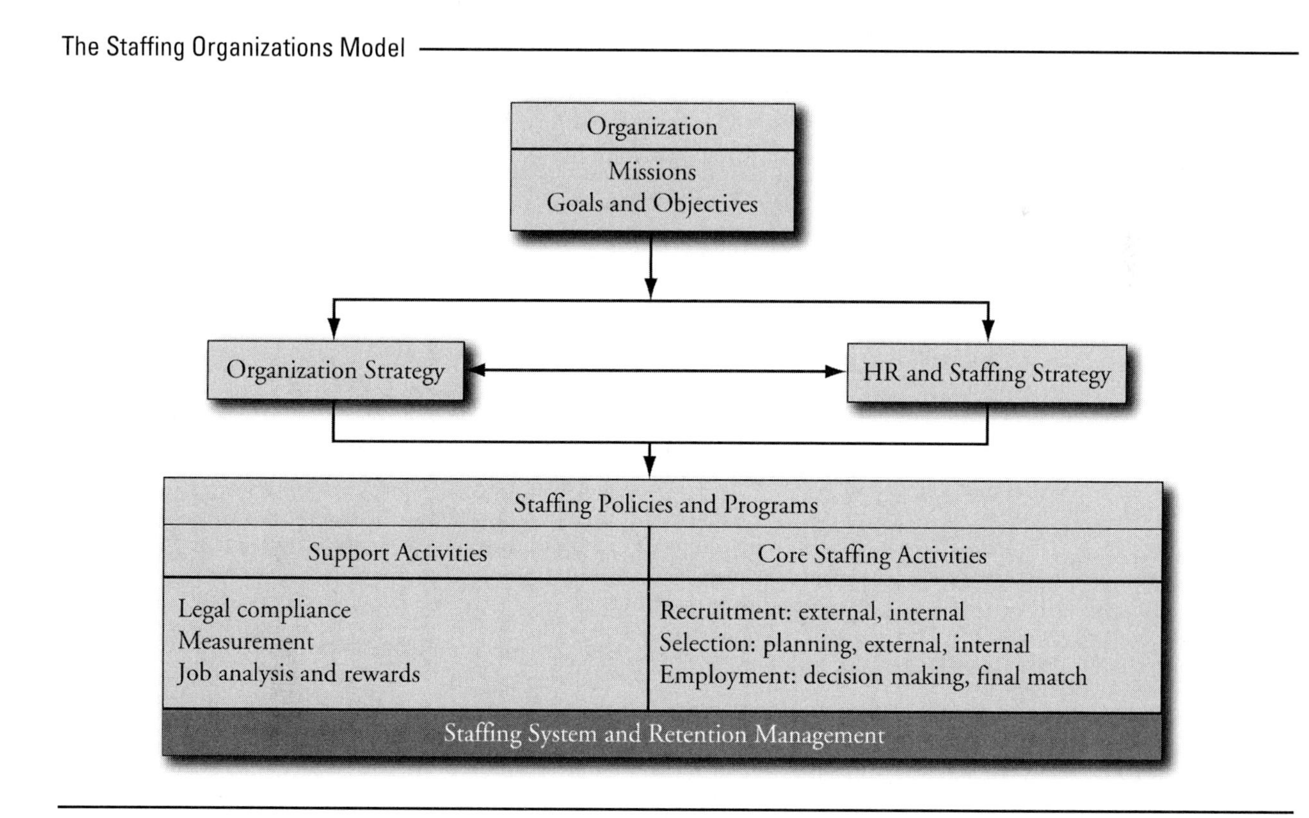

CHAPTER 11

Retention Management

CHAPTER OBJECTIVES

After reading this chapter, you will be able to:

- Understand the importance of an organization's ability to retain enough employees with important KSAOs to generate future success
- Define the three types of turnover and identify the causes and drivers for each type
- Explain how retention management is based on thorough analysis factors that affect an organization's turnover
- Give examples of voluntary, termination, and downsizing turnover and the impact of each on the organization
- Use the sample exit interview questions and practice conducting an exit interview
- Identify the laws and regulations to be aware of and incorporate into its retention strategy when making decisions on an employee's separation from the organization
- Discuss the legal recommendations to ensure that a performance management system is fair and equitable to employees during separation

AEGON Canada Inc. is an insurance company that has experienced compounded annual double-digit growth over the last decade. In 2001, AEGON decided to invest more resources into "getting the right people and keeping them after reviewing results of employee satisfaction surveys, as well as turnover levels," stated George Kralidis, assistant vice-president of human resources.

To try to improve employee retention, an area of focus was looking at the issue of employees quitting because of their boss. The methodology used to understand the impact was comparing job profiles that were developed using the McQuaig Institute behavioural job profiling method where the focus in creating the job profile is primarily on the soft skills and less on the hard skills for the managers and their employees. The purpose was to determine behavioural fits in areas such as decision-making approaches, sense of urgency, delegating styles, and need for structure.

Using the McQuaig profiles and comparing manager/employees styles had a significant impact on retention. "In 2000, AEGON Canada (then Transamerica Life) posted a staff turnover rate of 16 percent. In 2004, turnover came in at 9 percent, a 44 percent reduction. This decrease in turnover had a tremendous impact on the bottom line," stated Kralidis.

Another area of concentration was addressing generational differences between employees. AEGON developed a flexible employee-centric approach to different reward systems, growth opportunities, and benefit programs.

By implementing a recruitment strategy with the ability to profile the job to the candidate and the candidate to boss, and implementing flexible options to meet generational needs, AEGON reduced turnover, increased retention rates, and had fewer employee relations issues, and employees demonstrated greater satisfaction with their job and managers.[1]

Retention of employees is the final component of an overall staffing system. While some loss of employees is both inevitable and desirable, retention management seeks to ensure that the organization is able to keep enough employees with important KSAOs to generate future success.

In this chapter, turnover and its causes are first discussed. Three types of turnover are identified—voluntary, termination, and downsizing. Each type of turnover has different causes or drivers, and these are identified and discussed. Particular attention is paid to voluntary turnover and its three primary causes, namely, ease of leaving, cost of leaving, and alternatives.

Retention management must be based on a thorough analysis of the organization's turnover. The analyses discussed are measuring turnover, determining employees' reasons for leaving, and assessing the costs and benefits of turnover.

Attention then turns to retention initiatives, with the first discussion focused on ways of enhancing retention by reducing voluntary turnover. Examples of current organization practices and a decision process to follow for deciding whether to move forward with such practices are presented. This is followed by numerous examples of how to increase retention by attacking its underlying causes.

The next retention initiative discussed is that of reducing the occurrence of employee terminations by using performance management and progressive discipline initiatives.

The final retention initiative is the matter of downsizing. Here, the first concern is with keeping a sufficiently high number and quality of employees that the organization does not go overboard, shedding so many employees that the ability to rebound back is threatened. Also, there are many alternatives to downsizing that might be used. How to treat employees who survive a downsizing is also discussed.

The final topic is that of legal issues. The first issue is a complex one, reminding those responsible for staffing of the myriad laws and regulations pertaining to employee separation from the organization. The second issue is that of performance appraisal, a matter of critical importance for organizations seeking to retain their best performers.

TURNOVER AND ITS CAUSES

Nature of the Problem

retention strategy

Focus on number and value of employees an organization tries to keep

The focus of this book so far has been on acquiring and deploying people in ways that contribute to organizational effectiveness. Attention now shifts to retaining employees as another part of staffing and how it contributes to organizational effectiveness. Although turnover is often seen exclusively as a detriment to organizational performance, there are several positive, functional outcomes. An extremely important part of employee **retention strategy** and tactics thus must involve careful assessment of both retention costs and benefits and the design of retention initiatives that provide positive benefits at reasonable cost to the organization. Moreover, retention strategies and tactics must focus not only on how many employees are retained but exactly who is retained. Both within and between jobs and organization levels, some employees are "worth" more than others in terms of their contributions to job and organizational effectiveness. Another important matter for the retention agenda is thus making special efforts to retain what we call "high value" employees.

Retention must be tackled realistically, however, since some amount of employee turnover is simply inevitable.[2] People constantly move out of organizations voluntarily, and organizations shed employees as well. For example, for employees between the ages of 28 and 40 (Generation

Xers), the median number of years they have been with their current employer (called tenure) is four years, and it is "estimated that those who entered the workforce in the 1990s will change jobs nine times before they reach the age of 32."[3] While job-hopping decreases and median tenure increases with age, some amount of turnover persists throughout workers' careers. In some industries, high voluntary turnover is a continual fact of life and cost of doing business. Turnover among sit-down restaurant managers, for example, hovers around 50 percent annually year after year. It is not clear that even costly retention initiatives, such as substantial pay level increases or converting managers to franchisees, can reduce this turnover.

When people voluntarily leave an organization, they do so for a variety of reasons, only some of which are potentially avoidable (controllable) by the organization. Sound retention management thus must be based on a gathering and analysis of employees' reasons for leaving. Specific retention initiatives then must be tailor-made to address these reasons and hopefully neutralize them and take them "out of play," but in a cost-effective way. Against this backdrop we now turn to a more detailed discussion of types of turnover and their causes.

avoidable voluntary turnover
Turnover that can potentially be prevented by certain organization actions

unavoidable voluntary turnover
Turnover that an organization probably can not prevent

high-value employees
Difficult-to-replace employees with high job performance, strong KSAOs, key intellectual capital, high promotion potential, high training and development invested in them, and high experience

involuntary turnover
Turnover caused by termination, due to discipline and/or job performance, or downsizing

downsizing
Involuntary turnover that typically targets groups of employees and is also known as reduction in force (RIF)

Types of Turnover

There are many different types of employee turnover. Exhibit 11.1 provides a basic classification of these types.[4] It can be seen that turnover is either voluntary, being initiated by the employee, or involuntary, being initiated by the organization.

Voluntary Turnover Voluntary turnover, in turn, is broken down into **avoidable** and **unavoidable turnover**. Avoidable turnover is that which potentially can be prevented by certain organization actions, such as a pay raise or a new job assignment. Unavoidable turnover represents employee quits that the organization probably can not prevent, such as people who quit and withdraw from the labour force through retirement or returning to school. Other examples of unavoidable turnover are people who quit due to dual career problems, pursuit of a new and different career, health problems that require taking a different type of job, child care and elder care responsibilities, or leaving the country. The line of demarcation between avoidable and unavoidable is fuzzy and depends on decisions by the organization as to exactly what types of voluntary turnover it thinks it could potentially prevent.

A further line of demarcation involves just avoidable turnover, in which the organization explicitly chooses to either try to prevent or not try to prevent employees from quitting. As shown in Exhibit 11.1, the organization will try to prevent **high-value employees** from quitting—those difficult-to-replace employees with high job performance, strong KSAOs, key intellectual capital, high promotion potential, high training and development invested in them, and high experience. Retention attempts for low-value employees are less likely to be made—this is a specific decision the organization must make.

To minimize the costs created by involuntary turnover, managers need to be trained to be aware of the warning signs and put in place plans to deter high-value employees from leaving. Some signs that managers should watch for are employees suddenly dressing up for work, an increase in the number of personal phone calls, a change in behaviour from engaged to aloof, absenteeism, and lateness.[5]

RPC 5.2

Involuntary Turnover **Involuntary turnover** is split into termination and downsizing types. Termination turnover is aimed at the individual employee, due to discipline and/or job performance problems. **Downsizing** turnover typically targets groups of employees and is also known as reduction in force (RIF). It occurs as part of an organizational restructuring or cost-reduction program to improve organizational effectiveness and increase shareholder value (stock price). RIFs may occur as permanent or temporary layoffs for the entire organization, or as part of a plant or site closing or relocation. RIFs may also occur as the result of a merger or acquisition, in

EXHIBIT 11.1 Types of Employee Turnover

A. Voluntary (employee initiated)

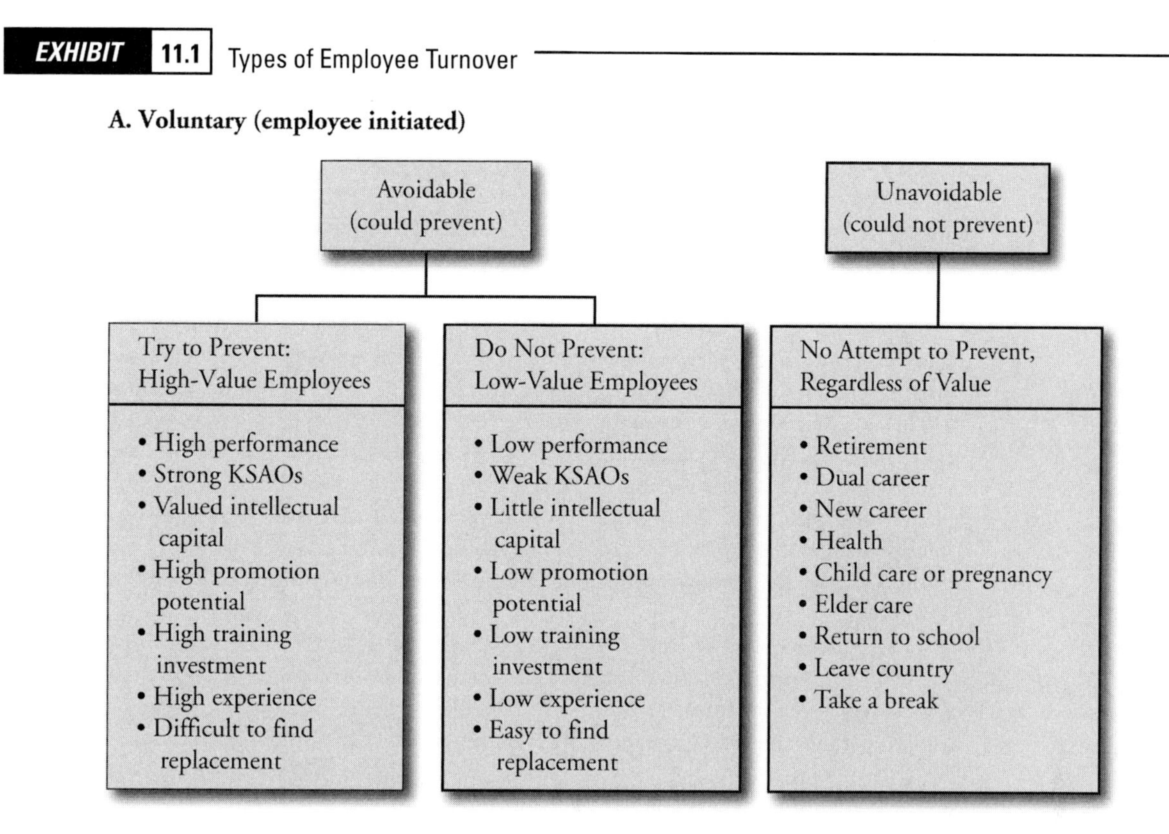

B. Involuntary (organization initiated)

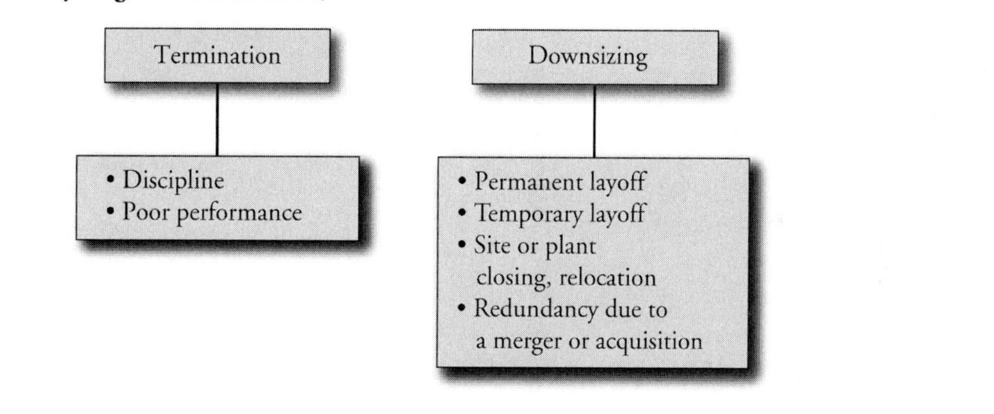

which some employees in the combined workforces are viewed as redundant in the positions they hold. It is important to recognize that even though the organization is considering terminating employees through termination and downsizing, it can take many steps to lessen or eliminate terminations or downsizing, thereby having positive employee-retention impacts.

It is apparent that there are many different types of turnover, and these types have different underlying causes. Because of this, the organization must think very selectively in terms of the different types of retention strategies and tactics it wishes to deploy. It is first necessary to explore the underlying causes of turnover, since knowledge of those causes is necessary for developing and implementing those retention strategies and tactics.

Causes of Turnover

Separate models of turnover causes are presented next for each of the three turnover types that the organization may seek to influence with its retention strategies and tactics. These are voluntary, termination, and downsizing turnover.

Causes of Voluntary Turnover Through considerable research, various models of voluntary turnover have been developed and tested.[6] The model shown in Exhibit 11.2 is a distillation of that research.

The employee's intention to quit depends on three general factors: the perceived desirability of leaving, the perceived ease of leaving, and alternatives available to the employee. The perceived desirability of leaving is often an outgrowth of a poor person/job or person/organization match. One form of the mismatch may be a difference between the rewards provided by the job and rewards desired by the employee, leading to job dissatisfaction. In addition to mismatches, certain shocks may occur to the employee that trigger a more impulsive intention to quit, such as finding out that the organization is being acquired and one's job might be eliminated. Interpersonal conflicts with co-workers or supervisors are another type of shock that could lead to turnover. Finally, employees may find it desirable to leave for personal, nonjob reasons that are unavoidable.

The perceived ease of leaving represents a sense of lack of barriers to leaving and of the likelihood of being able to find a new job. Labour market conditions, specifically the tightness or looseness of the labour market, are very important types of information for the employee in helping to frame an intention to quit. Tight labour markets fuel the intention-to-quit flames, and loose labour markets douse the flames. The flames may also be doused by the employee knowing

EXHIBIT 11.2 Causes (Drivers) of Voluntary Turnover

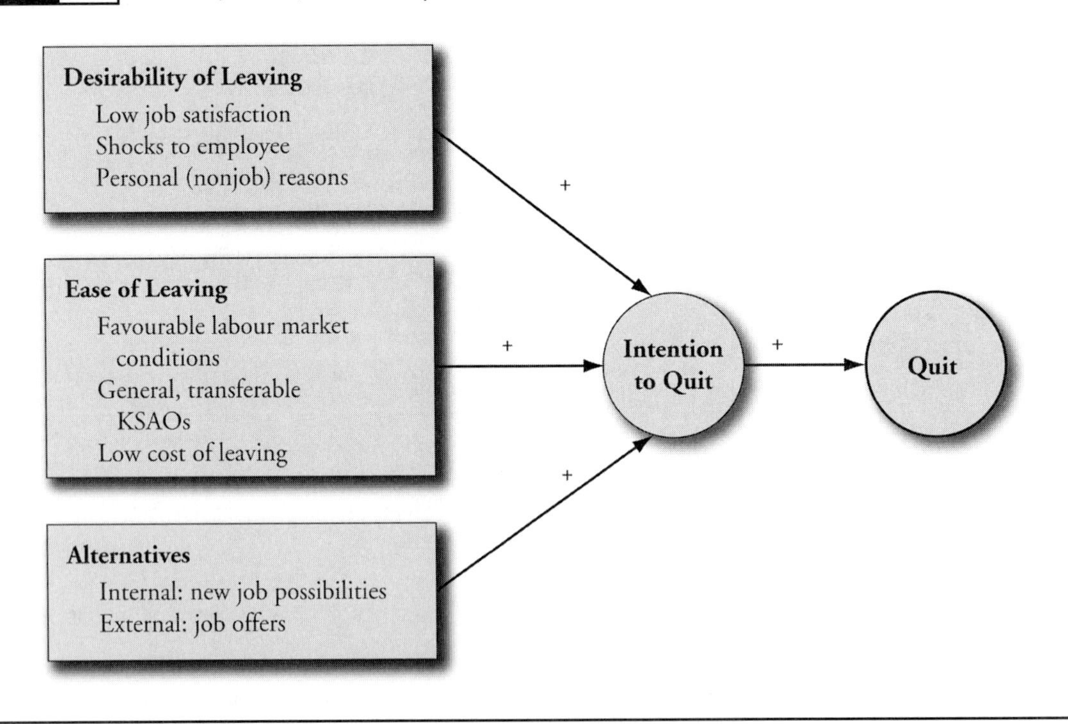

Note: The relative importance of the drivers and how they interact to determine the decision to quit varies across situations.

that many of his or her KSAOs are specific and useful only to the current employer. Ease of leaving may also be heightened by a low cost of leaving, such as not having to give up valuable benefits because none were provided by the organization. In short, the ease of leaving will be higher when labour market conditions provide plentiful job opportunities with other organizations, when the employee possesses KSAOs that are transferable to other organizations, and when leaving is not a very costly proposition for the employee.

Finally, the intention to quit will depend on other job alternatives available to the employee within and outside the organization. Specifically, availability of promotion, transfer, and relocation alternatives may lessen or eliminate any intentions to quit by the employee, even though the employee is very dissatisfied with the current job. Also, actual or potential receipt of a job offer from another employer represents a clear external alternative for the employee.

The final stage of the turnover process is the formation of intention to turnover, which is accompanied by a search for alternatives. Job searching has been empirically identified as a close correlate of turnover. However, employers should not assume that it is too late to make efforts to keep an employee who is seeking another job. Directly addressing what changes would be necessary to keep an employee is a good strategy in this case. Many employees who are looking for alternative jobs would be willing to stay with their current employers if their jobs were modified sufficiently.

The model in Exhibit 11.2 illustrates both avoidable and unavoidable turnover. Retention initiatives must be directed toward the avoidable types of turnover, such as turnover due to job dissatisfaction; employee possession of general, transferable KSAOs; a low cost of leaving; the availability of other job opportunities within the organization; and the employee's receipt of a job offer.

Causes of Termination Turnover Termination turnover is due to extremely poor person/job matches, particularly the mismatch between job requirements and KSAOs. One form of the mismatch involves the employee failing to follow rules and procedures. These requirements range from the relatively minor (e.g., dress code violations, horseplay) to the very serious (e.g., theft). Often it is the cumulative effect of multiple incidents that results in the termination.

The other form of termination turnover involves unacceptable job performance. Here, the KSAOs–job requirements mismatch is severe. In fact, the employee's performance is so deficient that the organization has decided that it is intolerable and the only solution is termination.

Causes of Downsizing Turnover Downsizing turnover is a reflection of a staffing level mismatch in which the organization actually is, or is projected to be, overstaffed. In other words, the head count available exceeds the head count required. Overstaffing may be due to a lack of forecasting and planning, inaccuracies in forecasting and planning, or unanticipated changes in labour demand and/or labour supply. For example, optimistic forecasts of demand for products and services that do not materialize may lead to overstaffing, as may sudden unanticipated downturns in demand that create sudden excess head count. Or, increasing looseness in the labour market may reduce the ease of movement, causing fewer employees to leave the organization—an unanticipated decrease in the voluntary turnover rate and thus increase in workforce head count available. Quite naturally, these types of demand/supply imbalances create strong downsizing pressure on the organization to which it must respond.

ANALYSIS OF TURNOVER

Analysis of turnover requires that the three types be measured and benchmarked, that specific reasons for employees' leaving be identified, and that costs and benefits of each type of turnover be assessed.

Measurement

Formula Since turnover involves the discrete action of leaving or staying with the organization, it is expressed as the proportion or percentage of employees who leave the organization in some time period. Thus:

$$\text{turnover rate} = \frac{\text{number of employees leaving}}{\text{average number of employees}} \times 100$$

Use of this formula to calculate turnover rates will require data on, and decisions about, (1) what is the time period of interest (e.g., month, year), (2) what is an employee that "counts" (e.g., full time only? part time? seasonal?), and (3) how to calculate the average number of employees over the time period, such as straight or weighted average.

Breakouts and Benchmarks Analysis and interpretation of turnover data is aided by making breakouts of the data according to various factors, including the following:

1. Type of turnover: voluntary—avoidable; involuntary—termination; involuntary —downsizing
2. Type of employee (e.g., permanent–nonpermanent, demographics, KSAOs, performance level)
3. Job category
4. Geographic location

Such breakouts help in identifying how much variation in turnover there is around the overall average and pockets of the most and least severe turnover. Such data are the foundation for development of strategic retention initiatives.

It is also useful to benchmark turnover data in order to have comparative statistics that will aid in interpretation of the organization's turnover data. One benchmark is an internal one, looking at the trends in the organization's own turnover data over time. Such trend analysis is very useful for identifying where turnover problems are worsening or improving and for evaluating the effectiveness of retention initiatives. Internal benchmarking requires a commitment to a sustained data collection process.

The other form of benchmarking is external, in which the organization compares its own data to the current rates and turnover trends of other organizations. One major external benchmarking source is Labour Force Survey (LFS) data, collected and published by Statistics Canada (www.statcan.ca/english/Subjects/Labour/LFS/lfs-en.htm). It provides data on total employment increases, monthly unemployment rates, rate of employment growth, increase in full-time employment, and provincial highlights. Exhibit 11.3 provides a representation of data from the Labour Force Survey for the month of August between 2001 and 2005. It should be noted that on the website the data is broken down by province, industry based on NAICS codes, sex, and age.

Reasons for Leaving

5.3

It is important to ascertain, record, and track the various reasons for why employees are leaving the organization. The data are essential for measuring and analyzing turnover. At a minimum, the exit of each employee should be classified as a voluntary, termination, or downsizing exit, thus permitting the calculation of turnover rates for these three major types of turnover. In order to learn more about the specific reasons underlying exit decisions, however, more in-depth probing of employees is necessary. Three tools for conducting such probing are exit interviews, postexit surveys, and employee satisfaction surveys.[7] All three tools can be used to help gauge whether the decision to leave was voluntary or not, and if voluntary, the specific reasons—thus allowing a determination of avoidable and unavoidable turnover.

EXHIBIT 11.3 Monthly Data on Labour Force Fluctuations

August	Total Employment	Monthly Employment Increases	Unemployment Rate	Year to Date Rate of Growth
2001	15.4 million	(–8,000)	7.2%	(–3%)
2002	15.4 million	59,000	7.5%	2.6%
2003	15.7 million	(–19,000)	8.0%	.03%
2004	16 million	(–7,000)	7.2%	.07%
2005	16.2 million	28,000	6.8%	1.5%

exit interviews
Formally planned interviews conducted with departing employees, which are used to understand employees' reason for leaving and to explain rehiring rights, benefits, and confidentiality agreements

Exit Interviews **Exit interviews** are formally planned and conducted interviews with departing employees. In addition to help learn about the employee's reasons for leaving, exit interviews are used to explain such things as rehiring rights, benefits, and confidentiality agreements.

It is important to ensure that exit interviews are conducted carefully. Research suggests that there are differences between the reasons for turnover employees provide in exit interviews and reasons employees provide in anonymous surveys.[8] Departing employees are reluctant to complain about their former employers because they will want to avoid burning bridges and don't want to jeopardize future references. In response, employees may claim that they are leaving for higher pay, when in fact they are leaving because of poor working conditions or interpersonal conflicts with supervisors and co-workers.

The following are suggestions for conducting an appropriate interview that will hopefully elicit truthful information from the interviewee:

1. The interviewer should be a neutral person (normally from the HR department or an external consultant) who has been trained in how to conduct exit interviews.
2. The interviewer should put the employee at ease and explain the purposes of the interview, follow a structured interview format and avoid excessive probing and follow-up questions, take notes, and end the interview on a positive note.
3. There should be a structured interview format that contains questions about unavoidable and avoidable reasons for leaving. For the avoidable category, questions should focus on desirability of leaving, ease of leaving, and job alternatives. (Exhibit 11.4 contains an example of structured exit interview questions, with questions focused on desirability of leaving, ease of leaving, and alternatives.)
4. The interviewer should prepare for each exit interview by reviewing the interview format and the interviewee's personnel file.
5. The interview should be conducted in a private place, before the employee's last day.
6. The interviewee should be told that the interview is confidential and that only aggregate results will be used to help the organization better understand why employees leave and to possibly develop new retention initiatives.

Too often, exit interviews are filed and forgotten instead of linking the information gathered back into strengthening organizational effectiveness by sharing changes suggested with the appropriate departments.[9]

The organization must decide whether to conduct exit interviews with all departing employees or with only those who are leaving voluntarily. The advantages of including all departing employees are that it expands the sample from which information is drawn and even employees leaving involuntarily can provide useful information.

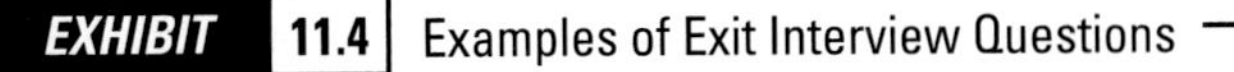

EXHIBIT 11.4 Examples of Exit Interview Questions

1. Current job title ________ Department/work unit ________
2. Length of time in current job ________ Length of time with organization ________
3. Are you leaving for any of the following reasons?
   retirement ________ dual career ________ new career ________ health ________
   child care or pregnancy ________ elder care ________ return to school ________
   leave the country ________ take a break ________
4. Do you have another job lined up? ________ New employer ________
5. What aspects of your new job will be better than current job? ________
6. Before deciding to leave did you check the possibility of any of the following?
   job transfer ________ promotion ________ relocation ________
7. Was it easy to find another job? ________ Why? ________
8. Did many of your current skills fit with your new job? ________
9. What aspects of your job have been most satisfying? ________
   least satisfying? ________
10. What could the company have done to improve your job satisfaction? ________
11. How satisfactory has your job performance been since your last review? ________
12. What are things the company or your manager could have done to help you improve your performance? ________
13. If you could have had a different manager, would you have been more likely to stay with the company? ________
14. Are you willing to recommend the company to others as a place to work? ________
15. Would you be willing to hire back with the company? ________
16. Is there anything else you would like to tell us about your decision to leave the company? ________

Postexit Surveys To minimize departing employees' concerns about exit interviews regarding confidentiality and possible employer retaliation, postexit surveys might be used. It is unknown what types of response rates are typical for postexit surveys. It is recommended that:

1. The survey covers the same areas as the exit interview
2. The survey be sent shortly after the employee's last day
3. A cover letter explain the purpose of the survey, use of only aggregate results, and confidentiality of individual responses
4. A stamped, pre-addressed envelope be included for return of the survey

employee satisfaction surveys
An important way to discover the types of job rewards that are most dissatisfying to employees and might therefore become reasons for leaving

Employee Satisfaction Surveys Since employee job dissatisfaction (desirability of leaving) is known to be a potent predictor of voluntary turnover, conduct of **employee satisfaction surveys** is an important way to discover the types of job rewards that are most dissatisfying to employees and might therefore become reasons for leaving. Conducting job satisfaction surveys has the advantage of learning from all employees (at least those who respond to the survey), rather than just those who are leaving. Satisfaction survey results also give the organization information it can use to hopefully pre-empt turnover by making changes that will increase job satisfaction. FedEx Canada employs 5,000 employees in 60 locations across Canada and it takes part in regular employee satisfaction surveys along with FedEx businesses in 210 countries. The surveys ask questions to measure "employee engagement, career development, reward, organizational identification, job security, and product quality." Managers need to submit action plans for any of their areas that have a low score, and improvement in future survey results is linked to the manager's performance appraisal and variable pay.[10] Designing, conducting, analyzing, and interpreting results from these surveys require substantial organizational resources and should only be undertaken with the guidance of a person explicitly trained in job satisfaction survey techniques. Often there will be a consultant retained for this purpose.

Costs and Benefits

Costs and benefits may be estimated for each of the three turnover types. These costs are both financial and nonfinancial in nature. Most involve actual costs or benefits, though some are potential, depending on how events transpire. Some of the costs and benefits may be estimated financially, a useful and necessary exercise. Such financial analysis must be supplemented with a careful consideration of the other costs and benefits to arrive at a reasonable estimate of the total costs and benefits of turnover. It may well turn out that the nonfinancial costs and benefits outweigh the financial ones in importance and impact for the development of retention strategies and tactics. For example, the development of retention strategies known as alternative work practices (e.g. teamwork, flexible job design, performance-based pay systems, and formal training) will lead to higher productivity and a reduction in labour turnover, particularly in firms that employ a highly skilled workforce.[11]

Costs and Benefits of Voluntary Turnover Exhibit 11.5 shows the major types of costs and benefits that can occur when an employee leaves the organization.[12] An assessment of these costs and benefits could be used in the case of an individual employee who is threatening to leave for avoidable reasons; the assessment will help frame decisions about whether a retention attempt should be made, and if so, how far the organization is willing to go in that attempt. Or, at the aggregate level the costs and benefits assessment could be developed for the work or business unit, division, or total organization. Results may then be used to communicate with top management about the nature and severity of employee turnover and to help fashion the development of retention strategies and tactics.

Inspection of Exhibit 11.5 shows that on the cost side there are separation, replacement, and training costs, both financial and nonfinancial. The financial costs mainly involve the cost of people's time, cost of materials and equipment, cash outlays, and productivity losses. The other costs are less discernable and harder to estimate but may entail large negative impacts on organizational effectiveness, such as loss of clients. On the benefits side, a number of positive things may occur, including finding a higher-quality, less-expensive replacement for the departing employee(s).

Accurate cost and benefit calculations require diligence and care in development, particularly those involving people's time. To estimate time costs, it is necessary to know the average amount of time spent by each person in the specific activity, plus each person's compensation (pay rate plus benefits). Consider a case that identifies the cost of conducting an exit interview, assuming the following:

1. The HR specialist spends one hour conducting the interview and writing up a brief summary to add to the voluntary turnover data file.
2. The HR specialist's salary is $46,000 ($23/hour).
3. The exiting employee's salary is $50,000 ($25/hour).
4. Cost of benefits are 30 percent of salary ($6.90/hour for HR specialist and $7.50/hour for employee).
5. The time cost of the exit interview is $62.40.

At the aggregate level, if the HR specialist conducts 100 exit interviews annually, and the average pay rate of those interviewed is $20 per hour, the annual time cost of exit interviews is $5,590:

Portion of HR specialist's salary = $2,300 + benefits = $690
Portion of employees' salary = $2,000 + benefits = $600
Total cost: $5,590

Materials and equipment costs are likely to be most prevalent in replacement and training costs. For example, they will be a part of staffing costs in such things as recruitment brochures and testing materials, orientation program materials, and induction materials such as benefits enrolment forms. Formal training may involve the use of both materials and equipment that must be costed. Cash outlays include paying for the departing employee's accrued but unused vacation pay, possible temporary coverage for the departed employee, and hiring inducements for the replacement employee.

On the benefits side, the primary immediate benefit is the labour cost savings from not having the departing employee on the payroll until a permanent replacement is hired (if ever),

EXHIBIT 11.5 Voluntary Turnover: Costs and Benefits

I. Separation Costs

A. Financial Costs

HR staff time (e.g., exit interview, payroll, benefits)
Manager's time (e.g., retention attempts, exit interview)
Accrued paid time off (e.g., vacation, sick pay)
Temporary coverage (e.g., temporary employee, overtime for current employees)

B. Other Costs

Production and customer service delays or quality decreases
Lost or unacquired clients
Leaves—goes to competitor or forms competitive business
Contagion—other employees decide to leave
Teamwork disruptions
Loss of workforce diversity

II. Replacement Costs

Staffing costs for new hire (e.g., cost-per-hire calculations)
Hiring inducements (e.g., bonus, relocation, perks)
Hiring manager and work-unit employee time
Orientation program time and materials
HR staff induction costs (e.g., payroll, benefits enrolment)

III. Training Costs

Formal training (trainee and instruction time, materials, equipment)
On-the-job training (supervisor and employee time)
Mentoring (mentor's time)
Socialization (time of other employees, travel)
Productivity loss (loss of production until full proficient employee)

IV. Benefits

Replacement employee better performer and organization citizen than last employee
New KSAO and motivation infusion to organization
Opportunity to restructure work unit
Savings from not replacing employee
Vacancy creates transfer or promotion opportunity for others
Replacement less expensive in salary and seniority-based benefits

or of hiring a temporary replacement at a lower pay rate until a permanent replacement is acquired. And the hired permanent replacement may be hired at a lower wage or salary than the departing employee, resulting in additional pay and benefit savings. The other benefits shown in Exhibit 11.5 are less tangible but potentially very important in the long run, with the possibility of improved work-unit and organizational effectiveness.

Exhibit 11.6 shows the cost estimates for a single incident of voluntary turnover for a hypothetical industrial supplies organization that employs 40 salespeople who receive $20 per hour on average and who bring in approximately $8 million in total annual sales. The three categories of the turnover and replacement process (separation, replacement, and training) are described in terms of their time costs, materials and equipment costs, and other costs.

Separation costs include the time of employees who process turnover ($25 + $15) and the former employee's manager ($120). There is also accrued time off paid to the departing individual ($160). Replacement costs include both a temporary fill-in and a permanent replacement. It takes an average of four weeks to find a permanent replacement. During these four weeks (160 hours), a temporary replacement is hired from a staffing firm for $15 per hour plus a 33.3 percent markup. While this temporary employee is paid less than the average salesperson, temporary salespeople typically make $2,000 less in sales over the four-week period. A permanent new hire

EXHIBIT 11.6 Example of Financial Cost Estimates for One Voluntary Turnover

	Time			
	Hours	**Cost ($)**	**Materials and Equipment ($)**	**Other Costs ($)**
A. Separation Costs				
Staffing manager	1	25		
HR staff	1	15		
Employee's manager	3	120		
Accrued paid time off	160	2,400		
Processing			30	
B. Replacement Costs				
Temporary replacement				
Compensation difference	160	(800)		
Staffing manager	1	25		
Employee's manager	1	40		
Staffing firm fee (markup)				800
Permanent replacement				
Compensation difference	960	(4,800)		
Cost-per-hire				4,500
Hiring bonus				3,000
Laptop computer				2,000
Employee's manager	3	120		
Orientation	8	160		
C. Training Costs				
Training program			1,000	
Trainee	80	1,200		
Instructor	100	1,600		
Mentor	52	1,040		
Productivity/sales loss				
Permanent replacement				50,000
Temporary replacement				2,000
D. Total Costs		1,545	1,030	62,300

receives an average of \$15 per hour less for the first six months of employment until he or she gets up to speed (\$5/hour less × 960 hours = \$4,800 in savings). However, each new hire costs \$4,500, and newcomers receive a hiring bonus of \$3,000 and a laptop computer worth \$2,000. Each new salesperson's manager typically devotes an additional three hours to orienting the newcomer, along with an eight-hour organizational orientation session.

Training costs include the materials and equipment required for the program (\$1,000), two weeks (80 hours) of paid time in the class, and the pay for an instructor who devotes 100 hours to the program. Additionally, an experienced salesperson acts as a mentor during the transition period, averaging one hour per week over the course of a year. It takes the new permanent replacement 24 weeks (24 weeks × 40 hours = 960 hours) to reach the average sales proficiency of \$200,000; this means that \$50,000 in sales is lost during this period. Overall, the estimated total costs for this organization for a single salesperson turnover incident come to \$62,300. The data for this organization also suggest that time costs and material costs are a fairly trivial contribution to the total expense of turnover. Lost productivity makes up 80 percent of the cost of turnover. (i.e., 50,000/62,300 = 80%). This figure will, of course, vary considerably depending on the job under consideration.

It should be recognized that turnover cost estimates require considerable judgment and guesstimate. Nonetheless, the example above illustrates that many turnover costs are hidden in the time demands placed on the many employees who must handle the separation, replacement, and training activities, and the sales or productivity losses experienced. Such costs might be offset at least in part, however, through the acquisition of less-expensive temporary and permanent replacement employees, at least for a while. It should also be noted that when turnover costs for a single employee loss are aggregated to an annual level for multiple losses, the costs can be substantial. In the above example, if the sales unit experienced just a 20 percent annual voluntary turnover rate, it would lose eight employees at a total cost of \$519,000, or 6.5 percent of annual sales.

5.3

Costs and Benefits of Termination In the case of an employee being terminated, some of the costs and benefits are the same as for voluntary turnover. Referring to Exhibit 11.7, it can be seen that separation, replacement, and training costs are still incurred. There may be an additional

EXHIBIT 11.7 Termination: Costs and Benefits

I. Separation Costs

A. Financial Costs

- Same as for voluntary turnover plus
- Contract buyout (salary, benefit, perks)

B. Other Costs

- Manager and HR staff time handling problem employee
- Grievance, alternative dispute resolution
- Possibility of lawsuit, loss of lawsuit, settlement or remedy
- Damage to harmonious labour–management relations

II. Replacement Costs

- Same as for voluntary turnover

III. Training Costs

- Same as for voluntary turnover

IV. Benefits

- Departure of low-value employee
- High-value employee replacement possibility
- Reduced disruption for manager and work unit
- Improved performance management and disciplinary skills

separation cost for a contract buyout of guarantees (salary, benefits, perks) made in a fixed-term contract. Such buyouts are very common for high-level executives and public sector leaders such as school superintendents. These guarantees are negotiated and used to make the hiring package more attractive and to reduce the financial risk of failure for the new hire. Such guarantees can drive up the costs of termination substantially and reinforce the need for careful selection decisions followed by support to help the new hire turn out to be a successful performer who will remain with the organization for at least the full term of the contract.

It is the other costs that are potentially very large. A termination is usually preceded by the manager and others spending considerable time, often unpleasant and acrimonious, with the employee in seeking to change the person's behaviour through progressive discipline or performance management activities. Many times these attempts fail, an actual termination is threatened or made, and it is decided to submit the issue to an alternative dispute resolution (ADR) forum for handling. The ADR process will often consume considerable time costs and cash outlays. Instead of using ADR, the termination may be made and followed by a lawsuit, such as a claim that the termination was tainted by discrimination based on the race or sex of the person terminated. In turn, the time costs for handling the matter, and the potential cash outlays required in a settlement or court-imposed remedy, can be substantial.[13] In short, compared to voluntary turnover, termination is a more costly, and unpleasant, type of turnover to experience. Moreover, in unionized settings, termination problems may pose a serious threat to labour–management relations.

Against these often large costs are many potential benefits. First and foremost is that the organization will be rid of a truly low-value employee whose presence has caused considerable disruption, ineffective performance, and possibly declines in organizational effectiveness. A following benefit is the opportunity to replace the discharged employee with a high-quality new hire that will hopefully turn out to be a high-value employee. A side benefit of a discharge experience is that many members of the organization will gain improved disciplinary and performance management skills, and the HR department's awareness of the need for better discipline and performance management systems may be heightened and lead to these necessary changes.

Costs and Benefits of Downsizing Downsizing costs are concentrated in separation costs for a permanent RIF (reduction in workforce) since there will presumably be no replacement hiring and training. These costs are shown in Exhibit 11.8, along with potential benefits.[14] For economic costs, the major cost areas are time costs, cash outlays for various severance and buyout packages, and increased unemployment compensation insurance premiums. The time costs involve both HR staff and managers' time in planning, implementing, and handling the RIF.

Severance costs may take numerous forms. First, employees can be paid for accrued time off. Second, early retirement packages may be offered to employees as an inducement to leave early. Third, employees ineligible for early retirement may be offered a voluntary severance package as an inducement to leave without being laid off. A typical severance package includes one week's pay for each year of service, continued health insurance coverage and premium payment, and outplacement assistance. More generous terms may be provided to key executives, such as two weeks pay for each year of service and a lump-sum exit bonus. A danger with both early retirement and voluntary severance packages is that their provisions may turn out to be so attractive that more employees take them and leave than had been planned for in the RIF.

If the early retirement and voluntary severance packages do not serve as an adequate inducement to sufficient numbers of employees, the organization may also institute an involuntary RIF with a severance package, oftentimes not as generous as the voluntary package offered. It is customary to inform employees of the content of both the voluntary and involuntary packages at the time the RIF is announced so that they may decide which to take. Some employees may decide to take their chances by not accepting the voluntary package and gambling that they won't be laid off (or if they are, being willing to live with the involuntary severance package).

EXHIBIT 11.8 Downsizing: Costs and Benefits

I. Separation Costs

A. Financial Costs

- HR staff time in planning and implementing layoff
- Managers' time in handling layoff
- Accrued paid time off (e.g., vacation, sick pay)
- Early retirement package
- Voluntary severance package (e.g., one week pay/year of service, continued health insurance, outplacement assistance)
- Involuntary severance package
- Contract buyouts for fulfillment of guarantees
- Higher unemployment insurance premiums
- Change in control (CIC) guarantees for key executives during a merger or acquisition

B. Other Costs

- Shareholder value (stock price) may not improve
- Loss of critical employees and KSAOs
- Inability to respond quickly to surges in product and service demand; restaffing delays and costs
- Contagion—other employees leave
- Threat to harmonious labour–management relations
- Possibility of lawsuit, loss of lawsuit, costly settlement or remedy
- Decreased morale, increased feelings of job insecurity
- Difficulty in attracting new employees

II. Benefits

- Lower payroll and benefit costs
- Increased production and staffing flexibility
- Ability to relocate facilities
- Improved promotion and transfer opportunities for stayers
- Focus on core businesses, eliminate peripheral ones
- Spread risk by outsourcing activities to other organizations
- Flatten organization hierarchy—especially among managers
- Increase productivity

Some employees may receive special severance consideration. For those on a fixed-term contract, a contract buyout will be necessary. Others, usually key executives, may have change in control (CIC) clauses in their contract that must be fulfilled if there is a merger or acquisition; CICs are also known as "golden parachutes." In addition to the terms in typical severance packages, a CIC may provide for immediate vesting of stock options, (a) retirement payout sweetener or buyout, (b) bonus payments, continuation of all types of insurance for an extended time period, and maintenance of various perks.

Bell Canada implemented an initiative called "Bell People First" that deployed 1,500 workers who could have been downsized and saved about $36 million in severance costs in a two-year period.[15]

Other costs of downsizing shown in Exhibit 14.8 may also be considerable. Shareholder value (stock price) may not improve, suggesting the stock market views the probable effectiveness of the restructuring as low. There will be a critical talent loss and an inability to respond quickly to need for workforce additions to cover new demand surges. And a reputation for job instability among job seekers will create added difficulties in attracting new employees. Terminated employees may pursue legal avenues, claiming, for example, that decisions about whom to layoff were tainted by age discrimination. Employees who survive the job cuts may have damaged morale and fear even more cuts, which may harm performance and cause them to look for another job with a more secure organization. Finally, as with terminations, downsizing may place great strains on labour–management harmony.

Against this backdrop of heavy costs are many potential benefits. There will in fact be lower payroll and benefits costs. The organization may gain production and staffing flexibility, an ability to outsource parts of the business that are not mission critical, and opportunities for facilities redesign and relocation. The restructuring may also entail a flattening of the organization hierarchy through elimination of management layers, leading to increased speed in decision making and productivity boosts. Finally, new promotion and transfer opportunities may open up as the restructuring leads to the hoped-for rebound in organizational effectiveness.

Summary of Costs and Benefits Despite their many potential benefits, voluntary turnover, terminations, and downsizing are typically costly propositions. Time costs, materials costs, performance and revenue losses, severance costs, legal costs, and so forth can create substantial cost challenges and risks for the organization. Potentially even more important are the human costs of frayed relationships, critical talent losses, performance declines, disruptive discipline, the contagion effect of other employees leaving along with the departing employee, and the risk of not being able to locate, attract, and hire high-quality replacements.

The organization must carefully weigh these costs and benefits generally for each type of turnover, as well as specifically for separate employee groups, job categories, and organizational units. Clear cost-benefit differences in turnover will likely emerge from these more fine-grained analyses. Such analyses will help the organization better understand its turnover, where and among whom it is most worrisome, and how to fashion tailor-made retention strategies and tactics.

RETENTION INITIATIVES: VOLUNTARY TURNOVER

For most organizations, of the three types of turnover, voluntary turnover is the most prevalent and the one they choose to focus on in the continual "war for talent." Described first below are examples of retention initiatives undertaken by organizations to increase retention. These are vast in number, but little is known about how organizations actually decide to act on a turnover problem and go forth with one or more retention initiatives. To fill this void, a retention decision process is described that will help the organization more systematically and effectively pursue the right retention initiatives. Based on the causes of turnover model (Exhibit 11.2), ways to influence the three primary turnover drivers—desirability of leaving, ease of leaving, and alternatives—are suggested for retention initiatives.

Current Practices and Deciding to Act

Turnover analysis does not end with the collection and analysis of data. These activities are merely a precursor to the critical decisions of whether or not to act to solve a perceived turnover problem, and if so, how to intervene to attack the problem and ultimately assess how effective the intervention was. Presented first are some examples of organization retention initiatives that illustrate the breadth and depth of attempts to attack retention concerns. Then a systematic decision process for retention initiatives is provided as a framework to help with deciding to act or not act. Such decision guidance is necessary given the complexity of the retention issue and the lack of demonstrated best practices for improving retention.

Survey Analysis Several descriptive surveys provide glimpses and hints of what actions organizations decide to take to attack retention. These examples come mostly from relatively large organizations, so what happens in small organizations is more of an unknown. Nonetheless, the data provide interesting illustrations of organization tenacity and ingenuity, along with a willingness to commit resources, in their approaches to retention.

- The Conference Board of Canada publishes an annual "Compensation Planning Outlook." The 2005 report was compiled from surveys received from 294 respondents from large and mid-sized Canadian companies. The average voluntary turnover for the organizations surveyed was 6.6 percent overall, with higher percentages for the following sectors: finance, insurance, and real estate (7.1%); retail trade (12%); not-for-profit (8.1%); and services (12.6%).[16]
- In 2003, a policies and practices survey conducted by Mercer Human Resource Consulting reported an overall turnover rate, including voluntary and involuntary, of 14.8 percent. The breakdown by industry was wholesale/retail, 35.9 percent; high tech and telecom, 18.6 percent; natural resources, 16.7 percent; services and insurance, 14.2 percent; banking/finance, 13.8 percent; durable manufacturing, 10.8 percent; non-durable manufacturing, 9.8 percent; non-profit, 10.4 percent; and transportation/utilities/real estate, 6.7 percent.[17]
- From a Society of Human Resource Management (SHRM) survey in 2000 of HR professionals in 473 organizations in the United States, the top ten reasons for employees leaving are the following: pursuit of career opportunities elsewhere (78%), better pay and benefits package (65%), poor management (21%), relocating spouse/partner (18%), return to school (15%), retire (14%), job security fears (10%), poor relationships with co-workers (10%), child care issues (8%), and perceived discriminatory treatment (5%). Survey respondents stated that the three biggest threats to employee retention were higher salaries obtainable elsewhere, lack of career development opportunities, and the rising acceptability of job hopping.[18] These results suggest pay is an overcited reason for turnover in exit surveys.
- WorldatWork surveyed HR professionals in 2,554 organizations, of which 72 percent indicated they had concerns about the attraction and retention of talent.[19] Retention problems varied substantially among job categories. In response to retention problems, the organizations had developed numerous attraction and retention initiatives. The top ten initiatives in percentage usage were market adjustment/base salary increase (62%); hiring bonus (60%); work environment—including flexible work schedules, compressed work weeks, related dress code, and telecommuting (49%); retention bonus (28%); promotion and career development opportunities (27%); paying above market (24%); special training and education opportunities (22%); individual spot bonuses (22%); stock programs (19%); and project milestone/completion bonuses (15%).
- Each year *The Globe and Mail's Report on Business* magazine publishes a list of the 50 Best Employers in Canada. More than 2,500 organizations are invited to participate, and in 2004, 129 responded, representing "64,000 employees and more than 1,200 leaders." Employees from the participating organizations completed surveys on their organization's best practices in human resources that met the employees' and the business's needs. The key areas assessed were leadership aligned with employees, employee engagement, people-management practices, communication and execution of human resources practices, and employees' connection to the business. BC Biomedical Laboratories ranked first in 2004 (its employees scored 96% on the engagement rating) and holds the prestigious honour of being the first company that has earned this spot more than once.[20] The reader should consult the 50 Best Employers list each year to gain glimpses about what organizations are doing to make themselves attractive to job applicants and employees, which may aid in retention enhancement.

Unfortunately, the *Report on Business* study did not provide specific information on patterns of usage and effectiveness of retention initiatives among the 50 organizations. But Hewitt Associates, which conducted the survey, did provide information on succession planning, which is a major component of a progressive retention program:

"74 percent of senior leadership team members at Best Employers believe that their organization is investing enough to develop the next generation of leaders, while that figure is 65 percent for non-Best participants. In addition, 64 percent of Best Employers' senior leaders believe that their organizations have an excellent succession planning process for developing leaders. At non-Best Employers, only 46 percent think their organization has an excellent succession planning process."[21]

What do these organizations do about retention problems and threats? Exhibit 11.9 shows the percentage of organizations offering 36 different retention initiatives and the judged effectiveness of each one. It can be seen that base and variable pay, benefits, hours of work, and training and development practices dominated in terms of usage. Also apparent is a fairly less-than-perfect relationship between usage and effectiveness overall, though the top ten most effective initiatives also had high usage.

Although few intrinsic rewards were mentioned in the SHRM survey, this does not mean that such rewards do not reduce turnover in the aggregate. In fact, research generally suggests that there is a strong relationship between job enrichment efforts from organizations and employee satisfaction. Employee perceptions that their jobs provide them with high levels of intrinsic satisfiers are consistently related to job satisfaction across multiple studies.[22] In addition, research suggests that individuals who hold jobs that are intrinsically satisfying are less likely to turnover.[23]

Retention Bundles. The retention initiatives described up to this point have been described in terms of individual practices, such as providing rewards linked to tenure or matching offers from other organizations. This should not be taken to suggest that retention initiatives should be offered in isolation. To be effective, retention practices need to be integrated into a comprehensive system, or as a "**retention bundle**" of practices. One study grouped steel minimills into those that used a bundle of commitment-oriented staffing practices (including programs to foster social relationships, employee participation, and general training) as opposed to minimills that used control-oriented practices (including programs that focused on reducing employment costs through minimal investment in employee programs). Turnover was two times higher in control-oriented organizations relative to commitment oriented organizations.[24] A study examining a more diverse set of firms focused on alternative effective set of bundles, including extensive recruiting, careful use of validated selection strategies, attitude assessments, incentive compensation, organizational communication, and use of formal job analysis procedures. Each standard deviation increase in the use of this bundle of high-performance work practices resulted in a 7 percent decrease in the turnover rate relative to the average turnover rates.[25]

retention bundles
Retention practices integrated into a comprehensive system

In practical terms, managers need to examine all the characteristics in the work environment that might lead to turnover and address them in a comprehensive manner. Organizations that provide strong investments in their staffing methods may find their investments are lost if they do not support this strategy with an equally strong commitment to providing newcomers with sufficient orientation material to become adjusted to their new jobs. Organizations that provide numerous benefits in a poorly integrated fashion may similarly find that the intended effects are lost if managers and employees believe that the programs fail to address their needs.

Specific Retention Initiatives. To further illustrate policies that organizations might adopt to control turnover, Exhibit 11.10 summarizes practices from "Canada's Top 100 Employers 2006," reported the *Financial Post,* that have been able to significantly improve retention outcomes. The report compiled by Mediacorp Canada Inc. lists best practices in recruiting and retaining employees from over 1,200 workplaces across Canada who elect to take part in the complex application process.[26]

Professor Dan Ondrack of the Rotman School of Management suggests that top 100 companies have much less turnover (4% compared with 8% in most industries), so they have much lower training and development costs associated with integrating new staff. Professor Ondrack's research identified that it costs $50,000 to recruit, train, and assimilate a new semi-professional employee within an organization.[27]

EXHIBIT 11.9 Retention Initiatives: Usage and Effectiveness

Scale: 1 = very effective; 5 = not effective at all

	Effectiveness Average	Offer the Initiative? Yes	No	Plan To
1. Health care benefits	1.96	94%	3%	—
2. Competitive salaries	2.02	83%	8%	5%
3. Competitive salary increases	2.05	75%	15%	6%
4. Competitive vacation/holiday benefits	2.09	92%	4%	1%
5. Regular salary reviews	2.11	89%	6%	4%
6. Defined contribution retirement	2.21	73%	21%	2%
6. Paid personal time off	2.21	75%	20%	2%
8. Flexible work schedules	2.25	60%	32%	4%
9. Training and development opportunities	2.26	88%	4%	4%
10. Open door policy	2.32	93%	3%	2%
10. New hire orientation	2.32	92%	2%	3%
10. Defined benefit plan	2.32	52%	41%	2%
13. Child care paid/on-site	2.4	3%	89%	5%
14. Early eligibility for benefits	2.41	40%	54%	2%
14. Workplace location	2.41	59%	23%	—
16. Tuition reimbursement	2.42	77%	17%	3%
17. Retention bonuses	2.43	22%	71%	4%
18. Child care subsidies	2.46	8%	84%	4%
19. Spot cash	2.48	43%	47%	6%
20. Stock options	2.53	27%	66%	3%
21. Succession planning	2.54	32%	46%	16%
22. Non- or low-cash rewards	2.56	63%	25%	8%
23. Casual dress	2.59	76%	18%	1%
24. 360-degree feedback	2.6	31%	51%	14%
25. On-site parking	2.64	86%	10%	1%
26. Domestic partner benefits	2.66	12%	74%	4%
26. Eldercare subsidies	2.66	4%	89%	2%
28. Attitude surveys/focus groups	2.67	46%	41%	10%
28. Alternative dispute resolution	2.67	31%	60%	5%
30. Transportation subsidies	2.74	16%	75%	4%
31. Fitness facilities	2.75	26%	62%	8%
32. Severance package	2.77	56%	38%	1%
33. Sabbaticals	2.78	12%	82%	2%
34. Telecommuting	2.79	26%	64%	7%
35. Noncompete agreements	2.84	46%	48%	—
36. Concierge services	2.92	5%	87%	4%

Note: Data in row may not add up to 100% due to missing data.
Source: Society for Human Resource Management, *Retention Practices Survey* (Alexandria, VA: author, 2000), p. 12. Used with permission.

EXHIBIT 11.10 Retention Initiatives for Top 6 Companies in Financial Post 100 Companies to Work for in Canada 2006

Organization Name	Initiatives
Dofasco Inc.	Profit-sharing payments of at least $9,000 for each employee last year; holiday party for over 30,000 employees, retirees, and families; $15 million spent in training in last year
Ernst & Young LLP	Wide range of cash bonuses; maternity leave top-up (100% for 17 weeks); adoption assistance (to $5,000); emergency day care services; three additional paid days off
General Dynamics	Free turkeys to employees at Christmas; in-house hockey teams; two-month compassionate leave top-up; recognition awards of up to $750
The Great Little Box Company Ltd.	Mexico or Las Vegas trip incentives; employer that opens its books to employees each month; monthly profit-sharing payments; maternity and adoptive parent top-up payments
L'Oreal Canada Inc.	Tuition subsidies, online courses, and international training opportunities in Paris and New York; maternity and adoptive parent top-up payments (100% for 17 weeks); on-site day care centre
North Atlantic Refining Ltd.	Employee discounts on gas, propane, and heating equipment; training through tuition subsidies, bonuses, and scholarship program for post-secondary students

Decision Process. Decisions about whether to try to improve retention and how to do so should not be made lightly. The following are critical considerations in the decision-making process:

1. On average, organizations experience extensive voluntary turnover.
2. Organizations vary considerably in how much turnover they have.
3. Organizations think their turnover is due to many different causes.
4. Organizations commit substantial resources to multiple retention initiatives.
5. Organizations view retention initiatives as varying in effectiveness.

There is much that must be carefully thought through prior to actual action. Provided in Exhibit 11.11 is a suggested decision process to follow.

As shown in Exhibit 11.11 there are five sequential questions to ask and analyze. Listed with each question are several factors to consider when addressing that question.

1. Do We Think Turnover Is a Problem? Several types of data need to be considered and analyzed. First and most important is what percentage of turnover is voluntary and avoidable, followed closely by what the relevant organization units are for looking at the data. A breakout of voluntary avoidable turnover should be available for each unit. Then, it is necessary to judge whether the turnover rate(s) are increasing and/or high relative to internal and external benchmarks such as industry or direct competitor data. If turnover is relatively high or getting higher, this is cause for concern. Now additional digging is necessary, such as whether managers are complaining about retention problems, if mostly high-value employees are leaving, and whether there are demographic disparities among the leavers. If these indicators also show trouble signs, then it is likely that turnover is a problem. The final analysis should involve the type of costs/benefits described earlier. Even though turnover may be high and so forth, in the final analysis it is only a problem if its costs are judged to exceed the benefits it provides at its current rate, or future projected rate.

2. How Might We Attack This Problem? Key consideration areas are desirability of leaving, ease of leaving, and alternative turnover. Also, within each of these areas, which specific

EXHIBIT 11.11 Decision Process for Retention Initiatives

Do We Think Turnover Is a Problem?	How Might We Attack the Problem?	What Do We Need to Decide?	Should We Proceed?	How Should We Evaluate the Initiatives?
• Proportion of turnover that is available is high • Turnover calculated for separate units • Turnover high or increasing relative to internal and external benchmarks • Managers complain about retention problems • High-value employees are leaving • Demographic disparities among leavers • Overall costs exceed benefits of turnover	• Lower desirability of leaving? Increase job satisfaction—yes Decrease shocks—no Personal reasons—no • Lower ease of leaving? Change market conditions—no Provide organization-specific KSAOs—yes Make leaving more costly—yes • Change alternatives? Promotion and transfers—yes Respond to job offers—yes	• Turnover goals • Targeted to units and groups • High-value employees • General and targeted retention initiatives • Lead, match, or lag the market • Supplement or supplant • HR and managers' roles	• Feasibility • Probability of success • Timing	• Lower proportion of turnover if avoidable • Turnover low or decreasing compared to benchmarks • Fewer complaints about retention problems • Fewer high-value employees leaving • Reduced demographic disparities • Lower costs relative to benefits

factors is it possible to change? Referring to Exhibit 11.11, for desirability of leaving it shows that increasing job satisfaction is possible, while it is likely not possible to change personal shocks or personal reasons for leaving. Likewise, for ease of leaving it is possible to provide organization-specific KSAOs and to increase the cost of leaving for the organization.

3. What Do We Need to Decide? Decisions now need to be made to cross the boundary from consideration to possible implementation. In working through this question, the first decision is the specific numerical turnover (retention) goals in the form of desired turnover rates. Retention programs without retention goals are bound to fail. Next, consideration needs to be given to whether the retention goals and programs will be across the board or targeted to specific organization units and/or employee groups. Examples of target groups include certain job categories in which turnover is particularly troublesome or where there is traditionally high turnover (e.g., women and minorities, first-year employees, newcomers).

Then the consideration becomes if and how high-value employees will be treated. If the organization has not previously identified high-value employees, then an employee assessment system for guiding such a determination will be the necessary first step. Many organizations develop special retention initiatives for high-value employees, on top of other retention programs, and it will have to be decided whether to follow this path of special treatment for such employees.[28]

Having identified and established turnover goals for organizational units, targeted groups, and high-value employees, the retention program specifics must be designed. They may be general (across-the-board) initiatives applicable to all employees, or they may be targeted ones. For each initiative it must be decided how to position the organization's initiative relative to the marketplace and whether it will seek to lead, match, or lag the market.

An example would be considering how base pay and variable pay plans should be positioned to attract candidates with the required skill sets. Will base pay on average be set higher than the market average (lead), the same as the market average (match), or lower than the market average (lag)? Also, will new variable pay plans try to outdo competitors by providing, for example, a more favourable stock option plan, simply try to match competitors, or be less competitive?

Add to the complexity the delicate issue of whether new retention initiatives will supplement (add on to) or supplant (replace) existing rewards and programs. If the decision is replacement, the organization should be prepared for the possibility of employee backlash against what employees may perceive as "take-backs" of rewards they currently have and must give up.

Finally, the respective rules of HR and individual managers will have to be worked out, and this may vary among the retention initiatives. If the initiative involves responding to job offers, for example, line managers may demand a heavy or even exclusive hand in making them. Alternatively, some initiatives may be driven by HR; examples include hours of work and variable pay plans.

4. Should We Proceed? It will depend on judgments about feasibility, such as ease of implementation. Judgments about probability of success will also enter in, and having specific turnover (retention) goals will be of immense help in making the decision. Finally, matters of timing should enter in. Even if judged to be feasible and a likely success, a retention program may not be launched immediately. Other HR problem areas and initiatives may have emerged and taken on higher priority. Or, turnover problems may have lost urgency because looser labour markets may have intervened to reduce turnover at the very time the retention initiatives were being planned.

5. How Should We Evaluate the Initiatives? This question may be quite hypothetical since the decision to proceed with the intervention has not yet been made. Answers will provide focus to the design of the intervention and the agreed upon criteria, which will be the basis used to judge the intervention's effectiveness. Ideally, the same criteria that led to the conclusion that turnover was a problem (question #1) will be used to determine whether the solution that has been chosen actually works (question #5). For this reason, the same criteria as shown under question #1 are shown under question #5.

Desirability of Leaving

desire to leave
Decision depends on employee job satisfaction, shocks they experience, and personal (nonjob) reasons

Employees' **desire to leave** depends on their job satisfaction, shocks they experience, and personal (nonjob) reasons. Of these, only job satisfaction can usually be meaningfully influenced by the organization. So the first strategy for improving retention is to improve job satisfaction. The myriad examples of retention initiatives used by organizations described above represent mostly attempts to improve job satisfaction through delivery of various rewards to employees. Indeed, refer back to the multitude of job rewards displayed in Exhibits 4.24 and 4.25. These include direct compensation (base and variable pay), indirect compensation (benefits), hours of work, career advancement, job security, and several intrinsic rewards. Providing either greater amounts of these rewards or adding them to the set of rewards already provided to employees represent key strategies for improving job satisfaction and hopefully retention.

It is critical to understand that merely "throwing" more or new rewards at employees is not a sound retention initiative. Which rewards are chosen, and how they are delivered to employees, will determine how effective they are in improving job satisfaction. Accordingly, guidelines for reward choice and delivery are also described.

Guidelines for Increasing Job Satisfaction and Retention Recalling our discussion in Chapter 4, there are a variety of extrinsic and intrinsic rewards that can be brought to bear on the question of job satisfaction. Rather than reiterating these specific rewards here, we instead discuss the manner in which organizations can provide both categories of rewards consistent with the best practices identified by research and experience (see Exhibit 11.12).

EXHIBIT 11.12 Guidelines for Increasing Job Satisfaction and Retention

A. Extrinsic Rewards
- Reward must be meaningful and unique.
- Reward must match individual preferences.
- Link rewards to retention behaviours.
- Link reward to performance.

B. Intrinsic Rewards
- Assign employees to jobs that meet their needs for work characteristics.
- Provide clear communications with employees.
- Design fair reward allocation systems.
- Ensure supervisors provide a positive environment.

job satisfaction
Results from a match between the rewards desired by employees and the rewards provided by the job

One important point must be borne in mind for both intrinsic and extrinsic rewards. The person/job match model emphasizes that **job satisfaction** results from a match between the rewards desired by employees and the rewards provided by the job. It is also important to provide rewards large enough to be meaningful to the recipient. For example, an employee earning $50,000 who receives a gross 4 percent raise of $2,000 will realize a raise of 2.8 percent if inflation and taxes combined are at 30 percent. Such a net raise may not be very meaningful.

Employee reward preferences may be assessed at all stages of the staffing process by doing the following:

1. Asking applicants what attracted them to the organization
2. Asking current employees about the most important sources of job satisfaction
3. Assessing reasons for turnover during exit interviews

extrinsic rewards
Rewards that are unique and unlikely to be offered by competitors with base pay levels as an important component of these rewards

Extrinsic Rewards. To have attraction and retention power, extrinsic rewards must be unique and unlikely to be offered by competitors. The organization must benchmark against its competitors to determine what others are offering. Base pay levels are an important component in this process. Organizations may attempt to lead the market by providing wages above the market level. This leader strategy allows the organization to attract a higher-quality workforce, provides a workforce that is very satisfied with its pay, and minimizes the attractiveness of alternatives because employees cannot find comparable salaries elsewhere.[29] This market leader strategy can be pursued for any reward, and can be tailored to particular employee and industry demands. For example, if an organization is a seasonal employer in the recreation and tourism industry, it may concede pay leadership and lead with benefits such as free use of equipment (e.g., boats, bikes), clothing at cost, and free passes for use of facilities.

In providing extrinsic rewards, it is important to remember that employees will differ in their preference for compensation, benefits, and other potential positive outcomes. Employees with heavy family commitments may place a greater value on reductions in working hours or the opportunity to work from home. On the other hand, employees without such commitments may prefer opportunities for travel in their work. Other employees may be more concerned about increases in their base compensation levels. It is important for supervisors to carefully assess employee preferences to maximize the positive outcomes of rewards.

Rewards can be even more powerfully attached to employee retention if they explicitly take seniority into account. For example, employees who have been with the organization longer may receive more vacation hours, career advancement opportunities, and increased job security. A more subtle way of rewarding employee retention is to make the reward contingent on the person's base pay level. Base pay levels typically increase over time through a combination of promotions and merit pay increases. Defined benefit retirement plans, for example, typically calculate retirement pay as some percentage (say, 50%) of the average person's three highest years of pay multiplied by years of service. Specific retention bonuses are also used to encourage longer-term relationships.

Rewards can also be linked to employee job performance. Organizations with a strong performance management culture thrive on high performance expectations, coupled with large rewards (e.g., base pay raises, bonuses, commissions, and stock options) for high performers. Because lesser performers receive lower wages in these organizations, they are more likely to leave, whereas superior performers are more likely to stay.[30] Organizations may even more specifically target key performers by providing special retention bonuses, new job assignments, and additional perks if it appears that top performers are likely to leave.[31]

intrinsic rewards
Rewards that revolve around job quality and work environment, and are of value to employees

Intrinsic Rewards. The **intrinsic rewards** described in Exhibit 11.12 should not be overlooked. There is consistent evidence that employee dissatisfaction with the intrinsic quality of their jobs is strongly related to turnover.[32]

Improving the work environment involves assigning employees to jobs that better meet their intrinsic-reward preferences. For example, employees with high needs for skill variety could be assigned to more complex jobs or projects within a work unit, or employees with high autonomy needs could be assigned to supervisors with a very "hands-off" style of leadership. Job redesign can also improve the work environment. To increase skill variety, managers may broaden the scope of tasks and responsibility for longer-term employees, allowing for personal growth on the job. Job rotation programs also help to reduce perceived monotony on the job. Some organizations combine intrinsic and extrinsic rewards through the development of formal knowledge- and skill-based plans. In these plans, specific knowledge or skills are designated as critical, and employees receive a predetermined increase in base pay for demonstrated proficiency or acquisition of the knowledge or skill. For example, many school boards provide teachers with increases in their base compensation level for receiving masters' degrees. Enhancing job autonomy might be facilitated by establishing formal performance goals for the job, but giving employees minimal direction or oversight for the methods required to achieve these goals. Similar methods for improving task identity, task significance, and feedback should also be considered.

distributive justice
Perceptions that individual reward levels are consistent with employees' contributions to the organization

procedural justice
Perceptions that the process for allocating rewards and punishments is administered consistently, following well-defined guidelines, and is free from bias

One of the closest correlates of employee commitment is the perception that the organization engages in fair treatment of its employees and provides them with support. Two forms of justice are necessary.[33] **Distributive justice** refers to perceptions that the individual reward levels are consistent with employee contributions to the organization. **Procedural justice** refers to perceptions that the process for allocating rewards and punishments is administered consistently, follows well-defined guidelines, and is free from bias. A sense that these justice principles have been violated can create dissatisfaction and may result in turnover or a lawsuit.

A crucial component to increasing employees' perception of justice is clear communication. Communication must begin early in the staffing process by providing employees with honest information about their job conditions. Evidence suggests that employees who receive adequate information regarding job conditions perceive their employers as more honest and may be less likely to turnover.[34] If reward systems are going to increase satisfaction, employees must know why the system was developed, the mechanics of the system, and the payouts to be expected. Such knowledge and understanding require continuous communication. Research shows that a very common form of employee dissatisfaction with reward systems is a failure to understand them, or actual misinformation about them.[35] Any retention initiative designed to increase job satisfaction must have a solid communication component. On a broader level, communication regarding the organization's strategic direction can reduce turnover. Surveys at SAP Software indicated that employees who felt that the organization had a clear vision for the future and believed that top management supported them were more likely to report that they were engaged in their work.[36]

Justice perceptions are also strongly influenced by reward system design. Distributive justice requires that there be a rational and preferably measurable basis for reward decisions. Seniority-based rewards score high here because many employees believe seniority is a legitimate way to distinguish employees, and because it can be objectively measured. Objective measures of job performance, such as sales figures, are also likely to be accepted as legitimate. Rewards based on managerial performance reviews may be more problematic if employees question the legitimacy of the performance measurement system, or if they believe that these rewards create divisive comparisons among employees. When managerial reviews are part of the rewards process, the procedures involved in the review should be clearly communicated to employees.

It is said that employees don't quit their jobs, they quit their bosses. Thus, interpersonal compatibility or chemistry between the employee and supervisor can be a critical part of the employee's decision to stay or leave. The same could be said for co-workers. Employees who believe that they fit with the social environment in which they work are more likely to see their jobs as a source of significant social rewards. The resultant sense of camaraderie with the supervisor and co-workers may make them reluctant to leave the organization.

The supervisor also is a source of justice perceptions because of his or her role as a direct source of reward or punishment. The supervisor functions as an intermediary between the employee and the organization's compensation and promotion systems. This is because they decide the process for assessing employees, as well as the amount of rewards to be provided on the basis of these assessments. The supervisor will also serve as a key communication conduit regarding reward systems. If supervisors communicate the purpose and mechanics of the system, employees will be able to understand the process of reward distribution, and also understand what they need to do if they wish to receive rewards in the future.

Supervisors and co-workers in the social setting can also engage in abusive or harassing behaviours that are threatening or discomforting to the employees. Research suggests that employees who believe that their supervisors are abusive are more likely to turnover, as indicated in the AEGON story at the beginning of this chapter.[37] Examples of abusive supervisor behaviours that are frequently cited in surveys include "tells me my thoughts and feelings are stupid," "puts me down in front of others," and "tells me I'm incompetent." More extreme behaviours, such as sexual harassment, will have even stronger negative impacts on employee's desire to remain on the job. Turnover due to interpersonal conflicts at work tends to come especially quickly; many employees who have such conflicts will bypass the process of intentions to turnover and job search and will instead quit immediately.

Ease of Leaving

The decision process (Exhibit 11.11) indicates two points of attack on ease of leaving—providing organization-specific training and increasing the cost of leaving. The third possible factor, changing labour market conditions, cannot be influenced and represents a variable that will continuously influence the organization's voluntary turnover.

Organization-Specific Training Training and development activities provide KSAOs to employees that they did not possess at the time they entered the organization as new hires. Training and development seek to increase labour quality in ways that will enhance employees' effectiveness. As shown previously, training represents a substantial investment (cost) that evaporates when an employee leaves the organization.

The organization may invest in training to provide KSAOs that vary along a continuum of general to organization specific. The more general the KSAOs, the more transferable they are to other organizations, thus increasing the likelihood they improve the employee's marketability and raise the probability of leaving. Organization-specific KSAOs are not transferable, and possession of them does not improve employee marketability. Hence, it is possible to lower the employee's ease of leaving by providing, as much as possible, only organization-specific training content that has value only as long as the employee remains with the organization.

This strategy needs to be coupled with a selection strategy in which any general KSAOs required for the job are assessed and selected so that they will not have to be invested in once the employee is on the job. For example, applicants for an entry-level sales job might be assessed and selected for general sales competencies such as written and verbal communication and interpersonal skills. Those hired may then receive more specialized training in such areas as product knowledge, specific software, and knowledge of territories. To the extent such organization-specific KSAOs become an increasingly large proportion of the employee's total KSAO package over time, they help restrict the employee's mobility.

This strategy entails some risk. It assumes the general KSAOs are available and affordable among applicants. It also assumes these applicants will not be turned off by the job if they learn about the organization-specific training and development they will receive.

Increased Cost of Leaving Driving up the cost of leaving is a way to make it less easy to leave. Providing above-market pay and benefits is one way to do this since employees will find it difficult to find better-paying jobs elsewhere. Any form of deferred compensation, such as deferred bonuses, will also raise the cost of leaving since the compensation will be lost if the employee leaves prior to being eligible to receive it.

Retention bonuses might also be used. Normally, these are keyed to high-value employees whose loss would wreak organizational havoc. Such may be the case during mergers and acquisitions, when retention of key managers is essential to a smooth transition. For example, when Canadian Imperial Bank of Commerce (CIBC) purchased Merrill Lynch's stockbroker retailer network, 1,000 stockbrokers were given a one-time retention bonus equal to 110 percent of their take-home pay in the year 2000. This was a considerable amount considering that about 75 of the stockbrokers had income of more than $1 million a year.[38]

Another long-term way to make leaving costly is to locate the organization's facilities in an area where it is the dominant employer and other amenities (housing, schools, health care) are accessible and affordable. This may entail location in the outer rings of suburban areas or relatively small and rural communities. Once employees move to and settle into these locations, the cost of leaving is high because of the lack of alternative jobs within the area and a need to make a costly geographic shift in order to obtain a new job.

Alternatives

In confronting outside alternatives available to employees, the organization must fashion ways to make even better internal alternatives available and desirable. Two key ways to do this involve internal staffing and responding to outside job offers.

internal staffing

Creates opportunities for employees to look internally for new job opportunities and for managers to benefit by seeking internal candidates rather than going to the outside

Internal Staffing The nature and operation of **internal staffing** systems have been explored already. It is important to reiterate that open systems serve as a safety value, retentionwise, in that employees are encouraged to look internally for new job opportunities and managers benefit by seeking internal candidates rather than going to the outside. The organization should also think of ways outside the realm of its traditional internal staffing systems to provide attractive internal alternatives to its employees.

For example, Mercer Management Consulting has developed a rotational externship program for some of its consultants. These consultants are allowed to take on a full-time operational role for a client for 6 to 24 months, rather than handle multiple clients, allowing the consultant the satisfaction of seeing a project through to completion and to gain valuable operating experience. It is hoped that these consultants will return to Mercer at the end of the project, based on the bird-in-the-hand theory—if you love it, let it go; if it loves you, it will come back. Another example is a temporary internal transfer system used by Interbrand Group, Inc., a unit of Omnicom Group, Inc. Certain high-performance employees are offered short-term transfers to any of its 26 offices worldwide. The lateral moves last from three months to one year. The transfers allow employees to get a change in life without having to quit their jobs.[39]

Response to Job Offers When employees receive an actual outside job offer, or are on the verge of receiving one, they clearly have a solid job alternative in hand. How should the organization respond, if at all, in order to make itself the preferred alternative?

The organization should confront this dilemma with some carefully thought through policies in advance. This will help prevent some knee-jerk, potentially regrettable actions being taken on the spot when an employee brings forth a job offer and wants to use it for leverage.

First, the organization should decide whether it will or will not be willing to respond to job offers. Some organizations choose not to, thereby avoiding bidding wars and counteroffer games; and even if the organization successfully retained the employee, the employee may now lack commitment to the organization, and other employees may resent the special retention deal that was cut. Other organizations choose to respond to job offers, not wanting to automatically close out an opportunity to at least respond to, and hopefully retain, the employee. Other times, job offers are welcomed because they help the organization sort out who its stars are and what kinds of offer packages it may have to give other recruits in order to lure them into the organization's fold. There is even an example of an organization that pays $1,000 "notification bonuses" to employees who disclose receiving an outside offer so that it can learn its content and have the option of being able to respond to it.[40] The price for such an openness to outside offers is that it may encourage employees to actively solicit them in order to try to squeeze a counteroffer out of the organization, thus improving the "deal."

The second major policy issue is for which employees will the organization respond to outside offers. Will it be all employees, or only select ones, and if so, which select ones? Here, the focus should likely be on high-value employees.

A third set of policy issues pertains to who will put together the counteroffer, and what approval process must be followed. While individual managers will likely want wide latitude over these issues, the HR function will need to be an important player for cost control purposes, as well as for ensuring procedural and distributive justice overall.

RETENTION INITIATIVES: TERMINATION

Performance Management

RPC 5.4

performance management
System used by many organizations to help ensure that the initial person/job match made during staffing yields an effectively performing employee, to facilitate employee performance improvement and competency growth, and to detect and hopefully remedy performance problems

Performance management is used by many organizations to help ensure that the initial person/job match made during staffing yields an effectively performing employee, to facilitate employee performance improvement and competency growth, and to detect and hopefully remedy performance problems. Performance management systems focus most of their attention on planning, enabling, appraising, and rewarding employee performance.[41] Having a performance management system in place, however, also allows the organization to systematically detect and treat performance problems employees exhibit before those problems become so harmful and intractable that termination is the only recourse. The termination prevention possibilities of a performance management system make it another important retention initiative to use within an overall retention program. Also, a sound performance management system can be very useful in helping organizations successfully defend itself against legal challenges to terminations that do occur.

Exhibit 11.13 portrays the performance management process. Organization strategy drives work-unit plans, which in turn become operational and doable for employees through a four-stage process.

- **Stage 1: Performance planning** involves setting performance goals for each employee and identifying specific competencies the employee will be evaluated on.
- **Stage 2: Performance execution** focuses on the employee actually performing the job. Assistance to the employee could or should be made in the form of resources to aid in job performance, coupled with coaching and feedback from the employee's manager, peers, and others, which often occurs quarterly or yearly.
- **Stage 3: Formal performance review** is conducted usually by the manager. An assessment is made of the employee's success in reaching established goals, ratings of the employee's competencies are made, written comments are developed to explain ratings and provide

suggestions for performance improvement, and feedback of the assessment is provided to the employee. Collectively, these actions are known as performance appraisal.

- **Stage 4: Decision making** involves using the information developed during the performance review to help make decisions that will affect the employee. Most likely, these decisions pertain to pay raises and to training and career plans. They may also pertain to formal identification of performance problems, where the employee either has shown, or is headed toward, unacceptable performance. After decisions are made, the performance cycle is complete, and performance planning begins again.

It should be noted that the design, implementation, and operation of a performance management system is a complex undertaking, and the specific ways that the four stages described above are actually carried out vary among organizations.[42] For purposes here, however, the performance management system depicted in Exhibit 11.13 shows how such a system can be a critical retention tool for the organization when it is confronted with employees who are having severe performance problems that place them on the cusp of termination.

Specifically, it may be decided that an employee has severe performance problems (stage four), and this can then set in motion a focused performance-improvement process throughout the next performance management cycle. To begin, performance directions and standards are established for the performance problem employee. These are the critical yardsticks that can be used to communicate performance expectations to employees and later laid against the employee's performance to determine actual performance attainments. Employees who are experiencing performance problems will thus have clear indications of performance expectations and needed performance improvements. It is unwise to then simply "turn the employee loose" to perform unaided. There is no reason to recycle and repeat past actions. Instead, assistance in the form of resources to do the job and particularly attentive coaching and feedback from the manager are ingredients for performance improvement by the employee. During performance review, special attention will have to be paid to those areas in which the employee's performance was deemed to be a problem, and a very thorough documentation and review of all the performance data will

EXHIBIT 11.13 Performance Management Process

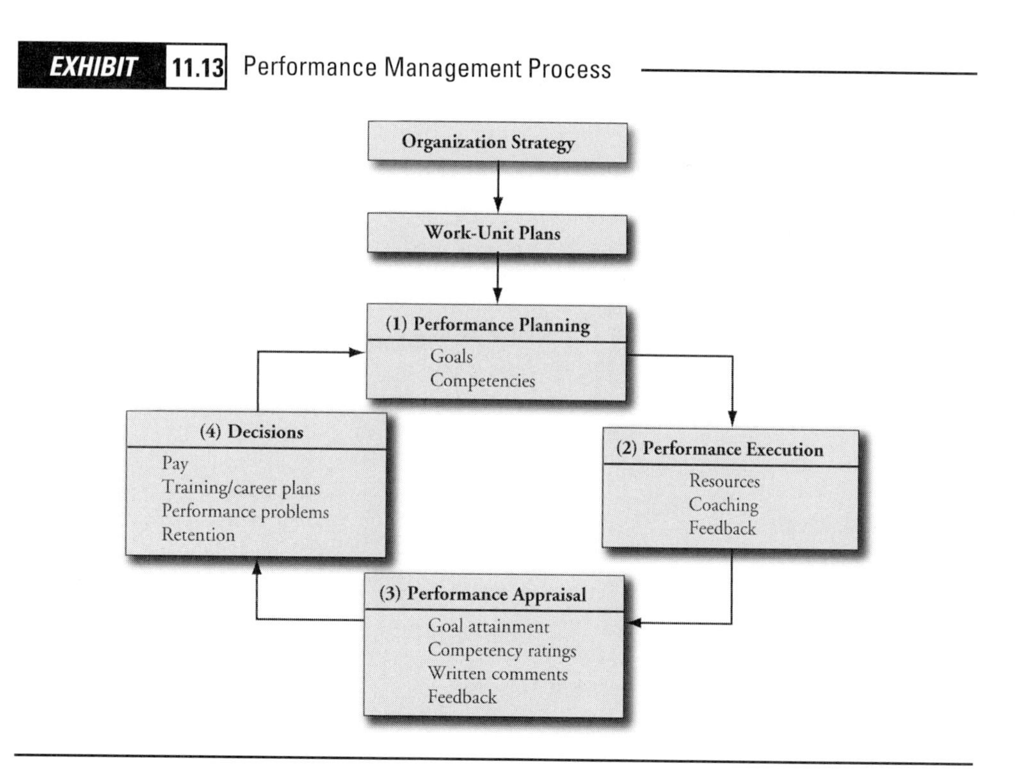

be necessary. Based on the analysis and evaluation of the data, it will then have to be decided whether sufficient performance improvement has occurred to warrant continued retention of the employee.

Manager Training and Rewards There are many components required for a successful performance management system. None are probably more critical than training and rewards for the managers who will be users of the performance management system with employees in their work units.[43]

Performance management requires a complex set of knowledges and skills that managers must possess, particularly for the performance execution and performance appraisal stages. Training for managers is essential to provide them these requisites to being effective performance managers. Examples of training content include purposes of performance management, policies and procedures of the performance management system, appraisal forms and how to complete them, keeping records of employee performance incidents, rating accuracy, coaching techniques, finding and providing resources, methods of providing feedback, goal setting, and legal compliance requirements. It is especially important to stress exactly why and how performance management is to be used as a retention initiative that seeks to prevent termination through intensive performance improvement attempts.

Managers must also be provided incentives for using these new knowledges and skills to effectively conduct performance management. At a minimum it is necessary to formally make performance management a part of the manager's job, during the performance planning stage for the manager, so that the manager will have performance management as an area of responsibility requiring attention and that the manager's own performance appraisal results will depend on how well the manager practices performance management. Of course, reward decisions such as pay raises can then be driven at least in part by this portion of the performance appraisal. One of the manager's most important rewards will be an intrinsic one, namely, the experience of helping a performance problem employee improve sufficiently that the employee is retained by the organization.

Another important part of training should be concerned with employee termination. Here managers must come to understand that a decision to terminate an employee for performance problems falls outside of the normal performance management process (Exhibit 11.13) and is not a decision that can or should be made alone by the individual manager. Terminations require separate procedural and decision-making processes.[44] These could also be covered as part of a regular performance management training program, or a separate program devoted to termination could be conducted.

Progressive Discipline

Employee discipline pertains to problems of behavioural conduct that violate rules, procedures, laws, and professional and moral standards.[45] Discipline may also come into play for performance problem employees. Progressive discipline has a series of penalties for misconduct that increase in severity if the misconduct is repeated, starting with an informal warning and going all the way up to termination. The goal of progressive discipline is retention, except in circumstances of repeated misconduct or extreme misconduct that warrant termination. In progressive discipline, employees are given notice of their misconduct and are provided the opportunity (and often the assistance) to change their behaviour; termination is a last resort. Exhibit 11.14 outlines the steps in progressive discipline systems, which are rooted in major principles of fairness and justice.[46]

Failure to incorporate the requirements shown in Exhibit 11.14 into the organization's discipline process can result in very negative reactions of employees—work-unit disruption, job actions such as work slowdowns, sabotage, and turnover—because employees feel justice is being meted out unfairly.

EXHIBIT 11.14 Steps in a Progressive Discipline System

1. Give employees notice of the rules of conduct and misconduct.
2. Give employees notice of the consequences of violation of the rules.
3. Provide equal treatment for all employees.
4. Allow for full investigation of the alleged misconduct and defence of the employee.
5. Provide employees the right to appeal a decision.

EXHIBIT 11.15 Progressive Discipline Examples: Misconduct and Penalties

A. Misconduct

Minor Offence	Moderate Offence	Major Offence
• Punctuality	• Equipment damage	• Dishonesty
• Horseplay	• Misdemeanour (on job)	• Felony
• Cleanliness	• Harassment	• Sabotage
• Computer—personal use	• Unsafe behaviour	• Theft
• Smoking	• Hostile work environment	• Drug/alcohol on job
• Dress code	• Professional standards breach	• Firearms/explosives

B. Penalties

Minor Offence

First Time	Second Time	Third Time	Fourth Time
Oral warning or written reprimand	Written reprimand or suspension	Suspension or termination	Discharge Termination

Moderate Offence

First Time	Second Time	Third Time	Fourth Time
Written reprimand	Suspension	Longer suspension	Termination

Major Offence

First Time	Second Time	Third Time	Fourth Time
Suspension or termination	Termination	Not applicable	Not applicable

Actions to Take To address those fairness requirements, several things should be done. First, establish what constitutes misconduct and the penalties for misconduct. Exhibit 11.15 provides examples of various forms of misconduct, grouped according to severity (minor, moderate, major). Also shown are examples of penalties for each category of severity. The penalties start with an oral warning and progress through a written warning, suspension, and termination. Second, provide training to employees and managers so that they are aware of the types of misconduct, penalties, investigation and documentation requirements, and appeal rights. Third, work with managers to ensure that there is consistency of treatment (no favouritism) of employees, meaning that similar misconduct results in similar penalties for all employees. Finally, establish an appeals procedure in which employees may challenge disciplinary actions if one is not already in place. This could be based on a variety of alternative dispute resolution procedures described in Chapter 12.

Documentation by the manager is critical in all but the least severe instances of misconduct (e.g., first-time minor offence with an oral warning).[47] Thus, the manager must investigate allegations of misconduct, gather evidence, and write down and keep records of what was learned. Allegations of tardiness, for example, might involve inspection of time cards and interviews with other employees. The time cards and interview notes should then be kept as part of the documentation record. Employees should have the right to see all documentation and provide written documentation in self-defence.

Though not shown in Exhibit 14.15, performance problems could be incorporated into, or dovetailed with, the progressive discipline system.[48] Here, it would be wise if possible to first adhere to the normal performance management cycle, so that correction of performance deficiencies is done in a consultative way between the employee and the manager, and the manager assumes major responsibility for providing resources to the employee, as well as for attentive coaching and feedback. If performance improvement is not forthcoming, then shifting to the progressive discipline system will be necessary. For very serious performance problems, it may be necessary for the manager to address them with an expedited performance management cycle, coupled with a clear communication to the employee that failure to correct performance problems could lead immediately to the beginning of formal disciplinary actions.

5.5

Employee termination is the final step in progressive discipline, and ideally it would never be necessary. Rarely, if ever, will this be the case. The organization thus must be prepared for the necessity of conducting terminations. Termination processes, guidelines, training for managers, and so forth must be developed and implemented. Considerable guidance is available to help the organization in this regard.[49]

RETENTION INITIATIVES: DOWNSIZING

Downsizing involves reduction in the organization's staffing levels through layoffs (RIFs). Many factors contribute to layoff occurrences: decline in profits, restructuring of the organization, substitution of the core workforce with a flexible workforce, obsolete job or work unit, mergers and acquisitions, loss of contracts and clients, technological advances, productivity improvements, shortened product life cycles, and financial markets that favour downsizing as a positive organizational action.[50] While downsizing obviously involves the elimination of jobs and employees, it also encompasses several retention matters. These involve balancing the advantages and disadvantages of downsizing, staffing levels and quality, alternatives to layoffs, and dealing with employees who remain after downsizing.

Weighing Advantages and Disadvantages

There are multiple advantages (benefits) and disadvantages (costs) of downsizing; refer back to Exhibit 11.8 for a review. A thoughtful consideration of these makes it clear that if downsizing is to be undertaken, it should be done with great caution. It is simply not usually an effective "quick fix" to financial performance problems confronting the organization.

Moreover, research suggests that the presumed and hoped-for benefits of downsizing may not be as great as it might seem.[51] For example, one study looked at how employment level changes affected profitability and stock returns of 537 organizations over a 14-year period. Downsizing did not significantly improve profitability, though it did produce somewhat better stock returns. But organizations that combined downsizing with asset restructuring fared better. Another study looked at the incidence of downsizing across the regional sales offices of a large financial services organization and found layoffs ranged from 0 to 29 percent of the workforce, with an average of 7 percent. It was also found that the amount of downsizing had a significant negative impact on sales offices' profitability, productivity, and customer satisfaction. Additional research has found that downsizing has negative impacts on employee morale and health, workgroup creativity and communication, and workforce quality.[52]

In short, downsizing is not a panacea for poor financial health. It has many negative impacts on employees and should be combined with a well-planned total restructuring if it is to be effective. Such conclusions suggest the organization should carefully ponder if in fact it wants to downsize; if so, by how much; and which employees should it seek to retain.

Staffing Levels and Quality

Reductions in staffing levels should be mindful of retention in at least two ways. First, enthusiasm for a financial quick fix needs to be tempered by a realization that once lost, many downsized employees may be unlikely to return later if economic circumstances improve. It will then have to engage in costly restaffing, as opposed to potentially less costly and quicker retention initiatives. At a minimum, therefore, the organization should consider alternatives to downsizing simultaneous with downsizing planning. Such an exercise may well lead to lesser downsizing and greater retention.

Staffing level reductions should also be thought of in selective or targeted terms, rather than across the board. Such a conclusion is a logical outgrowth of human resource planning, through which it is invariably discovered that the forecasted labour demand and supply figures lead to differing human resource head-count requirements across organizational units and job categories. Indeed, it is possible that some units or job categories may be confronting layoffs while others will actually be hiring. Such an occurrence is increasingly common in organizations.[53]

If cuts are to be made, who should be retained? Staffing quality and employee acceptance concerns combine to produce some alternatives to choose from. The first alternative would be to retain the most senior employees, and cut the least senior employees, in each work unit. Such an approach explicitly rewards the most senior employees, thus likely enhancing long-run retention efforts by signalling job security commitments to long-term employees. Such seniority-based retention also likely meets with strong employee acceptance. On the downside, the most senior employees may not be the best performers, and looking ahead, the most senior employees may not have the necessary qualifications for job requirements changes that will be occurring as part of the restructuring process. In addition, seniority-based layoffs raise important but thorny procedural internal labour market issues, such as how to exactly count seniority and what (if any) "bumping" rights employees targeted for layoff might have. **Bumping** is a process by which an employee may avoid layoff by taking over the job of another employee, usually one with less seniority, who will be laid off instead. In unionized settings, such issues are typically spelled out at length in the labour contract.[54]

bumping
A process by which an employee may avoid layoff by taking over the job of another employee, usually one with less seniority, who will be laid off instead

A second alternative would be to make performance-based retention decisions. Employees' current and possibly past performance appraisals' would be consulted in each work unit. The lowest-performing employees would be designated for layoff. This approach seeks to retain the highest-quality employees, those who through their performance are contributing most to organizational effectiveness. It may meet with less employee acceptance than the first alternative among some employees because of perceived injustice in the performance appraisal process. It also assumes that the current crop of best performers will continue to be so in the future, even though job requirements might be changing. And legal challenges may arise, as discussed later.

A third alternative focuses on retaining what were called "high-value employees" and concentrating layoffs on "low-value employees" (Exhibit 11.1). Here, multiple criteria of value are used, rather than a single one such as seniority or performance, though both of these value indicators would likely be included in the value assessments of employees. Recognition of multiple indicators of value is more encompassing in terms of employees' likely future contributions to organizational effectiveness, and because of this it may also meet with high employee acceptance. Use of this approach, however, requires a complex and potentially burdensome process. Indeed, the process is directly akin to an internal selection system in which the value indicators must be identified, assessed, scored, and weighted to come up with a composite value score for each employee that would then be used as the basis for the retention decision. Cut scores are also probably required.

Alternatives to Downsizing

A no-layoffs or a guaranteed employment policy as an organization strategy is the most dramatic alternative to downsizing. Several major organizations pursue this strategy, including S.C. Johnson, Pella, Nucor, Northwestern Mutual, Enterprise Rent-A-Car, Erie Insurance, and Lincoln Electric.[55] At Lincoln Electric, every employee who has three or more years of continuous service is guaranteed a minimum of 75 percent of a normal workweek. This guarantee is for a job, not a specific position, so cross-training with flexible internal mobility is practical. To create a staffing buffer, during peak times overtime is paid rather than staffing up with new employees; then during downturns, overtime hours, but not employees, are cut. Incentive pay systems are used, along with letting go of people who don't meet performance expectations. Senior executives have a higher percentage of their pay in profit sharing than the rest of the workforce, which functions as an economic buffer during downturns.

No-layoff strategies require considerable organization and HR planning, along with a commitment to a set of programs necessary for successfully implementing the strategy. The strategies also require a gamble and bet that, if lost, could severely damage employee loyalty and trust.

Other organizations are unwilling to make a no-layoff guarantee but pursue layoff minimization through many different programs. Exhibit 11.16 provides an example, based on a survey of 226 organizations. It can be seen that multiple steps were taken prior to layoff, headed by attrition (not replacing employees who leave), employment freezes, and nonrenewal of contract workers. A series of direct and indirect pay changes (e.g., salary reduction, early retirement) also played some role in their layoff minimization. Other actions are also possible, such as temporary layoff with some proportion of pay and benefits continued, substitution of stock options for bonuses, conversion of regular employees to independent contractors, temporary assignments at a reduced time (and pay) commitment, and off-site Internet employees who temporarily convert to work-at-home on a reduced time (and pay) basis.[56]

Employees Who Remain

Employees who remain either in their prelayoff or in a redeployed job after a downsizing must not be ignored. Doing otherwise creates a new retention problem—survivors who are stressed and critical of the downsizing process. One study of survivors found that less than 50 percent of them rated management's honesty as positive in regard to layoffs, felt support for remaining staff was adequate, and thought their organizations recognized the value of remaining employees. Moreover, almost half of the survivors learned about the downsizing through rumours or word of mouth.[57] In terms of stress, it is heightened by loss of co-workers and friends, higher workloads, new locations and work hours, new and/or more responsibilities, and fear of job loss just around the corner.

These many examples of "survivor sickness" suggest a need to anticipate and attack it directly within downsizing planning. One survey reported that organizations sought to meet survivors' needs through enhanced communication programs, morale-boosting events, promotion of the employee assistance program, and stress-related training. Surprisingly, 30 percent of organizations surveyed reported they took no steps to deal with survivors.[58] Unless steps are taken to help survivors plan for and adjust to the new realities they will confront, heightened job dissatisfaction seems inevitable. In turn, voluntary turnover may spike upward, increasing even more the cost of downsizing.

LEGAL ISSUES

Retention initiatives are closely intertwined with the occurrence of employee separations, since the result of an unsuccessful retention initiative is the voluntary or involuntary separation of the employee from the organization. The organization's retention initiatives thus must be guided in part by the laws and regulations governing separations. A brief overview of these is provided.

EXHIBIT 11.16 Layoff Minimization Examples

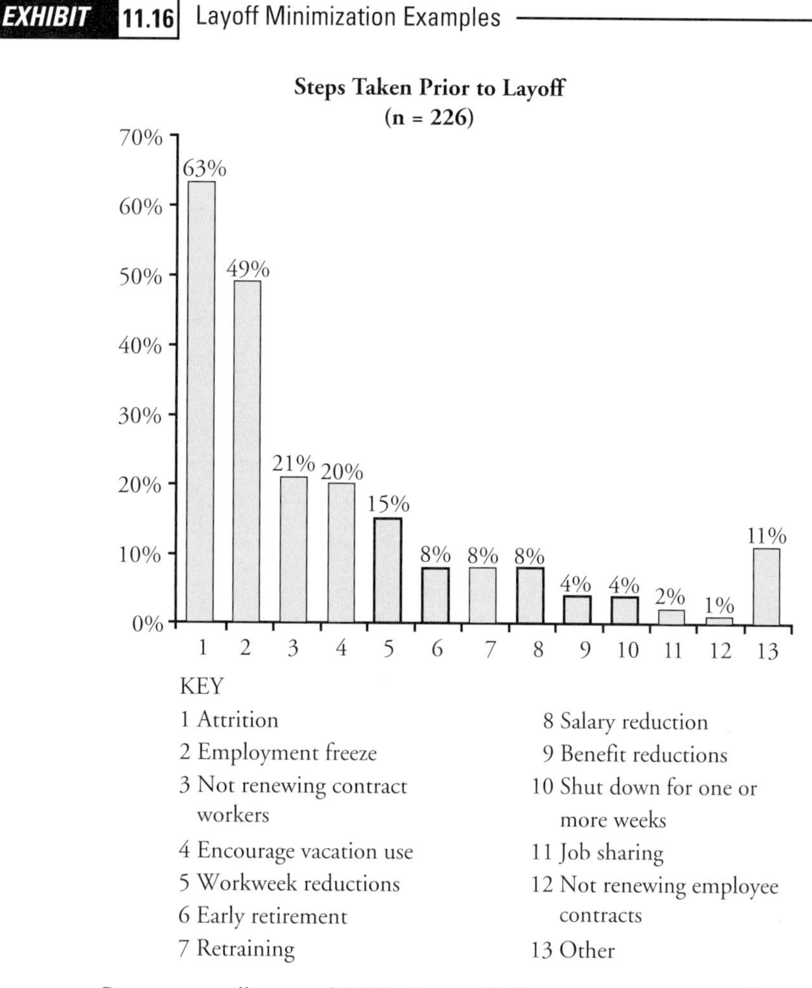

Source: Society for Human Resource Management, *Layoffs and Job Security Survey* (Alexandria, VA: author, 2001), p. 9. Used with permission.

Then a detailed look at the role of performance appraisal in separation is presented since a thrust of this chapter has been performance-based retention.

Separation Laws and Regulations

A desire to provide protection and safeguards to employees leaving the organization, especially for discharge and downsizing, has led to a myriad of laws and regulations governing the separation process.[59] These include federal and provincial human rights codes, provincial employment standard acts, employment contracts, and labour contract provisions. The Web sites for the provincial employment standards related to employee separations can be found at the end of this chapter under the heading "Relevant Web Sites."

A basic tenet underlying restrictions on employee separation is the need for fair and consistent treatment of employees. Included here are concerns for ensuring procedural fairness and for basing separations on legitimate bases, such as merit, seniority, or performance. The organization should be thoroughly familiar with these numerous laws and regulations, and their underlying principles, as it designs and administers its retention initiatives.

Performance Appraisal

Organizations often favour retention and separation systems and decisions being driven by employee performance. Laws and regulations generally uphold or even encourage such a role for performance. However, the law as interpreted also insists that the performance appraisals, and the performance appraisal system generally, be fair and equitable in application to employees undergoing separation. Interpretations come about from a combination of court decisions and governmental regulations that have evolved around the issue of performance appraisal in practice.

Based on these decisions and regulations, numerous specific suggestions have been put forth to guide the organization in the design and use of its performance appraisal (or management) system.[60] The recommendations include the following:

- Appraisal criteria should be job related, specific, and communicated in advance to the employee.
- The manager (rater) should receive training in the overall performance appraisal process and how to avoid common rating errors.
- The manager should be familiar with employee's job description and actual performance.
- There should be agreement among different raters in their evaluation of the employee's performance.
- Evaluations should be in writing.
- The employee should be able to review the evaluation and comment on it before it becomes final.
- The employee should receive timely feedback about the evaluation and an explanation for any outcome decision (e.g., retention or separation).
- There should be an upward review of the employee's appraisal.
- There should be an appeal system for employees dissatisfied with their evaluation.

Conforming to the above recommendations will help (not guarantee) to provide a fair evaluation process and the defensible evaluation decisions pertaining to retention and separation. If the organization wants to manage a performance-driven retention system, it would be wise to ensure the adequacy of its performance appraisal system relative to the above recommendations.

SUMMARY

Retention management seeks to control the numbers and types of employees who leave and who remain with the organization. Employee loss occurs via voluntary turnover or involuntary turnover in the form of termination or downsizing. Voluntary turnover is caused by a combination of perceived desirability of leaving, ease of leaving, and alternatives to one's current job. Some of these reasons are avoidable, and others are not. Avoidable turnover can also be said to occur among high- and low-value employees. Termination occurs for performance- and discipline-related problems. Downsizing, or reduction in force (RIF), comes about because the organization is, or is projected to be, overstaffed in head-count terms.

It is important for the organization to conduct thorough analyses of its turnover. Using a simple formula, turnover rates can be calculated, both overall and broken down by types of turnover, types of employees, job categories, and geographic location. It is also useful to benchmark the organization's turnover rates internally and externally. Another form of analysis is determining reasons that people leave. This can be done via exit interviews, postexit surveys, and employee satisfaction surveys. Analysis of costs and benefits of each of the three types of turnover should also be done. The three major cost categories are separation, replacement, and training. Within each category numerous costs, both financial and nonfinancial, may be estimated. Likewise, each type of turnover has both financial and nonfinancial benefits associated with it that must be weighed against the many costs. A thorough understanding of costs and benefits will help the organization determine where and among whom turnover is the most worrisome, and how to fashion retention strategies and tactics.

To reduce voluntary turnover, organizations engage in numerous retention initiatives centred around direct and variable pay programs, benefits, hours of work schedules, and training and development. Little is known about attempts to increase intrinsic rewards. A decision process may be followed to help decide which, if any, of such retention initiatives to undertake. The process follows five basic questions: Do we think turnover is a problem? How might we attack this problem? What do we need to decide? Should we proceed? How should we evaluate the initiatives? To influence the desirability of leaving, the organization must raise job satisfaction by providing both extrinsic and intrinsic rewards. Ease of leaving can possibly be reduced by providing organization-specific training and by increasing the costs of leaving. Finally, retention might be improved by providing more internal job alternatives to employees and by responding forcefully to other job offers they receive.

Termination might be reduced via formal performance management and progressive discipline systems. The performance management system involves four stages—performance planning, performance execution, performance appraisal, and decisions about the employee. This system helps prevent, and correct, performance problems. A progressive discipline system addresses problems of behavioural conduct that violate rules, procedures, laws, and professional and moral standards. It has a series of penalties for misconduct that progress up to termination, which the system seeks to prevent if at all possible. The system should be based on five important principles of fairness and justice.

Downsizing involves layoffs, but also retention issues. While downsizing seems to have some obvious benefits, research indicates that there are many costs as well, so the organization should carefully consider whether it really wants to downsize, and if so by how much in terms of employee numbers and quality. Staffing levels should be achieved in a targeted way, rather than across the board. From a staffing quality perspective, cuts could be based on seniority, job performance, or a more holistic assessment of who are the high-value employees the organization desires to retain. There are also many alternatives to downsizing that could be pursued. Attention must be paid to employees who survive a downsizing, or they might create a new retention problem for the organization by starting to leave.

Legally, employee separation from the organization, especially on an involuntary basis, is subject to myriad laws and regulations the organization must be aware of and incorporate into its retention strategy and tactics. If the organization wishes to base retention decisions on employees' job performance, it should recognize that laws and regulations require performance management systems to be fair and equitable to employees during separation. Based on regulations and court decisions, there are numerous recommendations to be followed for a performance management system to have a chance at withstanding legal challenges and scrutiny.

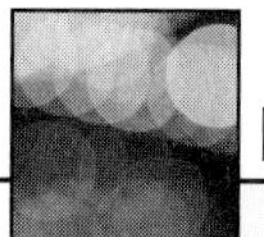

KEY TERMS

RELEVANT WEB SITES

Labour Force Survey Statistics

www.statcan.ca/english/Subjects/Labour/LFS/lfs-en.htm

Employment Standards Acts

Alberta: http://bsa.cbsc.org/gol/bsa/site.nsf/en/su07090.html

British Columbia: http://bsa.cbsc.org/gol/bsa/site.nsf/en/su07091.html

Manitoba: http://bsa.cbsc.org/gol/bsa/site.nsf/en/su07092.html

New Brunswick: http://bsa.cbsc.org/gol/bsa/site.nsf/en/su07093.html

Newfoundland and Labrador: http://bsa.cbsc.org/gol/bsa/site.nsf/en/su07094.html

Northwest Territories: http://bsa.cbsc.org/gol/bsa/site.nsf/en/su07095.html

Nova Scotia: http://bsa.cbsc.org/gol/bsa/site.nsf/en/su07096.html

Nunavut: http://bsa.cbsc.org/gol/bsa/site.nsf/en/su07097.html

Ontario: http://bsa.cbsc.org/gol/bsa/site.nsf/en/su07098.html

Prince Edward Island: http://bsa.cbsc.org/gol/bsa/site.nsf/en/su07223.html

Quebec: http://bsa.cbsc.org/gol/bsa/site.nsf/en/su07224.html

Saskatchewan: http://bsa.cbsc.org/gol/bsa/site.nsf/en/su07225.html

Yukon: http://bsa.cbsc.org/gol/bsa/site.nsf/en/su07226.html

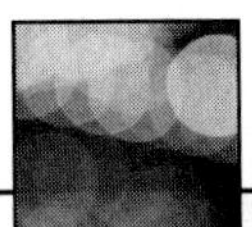

DISCUSSION QUESTIONS

1. For the three primary causes of voluntary turnover (desirability of leaving, ease of leaving, alternatives), might their relative importance depend on the type of employee or type of job? Explain.
2. Which of the costs and benefits of voluntary turnover are most likely to vary according to type of job? Give examples.
3. If a person says to you, "It's easy to reduce turnover, just pay people more money," what is your response?
4. Why should an organization seek to retain employees with performance or discipline problems? Why not just fire them?
5. Discuss some potential problems with downsizing as an organization's first response to a need to cut labour costs.

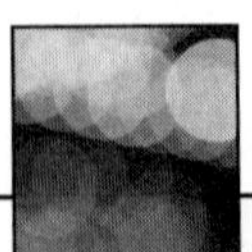

ETHICAL ISSUES

1. Consider a circumstance where your organization is doing exit interviews and has promised confidentiality to all who respond. You are responsible for conducting the exit interviews. Your supervisor has asked you to give her the name of each respondent so that she can assess the information in conjunction with the person's supervisor. What obligation do corporate HR employees have to keep information confidential in such circumstances?

2. There are numerous negative organizational consequences to firing employees, including the discomfort of the supervisor who needs to deliver the termination information, conflict or sabotage from the departing employee, and the potential for a lawsuit. In response, many supervisors provide problem employees unpleasant work tasks, reduce working hours, or otherwise negatively modify their jobs in hopes that the problem employees will simply quit. What are the ethical issues raised by this strategy?

APPLICATIONS

Managerial Turnover: A Problem?

HealthCareLaunderCare (HCLC) is a company that specializes in picking up, cleaning, and delivering all the laundry for health care providers, especially hospitals, nursing homes, and assisted-care facilities. Basically, these health care providers have outsourced their laundry operations to HCLC. In this very competitive business, a typical contract between HCLC and a health care provider lasts only two years, and HCLC experiences a contract nonrenewal rate of 10 percent. Most nonrenewals occur because of dissatisfaction with service costs and especially quality (e.g., surgical garb that is not completely sterilized).

HCLC has 20 laundry facilities throughout the country, mostly in large metropolitan areas. Each laundry facility is headed by a site manager, and there are unit supervisors for the intake, washing, drying, inspection and repair, and delivery areas. Each site employs an average of 100 full-time employees.

Operation of a facility is technologically sophisticated and very health and safety sensitive. In the intake area, for example, employees wear protective clothing, gloves, and eyewear because of all the blood, gore, and germs on laundry that comes in. The washing area is comprised of huge washers in 35-foot stainless steel tunnels with screws that move the laundry through various wash cycles. Workers in this area are exposed to high temperatures and must be proficient in operation of the computer control systems. Laundry is lifted out of the tunnels by robots and moved to the drying room area, where laundry is dried, ironed, and folded by machines tended by employees. In the inspection and repair area, quality inspection and assurance occurs. Laundry is inspected for germs and pinholes (in the case of surgical garb—pinholes could allow blood and fluids to come into contact with the surgeon), and other employees complete repairs on torn clothing and sheets. In the delivery area, the laundry is hermetically sealed in packages and placed in delivery vans for transport.

HCLC's vice president of operations, Tyrone Williams, manages the sites, and site and unit managers, with an iron fist. Mr. Williams monitors each site with a weekly report of a set of cost, quality, and safety indicators for each of the five areas. When he spots what he thinks are problems or undesirable trends, he has a conference telephone call with both the site manager and the area supervisor. In the decidedly one-way conversation, marching orders are delivered and are expected to be fulfilled. If a turnaround in the "numbers" doesn't show up in the next weekly report, Mr. Williams gives the manager and supervisor one more week to improve. If sufficient improvement is not forthcoming, various punitive actions are taken, including demotions, reassignments, and terminations. Mr. Williams feels such quick and harsh justice is necessary to keep HCLC competitive and to continually drive home to all employees the importance of working "by the numbers." Fed up with this management system, many managers have opted to say, "Bye-bye numbers!" and leave HCLC.

Recently, the issue of retention of site and unit managers came up on the radar screen of HCLC's president, Roman Dublinski. Mr. Dublinski glanced at a payroll report showing that 30 of the 120 site and unit managers had left HCLC in the past year, though no reasons for leaving were given. In addition, Mr. Dublinski had received a few copies of angry resignation letters written to Mr. Williams. Having never confronted or thought about possible employee retention problems or how to deal with them, Mr. Dublinski calls you (the corporate manager of staffing) to prepare a brief written analysis that will then be used as the basis for a meeting between the two of you and the vice president of HR, Debra Angle (Ms. Angle recommended this). Address the following questions in your report:

1. Is the loss of 30 out of 120 managers in a single year cause for concern?
2. What additional data should we try to gather to learn more about our managerial turnover?
3. What are the costs of this turnover? Might there be any benefits?
4. Are there any lurking legal problems?
5. If retention is a serious problem for HCLC, what are the main ways we might attack it?

Retention: Deciding to Act

Wally's Wonder Wash (WWW) is a full-service, high-tech and high-touch, car wash company owned solely by Wally Wheelspoke. Located in a city of 200,000 people in central Canada (with another 100,000 in suburbs and more rural towns throughout the county), WWW currently has four facilities within the city. Wally has plans to add four more facilities within the city in the next two years, plus plans a little farther out to begin placing facilities in suburban locations and the rural towns. Major competitors include two other full-service car washes (different owners), plus three touchless automatic facilities (same owner) in the city.

Wally's critical strategy is to provide the very best to customers who want and relish extremely clean and "spiffy" vehicles and to have customers feel a positive experience each time they come to WWW. To do this, WWW seeks to provide high-quality car washes and car detailing and to generate considerable repeat business through competitive prices combined with attention to customers. To make itself accessible to customers, WWW is open seven days a week, 8 a.m. to 8 p.m. Peak periods, volumewise, are after 1 p.m. on weekdays and between 10 a.m. and 5 p.m. on weekends. In addition, Wally uses his workforce to drive his strategy. Though untrained in HR, Wally knows that he must recruit and retain a stable, high-quality workforce if his current businesses, let alone his ambitious expansion plans, are to succeed.

WWW has a strong preference for full-time employees, who work either 7 a.m. to 4 p.m. or 11 a.m. to 8 p.m. Part-timers are used occasionally to help fill in during peak demand times and during the summer when full-timers are off on vacation. There are two major jobs at WWW—attendant (washer) and custom service specialist (detailer). Practicing promotion from within, all specialists are promoted from the attendant ranks. There are currently 70 attendants and 20 customer service specialists at WWW. In addition, each facility has a manager. Wally has filled the manager's job by promotion-from-within (from either attendant or custom service specialist ranks) but is unsure if he will be able to continue doing this as he expands.

The job of attendant is a demanding one. Attendants vacuum vehicles front and rear (and trunk if requested by the customer), wash and dry windows and mirrors, dry vehicles with hand towels, apply special cleaning compounds to tires, wipe down the vehicle's interior, and wash or vacuum floor mats. In addition, attendants wash and fold towels, lift heavy barrels of cleaning compounds and waxes, and perform light maintenance and repair work on the machinery. Finally, and very importantly, attendants consistently provide customer service by asking customers if they have special requests and by making small talk with them. A unique feature of customer service at WWW is that the attendant must ask the customer to personally inspect the vehicle before leaving to ensure that the vehicle is satisfactorily cleaned (attendants also correct any mistakes pointed out by the customer). The attendants work as a team, with each attendant being expected to be able to perform all of the above tasks.

Attendants start at a base pay of $8 per hour, with automatic 50-cent raises at six months and one year. They receive a brief training from the manager before starting work. Custom service specialists start at $9 per hour, with 50-cent raises after six months and one year. Neither attendants nor custom service specialists receive performance reviews. Managers at each facility all receive a salary of $27,000, plus an annual "merit" raise based on a very casual performance review conducted by Wally (whenever he gets around to it). All attendants share equally in a customer tip pool; custom service specialists receive individual tips. The benefits package is comprised of (1) major medical health insurance with a 20 percent employee co-pay on the premium, (2) paid statutory holidays, and (3) a generous paid sick pay plan of two days per month (in recognition of high illness due to extreme working conditions).

In terms of turnover, Wally has spotty and general data only. WWW experienced an overall turnover rate the past year of 65 percent for attendants and 20 percent for custom service specialists; no managers left. Though lacking data further back, Wally thinks the turnover rate for attendants has been increasing. WWW's managers constantly complain to Wally about the high level of turnover among attendants and the problems it creates, especially in fulfilling the strong customer-service orientation for WWW. Though the managers have not conducted exit interviews, the major complaints they hear from attendants are (1) pay is not competitive relative to the other full-service car washes or many other entry-level jobs in the area, (2) training is hit-or-miss at best, (3) promotion opportunities are limited, (4) managers provide no feedback or coaching, and (5) customer complaints and mistreatment of attendants by customers are on the rise.

Wally is frustrated by attendant turnover and its threat to his customer service and expansion strategies. Assume that he calls on you for assistance in figuring what to do about the problem. Use the decision process shown in Exhibit 11.11 to help develop a retention initiative for WWW. Address each of the following questions in the process:

1. Do we think turnover is a problem?
2. How might we attack this problem?
3. What do we need to decide?
4. Should we proceed?
5. How should we evaluate the initiatives?

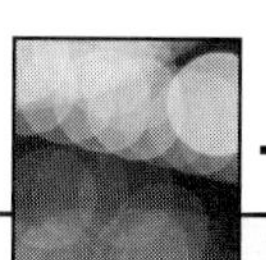

TANGLEWOOD STORES CASE

The final stage of the staffing process is ensuring that you are able to retain those individuals you have carefully recruited and selected. This chapter described some of the most well-documented correlates of employee turnover, including perceptions of organizational reward systems, the work environment, communication and justice, and the social environment.

The Situation

Although some retail organizations are comfortable with fairly high turnover, Tanglewood is very concerned about losing the talent and cultural knowledge of its managerial employees. The leaders of the organization are especially worried that competing retail firms have recognized the quality of Tanglewood's employee development plans, and are enticing away the best store managers with large salary offers. Corporate staffing representatives have collected information regarding turnover rates and job satisfaction scores for all of its stores. In addition to the raw turnover rates, they also have provided you with data on those employees who have left, including their job performance levels and exit interviews.

Your Tasks

First and foremost, Tanglewood wants you to find out whether turnover is a serious concern by looking at the relationship between performance and turnover. Once you have determined how much of a concern turnover is, you will investigate why employees are leaving. You will assess what the available information tells you about the reasons for turnover, and also assess what new information Tanglewood might gather in the future to improve their understanding of why turnover occurs. Using Exhibit 11.12 as a guide, you will develop recommendations for how Tanglewood can improve retention with a combination of intrinsic and extrinsic rewards. The background information for this case, and your specific assignment, can be found at www.mcgrawhill.ca/OLC/heneman.

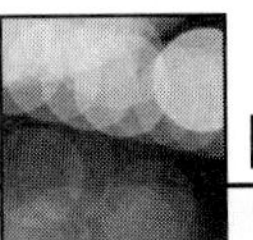

ENDNOTES

1. *HR Professional,* "About Staff: Hire Right: How AEGON improved employee satisfaction," October/November 2005.
2. U.S. Department of Labor, "Employee Tenure Study," *News,* August 29, 2000; U.S. Department of Labor, "Mass Layoffs in October 2001," *News,* November 30, 2001; U.S. Department of Labor, "Number of Jobs Held, Labor Market Activity, and Earnings Growth over Two Decades: Results from a Longitudinal Survey Summary," *News,* April 25, 2000; B. Wysocki Jr., "When the Job Is from Hell, Recruiting Is Tough," *Wall Street Journal,* July 10, 2001, p. B1.
3. K. Shinn, "Juggling the generation," *Jacksonville Business Journal,* March, 2001, p. 1.
4. P. W. Hom and R. W. Griffeth, *Employee Turnover* (Cincinnati, OH: South-Western, 1995), pp. 1–12; Saratoga Institute, *Human Capital Benchmarking Report* (Santa Clara, CA: author, 2001).
5. F. Callocchia and M. Ramsay, "Employers we love, employers we leave," *Canadian HR Reporter,* April 23, 2001.
6. R. W. Griffeth, P. W. Hom, and S. Gaertner, "A Meta-Analysis of Antecedents and Correlates of Employee Turnover," *Journal of Management,* 2000, 26, pp. 463–488; Hom and Griffeth, *Employee Turnover,* pp. 51–107; J. D. Kammeyer-Mueller, C. R. Wanberg, T. M. Glomb, and D. A. Ahlburg, D. A. "Turnover Processes in a Temporal Context: It's About Time." *Journal of Applied Psychology* (in press); T. W. Lee and T. R. Mitchell, "An Alternative Approach: The Unfolding Model of Employee Turnover," *Academy of Management Review,* 1994, 19, pp. 51–89; J. G. March and H. A. Simon, *Organizations* (New York: Wiley, 1958); T. R. Mitchell, B. C. Holtom, and T. W. Lee, "How to Keep Your Best Employees: Developing an Effective Retention Policy," *Academy of Management Executive,* 2001, 15(4), pp. 96–107; C. O. Trevor, "Interactions Among Actual Ease of Movement Determinants and Job Satisfaction in the Prediction of Voluntary Turnover," *Academy of Management Journal,* 2001, 44, pp. 621–638.
7. N. Drake and I. Robb, "Exit Interviews," 2001 (www.shrm.org/whitepapers); R. W. Griffeth and P. W. Hom, *Retaining Valued Employees* (Cincinnati, OH: Southwestern, 2001), pp. 203–222.

8. M. A. Campion, "Meaning and Measurement of Turnover: Comparison and Recommendations for Research," *Journal of Applied Psychology,* 1991, 76, pp. 199–212; H. R. Nalbantian and A. Szostak, "How Fleet Bank Fought Employee Flight," *Harvard Business Review,* April 2004, pp. 116–125.
9. J. Jackson, "Are exit interviews your best kept secret?" *Canadian HR Reporter,* August 9, 2004.
10. G. Burket, "HR leaders talk about employee engagement," *Canadian HR Reporter,* September 12, 2005.
11. R. Morissette and J. M. Rosa, "Alternative Work Practices and Quit Rates: Methodological Issues and Empirical Evidence for Canada," Statistics Canada, March 2004, pp. 23–24.
12. W. F. Cascio, *Costing Human Resources,* fourth ed. (Cincinnati, OH: South-Western, 2000), pp. 23–57; Griffeth and Hom, *Retaining Valued Employees,* pp. 10–22; Hom and Griffeth, *Employee Turnover,* pp. 13–35.
13. Cascio, *Costing Human Resources,* pp. 83–105; P. C. Gibson and K. S. Piscitelli, *Basic Employment Law Manual for Managers and Supervisors* (Chicago: Commerce Clearing House, 1997); E. E. Schuttauf, *Performance Management Manual for Managers and Supervisors* (Chicago: Commerce Clearing House, 1997).
14. J. N. Barron and D. M. Kreps, *Strategic Human Resources* (New York: Wiley, 1999), pp. 421–445; Cascio, *Costing Human Resources,* pp. 23–57; J. A. Schmidt (ed.), *Making Mergers Work* (New York: Towers, Perrin, Foster and Crosby, 2001), pp. 257–268.
15. J. Mullich, "Looking Inward at Bell Canada," *Workforce Management,* March 2005, 84(3), pp. 50–51.
16. The Conference Board of Canada, "Compensation Planning Outlook 2005: Holding the Line on Pay Increases."
17. V. Uyen, "What's your turnover rate?" *Canadian HR Reporter,* October 20, 2003, 16(18), p. 1.
18. Society for Human Resource Management, *Retention Practices Survey* (Alexandria, VA: author, 2000).
19. B. Parus and J. Handel, "Companies Battle Talent Drain," *Workspan,* September 2000, pp. 16–72.
20. *Canadian HR Reporter,* "The top 50 employers in Canada," January 5, 2005.
21. CNW Group, "From Attraction/Retention to Financial Results, 50 Best Employers Competition, Says Hewitt Associates" January 3, 2005, www.newswire.ca/en/releases/archive/January2005/03/c9367.html.
22. T. A. Judge, J. E. Bono, and E. A. Locke, "Personality and Job Satisfaction: The Mediating Role of Job Characteristics," *Journal of Applied Psychology,* 2000, 85, pp. 237–249; B. T. Loher, R. A. Noe, N. L. Moeller, and M. P. Fitzgerald, "A Meta-Analysis of the Relation of Job Characteristics to Job Satisfaction," *Journal of Applied Psychology,* 1985, 70, pp. 280–289.
23. M. A. Campion and M. M. Mitchell, "Management Turnover: Experiential Differences Between Former and Current Managers. *Personnel Psychology,* 1986, 39, pp. 57–69; Kammeyer-Mueller, Wanberg, Glomb, and Ahlburg, "Turnover Processes in a Temporal Context: It's About Time"; P. E. Spector and S. M. Jex, "Relations of Job Characteristics from Multiple Data Sources with Employee Affect, Absence, Turnover Intentions, and Health," *Journal of Applied Psychology,* 1991, 76, pp. 46–53.
24. J. B. Arthur, "Effects of Human Resource Systems on Manufacturing Performance and Turnover," *Academy of Management Journal,* 1994, 37, pp. 670–687.
25. M. A. Huselid, "The Impact of Human Resource Management Practices on Turnover, Productivity, and Corporate Financial Performance," *Academy of Management Journal,* 1995, 38, pp. 635–672.

26. P. Evans, "How 'the best' was done," *National Post,* October 25, 2005, FP Working section, p. 8.
27. P. Evans, "Best of the best know how to invest in staff," *National Post,* October 22, 2005, FP Working section, p. 2.
28. H. Axel, "Strategies for Retaining Critical Talent," *The Conference Board,* 1998, 6(2), pp. 4–18.
29. P. Cappelli, "A Market-Driven Approach to Retaining Talent," *Harvard Business Review,* January–February 2000, pp. 103–111; T. Wilson, "Brand Imaging," *ACA News,* May 2000, pp. 44–48.
30. C. O. Trevor, B. Gerhart, and J. W. Boudreau, "Voluntary Turnover and Job Performance: Curvilinearity and the Moderating Influences of Salary Growth and Promotions," *Journal of Applied Psychology,* 1997, 82, pp. 44–61.
31. Cappelli, "A Market-Driven Approach to Retaining Talent." L. Gomez-Mejia and D. Balkin, *Compensation, Organization Strategy, and Firm Performance* (Cincinnati, OH: Southwestern, 1992), pp. 290–307; B. Klaas and J. McClendon, "To Lead, Lag, or Match: Estimating the Financial Impact of Pay Level Policies," *Personnel Psychology,* 1996, 49, pp. 121–140.
32. J. Cohen, "I/Os in the Know Offer Insights on Generation X Workers," *Monitor on Psychology,* February 2002, pp. 66–67; Griffeth and Hom, *Retaining Valued Employees,* pp. 31–45; Kammeyer-Mueller, Wanberg, Glomb, and Ahlburg, D. A. "Turnover Processes in a Temporal Context: It's About Time."
33. R. Folger and R. Cropanzano, *Organizational Justice and Human Resource Management* (Thousand Oaks, CA: Sage, 1998).
34. Hom and Griffeth, *Employee Turnover,* pp. 93–103.
35. S. Fournier, "Keeping Line Managers in the Know," *ACA News,* 2000, 43(3), pp. 1–3; K. D. Scott, D. Morajda, and J. W. Bishop, "Increase Company Competitiveness," *WorldatWork Journal,* 2002, 11(1), pp. 35–42.
36. T. Rutigliano, "Tuning Up Your Talent Engine," *Gallup Management Journal,* Fall 2001, pp. 12–14.
37. B. J. Tepper, "Consequences of Abusive Supervision," *Academy of Management Journal,* 2000, 43, pp. 178–190.
38. C. Alphonso, "Top staff gain clout in mergers," *The Globe and Mail,* May 29, 2002, p. C1.
39. E. R. Silverman, "Mercer Tries to Keep Its Employees Through Its 'Externship' Program," *Wall Street Journal,* November 7, 2000, p. B18.
40. J. S. Lublin, "In Hot Demand, Retention Czars Face Tough Job," *Wall Street Journal,* September 12, 2000, p. B1.
41. M. Armstrong, *Performance Management,* second ed. (London: Kogan-Page, 2000); D. Grote, *The Complete Guide to Performance Appraisal* (New York: AMACOM, 1996); G. P. Latham and K. N. Wexley, *Increasing Productivity Through Performance Appraisal,* second ed. (Reading, MA: Addison-Wesley, 1994); E. E. Schuttauf, *Performance Management Manual for Managers and Supervisors* (Chicago: Commerce Clearing House, 1997).
42. Grote, *The Complete Guide to Performance Appraisal;* Society for Human Resource Management, *Performance Management Survey* (Alexandria, VA: author, 2000).
43. G. A. Stoskopf, "Taking Performance Management to the Next Level," *Workspan,* February 2002, pp. 26–33.
44. F. T. Coleman, *Ending the Employment Relationship Without Ending Up in Court* (Alexandria, VA: Society for Human Resource Management, 2001); J. G. Frierson, Preventing Employment Lawsuits (Washington, DC: Bureau of National Affairs, 1997); Gibson and Piscitelli, Basic Employment *Law Manual for Managers and Supervisors.*

45. Gibson and Piscitelli, *Basic Employment Law Manual for Managers and Supervisors,* pp. 51–53.
46. Frierson, *Preventing Employment Lawsuits,* pp. 140–141.
47. Schuttauf, *Performance Management Manual for Managers and Supervisors,* pp. 43–45.
48. Frierson, *Preventing Employment Lawsuits,* pp. 358–365; Gibson and Piscitelli, *Basic Employment Law Manual for Managers and Supervisors,* pp. 48–53.
49. Coleman, *Ending the Employment Relationship Without Ending Up in Court,* pp. 51–84.
50. Barron and Kreps, *Strategic Human Resources,* pp. 421–443; Society for Human Resource Management, *Layoffs and Job Security Survey* (Alexandria, VA: author, 2001).
51. W. F. Cascio, L. E. Young, and J. R. Morris, "Financial Consequences of Employment-Change Decisions in Major U.S. Corporations," *Academy of Management Journal,* 1997, 40, pp. 1175–1189; J. C. McElroy, P. C. Morrow, and S. N. Rude, "Turnover and Organizational Performance: A Comparative Analysis of the Effects of Voluntary, Involuntary, and Reduction-in-Force Turnover," *Journal of Applied Psychology,* 2001, 86, pp. 1294–1299.
52. Barron and Kreps, *Strategic Human Resources,* pp. 424–430.
53. P. Barta, "In This Expansion, As Business Booms, So Do the Layoffs," *Wall Street Journal,* March 13, 2000, p. A1; L. Uchitelle, "Pink Slip? Now It's All in a Day's Work," *New York Times,* August 5, 2001, p. BU1.
54. Bureau of National Affairs, *Basic Patterns in Union Contracts,* pp. 67–88; J. A. Fossum, *Labor Relations,* eighth ed. (Burr Ridge, IL: McGraw-Hill/Irwin, 2002), pp. 126–127.
55. M. Conlin, "Where Layoffs Are a Last Resort," *Business Week,* October 8, 2001, p. 42; Q. Hardy, "Cease Firing," *Fortune,* November 26, 2001; "How No Layoffs Can Work," November 6, 2001 (www.businessweek.com/careers).
56. F. Crandall and M. J. Wallace Jr., "Down(sized) but Not Out," *Workspan,* November 2001, pp. 31–35.
57. A. Freedman, "Serving the Survivors," *Human Resource Executive,* December 2001, p. 47.
58. Freedman, "Serving the Survivors."
59. Coleman, *Ending the Employment Relationship Without Ending Up in Court; Frierson, Preventing Employment Lawsuits;* S. C. Kahn, B. B. Brown, and M. Lanzarone, *Legal Guide to Human Resources* (Boston: Warren, Gorham and Lamont, 2001), pp. 9–3 to 9–82; D. P. Twomey, *Labor and Employment Law,* 11th ed. (Cincinnati, OH: West, 2001).
60. Kahn, Brown, and Lanzarone, *Legal Guide to Human Resources,* pp. 6–2 to 6–58; D. C. Martin, K. M. Bartol, and P. E. Kehoe, "The Legal Ramifications of Performance Appraisal," *Public Personnel Management,* 2000, 29, pp. 379–406; J. M. Werner and M. C. Bolino, "Explaining U.S. Courts of Appeals Decisions Involving Performance Appraisals: Accuracy, Fairness, and Validation," *Personnel Psychology,* 1997, 50, pp. 1–24.

CHAPTER 12

Staffing System Management

CHAPTER OBJECTIVES

After reading this chapter, you will be able to:

- Describe the structure of a human resource department with identifiable staffing or employment functions
- Use examples of job descriptions to determine level of responsibility, education, and KSAOs required for an entry-level staffing position
- Understand the importance of clear HR policies and procedures to minimize inconsistent and potentially illegal staffing practices
- Discuss the advantages and disadvantages of using electronic systems to conduct a wide range of staffing tasks
- Define outsourcing and professional employer organization (PEO) and list the factors driving organizations to consider outsourcing HR activities
- Explain the key factors used to evaluate the effectiveness of a staffing system
- Understand the legal ramifications of maintaining employee records as pertaining to human rights and privacy legislation
- Discuss the importance of employment law training for managers and employees and establishing alternate dispute resolution procedures to address employment disputes

Staffing systems involve complex processes and decisions that require organizational direction, coordination, and evaluation. Most organizations must create mechanisms for managing their staffing system and its components. Such management of staffing systems requires consideration of both administration and evaluation, as well as legal issues.

Regarding administration, this chapter shows how the staffing (employment) function is one of the key areas within the HR department. It provides illustrations of a typical organizational chart within a staffing department. Examples of staffing positions available to people interested in human resources are also described. The importance and role of policies and procedures is explained, as well as how the use of technology and software enhances the efficient operation of staffing systems. Finally, a discussion on the effectiveness of outsourcing-specific staffing activities is described as a way to streamline the staffing function.

Presented next is a discussion of ways to evaluate the effectiveness of standardizing the staffing process. A way to gauge effectiveness is demonstrated through a flow chart of a process to guide identification of practices that deviate or cause bottlenecks from the standardized format. Results from this process are examined to gauge the effectiveness of staffing systems. Compilation and analysis of staffing system costs are also suggested as an evaluation technique. Assessment of customer (hiring managers, applicants) satisfaction is presented as a new, innovative approach to the evaluation of staffing systems.

The discussion then focuses on the importance of compiling various records and reports and of conducting legal audits of staffing activities. Training for managers and employees and mechanisms for dispute resolution are also discussed.

ADMINISTRATION OF STAFFING SYSTEMS

Organizational Arrangements

organizational arrangements
How an organization structures itself to conduct human resources and staffing activities

Organizational arrangements refers to how an organization structures itself to conduct human resources and staffing activities, often within the human resources (HR) department. The arrangements vary considerably, and both organization size and type (integrated or multiple business) make a difference in the likely type of organizational arrangement used.

Consider the following data from Industry Canada on the Canada's small business community. Ninety-eight percent of organizations have fewer than 100 employees, and 99 percent of the 2.2 million businesses in Canada are considered small or medium enterprises (SMEs) and have less than 500 employees. According the Industry Canada, approximately 1 million small enterprises provide one out of every three jobs in Canada, employing almost 5 million people, or 47 percent of the private labour force.[1]

In organizations with fewer than 100 employees, regardless of purpose, research suggests that staffing is most likely to be conducted by the owner, president, or work unit manager. Only a small percentage (13%) of organizations will have an HR department in which responsibility for staffing might be housed. And staffing activities are quite varied among these small organizations in terms of establishing job requirements, recruitment sources, recruitment communication techniques, selection methods, decision making, and job offers. The presence of an HR department leads these organizations to adopt staffing practices different from those without an HR department.[2]

integrated business organization
Comprised of business units pursuing a common business product or service

multiple-business organization
Comprised of business units offering a diverse set of products or services

As organization size increases, so does the likelihood of there being an HR department and a unit within it responsible for staffing. But the exact configuration of the HR department and staffing activities will depend on whether the organization is an integrated business organization or a multiple-business organization.[3] An **integrated business organization** is comprised of business units pursuing a common business product or service. A **multiple-business organization** is comprised of business units pursuing a diverse set of products or services. Because of its diversity, the multiple-business organization will likely not try to have a major, centralized corporate HR department. Rather, it will have a small corporate HR department, with a separate, decentralized HR department within each business unit. In a multiple-business organization, staffing activities will be decentralized and focused on the local HR needs, with guidance and expertise provided by the corporate HR department.

In an integrated-business organization, there will likely be a highly centralized HR department at the corporate level, with a much smaller HR presence at the plant or site level. As pertains to staffing, such centralization creates economies of scale and consistency in staffing policies and processes, as well as hiring standards and new hire quality.

SunTrust Bank in Atlanta provides an excellent example of an organization that moved from a decentralized to a centralized HR function and created a new corporate employment department to manage staffing throughout its 1,200 branches.[4] Previously, SunTrust operated with 28 regional charters, and each region had its own HR department and staffing function. This created a muddle of inconsistency in technologies, services, and expertise, as well as quality of its job candidates. Through centralization, the bank sought to achieve greater consistency, along with a common vision and strategic focus, while still allowing some flexibility in operation among the regions. HR managers from the regional HR departments who had served as generalists were moved into specialist roles, some of them in the new employment department, with the assistance of considerable training in new policies and procedures. Job descriptions, qualifications, and recruitment strategies were standardized, and competency models were created to identify ideal candidates' personality traits, interests, and skills. Also, standardized guidelines, checklists, and candidate evaluation tools were developed. But some latitude was allowed for individual banks and staffing managers, such as decisions on how and when to recruit within their own territory. It appears as though the centralization worked well. The new head of the HR function said, "We tried to balance the push-pull between the corporate vision and the real-world banking realities. We did not want one side or the other to hold all the cards.... The bank managers unanimously say they are now getting better candidates and our new, more precise recruiting system has enabled us to reduce advertising and sourcing expenditures, while increasing the amount of assessments on each candidate. So in effect we end up spending less but getting more." It is also reported that full-time teller turnover was decreased, the average time to fill a position dropped, and the average cost to fill an hourly position was reduced.

A more detailed example of a centralized organizational chart for an integrated-business, multiplant manufacturing organization is shown in Exhibit 12.1. At the corporate level, the HR department is headed by the vice president of human resources. Reporting to the vice president are directors of employment and legal affairs, compensation and benefits, training and development, labour relations, and HR information systems. These directors, along with the vice president, formulate and coordinate HR strategy and policy, as well as manage their own functional units.

The director of employment and legal affairs has three direct reports: the managers of salaried employment, hourly employment, and legal affairs. Each manager, in turn, is responsible for the supervision of specialists and assistants. The manager of salaried employment, for example, handles external and internal staffing for managerial and professional jobs. There are two specialists in this unit, university recruiter and internal placement specialist, plus an administrative assistant. The manager of hourly employment is responsible for external and internal staffing for hourly paid employees. Reporting to this manager are four specialists (recruiter, interviewer, testing specialist, and consultant) plus two administrative assistants. The manager of legal affairs has a consultant plus an administrative assistant as direct reports. The consultants are individuals who serve in liaison roles with the line managers of units throughout the organization when hiring is occurring. Functioning as internal customer service representatives to these managers, the consultants help the managers understand corporate employment policies and procedures, determine specific staffing needs, handle special staffing problems and requests, and answer questions.

At the plant level, there is a single HR manager, plus an administrative assistant, who performs all HR activities, including staffing. This HR manager is a true generalist and works closely with the plant manager on all issues involving people concerns. Regarding staffing, the dotted line shows that the HR manager has an indirect reporting relationship to the director of employment and legal affairs (as well as the other corporate-level HR directors, not shown). A crucial responsibility for these directors is to work with the HR manager to develop policies and programs, including staffing, that are consistent with corporate strategy while allowing the opportunity to tailor make programs and strategies that fit the particular needs and workforce of the plant.

The above example shows staffing to be a critical area within the HR department, and research confirms this importance. For example, the staffing function typically receives a greater percentage of the total HR department budget than any other function, averaging about 20 percent of the total budget. A study of HR departments in large organizations found that the focus on recruitment and selection activities had increased significantly over the past several years, more

Example of HR Department and Employment (Staffing) Function

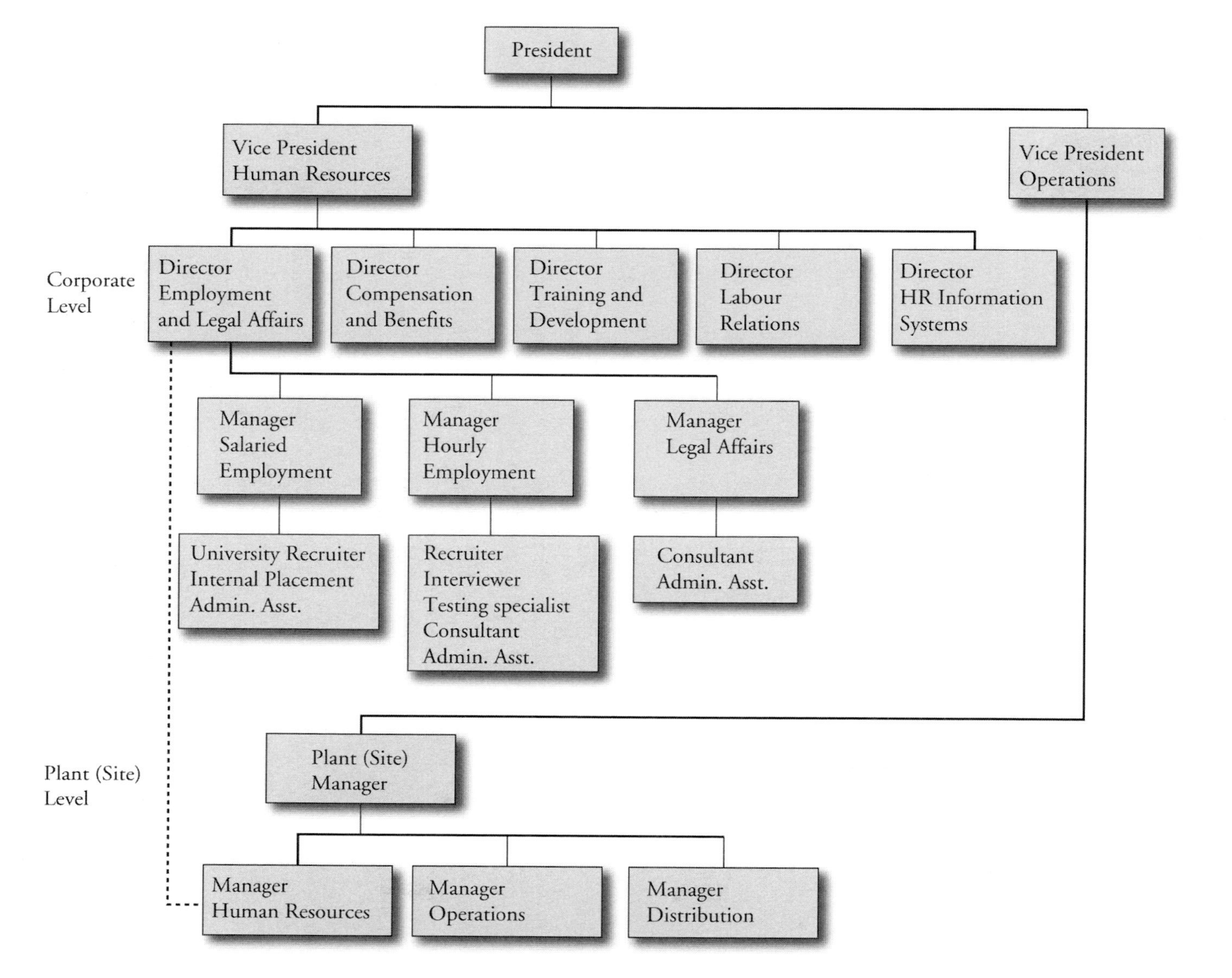

so than for any other HR activity.[5] Salaries for people in the staffing function are comparable to those in the other HR functions. Increasingly, employees in all HR areas are becoming eligible for short-term incentives and bonuses.[6]

Those employed within the staffing function must work closely with members of all the other functional HR areas. For example, staffing members must coordinate their activities with the compensation and benefits staff in developing policies on the financial components of job offers, such as starting pay, hiring bonuses, and special perks. Staffing activities must also be closely coordinated with the training and development function. This will be needed to identify training needs for external, entry-level new hires, as well as for planning transfer and promotion-enhancing training experiences for current employees. The director of labour relations will work with the staffing area to determine labour contract language pertaining to staffing issues (e.g., promotions and transfers) and to help resolve grievances over staffing procedures and decisions. Record keeping, staffing software, and legal statistics requirements will be worked out with the director of HR information systems.

It should also be noted that although staffing activities tend to be concentrated within the HR department, anyone involved in staffing for specific organizational units would also play a role in the overall staffing process. The unit manager will submit the hiring authorization request, work closely with HR in developing KSAOs required/preferred for the vacant position, and actively participate in making discretionary assessments and job offers. Other members of the unit may provide input to the unit manager on KSAOs sought, formally meet and interact with candidates for recruiting and attracting purposes, and provide inputs to the unit manager on their preferences about who should receive the job offer. In team-based work units, team members may play an even more active role in all phases of the staffing process. Each organization needs to develop its own organizational structure that best fits with staffing strategy to achieve its employment requirements.

Jobs in Staffing

Jobs in staffing are quite varied. In the private sector, most are housed within the HR department (corporate, plant, or office site level). In the public sector, they are found within the central personnel or HR office, as well as in various specified agencies, such as transportation or human services.

The types and scope of tasks and responsibilities in staffing jobs varies depending on the level or specialization of the position. Jobs that are more specialized usually involve a functional specialty such as interviewing, recruiting, or university relations. These tend to be entry-level positions into the HR field. Other jobs may have a more generalist flavour to them, particularly in smaller organizations or smaller units (plant or office) of a larger organization. In such units, one person may handle all staffing-related activities. At higher organizational levels, both specialist and generalist jobs are found. Examples of specialist positions include test development and validation, executive assessment, and employment equity. Generalists usually have broader managerial responsibilities that cut across specialties; the job of staffing manager is one example.

Exhibit 12.2 provides examples of job descriptions for two staffing jobs—a recruiter/staffing coordinator and a staffing manager. Human Resources and Social Development Canada gives examples of job profiles for human resources specialist, recruitment specialist, human resources manager, and human resources assistant positions in the National Occupational Classification 2001 (NOC 2001) that can be adapted to specific organizational structures.[7]

Entry into staffing jobs normally occurs at the specialist rank in the areas of recruiting and interviewing, in both private and public organizations. Staffing of these jobs can come from new hires, from an internal transfer (e.g., management training program, line management job), or from another HR function. There is no fixed point or method of entry into staffing jobs.

EXHIBIT 12.2 Examples of Staffing Jobs

A. Recruiter/Staffing Coordinator

Job Description:

Respond to current and prospective staffing requirements by preparing internal postings and external advertisements; collect and screen applications to identify candidates who meet the requirements of positions. Responsibilities include creating a short list of candidates; contacting potential candidates to arrange interviews; recruiting graduates from colleges, universities, and other educational institutions; coordinating with hiring managers on scheduling and conducting interviews; conducting reference checks; and arranging staff training.

Education:

Completion of Human Resources Diploma program or a university degree or college diploma related to human resources (e.g., business administration, industrial relations, business, or psychology). Certification as a Certified Human Resources Professional (CHRP) is highly desired.

Required Skills:

One to three years of experience. Must have the ability to maintain a high level of confidentiality; have excellent interpersonal and communication skills; be an effective team player; and have the ability to prioritize and manager multiple tasks. Proficiency in MS Office (Word, Excel, PowerPoint, and Outlook) is required.

Desired Skills:

Experience recruiting for plant positions including assemblers, material handlers, and shipping/receiving personnel.

Job Category: Human Resources
Location: Halifax, Nova Scotia
Job Status: Full-time

B. Staffing Manager

Job Description:

Provides strategic staffing leadership support to the line managers in both administrative and manufacturing units. Key responsibilities are developing, analyzing, implementing, and evaluating the effectiveness of the recruitment and selection process, both internally and externally, and ensuring that practices meet legal and corporate compliance requirements. The incumbent manages three recruiters who coordinate college and university job fairs, develop print and Internet job advertisements, screen and short list candidates who meet the KSAO job requirements, and provide support to line managers from first interview to job offer stages.

The incumbent is also responsible for developing and implementing tools and processes to improve organizational profitability by optimizing recruiting strategies; developing, monitoring, and implementing budget for staffing department; and providing monthly variance reports to senior management. The incumbent is also responsible for staff development including performance management, training, and coaching.

Education:

BA in relevant field and certification as Certified Human Resources Professional (CHRP).

Required Skills:

Must have minimum five years experience leading a successful high-volume recruiting team. Must have high-level oral and written communication skills; strong interpersonal skills with the ability to gain trust and confidence from others; project management experience to design, plan, and carry out multiple projects from start to finish with well-defined benchmarks and outcomes; and ability to multitask in a time-sensitive environment.

Desired Skills:

Prefer experience in managing the recruitment and selection function within a mid-size, unionized automotive parts environment.

Job Category: Human Resources
Location: Halifax, Nova Scotia
Job Status: Full-time

Mobility within staffing jobs may involve both traditional and nontraditional career tracks. In a traditional track, the normal progression is from entry-level specialist up through the ranks to staffing manager, with assignments at both the corporate and operating unit level. A nontraditional track may involve entry into a staffing specialist job, lateral transfer after a year to another functional HR area, rotation from there into an entry-level supervisory position, advancement within the supervisory ranks, and then promotion to the job of staffing manager. In short, there is often no established upward mobility track. One should expect the unexpected.

If a person advances beyond or outside of the staffing function, this will usually serve the person well for advancement to the highest HR levels (director or vice president). At these levels, job occupants have typically held varied assignments, including working outside HR in managerial or professional capacities. The work outside HR has been in diverse set of areas, including customer service, operations, finance, sales/marketing, and HR consulting.[8]

It should be noted that jobs in staffing (and other areas of HR) are becoming increasingly more customer focused and facilitative in nature. As staffing activities become more decentralized and subject to line management control, holders of staffing jobs will provide requested services and act as consultants to the service requesters. This will be a challenge because many of those newly responsible for staffing (line managers and team leaders) will be untrained and inexperienced in staffing matters.

Increasing numbers of staffing jobs are found in staffing firms. One such firm is Express Personnel Services, a large, diversified staffing firm with offices in Ontario, Alberta, and British Columbia (www.expresspersonnel.com). Services offered by Express include temporary staffing (short and long term), direct hire, professional search, on-site management programs, and training programs. Exhibit 12.3 provides a job description for an entry-level staffing consultant for Express. More advanced jobs include professional search specialist, associate services coordinator, on-site recruitment manager, associate services manager, and client services manager. Individuals in on-site staffing roles work directly with the client's HR department to conduct all phases of staffing. Use of such specialists occurs when the client lacks staffing expertise or is seeking to hire large numbers of new employees quickly.[9]

Another new type of staffing job is that of chief talent officer or vice president for talent acquisition. Organizations that are critically dependent on talent, such as technology and entertainment ones, and that need to conduct specialized talent searches outside the mainstream of the normal staffing processes, are creating such positions. One organization, America Online, went even further and created a special talent acquisition department with 35 people who conduct both external and internal searches. It is suggested that such individuals have a background in recruiting, understand accountability in organizations, possess some marketing experience to help sell the organization and build relationships, and can draw on an ability to think "outside the box" and devise a strategic vision for recruits and their roles within the organization.[10]

Policies and Procedures

policy RC 4.1
An objective or guiding principle to be sought through appropriate actions

procedure
A prescribed routine or way of acting in similar situations that provides rules to govern a particular course of action

It is highly desirable to have written policies and procedures to guide the administration of staffing systems. Understanding the importance of policies and procedures first requires definition of these terms.

A **policy** is a selected course or guiding principle. It is an objective to be sought through appropriate actions. For example, the organization might have a promotion-from-within policy as follows: It is the intent of XXX organization to fill from within all vacancies above the entry level, except in instances of critical, immediate need for a qualified person unavailable internally. This policy makes it clear that promotion from within is the desired objective; the only exception is the absence of an immediately available qualified current employee.

A **procedure** is a prescribed routine or way of acting in similar situations. It provides the rules that are to govern a particular course of action. To carry out the promotion-from-within policy, for example, the organization may have specific procedures to be followed for listing and communicating the vacancy, identifying eligible applicants, and assessing the qualifications of the applicants.

EXHIBIT 12.3 Staffing Job at Express Personnel Services

Job Title: Staffing Consultant

Reports To: Franchisee/Manager

Principal Accountabilities of Position: To assist in accomplishing the goals and objectives of the office by exercising multi-tasking, decision-making, and problem-solving skills.

Role of the Staffing Consultant: The Staffing Consultant consistently exercises discretionary judgment in administering Express systems and procedures in recruiting, hiring, and assigning associates to clients within the franchise territory. The Staffing Consultant is also responsible for retaining qualified associates and for inside sales, including responsibility for increasing sales and hours by making telephone sales calls for a portion of each day.

If a Staffing Consultant can assign a high percentage of associates and keep a greater number of associates working longer, the results are increased revenue, reduced recruiting costs, and better service to clients.

Clients appreciate and come back for quality service. It is the Staffing Consultant who takes the job order, assigns the associate, and follows up to ensure client satisfaction. It is the quality of service that causes a client company to select one staffing service over another.

Service is based on people, and people are not perfect. However, a good Staffing Consultant can smooth out difficulties resulting from human imperfections and can assure both quality and quantity in terms of associates and assignments.

Essential Functions:

1. Recruiting and Employment:
   - Develops and maintains recruiting sources to ensure consistent applicant flow
   - Receives and processes inquiry calls from applicants and associates
   - Conducts job interviews, administers and scores tests, evaluates applicant skills, abilities, and availability
   - Verifies professional/personal references and employment history through written and verbal communications with all available reference sources
   - Verifies degrees, certifications, and qualifications
   - Determines applicant suitability
   - Completes employment process by auditing all applicant-completed documents and conducts orientations about Express policies, procedures, compensations, benefits, and the employer/employee relationship
   - Determines associate compatibility and availability and assigns to client
   - Assures that reasonable accommodations are made to provide access to the Express employment process for individuals with limitations, and ensures that clients also provide reasonable accommodation for worksite needs
   - Assigns associates to client accounts, advising associates of client's location, the person to whom they will report, working conditions, essential job functions, work schedule, pay rate, and all other pertinent information
2. Client Relations:
   - Conducts periodic sales and service calls (*must maintain a valid driver's licence*) on existing and potential clients to identify and solve problems as well as stimulate greater business opportunity
   - Analyzes client's operation and develops and presents alternative staffing strategies suited to client-specific needs
   - Receives and processes inquiry calls from clients and prospects
   - Receives job orders and ascertains client's essential job function requirements and assignment details
   - Tours client facilities periodically to observe working conditions, production requirements, presence of legal posters, and Material Safety Data sheets
   - Advises clients concerning bill rates and pertinent assignment-related information
   - Researches issues and is able to advise clients about employment laws and practices relevant to co-employment and effective employee relations practices

Continued

EXHIBIT 12.3 *Continued*

3. Employee Relations:
   - Gathers associate work performance data from clients in accordance with Express quality assurance procedures
   - Monitors and records associate performance and provides necessary feedback
   - Provides associate counselling and appropriate disciplinary action to correct performance problems
   - Terminates unsatisfactory associates
   - Receives, investigates, and processes associate complaints and allegations of discrimination, harassments, and other worksite problems
   - Ensures the local Express office complies with federal, provincial, and municipal statutes and regulations governing the employment process and co-employment relationships
4. Administration:
   - Applies Express policies and procedures in resolving time card errors and client billing discrepancies to ensure the accurate and timely delivery of pay cheques and invoices
   - Meets with Sales Representative daily to review progress on accounts and other pertinent client information
   - Maintains client goodwill and helps collect delinquent accounts, including negotiating payment with client decision makers
5. Sales:
   - Spends a portion of each day making telephone sales calls to fill client needs and provide assignments for quality associates and candidates
   - Shares information with outside sales representatives to increase sales and hours

Other Duties:

- Maintains reference materials on applicable employment laws
- Maintains awareness of local labour market, business conditions, activities of competing companies, and industry-related trends
- Prepares and submits activity reports, ideas, and articles for the Express associate newsletter
- Other projects and activities as assigned

Working Conditions and Physical Requirements:

- Primary activities are conducted within a well-lit, climate-controlled office
- Occasional trips to client locations require travel and potential exposure to unpleasant weather conditions
- Ability to sit for extended periods and maintain the normal range of body motion
- Must be able to work effectively under the stress of multiple daily deadlines and commitments
- Occasional out-of-town trips may be required to attend special events and training sessions

Minimum Education:

Bachelor's degree in business, marketing, or related field suggested, or equivalent education and experience in business, sales, customer services, or public relations

Knowledge and Skills:

- Must have a working knowledge of the co-employment relationship and applicable federal and provincial employment laws including Employment Standards Act and Human Rights Code
- Should have thorough knowledge of the staffing and placement services offered by Express as well as pricing techniques and strategies
- Should possess strong interpersonal, communication, conflict resolution, and problem-solving skills
- Must be able to compose routine correspondence and reports

Source: Express Personnel Services. Used with permission.

EXHIBIT 12.4 HRVS.ca Policies and Procedures on Common HR Topics

Alternative Work Arrangements
- Code of Conduct
- Compensation
- Confidentiality
- Conflict Resolution
- Contract Workers & Employment Status
- Discipline
- Employee Benefits
- Harassment

Hiring
- Hiring – Recruitment and Selection
- Hiring – Offer of Employment
- Hiring – Probation
- Hiring – Orientation
- Hiring – Employment of Relatives
- Hiring – Filling of Temporarily Vacant Positions

Holidays
Hours of Work
Internet and E-mail Use
Job Evaluation
Leaves
- Leaves – Bereavement & Compassionate
- Leaves – General & Educational
- Leaves – Jury & Witness Duty
- Leaves – Maternity, Parental & Adoption
- Leaves – Sick & Personal
- Leaves – Time Off to Vote

Occupational Health and Safety
Overtime
Pay Administration
Performance Management
Professional Development
Recognition and Reward
Retirement
Termination
Vacation
Workplace Diversity

Source: Reprinted with permission, HRVS.ca (**www.hrvs-rhsbc.ca/policies/pg003_e.cfm**).

Policies and procedures thus indicate desirable courses of action and the steps to be taken to carry out the action. Without staffing policies and procedures, staffing becomes an ad hoc, casual, whimsical process. Such a process is fraught with possibilities of hurried and catch-up recruiting, nonstandardized and nonvalid assessments of applicants, decision making based on non-job-related qualification considerations (such as personal or political preferences), and job offers that exceed allowable limits on salary (and other terms) and create internal equity problems between the new hires and job incumbents. Lack of policies and procedures may also lead to practices that may foster negative applicant reactions, as well as run afoul of applicable laws and regulations.

The scope of staffing actions and practices is large, ranging across a broad spectrum of recruitment, selection, and employment issues, both external and internal. Consequently, the organization's staffing policies and procedures also need to be broad in scope. To illustrate this, Exhibit 12.4 provides a list of HR policies and procedures on common human resources topics created by HRVS.ca, which was developed in 2002 under the joint leadership of Community Foundations of Canada and United Way of Canada to provide human resources tools and information to non-profit organizations. The list is available online at www.hrvs-rhsbc.ca/policies/pg003_e.cfm, providing links to further information about each topic.

Technology

Staffing activities generate and use considerable information, often in paper form. Job descriptions, application materials, resumés, correspondence, applicant profiles, applicant flow and tracking, and reports are examples of the types of information that are necessary ingredients for the operation of a staffing system. Naturally, problems regarding what types of information to generate, and how to file, access, and use it, will arise when managing a staffing system. Addressing and solving these problems have important implications for paperwork burdens, administrative processing costs, and speed in filling job vacancies. Thus, management of a staffing system involves management of an information system.

For many organizations, the information system will continue to be primarily a paper-based and manual system. This will most likely occur in smaller organizations, single-site organizations, and organizations where there is a limited amount of staffing activity (few vacancies to fill) in a given time period. For such systems, a careful scrutiny should be done to determine if they are requiring excessive and duplicative paper documents, as well as unnecessary files and logs.

As organizations increase in size, complexity (e.g., multiple sites), and level of staffing activity, the paperwork, paper flows, and manual handling become expensive and burdensome. Moreover, the number of individuals needed to operate the staffing system and its paper become excessive. These problems cause the organization to seek staffing system efficiencies through adoption of staffing technology.

The primary improvements come about through a combination of conversion to electronic information and automation of staffing tasks and processes. A central feature is the creation of electronic databases of applicant and employee information. Computer systems will also be needed to provide data entry, access, and manipulation. Also, relevant software will need to be developed or purchased commercially through vendors. These information system requirements naturally mean that HR information system specialists will need to work closely with members of the staffing function.

Armed with the above ingredients, a myriad of staffing tasks can be performed. A suggestive listing of these tasks is provided in Exhibit 12.5. As can be seen, the tasks run the full gamut of staffing activities.

Scores of vendors and consultants are available to provide hardware, software and software product, and system design and installation services to the organization. One example is Resumix. With Resumix Hiring Gateway software, applicant resumés are received via scanning, e-mail, or fax. Key KSAO information is then extracted from the resumé and used to create a resumé summary database, which may be accessed instantly. The resumé summary includes contact information, education data, working history, and up to 80 job skills. A manager with a vacancy to fill can then create an electronic job order that specifies KSAO requirements (both necessary and preferred). The system then automatically conducts keyword searches among the resumé summaries, yielding one or more person/job matches that are rank-ordered based on the number of successful matching criteria. Another feature is that a recruiter can look up and identify all currently unfilled job orders, so that a candidate the recruiter is working with can then be matched against all such job orders. Also, as new resumé summaries are entered into the database they are automatically matched against all open job orders and "flagged" for recruiter attention if there is a

EXHIBIT 12.5 Computerized Staffing Tasks

- Forecasting workforce supply and demand
- Employee succession planning
- Applicant/employee KSAO database
- Job requisitions
- Job posting reports
- Applicant logs, status, and tracking reports
- Correspondence with applicants
- New hire reports (numbers, qualifications, assignments)
- Employment activity (vacancies, requisitions, positions filled)
- Legal data analysis and reports
- Selection (keyword search criteria, testing)
- Electronic resumé routing
- Recruitment source effectiveness

potential match. Other features of Resumix are generation of standard letters (acknowledgments, interview invitation, etc.), preparation of reports and staffing metrics, shipment of resumés and resumé summaries to interested parties via fax and e-mail, creation of an employment folder that adds documents (e.g., interviewer's notes) to the resumé summary, and operation of a job posting system. The city of Toronto, for example, uses Resumix to store and retrieve resumés electronically for staffing purposes, and assists applicants with instructions on how to prepare a scannable resumé to optimize the resumé's opportunity to be matched for suitable jobs once it is downloaded into Resumix (www.toronto.ca/employment/resume_help.htm).

Web-based staffing management systems are also available from application service providers (ASPs). With such systems, the vendor provides both the hardware (e.g., servers, scanners) and the software, as well as day-to-day management of the system. Recruiters and hiring managers access the system through a Web browser. One example of such a system is Taleo Business Edition (www.taleo.com). The company has Canadian offices in Toronto and Quebec City and serves 350 organization and 500,000 registered users with 29 million candidates in 100 countries. It has worked with large companies such as Dow Chemical and Hewlett-Packard "designing and developing recruitment and talent management software to meet the needs of these sophisticated, complex, and dynamic companies. Mosiac Sales Solutions, with operations throughout Canada cut time to hiring by 33 percent, decreased hiring managers' time requirements by 75 percent, and reduced advertising costs by 90 percent using the Taleo system." The system accepts resumés, scans and codes them, and stores them in a relational database on a secure server. The system has a candidate management component for managing resumés and searches, auto-response e-mails, contact and communication logs, interviews, offer letters and approval, and historical activity trail. It also has a requisition management component for real-time job posting, prescreening questions, job-specific candidate ranking, e-mail-based approval process, agency access, job-specific application form, multiple career site posting, and job board posting. Numerous reports, customized for the users, gauging the effectiveness of process, can be generated.[11]

There are many other staffing software providers, including the following:

- PeopleSoft (www.peoplesoft.com)
- recruiterSoft (www.recruitersoft.com)
- Vurv (formerly Recruitmax; www.vurv.com)
- Webhire (www.webhire.com)
- HRsmart (www.hrsmart.com)

How to evaluate, and make choices from among, the myriad software providers is beyond the scope of this book. For-fee buyers' guides, however, are available that describe the vendors and products and make product comparisons (see www.hr.com and www.rocket-hire.com).

Effectiveness Surveys of organizations' experiences with new staffing technologies and case studies of their adoption, implementation, and operation provide a comprehensive overview of how well the new technologies are working.[12] What emerges from the data is a very "mixed bag" of evidence, with numerous positive and negative experiences being reported. Based on these reports, Exhibit 12.6 provides a summary of the potential advantages and disadvantages of staffing technology.

From Exhibit 12.6 it is clear that staffing technologies may have a multitude of positive and negative effects. Many of these effects extend beyond process improvement (e.g., speed of staffing) and cost reduction. While these two potential advantages are very important ones, they need to be considered within the context of other potential advantages, and especially the myriad potential disadvantages. Based on the evidence, it is very clear that the organization should proceed with caution and due diligence in deciding whether to move toward use of new staffing technologies, evaluating products and vendors, establishing service agreements with vendors, and conducting careful planning prior to implementation. It is also clear that even once implemented, monitoring and system improvement will need to be periodically undertaken.

EXHIBIT 12.6 Staffing Technology: Potential Advantages and Disadvantages

A. Potential Advantages

- Reduced time to fill positions
- Reduced costs: less and cheaper advertising; reduced use of staffing firms and fees; reduced use of executive search firms and fees; fewer recruiters due to elimination or consolidation of positions
- Improved applicant satisfaction due to improved staffing process speed and feedback about hiring status
- Improved recruiter performance and monitoring
- Improved person/job and person/organization matches
- Improved staffing reports generation—number, speed, accuracy
- Improved employment brand
- Expanded applicant visibility, especially for internal staffing

B. Potential Disadvantages

- Most useful in large organizations and in high-volume staffing situations
- Impersonal and difficult to build meaningful, sustained relationships with candidates and finalists
- Costs of switching to new system (e.g., implementation, downtime)
- Applicant dishonesty (e.g., providing false information, cheating on test)
- Costs of training recruiters and managers to use the new system
- Difficulties in motivating recruiters and managers to continue to use the system
- Process bottlenecks (e.g., system downtime, manager delays in using the system)
- Management of relationship with vendor (e.g., negotiate service agreement, monitor performance)
- "Lock in" to vendor—difficult to switch vendors
- Vendor survival in the long run
- Incompatibility with other HR systems and technology

Outsourcing

outsourcing
Contracting out work to a vendor or third-party administrator

Outsourcing refers to contracting out work to a vendor or third-party administrator. There are many examples of the outsourcing of specific staffing activities. These include seeking temporary employees, executive searches, drug testing, skill testing, background checks, conducting job fairs, employee relocation, assessment centres, and employment equity planning. Other examples continue to emerge. For example, on-demand recruiting services provide short-term assistance in conducting executive searches, but payment for these services is based on a fixed fee or time rate, rather than on a percentage of the new hire's salary.[13]

An emerging type of vendor is the professional employer organization (PEO), formerly referred to as an employee leasing firm. It is similar to a staffing firm, but differs from it by providing a wider range of HR services and having a long-term commitment to the client. Under a typical arrangement, the client organization enters into a contractual relationship with a PEO to conduct some or all HR activities and functions. The client and the PEO are considered co-employers of record. A PEO is particularly appealing to small employers because it can perform the following:[14]

- Provides special HR expertise and technical assistance
- Conducts the administrative activities and transactions of an HR department
- Provides more affordable employee benefits

- Meets legal obligations (payroll, withholding, workers' compensation, employment insurance)
- Manages legal compliance

There is also experimentation with total outsourcing of the staffing function. An example is Kellogg (cereal and convenience foods), which selected a single vendor to which the entire staffing process was outsourced. Kellogg worked with the vendor at the outset to develop a staffing strategy and fit it into the vendor's staffing technology, implement the total staffing solution, and then modify the system as experience with it revealed problems requiring adjustment. Assessment and hiring of finalists, however, remained in the hands of the hiring manager. Within three years, over 95 percent of jobs available at Kellogg were being filled by the vendor.[15]

An example of a company who outsourced the recruitment function and then brought it back in-house is RBC Financial Group. RBC outsourced its recruitment function in 1997 and then decided to return to doing it in-house in 2001. The outsourcing company managed external recruitment effectively but managers and employees were unhappy with the internal recruitment process, and approximately 60 percent of all hires throughout the organization are internal. The outsourced recruiters were not able to determine effectively the fit between internal candidates and the job and could not sell the benefits of the job as well as internal recruiters.[16]

Many factors are driving organizations to consider outsourcing HR activities generally, including the following:

- Cost reduction
- Growing cost of technology acquisition
- Maintenance and upgrading
- Need for improved service quality
- Resource availability from vendors
- Special expertise of vendors
- Flexibility to meet changing needs

Despite these driving forces, there is also resistance within the organization to outsourcing. Among these internal barriers are a questionable cost-benefit justification, resistance within HR and from line management, inadequate readiness of people or systems, fear of a lack of control, and lack of outsourcing experience.

As the above forces for change and resistance to them suggest, a decision to outsource staffing activities should not be made without careful planning and forethought, and recognition that there will be perceived downsides to outsourcing that will likely be pointed out. Should the decision to outsource be made, it will then be necessary to select a vendor or service provider. An example of such a selection, involving the choice of a staffing firm, was given in Chapter 2 (see Exhibit 2.3). That example is a useful starting point for a more general set of recommendations about vendor or service provider selection.

At the outset, it is important to remember that the agreement (often called a service-level agreement, or SLA) with the vendor is almost always negotiable, and that flaws in the negotiating stage are responsible for many problems that may subsequently occur in the relationship. Using some form of legal or consulting assistance might be desirable, especially for the organization that has little or no staffing outsourcing experience.

There are many issues to discuss and negotiate. Awareness of these factors and advance preparation with regard to the organization's preferences and requirements are critical to a successful negotiation with a potential vendor. These factors include the following:

- The actual staffing services sought and provided
- Client control rights (e.g. monitoring of the vendor's personnel, software to be used)
- Fees and other costs
- Guaranteed improvements in service levels and cost savings

- Benchmarking metrics and performance reviews
- Willingness to hire the organization's own employees to provide expertise and coordination

On top of these factors, the choice of vendor should take into account the vendor's past track record and familiarity with the organization's industry.[17]

EVALUATION OF STAFFING SYSTEMS

3.5

evaluation of staffing systems
Focuses on the operation of the staffing process, the results and costs of the process, and the satisfaction of customers of the staffing system

Evaluation of staffing systems refers to the effectiveness of the total system. The evaluation should focus on the operation of the staffing process, the results and costs of the process, and the satisfaction of customers of the staffing system.

Staffing Process

The staffing process establishes and governs the flow of employees into, within, and out of the organization. Evaluation of the process itself requires a mapping out of the intended process, identifying any deviations from the intended process, and planning corrective actions to take to reduce or eliminate the deviations. The intent of such an evaluation is to ensure standardization of the staffing process, remove bottlenecks in operation, and improve speed of operation.

standardization
Consistency of operation of the organization's staffing system

Standardization refers to the consistency of operation of the organization's staffing system. Use of standardized staffing systems is desirable for several reasons.

1. Standardization ensures that the same KSAO information is gathered from all job applicants, which, in turn, is a key requirement for reliably and validly measuring these KSAOs.
2. Standardization ensures that all applicants receive the same information about job requirements and rewards. Thus, all applicants can make equally informed evaluations of the organization.
3. Standardization will enhance applicants' perceptions of the procedural fairness of the staffing system and of the decision made about them by the organization. Having applicants feel they were treated fairly and got a "fair shake" can reap substantial benefits for the organization. Applicants will speak favourably of their experience and the organization to others, they may seek employment with the organization in the future (even if rejected), they may be more likely to say "yes" to job offers, and they may become organizational newcomers with a very upbeat frame of mind as they begin their new jobs.
4. Standardized staffing systems are less likely to generate legal challenges by job applicants; if they are challenged, they are more likely to successfully withstand the challenge.

Mapping out the staffing process involves construction of a staffing flowchart. An example of a staffing flowchart is shown in Exhibit 12.7. It is a flowchart that depicts the staffing system of a medium-sized (580 employees) high-tech printing and lithography company. It shows the actual flow of staffing activities, and both organization and applicant decision points, from the time a vacancy occurs until the time it is filled with a new hire.

A detailed inspection of the chart reveals the following sorts of information about the organization's staffing system:

1. It is a generic system used for both entry-level and higher-level jobs.
2. For higher-level jobs, vacancies are first posted internally (thus showing a recruitment philosophy emphasizing a commitment to promotion from within). Entry-level jobs are filled externally.
3. External recruitment sources (colleges and universities, newspaper ads, employment agencies) are used only if the current applicant file yields no qualified applicants.

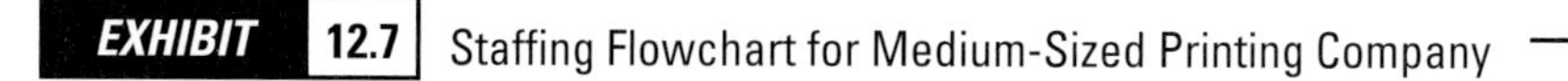

EXHIBIT 12.7 Staffing Flowchart for Medium-Sized Printing Company

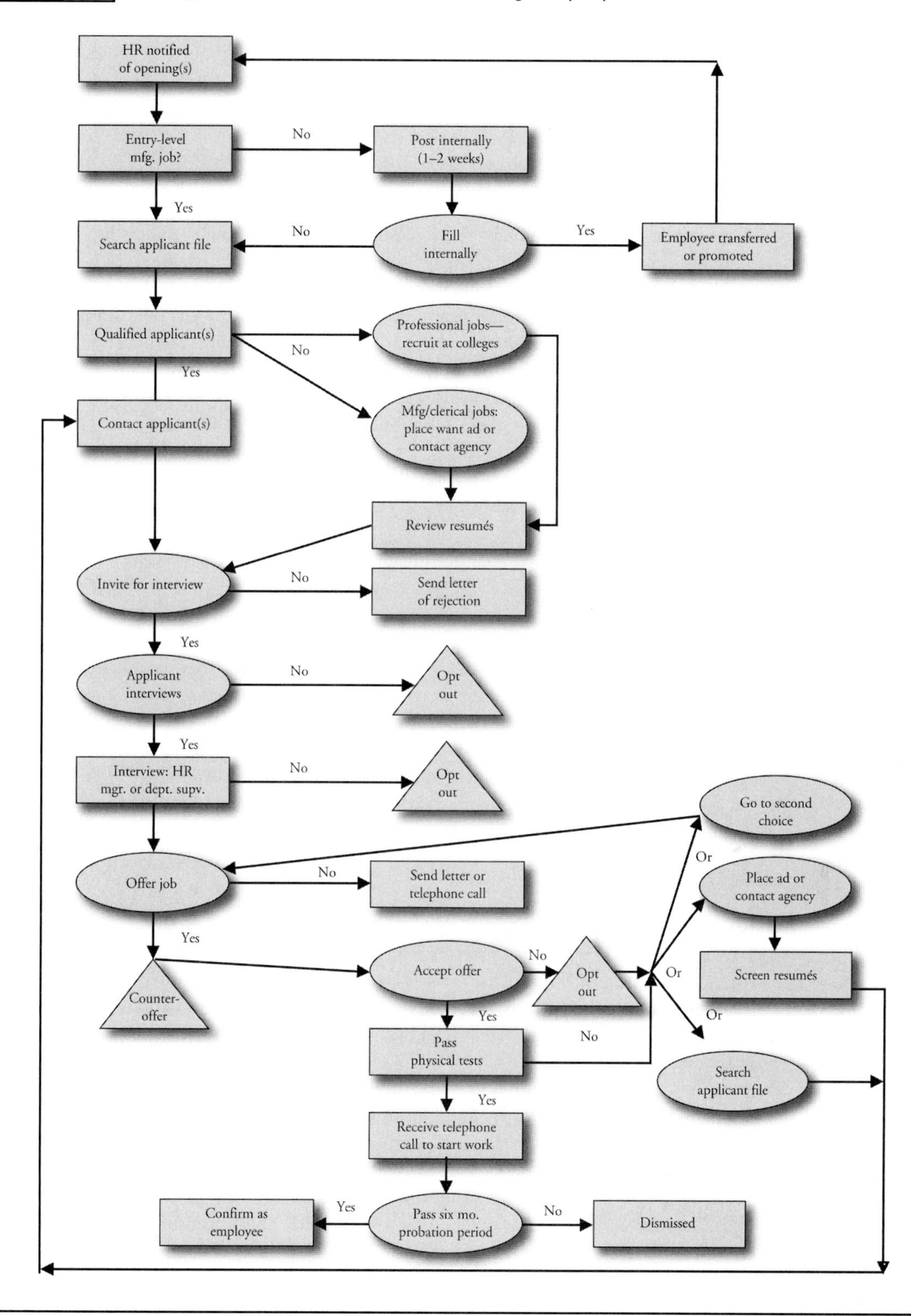

4. Initial assessments are made using biographical information (application blanks, resumés), and results of these assessments determine who will be interviewed.
5. Substantive assessments are made through the interview(s) conducted by the HR manager and the hiring supervisor, and results of these assessments determine who receives the job offer.
6. The applicant may counteroffer, and acceptance by the applicant of the final offer is conditional on passing physical tests.
7. The new hire undergoes a six-month probationary employment period before becoming a permanent employee.

A more fine-grained analysis is then conducted to indicate the specific steps and actions that should be taken throughout the staffing process. For example, it can be seen in Exhibit 12.7 that non-entry-level manufacturing jobs are posted internally, so the more fine-grained analysis would involve a description of the job-posting process—content of the posting, timing of the posting, mechanisms for circulating and displaying the posting, and person responsible for handling the posting. As another example, the staffing process involves contacting qualified applicants for an interview, inviting them for an interview, and interviewing them. The more fine-grained analysis would involve identification of the amount of time between the initial contact and completion of interviews, who conducts the interview, and the nature/content of the interview (such as a structured, situational interview). After the fine-grained analysis is complete, there would be a detailed specification of the staffing process in flow terms, along with specific events, actions, and timing that should occur over the course of the process.

Once the staffing process has been mapped out, the next step is to check for deviations from it that have actually occurred. This will require an analysis of some past staffing "transactions" with job applicants, following what was done and what actions were taken as the applicants entered and flowed through the staffing system. All identified deviations should be recorded. It might be found, for example, that the content of the job postings did not conform to specific requirements for listing tasks and necessary KSAOs; or that interviews were not being conducted within the required one-week period from date of first contact with a qualified applicant; or that interviewers were conducting unstructured interviews rather than the required structured, situational interview.

The next step is to analyze all discovered deviations and determine the reason(s) for their occurrence. The final step is to determine and make changes in the staffing system in order to reduce deviations, enhance standardization, and remove bottlenecks.

Staffing Process Results

Over the course of the staffing process it is possible to develop quantitative indicators that show how effectively and efficiently the staffing system is operating. For example, how many applicants does a given vacancy attract, on average? Or, what percentage of job offers are accepted? What is the average number of days it takes to fill a vacancy? What percentage of new hires remain with the organization for one year post hire? Answers to such questions can be determined by tracking and analysis of applicant flows through the staffing pipeline.

Exhibit 12.8 shows the required layout for this tracking and analysis, as well as some staffing process results that may be easily calculated. In the upper part (A) of the exhibit, the steps in the staffing process start with announcement of a vacancy and run through a sequential flow of selection, job offer, offer acceptance, start as new hire, and retention. Also shown is a timeline, in average number of days, for completion of each step. For illustration purposes, it is assumed there are 25 vacancies that have been filled and that these vacancies attracted 1,000 applicants who then proceeded through the staffing process. Ultimately, all 25 vacancies were filled, and these new hires were then tracked to see how many of them remained with the organization for six months and one year post hire.

EXHIBIT 12.8 Evaluation of Staffing Process and Results: Example

A. Staffing Process Example

No. of vacancies filled = 25

Process step	Vacancy announced (1)	Applicants (2)	Candidates (3)	Finalists (4)	Offer receiver (5)	Offer acceptance (6)	Start as new hire (7)	On the job: Six months (8)	One Year (9)
No. of people	0	1,000	200	125	30	25	25	20	13
Process time Avg. no. of days	0	14	21	28	35	42	44		

B. Staffing Process Results

Applicants/Vacancy = 1,000/25 = 40

Yield ratio: candidates/applicant = 20%; new hires/applicant = 2.5%; offers accepted/received = 83.3%

Time lapse: avg. days to offer = 35; avg. days to start = 44
(cycle time)

Retention rate: $\frac{\text{on job six months}}{\text{new hires}}$ = 80% for six months; $\frac{\text{on job one year}}{\text{new hires}}$ = 52% for first year

At the bottom (B) of Exhibit 12.8 are staffing process results indicators, also referred to as metrics, along with calculations of them for the example. The first indicator is applicants per vacancy, which averaged 40. This is an indication of the effectiveness of recruitment activities to attract people to the organization. The second indicator is the yield ratio; it indicates the percentage of people who moved on to one or more of the next steps in the staffing process. For example, the percentage of applicants who became candidates is 20 percent; the percentage of job offers accepted is 83.3 percent. The third indicator, time lapse (or cycle time), shows the average amount of time lapsed between each step in the staffing process. It can be seen that the average days to fill a vacancy is 44. The final indicator is retention rate; for the new hires it can be seen that the six-month retention rate was 80 percent, and the one-year rate fell to 52 percent.

These types of metrics are very useful barometers for gauging the pulse of the staffing flow. They have an objective, "bottom-line" nature that can be readily communicated to managers and others in the organization. These types of data are also very useful for comparative purposes. For example, the relative effectiveness and efficiency of staffing systems in two different units of the organization could be assessed by comparing their respective yield ratios and so forth. Another comparison could be the same staffing system compared to itself over time. Such time-based comparisons are useful for tracking trends in effectiveness and efficiency. These comparisons are also used to help judge how well changes in staffing practices have actually worked to improve staffing process performance.

For example, Mirage Resorts in Las Vegas was going to conduct a mass, one-time staffing process to hire 9,600 employees for the opening of Bellagio, its new luxury resort. Mirage Resorts' previous mass hire had taken nine months; it sought to design a staffing process that would shorten that staffing time and cost. A new, computerized staffing process was developed that accomplished the staffing objective within five-and-one-half months, at a cost savings of $600,000. The system operated as follows:

- Based on a newspaper help-wanted ad, interested applicants called a toll-free number to schedule an appointment to apply in person.
- Up to 1,200 applicants daily completed an application on a computer screen, and then went to an HR checkout desk to make sure they had completed the application appropriately. At the desk, applicants had their appearance and behaviour noted.

- Applicant data was placed in a database, which was searched by individual hiring departments.
- Viable candidates were interviewed by one of 180 specially trained interviewers.
- Interview results were fed back into the database.
- Background checks were then conducted, and those chosen as finalists by hiring managers in the hiring departments took a drug test.
- Job offers were then extended by departments, though this took up to a few months after the interview.

Only 3 percent of the initial applicants that were favourably evaluated by Mirage withdrew somewhere along the staffing process.[18]

Increasingly, organizations are emphasizing time to fill vacancies as a key indicator of staffing effectiveness based on the reasonable assumption that the shorter the vacancy time, the less the employee contribution foregone. Vacancies in sales jobs, for example, often mean lost sales and revenue generation, so shortening the time to fill means lessening the revenue foregone. Reducing time to fill vacancies has led organizations to develop "speed hiring" and continuous hiring programs, which in turn causes them to redesign their staffing systems to eliminate any excessive delays or bottlenecks in the process.[19]

It is possible to compare the organization's own staffing metrics with those of other organizations. Results from two staffing metrics surveys might be consulted for this purpose, from Staffing.org (www.staffing.org) and the Saratoga Institute (www.saratogainstitute.com). The Saratoga Institute, for example, annually collects and compiles HR metrics data, including staffing from over 900 organizations. Some examples of the staffing metrics from the Saratoga Institute are shown in Exhibit 12.9. The data are shown separately for external and internal hires, and for salaried and hourly employees. It can be seen, for example, that for salaried employees the average time to fill a position was 64 days and the average days to start was 83 days. It should be noted that these results will vary in a given time period by such factors as organization size and industry. They will also vary over time according to tightness of the labour market, with tighter labour markets having larger average times. Finally, surveys of organizational practice in calculating staffing metrics should be consulted to learn about the many nuances involved.[20]

Staffing Costs

Though staffing costs are an obviously important concern for evaluating staffing activities, actually deriving the cost estimates is difficult. There is no commonly used way of costing out the staffing process. One suggested way for doing so is provided by the Saratoga Institute; Staffing.org also might be consulted.

The previously mentioned survey by the Saratoga Institute is also used to collect organizations' estimates of staffing costs and then report a cost-per-hire estimate. The staffing cost estimates are composed of (1) advertising, employment agency, and search firm fees; (2) employee referral bonuses; (3) travel costs for recruiter and applicants; (4) relocation costs; (5) recruiter salary and benefit costs; and (6) a 10 percent add-on to approximate costs of testing, reference checking, bonding, hiring unit staff time, administrative support, and minor expenses. Based on these cost estimates, the average cost per hire is shown in Exhibit 12.9. It can be seen that for external hires, the average cost was $8,924 for salaried employees and $865 for hourly employees; costs were less for internal hires. These cost data also vary by organization size, industry, and labour market tightness. Other cost data, and how to calculate them, are also available.[21]

Another staffing cost metric is the staffing cost or efficiency ratio.[22] It takes into account that recruiting applicants for higher compensation level jobs might cost more, due to such costs as executive search fees, recruitment advertising, relocation, and so forth. The formula for the staffing cost ratio is total staffing cost ratio = total staffing costs/total compensation recruited. Though the cost per hire may be greater for one job category than another job category, their staffing cost ratios may be the same. This is illustrated in Exhibit 12.10. It can be seen that if

EXHIBIT 12.9 Staffing Metrics: Average Time and Cost

	Days to Fill	Days to Start	Cost/Hire
A. External Hires			
Salaried	64	83	$8,924
Hourly	42	59	$865
B. Internal Hires			
Salaried	43	63	$930
Hourly	35	50	$456

Source: Saratoga Institute, *Human Capital Benchmarking Report*, Santa Clara, CA, 2001. Used with permission.

EXHIBIT 12.10 Comparison of Cost Per Hire and Staffing Cost Ratio

Job Category	New Hires	Staffing Cost	Cost Per Hire	Compensation Per Hire	Staffing Cost Ratio
Repair	500	$500,000	$1,000	$20,000	5%
Sales Manager	100	$300,000	$3,000	$60,000	5%

just cost per hire is considered, it appears that recruitment for the repair job is more effective than for the sales manager job. But by also calculating the staffing cost ratio, it can be seen that recruitment is at the same level of efficiency for both job categories—that is, recruitment for each source is incurring the same relative expense to "bring in" the same amount of compensation via new hires.

Customer Satisfaction

Staffing systems, by their very nature, influence users of them. Such users can be thought of as customers of the system. Two of the key customers are managers and job applicants. Managers look to the staffing system to provide them the right numbers and types of new hires to meet their own staffing needs. Job applicants expect the staffing system to recruit, select, and make employment decisions about them in ways that are fair and legal. For both sets of customers, therefore, it is important to know how satisfied they are with the staffing systems that serve them. Detection of positive satisfaction can reinforce the usage of current staffing practices. Discovering areas of dissatisfaction, alternately, may serve as a trigger for needed changes in the staffing system and help pinpoint the nature of those changes.

Customer satisfaction with staffing systems is of fairly recent origin as an organizational concern. Rarely in the past were managers and job applicants even thought of as customers, and rarer yet were systematic attempts made to measure their customer satisfaction as a way of evaluating the effectiveness of staffing systems. Recently, that has begun to change. Described next are examples of measures of customer satisfaction for managers and for job applicants.

Managers The state of Wisconsin Department of Employment Relations houses the Division of Merit Recruitment and Selection (DMRS), which is the central agency responsible for staffing the state government. Annually, it helps the 40 state agencies to fill about 4,000 vacancies through hiring and promoting. Managers within these agencies, thus, are customers of the DMRS and its staffing systems.

To help identify and guide needed staffing system improvements, the DMRS decided to develop a survey measure of managers' satisfaction with staffing services. Through the use of focus groups, managers' input on the content of the survey was solicited. The final survey had 53 items on it, grouped into five areas: communication, timeliness, candidate quality, test quality, and service focus. Examples of the survey items are shown in Exhibit 12.11.

The survey was administered via internal mail to 645 line and HR managers throughout the agencies. Statistical analyses provided favourable psychometric evidence supporting usage of the survey. Survey results served as a key input to implementation of several initiatives to improve staffing service delivery. These initiatives led to increases in the speed of filling vacancies, elimination of paperwork, higher reported quality of job applicants, and positive applicant reactions to the staffing process.[23]

Job Applicants As with managers, it is best to develop a tailor-made survey for job applicants, one that reflects the specific characteristics of the staffing system being used and the types of contacts and experiences job applicants will have with it. Consultation of a staffing flowchart (Exhibit 12.7) would be helpful in this regard. If possible, the survey should

EXHIBIT 12.11 Examples of Survey Items for Assessing Manager's Satisfaction with Staffing Services

Communication: How well are you kept informed on the staffing process?

How satisfied are you with:

1. The clarity of instructions and explanation you receive on the staffing process
2. Your overall understanding of the steps involved in filling a vacancy
3. The amount of training you receive in order to effectively participate in the total staffing process

Timeliness: How do you feel about the speed of recruitment, examination, and selection services?

How satisfied are you with the time required to:

1. Obtain central administrative approval to begin the hiring process
2. Score oral and essay exams, achievement history questionnaires, or other procedures involving scoring by a panel of raters
3. Hire someone who has been interviewed and selected

Candidate Quality: How do you feel about the quality (required knowledges and skills) of the job candidates?

How satisfied are you with:

1. The number of people you can interview and select from
2. The quality of candidates on new register
3. Your involvement in the recruitment process

Test Quality: How do you feel about the quality of civil service exams (tests, work samples, oral board interviews, etc.)?

How satisfied are you with:

1. Your involvement in exam construction
2. The extent to which the exams assess required KSAOs
3. The extent to which the exams test for new technologies used on the job

Service Focus: To what extent do you believe your personnel/staffing representatives are committed to providing high-quality service?

How satisfied are you with:

1. The accessibility of a staffing person
2. The expertise and competence of the staffing representative
3. Responses to your particular work unit's needs

Source: H. G. Heneman III, D. L. Huett, R. J. Lavigna, and D. Ogsten, "Assessing Managers' Satisfaction with Staffing Services," *Personnel Psychology*, 1995, 48, pp. 170–173. © *Personnel Psychology*, 1995. Used with permission.

be given to three different applicant groups: candidates who were rejected, candidates who accepted a job offer, and candidates who declined a job offer. Examples of questions that might be included on the survey are in Exhibit 12.12. Separate analysis of responses from each group should be done. Online assistance in survey design, survey administration, and analysis of results is available from SurveyMonkey (www.surveymonkey.com) and Zoomerang (www.zoomerang.com).

EXHIBIT 12.12 Sample Job Applicants Satisfaction Survey Question

1. What prompted you to apply to Organization X?

____ company Web site ____ advertisement ____ employee referral
____ job fair ____ campus recruitment ____ other (indicate)

2. Was the information you got from this source valuable?

____ very ____ somewhat ____ no

3. Please indicate your level of agreement with each of the following on the 1–5 scale, where 1 = strongly disagree and 5 = strongly agree

	strongly disagree			strongly agree	
The applicant process was easy to use.	1	2	3	4	5
I received a prompt response to my application.	1	2	3	4	5
My first interview was promptly scheduled.	1	2	3	4	5
My first interview covered all my qualifications.	1	2	3	4	5
The test I took was relevant to the job.	1	2	3	4	5
The test process was fair.	1	2	3	4	5
I received prompt feedback about my test scores.	1	2	3	4	5
I always knew where I stood in the selection process.	1	2	3	4	5
My interview with the hiring manager was thorough.	1	2	3	4	5
The hiring manager represented Organization X well.	1	2	3	4	5
I was treated honestly and openly.	1	2	3	4	5
Overall, I am satisfied with the selection process.	1	2	3	4	5
I would recommend Organization X to others as a place to work.	1	2	3	4	5

4. Please describe what you liked most about your experience seeking a job with Organization X.

5. Please describe what you liked least about your experience seeking a job with Organization X.

LEGAL ISSUES

Record Keeping, Privacy, and Reports

In staffing systems, substantial information is generated, used, recorded, and disclosed. There are numerous legal constraints and requirements surrounding staffing information. These pertain to record keeping, privacy concerns, and preparation of reports.

Record Keeping A wide range of information is created by the organization during staffing and other HR activities. Examples include personal data (name, address, date of birth, dependents, etc.), KSAO information (application blank, references, test scores, etc.), medical information, performance appraisal and promotability assessments, and changes in employment status (promotion, transfers, etc.). Why should records of such information be created?

Basically, records should be created and maintained for two major legal purposes in staffing. First, they are necessary for legal compliance. Federal and provincial laws specify what information should be kept, and for how long. Second, having records allows the organization to provide documentation to justify staffing decisions or to defend these decisions against legal challenge. For example, performance appraisal and promotability assessments might be used to explain to employees why they were or were not promoted. Or, these same records might be used as evidence in a legal proceeding to show that promotion decisions were job related and unbiased.

The documents kept in an employee's file should comprise only documents that relate directly to the job and the employee's performance of it. To determine which documents to place in the employee file, ask whether it is a document on which the organization could legally base an employment decision. If the answer is "no," "probably not," or "not sure," the document should not be placed in the employee's personnel file.

Any document that is to be placed in an employee's personnel file should be reviewed before it becomes part of that record. Examine the document for incomplete, inaccurate, or misleading information, as well as potentially damaging notations or comments about the employee. All such information should be completed, corrected, explained, and, if necessary, eliminated. Remember that any document in the personnel file is a potential court exhibit that may work either for or against the employer's defence of a legal challenge.[24]

As a general rule, most records must be kept for a minimum of one year from the date a document is made or a staffing action is taken, whichever is later. Exceptions to the one-year requirements all provide for even longer retention periods. If a charge of discrimination is filed, the records must be retained until the matter is finally resolved.

Privacy Concerns As discussed in Chapter 2, protection of privacy is a relatively new issue with the enactment of the Personal Information Protection and Electronic Documents Act (PIPEDA) in 2001. The Act applies to the collection, use, and disclosure of personal information by organizations under federal jurisdiction. It also applies to non-federally regulated organizations that sell, use, or disclose personal information outside of the province in which it was gathered, and organizations that collect, use, or disclose personal information in connection with the operation of a federally regulated private sector business. The purpose of the Act is to protect the privacy of individuals with respect to personal information about themselves held by government institutions, and to provide individuals with the right of access to that information.

Several (not all) provinces have laws guaranteeing employees reasonable access to their personnel files. The laws generally allow the employee to review and copy pertinent documents. The employee has the right to seek to correct erroneous information on the file or to have a notation attached to any information for which a correction was requested but not made. At the federally regulated level, the employer must identify the reason for collecting personal information and gain the consent of the employee as to the use, disclosure, and retention of the employee's information.

Audits

It is highly desirable to periodically conduct audits or reviews of the organization's degree of compliance with laws and regulations pertaining to staffing. The audit forces the organization to study and specify what in fact its staffing practices are and to compare these current practices against legally desirable and required practices. Results can be used to identify potential legal trouble spots and to map out changes in staffing practices that will serve to minimize potential liability and reduce the risk of lawsuits being filed against the organization.

The audit could be conducted by the organization's own legal counsel. Alternately, the HR department might first conduct a self-audit, and then review its findings with legal counsel. Conducting an audit after involvement in employment litigation is also recommended.[25]

Not only is it desirable that legal audits be conducted, but they should be done on a recurring basis. The appearance of new laws or amendments to them, issuance of new policy guidance and regulations by federal agencies, and changing court interpretations all mean that the line of demarcation between permissible and impermissible staffing practices is fuzzy and in need of periodic re-examination.

Training for Managers and Employees

Training for managers and employees in employment law and compliance requirements is not only a sound practice, but increasingly a defence point for the organization in employment litigation. The following statement illustrates this: "Recent judicial and agency activity make clear that training is no longer a discretionary HR activity—it is essential. The question is not whether your company is going to provide it, but how long will it have to suffer the costly consequences of neglect. A carefully crafted, effectively executed, methodically measured, and frequently fine-tuned employment practices training program for managers and employees is a powerful component of a strategic HRD (human resource development) plan that aligns vital corporate values with daily practices. The costs of neglect are serious. The benefits are compelling and fundamental to long-term success.... Adequate, effective, and regularly scheduled employment law and practices training is now the rule, not the exception."[26] While this need for training arose from within the realm of sexual harassment prevention, it has gradually encompassed all forms of discrimination, including that which might occur in staffing the organization.

Though the requirements for employment law training are still developing, it appears as though there are several desirable components to be incorporated into it:[27]

1. The training should be for all members of the organization.
2. Basic harassment and discrimination training should be given immediately to new employees, managers should receive additional training, and refresher training should occur periodically and when special circumstances arise, such as a significant change in policy and practice.
3. The trainers should have special expertise in employment law and practice.
4. The training content should be substantive and cover human rights practices in several staffing areas—such as recruitment, hiring, succession planning, and promotion—as pertains to the numerous human rights laws and regulations; training in other areas of HR—such as compensation and benefits—should also be provided.
5. The training materials should also be substantive, incorporate the organization's specific harassment and discrimination policies, and allow for both information presentation and active practice by the participants.

Dispute Resolution

Employment laws and regulations naturally lead to claims of their violation by job applicants and employees. If the claim is filed with an external agency, such as the Canadian Human Rights

EXHIBIT 12.13 Alternative Dispute Resolution Approaches

Approach	Description
Negotiation	Employer and employee discuss complaint with goal of resolving complaint.
Fact finding	A neutral person, from inside or outside the organization, investigates a complaint and develops findings that may be the basis for resolving the complaint.
Peer review	A panel of employees and managers work together to resolve the complaint.
Mediation	A neutral person (mediator) from within or outside the organization helps the parties negotiate a mutually acceptable agreement. Mediator is trained in mediation methods. Settlement is not imposed.
Arbitration	A neutral person (arbitrator) from within or outside the organization conducts formal hearing and issues a decision that is binding on the parties.

Commission, the dispute resolution procedures described in Chapter 2 are applied. In the case of the Canadian Human Rights Commission, it seeks to settle disputes quickly and without formal investigation and Canadian litigation, by providing mediation as an alternative dispute resolution (ADR) procedure (www.chrc-ccdp.ca). The Canadian Human Rights Commission provides, without fee, a trained mediator to help the employer and job applicant (or employee) reconcile their differences and reach a satisfactory resolution. The process is confidential, any records or notes are destroyed at its conclusion, and nothing that is revealed may be used subsequently in investigation or litigation should the dispute not be resolved. Most disputes are resolved through mediation, though employers are generally less willing than applicants or employees to accept an offer of mediation.[28]

For claims of discrimination (or other grievances) made internally, the organization will likely offer some form of ADR to resolve the dispute.[29] Exhibit 12.13 shows the numerous approaches to ADR that might be used. Research shows that most organizations do in fact use one or more of these procedures, with negotiation and fact finding being the most prevalent by far. Peer review and mediation are used substantially less, and arbitration is the least used.[30]

Organizations are experimenting with more formal ADR systems that combine elements of all the approaches shown in Exhibit 12.13. An example of such an ADR with five sequential steps is shown in Exhibit 12.14. Step 1 corresponds to negotiation, step 2 to fact finding, steps 3 and 4 to peer review and mediation, and step 5 to arbitration. It should be noted that such ADRs are highly experimental; their effectiveness and legality is open to question. Also, many guidelines are being suggested for their establishment and use.[31]

The Special Case of Arbitration With arbitration as the ADR procedure, the employer and job applicant (or employee) agree in advance to submit their dispute to a neutral third-party arbitrator, who will issue a final and binding decision. Such arbitration agreements usually include statutory discrimination claims, meaning that the employee agrees to not pursue charges of discrimination against the employer by any means (e.g., lawsuit) except arbitration. The courts have ruled that such arbitration agreements generally are legally permissible and enforceable. However, if the organization decides to require mandatory arbitration agreements from job applicants and employees, it should be aware that there are many specific, suggested standards that the arbitration agreement and process must meet in order to be enforceable.[32]

EXHIBIT 12.14 Example of Alternative Dispute Resolution (ADR) Procedure

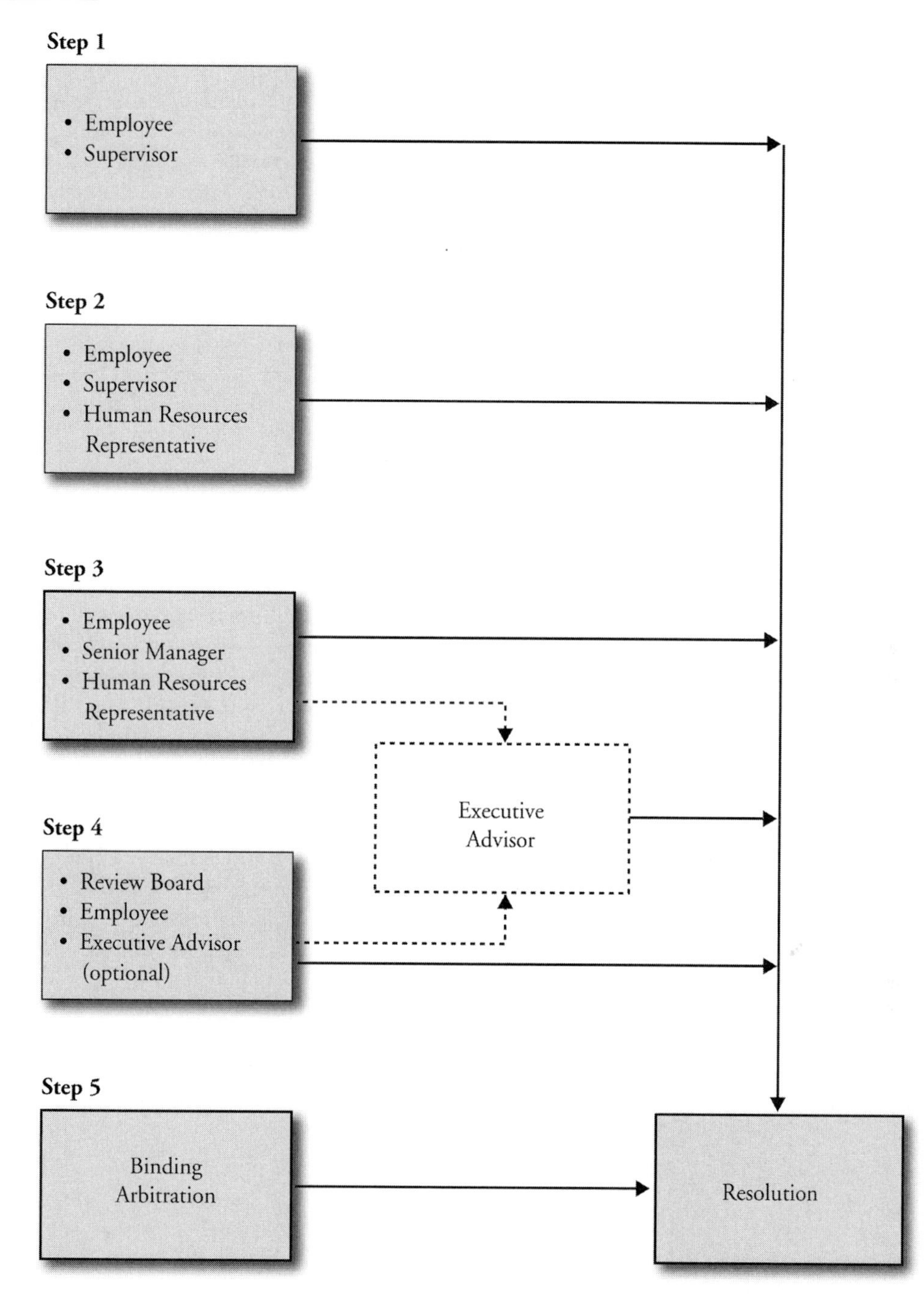

Source: U.S. Government Accounting Office, *Employment Discrimination: Most Private Sector Employers Use Alternative Dispute Resolution*, Report 95–150 (Washington, DC: author, 1995), p. 9.

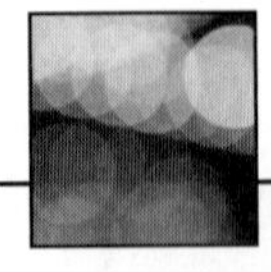

SUMMARY

The multiple and complex set of activities collectively known as a staffing system must be integrated and coordinated throughout the organization. Such management of the staffing system requires both careful administration and evaluation, as well as compliance with legal mandates.

To manage the staffing system, the usual organizational arrangement in all but very small organizations is to create an identifiable staffing or employment function, and to place it within the HR department. That function then manages the staffing system at the corporate and/or plant and office level. Numerous types of jobs, both specialist and generalist, are found within the staffing function. Entry into these jobs, and movement among them, is very fluid and does not follow any set career mobility path.

The myriad staffing activities require staffing policies to establish general staffing principles and procedures to guide the conduct of those activities. Lack of clear policies and procedures can lead to misguided and inconsistent staffing practices, as well as potentially illegal ones. Staffing technology can help achieve these consistencies and aid in improving staffing system efficiency. Electronic systems are increasingly being used to conduct a wide range of staffing tasks; they have a mixed bag of advantages and disadvantages. Outsourcing of staffing activities is also being experimented with as a way of improving staffing system operation and results.

Evaluation of the effectiveness of the staffing system should proceed along several fronts. First is assessment of the staffing system from a process perspective. Here, it is desirable to examine the degree of standardization (consistency) of the process, as well as a staffing flowchart in order to identify deviations in staffing practice and bottlenecks. The results of the process according to indicators such as yield ratios and time lapse (cycle time), and costs of staffing system operation, should also be estimated. Finally, the organization should consider assessing the satisfaction of staffing system users, such as managers and job applicants.

Considerable attention should be devoted to legal issues. Various laws require maintenance of numerous records and compilation of reports, especially as pertains to human rights. Care must be taken to guard privacy rights and access to information maintained in files. It is desirable to periodically conduct an actual legal audit of all the organization's staffing activities. This will help identify potential legal trouble spots that require attention. Employment law training for managers and employees is increasingly necessary. Methods for addressing employment disputes, known as alternative dispute resolution procedures, should be explored.

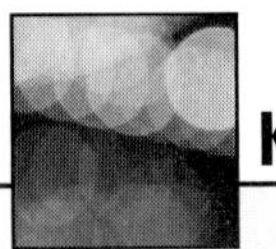

KEY TERMS

evaluation of staffing systems 426
integrated business organization 413
multiple-business organization 413
organizational arrangements 413
outsourcing 424
policy 418
procedure 418
standardization 426

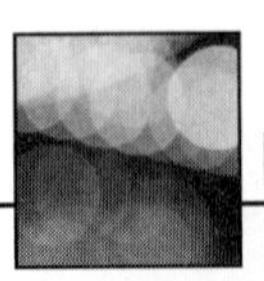

RELEVANT WEB SITES

HR Council: Human resource tool kit for the voluntary/non-profit sector

www.hrvs-rhsbc.ca

Personal Information Protection and Electronic Documents Act (PIPEDA), also called Privacy Act

http://lois.justice.gc.ca/en/P-21/index.html

Canadian Human Rights Commission: Alternative dispute resolution (ADR)

www.chrc-ccdp.ca/adr/default-en.asp

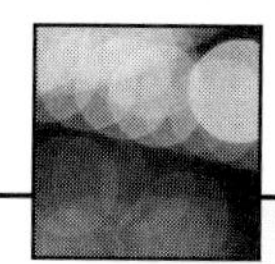

DISCUSSION QUESTIONS

1. What are the advantages of having a centralized staffing function, as opposed to letting each manager be totally responsible for all staffing activities in his or her unit?
2. What are examples of staffing tasks and activities that cannot or should not be simply delegated to a staffing information system for their conduct?
3. What would be the advantages and disadvantages of outsourcing the entire staffing system to a vendor?
4. In developing a report on the effectiveness of the staffing process being conducted for entry-level jobs, what factors would you address and why?
5. How would you try to get individual managers to be more aware of the legal requirements of staffing systems and to take steps to ensure that they themselves engage in legal staffing actions?

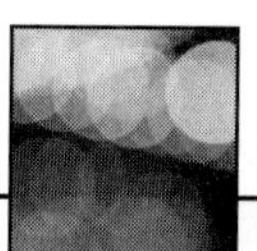

ETHICAL ISSUES

1. It has been suggested that the use of staffing technology and software is wrong because it dehumanizes the staffing experience, making it nothing but a mechanical process that treats applicants like digital widgets. Evaluate this assertion.
2. Since there are no standard ways of creating staffing process results and costs metrics, is there a need for some sort of oversight of how these data are calculated, reported, and used within the organization? Explain.

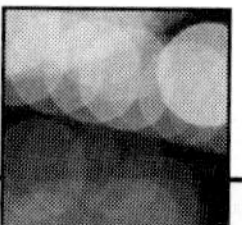

APPLICATIONS

Learning About Jobs in Staffing

The purpose of this application is to have you learn in detail about a particular job in staffing currently being performed by an individual. The individual could be a staffing job holder in the HR department of a company or public agency (provincial or local government), a nonprofit agency, a staffing firm, an employment agency, a consulting firm, or the federal employment (job) service. The individual may perform staffing tasks full time, such as a recruiter, interviewer, counsellor, employment representative, or employment manager. Or, the individual may perform staffing duties as part of the job, such as the HR manager in a small company or an HR generalist in a specific plant or site.

Contact the job holder and arrange for an interview with that person. Explain that the purpose of the interview is for you to learn about the person's job in terms of job requirements (tasks and KSAOs) and job rewards (both extrinsic and intrinsic). To prepare for the interview, review the examples of job descriptions for staffing jobs in Exhibit 12.2 and 12.3, obtain any information you can about the organization, and then develop a set of questions that you will ask the job holder. Either before or at the interview, be sure to obtain a copy of the job holder's job description if one is available. Based on the written and interview information, prepare a report of your investigation. The report should cover the following:

1. The organization's products and services, size, and staffing (employment) function
2. The job holder's job title, and why you chose that person's job to study
3. A summary of the tasks performed by the job holder and the KSAOs necessary for the job
4. A summary of the extrinsic and intrinsic rewards received by the job holder
5. Unique characteristics of the job that you did not expect to be a part of the job

Evaluating Staffing Process Results

The Keepon Trucking Company (KTC) is a manufacturer of custom-built trucks. It does not manufacture any particular truck lines, styles, or models. Rather, it builds trucks to customers' specifications; these trucks are used for specialty purposes, such as snow removal, log hauling, and military cargo hauling. One year ago KTC received a new, large order that would take three years to complete and would require the external hiring of 100 new assemblers. To staff this particular job, the HR department manager of hourly employment hurriedly developed and implemented a special staffing process for filling these new vacancies. Applicants were recruited from three different sources: newspaper ads, employee referrals, and a local employment agency. All applicants generated by these methods were subjected to a common selection and decision-making process. All offer receivers were given the same terms and conditions in their job offer letters and told there was no room for any negotiation. All vacancies were eventually filled.

After the first year of the contract, the manager of hourly employment, Dexter Williams, decided to pull together some data in an attempt to determine how well the staffing process for the assembler jobs had worked. Since he had not originally planned on doing any evaluation, Dexter was able to retrieve only the following data to help him with his evaluation:

EXHIBIT
Staffing Data for Filling the Job of Assembler

Method	Applicants	Offer receivers	Start as new hires	Remaining at six months
Newspaper ads				
No. apps.	300	70	50	35
Avg. no. days	30	30	10	
Employee referral				
No. apps.	60	30	30	27
Avg. no. days	20	10	10	
Employment agency				
No. apps.	400	20	20	8
Avg. no. days	40	20	10	

1. Determine the yield ratios (offer receivers/applicants, new hires/applicants), time lapse or cycle times (days to offer, days to start), and retention rates associated with each recruitment source.
2. What is the relative effectiveness of the three sources in terms of yield ratios, cycle times, and retention rates?

3. What are possible reasons for the fact that the three sources differ in their relative effectiveness?
4. How do these data compare to national staffing metrics data (Exhibit 12.9)?
5. What would you recommend that Dexter do differently in the future to improve his evaluation of the staffing process?

ENDNOTES

1. Industry Canada, *Small Business Policy Branch Strategic Plan 2003–04 to 2005–06,* "The Importance of Small Business in Canada," June 2005, http://strategis.ic.gc.ca/epic/internet/insbrp-rppe.nsf/en/rd00022e.html.
2. H. G. Heneman III and R. A. Berkley, "Applicant Attraction Practices and Outcomes Among Small Businesses,"*Journal of Small Business Management,* January 1999, pp. 53–74.
3. E. E. Lawler III and A. A. Mohrman, *Creating a Strategic Human Resources Organization* (Stanford, CA: Stanford University Press, 2003), pp. 15–20.
4. M. Hammers, "SunTrust Bank Combines 28 Recruiting and Screening Systems into One," *Workforce,* December 3, 2003.
5. Lawler and Mohrman, *Creating a Strategic Human Resources Organization,* p. 33.
6. J. Vocino, "HR Compensation Continues to Rise," *HR Magazine,* November 2004, pp. 72–88.
7. Human Resources and Social Development Canada, *National Occupational Classification* 2001, www23.hrdc-drhc.gc.ca/2001/e/generic/welcome.shtml.
8. Mercer Human Resource Consulting, *Transforming HR for Business Results* (New York: author, 2004), p. 9.
9. A. Rosenthal, "Hiring Edge," *Human Resource Executive,* April 2000, pp. 96–98.
10. J. S. Arthur, "Title Wave," *Human Resource Executive,* October 2000, pp. 115–118; K. J. Dunham, "Tapping Talent," *Wall Street Journal,* April 10, 2001, p. B14.
11. D. Podnoroff, "Taleo: Comprehensive Recruiting and Talent Management," *HRBrief.com,* 2005, www.hrbrief.com/a/66-Taleo-Software-Review.asp.
12. *BrassRing,* "Measuring the Value of a Talent Management System," January 7, 2005, www.brassring.com; P. Buckley, K. Minette, D. Joy, and J. Michaels, "The Use of an Automated Employment Recruiting and Screening System for Temporary Professional Employees: A Case Study," *Human Resource Management,* 2004, 43, pp. 233–241; D. Chapman and J. Webster, "The Use of Technologies in the Recruiting, Screening, and Selection Processes for Job Candidates," *International Journal of Selection and Assessment,* 2003, 11, pp. 113–120; S. Greengard, "Seven Myths About Recruiting Technology," *Workforce,* August 10, 2004, www.workforce.com; J. W. Jones and K. D. Dages, "Technology Trends in Staffing and Assessment, A Practical Note," *International Journal of Selection and Assessment,* 2003, 11, pp. 247–252; B. Roberts, "A Sure Bet," *HR Magazine,* August 2004, pp. 115–119.
13. M. Frase-Blunt, "A Recruiting Spigot," *HR Magazine,* April 2003, pp. 71–79.
14. B. S. Klaas, J. McClendon, T. Gainey, and H. Yang, *HR Outsourcing in Small and Medium Enterprises: A Field Study of the Use and Impact of Professional Employer Organizations* (Alexandria, VA: Society for Human Resource Management Foundation, 2004).
15. B. Siegel, "Outsourced Recruiting," in N. C. Burkholder, P. J. Edwards, and L. Sartain (eds.), *On Staffing* (Hoboken, NJ: Wiley, 2004), pp. 116–132.
16. D. Brown, "RBC Financial Group brings recruitment back into the fold," *HR Reporter,* April 21, 2003, p. 1.
17. P. Babcock, "Slicing Off Pieces of HR," *HR Magazine,* July 2004, pp. 71–76; J. C. Berkshire, "Seeking Full Partnership," *HR Magazine,* July 2004, pp. 89–96;

D. Dell, *HR Outsourcing* (New York: The Conference Board, 2004); E. Esen, *Human Resource Outsourcing* (Alexandria, VA: Society for Human Resource Management, 2004); S. Greengard, "Pulling the Plug," *Workforce Management,* July 2004, pp. 43–46; R. J. Grossman, "Sticker Shock," *HR Magazine,* July 2004, pp. 79–86; T. Starner, "Measuring Success," *Human Resource Executive,* October 16, 2004, pp. 49–50.

18. E. P. Gunn, "How Mirage Resorts Sifted 75,000 Applicants to Hire 9,600 in 24 weeks," *Fortune,* October 12, 1998, p. 195.
19. L. Micco, "Lockheed Wins the Best Catches," *Employment Management Association Today,* Spring 1997, pp. 18–20; E. R. Silverman, "The Fast Track," *Human Resource Executive,* October 1998, pp. 30–34.
20. L. Klutz, *Time to Fill/Time to Start: 2002 Staffing Metrics Survey* (Alexandria, VA: Society for Human Resource Management, 2003).
21. Society for Human Resource Management, *2002 SHRM/EMA Staffing Metrics Study* (Alexandria VA: author, 2003); Staffing.org, *2003 Recruiting Metrics and Performance Benchmark Report* (Willow Grove, PA: author, 2003).
22. K. Burns, "Metrics Are Everything: Why, What and How to Choose," in Burkholder, Edwards, and Sartain (eds.), *On Staffing* (Hoboken, NJ: Wiley, 2004), pp. 364–371.
23. H. G. Heneman III, D. L. Huett, R. J. Lavigna, and D. Ogsten, "Assessing Managers' Satisfaction with Staffing Service," *Personnel Psychology,* 1995, 48, pp. 163–172.
24. H. P. Coxson, "The Double-Edged Sword of Personnel Files and Employee Records," *Legal Report* (Alexandria, VA: Society for Human Resource Management, 1992).
25. J. W. Janove, "It's Not Over, Even When It's Over," *HR Magazine,* February 2004, pp. 123–131.
26. W. K. Turner and C. S. Thrutchley, "Employment Law and Practices Training: No Longer the Exception—It's the Rule," *Society for Human Resource Management Legal Report,* July–August 2002, p. 3.
27. S. K. Williams, "The New Law of Training," *HR Magazine,* May 2004, pp. 115–118.
28. M. Barrier, "The Mediation Disconnect," *HR Magazine,* May 2003, pp. 54–58; "EEOC's Efforts to Expand Mediation Gain Momentum" (no author), *HR Magazine,* May 2003, pp. 32–34;
29. M. W. Bennett, D. J. Polden, and H. J. Rubin, *Employment Relationships: Law and Practice* (New York: Aspen, periodically updated), pp. 13–1 to 13–33.
30. U.S. Government Printing Office, *Employment Discrimination: Most Private Sector Employers Use Alternative Dispute Resolution* (Washington, DC: author, 1995).
31. L. B. Bingham, "Employment Arbitration and the Courts," *Industrial Relations Research Association Perspectives on Work,* 1998, 2(2), pp. 19–23; U.S. Government Printing Office, *Employment Discrimination: Most Private Sector Employers Use Alternative Dispute Resolution;* C. Wittenberg, S. MacKenzie, M. Shaw, and D. Ross, "And Justice for All," *HR Magazine,* September 1997, pp. 131–137.
32. M. E. Bruno, "The Future of ADR in the Workplace," *Compensation and Benefits Review,* November–December 2001, pp. 46–59; C. Hirschman, "Order in the Hear," *HR Magazine,* July 2001, pp. 58–64; L. P. Postol, "To Arbitrate Employment Disputes or Not, That Is the Question," *Society for Human Resource Management Legal Report,* September–October 2001, pp. 5–8.

Name Index

Subject Index